HOUGHTON MIFFLIN COMPANY
BOSTON

NEW YORK · ATLANTA · GENEVA, ILL. · DALLAS · PALO ALTO

Industrial

Organization and

Economic

Development,

In Honor of E. S. Mason .

Edited by

Jesse W. Markham

Gustav F. Papanek

Both of Harvard University

Printed in the U.S.A.

To Ed

Preface

At a session of the annual meeting of the American Economic Association two decades ago, the chairman introduced what appeared to be over half of the participants as members of the "Masonic" school. The full import of this collective appellation has become clearer since then. In the early 1930's the stream of literature concerned with the monopoly problem and the public policies designed to cope with it was redirected: the qualitative and conjectural pronouncements of an earlier era gave way to model building and factual analysis; the field of economic inquiry bearing such titles as Trusts and Public Regulation was reborn Industrial Organization. The name most inseparably identified with the redirection of the intellectual effort and the rebirth of the field clearly is that of Professor Edward S. Mason.

Characteristically, Ed Mason has attributed much of this to others. In the General Introduction of his *Economic Concentration and the Monopoly Problem,* he identified the sources of the shift in direction as follows:

> A re-examination of the position of large firms in the American and other industrial economies, and the monopolistic and other consequences thereof, may be said to have begun with the almost simultaneous appearance in 1932–33 of Chamberlin's *Theory of Monopolistic Competition,* Robinson's *The Economics of Imperfect Competition,* and Berle and Means' *The Modern Corporation and Private Property.* These studies not only have initiated subsequent inquiry, but also serve to point out fairly clearly the area with which we are concerned. On one side is a re-examination of market 'models' and the theory of the firm; on the other, factual and statistical studies of economic concentration, market structure, and business policies.

No one, and certainly none of Mason's students, would deny that these cited works were of ground-breaking importance. But in the interest of historical accuracy it must be noted that Mason's *The Street Railway in Massachusetts* also appeared in 1932, and that Chamberlin in his preface to *Monopolistic Competition* acknowledged his very large indebtedness to Professor Mason, then a year or two Chamberlin's senior in the Harvard

Economics Department. Thus began Professor Mason's steady flow of distinguished publications and — more as a tribute to him than as a reflection of our own immodesty — distinguished students, that comprised the birth and subsequent development of the discipline of industrial organization.

The flow, of course, was not confined to industrial organization. The agile and productive mind turns to the pressing and unsolved problems of its time. Economic development became one of the most popular fields in economics in the late 1950's, when the challenge of problems in this subject became evident. As usual, Edward Mason had been half a decade ahead of the crowd. His particular combination of qualities was as effective in economic development as it had been in his earlier industrial organization incarnation — sharp analytical abilities, a concern with the crucial economic policy issues and an uncanny ability to convince others about the important issues of development policy.

Within a few years after Mason's shift to the development field, his influence was strongly felt. Harvard became one of the major centers for research and training in development economics. Over a hundred government officials from the less developed world had gone through a training program he had initiated and were beginning to appear as cabinet members and heads of planning agencies. Ed Mason was the one academic with whom governments and international organizations invariably wanted to consult about complex economic development problems. The advisory group he had set up for Pakistan had completed its metamorphosis into a major university advisory service to governments of less developed countries. In universities and governments throughout much of the world a large proportion of the professionals concerned with development turned out to be students of Ed Mason in the true sense of the word. Former participants in his courses or former colleagues had all learned from him about economic analysis, about organization and, perhaps most important, how to approach realistically and yet humanely the crushing problems of the less developed world.

The articles, written expressly for this volume, are expressions of the high esteem and deep affection we, who have been fortunate enough to be his students, hold for Edward Mason. We shall forgo the temptation to provide an introduction to the substantive content of each contribution, bearing in mind the admonition of a little older and much wiser former colleague on the occasion of returning a manuscript submitted to him for his critical comments: "You should eliminate those little chapter introductions telling what each chapter is all about. If your writing and analysis do not clearly accomplish this, the promises you make at the outset will not remedy the essential deficiency." Individually, we believe each selection speaks clearly and effectively for itself. Viewed as a whole, the articles mirror the unresolved problems of economic development and the richness and variety of industrial organization problems that still persist: the role of trade, capital movements, and technical assistance in economic development; the relationships among market structure, conduct and performance; economies of scale; the scope of antitrust and other regulatory policies; the theory of the firm; analyses of particular industrial markets concentrating especially, and we suspect inevitably, on the oil industry. But then if it had not been oil it most certainly would have been steel.

We have discovered, not to our great surprise, that the timing of such a volume inevitably conflicts with the schedules of some. Essays we had hoped would appear in this volume for a variety of reasons were not, or could not, be undertaken or completed. We regret, therefore, that several of Mason's distinguished students are not represented.

Festschrifts, by the canons of academia, generally commemorate the arrival of the honored scholar's and teacher's 60th or 65th birthday. Whatever a close accounting in terms of the calendar may reveal, none of us who have been privileged to maintain close contacts with him in recent years could be persuaded that Professor Mason conforms to the mien or the schedule of a scholar in his sixties. Indeed, had it not been for the fact that some of his students were beginning to show signs of entering their sixties, this volume may well have waited.

Jesse W. Markham
Gustav F. Papanek

Cambridge, Massachusetts

Table of Contents

PART TWO

Economic Development and International Trade

PART ONE

Industrial Organization and Public Policy

James W. McKie

Almarin Phillips

Joe S. Bain

Raymond Vernon

Donald F. Turner

Richard H. Holton

Jesse W. Markham

M. A. Adelman

Samuel M. Loescher

Robert L. Bishop

John Lintner

Merton J. Peck

Richard Caves

Market Structure and Function:

Performance versus Behavior

James W. McKie[*]

Industrial organization as a discipline of applied economics was largely created and developed by Edward S. Mason and his students during the 1930's. Earlier study of the organization of industry and business behavior and of public policy toward them, had been almost entirely "institutional" in approach. The appearance of the theories of monopolistic competition and oligopoly sparked a new effort to understand and analyze economic activities that did not conform very well to the models of the market then available and to develop a larger body of factual knowledge about industry and markets. Like most applied disciplines, industrial organization has taken many forms in different hands and has followed multiple lines of development difficult to characterize by a single label. To some economists, it consists merely of verifying and testing theoretical models of markets, while to others it is a means of constructing new syntheses of theory and empirical fact.

Most students of industrial organization have found it useful to organize their inquiries around the relationships among industrial *structure,* the *behavior* of firms and other organizations, and economic *performance* judged in terms of ultimate norms of economic welfare. It would be very convenient if this analytical schema formed a completely connected system, enabling us to begin at any point and demonstrate all of the relationships with any other. Studies of the market might begin with details of structure, predict behavior uniquely and completely from these, move forward to infer performance from behavior, and show how well this performance met the relevant norms of economic organization. Or it might move in reverse,

* Vanderbilt University

starting with a norm, deducing from it "good" performance, and ending with the structure that would produce such results. Studies of individual industries have illuminated particular aspects of these relationships, but research aimed at a higher level of generalization has not fully connected structure, behavior, and performance in a linear or stepwise sequence. It seems instead to have produced two kinds of generalizations: those linking structure and performance directly and those linking structure and behavior.[1]

Investigations of economic performance have usually bypassed behavioral problems. In this they resemble the abstract theoretical models of the firm and the market under conditions of pure competition and pure monopoly, for which profit maximization is the only behavioral principle necessary: *price policy* is what produces maximum profits. Questions of behavior become interesting in equilibrium analysis only when there is some uncertainty about the theoretical prediction of results. Performance, on the other hand, is more directly dependent upon the properties of the predicted equilibrium.

Structure and Performance: A Survey of the Findings

Influence of concentration.   The empirical relationships between structure and performance are not fully known, but extensive research has yielded some tentative results. For this purpose, a fairly simple specification of the market's or "industry's" structure seems to be sufficient. (In this respect, as well as in its indifference to behavioral questions, the analysis resembles the polar models of theory.) The simplest of all specifications is *concentration in one dimension* — the largest-4- or 8-firm concentration ratio or the Herfindahl index $\Sigma\sigma^2$.[2] This may be supplemented by a measure of entry, though barriers to entry usually accompany persisting high concentration. The preferred dimension of performance in these surveys is the rate of profit or a variation of it. Perhaps the best known of these relationships between summary measures of structure and profits performance is that discovered by Bain, who found a significant difference between profit rates in industries having an industry concentration ratio for the largest 8 sellers above 70 percent and profit rates in industries having

---

[1] By "structure" is meant those aspects of an industry's environment that are relatively fixed and objective; "behavior" means the pattern of decisions made by the managements of the component firms (including reactions to structural influences) and usually capable of alteration in the short run. "Conduct" here means the same thing as behavior. The attributes of structure and behavior are detailed below. For a further suggestion on "closing" the system, see the paper by Almarin Phillips in this volume.

[2] The concentration ratio is the ratio of the sales of the largest 4 (or 8) sellers, added together, to total sales in the market. (Value of shipments or total employment are sometimes used instead of sales.) The Herfindahl index is calculated by finding the share of each seller in the market as a decimal fraction, squaring it, and summing the results for all sellers.

lower concentration ratios.[3] Bain inferred that this line roughly marked the breaking point below which tacit collusion among oligopolists was not effective.[4] The class of *highly concentrated* oligopolies thus calls for a particular class of applicable models.

Other investigators have used concentration as a predictive variable for performance. Without going into details, we may recognize two or three examples. George Stigler found a relationship, though a rather weak one, between profitability and concentration when the Herfindahl index exceeded .25 or when the share of the *4* largest firms in total sales exceeded 80 percent.[5] The distinction of an effectively collusive or highly concentrated oligopoly is again implied, though the cutoff is considerably higher than in Bain's formulation. In 1963, for example, the number of 4-digit Census manufacturing industries showing largest-*4* concentration ratios higher than 79 percent was only 27 out of 417, while the number showing largest-*8* concentration ratios higher than 69 percent was 104. Because nonspecialists may not be fully acquainted with data on concentration, the "highly concentrated" industries in 1963, according to Stigler's criterion of 80 percent for the largest 4, are shown in the Appendix Table.

Using a somewhat different measure of concentration, David Schwartzman investigated the same problem. He distinguished between "monopolistic" industries in which the 4 largest firms accounted for 50 percent or more of total *employment* and other industries in which the 4 largest had less than 50 percent.[6] He found that the former exhibited a significantly higher ratio of gross product value to direct cost than the latter, that is, a higher ratio of price to average variable cost. The size of the monopoly's effect on price was estimated at 8.3 percent of average variable cost. Schwartzman did not detect significant differences in this ratio *within* the "monopoly" group.

Influence of entry conditions. Conditions of entry as an independent influence on profits have also been tested by Bain and others. Though the

[3] Joe S. Bain, *Barriers to New Competition* (Cambridge: Harvard University Press, 1956), pp. 192–201.

[4] Joe S. Bain, *Industrial Organization,* Second Edition (New York: John Wiley & Sons, Inc., 1968), p. 448.

[5] George J. Stigler, "A Theory of Oligopoly," *Journal of Political Economy,* LXXII (February, 1964), 41–61. These findings succeeded an earlier study by Stigler which found "ambiguous, but on the whole negative" relations between profits and concentration. *Capital and Rates of Return in Manufacturing Industries* (Princeton: Princeton University Press, 1963), p. 68.

[6] David Schwartzman, "The Effect of Monopoly on Price," *Journal of Political Economy,* LXVII (August, 1959), 352–362. Because measures of employment typically show lower percentages of concentration in the largest firms than do percentages of total sales or output (the Census measures), Schwartzman's largest-4-with-50-percent-of-employment probably reflects a concentration level for most cases at least as high as a dividing line of 70 percent (in terms of value of output) for the largest 8.

evidence is sketchy, it does at least indicate that very high barriers to entry do have some influence in addition to high concentration.[7] Michael Mann found further support for this hypothesis in his investigation of thirty industries during the 1950's.[8] The highly concentrated industries with very high entry barriers showed greater average profits than the highly concentrated industries with only substantial or moderate entry barriers. It is not clear from such limited samples whether this generalization would survive a redefinition of the "highly concentrated" class on a more restricted basis, such as the largest 4 sellers having 80 percent or more instead of the largest 8 sellers having 70 percent or more.[9] In other words, raising the cutoff for the highly concentrated group probably eliminates some of the independent influence of the entry condition, since concentration and very high barriers to entry become more closely associated in the upmost reaches of the scale.

Tests by Collins and Preston. Norman R. Collins and Lee Preston made further tests for relationships between price-cost margins and concentration in manufacturing industries.[10] They detected a ". . . statistically significant, but not always strong, association between concentration and indicators of profitability in manufacturing industries." The association seemed to be a continuous one, lacking the breaking point that other investigators had found in similar relationships.

In their statistical investigation Collins and Preston included structural variables additional to concentration and entry conditions. Their multiple-correlation analysis produced significant coefficients of regression for a capital-output ratio, and an "index of geographical dispersion" — a more accurate definition of market size for dispersed industries — against price-cost ratios in 4-digit Census industries. In a subsequent refinement, they found that the relationship linking concentration and profit margins in consumer goods industries was distinctly different from the one in producer

---

[7] Bain, *Barriers to New Competition*, p. 199.

[8] H. Michael Mann, "Seller Concentration, Barriers to Entry, and Rates of Return in Thirty Industries, 1950–1960," *Review of Economics and Statistics,* XLVIII (August, 1966), 296–307.

[9] It is interesting to note that of the groups studied by Mann and having high measures in both concentration and entry barriers, 6 of the 8 industries would be highly concentrated under the 4/80 percent criterion, while a seventh had below-average profits. In the groups having over 8/70 percent concentration but with merely substantial or moderate barriers, only 4 of the 13 industries would meet the 4/80 percent high-concentration test, of which one had above-average profits. Regrouping on the basis of the 80 percent criterion alone shows a difference in average profit rates above and below the 4/80 percent level for the 21 industries meeting the 8/70 criterion for high concentration, though the difference (14.4 percent versus 12.3 percent) is not as significant as between Mann's high/very high group (16.4 percent) and his high/substantial group (11.1 percent).

[10] N. R. Collins and L. E. Preston, *Concentration and Price-Cost Margins in Manufacturing Industries* (Berkeley: University of California Press, 1968), p. 107.

goods industries. The relationship was much stronger for consumer goods industries, whether differentiated or not, than for producer goods industries, perhaps owing to differences in buyers' bargaining power and in market organization. Collins and Preston also reported that concentration did not seem to affect profitability in industries in which concentration is declining, whether or not new entry was responsible for the decline.[11]

Evidently the statistical search for influence of structural variables on profit performance is likely to exhibit diminishing returns as more elements of structure are brought into the picture.[12] The variables that have been investigated do not by any means fully describe or specify industrial structure as a specialist in industrial organization understands that term. They do, however, include the most fundamental ones: concentration among sellers and the condition of entry, an element which is itself correlated with concentration. We have, in addition, rudimentary indications that the nature of the buyers, the rate of increase in concentration, the industry's growth rate, and the absolute size of the firm may affect profit performance and, by implication, allocative efficiency. Some studies locate a breaking point between highly concentrated oligopolies and other industries at different places in the scale of concentration, while others find no distinct cleavage but rather an intensification of monopolistic results as concentration becomes very high.[13]

Other criteria of performance.   The relations of the principal structural elements — concentration and conditions of entry — with criteria of performance other than profits have not been tested to the same extent. Technological innovation as a dimension of performance has received increasing attention of late, but its dependence upon structural variables remains obscure. The predicted relationship is inverse: more innovation is associated with higher concentration and barriers to entry. We cannot stop to survey the evidence here; all it really shows is that atomistic industries do

---

[11] Collins and Preston, "Price-Cost Margins and Industry Structure," *The Review of Economics and Statistics*, Vol. LI, No. 3 (August, 1969). The stronger association for consumer goods industries is not confined to those making extensive use of advertising.

[12] A multiple-variable study by D. R. Kamerschen also deserves notice: "The Influence of Ownership and Control on Profit Rates," *American Economic Review*, LVIII 3 (June, 1968), 432–447. After extensive simple- and multiple-correlation analysis, he concludes that the most important structural variables influencing the rate of return are: (1) barriers to entry, (2) the industry's growth rate, and (3) total assets, that is, size of firm. He did not find a concentration variable (a largest-8-firm measure) to be significant, but that result may have been due to the high collinearity between the concentration variable and the barriers-to-entry variable, and perhaps also between concentration and capital requirements (total assets).

[13] These findings are subject to all of the well-known anomalies between the Standard Industrial Classification as used by the Bureau of the Census (the fountainhead of most of the data) and the economic definition of markets. For further discussion, see Appendix.

not seem to innovate rapidly while oligopolistic ones often do. So far it has not demonstrated a functional relationship between innovation and degrees of monopoly.

It is usually assumed that market pressures in unregulated industries are generally great enough to effect an approximation of efficiency in cost. Contrary examples exist, but no systematic association between the degree of monopoly and cost inefficiency is now known. Selling costs are always an equivocal test of poor performance, since they seem to be rooted in consumers' attitudes and wants, and our models of equilibrium do not tell us how to evaluate them in assessing performance. That some consumer goods industries with differentiated products have high selling costs is undeniable. The oligopolistic firms in these industries make these outlays in order to realize high profits, and from the point of view of the profits test, selling costs are simply a "barrier to entry." Perhaps they are a special kind of barrier and should be added to the profits test as an extra measure of allocative inefficiency, but the profits test at least indicates their presence and effect.[14]

Theoretical models of monopoly already assure us that abnormal profits can be expected from monopoly safeguarded by barriers to entry. The studies mentioned above are not designed to prove this proposition but to identify the industries that qualify as monopolies by a profits test. If the 80-percent-concentration-ratio test or other similar groupings are statistically reliable for general application, we may conclude that oligopolies in the high-concentration bracket usually succeed in getting systematically closer to joint monopoly than do oligopolies with a looser structure whose profits do not differ appreciably from profits in structurally competitive industries. If rates of profit increase in a linear relationship with concentration, without a distinct break, then the degree of concentration might be said to predict after the fashion of Cournot the degree of approximation to joint monopoly profits. But in either case the relationship is a static equilibrium relationship like that in the theoretical models they resemble. The results do not depend on an analysis of behavior, nor do they need to. *How* firms in concentrated industries achieve what appears to be a joint monopoly, at least to a degree; why some highly concentrated industries are exceptions to the rule; why oligopolies with looser structures fail to achieve similar results or whether they behave like structurally competitive industries, — these questions have held little interest in the analysis of performance as it has been carried on up to now.

[14] After an extensive study, William S. Comanor and Thomas A. Wilson concluded, "Industries with high advertising outlays earn, on average, a profit rate which exceeds that of other industries by nearly four percentage points. . . . It is likely, moreover, that much of this profit rate differential is accounted for by the entry barriers created by advertising expenditures and by the resulting achievement of market power." From "Advertising Market Structure and Performance," *Review of Economics and Statistics,* LXIX (November, 1967), 423–440.

Structure and Behavior

Relevant structural elements. A very much more complex specification of an industry's structure is needed for analyzing behavior than for predicting performance in terms of the profit rate or other simple tests of performance. Indeed, the investigator who studies industrial behavior very quickly finds himself in the classic dilemma of applied research: to reconcile general theorems with particular facts, if possible, in an optimum combination. To particularize too much is to run the risk of *ad hoc* theorizing or of finding "generalizations" that apply only to a particular case. The temptation to do this is strong, and even the most scientific industrial study tends to become anecdotal. A list of general instructions to guide such studies can easily run to hundreds of questions whose answers would be interesting.[15] Although a thorough understanding of all the behavior exhibited by an industry undoubtedly requires this sort of investigation, it is nevertheless possible to group certain outstanding patterns in market behavior and to essay predictions of their occurrence in terms of a limited set of structural characteristics. For at least the last thirty years, students of industry have generally found serviceable the following set, or some near variant of it.[16] It represents a workable compromise between the excess of facts in *ad hoc* analysis and the bare skeletons of the austere models of market theory.

1. Distribution of sellers by number and size — seller concentration.
2. Relative ease of entry to, and exit from, the industry or market.
3. Conditions of demand and nature of the product
   Differentiated or homogeneous
   Consumer good or producer good; durable or perishable
   Unit value
   Methods of distribution
   Intermittent or continuous demand
   Price elasticity
   Short-run income elasticity
   Long-run rate of growth
4. Cost conditions and technology
   Shape of marginal and average cost curves; weight of overhead costs; cost flexibility
   Economies of scale

---

[15] See, for example, E. E. Hagen's *Handbook for Industry Studies* (Cambridge: Massachusetts Institute of Technology, 1955), for study of industry development, which comprises 103 main questions or points for study organized under 15 rubrics, and includes almost 400 subsidiary questions for the guidance of the investigator.

[16] It is a somewhat expanded version of the structural features described in Mason's famous article, "Price and Production Policies of Large-Scale Enterprise," *American Economic Review*, Supplement, (March, 1939). That article gave mature expression to the "structural-functional" approach under discussion here, possibly for the first time.

Vertical integration

Joint or common products

Technological complexity; the underlying rate of technical advance

5. Factor-market influences; relative factor costs; monopoly and competition in factor markets.

6. Locational influences — materials, labor, markets.

7. Governmental regulation of prices, inputs, and outputs and specific taxation.

8. Distribution of buyers by number and size — buyer concentration.

Possible combination of structural elements. These basic structural elements can be rearranged and given other labels, but most would turn up on any industrial economist's list of primary structural influences on behavior. Not all of them are relevant in every case — in fact, only a few may be of any particular importance in a given industry or market. Even though the list is limited, the number of possible combinations, including varying characteristics of the structural features enumerated here, is enormous. Not even *ad hoc* investigation could supply actual cases for all of these possibilities. The list encompasses the classical structural assumptions for the polar models of market theory — pure competition, for example, assumes numerous atomistic sellers, free entry, homogeneous product, and numerous atomistic buyers: the other elements, such as demand elasticity and technology, are not relevant to its prediction of a static equilibrium. In less perfect cases, different combinations of structural characteristics are useful.

Two examples follow. A combination of structural elements that occurs fairly frequently comprises the following: many producers of small size, though not necessarily atomistic, easy entry, difficult exit (immobile capital investment), undifferentiated product, price-inelastic demand, high overhead costs, and relatively stagnant technology. Secondary characteristics may vary, but the primary ones spell trouble. The industry invites entry when prices and profits are attractive, but excess numbers and superfluous resources cannot leave again when demand turns unfavorable. The high overhead costs produce a considerable margin between average and marginal costs at less-than-capacity operation for the individual producer, while the low price-elasticity of demand ensures that excess production will drive prices well down into this range. The firms are unable to protect themselves by differentiating their product. Because of their numbers, they cannot reach any kind of tacit agreement on prices or output. The result is chronic depression, unremunerative prices, persisting distress in the industry, and a failure of the equilibrating mechanisms of the market. This pattern has sometimes been called the "cartel syndrome," since it usually prompts the producers to form a cartel that limits output and stabilizes prices and to call Government to their aid. Instances are found in many extractive industries, such as soft coal, tin, coffee, sugar, and the like.

Another group of cases occurs when oligopolistic industries are subject to strong locational influences from dependency on material or resource, or to large economies of scale which require that establishments seek distant markets for some of their output, or to both conditions, and when transportation costs are high relative to unit value and the product is undifferentiated. This combination of structural elements is reliably predictive of delivered-price systems. These systems may vary from simple freight absorption to highly collusive basing-point systems, depending on further environmental details, but the family resemblance among them is strong.

Many other similarities occur. Not every observed form of market behavior can be grouped and demarcated with unique predictive factors. Some are *sui generis* and hence not worth attempting to predict; but even these can be better understood in terms of the particular set of structural circumstances that give rise to them. Those forms observed with some frequency cover the whole range of possibilities, including almost-pure competitive behavior and almost-pure monopoly. The following are some points in that range:

1. Profit-maximizing behavior by single-firm monopoly, including monopolistic discrimination
2. Joint-profit maximizing behavior in oligopoly through near-perfect tacit collusion
3. Delivered pricing systems
   a) Basing-point systems (sometimes combined with price leadership)
   b) Freight equalization
4. Market-sharing
5. Nonprice competition with price stabilization in oligopoly
   a) Selling-cost rivalry
   b) New-product competition
6. Price leadership
   a) Dominant-firm leadership
   b) Oligopolistic leadership with imperfect coordination
   c) Barometric leadership
7. Nonleadership oligopoly pricing patterns involving sporadic discrimination
8. Price warfare in oligopoly — intermittent or permanent
9. Excessive or disorderly competition — the "cartel syndrome"
10. Formula pricing and other mechanisms of monopolistic competition
11. Simple profit-maximizing behavior by firms constrained by atomistic conditions in the market

Behavior of oligopolies. Specialists in industrial organization have always been mainly interested in the oligopoly cases. If it were not for the problem of oligopoly, "industrial organization" would probably not have emerged as a special subject at all. Of course, if the result of oligopoly usually approximated that of joint monopoly, analysis of oligopolistic behavior would hold little interest. It is when we observe or assume rivalry that behavioral questions become important. Oligopolistic rivalry is not necessarily resolved in a joint-monopoly solution, but it is not "competition" either. How are independent decisions in an interdependent market situation coordinated, made consistent, and brought to some kind of equilibrium or balance? We do not usually observe chaos in these markets, though price warfare does break out in some of them. The patterns of orderly coordination commonly take the forms enumerated above. Structural configurations help us to predict them and also to identify the causes of bizarre or disorderly cases of oligopoly which fail to reach a stable condition of balance.[17]

The highly-concentrated oligopolies (by various definitions) include some which are much more dominated by rivalry than others, even others less concentrated and less protected against entry. Structural variations of a rather detailed sort should account for such anomalies. Electrical generating equipment is an illustrative case. It is a highly concentrated industry.[18] In turbines, at the time of the electrical equipment conspiracies of the 1950's, there were only three significant producers (since reduced to two) and in heavy-duty switchgear and transformers only four or five. There were high barriers to entry. One would have expected a tight oligopolistic discipline — effective tacit collusion with results approximating maximum joint profits. If the pattern were to take the form of price leadership, General Electric (GE), the largest seller, overall, would be the logical leader. Instead, there have been alternating periods of overt collusion and price warfare; tacit coordination never took hold of the markets, at least

---

[17] The modes of oligopolistic behavior included in the above list do not include direct agreement, enforceable cartel arrangements, order imposed on the industry by Government fiat, and so forth. They assume independent decisions, though in a milieu of interdependence produced by the oligopoly's structure. If there is explicit agreement or control, an additional institutional determinant supersedes the kind of prediction that follows from structure, but the latter does not entirely disappear; it is transformed into a prediction of the stability or effectiveness of the agreement. This is not to say that results will be the same whether there is an overt agreement or not but merely that the circumstances determining the effectiveness of tacit coordination of independent decisions among rival firms also affect the kind of agreement they can form and the strength of their adherence to it.

[18] The 4-digit industry 3511 (steam engines and turbines) has a 4-digit primary-product concentration ratio over 80 and an industry concentration ratio over 90, but it is somewhat overaggregated from an economic point of view. The 5-digit product class 35111 (Units and parts of steam, gas, and hydraulic turbine generator sets) undoubtedly has a 4-firm ratio of 100, though the Census withholds the figure to avoid disclosing information for individual firms. Power transformers had a largest-4 concentration ratio in 1963 of 76 percent, and circuit breakers 71 percent, but these may have included types other than the main-line equipment of power utilities.

not before the traumatic event of the trials for conspiracy. GE never exercised price leadership and was just as prone to instigate price warfare as its rivals.

The reasons for the observed results lie in aspects of structure other than concentration, aspects which in this case were strong enough to override the cohesive tendency of highly concentrated oligopoly. Conditions of demand elasticity were troublesome in themselves, as was the presence of large and powerful buyers who were utilities; but the really decisive factor was the intermittent character of the demand, associated with the high value (unit or combined) of the intermittent orders. If a supplier did not obtain a given contract, he might have to wait several years for another chance at a large order, keeping his plant idle or working well under capacity on repair business and overall replacements. The only possibility of operation at capacity lay in getting the large contracts. The internal managerial response of the suppliers was to put heavy pressure on their electrical equipment divisions to get these contracts by any available means. The divisions in turn alternated between unrestrained price-cutting against rivals and direct agreement with rivals to allocate business. These agreements were inherently unstable, of course. Nothing like an equilibrium appeared in these markets during the postwar years.

If GE or some other firm had attempted to establish itself as a price leader, it would have had to forego price-cutting and lose many contracts to its rivals over a number of years until the rivals at last became convinced that the leader would not undercut its preferred price and would provide a firm basis for tacit coordination of policies. But the would-be leader would have had no assurance that its rivals would ever decide to become followers, since their relative advantage might have remained greater with the leader removed from the scene, while it could remove itself permanently by protracted self-denial of business. The alternative tactic of disciplining recalcitrant followers was not really of much use to a would-be leader, since intermittent price warfare actually did occur but did not lead to emergence of a stable pattern of tacit coordination.[19]

If there were a general theory of oligopoly, concern for behavior would no doubt be unnecessary. We have instead a great many models of oligopoly based on special assumptions. Some of them are no more than

---

[19] To explain cases like this, Oliver Williamson has constructed an ingenious dynamic model expressed in terms of (1) adherence of oligopolists to the group goal of profit maximization, (2) communication among the sellers, (3) changes — both favorable and unfavorable — in the "environment." Periods of close adherence alternate with periods of "competition," in which adversity causes the internal goals of the individual members to displace collective considerations. "A Dynamic Theory of Interfirm Behavior," *Quarterly Journal of Economics*, LXXIX (November, 1965), 579–607. It is a cyclical model with properties of persistence which turn it into a two-state pattern. Williamson offers a broad definition of the critical environmental factors instead of the narrow demand conditions specified above as critical in the electrical equipment case.

pictorial representations of certain patterns in behavior, while others are abstract constructions of equilibrium. The proliferation of partial and special oligopolistic models has been very helpful to the student of industrial organization who is always on the lookout for tools and spare parts that he can use in his quest, but it has undoubtedly encouraged an eclectic approach in applied research into oligopolistic markets.

The Oligopolistic Models: Equilibrium and Behavior

Significance attributed to behavior. Allocative efficiency depends directly on the results in terms of prices, costs, and output achieved in a market; hence equilibrium models provide the theoretical counterpart of certain types of performance analysis. The significance they attribute to behavior or the process of reaching equilibrium — or disequilibrium — varies considerably. "Oligopolistic behavior" obviously must describe a means of coordination or convergence, in addition to simple maximizing of profits, if an equilibrium is to result.

It seems that these two parts of the problem — equilibrium and behavior — to a large extent make competing demands on the models that explain them. Models that include a consistent equilibrium solution have little to say about behavior, while those that purport to predict an oligopoly's behavior frequently essay no prediction of universally valid equilibrium results.[20] The simplest example of the former is the Chamberlin case of "mutual dependence recognized" or simple duopoly with perfect symmetry, instantaneous reactions, and perfect information.[21] The equilibrium solution is joint-profits maximization. This "recognition" of mutual dependence or of "direct and indirect influence" is the only behavioral element included in the model. Although Chamberlin went on to say that "uncertainty" could prevent attainment of joint monopoly and produce a solution somewhere between monopoly and competition, he did not perceive that this "uncertainty" contained the whole problem of oligopoly as we now understand it.

Models with rudimentary behavioral machinery. Fellner's elaboration of the joint-monopoly solution[22] attempted to specify a kind of oligopolistic

[20] A similar observation about the theory of competitive markets itself was made recently by Paul J. McNulty: "There is a striking contrast in economic literature between the analytical rigor and precision of competition when it is described as a market structure, and the ambiguity surrounding the idea of competition whenever it is discussed in behavioral terms." "The Meaning of Competition," *Quarterly Journal of Economics,* LXXXII (November, 1968), 640. Competitive "behavior" seems to appear only when competition is imperfect.

[21] Edward Chamberlin, *The Theory of Monopolistic Competition,* Sixth Edition (Cambridge: Harvard University Press, 1950), pp. 46 ff.

[22] William Fellner, *Competition Among the Few* (New York: Alfred A. Knopf, 1949).

behavior missing from the Chamberlinian formulation but at the inevitable cost of some fuzziness and unpredictability in the equilibrium solutions. Because price is multidimensional, because demand and cost conditions change over time and technological advance and product development are not fully predictable, because firms differ in their basic structural characteristics and have interests not identical with those of the group collectively, they are unwilling to surrender sovereignty to a joint monopoly. Coordination of policies among the oligopolists will be less than complete. Joint tacit collusion will have more effect on price, or at least on some aspects of price, and on output than on investment policy and technological change, which are likely to remain relatively independent. Full joint monopoly, on the other hand, requires complete joint control of *every* dimension of policy, long-run as well as short-run. These conclusions certainly correspond better than Chamberlin's to what we observe in the real world, but the theory is not predictive in the sense of telling us how much deviation from the results of complete joint monopoly can be expected in each dimension as a result of the various configurations of structural influences in different possible oligopolistic situations.

Stigler has suggested a means of predicting collusion in oligopoly.[23] He calculates the feasibility of collusion in terms of several variables, such as the number of buyers, the probability of repeat purchases, and the relative sizes of firms. The key operational factor is information on price-cutting, information which is essential to maintenance of effective tacit collusion and which varies with these structural conditions. The most effective means of preventing secret price-cutting would be market-sharing under enforceable quotas, but tacit collusion can at least approximate the same result if the oligopolists have information just about as good. A joint-monopoly relationship of tacit collusion is likely to exist only in the highly concentrated oligopolies.

Among the oligopolistic models that include rudimentary behavioral machinery are the Cournot formulation and other theories of the same family. They depend on assumed or deduced reactions of oligopolistic firms to each other. Cournot's theory, of course, is based on pure assumption, and we need not recapitulate the self-contradictory nature of that assumption. Other theories of this family also attempt to derive oligopolistic solutions that do not approximate maximization of joint profits from simple behavioral reactions or rules. They too may depend on arbitrarily assumed conjectural reactions. Many of the leadership models have this characteristic.[24] Without some independent means of explaining why the firms follow

---

[23] "A Theory of Oligopoly," *loc. cit.*

[24] We should recognize Stackelberg's attempt to catalogue all of the possible leadership-followership combinations, as he understands them, for both price and output variables. It is almost the apotheosis of "classical" oligopoly theory. See Fellner, *op. cit.*, Chapters 2 and 3.

these reactions or why a "leadership-followship" relation must develop, sellers' expectations can be mutually consistent only by accident. In other words, the behavior is assumed merely to prove the existence of equilibrium and is completely subordinated to its formal properties. A similar approach, which barely escapes this characterization, is the Theory of Games — the zero-sum branch.[25] Its behavioral theory reduces to an assumption about motivation. The *Maximin principle* — choosing the least unfavorable outcome from a range of profits and losses that is affected by adverse possibilities — may be a useful description of some actual motives overlooked when we assume that firms have a single-valued goal of maximizing profits. Within the model of zero-sum games, however, the maximin assumption is as subordinate to the formal equilibrium as the constant-output assumption in the Cournot model. The nature of a zero-sum game itself, of course, eliminates the mixture of convergent and divergent interests characteristic of oligopolistic rivals in the real world.

Bain's entry-limit principle of oligopoly[26] is grounded in observed fact rather than in *a priori* assumptions about behavior. It neatly demonstrates the upper limit to price when sellers adapt their price strategies to forestalling entry, that is, "long-run" maximization of joint profits.

The difficulties with this theory are stepped-down versions of the difficulties with the joint-maximum-profit solutions. Tacit collusion among sellers must solve the problem of interdependence, which requires a co-ordinating device except in the limiting case of the *Sylos postulate* mentioned in footnote 26. The entry-limiting price is a fact of the environment which each firm can recognize and on which each can base its own behavior. The practical obstacles to doing this are undoubtedly less than the obstacles to coordinating behavior through maximizing joint-profits, since the potential conflicts and divergence of interests among the established firms are less with respect to the objective of forestalling entry. Obstacles do exist, however. The theory does not predict results in those cases where tacit collusion or recognition of interdependence is not effective enough to keep actual

[25] Bain has aptly commented that this theory has ". . . shown us how to reach a Cournot duopoly solution the hard way." "Chamberlin's Impact on Microeconomic Theory" in R. Kuenne, ed., *Monopolistic Competition Theory: Studies in Impact* (New York: John Wiley & Sons, Inc., 1967), p. 165.

[26] The most recent version is in *Industrial Organization*, Second Edition, pp. 255–269, though previous formulations were published more than a decade earlier. (*Barriers to New Competition,* 1956.) The similar theory of P. Sylos-Labini in *Oligopoly and Technical Progress* (Cambridge: Harvard University Press, 1962) is based entirely on a restrictive assumption that potential entrants to an oligopolistic market act on the expectation that established firms will maintain their existing output while reducing price. Donald Farrar and Charles F. Phillips, Jr. have pointed out that this is very similar to Cournot's assumption. "New Developments on the Oligopoly Front: A Comment," *Journal of Political Economy,* LXVII (August 1959), 414–417. Bain deals with this case, but his analysis is not confined to it. See also F. Modigliani, "New Developments on the Oligopoly Front," *Journal of Political Economy,* LXVI (June 1958), Part VIII.

price up to the level that would just fail to induce entry. But the theory probably does apply to many "highly concentrated" industries, and this complements the analysis of their performance referred to earlier.

The hypothesis that firms try to maximize total revenues subject to a constraint of minimum profit — the "sales-maximization hypothesis" — is purely a principle of behavior, more specifically, of motivation, which does not purport to be a model of oligopolistic equilibrium.[27] The hypothesis has at least one foot in managerial economics, but its predictions could also embrace market equilibrium in oligopoly by incorporating appropriate assumptions about the minimum rate of return and the distribution of firms by size. If the rate-of-return constraint for established firms were determined by conditions of entry and the minimum size of the firm by economies of scale, as in one variant of Bain's model, the sales-maximization policy would result in a market equilibrium quite different from the joint-profits maximum.[28]

Highly developed behavioral models.   A highly developed behavioral approach to oligopoly stems from the branch of games theory that deals with games of mutual dependence, or nonzero-sum games. Prominent among the writings on this subject are those of T. C. Schelling.[29] They are extraordinarily fruitful of suggestions and insights into the nature of oligopolistic behavior. Two contributions stand out in particular: (1) Analysis of a bargaining *sequence,* which can have different results depending on the path it follows, seems to provide the key to explaining a number of loosely structured oligopolistic situations in which the firms could not plausibly reach a joint-monopoly solution, or indeed any kind of equilibrium, through static or "timeless" recognition of mutual interdependence. In a sequence of behavioral moves the firms may make threats, bluffs, tacit offers, and partial or total tacit commitments; they may offer or take hostages; and they

[27] William J. Baumol, *Economic Theory and Operations Analysis,* Second Edition (Englewood Cliffs, New Jersey: Prentice-Hall, Inc., 1965), pp. 301–304.

[28] A profit constraint resulting from an entry-forestalling price lower than the price that would yield maximum short-run profits suggests the possibility of a trade-off between a larger number of sellers operating at minimum average cost and a smaller number operating at the sales-maximizing output (subject to the profit constraint). Perhaps the latter is more effective for restraining entry in actual situations, since the potential entrant is unlikely to suppose that each established seller will reduce his share of the market in order to maintain prices. In either case a U-shaped long-run cost curve or some convention for limiting each firm's output is necessary for a definite group equilibrium. William G. Shepherd has shown that under oligopolistic interdependence, the sales-maximization assumption does not predict equilibrium for the market. Interdependence may generate a kinked-demand-curve reaction, producing results little or no different from profit maximization. "On Sales-Maximizing and Oligopoly Behavior," *Economica,* XXIX (November, 1962), 420–424.

[29] Thomas C. Schelling, *The Strategy of Conflict* (Cambridge: Harvard University Press, 1960). Most of Schelling's work concerns problems of strategy in other fields than the strictly economic one of oligopoly, but the analogies among the various fields of application are striking.

may engage in various kinds of communication or else refuse communications from others. Static-equilibrium solutions have no place for these attributes of behavior. (2) The analysis of convergence shows how various means of coordinating decisions without overt communication among the parties may appear in an oligopolistic market — how an environment which apparently contains little or no "information" actually provides signals for coordinating behavior. The past experience of firms with similar situations, or the long-standing use of a particular set of managerial policies,[30] may enter into such patterns of coordination along with the conventional structural attributes of a market.

Behavioral models and elements of market structure. In its present stage of development, the theory of mutual-dependence games does not yet yield the predictions of prices and outputs that we expect of an oligopolistic theory pretending to be universal. Equilibrium is entirely subordinated to behavioral mechanisms. The large variety of these mechanisms does, of course, correspond to reality in a wide sector of industrial organization, and they could be fitted into our analytical framework by linking them to attributes of structure. Whether maximin behavior is likely or unlikely; whether the bargaining situation favors convergence on a single solution or an unstable diffusion among conflicting bases of decision; whether firms can use positions or events in one market as levers to produce certain preferred results in others; whether threats are feasible and effective; and so forth, could be predicted from the more or less detailed facts of market structure outlined above on pages 9–10. This branch of oligopoly theory would then become a useful part of the structural-functional approach.

Two additional factors help explain observed results in oligopolistic markets. When we work backward from its behavioral analysis to structural configurations, we find that many market patterns require a consideration both of the past history of the markets and the firms in it, and at the internal organization and motivations of the oligopolistic suppliers. These two factors increase the danger of *ad hoc* theorizing about behavior, since both tend to be anecdotal or at any rate less capable of generalizing and testing for alternatives than the objective elements of structure already summarized. Yet they aid understanding. For example, it is not easy to see without reference to the industry's history why price leadership has held up so well in the steel industry during the post-war period. It is only on the borderline of "highly concentrated" industries, according to the most inclusive definition of that group. Although entry barriers to basic steel[31]

---

[30] Pricing formulas that are simple, stable, and appealing may produce such a convergence if the correct numbers can be communicated overtly or tacitly. Sometimes, of course, adverse structural circumstances can nullify or prevent emergence of a coordinating focus, as shown by the electrical equipment case discussed above.

[31] Including semi-finished steel, such as rolling mill products.

are undoubtedly substantial, the industry's success in keeping prices up to, or near, that barrier has been remarkable. Indeed, both relative prices and profitability moved up during the twenty years following World War II while the break-even point moved down. One would not have expected such tight discipline in an industry in which the largest four producers controlled 50 percent of output and the largest eight, 70 percent. U.S. Steel's output would not have been large enough in the late 1950's relative to the rest of the industry — 28–30 percent of total steel ingot production — to exercise dominant-firm leadership. Its position of authority was a relic of *past* dominance and of the habit of followership inculcated in other producers during the long years that U.S. Steel was the natural and authoritative price leader. The historical need for price discipline and the demonstrated benefits of dependable price leadership were graven in the memory of all steel executives. Other circumstances also strengthened leadership, such as the simplification of a pricing and mark-up formula based on steel wages after the labor market became unionized; bilateral oligopoly in factor markets often has this effect. The historical roots of structure are a necessary part of the explanation, however. Only after imports from sources not observing the domestic price policies or pattern of leadership began to invade the market did this leadership start to crumble.

The decline in U.S. Steel's position as a leader has been reinforced by changes in pricing largely provoked by public policy: substitution of pricing according to product classes for across-the-board pricing of all steel products. The former is, of course, much less amenable to control through tacit coordination of policies than the latter. The problem of "focus" has become much more difficult. Nevertheless, the leadership pattern persists in a somewhat eroded form.[32]

The second factor supplementing the standard structural elements that is sometimes useful in explaining observed behavior is the internal organization and motivation of firms. In the long run this factor is probably not of much significance: the ordinary profit motive and the pressure toward efficient organization will win out in most unregulated industries. On the other hand, it may be important in some short-run developments in concentrated oligopolies, precisely because they include only a few firms. With only a few firms, the adoptive mechanism of the market sometimes fails to work because there are not enough trials, and managerial idiosyncrasies can lead the industry in several "wrong" directions without immediate external check or feedback of corrective information. A single-firm monopoly can obviously do this; it is one reason why public utility commissions find it so difficult to control quality of performance by regulated monopolies. Perhaps an illustrative case from highly-concentrated oligopoly is the policy of the

---

[32] For analysis of the relations among prices, imports, and vertical integration, see Walter Adams and J. B. Dirlam, "Steel Imports and Vertical Oligopoly Power," *American Economic Review,* LIV (September, 1964), 626–655.

leading firms in the automobile industry in the late 1950's, a policy which prevented their detecting the shift in public taste — until the upsurge of imports woke them to the need for producing more compact and less expensive automobiles. The internal organization of the firm can also affect responses to the market's opportunities and shifting parameters. Managerial "satisficing" — the focusing on fulfillment of management's wants — can lead to different price-output responses than profit-maximizing, at least in the short run.[33] Decentralized organizations behave differently from centralized ones because of differences in attitudes and behavior of individual departments toward the central goals of the firm ("sub-optimizing responses") and differences in the internal flow of information.[34] And so on. These responses can even make a difference in the long run in concentrated industries if they have a feedback effect on structure itself, as they occasionally might — witness what happened in the soap industry and in civil aircraft manufacture as a result of some key managerial aberrations.[35] We normally expect that the environment itself will select profit-maximizing managers and force them to make efficient decisions, but contrary examples do occur. With the growth of large conglomerates that substitute in some degree internal organization for that of the market, the managerial organizational factors may become more significant in the behavior of oligopolistic industries.

Summary: Implications for Policy

Up to now, the study of industrial organization has followed two parallel paths instead of one that links structure, behavior, performance and ultimate norms in a single system. It has investigated the connections between structure and performance. These relationships are known, in part, on the basis of a fairly simple definition of structure, emphasizing concentration and entry conditions. It has also investigated the connections between structure and behavior. These relationships depend on a much more complex definition of structure, embracing a large range of possible configurations. The oligopolistic industries are the chief arena of interest in both lines of inquiry. Though theoretical models have been of some help in defining the relationships — the connection between structure and performance and the connection between structure and behavior — no single general model

[33] Williamson suggests that management shifts between managerial-satisficing goals and profit-maximizing goals ". . . as the environment alters between munificent and penurious conditions." "A Dynamic Stochastic Theory of Managerial Behavior" in *Prices: Issues in Theory, Practice, and Public Policy,* ed. Almarin Phillips and O. E. Williamson (Philadelphia: University of Pennsylvania Press, 1967), p. 28. "Sales-maximization" in its pure form could also be regarded as a kind of managerial goal.

[34] Alfred D. Chandler's *Strategy and Structure* (Cambridge: The M.I.T. Press, 1962) provides an excellent historical and analytical survey of the growth of large decentralized business organizations and the managerial role in their creation and use.

[35] This refers to the decisive change in the position of Lever Brothers in the late 1940's, and to the weakening of General Dynamics (Convair) in the 1960.

of oligopoly exists. Moreover, the available theory has not developed a definitive relationship between behavior and performance. The various oligopoly models seem to exhibit a kind of trade-off between behavior and equilibrium properties of the kind that measure allocative efficiency: the more they are concerned with explaining one, the less definite are their findings on the other.

Performance analysis has identified a group of industries whose profit performance indicates monopolistic distortions of optimum allocation of resources. The structural characteristics that produce this result are, principally, high concentration — the largest 8 sellers having over 70 percent of output or sales is one test of concentration — and entry barriers. If within this group we demarcate a more restricted group of very highly concentrated industries — for example, those with concentration ratios upwards of 80 percent for the largest 4 sellers — the entry-barriers test converges with the concentration criterion. It is in this group of industries that we are most likely to find the structural causes of monopoloid restrictions on allocative efficiency. As we move into lower ranges of concentration and entry barriers, performance becomes more "competitive" in nature, but behavior presents more complex patterns for explanation and analysis. This may be because tacit collusion for joint monopoly profits, or joint maintenance of the entry-forestalling price, becomes very unlikely below certain levels of concentration or entry barriers.

Of the two kinds of inquiry, that into performance and that into behavior, the former is doubtless the more important. The main problem of concern has been the circumstances of organization that produce good and bad performance when judged by some norms or other. Prescriptions of policy depend on such findings. Structure-performance analysis thus leads to a tentative conclusion that public policy should try to improve performance in the highly concentrated industries — including, but not limited to, those mentioned in the Appendix Table. If need be, public policy should try to reduce concentration sufficiently to bring performance within the acceptable range. If it cannot do that because economies of scale defeat the purpose, it should find a surrogate for market compulsion of good performance, such as public regulation.

This type of prescription for policy would find a good many adherents, among economists and others. The most concentrated industries in the economy are natural targets for antitrust action.[36] The general public sup-

---

[36] This view is supported by the "White House Task Force Report on Antitrust Policy" of July 5, 1968, released May 21, 1969. That report advocates legislation to permit legal proceedings against highly concentrated industries in order to reduce concentration by divestiture and other forms of relief. A concentrated or "oligopoly" industry is defined as a market in which any four or fewer firms have an aggregate market share of 70 percent or more during 7 of the last 10 years and 4 of the last 5 years, with certain supplementary tests. Such an antitrust law would set up a purely structural test beside the behavioral tests that now seem to be required by the Sherman Antitrust Act. See Bureau of National Affairs, *Antitrust & Trade Regulation Report* No. 411, Special Supplement, Part II, May 27, 1969.

ports this view for a variety of reasons, including economic ones. Economists who believe that another norm, progressiveness or technological innovation, has a value equal to allocative efficiency and that it is promoted by oligopoly might have reservations, but a remedial policy aiming simply at reducing concentration somewhat in the highly concentrated industries is not likely to dry up the wellsprings of innovation and may even stimulate them.

The findings reviewed above help us to identify correctly the industries whose structure and performance are likely to prove troublesome. They enable policy-makers to avoid a too-broad definition of structurally unsatisfactory markets.[37] Insofar as structural criteria are usable, they provide a useful guide for antitrust policy. But, in the United States at least, the antitrust laws focus on conduct rather than structure. Acts, rather than conditions, are offenses under the law. There are exceptions, such as the sanctions in the Public Utility Holding Company Act of 1935, but a principle of structural tests has not found its way into the general antitrust law, notwithstanding that many economists advocate such a principle. Nor does antitrust policy give much weight to tests for performance. The existing sanctions against price conspiracy, restrictive practices, and mergers having monopolistic effects do limit monopoly, but it is a policy of containment rather than correction of preexisting monopolistic structure. Moreover, the attitude of the law toward less clear-cut forms of conduct in oligopolistic industries is ambivalent at best, and often contradictory.

The weakness of the links in economic analysis between behavior and performance thus creates difficulties for a rational policy toward industrial organization. Public policy often proceeds with its judgments and sanctions of behavior without any guidance from economic science. Nor has research in industrial organization yet produced entirely satisfactory knowledge of the relations between structure and behavior, even though it has found how behavioral decisions by business firms are likely to be affected by certain key structural constraints. To prescribe alternatives to conduct that is

---

[37] The definitions in the Kaysen-Turner volume of "Type I oligopoly" (the first 8 firms have at least 50 percent of total market sales and the first 20 firms at least 75 percent) and "Type II oligopoly" (the largest 8 firms have at least 33 percent, while the rest of the market is unconcentrated) are at best ambiguous. Carl Kaysen and Donald F. Turner, *Antitrust Policy* (Cambridge: Harvard University Press, 1959), p. 27. The definition for Type I is justified on the basis that "recognition of interdependence by the leading firms is extremely likely." But the criterion seems too broad to predict monopolistic performance as a result of that recognition, while the structural criterion of Type II is so low that it hardly seems to qualify as oligopoly at all. However, Kaysen and Turner do not base their policy recommendations directly on these foundations. Instead, they suggest as one possible policy against unreasonable market power, that "Market power shall be conclusively presumed where, for five years or more, one company has accounted for 50 percent or more of annual sales in the market, or four or fewer companies have accounted for 80 percent of such sales." (P. 98.) These quantitative criteria are virtually the same as those used by Stigler, *supra*.

deemed unsatisfactory, economics needs to strengthen both its means of predicting performance from behavior and its knowledge of what structural alterations will do to behavioral patterns. A better understanding of market behavior — especially in oligopoly — is a principal mission of future research in industrial organization.

APPENDIX: THE HIGHLY CONCENTRATED INDUSTRIES

The industries in the Standard Industrial Classification, which are the building blocks for the statistical analyses described above, do not take account of imports nor of certain kinds of vertical integration, and they confuse market boundaries when establishments are grouped on the basis of inputs or processes and not on the basis of product similarity and substitutability. Firms reporting data on profits do not usually allocate them among products or markets. Some industries in the SIC are underaggregated from the point of view of the market analyst because they do not include important substitutes, while others are overaggregated because they include products sold in different markets. Either deviation can cause trouble for a statistical analysis that attempts to predict profit performance from data on concentration.

A rough indication of the extent of these difficulties in the Stigler version of high-concentration industries is given by the Appendix Table, which lists all of the 4-digit manufacturing industries that had largest-4 concentration ratios over 79 percent in 1963. Only a few of these industries fail to include important close substitutes. Thus cellulosic fibres (2823) and non-cellulosic organic fibres (2824) could substitute for each other, as well as for natural fibres outside the chemical group. Aluminum (3334) faces substitution from copper (which also has a high concentration ratio) in some uses, and from steel in others. Cereal preparations (2043) have limited substitutes, and hard-surface floor coverings (3982) face competition from carpets and rugs. The other 22 industries are pretty much self-contained, except that different basic fibres can find their way into tire cord and fabric (2296). On the other hand, some are doubtless overaggregated. Five-digit product groups are sometimes, though not always, better aggregates for defining a market than the 4-digit industries or the 4-digit product group constituting the primary products of an industry. The table shows the number of 5-digit classes in each 4-digit product group and the available concentration ratios in shipments of 4-digit primary product groups for comparison with the industry's concentration ratios in this select list. The 5-digit concentration ratios are not shown; in almost all cases they are higher than the 4-digit ratios.

Over half the industries have only one 5-digit group for their primary products, which at least hints that they are not overaggregated on the basis of products. The others can be split into 2 or more product classes having concentration ratios that are typically somewhat higher than the 4-digit ratio. A comparison of the concentration ratio for all shipments by establishments classified within the industry and the ratio for shipments of products primary to the industry reveals few major anomalies; the only noteworthy ones are in nonferrous forgings (3392) and household vacuum cleaners (3636). These differences

Appendix Table   The "Highly Concentrated" 4-Digit SIC Industries in 1963

Concentration Ratios for Largest 4 Sellers Over 79 percent

SIC Number	Name of Industry	Industry Concentration Ratio (Largest 4)	Primary Product Concentration Ratio (Largest 4)	Number of 5-Digit Product Classes in Industry[1]
2043	Cereal preparations	86%	82%	1
2073	Chewing gum	90	86	1
2111	Cigarettes	80	D[2]	1
2296	Tire cord and fabric	79	71	1
2814	Cyclic (coaltar) crudes	D[2]	95	1
2823	Cellulosic man-made fibers	82	79	2
2824	Organic fibers, noncellulosic	94	D[2]	2
3031	Reclaimed rubber	93	73	1
3211	Flat glass	94	NA	4
3275	Gypsum products	84	82	3
3332	Primary lead	D[2]	D[2]	2
3334	Primary aluminum	D[2]	93	2
3392	Nonferrous forgings	84	56	1
3492	Safes and vaults	D[2]	D[2]	1
3511	Steam engines and turbines	93	83	2
3624	Carbon and graphite products	83	82	1
3635	Household vacuum cleaners	81	64	1
3636	Sewing machines	D[2]	82	1
3641	Electric lamps	92	89	1
3661	Telephone and telegraph apparatus	92	D[2]	3
3671	Electron tubes, receiving types	87	83	1
3672	Cathode ray picture tubes	91	81	1
3692	Primary batteries, dry and wet	89	83	1
3717	Motor vehicles and parts	79	NA	8
3723	Aircraft propellers and parts	D[2]	87	1
3741	Locomotives and parts	97	92	1
3982	Hard-surface floor coverings	87	85	3

Source: U.S. Bureau of the Census, *Concentration Ratios in Manufacturing Industry*, 1963 (Washington: U.S. Government Printing Office, 1966).

[1] Number of 5-digit product classes among products primary to the industry.

[2] Figures withheld to avoid disclosure of information for individual sellers, but almost certainly over 80 percent.

338 In2m
c. 1

arise from low specialization, low coverage, or skewness in the product-mix among large and small establishments, or from all three characteristics. The lower product-concentration ratio for these two industries would lead us to expect a more competitive performance in them than the industry-concentration ratio predicts.

A number of industries with concentration ratios well under 80 percent have buried in them product classes with ratios over 80 percent. There are about 84 5-digit product classes in 4-digit industries *not* included among the highly-concentrated ones in the Table that had concentration ratios over 79 percent for the largest 4 sellers in 1963. Added to the 5-digit classes included in the Table that have concentration ratios over 79 percent, there are in this highly-concentrated category about 130 out of a total of 1,318 5-digit product groups in manufacturing — some 10 percent of the total. To the extent that these classes are economic "industries" with monopoloistic profits, they undoubtedly create difficulties for statistical tests of the hypothesis when the tests use only 4-digit ratios and data on profits. If the relationship did indeed hold, it could be verified for those product classes as well if the principal producers could be identified and their sales and profit figures allocated to product groups. Examples are baking powder and yeast (20994), acetylene (28132), synthetic organic detergents, packaged (28415), razor blades and razors except electric (34212), vacuum and insulated bottles, jugs and chests (34293), and photographic sensitized film and plates (38615). These are probably closer to economic "industries" than the 4-digit SIC industries that contain them, and their general properties would lead the observer to expect a considerable departure from competitive performance in them. Unfortunately, most of the relevant Census data and profit figures are available only for 4-digit industries at best. The problem becomes more troublesome as large firms become more conglomerate.

2

Structure, Conduct, and Performance — and Performance, Conduct, and Structure?

*Almarin Phillips**

I. Introduction

More than three decades ago, Edward S. Mason provided a challenge to economists interested in problems of microeconomic analysis. "[I]f economics is to put itself in a position to contribute to the formulation of public policy," he wrote, "it must conceive the monopoly problem in a more extensive way than is at present customary. It is not enough to find evidence of the existence of market controls, nor is it sufficient to conduct purely analytical and descriptive studies of various types of control situations. While this is important, the formulation of public policy requires a distinction between situations and practices which are in the public interest and those which are not . . . A further study of different types of industrial markets and business practices and of the effects on prices, outputs, investment and employment designed to indicate means of distinguishing between socially desirable and undesirable situations . . . is . . . the only way in which economics can contribute directly to the shaping of public policy."[1]

The challenge was accepted. The "different types" of markets covered by the studies came to be classified within the general heading *market structure.* "Business practices" were enumerated under the heading *market conduct;* "effects on prices, outputs," and so forth, under the label *market perform-*

* University of Pennsylvania

[1] E. S. Mason, "Monopoly in Law and Economics" *Yale Law Journal* (November 1937), p. 49.

ance. And, indeed, economists using the technique suggested by Professor Mason have had an effect on policy.

It is not the intention of this paper to gainsay the usefulness of the structure-conduct-performance approach to antitrust problems. It is its intention, however, to point to severe limitations of the approach in the context of the full gamut of current microeconomic problems. It is also its intention to suggest a more complete and closed schema of markets within which to view the interactions among structural, behavioral, and performance variables. Section II has been written to show the dominance in most present work on industrial organization of what is conceptually a narrow approach in terms of structure, conduct, and performance. Section III deals with some generally ignored relations between performance and conduct; section IV, with some equally disregarded relations between performance and structure. The fifth section discusses a number of other hypotheses and their relations to the structure-conduct-performance approach.

II.   *The Structure-Conduct-Performance Tradition*

The structure-conduct-performance tradition in industrial organization has been strongly affected by simple and static microeconomic theory. Indeed, one might say that the corpus of the dominant analytic method in studies of industrial organization is nothing more than a naive, Cournot-like model of a market. First, a specific structure is assumed to exist. In Cournot's duopoly case, this is two sellers of a homogeneous product, each with adequate capacity to meet total market demand. Cournot implicitly assumed that entry was barred. Second, a mode of sellers' behavior is hypothesized. In the Cournot case, each seller is assumed to set his own output so as to maximize profits under the condition that the other seller's output will be unaffected by the decision. Third, implicitly or explicitly, the market's technology and conditions of input are specified so as to yield cost functions. In the better-known of the Cournot models, zero costs are assumed. Finally, a demand function is assumed. In the Cournot case, demand is taken as a simple, linear function of price. From these assumptions, market performance is deduced. In Cournot's case, the resulting output is $\frac{n}{n+1} (X_c)$, where n is the number of firms and X_c is the zero-priced output of a competitive equilibrium.

The similarity between this approach and the method of industrial organization is quite clear. As Joe Bain expresses it, "[W]e look initially to the characteristics of market structure and of market conduct as primary determinants of the market performance of enterprises, or of groups or industries of business firms."[2] Richard Caves gives a somewhat different variant

[2] J. S. Bain, *Industrial Organization,* second edition (1968), p. 3.

of the same theme: "Market structure is important because the structure determines the behavior of firms in the industry, and that behavior in turn determines the quality of the industry's performance."[3]

Viewed in generality, this is a naive, Cournot-like approach. In such a fully open system, exogenously determined industrial structure and conduct, along with exogenously given technology and demand, determine performance. Nothing about the latter, it seems, including possible reactions by entrepreneurs to their achievements in the existing structure-conduct-performance complex, leads to their adaptively responding so as to alter either conduct or structure.

The mode of analysis is not limited to economists. The courts — perhaps less fully — have also come to judge the social desirability of particular market structures or particular forms of conduct in terms of the inferred effects on performance.[4] Overt agreements to fix prices or market shares have, of course, been held to be per se illegal for many years. As Mason has noted, such rules make "economic sense when, and only when, the facts — i.e., the market situation or course of conduct complained of — permit a legitimate inference as to the effects."[5] There was also a period following the *Alcoa* and *American Tobacco* decisions when, in addition to overt agreements, homogeneous oligopoly appeared very close to being considered presumptively or even per se illegal.[6] Although this view of monopolization may have waned in the intervening years, present merger policy does rest on the view that increasing market concentration is very likely to be the cause of socially less desirable market performance.[7] All these illustrations involve a simple line of causation from structure and conduct to the determination of performance.

That performance can be inferred with confidence from knowledge of structure and conduct is, nonetheless, rather uniformly denied in all save the

[3] R. E. Caves, *American Industry: Structure, Conduct, Performance*, second edition (1967), p. 17.

[4] This has been true for some time. E. S. Mason, "The Current Status of the Monopoly Problem in the United States," *Harvard Law Review* (June 1949), observed that "the courts have moved a substantial distance in the direction of accepting the presence or absence of the market conditions associated with the notion of workable competition as appropriate tests. On all four of the important desiderata, number of firms, share of the market, collusion and the conditions of entry, previous doctrine has been altered or extended."

[5] E. S. Mason, "Market Power and Business Conduct: Some Comments on the Report of the Attorney General's Committee on Antitrust Policy," *American Economic Review* (May 1956), p. 476.

[6] For a discussion of such views, see J. B. Dirlam and A. E. Kahn, *Fair Competition* (1954), pp. 30–31, 70–71.

[7] Perhaps the clearest statement is in *United States* v. *Philadelphia National Bank*, 374 U.S. 321 (1963). "Specifically, we think that a merger which produces a firm controlling an undue percentage share of the relevant market, and results in a significant increase in the concentration of firms in that market, is so inherently likely to lessen competition substantially that it must be enjoined in the absence of evidence clearly showing that the merger is not likely to have such anticompetitive effects . . ."

polar and static cases of pure competition and pure monopoly. Carl Kaysen and Donald Turner, for example, acknowledge that, "In practice our analytic apparatus is inadequate to the task of providing such correlations in the study of actual markets . . . We can neither predict market performance from market structure, nor can we tell from structure alone how competitive the processes of the market are."[8] Such confessions of inadequacy have as yet had little impact on the development of extensions to, or alternatives for, the structure-conduct-performance tradition.

III. Performance and Conduct

The Cournot model has been widely criticized — largely for its lack of realism. If in the duopolistic solution each firm accumulates profits at a rate only four-ninths of the monopoly rate, why do they not combine or collude with respect to price and output so that each would receive one-half of the monopoly rate? If the monopoly (or duopoly, and so forth) rate is above the competitive rate, why does entry not occur? If, in the process of reaching the Cournot equilibrium, each firm repeatedly discovers its assumption concerning the response of the other to its moves is incorrect, why does it not learn therefrom and assume more "realistic" patterns of behavior?

These questions suggest a theoretical system very different from that of the Cournot model. In one phase of the suggested system, structure and conduct are determinants of performance; in another phase, they are themselves determined by performance. That is, the system views market conduct and market structure as at least partially the result of adaptive response by firms to their existing conditions and perceived alternatives.

A rapid examination of a simple system of this type may be helpful. Adopting from, and expanding on, March and Simon,[9] S is defined as the level of satisfaction deriving from the profits accruing to, and distributed among, a set of oligopolistic firms, and $\bar{S}$ is the desired or "satisficing" level of S.[10] Aspired profits are denoted by A. The profits perceived as flowing from the system, given its conditions at any time, are R; and L is the rate (or time and money costs) of search for alternative (and mutually acceptable) rules of conduct. E is the "friendliness" of the firms' environment, and $\bar{N}$ is taken as a shift parameter reflecting fully exogenous environmental conditions. With this nomenclature, the hypothesized relations are:

[8] C. Kaysen and D. F. Turner, *Antitrust Policy* (1959), pp. 60–61.

[9] See J. G. March and H. A. Simon, *Organizations* (1958), pp. 48–50, where a four-equation model of adaptive response, apparently representing the behavior of a group of employees, is given.

[10] A "satisficing" rather than a maximizing form has been chosen because of the difficulties of achieving full joint-profit maximization in oligopolistic situations. The "satisficing" approach may conceptually be viewed as limited joint-profit maximization in the Fellner sense.

(1) $$\frac{dA}{dt} = f(R - A), \text{ where } \frac{\partial\left(\frac{dA}{dt}\right)}{\partial(R - A)} > 0$$

(2) $$S = R - A$$

(3) $$L = F(\overline{S} - S), \text{ where } S > 0, \frac{\partial(L)}{\partial(\overline{S} - S)} > 0$$

(4) $$\frac{dR}{dt} = \Phi(L, E), \text{ where } \frac{\partial\left(\frac{dR}{dt}\right)}{\partial L} \geq 0, \frac{\partial\left(\frac{dR}{dt}\right)}{\partial E} > 0$$

(5) $$E = \Psi(N, L), \text{ where } \frac{\partial E}{\partial L} \geq 0.$$

The structure of the oligopoly — the number of firms, their relative sizes, conditions of entry, and the like — is taken as given at this point, though it would be preferable expressly to include structural variables. As explained below, different functional forms will be involved with different structural conditions.

According to equation (1), aspired profits tend to rise as the difference between the profits perceived as coming from the current state of the system and currently aspired profits increases. In other words, the aspirations of the oligopolists adapt to their circumstances. Equation (2) posits that the levels of their satisfactions at any time depend directly on the difference between expected profits and aspired profits. Search for new rules of conduct, according to equation (3), is a direct function of the difference between the "satisficing" and the actual level of achievements. More (less) search occurs as actual satisfactions fall short of (exceed) the "satisficing" level. Conduct, in this sense, is a function of the system's performance. Equation (4) states that perceived profits change over time as a function of search and the demand environment. As stated, search is restricted to types of conduct that have no negative effects on profit levels — with rational managers in the system, a sort of long-run necessary condition for search. Increases in the "friendliness" of the environment, E, cause increases in profits. Finally, equation (5) ties profits to the environment and to factors in the state of nature outside the system, that is, constraints deriving from the tastes and incomes of consumers and constraints on behavior imposed by the government. As formulated, the firms may be able through search to find rules of conduct which will tend to make the environmental factors less restrictive. These might pertain, for example, to activities in sales promotion. They might also, however, take the form of activities aimed at altering the nature of the government's constraints.

It should be noted that performance as viewed by the oligopolists in this system is not valued in the same way as it is in traditional welfare economics. At least in terms of the price and output dimensions of performance, moves away from the monopolistic price-output combination and toward the competitive one would be viewed as deteriorations in performance by the oligopolists and as improvements in performance from a welfare standpoint. Although the latter view may affect governmental constraints on behavior, it is performance as viewed by the firms that determines their search for changes in conduct.

Oliver E. Williamson has developed a dynamic theory about the collusiveness of oligopolists, a theory that is within the general class of models indicated above.[11] His model offers, among other things, explanations of the oscillatory nature of collusive agreements in terms of shifting environmental conditions. Collusive behavior with respect to price is far from the entire picture, however. The more general argument advanced here is that conduct — taken very generally — is functionally related, though not fully determined, by market performance and by the achievements of firms within the confines of that performance.

Aside from price-fixing and market-sharing agreements, what other forms of conduct may be involved? Look at some of the better known cases. In the bituminous coal industry of the late 1920's and early 1930's, such things as joint advertising and research, establishment of uniform grades of coal, and the common classification of wholesale and retail customers were as much a direct response to the performance of the market as was the creation of joint selling agencies.[12] So, too, it should be emphasized, was the Bituminous Coal Conservation Act. Search for privately policed rules of conduct which would remedy low levels of achievement failed; policing by the state was then found to be a possible alternative.

In the more recent history of the industry, agreements between the major operators and the United Mine Workers — whether or not a violation of the antitrust laws — seem clearly to be an adaptive response in conduct flowing directly from threats to achievements caused by the smaller and often nonunionized mines.[13] The list is easy to lengthen. For example, consider the increasing formality in price formation in steel from the period of informal price leadership, to the Gary Dinners, to the use of the basing point pricing system. Each shift in conduct followed depressions or the development of internal modes of conduct which lowered the firms' achievements. But there are less obvious examples. Why are nuts and bolts standardized by types and threads? Why might fire extinguisher manufacturers agree on models with common characteristics? Why should milk distributors press for legislation defining the maximum butterfat content as well as the minimum prices for various grades of milk? Why did cigarette manufacturers establish a cancer research program in the early 1960's? Why did the major refiners of gasoline, beginning many years ago, com-

[11] O. E. Williamson, "A Dynamic Theory of Interfirm Behavior," *Quarterly Journal of Economics* (November 1965).

[12] *Appalachian Coals, Inc. v. United States,* 288 U.S. 344 (1933).

[13] *United Mine Workers v. Pennington,* 381 U.S. 657 (1967).

monly behave so as virtually to eliminate the multiple-brand "split-pump" stations? Why do steel companies bargain as a unit with United Steel Workers? Why do airlines form profit-sharing pools between struck carriers and those not struck?

It is submitted that all these responses emanate from search instigated because of aspects of market performance — an explanation that seems obvious, yet one that tends to be ignored. Two additional illustrations may help make this point. The first concerns John Kenneth Galbraith's "theory of countervailing power"; the second, exemptions from the antitrust law.

When Galbraith advanced the notion of countervailing power, one reaction was to pass it off as simply a verbal exposition of the static theory of bilateral monopoly.[14] It is not that at all. What Galbraith has observed is that, when some groups in society — farmers and workers, for instance — find their rewards low relative to those perceived to flow from alternative behavioral arrangements, the low achievements cause them to search for means to institute new modes of conduct or to search for new organizational forms. The *end* of the process may be bilateral monopoly, but the process itself is a feedback from market performance to either conduct or structure. Galbraith, it seems, claimed too much concerning the social value of the process, but he was describing a system of dynamic, adaptive response that was not a part of the then current body of static theory.

The second illustration concerns so-called exemptions from antitrust, which economists with specialties in antitrust matters often regard as anomalies. In its regulation of conduct, antitrust law attempts to prevent privately established and privately enforced codes of behavior which tend, according to the traditional view, to affect performance in socially adverse ways. Many of the legal exemptions from antitrust permit or enforce behavior of precisely the sort antitrust attempts to stop. In both cases, however, the behavior of firms can be better understood when viewed as adaptive responses.

For reasons that will become clearer in the next section, the legal exemptions have tended to occur in markets in which structure and conduct produce low levels of achievement for participating enterprises. They have tended to occur where — in terms of equations (4) and (5), above — the responsiveness of the environment and of profits to search for privately sanctioned rules of conduct is essentially zero and where the structure of the market cannot easily become more concentrated in short periods of time. That is, viewed in a more complete system, exemptions are the vehicles which mitigate competitive performance in one set of industries; privately established rules of conduct or concentrated market structures (or some combination of the two) which produce less competition do the same thing

[14] See for example, G. J. Stigler, "The Economist Plays With Blocs," *American Economic Review* (May 1954), p. 7.

in another set. In both sets, the results derive from the feedbacks from performance.[15]

IV. Performance and Structure

There are also relations between performance and structure in addition to those inherent in the traditional structure-conduct-performance triad. As suggested above, these relations are intertwined with the relations between performance and conduct. It was because of such interrelations that it was necessary to assume that structural variables were given in the description of the model presented in the previous section.

What sort of tenable hypotheses are there concerning the ways in which the functions in the behavioral model may be associated with structure?[16] Consider a simple structural variable, the number of firms. With a large number of firms, *ceteris paribus, each* would be likely to view $\partial E/\partial L$, from equation (5), as being less than is the case where the number of firms is small. This situation is partly because the larger number of firms implies, given market demand, that each is smaller in relation to its environment and hence less able to influence it by independent action. It is partly because cohesive group action that might favorably affect the environment is more difficult as the group becomes larger.[17] Firms which fail to cohere may obtain larger short-term benefits than do those which do cohere. In other words, "cheating" pays. At the same time the firms which fail to cohere may undermine the efforts of other firms to improve the nature of the environment.

In equation (4), dR/dt is likely to be of a different order of magnitude, given other factors, when the number of firms is large than when the number is small. It follows from the comments immediately above that, as E depends on L, the effects from E may be less. More directly, each firm would probably view search for alterations in conduct as less productive when the number of firms was large than when it was small. One reason for this is the problem of "internalizing" the rewards. A larger number of firms implies smaller market shares; smaller market shares mean, for example, that independent search yielding a more beneficial environment does so with less absolute return to the responsible firm because the firm receives benefits

---

[15] In terms of what might be called *ad hoc* second-best theorizing, it may be argued that the exemptions tend to increase welfare by creating for the exempted markets ratios of marginal cost to price closer to those of the nonexempted markets than would otherwise prevail. Is Congress wiser than has been thought in its policy of exemptions?

[16] Williamson, *op. cit.* takes into account the influence of structure. It remains, however, an area in which more work should be done to put changes in structural variables into a formal dynamic model of markets.

[17] On this point, see my *Market Structure, Organization and Performance* (1961), pp. 29–30, and Williamson, *op. cit.,* p. 600 fn. 3.

more or less in proportion to its market share.[18]   Another reason is that, where the number of participants is large, it is more difficult — more costly — to find and achieve a new mode of conduct which will improve profits.

A possible result of this situation is that equation (3) may be different when the number of firms is large than when it is small. Given the difference between actual and satisfactory profits, as well as other variables in the system, less search for alternative rules of conduct may occur as the number of firms increases. It must be emphasized, however, that stated in this partial form, the hypothesis has not taken into consideration the effects of differences in profit levels between the cases of large and small numbers of firms. Following from equation (3), firms in the markets with large numbers of firms and low profits may search very extensively. On the other hand, if L proves over time to be particularly nonproductive, there are behavioral hypotheses suggesting that $\overline{S}$ and A — satisfactory achievements and aspired profits — may themselves fall as individuals become resigned to the niggardliness and nonresponsiveness of their circumstances.[19]   This type of behavior, of course, would alter the basic form of the system.

The number of firms is only one of various structural considerations. Its effect on the functional forms in the model seems reasonably straightforward and, indeed, this factor might be explicitly added to the system. An additional equation showing entry and exit as behavioral responses to level of performance would be all that is necessary. It is less obvious that such structural variables as concentration (or, in this context, asymmetries in the distribution of power among firms) and the degree of product homogeneity could as easily be incorporated. These variables do, however, affect things like the ease of achieving adherence to behavioral codes, and so forth.

In a fully developed version of such a dynamic system, some aspects of structural response to performance would be essentially substitutes for certain responses in conduct. For example, the low levels of achievement and, by most standards, the socially good performance associated with the structural and behavioral conditions of competitive markets could be altered by the adoption of new rules of conduct — a price-fixing conspiracy, for instance — or by a change in market structure — a series of mergers, for instance.[20]   Which is "best" from the view of the firms will depend on the constraints of the environment — antitrust consequences, for example; the costs and benefits of the alternatives; and the time distribution of the costs

---

[18] This assumes, of course, that the market is defined to include only firms whose products are substitutes so that they have a common demand environment.

[19] On such behavior, see N.R.F. Maier, *Frustration* (1949).

[20] Thus, while structure remains relevant in considering the competitiveness of markets in which public regulation imposes constraints on conduct, its effects will be different depending on the nature of the regulation. It seems to follow that the doctrine that "Immunity from the antitrust laws is not lightly implied" is correct only if interpreted to mean that the effects of structure and conduct are simultaneously analyzed.

and benefits. Price-fixing may typically be a short-term response to low achievements; mergers, a longer-term response.

A complete and succinct analysis of the conditions required for stability and of the paths to equilibrium of such a system under its many possible situations appears difficult. There are, however, two polar types of equilibria which, absent special governmental intervention, typify cases in the real world. One is that underlying the frequently observed stability in oligopolistic markets. As seen in the model given here, the "concentration movements" leading to these structures and the development by the involved firms of common conduct in pricing and sales promotion are the results of feedbacks from performance. They occur until a combination of structure and "acceptable" rules of conduct has arisen which, with entry barriers incorporated, places the firms in a relatively high achievement, quasi-monopolistic equilibrium. Once there, it might be noted, the group of firms is largely immune from antitrust prosecution under current law despite the on-going social consequences of the structure-conduct combination with respect to allocating resources. It might also be noted that for these firms managerial theories of behavior seem appropriate. The firms are at peace with their environment.[21]

The opposite pole of the observable equilibria is one with low levels of achievements for firms. The inability of firms to find behavioral rules which will at once raise the achievements of existing firms and bar the entry of new ones is primarily responsible for the performance. To the extent that antitrust laws prevent overt price-fixing agreements, entry-preventative conduct, and mergers among firms with small market shares, the laws contribute to a very obvious discrimination in the totality of competitive policy. Ethical judgments stemming from this discrimination and the differences in levels of achievement by firms in the two sets seem incontrovertibly to be the reason why requests for exemptions from antitrust policies are so often granted.[22]

V. *Other Matters Briefly Noted*

It has been argued that the objective of Galbraith's theory of countervailing power fit well within this general, interdependent and dynamic view of relations among structure, conduct, and performance. Whether the countervailing occurs through responsive adaptations in the conduct or in the structural aspects of the system, the theory can be seen as a part of a largely endogenous market system.

---

[21] On this, see O. E. Williamson, "A Dynamic Stochastic Theory of Managerial Behavior" and A. Phillips, "An Attempt to Synthesize Some Theories of the Firm," in *Prices: Issues in Theory, Practice and Public Policy,* Phillips and Williamson, (eds.) (1967), pp. 12 and 35, respectively.

[22] Might it not be better to strike at the opposite side?

The same generalization is true of a number of other variants of market theory. The theory of purely competitive markets — in a slightly dynamic cloak — is nothing but the naive Cournot model, with a large number of firms and with the feedbacks from performance restricted to capacity adjustments by existing firms and entry by new ones.[23] Chamberlinian monopolistic competition — and it is different from imperfect competition in this respect — adds dimensions of conduct. Thus, product differentiation and sales-promotion activities are considered along with price and output. Interestingly, however, Chamberlin retained just the same feedbacks from performance as are in the competitive model. Capacity adjustments and entry are covered; performance-responsive changes in product differentiation and sales promotion are not.

Schumpeter's theories can also be considered in terms of these arguments. Innovation in *The Theory of Economic Development* came as entrepreneurs "shocked" an existing competitive equilibrium by introducing a new product or process which had originated from the exogenous activities of inventors. But in *Capitalism, Socialism and Democracy,* the process is portrayed as endogenous. Large firms, operated by highly rationalized rules, innovate by organizing their research and development activities in a manner which is adaptive to variations in achievement and performance. In this system, innovation is added as a behavioral dimension which is itself at least partially determined by the performance of the market system.

Theories of entry-preventative behavior can be encompassed in this framework.[24] As Williamson has shown, limit price is a function, among other things, of such variables as wages and sales promotion.[25] Thus, fully considered, prices, wages and advertising can be seen as behavioral variables which not only directly affect performance and the achievements of firms, but also alter the feedbacks to entry and, hence, to market structure.

Finally, the analysis of regulation could be done in the same general framework. Stigler has argued that regulatory agencies are responsive to the objectives of those being regulated.[26] There are numerous instances in which it is clear that regulation has come about in the first instance because of the failure of firms to accomplish their own goals rather than because of their failure to perform in a socially beneficial way. Regulation may be viewed, then, as an adaptive response from performance — private response by firms or social response to firms or some mixture of the two. Additional

[23] Cournot, of course, extended the duopoly case to the competitive one in Chapter 8 of *Researches.*

[24] F. Modigliani, "New Developments on the Oligopoly Front," *Journal of Political Economy* (June 1958) is an extraordinarily good presentation of these theories.

[25] O. E. Williamson, "Selling Expenses as a Barrier to Entry," *Quarterly Journal of Economics* (February 1963) and "Wage Rates as a Barrier to Entry," *Quarterly Journal of Economics* (February 1968).

[26] G. J. Stigler and C. Friedland, "What Can Regulators Regulate? The Case of Electricity," *Journal of Law and Economics* (October 1962).

analysis of regulation, with attention to which of the structural and behavioral dimensions are regulated and which are not and to the concomitant
effects on performance and achievements might well be profitable.

VI. Conclusions

The formulation of public policy, as Mason noted, does indeed depend on
analysis leading to distinctions "between situations and practices which are
in the public interest and those which are not." It has been argued here that
industrial organization has fallen into a mold which prevents it from taking
the steps needed to fulfill the declared objective. One guess about why information on static conditions of structure and conduct has not been capable
of predicting performance is that the information has been used in an incomplete theoretical framework . Performance leads back to changes in structure
and conduct. Without consideration of the more complete and endogenous
relations among these variables, predictions covering any significant periods
of time are quite likely to be wrong.

3

The Comparative Stability
of Market Structures

*Joe S. Bain**

During the last twenty years, and especially in the latter part of the 1960's, a considerable number of economists have published the results of statistical tests — referring to private industries, markets, and even individual firms — for the association of market structure and market performance. Single-equation multiple regressions have typically been employed, most frequently with some measure of profit as the dependent variable and with some set of aspects of market structure, or proxies therefor, as the independent variables. Results have varied; but the preponderance of statistical experiments has found significant, though often weak, associations of structure and performance, as opposed to "no significant association." One typical, if not universal, characteristic of the a priori hypotheses tested in these experiments is that the dominant attributes of market structure used as independent variables are viewed as being, over substantial time periods, "comparatively immutable" determinants of market performance.

The general purpose of this essay is to appraise, from an a priori standpoint and empirically, the comparative stability over time of market structures, and then to consider the effects of any instability in market structures on experiments that test for structure-performance relations. First, however, it seems advisable to "clear the underbrush" of two fundamental issues involving a priori hypotheses to be tested — issues frequently left unresolved as econometric work proceeds.

Clearing Some Underbrush

Mason's hypothesis. The major impetus to the statistical experiments mentioned above seems to have come from the germinal work of Edward S.

* University of California, Berkeley

Mason, who during the 1930's in his classes, and in print in 1939,[1] advanced the general proposition that the performance of a firm was largely explained by the structure of the market in which it operated — and in fact that there was something like a deterministic association between market structure and performance. A little later I shall say more concerning the details of this proposition.

Debate over Mason's hypothesis. The first piece of "underbrush" to be considered is whether or not a deterministic association between market structure and performance is to be expected a priori. On this point, Mason encountered a forceful opponent in the person of Edwin G. Nourse, who had been approaching the question of the determinants of market performance from quite a different angle[2] It was one of Nourse's contentions that there was, or should be, substantially no deterministic association between market structure and performance. Rather, the idiosyncrasies of managers or managements were the dominant determinants of performance, regardless of market structures. Nourse went on to suggest that the idiosyncrasies of managers were systematically linked with their earlier occupational experiences. For example, Wall Street bankers would tend to follow quite different, and more conservative, price and related policies than would managers who had risen from production lines in manufacturing. This formulation further implied that there was more than one solution to a profit-maximizing problem, depending on the risk-aversion propensities of individual managers, and that the variance in solutions potentially overwhelmed associations of performance with market structure. Concerning the alleged attitudes of the manager who rose from the production line, we also seem to find the first seeds of the sales-maximization hypothesis.

Some debate between Mason and Nourse over the issue described above (the content of which is firmly imbedded in my notes of the time) is recalled by one of the principals thereto, but I have been unable to discover it in print. In any event, nobody won the debate, largely because it was on an a priori level and about ten years before the first statistical test of Mason's hypothesis appeared. In retrospect, we can say first that, if Nourse had been absolutely right, a lot of subsequent econometric experiments would have been conducted substantially to no point. Second, Mason's basic hypothesis has been confirmed to a considerable extent by such experiments. Third, if Mason and Nourse were both partly right — if, for example, there were a systematic and significant, but not strictly deterministic,

---

[1] E. S. Mason, "Price and Production Policies of Large-Scale Enterprise," *The American Economic Review,* Vol. XXXIX Suppl. 1939. Reprinted in A.E.A., *Readings in Industrial Organization and Public Policy,* ed., Heflebower and Stocking, (1958), pp. 190–204.

[2] See especially E. G. Nourse and H. B. Drury, *Industrial Price Policies and Economic Progress* (Washington, 1938) and E. G. Nourse, *Price Making in a Democracy,* (Washington, 1944).

association between structure and performance and if managerial idiosyncrasy also played quite a role — this circumstance would help explain the large amount of "statistical static" typically encountered in experiments relating structure to performance.

The possibility of applying statistical tests to Mason's hypothesis. The second piece of "underbrush," not wholly unrelated to the first, is the issue of whether or not the attributes of market structure that in Mason's system supposedly influence or determine market performance are few enough to make Mason's original hypothesis conceivably susceptible to statistical test — as in a cross-sectional analysis of industries. If, after all, the number of attributes of market structure is very large for any firm, statistical testing goes out the window. Nearly every industry or class of firms is then structurally unique in some respect (has a distinctive "mix" of significant structural attributes) and cross-sectional testing becomes unproductive. Every individual firm or industry becomes a case automatically self-explained by its singular total market structure or environment. In this event, the explanation of performances in terms of structures becomes at best an heuristic exercise, industry by industry, with no generalizations really in sight. That the original Mason hypothesis should have begun with this hidden blight is probably attributable to the fact that, when he propounded it, research in the nascent field of industrial organization centered on studying individual industries rather than on cross-sectional econometric experiments.

To trace the progress of the germinal Masonian doctrine, let us cite a few quotations. In his 1939 article, mentioned above,[3] when referring to the Chamberlinian model, he commented that

> ... The only part of that foundation which is likely to be found useable is composed of the ascertainable facts of numbers of sellers (and buyers) and product differentiation.[4]

To which he added:

> At least in the industrial area, the market, and market structure, must be defined with reference to the position of a single seller or buyer. *The structure of a seller's market, then, includes all those considerations which he takes into account in determining his business policies and practices. His market includes all buyers and sellers, of whatever produce, whose action he considers to influence his volume of sales.*[5]

And finally:

> The classification of market structures on the seller's side consists, then, in grouping together those firms, in whatever industry, which operate

[3] Mason, *op. cit.*, p. 195 in *Readings.*
[4] *Ibid.*, p. 195.
[5] *Ibid.*, p. 198. Italics added.

under the same or similar objective conditions. Among these conditions are the economic characteristics of the product; is it a producers or consumers good, is it durable or non-durable, is the product of an individual seller differentiated with respect to the products of other sellers in the same market or is it standardized? Another group of conditions relate to the cost and production characteristics of the firm's operation. The ratio of overhead to variable costs at given volumes of output and for given variations in volume of output, the flexibility of costs, locational factors, and the existence of joint costs are all important. A third class of considerations has to do with the numbers and relative sizes of buyers and sellers of whose action our given seller has to take account and with the relative ease of entry for new firms. Among the demand conditions which are empirically determinable may be mentioned the trend of sales, seasonal and cyclical fluctuations in sales, and, roughly, the knowledge possessed by buyers with respect to the quality and characteristics of the product. Differences in distribution channels provide another set of conditions of great importance for the policies and practices of a firm. The accurate specification and measurement of these and other market conditions with respect to an individual firm admittedly presents great, but not insuperable, difficulties. Properly used the available data should permit of an illuminating grouping of firms into classes exhibiting roughly the same type of market conditions. Under similar market conditions may not firms be expected to pursue similar policies and practices? A careful study of the empirically determinable differences in market structure may go far in explaining observable differences in policy and practice.[6]

This formulation of the Mason hypothesis was, and is, both stimulating and thought-provoking, however much tied to a view that research in the newly created field of industrial organization should center on individual firms or classes thereof. Regarding Mason's suggested grouping of firms into classes with roughly the same type of market structure, we tend to stumble on the same rock mentioned above on page 40. If we introduce into our classificatory system a large number of attributes of market structure, we rapidly approach the limit where there are only one or two instances of each "class" — especially given the reduction of the size of the sample for various extraneous reasons — and where statistical testing is fruitless. Despite this difficulty with too many independent variables, Mason's suggestion of a market-classification approach stands as a tall landmark in the development of a new field of industrial organization. The writer endorsed the original Masonian view for a number of years, as indicated in the following excerpt from a book published in 1944:

> A considerable acquaintance with the population of sellers and buyers in a market, with the source of the materials and the character of their productive techniques, with the geography of the market, and with the framework of law surrounding it is a prerequisite to the effective study of competition

[6] *Ibid.,* p. 198–199.

and price behavior within the market. This is true for both the author and the reader. The merits of such an analysis should not be confined, however, to its service as a preface to further work. A description, from the vantage point of economic analysis, of the environment of a principal industrial market may prove useful and perhaps illuminating to the economist and the general reader alike. It may further acquaintance with the extremely complex character of business institutions in the modern world, and may suggest hypotheses for investigation in the immediate or other industries.[7]

Even in the early 1960's, I endorsed the comparable views of my co-authors of a book, though in the special context of an exploratory study of structure-performance relations in a single public-enterprise industry, as follows:

"Market structure" encompasses those elements of the common environment of firms in a market which theoretical reasoning identifies as having a possible significant influence on their behavior. Elements of market structure that are customarily identified as theoretically significant include the number and size distribution of buyers and sellers in the market, the extent of barriers to the entry of new buyers and sellers, the presence or absence of product differentiation, the magnitude of fixed costs in the short run, the rate of growth of demand, and the presence of any special governmental regulations affecting the behavior of firms in the industry.[8]

By this time, however, I had certainly changed my mind about the original Mason hypothesis, and along the following line. First, if one poured into market structure as determinants of performance "everything but the kitchen sink," we were left with an hypothesis irrefutable a priori and not subject to statistical test, because we were approaching the limit at which nearly every industry was in a very significant degree structurally unique, in a different "class." And an hypothesis that is not conceivably susceptible to empirical refutation is not much of an hypothesis at all.

Second, the only way out of this trap — if one were to test for structure-performance relations — was to specify a very few, supposedly leading, structural variables that should be primarily associated with market performance — few enough to make cross-sectional testing meaningful. This would involve some revision, but no destruction, of the original Masonian hypothesis. The revision would simply adapt the hypothesis to a shift from the industry-study to the cross-sectional approach.

This revised approach is indeed not without its difficulties. No one ever supposed that the variance of dependent performance variables, especially within short or medium spans of time, was fully or in large part dependent on any selected few structural variables, whatever their names. In a limited

[7] Joe S. Bain, *The Economics of the Pacific Coast Petroleum Industry,* (Berkeley: 1944), Part I, p. vii.
[8] Bain, Caves, Margolis, *Northern California's Water Industry,* Baltimore: 1966, p. 5.

time period, the expectation — as supported by experiment — is that the variance in any dependent performance variable like a profit rate is proportionally much more influenced by "random" independent variables — such as demand variation, windfalls, and the like — than by a few specified structural variables — such as seller concentration and the condition of entry. Thus, in any experiment relating a few specified structural variables to performance, we encounter a great deal of "statistical static," or, in other words a large proportion of variance in the dependent performance variable not accounted for by the few specified structural variables. Hence enters first the dependence on statistical significance tests. And we find disappointingly low coefficients relating dependent to selected independent variables, and relatively low values of correlation coefficients.

Thus, we get into a box from which it is hard to escape. Being in this box is a price paid for trying to confirm a Masonian hypothesis with cross-sectional experiments. Either recognizing the dimensions of the box or just charging ahead without much thought, nearly all practitioners in the area of econometric tests of structure-performance relations have opted for specifying very few structural independent variables and then put the experiment in the "computer mill" to see what would fall out. Most interpretations of results have reflected a fairly sophisticated appreciation of the basic hypothesis and of the statistical problems involved. If we are interested in cross-sectional testing of the Masonian hypothesis, the counsel of wisdom seems to be that we should specify on a priori grounds or from experience a very few independent structural variables and deal with our statistical problems as they arise. One note might be added. In a more or less standard single-equation multiple regression (and elsewhere), every time we add an additional independent structural variable, we tend to enhance the problem of collinearity of independent variables — a result not generally to be desired.

The Comparative Stability of Market Structures

We now return to the main theme by inquiring into the comparative stability of market structure — and particularly into the stability of those few dimensions of structure usually emphasized in the sort of econometric tests referred to above. In these dimensions, I would include especially, but not exclusively, seller concentration, product differentiation, and the condition of entry. Some proxies for the preceding — such as ratios of selling cost to sales for product-differentiation barriers to entry or such as measures of plant concentration for plant scale economies and resulting barriers to entry — might be used.

The issue of structural stability is indeed crucial to any meaningful test of the central Masonian hypothesis, which rests fundamentally on the postulate that independent structural variables are comparatively immutable variables determining in the long run the values of dependent performance variables. If, after all, attributes of market structure were will-o'-the-wisps that moved quite significantly with the tides or seasons, there would not be much left to test, except in some very mechanical econometric context in which a number is just a number. Thus, we do need to inquire into comparative structural stability.

Not enough attention has been given to the issue for us to suggest conclusive answers, but we can offer some relevant a priori indications and evidence. As regards seller concentration, we might expect it to change at least slowly over time as surrounding circumstances vary. The record shows that *on the average* such concentration within industries has changed little for quite a while; for example, one Census publication indicates that from 1935 to 1947, with respect to 103 comparably defined 4-digit manufacturing industries, concentration as measured by the 4-firm concentration ratio increased perceptibly in 33 cases, decreased perceptibly in 34 cases, and was substantially unchanged in 36 cases. Subsequent studies, carrying us to 1958 or beyond, have revealed a similar sluggishness in the average of individual-industry concentration ratios. Still, there is evidently an appreciable variance in seller concentration within many individual industries, so that we cannot assume, for purposes of statistical testing, that individual-industry concentrations are in general practically immutable for periods as long as a decade.

It should be added to the preceding that, for a number of industries in this country, the actual degree of seller concentration has at once been overstated and made deceptively to appear stable because Census concentration data systematically disregard shipments or sales of foreign imports. After the period of postwar reconstruction, tariff reductions and comparable measures passed before World War II "took hold," thereby encouraging appreciable increases in foreign imports of a number of goods — for instance, steel, automobiles — with the result that actual seller concentration in the United States market moved more than Census statistics indicate.

What of the condition of entry? My observations suggest that, on the average among industries, the condition of entry tends to be comparatively stable over time, but it is a bit more of a will-o'-the-wisp than sellers' concentration, though selectively among industries. As regards absolute-cost barriers to entry, we need mainly note that patent expirations — or destruction of patent protection by antitrust decrees — sporadically lower such barriers significantly or even radically. As regards product-differentiation barriers to entry, we may note that in some significant cases — distilled liquors, for instance — relatively rapid shifts in consumer preferences, like that away from bourbon whiskey, have radically reduced entry barriers in less than a decade, as have product innovations in other cases. But the proportion of manufacturing industries appreciably affected is relatively small. As regards scale-economies barriers to entry, growth of the size of the market regularly reduces their impact; otherwise, there is relative stability. We must note, however, that scale-economy barriers in the United States market for a product may be significantly eroded if a foreign producer with a world market can exploit all scale economies while still exporting to the United States a minor fraction of his output. Think of the Volkswagen. Although this phenomenon is a long way from being ubiquitous, it must be taken into account.

Product differentiation within industries is sometimes fairly stable over time, but I conclude from observation that it is probably the least stable of the principal structural attributes of markets considered — this mainly of course with regard to consumer-good industries. Examples of instability in this regard include sellers of fountain pens, portable transistorized radios, typewriters, distilled liquor, and soft drinks. Here we seem to have a structural variable which often is disturbingly unstable over time.

My overall impression (very much of a guess-estimate) is that seller concentration is a variable which, on the average, is fairly stable over time, but not nearly as stable as we would like in order to get a very clear test of the central Masonian hypothesis. The condition of entry in general seems to have a roughly comparable stability. The stability of intraindustry product differentiation is probably a bit less.

These observations raise some serious statistical problems for cross-sectional testing of the hypothesis concerning the relation of structure to performance — problems that are not destructive but disturbing. Let us turn to some parts of these problems.

Structural Instability and Testing of Hypotheses

The basic hypothesis to be tested is that comparatively immutable dimensions of market structure have a *long-run* association with market performance. If we are really going to test this hypothesis, the market-structure variables ought to "hold still," or pretty still, for at least medium terms of time. For example, if at the one extreme the market-structure variables should be highly unstable from year to year, we could not test the hypothesis successfully, mainly because its a priori foundations would have been undercut rather thoroughly. Fortunately, we do not seem to be in this extreme situation.

But suppose that one or more of three or four basic structural variables are sufficiently unstable over time that we can only associate structure with performance for a succession of quite short-term periods — such as periods of three or four years. (Stigler, for example, apparently wary of the variability of his own dubiously devised concentration ratios, chopped the period 1938 to 1957 into six separate periods, each separately tested.)[9]

[9] See George J. Stigler, *Capital and Rates of Return in Manufacturing Industries* (Princeton, 1963). See especially p. 68.

Waiving the temptation to dissect Stigler's data and methodology in detail, I only point out that chopping up tests into three- or four-year intervals is almost as good as throwing the experiment away. Whatever is ostensibly picked up in statistical degrees of freedom is much more than cancelled by the very strong influence on the dependent performance variable — here profit rates — of short-run nonstructural influences on these rates, influences that are mostly unregistered in the formal statistical tests. From the standpoint of the basic hypothesis, "statistical static" tends to become so dominant that it is terribly difficult to ascertain any medium- or long-term associations of structure with performance.

More generally, where are we left in conducting experiments testing the long-run relation of structure to performance under conditions where the independent structural variables are appreciably mutable over time, even if not as mutable as Stigler might have suggested? In view of this mutability, it seems first that we need to look for the longest time period during which structural mutation has not been very large — I like about ten years on the average.

Having selected such a time period, the prevailing practice of assigning to each industry or firm a single measure of each structural variable, to be used as applicable to the whole test period, seems undesirable if the structural variable is appreciably mutable. This is because the statistically determined association of structure with performance will then be more or less arbitrarily weakened. It would be somewhat more desirable in a regression to use for each independent structural variable for every case a mean of the beginning and ending values of the variable. Greater statistical sins have been committed. One might also, in every case, complement the selected measure of each mutable structural characteristic with a matching independent variable that denotes roughly the direction and degree of structural change over the period of the statistical test. Use of these or comparably sensible statistical devices might help resolve some of the numerical difficulties that have been encountered in past experiments. As we continue to test the adapted Masonian hypothesis, this approach seems like a possibly rewarding track.

4

Organization as a Scale Factor
in the Growth of Firms

*Raymond Vernon**

Large firms in modern industry seem to be constantly engaged in trying to become larger still. Sometimes their efforts at sustained growth are directed simply toward making and selling more of what they already know how to make and sell. But just as often, the firms are intent on expanding into new products or new markets in which their experience is much more limited. On the surface, their efforts often appear successful, and their capacity to overcome the putative threat of "scale-diseconomies" — increased costs resulting from expansion in scope of operations — seems remarkably strong.

The object of this exploratory paper is to suggest that when industrial organizations are built on the copious use of skilled manpower, especially the use of general managers and technical personnel, major advantages of scale arise. Although this view is hardly new to economists, there was little basis until a few years ago for much more than a speculative approach to the issue.[1] As a result of the empirical work of recent years, however, the hypothesis takes on new interest for those concerned with the future of industrial organization.

* Harvard University

[1] Illustrative of early contributions of this kind are: R. F. Harrod, "The Law of Decreasing Costs," *Economic Journal,* Vol. XLI, No. 164 (December 1931), pp. 566–576; and Lionel Robbins, "Remarks upon Certain Aspects of the Theory of Costs," *ibid.,* Vol. XLIV, No. 173 (March 1934), pp. 1–18.

The preparation of this article was financed by a grant from the Ford Foundation to the Harvard Business School. I benefited enormously from the comments of L. E. Fouraker, William H. Gruber, Jesse W. Markham, R. R. Nelson, Nathan Rosenberg, and L. T. Wells, Jr.

Characteristics of Skill-Oriented Industries

Industries in the United States that make extensive use of skilled manpower have certain other characteristics in common. Such industries tend to be highly concentrated in structure; their leading firms are generally larger in terms of value added than the leading firms of other industries; and, as a rule, their involvement in foreign markets by way of trade and investment is considerably greater than that of other industries.

Table 4–1 reflects some of these relationships. Its three columns of data on the left-hand side represent alternative measures of the skilled manpower used in the industries listed. Note the marked degree of interrelation among the various measures. Where the percentage of total employment represented by scientists and engineers is relatively high, so are the other two measures of skilled-labor use. The remaining columns in the table indicate: (1) that the leading firms in the skill-oriented industries tend on the whole to be larger than those of the other industries; (2) that the degree of concentration in the skill-oriented industries tends to be higher than in the other industries;[2] and (3) that there is a significant relationship between the use of skilled manpower and the relative importance of exports. Other studies have demonstrated a similar correlation between skilled manpower and foreign investment.[3]

The exceptions to the patterns just described are also worth noting, however. Observe, for instance, the aberrant behavior of the tobacco industry. In this case, large scale and high degree of concentration are not accompanied by large inputs of skilled manpower. The size of both the leading tobacco firms and the leading transport firms (mostly the automobile industry) suggests that the propensity for large scale may be strengthened from other directions, especially from some capability associated with the selling function.

Nevertheless, the tendencies toward high concentration, large scale, and extensive foreign involvement are clearer for industries characterized by highly skilled labor than for capital-intensive industries. A classification of United States industry based on measures of capital intensity would not reveal as strong a set of relationships.[4]

---

[2] The coefficient of rank correlation between the figures in columns 1 and 5 of Table 1 is +.59; between columns 1 and 6, +.57. For further statistical evidence of the strong relationship between (1) employment of scientists and engineers and (2) degree of industrial concentration, see F. M. Scherer, "Market Structure and the Employment of Scientists and Engineers," *American Economic Review*, Vol. LVII (June 1967), p. 524. See also an excellent summary of the data on industrial concentration, size, and research in Daniel Hamberg, "Size of Firm, Oligopoly and Research: The Evidence," *Canadian Journal of Economics and Political Science*, Vol. XXX (February 1964), pp. 62–75.

[3] William H. Gruber, Dileep Mehta, and Raymond Vernon, "The R & D Factor in International Trade and International Investment of United States Industries," *Journal of Political Economy*, Vol. LXXV (February 1967), p. 20.

[4] See W. Gruber, D. Mehta, R. Vernon, *ibid.*, Table 6, p. 29.

Some Preliminary Speculation

The data in Table 4–1 suggest a number of possibilities regarding the role of organization as a scale factor in the growth of firms. To be sure, data like those in Table 4–1 give rise to substantial difficulties. First of all, the industrial classification in the table is very crude. Certain industries embrace a heterogeneous group of products and, as a result, seem to have a very diverse mix of organizational needs. Second, the data describe the industries at a single point in time, even though there is considerable evidence that organizational requirements undergo a pronounced change at different stages in any industry's existence.

It is not yet possible to disentangle these static and dynamic sources of variance in the data; the statistical basis for such decomposition does not exist. But various studies have developed enough fragments of the complex mosaic to provide some foundation for speculating about the pattern. Table 4–2 serves as a take-off for such speculation. It begins with a gross simplification, albeit a familiar one: a breakdown of products according to their stage of development. This sort of classification has been applied several times in empirical tests and found useful.[5]

Commencing at a point after the stage of "invention" in the Schumpeterian lexicon, Table 4–2 carries the product through three successive stages, specifying some of the changes in the roles of large and small firms. The table is, of course, rather a tour de force. All it claims to reflect is a typical set of sequences sufficiently important in total effect to have possible major influence on the shape of the data shown earlier in Table 4–1. Some of the empirical materials that suggest the sequence are presented in later sections. For the present, a more complete description of the patterns of change will be given in a few words.

Stage I in Table 4–2 represents a situation in which the relevant technology is closely held. Both the process of production and the product itself are in flux and the products are sold on a market in which the substitution elasticity of demand among producing firms is low. At this point, the innovative process — a process that includes not simply the research involved, but also a relatively expensive and prolonged period of developing the product and introducing it on the market — is usually in the domain of the large firm. Small firms are not inactive, but they generally serve as adjuncts to the larger organizations. They develop an innovation up to the point at which it has real proprietary value, then "sell out" by one means or another to a large organization; or they contribute to the activity of the large organization in some specialized ancillary role.

[5] G. C. Hufbauer, *Synthetic Materials and the Theory of International Trade* (London: Duckworth, 1966); Seev Hirsch, *Location of Industry and International Competitiveness* (Oxford: Clarendon Press, 1967); L. T. Wells, Jr., "A Product Life Cycle for International Trade?" *Journal of Marketing*, Vol. XXXII (July 1968); R. B. Stobaugh, Jr., *The Product Life Cycle, U.S. Exports and International Investment*, unpublished D.B.A. thesis, Harvard Business School, 1968.

Table 4-1 Selected Characteristics of Skill-Oriented and Other Industries in the United States

	1	2	3	4	5	6
Industry (SIC number)[a]	Scientists & engineers as % of total employment, 1964	Professionals, scientists, technical workers as % of labor force, 1960	Indirect labor as % of total employment, 1964	Exports as % of sales, 1962	Value added per firm of leading firms ($000,000), 1963	Measure of industrial concentration 1963
Aircraft (372)	13.0	12.2[b]	45.3	8.4	260.3	70.6
Office machines (357)	12.5	9.1[c]	40.9	13.3[c]	79.3	80.6
Drugs (283)	19.6	19.3	46.1	6.0	117.4	41.9
Chemicals (minus drugs) (other 28)	10.0	15.6[d]	38.0[d]	6.2	98.2	60.0
Electrical machinery (36)	7.9	15.2	32.9	4.1	95.7	58.9
Instruments (38)	8.4	16.2	36.1	6.7	58.0	60.0
Agricultural machinery (352)	6.6	9.1	29.0[e]	13.3[e]	92.9	55.0
Petroleum and coal (29)	10.7	—	35.7	1.2	184.4	54.2
Transport (minus aircraft) (other 37)	3.0	12.2[b]	31.0[b]	4.2	1072.7	66.3
Other machinery nonelectrical (other 35)	3.7	9.1[c]	29.0[c]	13.3[c]	30.6	41.6
Nonferrous metals (other 33)	3.1	7.3	20.0[e]	4.2	32.6	65.0
Rubber and plastics not elsewhere classified (30)	1.9	6.0	22.5	2.0	99.0	50.0
Ferrous metals (331 and 332)	2.6	5.0	20.0[e]	2.5	486.7	58.9[f]
Fabricated metals (34)	2.2	9.7	23.4	2.1	26.7	32.3
Stone, clay, glass (32)	1.5	5.0	19.3	1.9	25.5	48.5

Table 4-1 (continued)

Industry (SIC number)[a]	1	2	3	4	5	6
Paper (26)	1.9	3.9	20.9	2.1	38.1	46.3
Textiles (22)	0.8	2.1	10.0	3.4	26.4	43.3
Food (20)	1.2	—	33.1	0.9	45.1	45.4
Tobacco (21)	0.1	2.2	13.0	2.2	143.3	95.6
Furniture and fixtures (25)	0.7	2.0	17.0	0.7	11.2	24.5
Leather (31)	0.4	1.7	11.6	1.7	31.7	31.9
Printing and publishing (27)	0.3	—	35.8	1.7	46.8	27.1
Apparel (23)	0.1	1.0	21.6	0.7	10.5	23.8
Lumber and wood (24)	0.3	1.5	10.6	2.0	14.7	20.3

Sources: Col. 1—Data on scientists and engineers by industry are from U.S., Bureau of Labor Statistics, *Employment of Scientific and Technical Personnel in Industry*, Bulletin No. 1418 (Washington: U.S. Government Printing Office, 1964), Table A-14. Total employment by industry is from U.S., Bureau of Labor Statistics, *Employment and Earnings Statistics for the United States, 1909-1966*, Bulletin No. 1312-4 (Washington: U.S. Government Printing Office, 1964).
Col. 2—G. C. Hufbauer, "Commodity Composition of Trade in Manufactured Goods," unpublished manuscript, 1968, adapted from *U.S. Census of Population, 1960: Occupation by Industry* (Washington: U.S. Government Printing Office, 1963).
Col. 3—see Col. 1.
Col. 4—William H. Gruber, Dileep Mehta, and Raymond Vernon, "The R & D Factor in International Trade and International Investment of United States Industries," *Journal of Political Economy*, Vol. LXXV (February 1964), 23, Table 1.
Col. 5—U.S., Department of Commerce, *Concentration Ratios in Manufacturing Industry 1963*, Part II (Washington: U.S. Government Printing Office, 1967), adapted from Table 27. Average dollar value added of largest eight firms in each four-digit category is weighted by total value added of such four-digit category.
Col. 6—Calculated from *Census of Manufactures*: 1963. Each industry's measure is based upon the share of the industry's total shipments held by the largest firms. Four-digit SIC data are weighted by shipments and summed to create the variables at the two-digit and three-digit level in the study.
[a]SIC is the abbreviation for Standard Industrial Classification
[b]Based on SIC 37
[c]Based on SIC 35
[d]Based on SIC 28
[e]Based on SIC 33
[f]Based on SIC 331

Table 4–2   Roles of Large and Small Firms in the Post-Invention Period

Product Stage	Research & Development	Production and Distribution
Stage I: Innovation (from post-invention through industrial development)	Primarily large firms; smaller firms used peripherally as specialist contractors	Primarily large firms; smaller firms that have managed the early phases of this stage are commonly absorbed prior to stage II
Stage II: Dissemination and standardization	Relative increase in small-firm role, especially as specialist collectors and distributors of disseminated information	Continued dominance of large firms, with dominance even more pronounced in exports and in overseas subsidiary production than in domestic market
Stage III: Maturation and senescence	Indeterminate, but of reduced importance relative to production and distribution	Indeterminate; scale of existing firms may grow but new specialists may also emerge

Stage II is a phase in which others have begun to appropriate or imitate the technology, in which the process of production and the product's specifications have settled down, and in which price competition among rival firms has grown keener. At this point, the small firm emerges in a new role. As the original entrants begin to lose their hold over the relevant technology, the attention of present and prospective producers turns toward ensuring that their knowledge of the field is the best that can be obtained. A demand develops for the available knowledge in the field, suitably collated and digested for use by the producer. Firms specializing in R & D (research and development) appear whose function is to collect, improve, and disseminate such knowledge or to embody such knowledge in the form of designs for process and product and in the form of specialized machinery. At this stage, too, the established leaders in industry begin to build or extend their position in new markets, including foreign markets, hoping thereby to prolong the proprietary value of their innovations a little and to gain a head start in the intensified competitive race foreseen for such markets.[6]

In stage III, mass markets for the product have been widely developed.

[6] The motivations of large firms making investments in foreign productive facilities are explored to a greater extent in my article, "International Investment and International Trade in the Product Cycle," *Quarterly Journal of Economics,* Vol. LXXX (May 1966), pp. 190–207.

The technology, whether embodied in machinery or in the expertise of individuals, is available to anyone at a price. Any barriers to entry consist of capital rather than technology. The substitution elasticity of demand with respect to producing firms is very high in this stage. Because technology no longer presents a serious obstacle to entry, producers are greatly concerned in paring their costs and prices. Some gamble on a product-differentiating strategy by advertising, but some do not. To the extent that the process and product permit and when no further economies from scale of production are available, specialization in production occurs. If economies of scale exist in manufacturing components, as they usually do, specialists in components appear. The trend in average size of firms in the industry is not clear, since the outcome of the process of specialization produces indeterminate results.

In the sections that follow, we explore more thoroughly the rationalization for this crude model. Before doing so, however, one more complexity must be added to an already complex pattern. Table 4–2 purports to represent the course of a product from birth to old age. It does not trace the life of the initiating firm, a distinction vital to the thesis expounded here. Firms add new lines that contribute to growth and drop old ones that retard it. Certain kinds of firms, to be described later, do so more effectively than others. The more successful structures detect external opportunities and threats more readily. They fend off some of the factors contributing to diseconomies of scale, such as inadequate internal communication. The larger firms in the "newer industries" have characteristically achieved the organizational metamorphosis needed for such results. In the process, such firms leave behind a record of high expenditure for building up an organization, a record of high expenditure for development and organization of knowledge, and a record of extensive participation in foreign markets.

This paper expounds the thesis that the kind of organization efficient in mastering the problems of entering into the development of new products and new markets has certain explicit characteristics and that such an organization is associated with large-scale economies. The argument concerning scale is built up in three distinct steps. The first step is based on the lumpiness or indivisibility of skilled employees; it is assumed that, when business firms consider creating an organization composed of skilled employees, they think of themselves as taking on a large lumpy commitment akin to a capital investment rather than as purchasing a variable input, adjustable to the level of output. The second step requires the hypothesis that, in the industrial research process proper, the economies associated with such lumpy investments within the firm are likely to be very large. In the third step, the contention is that the full effectiveness of the research process is only achieved when it is intimately and continuously linked with the processes of marketing, production, and general planning.

These three elements "explain" the propensity toward large firms in skill-intensive industries.[7]

Lumpiness and Scale in the Use of Human Capital

Lumpiness defined. In handling many economic problems, one can reasonably regard labor as a factor available on an open market at a price equal to its marginal productivity. On the other hand, it may be inefficient and misleading to think of highly skilled labor in these terms, especially the kind of labor that achieves its peak productivity by adding to a base of general knowledge and experience the special knowledge and experience that is specific to the firm. In such cases, the kind of analysis associated with a capital investment may be more relevant than the kind associated with a variable factor input.[8]

The usefulness of the analogy to a capital investment stems from the fact that much of the terminal training of a high-level employee takes place inside the firm. In that case, the firm generally counts on paying initially more than the employee is currently worth, hoping to recoup later on. The beginning payment may be determined by the firm's requiring that, whatever the employee's productivity in any period, his level of compensation must correspond to his place in the firm's organizational pyramid. The longer the contemplated period of employment and the steeper the learning curve, the greater may be the deviation between payment and productivity for a given period during the term of employment. For a highly placed official, the anticipated pattern during his expected term of employment might look something like Figure 4–1.

Figure 4–1 is, of course, more plausible for some kinds of high-level activity than for others — more plausible, for instance, in activities demanding firm-specific knowledge than in activities based on industry-specific or occupation-specific knowledge; more plausible in tasks that depend on intricate teamwork than on tasks performed by independent actors. But a priori those qualifications would not seem to reduce by much the value of the analogy for high-level jobs and for scientifically based industries.

Risks from lumpiness. If the early payments to high-level personnel may be thought of as capital investment, they must also be thought of as

[7] Some of the ideas that follow are well developed, albeit from a slightly different viewpoint, in an admirable little book by Edith T. Penrose, *The Theory of the Growth of the Firm* (Oxford: Basil Blackwell, 1966).

[8] Gary S. Becker, *Human Capital,* (New York: National Bureau of Economic Research, 1964); E. B. Yudin, "Americans Abroad: A Transfer of Capital," in P. B. Kenen and Roger Lawrence (eds.) *The Open Economy* (New York: Columbia University Press, 1968) pp. 40–69; and R. L. Brummet, E. G. Flamholts, and W. C. Pyle, "Human Resource Measurement — A Challenge for Accountants," *The Accounting Review,* Vol. XLIII (April 1968), pp. 217–224.

Figure 4–1   *Prospective Cost and Benefit to the Firm from a High-Level Employee*

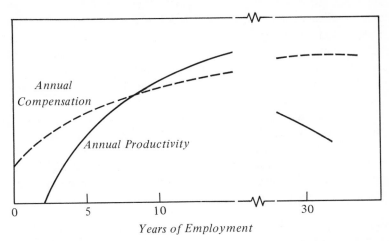

Years of Employment

investment at fairly high risk. The elements of risk include, for instance, the probability that the employee would die or quit in any period in the future; the probability, if he did not leave, that the anticipated increase in his productivity would not be realized; and the probability, if he did not leave, that the firm would have no need for the full output of which he was capable in each period. If the firm is acquiring a large number of employees, those elements of risk not interdependent among employees, such as the risk of premature death, would presumably be lower for the entrepreneur. It would not be surprising, however, if businessmen were to consider investment in employees as generally involving higher risks than investment in plant and equipment or in working capital. Viewed as a form of investment, the commitment involved in hiring a new division chief at $50,000 per annum, for example, might be perceived as involving a commitment of $60,000 in year 1 — the $50,000 salary plus net negative productivity of $10,000 — and $25,000 in year 2 — the excess of salary over productivity. At a 10 percent rate of discount, the discounted value of the "investment" at hiring, represented by the commitment to the end of the second year, would be on the order of $74,000.

If businessmen regarded the expenditures associated with the formation of organization as analogous to capital investments, would the "investment" add much to the barrier against entry in the industries concerned? By attaching the data underlying Table 4–1 to the ruminations above, one can gain some rough order-of-magnitude impressions on the point. Businessmen contemplating an investment in the employment of scientists and engineers would not be wholly unreasonable if they thought of that investment as amounting to $40,000 per head.[9] On that basis, an entrepreneur seeking to duplicate the staff of scientists and engineers in a leading firm in the eight most skill-oriented industries shown in Table 4–1 might be thought of as contemplating an investment in a 350-man staff, amounting to $14 million. The organizational requirements of the firm would also include a number of nontechnical general managers at somewhat higher pay. If those amounted to, say, half the number of scientists and engineers in the firm, a plausible assumption, then the total figure would rise to about $25 million.

Although the figure of $25 million can be treated only as an order of magnitude, it is worth observing that $25 million would represent about 30 percent of the net worth of the firms in the eight skill-oriented industries in 1964, or about 18 percent of their gross assets. This order of magnitude might well cause prospective entrepreneurs to pause in mobilizing their capital and assessing their risk.

Scale in the research function.   The argument, of course, still lacks a critical link. Why should the entrepreneur feel obliged to hire 350 scientists and engineers? Why not just one or two? If there is any answer, it must lie in some expectation of economies of scale by the entrepreneur.

That group research involves economies is not a view economists have found easy to accept. Historians, scientists, and businessmen, on the other hand, have generally seemed to accept the proposition without much demurrer. Historical interpretations commonly attribute the rise and fall of leadership in the applied sciences and in industrial innovation to the emergence of group research. For instance, some interpretations attribute to group research Germany's rise in industrial chemistry during the latter nineteenth century.[10] Likewise they attribute the subsequent decline in the preeminence of Germany, as well as the abortive performance of France, to the same factor operating in reverse — to the cultural inability of those countries to find a way of generating effective cooperation among their many narrowly-oriented research groups. Explanations of this sort are, by now, conventional wisdom in analyzing Europe's shortcomings in industrial research and innovation.[11]

[9] The median pay of scientists and engineers in United States industry in 1963 was about $13,000 per head; the annual cost to the firm per R & D scientist or engineer was about $38,000. National Science Foundation, *Basic Research, Applied Research and Development in Industry, 1963* (Washington: Government Printing Office, 1966), p. 130. If half of $38,000 is inseparably related to the productivity of the scientist or engineer, then $20,000 is approximately the relevant annual investment. Then, if the present value of the investment is taken as the equivalent of two years' cost, the computation produces the figure of $40,000 in the text.

[10] Joseph Ben-David, *Fundamental Research and the Universities* (Paris: OECD, 1968), p. 29. His interpretation is shared by many sources.

[11] E. Jantsch, *Technological Forecasting in Perspective* (Paris: OECD, 1967), p. 73; J.-J. Servan-Schreiber, *The American Challenge* (New York: Atheneum, 1968), p. 179 *et seq.*

The existence of important economies in large-scale research is usually so thoroughly taken for granted by businessmen and scientists that it is difficult to find an explicit rationalization for their assumption.[12] Whether or not businessmen are right is something on which I shall presently comment. Right or wrong, however, the belief need only be widely held, and widely acted upon, in order to constitute a barrier to entry.

Some bases for the view that economies exist in group research are fairly evident.[13] The most obvious basis, one derived from Adam Smith's classic explanation for economies of scale, is the advantages of specialized functions within the research team. A researcher confronted with a series of obstacles to the solution of a problem is likely to be less efficient in overcoming the obstacles than a group of researchers each of whom specializes in overcoming one type of obstacle.

A second reason, often alluded to in the literature of research, is the handling of risk. Here the insurance principle plays its usual role, although in two rather different ways.

One way in which the insurance principle applies relates to the usual problem of estimates based on small numbers. If the aggregate amount of research in an organization is large, the frequency with which any problem of a given sort will arise can be better estimated than if the aggregate amount of research is small. Accordingly, insofar as the combination of capabilities and equipment required for effective research is indivisible, large-scale research will exploit its internal capabilities and equipment more efficiently than small-scale research.

The other way in which the insurance principle is important relates to the variance associated with the outcome of research. Although small firms in the aggregate may have the same average record of research successes as large firms, the percentage of successes for any individual large firm will be more closely predictable than the percentage of successes for a given small firm. If investors prefer lesser risk for a given expected mean outcome, as they surely do, that preference will lead to larger research teams wherever the entrepreneur has a choice.

All of this, however, begs a critical question: Granted the large scale of many modern research projects, granted, too, the strength of large numbers in reducing the risks of research, why must all the research specialties required by the firm be brought inside its structure? Why is it not sufficient

[12] See, for instance, D. A. Schon, *Technology and Change* (New York: Delacorte Press, 1967), p. 53; Schon attributes the conviction in part to such successful demonstrations as the Manhattan Project and Sputnik. A typical reflection of this assumption is represented by an unpublished consensus of a group of experts in the pharmaceuticals industry that a "research based" pharmaceutical company should have at least 300 research workers and an annual research budget of $5 to $10 million.

[13] For an empirical analysis offering insights and illustrations, see W. J. J. Smith and Daniel Creamer, *R & D and Small Company Growth* (New York: The Conference Board, 1968). See also J. W. Watson, *The Double Helix* (New York: Atheneum, 1968).

that the specialties be available to the firm at a cost reflecting their productivity?

Let us acknowledge at once that, for some research purposes, it is neither necessary nor desirable for a specialized facility to be contained within the structure of the firm. Reverting to the terminology of Table 4–2 for a moment, the development of products still in stage I may require some specialized facility for research the use of which has not been anticipated and cannot easily be predicted. In such situations, the firm may prefer to call on an outside facility. The clusters of independent specialized laboratories and research-contracting firms found in several major centers in the United States and Western Europe depend to some extent on just this sort of business.[14]

Nevertheless, there appear to be powerful drives toward a firm's internalizing some of the external economies associated with the availability of research facilities, especially when the research is immediately related to industrial innovation. One, quite obviously, is the need for secrecy.[15] Another is the requirement of availability. When an outside facility has more business than it can handle, the firm cannot be sure of its influence over the outside facility's priorities. In averting risks, a firm that can picture the fruits of its future research imperilled by the unavailability of a critical outside facility at a critical time is likely to go to some lengths to bring such a facility under its control.

Some striking experimental evidence suggests still another very powerful force pushing the internalization of industrial research — the problem of effective communication among the participants. In such research, face-to-face communication is the preponderant means for transmitting information and ideas.[16] Although the evidence is still fragmentary, it provides strong indications that individuals are much more prepared to receive and accept messages emanating from those whom they consider part of "their organization" than from those whom they regard as "outsiders." Product managers will more readily accept the representations and estimates of their own business associates than of outsiders; engineers will more readily accept technical solutions generated inside their own laboratories than solutions from outside. Scientists, on the other hand, much more readily

---

[14] Data on the factors affecting the location of industrial research facilities are fragmentary. But see Max Hall (ed.), *Made in New York* (Cambridge, Mass.: Harvard University Press, 1959), pp. 291, 301–305; and Wilbur R. Thompson, "Locational Differences in Inventive Effort and Their Determinants," in R. R. Nelson (ed.), *The Rate and Direction of Inventive Activity* (Princeton: Princeton University Press, 1962), pp. 253–271 (hereafter cited as Nelson, *op. cit.*).

[15] The problem of protecting research output has taken on the dimensions of a major commercial problem in research-conscious industry. See: M. S. Barron, "Trade Secrets: What Price Loyalty?", *Harvard Business Review* (Nov.-Dec., 1968), pp. 66–71.

[16] See R. S. Rosenbloom and F. W. Wolek, *Technology, Information, & Organization* (Boston: Harvard Business School, 1967).

respond to signals from outside the firm and may be less responsive to signals from within, depending on the credentials of the sender; for them, the relevant "organization" is the scientific community with which they identify themselves.[17]

For some activities, the penalties of disregarding outside signals are less than for others. The stage of industrial innovation is generally the period of maximum secrecy in developing a product or process. In the stage prior to innovation, the "invention" on which the development is to be based is often widely known. In the stage following innovation, the diffusion of knowledge about the product or process is inevitable. It is in the innovational stage, therefore, that the complementarities engendered by skilled researchers working as a team have to express themselves within the firm. It is at this stage, therefore, that scale may afford an important advantage.

After the engineers have launched their marketable innovation, however, the communication needs of the producing firm are likely to change. At this stage a new development apparently sets in — a development that seems to confirm the importance of the communication pattern in determining the size of industrial research and developmental units. In the United States, if not elsewhere, there are strong indications that a field of industrial innovation originally developed by one or more of the firms using it eventually emerges as a separate industry, purveying its accumulated knowledge on a competitive basis to industrial users.[18]

In terms of the stages described in Table 4–2, this development can be thought of as taking place toward the end of stage I or in stage II — a point at which the original innovators have begun to lose their proprietary control over the body of existing technology. Outside purveyors of the relevant knowledge, or of the products in which the relevant knowledge is embodied have come into existence. More and more, the problem is one

---

[17] For a summary of the experimental evidence, see Edwin Mansfield, *The Economics of Technological Change* (New York: W. W. Norton, 1968), pp. 84–86; for added evidence, see Rosenbloom and Wolek, *op. cit.*, and T. J. Allen, "The Differential Performance of Information Channels in the Transfer of Technology," in W. H. Gruber and D. G. Marquis (eds.), *The Human Factor in the Transfer of Technology* (Cambridge: MIT Press, 1969), pp. 255–280. An underlying theoretical structure is proposed in Daniel Katz and R. L. Kahn, *The Social Psychology of Organizations* (New York: John Wiley & Sons, Inc., 1966); and in J. W. Brehm and A. R. Cohen, *Explorations in Cognitive Dissonance* (New York: John Wiley & Sons, Inc., 1962).

[18] This is a special case of the general phenomenon described in George J. Stigler, "The Division of Labor is Limited by the Extent of the Market," *Journal of Political Economy*, Vol. LIX, No. 3 (June 1951), p. 190 *et seq.* See also Edward Ames and Nathan Rosenberg, "The Progressive Division and Specialization of Industries," *Journal of Development Studies*, Vol. I, No. 4 (July 1965), pp. 1–21; and Nathan Rosenberg, "Technological Change in the Machine Tool Industry, 1840–1910," *Journal of Economic History*, Vol. XXIII, No. 4 (Dec. 1963), pp. 414–443. For recent illustrations, see Christopher Freeman, "Chemical Process Plant: Innovation and the World Market," *National Institute Economic Review*, No. 45 (Aug. 1968), pp. 29–58; and R. B. Stobaugh, Jr., *op. cit.*, Chapter V.

of assembling, collating, adapting, and applying the information being generated from an increasing number of sources. More and more, the communication problem is one that involves crossing the boundaries of individual firms, not remaining within them. At this stage, therefore, the communication efficiencies associated with large research organizations lose some of their force, and the smaller, specialist firm once more comes into its own, often as a spin-off from one of the original, larger innovators. This process helps explain the existence of much of the research community on Route 128 near Boston.[19]

To the extent that research conduces to large scale, therefore, one need not assume that it pushes the size of the original innovating firm upward without limit. The process of maturation may well lead to a spinning off of specialized research activities to outside firms. If the mother firms move on to other areas of industrial innovation, they retain a quality conducive to bigness, one that contines to place them in the industries at the top of Table 4–1. If, however, they spin off their research activities and throw in their lot with the maturing industries, they risk losing some of the stimuli for bigness that continue to operate in the "newer industries."

Research in relation to the firm's other functions. The final stage in the argument, however, is that the size of the skill-oriented firms is due in part to the communication needs between the function of research and the firm's other functions. Research activities, narrowly defined, are hardly important enough to explain the large size of the average firm in skill-intensive industries. Scientists and engineers engaged in "research" in United States industry constitute only a shade over one percent of the skilled labor force of that industry. For every scientist and engineer engaged in research in United States industry, there are five engaged in other activities.

Indeed, informed estimates of the relative importance of the research function in the complex process of industrial innovation usually assign the phase of research a comparatively small role, at least when measured in quantitative terms. For instance, one authoritative estimate indicates that R & D activity proper constitutes only 5 to 10 percent of the total cost of producing an industrial innovation. According to this estimate, engineering design represents 10 to 20 percent, tooling 40 to 60 percent, manufacturing start-up 10 to 15 percent.[20] It would be pushing plausibility to its outside limits, therefore, if one were to assume that the organizational requirements of the R & D activity proper were determining the large size of firms.

On the other hand, it is much less implausible to assign some importance

[19] E. B. Roberts, "Entrepreneurship and Technology," in W. H. Gruber and D. G. Marquis (eds.), *op. cit.*

[20] Panel on Invention and Innovation, *Technological Innovation: Its Environment and Management* (Washington: U.S. Department of Commerce, January 1967), p. 9.

to the common communication needs between researchers and non-researchers as a reason for the large size of firms associated with industrial innovation. The empirical work of organizational behaviorists seems to have established the fact that, where innovation is critical for achieving an organization's goals, a great deal of the organization's resources is devoted to integration and interaction among the units in the firm that perform different functions.[21] Effective industrial innovation requires an intimate communication link among those whose job consists of scanning the opportunities of the market, those who are concerned with understanding scientific possibilities, and those who have skills in converting laboratory-produced products to mass output.

Some reasons for this needed link are suggested by economic history.[22] Some emerge from contemporary studies of research-intensive industries.[23]

According to the old saw, necessity is invention's mother. New products and processes are not characteristically brought into being simply because they have become scientifically possible. They are created because, having become possible, they seem to promise a relatively riskless reward to the firm that brings them into being.[24] In some cases, to be sure, inventors have created useful products without much stimulus from the market, but products or processes of this sort often languished for long periods of time, were forgotten, and had to be resurrected or reinvented when the conditions of the market became more favorable.[25]

Despite the empirical evidence for these propositions, certain dangers are

[21] For evidence on this proposition, as well as a review of the related literature, see Edwin Mansfield, *The Economics of Technological Change* (New York: W. W. Norton & Co., 1968), especially pp. 68–98; this source is invaluable as a summary of the relevant literature to date. See also J. W. Lorsch and P. R. Lawrence, "Environmental Factors and Organizational Integration," to be published in *Proceedings of the American Sociological Association*, 1968; and David Allison (ed.), *The R & D Game* (Cambridge: MIT Press, 1969), pp. 212–235.

[22] For authoritative accounts of the economic history of innovation, see H. J. Habbakuk, *American and British Technology in the 19th Century* (Cambridge, England: University Press, 1962); W. P. Strassmann, *Risk and Technological Innovation* (Ithaca: Cornell University Press, 1959); and A. L. Levine, *Industrial Retardation in Britain 1880–1914* (New York: Basic Books, Inc., 1967). See also Jacob Schmookler, *Invention and Economic Growth* (Cambridge: Harvard University Press, 1966).

[23] Material suggestive of the generalizations that follow is found in three studies, all directed by Christopher Freeman and published in various issues of the *National Institute Economic Review*, as follows: No. 26, Nov., 1963, on the plastics industry; No. 34, Nov. 1965, on the electronics industry; No. 45, Aug. 1968, on the chemical process plant industry (previously cited). See also Nelson, *op. cit.*, Part III, pp. 279–359. The OECD also has developed extensive relevant materials for a dozen or so industrial sectors, much of it unpublished.

[24] An excellent treatment of this point is found in W. P. Strassmann, *Technological Change and Economic Development* (Ithaca: Cornell University Press, 1968), pp. 218–225.

[25] For illustrations in the synthetic materials field, see Hufbauer, *op. cit.*, pp. 86–87; in the 19th century machinery industry, Habbakuk, *op. cit.*, pp. 118–121; in the contemporary textile and machine tool industries, Schon, *op. cit.*, pp. 219–228.

involved in embracing too unequivocally the arguments in support of large-scale research. The connection between a firm's size and inventiveness is obscure; many major inventions seem to have originated in small producing firms rather than large.[26] Moreover, some data suggest that small producing firms in a given industry may be no less prone to use resources on research than large and that their use of such resources may be no less productive of research results.[27]

The relevant question here, however, is not whether firms of a given size are more efficient in producing innovative ideas; rather, the question is whether economies of scale result from the full multistage process which consists of generating an innovation, developing the innovation, and marketing the embodied output. Some evidence suggests that success in this process is not independent of the firm's size. The data indicate, for a selected group of inventions at least, that large firms apply new techniques more rapidly than small.[28] There is also support for the view that the amount of sales per unit of effort in research is greater for large firms than for small.[29]

The problems that small firms confront in converting an innovation to a marketable product are well documented. Fearful that they may be unable to protect the proprietary content of their ideas, small firms may be reluctant to offer the innovation for sale in the market. Large firms often reinforce this imperfection of the marketplace by a policy of rejecting the approaches of small firms, simply because the large firms are unwilling to be exposed to the risk of infringement claims. If the small firm decides to take on the post-innovative development of an idea, it enters upon a venture that is often prolonged and expensive, fraught with risk.[30] The possibility of an abortive or incomplete exploitation, therefore, seems higher for small firms than for large.

---

[26] See, for instance, Mansfield, *op. cit.,* pp. 107–110; also John Jewkes, David Sawers, and Richard Stillerman, *The Sources of Invention* (New York: St. Martin's Press, 1958).

[27] W. S. Comanor, "Market Structure, Product Differentiation, and Industrial Research," *Quarterly Journal of Economics,* Vol. LXXXI, No. 4 (Nov. 1967), p. 639; Daniel Hamberg, *R & D, Essays on the Economics of Research and Development* (New York: Random House, 1966).

[28] Edwin Mansfield, "The Speed of Response of Firms to New Techniques," *Quarterly Journal of Economics,* Vol. LXXVII, No. 2 (May 1963), pp. 290–311.

[29] See F. M. Scherer, "Firm Size and Patented Inventions," *American Economic Review,* Vol. LV, No. 5, Pt. 2, pp. 1097–1123. One wishes that the research effort in the firm and the sales generated by the firm could be more firmly linked by the statistics; unfortunately, the tie can only be inferred.

[30] One measure of the magnitude of the commitment confronting the firm that proposes to do its own development and introduction of a product is suggested by the generalization "seven years from conception to market" for new products. See D. A. Schon, *op. cit.,* p. 34. See also the Freeman chemical-process plant study, cited earlier, p. 46; and also J. L. Enos, "Invention and Innovation in the Petroleum Refining Industry," in Nelson, *op. cit.,* pp. 311–312. The innovative stage of major developments involves sums far in excess of $1,000,000 and periods of five to ten years.

The fact that the success of the innovative stage depends partly on ability to introduce a product or process effectively into the market indicates why Table 4–2 hypothesizes "sellouts" or mergers in the advanced phases of stage I. After an idea has been successfully carried beyond the test tube and demonstrably turned into something with proprietary value, the problem is to relate the half-tested asset to an organization that is efficient in completing the developmental process. The hypothesis behind the cryptic generalization in Table 4–2 is that large organizations frequently absorb smaller ones at this stage, with the one recognizing its opportunity and the other recognizing its need.

Organizational Adaptation in the Large Firm

If we return to the main observations stated above in connection with Table 4–2, one proposition still remains to be explored. The large firm, it was suggested, dominates skill-intensive industries more effectively than other industries of the United States. Achieving that domination involves a constant process of search and adaptation, a process which continually pushes the firm into new products and new markets while permitting it to slough off the more senescent activities in which it has been engaged. The evidence indicates that, whenever this process of adaptation and change is present in a firm, one also generally finds certain distinctive organizational characteristics. Organizational theorists have come to refer to the structures embodying these characteristics as "multidivisional product organizations."[31] This organizational form is characterized by substantially larger inputs of high-level managerial personnel per unit of output than the organizational structure it replaces.[32]

The need for larger inputs of high-level management in multidivisional organizations becomes clear as one looks at the change these organizations represent. In more primitive types of organization, specialization within the structure is primarily based on functional lines; there are production men, finance men, marketing men, and so on. In such organizations, general managerial decisions that require the synchronization of these functions are taken only at the top. Multidivisional structures, on the other hand, are designed to submerge the day-to-day business decisions of the firm to a level below the pyramidal top, that is, to a divisional level. Added high-level personnel are therefore needed to man the divisions. Moreover, as observed earlier in connection with research-oriented activities, a considerable investment has to be made in a coordinating and integrating apparatus,

[31] Evidence in support of the associations suggested in the last few sentences is found in L. E. Fouraker and J. M. Stopford, "Organizational Structure and the Multinational Strategy," *Administrative Science Quarterly*, Vol. 13, No. 1 (January 1968), pp. 47–64.

[32] See, for instance, A. D. Chandler, Jr., *Strategy and Structure* (Garden City, New York: Anchor, 1966); P. R. Lawrence and J. W. Lorsch, *Organization and Environment* (Boston: Harvard Business School, 1967).

capable of maintaining an effective flow of information among the divisions themselves, of identifying and negotiating conflicts, and of allocating the common resources of the firm, such as research capacity and financial capital.

The correlation between organizations of this sort and the propensity for change in products and markets is especially evident in the case of multinational enterprises. We have already referred to the strong association among size of firm, relative use of skilled manpower, and propensity to export and invest in foreign markets. The evidence is also quite clear that firms exhibiting all these characteristics have a high propensity to be organized on the multidivisional basis just described. In the mid-1960's, for instance, only 18 of 170 large United States firms, comprising practically all the major United States firms with substantial overseas investments in manufacturing, still retained the traditional functional basis of organization;[33] most of the others, having previously been organized on a more primitive basis, had adopted the multidivisional form.

Circumstantial evidence suggests that, once the basic change in structure is achieved, the diseconomies of scale which threaten any large organization are pushed off to a new, more distant level or, perhaps more accurately, that new economies appear sufficiently important to offset for an added period the diseconomies associated with large organizations. In the only extensive study of which I am aware that relates the business performance of the firm to organizational structure, a strong association is exhibited between high growth rates, high profit rates, and multidivisional organization.[34] An analysis of the profits of 136 large United States firms in 1965, for instance, shows that the median yield on investment was highest for multidivisional multinational firms and lowest for single-product domestic firms, with an exceedingly large gap between the two levels of performance.

What are the economies for which the multidivisional structure may be responsible? Some have already been suggested in the general discussion of research and research-related activities. The full exploitation of scale economies in research and research-related activities is helped by a constant succession of new products, or new markets, or both; but these new products and markets may require a structure that can handle efficiently the multifarious decisions about production and distribution associated with such a process. Among the expansive measures that help exhaust such economies are measures to sell in foreign markets. The penetration of foreign markets is especially attractive from the viewpoint of the research-intensive firm because such penetration may prolong the exploitation of proprietary technology. All proprietary technology has a certain perishability; the

[33] J. M. Stopford, *Growth and Organizational Change in the Multinational Firm,* unpublished doctoral thesis, Harvard Business School, 1966, p. 16.

[34] This study, unpublished as yet, was undertaken under the direction of Professor L. E. Fouraker.

longer it is applied in a given national market, the less likely it is to be relevant to the market's situation. And if still relevant after a long period, it is unlikely to be quite so proprietary. The drip-dry shirt, fresh-frozen food processing, the portable typewriter, numerically controlled machine tools — all of these had a period of proprietary exploitation in the United States, an exploitation whose power was eventually diluted by the diffusion of the relevant knowledge.

An organization's access to foreign markets can often prolong a little the proprietary value of such technology, thus spreading a sunk cost further. Even after the technology is well diffused within the market where it has first been introduced, it may still have lingering proprietary value in other markets. Evidence of a systematic lag in the introduction of new products and processes among different national markets is now fairly extensive.[35] That lag does not always result from ignorance or monopoly; it is often attributable to the fact that, because of differences in factor prices or consumer wants among different markets, wide-scale introduction of a product or process is not appropriate in that market until some time after its introduction elsewhere.[36] When the time for wide-scale introduction finally arrives, no more than a fraction of the producers in the first market may have the organization, the resources, or the contacts to exploit the opportunity for sale of the technology abroad. Thus, a firm's ready access to foreign markets may prolong the proprietary exploitation of an industrial innovation.

Another scale factor associated with multinational enterprises derives from the fact that the changes in demand confronting any group of related producing units are likely to be less synchronous for units located in different national markets than for units located in a single market. Firms having facilities in different markets, therefore, find themselves in a position to shuttle business among their various international units.[37]

Still another advantage of size associated with the multinational aspect of organization is the extension of an information grid whose antennae are placed in new market settings and new industrial milieux. This is a tricky issue from an economic point of view. The economic desirability of investing in the acquisition of knowledge usually cannot be determined a

[35] Hufbauer, *op. cit.*, Stobaugh, *op. cit.* In a less empirical vein, see Stephen Hymer, "La grande 'corporation' multinationale," *Revue Economique,* Vol. XIX, No. 6, pp. 949–973.

[36] For an elaboration of this thesis, see my "International Investment and International Trade in the Product Cycle," *Quarterly Journal of Economics,* Vol. LXXX, No. 2 (May 1966), p. 190. A theoretical model, accompanied by an empirical test in the computer industry, appears in A. J. Harman, *Innovations, Technology and The Pure Theory of International Trade,* unpublished Ph.D. thesis, MIT, September 1968.

[37] For a striking illustration, see Christopher Freeman's study of chemical process plants, cited earlier, p. 37: "But the large American contractors show great ingenuity and flexibility in switching work from one office to another anywhere in the world, in order to achieve an optimum loading of their total resources."

priori; some of the data needed to test the wisdom of the investment usually cannot be acquired except by making the investment itself.[38] Once capital has been sunk in a knowledge-gathering apparatus, however, there is a strong presumption of a positive incremental yield.

In the case of the multinational enterprise, its geographical spread may generate various kinds of information. One kind was referred to obliquely a little earlier. Food processors who acquire subsidiaries in foreign markets commonly learn of processes and products that can be used at once elsewhere; American automobile manufacturers, who have learned the skills of compact car manufacture through their European subsidiaries, carry that skill back to Detroit; and so on. Another kind of information obtained by multinational enterprises is knowledge about overseas suppliers whose unique skills or unique cost structure cannot be transferred across national boundaries. The specialization and cross-hauling that are beginning to appear so commonly among related subsidiaries of multinational firms partly result from unanticipated discoveries of this sort, such as the cheapness and skill of Mexican workers in the manufacturing of jigs and dies, the capacity of Brazilians to build economically aircraft engine parts to close tolerances, and so on.

The hypothesis that organizational structure is a source of major economies of scale seems consistent with a good deal of the evidence accumulated in recent years on the behavior of multinational enterprises and of enterprises in which highly-skilled manpower plays an important role. The advantages which such organizations enjoy, however, may be impaired when the rate of change slows up. Although the economies of scale associated with large organizations appear relevant to launching a new product or penetrating a new market, they seem less relevant to maintaining an already well-established position in a market for a well-known product. If the original advantages of the firm are based on proprietary information or esoteric skills, those advantages are always subject to the threat of diffusion and standardization. As diffusion and standardization occur, the advantages of the large skill-oriented firm probably begin to weaken. Then the productive process itself, based on standardized processes and products, derives its advantages of scale, such as they are, from the mechanical and physical aspects of the existing technology rather than from the integrating apparatus of the organization. Marketing becomes much more dependent on cost and price than on product differentiation, distinctive distribution, and service. Accordingly, although the organizational advantage may remain with the firm that is constantly rolling over its product line, the advantage may be lost to the firm that settles for what it has.

---

[38] For a stimulating elaboration, see Kenneth Arrow, "Economic Welfare and the Allocation of Resources for Invention," in Nelson, *op. cit.*, pp. 609–625.

5

The Scope of Antitrust and Other
Economic Regulatory Policies

*Donald F. Turner**

In this article,[1] I shall endeavor to set forth my general views on the proper scope of antitrust policy, of direct regulation, and of governmental subsidy and to discuss some of the basic policy questions raised by each. I do not of course attribute those views to Dean Mason, but I can and do acknowledge a great intellectual debt to him, as indeed must all of us in the legal profession who deal with these matters. As much as, or more than, any other, he has not only focused our attention on the essential role of economic analysis in the formulation of appropriate regulatory policies and legal rules; but in addition, with a fine awareness of the limitations of both law and economics, he has helped greatly in making economic research and analysis more directly useful to those lawyers, judges, and governmental officials who influence, and make critical decisions on, policy.

Most economists would probably view the actual results to date with reactions ranging from dissatisfaction to despair. And as will become evident, I do not see how one could look happily on the current state of the law in the economic regulatory area. Nevertheless, though improvements have perhaps been at best modest and in many areas wholly undetectable, there is little doubt in my mind that the law reflects considerably more awareness of economic issues than it did thirty years ago, and even a little more understanding.

A pervasive and overriding issue of domestic economic regulatory policy is when and to what extent we should rely on free competitive markets and

* Harvard University

[1] With the kind consent of the editors concerned, I have written this article both for inclusion in this volume in honor of Dean Mason and for publication, with only minor differences, in the April 1969 issue of the *Harvard Law Review*.

antitrust, and when and to what extent we should resort instead to regulation, exemption or governmental subsidy. Reliance on, and protection of, competition in the markets for goods and services has long been our declared general policy, but of course it has also long been subject to manifold exceptions. We have directly regulated entry, rates, and other aspects of economic performance in such industries as public utilities, transportation, and communication. We have interfered heavily in the markets for agricultural commodities. We permit collective bargaining over wage rates and other terms of employment. And we give direct or indirect subsidy or other forms of support to a wide range of economic activities.

Some departures from competitive policy have been plainly justifiable if not inevitable. We have always had certain markets where economies of size produce monopoly or extremely high concentration, where one firm or a very few firms of the most efficient size can supply the entire demand. The forced imposition of a competitive structure in such situations would be a costly and idle gesture. It has also been quite clear that, in some respects and in some situations, even vigorous and durable competition will not adequately satisfy important economic and social goals. Competition cannot insure cyclical stability, and in many areas, only governmental intervention in allocating private resources can redirect the use of resources so as to maximize aggregate economic wealth.

Granted, however, some situations in which competitive markets either do not allocate resources properly or perform inadequately in other respects and granted some markets in which economies of scale make a competitive structure undesirable, the question is when, as a matter of economic fact, do these considerations really apply and to what extent do they really require substantial interference with a policy of relying on, and promoting, competition. It seems reasonably clear to me that none of these problems are of such magnitude and character as to make antitrust policy largely obsolete. It also seems perfectly clear to me that in many instances we are regulating and subsidizing markets when there is no good reason to do so.

I. *Antitrust Issues*

A. The Proper Scope of Antitrust

As in the past, many currently contend that the useful scope of antitrust policy has been drastically diminished by the need to solve economic and social problems capable of being handled satisfactorily by the private market economy only if certain anticompetitive practices are allowed, and by the need for very large business firms and highly concentrated markets in order to achieve maximum economic efficiency and progress. The contention has little to support it. I will first consider improper allocation of resources.

Economists well know that there are some areas in which competitive markets do not produce an appropriate allocation of resources among various economic pursuits because the social costs of a particular activity or the social benefits it confers are not fully reflected in the private monetary costs and revenues of the individuals engaged in it. When an activity involves costs which the private producer does not have to pay, more resources will be devoted to that activity than should be. Similarly, when an activity confers benefits on others for which no payment is received, the amount of resources devoted to that activity will fall short of the economic ideal. Pollution of air and streams inflicts high economic costs on society that have not been reflected in the private costs borne by those whose activities contribute to it. So too will it be with the sonic booms of the Supersonic Transport. On the other hand, without governmental support, wholly inadequate resources would be devoted to education because the amounts actually paid to private suppliers would fall far short of the total benefits to society that education confers.

Obviously, efforts to direct resources away from some activities and toward others interfere with the resource-allocation pattern that would have been effected by the private market economy if left alone. On the other hand, such measures do not require direct interference with competitive structure — the number and size of firms — in particular markets or with competition in its main elements — cost of production, price, and quality of product. Nor do they require any far-reaching exemptions from the ordinary application of antitrust law.

The private market's departures from optimal allocation of resources can be substantially corrected by government-sponsored programs or by taxes, subsidies, or specific controls — zoning laws, safety standards, and the like — that can be designed so as to leave relatively free play for the operation of competition in the affected markets. To be sure, corrective measures may in some instances have an effect on the structure of the market. Any substantial increase in the cost of carrying on a particular activity is likely to reduce total output and, consequently, the number of supplying firms. Some firms may be less capable than others of bearing the cost of safety standards or of antipollution devices. Rarely if ever, however, would one expect these consequences to change market structure in kind as well as degree. In short, governmental measures to promote particular economic or social goals are largely independent of, or complementary to, competitive policy rather than in conflict with it.

There have been several recent instances in which the government has encouraged voluntary private cooperative measures to meet specific social problems. These measures have included organized solicitation of private loan funds for redeveloping blighted areas and organized efforts to procure property insurance for areas that would otherwise be denied it. The government has also encouraged a greater commitment of private resources, by individual or cooperative effort, to research on the causes and cures of air pollution. Private cooperation among competitors may raise problems of behavior conflicting with competitive policy that are not raised by direct governmental action.

If a substantial conflict were to arise in any proposed private course of action, I would question whether the plan was indeed a suitable way of meeting the particular objective of public policy involved. Serious conflicts seem unlikely to me, however.

No significant antitrust question is raised by a series of voluntary and individually-reached decisions by, say, insurance companies to insure property in high-risk areas that they would not ordinarily touch, or by lenders to participate in a program of granting funds for redeveloping ghettos. No antitrust problem is raised by the decision of individual business firms to make special efforts to hire and train disadvantaged workers. At first glance, that business firms condition their participation in such schemes on comparable commitments by their competitors may seem questionable. Agreement by various mortgage lenders to commit certain amounts to blighted areas at a rate of no more than eight percent might be called a maximum price-fixing agreement; an agreement by competing firms to allocate five percent of their new hirings to disadvantaged workers might be called a collective boycott of those who would otherwise be hired. It is hard to imagine that any such characterizations would lead to a governmental antitrust suit, however, or that private suits would get other than short shrift in the courts. Unlike the typical object of antitrust attack, these are actions contrary to the pecuniary interests of the parties concerned and thus do not pose the dangers normally associated with collaboration among competitors. In any event, if statutory authorization of antitrust exemption for such agreements were thought necessary, an exemption limited to the needs of the occasion would hardly make any significant inroad on general competition among the parties concerned.

Much the same can be said of joint research ventures in air pollution and the like. Here the approach of antitrust law is highly consistent with the aims of public policy that are at stake. Antitrust law has typically given appropriate leeway to the necessary joint venture — one enabling its participants to engage in economic activity which individually they either could not carry on or could carry on only much less effectively. At the same time, it seems highly probable that competition is as beneficial in research as in any other economic activity.[2] Consequently, antitrust might well be expected to view critically a complete pooling of research by all interested firms, not so much because this would eliminate all competition but because the elimination of competition is likely to lead to less productive research.

[2] See, e.g., Hitch, "Character of Research and Development in a Competitive Economy," in *Proceedings of a Conference on Research and Development and Its Impact on the Economy* 129, 133–34 (1958); Turner, "Patents, Antitrust and Innovation," 28 *U. Pitt. L. Rev.* 151, 158–59 (1966).

Yet this approach is precisely what anyone would take who is interested in maximum results in solving the problem of air pollution. Indeed, one might well wish to impose a wider range of obligations on joint ventures to make generally available the results of their research than past antitrust precedents might be thought to require.

Two arguments of a much broader nature have been advanced for sacrificing competitive policy to the pursuit of important social goals. One is that antitrust exemptions beyond those strictly necessary to enable desirable private cooperation should be granted in order to induce widespread private voluntary participation in designated programs. The other is that large business units are generally more responsive to serious social problems and, by virtue of larger resources, are more capable of making a contribution to their solution. Accordingly, so the argument goes, we should favor rather than disfavor large size and high concentration. With regard to these propositions, I can say only that if toleration of anticompetitive agreements and of business units far larger than economies of scale require is the price that must be paid for private organization to meet social goals, the price is far too great and we had best rely instead on direct governmental action.

Nor do I agree with the second ground for the contention that the useful scope of antitrust has been drastically diminished, namely, the claim that economies of scale dictate monopoly or a very small number of firms in most of our significant markets. I shall not review here in detail the recent debates on this subject, debates mainly stimulated by Professor Galbraith. I shall simply summarize what the available empirical studies suggest. They indicate that size of firms and market concentration are typically greater than economies of scale in production and distribution would require.[3] They show no evident correlation between innovation and either size of firms or concentration. It does indeed appear that more large firms (with 5,000 or more employees) do research than small firms (with less than 500 employees). But once we get firms large enough to do organized research at all, there seem to be no continuing economies of scale.[4] Similarly, there is little indication of any positive correlation between innovation and industrial concentration, and some indication to the contrary.[5]

Moreover, there are in general no adverse trends. From 1947 to 1963

[3] See, e.g., J. Bain, *Industrial Organization* 211–12 (2d ed. 1968); J. Bain, *Barriers to New Competition* 110–13 (1956).

[4] See Worley, "Industrial Research and the New Competition," 69 *J. Pol. Econ.* 183 (1961). See also Comanor, "Research and Technical Change in the Pharmaceutical Industry," 47 *Rev. Econ. & Statistics* 182 (1965).

[5] See J. Kendrick, *Productivity Trends in the United States* 179 (1961) (no significant correlation to cost-cutting innovations); Scherer, "Firm Size, Market Structure, Opportunity, and the Output of Patented Inventions," 55 *Am. Econ. Rev.* 1097, 1116–21 (1965) (slight position correlation in new products); Stigler, "Industrial Organization and Economic Progress," in *Business Organization and Public Policy* 125, 131–33 (H. Levin ed. 1958) (indications of negative correlation in cost-cutting innovations, 1899–1937).

significant decreases in four-firm concentration ratios in manufacturing industries were slightly more numerous than significant increases; and among producer-goods industries — where economies of large-scale production are usually most pronounced — significant declines of concentration were nearly twice as numerous as significant increases.[6]

Finally, Professor Galbraith's more recent comments indicate that not even he would claim that considerations of efficiency compel the kind of large size and high concentration that would permit producers to control their market rather than be controlled by it. Rather, his principal point appears to be that large firms and concentration are here to stay because no one is likely to do anything about them.[7] But whether we should do anything about unnecessary monopoly and unnecessarily high market concentration is of course, as it has long been, the critical question of policy, and the one to which I now turn.

B. The Treatment of Monopoly and Oligopoly

Given significant monopolistic and oligopolistic elements in the economy that are unwarranted by economies of scale, failure to do anything about them has raised, and will continue to raise, serious problems. For one thing, the existence of significant monopolistic power greatly stimulates claims by small, unorganized producers — farmers, gasoline dealers, automotive parts suppliers, and the like — that they too should receive protection or be allowed to protect themselves by collective action exempt from antitrust law.

In the main, such efforts should be strenuously resisted. As I have said elsewhere,[8] I believe Professor Galbraith is completely wrong in asserting that the failure of antitrust enforcement to break up existing monopoly power makes it pointless and immoral to prevent others from achieving comparable status by merger or even by price-fixing. The existence of monopoly or high concentration in some industries hardly makes it sensible to incur the economic cost of permitting other industries, now workably competitive, to go down the same road. And there is little reason to believe that the creation of "countervailing power" will typically lead to better economic results. Witness, for example, wage-price developments in the construction industry.

Moreover, arguments for a "collective-bargaining" or similar antitrust exemption are commonly made in situations where there is little or no

[6] *Staff of the Antitrust Subcomm. of the House Comm. on the Judiciary, 90th Cong., 1st Sess., Report on the Celler-Kefauver Act: Sixteen Years of Enforcement* 26–30 (Comm. Print 1967). The increases did, however, outnumber the decreases between 1958 and 1963. *Id.* at 27.

[7] "Hearing on Planning, Regulation, and Competition Before the Subcomms. of the Senate Select Comm. on Small Business," *90th Cong., 1st Sess.* 9–10, 31–32 (1967).

[8] *Id.* at 28–30.

direct exploitation in fact. Although monopoly and oligopoly are indeed frequent enough to worry about, most industrial markets are either workably competitive or competitive enough to prevent exorbitant profits, and one rarely finds significant situations in which unorganized suppliers must deal with, and are likely to be exploited by, only one or a very few buyers. Thus, the problem of the farmer is primarily one of excess production, not exploitation by those to whom he sells.[9] But these are not points easy to get across to those who feel abused, and the fact remains that the existence of significant degrees of monopoly power generates political pressures difficult to resist.

The second problem posed by failure to deal directly with monopoly and oligopoly is the pressure to augment the scope of other techniques of antitrust enforcement. For example, in the absence of direct dissolution of monopoly and oligopoly by divestiture, enforcement authorities are under heavy pressure to expand the scope of antimerger law so as to maximize the opportunity for deconcentration in the future. It has seemed desirable, even necessary, to place a high premium on preserving all significant potentialities of future competition and thus to discourage any substantial acquisition by a company at all likely to enter the industry by minor acquisition or internal expansion. Moreover, continued toleration of existing concentration makes a strong case for additional legislation imposing more sweeping prohibitions on acquisitions by large firms. Given such toleration, there is much to be said for legislation that would prohibit very large firms from acquiring any of the leading firms in other concentrated markets[10] or for legislation that would generally prohibit the eighty to one hundred largest firms in the country from growing substantially by any kind of merger.

I do not mean to suggest that there is no independent merit in a strong antimerger policy under section 7 of the Clayton Act or in additional legislation along the lines indicated. Nor do I mean to suggest that enforcement standards to date should necessarily be cut back if direct attacks on serious problems of monopoly and oligopoly were restored to the antitrust arsenal. Preventive measures are obviously less painful than major surgery. Moreover, preservation of a wide range of possibilities for future potential competition may be expected to improve performance in the many industries that would not be so economically significant or so highly concentrated as to warrant applying the remedies of dissolution and divestiture.

But the question is how far to move out the boundaries. A strong antimerger policy is not entirely costless. Part of the price we might pay for a greatly expanded antitrust attack on mergers would be to divert the merger movement into the economically less desirable channel of the pure con-

9 See H. Houthakker, *Economic Policy for the Farm Sector* 5–15 (1967).

10 See, e.g., *Council of Econ. Adv. Ann. Rep., in 1969 Economic Report of the President* 108 (1969).

glomerate. Other things being equal, we would generally prefer that an expansion-minded company buy into activities to which its skills have some direct economic relevance than into totally dissimilar businesses, because the chances of gains in efficiency would appear to be greater.

Moreover, for reasons that have been set forth at length elsewhere,[11] rational and effective antimerger law must depend primarily on generally-framed antimerger rules based largely on the relative size of the merging firms, and such general rules inevitably prevent some mergers that would have procompetitive effects. It is on the rules making marginal contributions to competition that judgment would be affected by the presence of direct measures for dealing with undue concentration. With a greater capacity to correct undue concentration as it appears, there would be less need to prevent mergers which present only remote possibilities of anticompetitive consequences.

Rather than couple a toleration of existing undue concentration with an extremely harsh antimerger policy, I believe it would be sounder economic policy to apply divestiture remedies to the most serious, persistent, and economically significant monopolies and oligopolies and to take a somewhat more conservative approach toward mergers likely to make a fair amount of economic sense. This policy would involve some toleration additional to that otherwise deemed appropriate of conglomerate mergers with relatively minor horizontal or vertical significance, and I suspect, some easing of the standards for size applied to horizontal and vertical mergers.

In my opinion, any costs of applying divestiture remedies to economically significant monopolies and highly concentrated industries would be far outweighed by prospective gains. That there would be substantial gains is of course subject to dispute, and the proposition cannot be proved beyond a reasonable doubt. It is certainly the fundamental premise of antitrust law that competitive markets will perform better than monopolies and highly concentrated markets.[12] If the premise is incorrect, much more of antitrust law than divestiture remedies should be tossed out the window.

---

[11] Bok, "Section 7 of the Clayton Act and the Merging of Law and Economics," 74 *Harv. L. Rev.* 226 (1960); Turner, "Conglomerate Mergers and Section 7 of the Clayton Act," 78 *Harv. L. Rev.* 1313, 1318–20 (1965).

[12] The premise was admirably explained by Judge Wyzanski:

[W]ell as a monopoly may have behaved in the moral sense, its economic performance is inevitably suspect. The very absence of strong competitors implies that there cannot be an objective measuring rod of the monopolist's excellence, and the test of its performance must, therefore, be largely theoretical. What appears to the outsider to be a sensible, prudent, nay even a progressive policy of the monopolist, may in fact reflect a lower scale of adventurousness and less intelligent risk-taking than would be the case if the enterprise were forced to respond to a stronger industrial challenge. Some truth lurks in the cynical remark that not high profits but a quiet life is the chief reward of monopoly power. And even if a particular enterprise seeks growth and not repose, an increased rate in the growth of ideas does not follow from an increased concentration of power. Industrial advance may indeed be in inverse proportion to

Empirical data appear to confirm the hypothesis underlying antitrust policy, namely, that at least some aspects of economic performance are worsened when effective competition is absent. Studies by Bain and by Collins and Preston have suggested a correlation between concentration of sellers and excess profits beyond what would appear to be accounted for by special circumstances like windfalls or rewards to innovation.[13] Empirical data on the relation of the market's structure to innovation are considerably less decisive, but they give no substantial reason for doubting that substitution of more effective competition for monopoly or tight oligopoly would improve economic performance in this dimension as well.[14]

As for the costs of restructuring, they might well be serious if there were any extensive campaign of atomization. We are not talking about that, however. What is at issue is divestiture applied only to firms much larger than necessary for economies of scale and applied only if viable successor firms of efficient size can be created. With these limitations, the disruptive effects of divestiture would have short-run consequences only, and in my opinion the disruptive effects are usually exaggerated anyway. Multiplant firms are commonly organized on a divisional basis, and there are frequent instances of substantial structural reorganizations within large firms, often in the direction of granting greater autonomy to divisional managers in order to minimize the inefficiencies of central control. Further, arrangements could be made for temporary contractual relationships among the successor firms during the transitional period in situations where, for example, production of a particular component had been concentrated in a single division.

The question remains whether the application of divestiture remedies to monopoly and oligopoly would have significant disincentive effects or other adverse effects on business decisions. Here, too, a great deal depends on the dimensions of divestiture policy. If, apart from cases involving plainly questionable conduct, divestiture is limited to substantial degrees of market power that have persisted for a considerable period of time — thus indi-

---

economic power; for creativity, in business as in other areas, is best nourished by multiple centers of activity, each following its unique pattern and developing its own esprit de corps to respond to the challenge of competition. The dominance of any one enterprise inevitably unduly accentuates that enterprise's experience and views as to what is possible, practical, and desirable with respect to technological development, research, relations with producers, employees, and customers.
United States v. *United Shoe Mach. Corp.*, 110 F. Supp. 295, 347 (D. Mass. 1953), aff'd per curiam, 347 U.S. 521 (1954).

[13] J. Bain, *Industrial Organization* 448 (2d ed. 1968); Collins and Preston, "Concentration and Price-Cost Margins in Food Manufacturing Industries," 14 *J. Indus. Econ.* 226 (1966). See also Weiss, "Average Concentration Ratios and Industrial Performance," 11 *J. Indus. Econ.* 237 (1963).

[14] See footnote 4, page 8 *supra*. See also Comanor, *supra* note 2 page 8 (diseconomies of scale encountered in even moderate sized firms).

cating the unlikelihood that anything other than direct action will provide a cure — it seems highly unlikely to me that any business firm would subdue its competitive efforts because of the possibility that it would be so successful for so long that divestiture would be applied. Even should it come to that, divestiture would leave untouched the monopolistic profits gained in the interim, and the only value destroyed by divestiture is the opportunity to obtain monopolistic profits from the same source in the future.

Without at this point going into a more elaborate discussion of the reasons, I shall simply state my own conclusion that the past inadequacies and periodic atrophy of antitrust in the monopoly and oligopoly areas have been unfortunate and that, as a matter of public policy, there ought to be at least a modest expansion. This statement leads to the question, "How?" As many readers are well aware, I at one time shared the view that, while section 2 of the Sherman Act is reasonably adequate for dealing with the kind of monopoly that ought to concern us, it is a legally inadequate instrument for dealing with oligopoly, and any interpretation that would make it adequate would be too much to ask of the courts.[15] Accordingly, I concluded that additional legislation was necessary and appropriate, and Professor Kaysen and I formulated a specific statutory proposal.[16]

Obviously, a well-drafted statute clearly setting forth the power of a divestiture court would be the most expeditious and effective method of enabling the job to be done. Among other things, it may well be desirable to establish a special court for cases of this kind, with special procedures and access to qualified technical assistance. Our proposal was suggestive; I do not doubt that it could be improved upon, for there are many issues that might be handled somewhat differently from the way we proposed. But I have come to believe, contrary to my earlier expressed views, that courts may fairly be asked to extend the scope of the Sherman Act's application to oligopoly and, further, to extend its application to single-firm monopoly beyond what past precedents, except possibly *Alcoa,*[17] have reached. I shall set forth my reasons, taking up first the case of monopoly.

1. Monopoly. My concern in the area of monopoly is with monopoly that has been legitimately obtained, by patents or superior performance, but, having been obtained, seems likely to persist for the foreseeable future unless the company encourages the entry and growth of competitors by affirmative help or by deliberately restricting capacity and output. Such cases are likely to be rare, but we have at times been faced with continuing monopoly power in important industries, and the economic interest in achieving an antitrust solution for those situations is considerable.

[15] C. Kaysen & D. Turner, *Antitrust Policy 21,* 110–11 (1959).
[16] *Id.* at 266–69.
[17] *United States* v. *Aluminum Co. of America,* 148 F. 2d 416 (2d Cir. 1945).

Specifically, the question is whether a firm may be held to have unlawfully monopolized a market simply by obtaining and retaining monopoly power over a substantial enough period of time to indicate that its power is relatively impervious to competitive erosion, excepting only those cases where the firm's size is attributable solely to economies of scale or where the power is still based on the unexpired patents that were its original source. Judge Hand's opinion in *Alcoa* comes very close to saying this; indeed, perhaps it does. After noting that Alcoa had retained its monopoly of primary aluminum for over three decades, Judge Hand commented:

> The only question is whether [Alcoa] falls within the exception established in favor of those who do not seek, but cannot avoid, the control of a market. It seems to us that that question scarcely survives its statement. It was not inevitable that it should always anticipate increases in the demand for ingot and be prepared to supply them. Nothing compelled it to keep doubling and redoubling its capacity before others entered the field. It insists that it never excluded competitors; but we can think of no more effective exclusion than progressively to embrace each new opportunity as it opened, and to face every newcomer with new capacity already geared into a great organization, having the advantage of experience, trade connections and the elite of personnel. Only in case we interpret "exclusion" as limited to manoeuvres not honestly industrial, but actuated solely by a desire to prevent competition, can such a course, indefatigably pursued, be deemed not "exclusionary." So to limit it would in our judgment emasculate the Act; would permit just such consolidations as it was designed to prevent.[18]

At an earlier point in the opinion, Judge Hand had suggested that not all monopoly was unlawful. Among the possible exceptions, he cited the producer who "may be the survivor out of a group of active competitors, merely by virtue of his superior skill, foresight and industry."[19] In such cases, he remarked,

> [A] strong argument can be made that, although, [sic] the result may expose the public to the evils of monopoly, the Act does not mean to condemn the resultant of those very forces which it is its prime object to foster. . . . The successful competitor, having been urged to compete, must not be turned upon when he wins.[20]

It is not readily apparent how these two passages can be reconciled. One would suppose that "skill, foresight and industry" — "those very forces which it is [the Sherman Act's] prime object to foster" — should be taken to mean the kind of competitive conduct and performance that ordinarily has unquestioned economic merit. This would include, as Judge Wyzanski

[18] 148 F. 2d at 431.
[19] 148 F. 2d at 430.
[20] *Id.*

later noted, the application of superior managerial skill, putting out superior products, economic or technological efficiency (including research), and low margins of profit maintained permanently and without discrimination.[21] One would think it also included expansion of capacity to meet existing or anticipated demand, which is obviously one of the most important responses that we expect a competitive market to generate. Yet this is precisely the kind of conduct which Judge Hand cited as the principal element in Alcoa's offense.

Accordingly, it has been commonly supposed that this latter aspect of Judge Hand's opinion could not be taken too seriously, that perhaps it was attributable to his reluctance to overturn lower court findings on the absence of unlawful conduct that he thought erroneous but not "clearly" so. In *Griffith,*[22] Mr. Justice Douglas at one point seemed to suggest even more than the implications of Judge Hand's opinion, namely, that not only the retention but the acquisition of monopoly power was itself a violation of section 2. But much more recently in *Grinnell* Justice Douglas, speaking for the Court, restated the offense:

> The offense of monopoly under §2 of the Sherman Act has two elements: (1) the possession of monopoly power in the relevant market and (2) the willful acquisition or maintenance of that power as distinguished from growth or development as a consequence of a superior product, business acumen, or historic accident.[23]

This formulation does not clarify the matter. The problem with it is much the same as with attempting to distinguish between "exclusionary" conduct and "skill, foresight and industry." Any highly successful competitive strategy tends to confer market power and tends to "exclude" competitors, and everyone who engages in such strategy knows this; thus, power obtained and maintained by any highly successful competitive strategy is "willfully" acquired. But *Grinnell* does suggest that, at least as to acquisition of power — "growth and development" — there is no offense where it is solely attributable to accident or competitive superiority.

As I see it, the result in *Alcoa* can be justified, even on the assumption that the company never indulged in any plainly questionable exclusionary tactics, by distinguishing between the acquisition of monopoly power on the one hand and the persistent retention of monopoly over a substantial period of time on the other. Alcoa could properly be held to have unduly "monopolized," not because it doubled and redoubled its capacity over a period of years in response to growing demands, but rather because the inability

---

[21] *United States* v. *United Shoe Mach. Corp.,* 110 F. Supp. 295, 342 (D. Mass. 1953), aff'd per curiam, 347 U.S. 521 (1954).

[22] *United States* v. *Griffith,* 334 U.S. 100, 106–07 (1948). The statement in question was clouded by reference to "purpose and intent."

[23] *United States* v. *Grinnell Corp.,* 384 U.S. 563, 570–71 (1966).

of competitors to break into the field — and the ability of Alcoa to hold the field to itself — reflected barriers to entry that were due not only to continuing "skill, foresight and industry," but also to Alcoa's original dominant position obtained long in the past. In short, it is appropriate to put a time limit on continuing monopoly power that rests in part on earlier success, regardless of how the early success was achieved.

In the first place, whatever the economic costs of continuing monopoly may be, they are the same regardless of the monopoly's origin. There is little reason to suppose that present performance would differ significantly depending on whether ten, twenty, or thirty years ago the monopoly position had been acquired by skill, foresight, and industry alone or in part by objectionable conduct. Second, dissolution of a monopoly that has existed for a substantial period of time is not punishing the early success but rather is simply putting a time limit on the reward for that success. Consequently, as I suggested earlier,[24] allowing a substantial period in which monopoly profits may be earned by the firm that has secured its monopoly by competitive superiority should minimize any disincentives to the kind of competitive behavior we seek to encourage. Third, for much the same reasons, imposition of the *Alcoa* rule as I have defined it raises no substantial question of fairness as long as it can be limited to governmental civil actions only, a question I shall discuss shortly. Statutory patent monopolies are limited to seventeen years. There is no apparent reason why any firm should have a right to enjoy indefinitely, or even for seventeen years, the fruits of monopoly from sources other than original unexpired patents or economies of scale.

So far, I have framed the rule to apply to persistent monopoly power that depends in part on advantages stemming from the original monopoly position, thus implying a defense that the original monopoly no longer had any causal relationship to the current monopoly, that the current position is entirely due to continuing and current skill, foresight, and industry. I would not hold open this defense, however, because it is nearly impossible to make and there is little point in encouraging anyone to try. An original monopoly position will have inevitably played a role in enabling a firm continually to attract top-flight managerial and research personnel. Relationships with customers and reputation, once they are established, will have made at least some contribution to continued success. Even in the case where a firm's later position is based primarily on significant patents developed well after the original position was secured, it is reasonable to presume that the firm would not have monopolized the new innovations but for the personnel that its original and continuing monopoly position enabled it to attract, and it is hard to see how that presumption could be disproved. Moreover, one can never be confident that a firm has perpetuated its monopoly solely by su-

---

[24] See pp. 14–17 *supra*.

perior skill, foresight, and industry when it has had no competitors to provide a market test. Thus, I would flatly state the rule as covering significant monopoly power that has persisted over a long enough time to indicate relatively impervious barriers to entry, regardless of how the monopoly was obtained or maintained, excepting only monopoly based on economies of scale or on the same unexpired patents that gave it birth.

Reasons might be advanced against such a rule in addition to those I have already dealt with. Three points merit discussion.

The first point is the possibility that the rule would lead to inferior economic performance by the monopolist after his monopoly had been acquired. Where circumstances indicate to a firm that its monopoly is likely to persist as long as it fully exploits its advantages, it can only escape eventual dissolution by taking deliberate steps to encourage the entry and growth of competitors. This, as such, is no cause for concern, because a more competitive market would be the goal of the antitrust suit in lieu of such conduct. If new companies cannot come in without access to the monopolist's later patents and technological know-how, such access would have to be facilitated. The problem arises if a monopoly firm without vital technological assets seeks to promote new competition simply by selling less and charging more than it otherwise would.[25] I suppose one must concede this as a possibility, that customers might in some instances pay more and obtain less during the period it takes to build up competitive capacity than they otherwise would. The cost would be substantial, if at all, however, only in those circumstances where the monopolist either deliberately idles a substantial part of his existing capacity or where he would be able to expand his own capacity to meet growing demand much more rapidly than new competitors could build theirs.

In a growing market there would be no need to idle a substantial amount of existing capacity. The monopolist could facilitate the entry of new competition simply by not building new capacity until his monopoly had been eradicated. If, on the other hand, market demand were static, it would appear to be less costly for the monopolist to sell his surplus plants directly to new competitors, for he would have no further use for them once the competitor's new capacity came into being. Accordingly, any costs in performance will probably lie in some delay in expanding capacity. I doubt that these costs would be substantial; in any event they would be relatively short-run costs and, like any short-run costs from divestiture, should be well outweighed by long-run gains.

The second problem with the *Alcoa*-type rule is a more "legal" one. As everyone knows, the Sherman Act carries criminal as well as civil sanctions. It would appear wholly inappropriate to impose criminal sanctions for the

---

[25] There is also the possibility that it might deliberately curb its investment in research and development. But this seems highly unlikely because of the risk that such a policy might lead not only to loss of monopoly but to loss of all or most of its market.

kind of "monopolizing" offense that I have described, namely, the mere retention of monopoly power for a substantial period of time without objectionable conduct of any kind. Hence, it doubtless would be urged that the proper reach of criminal sanctions should define the reach of the Act, even though, as a matter of practice, no enforcement agency would dream of bringing a criminal action for this kind of offense. It seems clear to me, however, that the existence of criminal sanctions has not had, and need not have, this effect. As early as the *Northern Securities* case[26] in 1904, Justice Holmes forcefully argued that the Sherman Act, as a criminal statute, should be strictly construed and confined more or less to those offenses recognized at common law when the Sherman Act was passed. Whatever the merits of the argument, it was made in vain. The Court has continually interpreted and reinterpreted the statute to apply to business practices not previously held to be unlawful; it has always viewed the Sherman Act as a flexible device for promoting competitive policy. Chief Justice Hughes described the Act as follows:

> As a charter of freedom, the Act has a generality and adaptability comparable to that found to be desirable in constitutional provisions. It does not go into detailed definitions which might either work injury to legitimate enterprise or through particularization defeat its purposes by providing loopholes for escape. The restrictions the Act imposes are not mechanical or artificial. Its general phrases, interpreted to attain its fundamental objects, set up the essential standard of reasonableness.[27]

This is hardly the way that courts typically interpret criminal statutes.

The opportunity to interpret the civil reach of the statute in this way has of course been facilitated by the virtually unbroken policy of the Justice Department to limit criminal prosecutions to such plain violations of the Act as price-fixing. But even if the enforcement agency were so reckless and so unwise as to bring a criminal action for monopolization devoid of moral dereliction, I see no reason why the courts could not explicitly take the position that criminal offenses under the Sherman Act are not, as a matter of substantive law, coterminous with civil offenses — that, in other words, some kinds of substantive offenses are civil offenses only.[28]

The final problem is somewhat similar to the one just discussed. Again as everyone knows, the Sherman Act is generally enforceable not only by the Government but also by private action. I believe that a private action should not lie for a charge of monopolization based solely on the fact that monopoly has been retained for a substantial period of time.

---

[26] *Northern Sec. Co.* v. *United States,* 193 U.S. 197, 401–04 (1904) (Holmes, J., dissenting).

[27] *Appalachian Coals, Inc.* v. *United States,* 288 U.S. 344, 359–60 (1933).

[28] Alternatively, it might be said that monopolizing devoid of unlawful conduct lacks the kind of "intent" or "willfulness" essential to a criminal violation. See P. Areeda, *Antitrust Analysis* 28–30 (1967); cf. *SEC* v. *Capital Gains Research Bureau, Inc.,* 375 U.S. 180, 192 & n. 40 (1963) (Investment Company Act of 1940).

Although it is important to be able to deal with persistent monopolistic power in significant markets, it would be unwise to bring every case that conceivably might be brought. Monopoly cases should not be lightly undertaken. The enforcement agency should be reasonably sure that the monopoly is substantial and economically significant and that remedial schemes which would improve matters can in fact be worked out. Clearly in the kind of monopoly case we are talking about, there is no public interest in proceeding unless an effective remedy is available. The decision whether or not to bring suit will commonly require sophisticated judgment. Private parties are unlikely to have comparable inhibitions. To be sure, private actions might be taken in some instances where the Government has failed to act for not very good reasons. But on balance, I would say that major monopoly suits raise issues of policy so important and so difficult that they should be left to public enforcement, at least in the absence of clearly objectionable conduct on the part of the companies concerned.

Can this be effected by interpretation? Here, as in the case of criminal sanctions, I see no barrier to the courts' holding that a private action for damages will not lie against a firm that has obtained and maintained the monopoly power without objectionable exclusionary behavior of any kind. Private litigants are entitled to treble damages. Treble damages are punitive enough in character to be little more or no more appropriate than criminal sanctions for the kind of monopolizing offense we are discussing.[29]

Furthermore, courts could properly refuse to grant dissolution or divestiture in a private equitable action.[30] A court of equity would have discretion to distinguish between public and private suits if there was a reasonable

---

[29] Cf. *SEC* v. *Capital Gains Research Bureau, Inc.,* 375 U.S. 180 (1963); P. Areeda, *supra* note 2, page 24, at 35–36 (general discussion of limitations on private damage actions).

[30] Section 16 of the Clayton Act, 15 U.S.C. § 26 (1964), provides that:

> Any person . . . shall be entitled to sue for and have injunctive relief . . . when and under the same conditions and principles as injunctive relief against threatened conduct that will cause loss or damage is granted by courts of equity . . . .

In comparison, section 15 of the Act, 15 U.S.C. § 25 (1964), which covers equitable actions by the United States provides that "[s]uch proceedings may be by way of petition setting forth the case and praying that such violation shall be enjoined or otherwise prohibited." The different language leaves room for the interpretation that such far-reaching relief as dissolution or divestiture is available in a governmental action but not in a private action, at least not in private cases other than those involving an unlawful merger. In *Graves* v. *Cambria Steel Co.,* 298 F. 761, 762 (S.D.N.Y. 1924), Judge Learned Hand said as much:

> The suit at bar, whatever else it is, is not a suit for an injunction; indeed, it is really a suit for the dissolution of a monopoly pro tanto. I cannot suppose that any one would argue that a private suit for dissolution would lie under section 16 of the Clayton Act.

I would not assert that the answer is so clear. "Injunctive relief" would normally, I suppose, be taken to refer to the range of equitable remedies that courts have power to impose. But the contrast between sections 15 and 16 would at least permit the courts to hold as Judge Hand did.

basis for doing so, which there quite plainly would be.[31] The courts have frequently been reluctant to grant divestiture or dissolution even in suits brought by the Government.[32] In general, unless combination or plainly unlawful conduct has been an essential element of the offense — and on occasion not even then — it has been thought inappropriate to grant divestiture or dissolution except where other measures are not likely to dissipate unlawful monopoly within a reasonable period of time. And given the far-reaching consequences of the remedy, it has been suggested that any petition for the divestiture have the approval of the Attorney General, thus indicating a considered official decision that the remedy would be in the public interest.[33]

As I have noted, private suits are much less likely to reflect a thorough assessment and dispassionate conclusions regarding the public interest. Moreover, the private litigant's interest in divestiture would often be tenuous or remote. This would be particularly clear in a suit brought against a monopolist by a small existing competitor or by an alleged potential competitor. Neither could be expected to derive any substantial private benefit from the more vigorous competition that carefully planned divestiture would be expected to achieve; indeed, they may well be biased toward relief that impaired the efficiency of the surviving firms.

Finally, although a private party quite evidently has a statutory right to seek injunctive relief for any violation, there is no conduct that may suitably be enjoined in a suit against a firm that has obtained and maintained monopoly power without any objectionable exclusionary behavior. It is possible that a private plaintiff might seek access to recent patents and technology from a firm whose present position of monopoly was substantially attributable to those sources. Here, too, a court of equity might reasonably decline to grant the requested relief on the grounds that the particular plaintiff is no more entitled to such relief than many others and that compulsory licensing to any "qualified" applicant raises questions that should not be resolved without governmental participation as a representative of the general public interest. But even if such relief is appropriate in a private action — and it may well be in some situations — we shall have brought the scope of private actions down to fairly modest dimensions, too small to cause concern about the substantive rule I have suggested.

---

[31] Thus, in *Switzer Bros.* v. *Locklin,* 297 F. 2d 39, 48 (7th Cir. 1961) (citations omitted), *cert. denied,* 369 U.S. 851 (1962), the court concluded:

> Even in the context of suits by the United States to restrain conspiratorial monopolies, divestiture as a remedy is not without proscription. . . . It seems certain to us that divestiture as a remedy in private antitrust litigation should be even more narrowly proscribed, especially in a case such as this where there is lacking a conspiratorial combine of giant economic units of industry. . . .

[32] See, e.g., *United States* v. *United Shoe Mach. Corp.,* 110 F. Supp. 295, 347–48 (D. Mass. 1953), *aff'd per curiam,* 347 U.S. 521 (1954).

[33] *Id.* at 348.

To sum up, I believe there is sound legal ground for interpreting section 2 of the Sherman Act to apply to monopoly power that has been persistently maintained over a substantial period of time, except where the power is based solely on economies of scale or where it arises out of, and still depends upon, the same unexpired patents.

2. Oligopoly.   Significant positions of individually-held monopoly power have been, and are likely to be, relatively infrequent. More frequent and more significant are instances of highly concentrated markets in which a relatively few sellers effectively share monopoly power. Forunately, these instances are not as common as some have suggested; we are a long way from being a tightly oligopolized economy, and many industries loosely oligopolistic in structure are workably competitive in behavior and performance. A fair number of industries, however, including some of our major ones, are highly concentrated and significantly noncompetitive; and although, as I pointed out earlier,[34] concentration has been declining in a good many markets, it has been relatively stable or increasing in many others, and anything other than direct measures will be most unlikely to lower concentration in such markets in the foreseeable future.

The economic reasons which have led the courts to impose stringent checks on individual monopolistic power are in most respects applicable to the shared monopolistic power of a tight oligopoly. Both situations are characterized by an absence of vigorous price competition, wider price-cost margins than would exist under effective competition, protection of inefficient firms, and a consequent misallocation of economic resources. Oligopoly is probably less likely than monopoly to have substantial adverse effects on technological competition, but here, too, fairly demonstrable instances of inferior performance are not unknown.[35] Moreover, oligopoly is often characterized, as are many European industries that have long operated under the protection of price cartels, by long-run excess capacity. In short, attack on shared monopolistic power is a highly important aspect of any effective competitive policy.

Here again, the best solution would be a suitably drafted new statute that not only clearly defined the circumstances in which courts were to effect the necessary relief, but also excluded criminal sanctions and private rights of action in cases devoid of "moral dereliction." But once again, I believe section 2 of the Sherman Act may fairly be interpreted to cover much more than it has in the past.

To begin with, as I have noted, the Act from very early on has been interpreted by the courts not merely as a proscription of offenses well-recognized in 1890, but as a flexible instrument for enforcing a public policy in

[34] See p. 9 *supra.*

[35] See, e.g., Adams & Dirlam, "Big Steel, Invention, and Innovation," 80 *Q. J. Econ.* 167 (1966).

favor of competition and against monopoly. In the landmark *Standard Oil* decision of 1912, the Court described the purpose of the statute as preventing the evils of monopoly:

> 1. The power which the monopoly gave to the one who enjoyed it, to fix the price and thereby injure the public; 2. The power which it engendered of enabling a limitation on production; and 3. The danger of deterioration in quality of the monopolized article which it was deemed was the inevitable resultant of the monopolistic control over its production and sale.[36]

And the Court said of section 2 that it was "intended to supplement the 1st, and to make sure that by no possible guise could the public policy embodied in the 1st section be frustrated or evaded."[37]

To date, there is little in the way of precedents that would reach the shared monopoly power of a few firms collectively dominating a market, beyond cases involving more or less explicit conspiracy to employ exclusionary tactics. Furthermore, it has generally been supposed that the "consciously parallel" noncompetitive pricing of firms in a classic oligopoly — the kind of behavior that reflects effectively shared monopoly power — is not the kind of "conspiracy" that, as such, could be reasonably subjected to attack, even though interdependent pricing appears to have legally sufficient aspects of tacit agreement. I agree with that conclusion.[38] Nor could mere parallel noncompetitive pricing reasonably be made the basis for charging firms with "conspiring" to monopolize, or with "combining" to monopolize, despite suggestions in recent decisions that "combination" is something a little different from, and a little more than, "conspiracy."[39] In addition to other difficulties, either approach would condemn firms whose market position was inevitable in the strictest sense — namely, where their position was attributable solely to economies of scale — and would thus in this and other situations impose wider sanctions on oligopolists than on outright monopolists.

On the other hand, neither these negative conclusions nor the limited scope of past precedents exhausts the possibilities for reaching shared monopoly power. Consider the implications of the *United Shoe Machinery* case.[40] United, with eighty to eighty-five percent of the shoe machinery market, was held to have unlawfully maintained its monopoly by courses of

---

[36] *Standard Oil Co.* v. *United States,* 221 U.S. 1, 52 (1911). See also *id.* at 58–60.

[37] *Id.* at 60. I should note, in all candor, that the Court also said the statue omitted any prohibition of "monopoly in the concrete," in the belief that market forces would eliminate monopoly not based on restraints of trade or other questionable conduct. *Id.* at 62.

[38] Turner, "The Definition of Agreement under the Sherman Act: Conscious Parallelism and Refusals to Deal," 75 *Harv. L. Rev.* 655, 663–71 (1962).

[39] See *Albrecht* v. *Herald Co.,* 390 U.S. 145, 149–50 (1968); *United States* v. *Parke, Davis & Co.,* 362 U.S. 29, 36–47 (1960).

[40] *United States* v. *United Shoe Mach. Corp.,* 110 F. Supp. 295 (D. Mass. 1953), *aff'd per curiam,* 347 U.S. 521 (1954).

conduct that unnecessarily restricted the opportunities of actual and potential competitors. The company distributed its machines by lease only; no machines were offered for sale. This prevented the creation of a second-hand market, which would have provided at least some check on its power to set the price on new machines. Moreover, the leases contained several provisions that deterred the users from disposing of a United machine and acquiring a competitor's; for example, a lessee desiring to replace a current United machine would get more favorable terms if replacement was by another United machine than by a competitor's machine. Third, United's leasing charges covered both the use of the machine and any necessary repairs, which were provided without any additional charge. This effectively prevented growth of independent service organizations and in turn compelled small competitors either to develop their own service organizations — which might well be too small to achieve economies of scale — or to operate under the disadvantage of trying to market their machines to customers who knew that repair service would be difficult to procure.

Except for earlier decisions involving the same company that appeared to hold otherwise, Judge Wyzanski concluded he would have ruled that:

> [I]t is a restraint of trade under §1 for a company having an overwhelming share of the market, to distribute its more important products only by leases which have provisions that go beyond assuring prompt, periodic payments of rentals, which are not terminable cheaply, which involve discrimination against competition, and which combine in one contract the right to use the product and to have it serviced.[41]

But he held that, even if not unlawful as such, these practices were an unacceptable course of behavior for a company possessing monopoly power:

> [T]hey are not practices which can be properly described as the inevitable consequences of ability, natural forces, or law. They represent something more than the use of accessible resources, the process of invention and innovation, and the employment of those techniques of employment, financing, production, and distribution, which a competitive society must foster. They are contracts, arrangements, and policies which, instead of encouraging competition based on pure merit, further the dominance of a particular firm. In this sense, they are unnatural barriers; they unnecessarily exclude actual and potential competition; they restrict a free market. While the law allows many enterprises to use such practices, the Sherman Act is now construed by superior courts to forbid the continuance of effective market control based in part upon such practices.[42]

Suppose that United Shoe had involved, not a single company with monopoly power, but two or three companies that were shown to have effectively shared monopoly power. It seems to me the result should be the same.

[41] *Id.* at 343.
[42] *Id.* at 344–45.

The result would be routine insofar as the defendants' individual and collective market positions were attributable to conduct that might properly be called illegal. If it is inappropriate for a single monopolist to employ long-term leases that are not terminable cheaply and that discriminate against competition because they are more restrictive than any acceptable business justification would warrant, I cannot see why the same should not be true of leading firms that share market dominance. Indeed, a practice that may be so characterized might reasonably be deemed unlawful without regard to market power of the company concerned, although in practice it is unlikely that exclusionary behavior of this kind could successfully be carried on by an insubstantial firm. Exclusionary behavior without adequate business justification may not only be classed as an unlawful restraint of trade under section 1 of the Sherman Act, but may also, where no contract or "agreement" is involved, be deemed an unlawful "attempt" to monopolize under section 2.

I will concede the possibility that market power may be an essential ingredient in determining the propriety of some kinds of conduct that may have a business justification. Distributing machines only by lease and not by sale may be used as an example. If one were dealing with an industry comprising twenty firms of more or less equal size selling virtually identical machines, there would be little ground for concern when one or a few firms were pursuing a lease-only policy. Any restrictive effect on customers wishing to purchase machines would be minimal in light of the ample sources of supply available. Accordingly, one might surmise that the firms which had adopted lease-only policies had done so for some legitimate business reason. Moreover, again supposing twenty companies offering comparable competing machines, it would not be completely clear that questionable conduct was involved even if all firms only leased. That no one offered machines for sale might simply reflect the fact that all customers preferred to lease. To establish the probability of unlawfully restrictive conduct, one would have to prove that there were some customers who would buy if they had the opportunity, thereby imposing upon the firms the burden of establishing why they uniformly declined to offer an option that some customers wanted.

In the situation I have just described, namely, a market of a substantial number of firms, the absence of any persuasive explanation for following a lease-only policy would suggest that there had been actual communicated agreement among the firms, for it is unlikely that a policy apparently against the interest of any single firm going it alone would have been commonly adopted without advance assurance that all would do the same. The smaller the number of firms — particularly when one gets down to two or three or four — the more likely that parallelism could evolve without overt communication; but with interdependence in decisions established, I see no difficulty in these circumstances — which are quite different from parallelism in basic prices — in reaching the conclusion that an unlawful "conspiracy" has taken place.[43]

There are difficulties, however, in applying precisely the same limitations of conduct to those who share monopoly power as are applied to the single monopolist. I am not particularly troubled where all the companies involved are doing the same thing. If it is appropriate to make conduct having relatively minor exclusionary effects the basis for illegality in the case of a single-firm monopoly — which is what I take the law now to be — it is no large step to extend the principle to shared monopoly. If the creation of a second-hand market for shoe machines was sufficiently important to justify the conclusion that United should have sold as well as leased, the same conclusion would be appropriate regarding three firms that had collectively monopolized the market. But if just one of the three was leasing, only, it would be harder to condemn it, especially if all three firms were of approximately equal size and were producing comparable machines. The facts may show that the two firms that did offer machines for sale in fact sold very few as compared to the number leased, which would mean that the second-hand market was of minimal consequence anyway. And if sales were substantial, this would tend to indicate that the firm that only leased had business reasons, other than limiting the second-hand market, for letting competitors take that part of the market. In addition, the restrictive effect of the policy would be less substantial, if not minimal, because there was a second-hand market consisting of machines sold by the other firms. Similar questions might arise in considering the consequences when only one out of three firms had "packaged" machines and servicing at a single charge.[44]

But setting this kind of situation aside, I believe that the law on shared monopoly may be brought virtually in line with the law on individual monopoly, and divestiture where feasible invoked as a remedy whenever it appears that injunctive relief will not adequately dissipate the power within a reasonable time. Where oligopolists sharing monopoly power have engaged in restrictive conduct lacking any substantial justification, they may appropriately be said to have unlawfully attempted to monopolize. Where it appears that their decisions to carry on particular exclusionary practices are interdependent — where one would not have carried on the practice unless the others had gone along — they may also be charged with a con-

[43] See Turner, *supra* note 3, page 30, at 677–78, 681, 683–84.

[44] Actually, I have great difficulty in understanding just what legitimate reason a firm would have for refusing to sell its machines to anyone who wanted to buy rather than lease. The only apparent additional expense is determining an appropriate price; but I would assume that expense to be negligible, and in any event it could be reflected in the price charged.

A wider range of considerations would appear to be involved in the packaging of servicing and machines, but given the resemblance to explicit tying arrangements and the exclusionary effects illustrated in *United Shoe,* it would be appropriate to ask for a clear showing that the practice serves legitimate purposes that would not be served by less restrictive alternatives.

spiracy or combination to monopolize. Finally, where each of the companies effectively sharing monopoly power has engaged in possibly justifiable conduct that nevertheless has unnecessary exclusionary effects, it seems logical and appropriate to me to charge each with having individually "monopolized" in violation of section 2. Each has obtained and maintained monopoly power — real, though shared — to which factors other than skill, foresight, industry, and the like have contributed.

The remaining question is whether one can fairly apply to shared monopoly power the prohibition of individual monopoly suggested by *Alcoa* — that, barring economies of scale or power still based on the unexpired patents that created it, monopoly becomes subject to judicial relief when retained over a sufficient period of time to indicate that it is substantially impervious to erosion by market forces. I would conclude that it is appropriate to do so if one accepts the *Alcoa* principle in the first place, because there is not enough difference between individual and shared monopoly to warrant different treatment.[45]

II. Direct Regulation

I turn now to some of the basic issues of policy that arise in direct economic regulation of various industries, whether such regulation is fairly complete, as in transportation, or partial, as in banking.

At the outset, it is by no means frivolous to ask whether direct control over entry, rates, and service — particularly as we have seen it in the past — is really worth the effort.[46] Direct regulation of economic performance poses intrinsic difficulties that run well beyond the problem of administrative ineptness, common as that has been. Among other things, regulatory constraint on profits tends to reduce incentives to efficiency and innovation by eliminating, or substantially reducing, the reward. The usual right of a regulated company to recover cost increases by rate increases tends to lessen resistance to unreasonable wage demands. Similarly, the right to a "fair"

---

[45] There is little doubt, however, that relief in a case of shared monopoly raises more complex problems and may require differing treatment of the firms concerned. I doubt that the feasibility of divestiture is generally less in oligopoly than in monopoly, since feasibility depends on the absolute size of the firm in relation to economies of scale rather than on market structure. But in some situations there may be a lack of symmetry. Suppose, for example, a three-firm industry in which the market shares are 50, 30, and 20 percent, respectively, and in which maximum economies of scale are reached at around 15 percent of the market. Divestiture would be appropriate for the larger two firms but not for the smallest.

Of course, I am also assuming that the case of effectively shared monopoly power has in fact been made out. In the example just given, there would be no case (unless there had been questionable exclusionary conduct) if the smallest firm was a recent entrant that had rather rapidly achieved its substantial share at the expense of the two leaders.

[46] For a negative answer and a penetrating critique see Posner, "Natural Monopoly and Its Regulation," 21 *Stan. L. Rev.* 548 (1969).

overall rate of return tends to encourage uneconomical pricing of some services and may encourage a bias toward more extensive investment of capital
than would otherwise be made. To varying degrees, these consequences
have proved beyond effective regulatory control.

This is not the place to discuss the ultimate question of whether direct
economic regulation, for these and other reasons, should be scrapped entirely. I doubt that it should; and there is no reasonable prospect that it will
be in the foreseeable future. But in any event, the difficulties and inadequacies of direct regulation, theoretical as well as practical, suggest that it
should be confined to cases in which strong elements of natural monopoly
are plainly present. They also suggest that even where some direct regulation is thought necessary, the regulatory agency should take advantage of
whatever competitive possibilities exist.

How far we have departed from those principles, and with what consequences, is most sharply brought home by the truly woeful results from
decades of regulating surface transportation. I do not see how we could
have ended up worse off than we did if there had never been any economic
regulation of surface transportation at all; in all likelihood we would now
have a vastly more efficient system. But even if there was, and still is, a
good case for maximum-rate regulation of railroads (the only mode of
transportation where significant monopoly positions have ever existed), we
have long had the requisite conditions for effective and workable competition over wide areas of surface transportation, potentialities which regulation has largely frustrated.[47]

There never was a sound economic case for regulating entry, rates, and
service in the motor carrier industry, and there is none now.[48] It is fairly
evident that regulation was imposed in 1935 in order to blunt the inroads
that motor-carriers were making on the railroads' business. Subsequent
regulation of motor common carriers not only prevented their capturing
traffic which they otherwise would have taken from other modes, but also
created such inefficiencies and high costs that truck traffic steadily moved
away from the common carriers to contract and private trucking. And in
more recent years, with contrary tendencies developing in intermodal competition, the efforts of railroads to recover lost traffic have been thwarted
by economically unsound minimum-rate regulation.[49]

Among other examples of unwarranted regulation, I would put limitations on entry into commercial banking, though the consequences have

[47] See, e.g., Peck, *"Competitive Policy for Transportation?,"* in *Perspectives on Antitrust Policy* 244 (A. Phillips ed. 1965).

[48] See, e.g., J. Meyer, M. Peck, J. Stenason & C. Zwick, *The Economics of Competition in the Transportation Industries* 211–22, 265 (1959).

[49] The overwhelming weight of expert economic opinion to the contrary, the I.C.C.
persists in using fully distributed costs as a proper basis for determining the low-cost
carrier of particular classes of traffic, and as a basis for rejecting rate reductions proposed by one regulated carrier that would divert traffic from another regulated carrier.

probably not been as dreary as in surface transportation.[50] Presumably, apart from a desire to insure minimum initial qualifications, entry has been limited on the theory that excessive competitive pressure on profit rates would lead to unsound banking practices, which would in turn increase the likelihood of bank failures, and on the further proposition that bank failures have consequences far less tolerable than failures in industrial markets generally. I believe we would be better off with free entry and more bank failures.

To begin with, control over entry has obvious costs. If control is in fact carried out to the point of minimizing the risk of bank failure, this necessarily implies protection of profit rates well in excess of competitive norms and consequently protection of inefficient banks. Also, limitations on entry increase concentration in local banking markets, and in banking as elsewhere there appears to be a correlation between concentration and price — here, interest rates.[51] In addition, restricted entry lowers the incentive to develop new banking services and provide new, more convenient locations; and it probably leads to a lending policy too conservative in terms of its general impact on the structure of markets. Typically considered to have the higher risks, the new firm and the relatively small firm will usually be the ones that find it most difficult to secure borrowed funds. Desirable as it may be from the banking standpoint that banks avoid higher-risk business loans, it is highly desirable from the standpoint of the economy in general that a substantial number of such risks be taken. In short, if banking is peculiar in that bank failures pose a particularly serious problem, it is also peculiar in that competition in lending performs a uniquely valuable function.

Moreover, it seems to me that the main source of concern about a higher rate of bank failures can be met without limitations on entry, at least without limitations for the sole purpose of restricting competition. The main concern about bank failure is losses to depositors, for there is no evident reason why the creditors or stockholders of a bank should get any more protection against failure than do creditors or stockholders of any other kind of enterprise. But this problem can be met, as it already has been for the vast majority of depositors, by federal deposit insurance. Given complete or nearly complete insurance coverage, the consequences of bank failure to depositors would be reduced to mere temporary inconvenience. Perhaps there remains a case for bank-entry limitations designed to keep out unqualified and inadequately financed new entrants. If so, those limited goals can be met by retaining minimum qualifications and conditions respecting experience and capitalization.

[50] *See generally* "Comment, Bank Charter, Branching, Holding Company and Merger Law: Competition Frustrated," 71 *Yale L. J.* 502 (1962).

[51] Edwards, "The Banking Competition Controversy," 3 *Nat'l Banking Rev.* 1, 19–22 (1965).

In my opinion, all these considerations suggest that there is much more to be gained than lost from abandoning economic controls over entry into commercial banking. I would also note, incidentally, that this should carry with it the elimination of restrictions on branch banking, leaving existing banks as free as any newcomer to establish facilities in any location dictated by their business judgment.

Obviously, a large part of the blame for misconceived and misapplied regulation of entry, rates, and other aspects of economic performance is attributable simply to wrong legislative judgment. Regulation has been imposed in situations where there was no excuse for it at all, and broader regulation has been imposed than the needs of the occasion have required. Moreover, the statutes conferring economic regulatory authority on commissions or agencies typically supply little more in the way of standards than "public interest, convenience and necessity"; often such vagueness reflects the fact that the legislatures have swept substantial disputes over policy under the rug, leaving the regulatory agency to respond to conflicting pressures as best it can.

But, generally speaking, surely the regulatory agencies could have done far better than they have. Broad, vague mandates indeed impose a heavy burden of responsibility; the other side of the coin is a broad opportunity to regulate wisely, which may well involve a decision to keep regulatory interference to a minimum. Nothing in the statutes granting it regulatory authority would have prevented the ICC (Interstate Commerce Commission) from being vastly more liberal in granting certificates to new motor carriers or to existing motor carriers seeking permission to carry additional products. Nothing in the statutes would have barred the ICC from letting trucks and railroads lower their rates as they pleased so long as the rates were "compensatory" in the sense that they covered long-run marginal cost.[52] Nothing in its statutes would have prevented the ICC from establishing a rule that it would disapprove any carrier merger likely to result in a substantial elimination of competition unless clear countervailing benefits were shown.

A fundamental difficulty is that the ICC and other regulatory agencies have failed adequately to recognize that regulation is at best a poor substitute for competition, not only insofar as efficiency and the development and provision of new improved services are concerned, but even with regard to rates. Much less incentive to efficiency and innovation exists where a company is both protected against competition and held to a maximum rate of return. Cost reduction increases profits only for the period it takes the regulatory agency to effect a corresponding rate reduction, and regulation

---

[52] Although there are some intimations to the contrary, I do not read the Supreme Court's decision in the ingot molds case, *American Commercial Lines, Inc.* v. *Louisville & N. R. R.*, 392 U.S. 571 (1968), as ruling otherwise. See *id.* at 594–97 Harlan, J., concurring).

can do little to compel a management to innovate, to develop new services, or to improve operating techniques. As for rates, regulatory commissions can only disallow rates that yield an unreasonably high rate of return. But reasonable rates occupy a zone, not a point. A rate may not be so unreasonably high as to warrant rejection and yet be considerably higher than the rate the regulated company would be willing to accept under the pressures of competition.

Moreover, there has been a failure adequately to appreciate the fact that, barring the situation where economies of scale are so substantial as to make any direct competition far too costly, few if any economic benefits to the public interest would not be readily served by competition. The problem of bank mergers is, I believe, a good example. Hardly any aspect of the "convenience and needs" justification of a bank merger[53] would not adequately be taken into account in a normal antitrust analysis, except insofar as it might be thought appropriate in considering bank mergers to give somewhat more weight to financial difficulties and more explicit recognition to economies of scale than would normally be done. The remarkably high correlation between the views of the Justice Department and of the Federal Reserve Board on specific bank-merger applications indicates that this view is not peculiarly that of an antitruster.

The "convenience and needs" of a community are normally fulfilled by having a range of banking alternatives sufficient to ensure that the banks are under competitive pressure to provide services the community wants at the lowest economical rates. In smaller banking markets, economies of scale may well lead to fewer banks than would be necessary for fully effective competition. And it is doubtless true that small banks are unable to participate in some loan markets or to provide some services that larger banks can. Limits on individual loans prevent small banks from handling larger loans singly (though not from participating in them), and by raising loan limits, the merger of two small banks might bring them more effectively into lending areas from which they have been partially foreclosed. Typically, however, the larger the loan or the larger the borrower, the wider the true geographic market, and the more likely it is that that particular market already offers the large borrower an adequate range of alternatives. Consequently, a balancing of anticompetitive consequences in the essentially local markets that merging banks serve against the procompetitive consequences in wider markets would rarely if ever lead to the conclusion that the

---

[53] The Bank Merger Act of 1966, 12 U.S.C. § 1828(c)(5) (Supp. III, 1968), provides that the responsible banking agency shall not approve:

(B) any . . . proposed merger transaction whose effect in any section of the country may be substantially to lessen competition, or tend to create a monopoly . . . unless it finds that the anticompetitive effects of the proposed transaction are clearly outweighed in the public interest by the probable effect . . . in meeting the convenience and needs of the community to be served.

"convenience and needs" of the community would be served by a merger of two substantial competitors.[54]

It has been urged in many proposals for a bank merger that the creation of a larger bank will stimulate economic development of the locality or area concerned. But no one has explained precisely how a significantly anti-competitive merger is going to do this, and there is at least as much reason to suppose that ordinarily a merger of that kind — by raising interest rates and leading to more conservative lending policies toward borrowers for whom local banks are the only real alternatives — will tend to curb economic development rather than promote it.

The Department of Justice has been subjected to unending criticism for its efforts to undo the decisions of specialized regulatory agencies. It is, however, the chronic failure of the regulatory agencies to pay due regard to the benefits of competition that has led the Department to seek a reversal in court of particular agency decisions. The poor record of the regulatory agencies has been one of the reasons why the Department has almost uniformly opposed the frequent efforts to attach new statutory antitrust exemptions to mergers or other activities subject to approval by regulatory agencies though often the primary reason has been that exemption from usual antitrust rules is simply unwarranted.

That a merger, for example, should be subject to attack on straight antitrust grounds after it has received the blessing of a regulatory agency is said to be unjust, inefficient, and inappropriate. Such matters, it is claimed, should be finally determined by the governmental body having a special expertise in all aspects of the industry concerned, subject only to the limited judicial review of an administrative agency's decisions. But there is no reason to suppose that, just because an administrative agency is best equipped to pass on some aspects of a merger or other proposed course of action, it is necessarily best equipped to determine other issues or to make a final determination. Expertise in the peculiar technical and other aspects of a particular industry does not necessarily carry with it a superior general economic expertise in evaluating effects on competition and the probable consequences of those effects. Indeed, although there have been some happy exceptions, the correlation has typically been poor. Dual jurisdiction is rather untidy. It can involve wasted motion. But given the past performance record of regulatory agencies, the retention of independent antitrust jurisdiction in such areas as radio and television, natural gas transmission, and bank mergers has in my opinion yielded better results than would have obtained without it.

[54] Nor does concern for the "floundering" bank necessitate any significant departure from conclusions that an antitrust approach would normally reach, except, as I noted, to give the risk of possible failure somewhat greater weight. Even then, the problems of the floundering bank can often be met by measures short of merger, or if by merger, by mergers less anticompetitive than an alliance with one of the bank's leading competitors. See *United States* v. *Third Nat'l Bank*, 390 U.S. 171 (1968).

Present procedures and allocation of decision-making could doubtless be greatly improved. Perhaps some rather radical changes would be in order. I suspect, for example, that a good many basic determinations of policy that have been given to regulatory agencies in the past would be better lodged in the executive branch, subject of course to congressional veto. I shall not pursue such questions here, however, for the simple reason that I have not really thought them out.

Assuming that we continue to operate more or less within the existing framework, there are nevertheless several ways in which the handling of regulatory matters might over the course of time be improved. First, we would certainly be better off with more explicit statutory standards that resolve at least some questions of policy and in the right way. For example, while I was not one of those who believed in any crying need for the Bank Merger Act, I believe its substantive standards for merger may well offer a useful model in such regulated industries as transportation, electric power, and natural gas. Much the same approach is reflected in proposed legislation that would immunize a merger of natural gas companies approved by the Federal Power Commission but would also provide that the Commission may certify the acquisition only if it finds that any adverse effect of the proposed transaction upon competition is insubstantial or is clearly outweighed by other considerations of public interest.[55] Statutory standards of this kind would considerably lessen the need for dual jurisdiction of those industries subject to pervasive economic regulation.

Second, as I suggested earlier,[56] the regulatory agencies commonly have ample authority to adopt presumptive rules of this kind without any specific statutory mandate. The Federal Maritime Commission, for example, adopted the principle that a shipping conference rule interfering with the policies of the antitrust laws would be approved only if the conference could:[57]

> bring forth such facts as would demonstrate that the . . . rule was required by serious transportation need, necessary to secure important public benefits or in furtherance of a valid regulatory purpose of the Shipping Act.

In upholding the rule, the Supreme Court stated that "[b]y its very nature an illegal restraint of trade is in some ways 'contrary to the public interest;' "[58] and it added: "The antitrust standard formulated here is in full accord with the kind of accommodation between antitrust and regulatory objectives approved by this Court in [other] cases."[59]

Third, I am convinced that, with or without revised statutory standards

[55] S. 1687, 90th Cong., 1st Sess. (1967).
[56] *See* p. 41 *supra.*
[57] *Federal Maritime Comm'n* v. *Aktiebolaget Svenska Amerika Linien,* 390 U.S. 238, 243 (1968).
[58] *Id.* at 244.
[59] *Id.* at 245 n.4.

creating a presumption in favor of competition, more extensive and systematic participation by the Executive branch via the Justice Department in proceedings before the regulatory agencies would effect significant and beneficial changes, not only in the weight given to competitive considerations but in the assessment of other aspects of the public interest as well. Without participation by the Executive branch, the burden of pressing these considerations is left to intervening private parties and to commission staffs. On many occasions, no private party appears to raise the kind of objections that ought to be raised; and where they do, the impact of their advocacy is inevitably reduced by the fact that their primary motivation is self-interest. Commission staffs do not suffer from the latter disability, and from time to time they perform admirably. On the other hand, they occupy an essentially dependent status; they are commonly viewed, rightly or wrongly, as having acquired rigid theological points of view; and for these and other reasons they cannot be expected adequately to carry the load. The Executive branch is in a vastly better position to bring resources and weight to bear in support of the public interest as it sees it; and more than any private party or any commission staff, it is in a better position to recognize and resolve, in the general public interest, the questions of policy that important agency-proceedings raise.

Finally, I am with deference compelled to say that in my opinion the courts could make a considerable contribution by demanding that the agencies display a higher standard of performance in analyzing, explaining, and justifying particular decisions than has been considered adequate in the past. I am not suggesting that the courts feel free to substitute their own opinions for those of the agency where what is involved is essentially a legislative or political policy judgment that the statute has compelled the agency to make. A good example of the latter is the question, faced by the FCC (Federal Communications Commission) in the earlier days of television, whether to issue UHF (ultrahigh frequency) licenses only or to adopt some combination of UHF and VHF (very high frequency). I shall oversimplify the case and perhaps hypothesize in some respects in order to make my point. At the time, VHF transmission was noticeably superior to UHF, and there was no near prospect that technological improvements would make UHF comparable. On the other hand, the paucity of VHF channels seriously limited the number of VHF stations that could operate in the various markets. Since UHF would be unable to compete effectively until improved and since even then it might face high barriers to entry into markets with entrenched VHF, the licensing of VHF threatened to limit future television competition rather severely. In deciding not to adopt an all-UHF system the FCC, among other things, placed a higher value on quick availability of high-quality television, which indeed was widely demanded, than on the dangers to future market structure from licensing

VHF. One might well have decided otherwise. If television had been limited to UHF, our remarkably proficient electronics industry might have been expected to produce rather rapid improvements in its quality. And a more competitive structure would have largely removed the case for direct controls over performance by the licensee, controls that have raised extremely vexing problems. But it would be hard to find fault with a court for refusing to impose a different assessment of the competing values than that made by the FCC.[60]

Nor do I suggest that the courts should upset agency decisions to the extent that their factual conclusions truly rest, or must be assumed to rest, on particular expertise. Thus, a banking commission's conclusion from a record with facts going both ways that a merging bank is in serious danger of failure may well reflect a judgment based on long experience with the banking business, and the judgment is entitled to weight in determining whether the factual conclusion is supportable by "substantial evidence on the record as a whole."

Obviously, however, much of the fact-finding and analysis that precedes an agency's ultimate decision involves either matters with which courts are reasonably familiar or matters requiring no peculiar expertise. It takes no more expertise to analyze the competitive consequences of a railroad merger or a pipeline merger or a bank merger than it does to analyze the consequences of a merger in many other industries, mergers that the courts have struggled with over the years. The courts are at least experienced enough in these matters to know the kind of analysis that must be made for a rational judgment, to know what economic issues are relevant, and to insist that the agency decision reflect adequate analysis and adequate attention to those issues. This standard is often not even remotely approached, even in some cases where the agency has been upheld.

I think it would not be amiss for the courts to go even somewhat further than this. If illegal restraints of trade and anti-competitive mergers are "in some ways contrary to public interest," or if it is appropriate for a regulatory agency, as did the FMC (Federal Maritime Commission), to adopt a rule outlawing acts contrary to the policies of the antitrust laws in the absence of a clear countervailing demonstration that the acts are necessary to secure important public benefits, might not the courts reasonably ask regulatory agencies which have declined to establish presumptions of this

---

[60] At the same time I am not suggesting that there are no limits to an agency's discretion in matters of this kind. *See* Justice Frankfurter's opinion (*dubitante*) in *Radio Corp. of America* v. *United States,* 341 U.S. 412, 421 (1951), where the Court declined to reverse an FCC decision authorizing the broadcasting of noncompatible color television even though work on a compatible system was well along (and in fact was perfected so quickly that the decision was withdrawn). Could not the Court have reasonably concluded that the effective date of the order should be delayed for a year or two, and the whole question reviewed at that time?

kind to explain why they should not? In a recent and pending appeal, the jurisdictional statement for the United States argued as follows:

> Before approving a merger of healthy carriers who represent the major source of rail competition in a vast area, the Commission should be required to show why the increased "proficiency" and profitability that these already effective and prosperous railroads may achieve by consolidation are likely to benefit shippers more than the cost reductions and rate reductions from new techniques that competitive pressures have historically produced. If it cannot do so, and cannot point to some strong countervailing public need or benefit, then approval of the merger violates the discretion entrusted to the Commission under the National Transportation Policy.[61]

Conceding that personal participation at an earlier stage of the proceedings may have colored my views, I concur.

III. Subsidy and Protectionism

I turn now to the basic issues raised by governmental efforts to protect particular activities or groups from the operation of market forces and to promote levels of activities beyond those that free markets would set. Instances of this kind of governmental economic policy are legion, and the list shows a remarkable incapacity to contract.

Producers of farm commodities have been the beneficiaries of both direct subsidies and the indirect subsidies afforded by artificial price supports. Producers of domestic crude oil are directly subsidized by high depletion allowances and indirectly subsidized by state rationing of production and by federal import quotas that together raise the domestic prices for crude oil far above the going prices in international markets. Similar devices have kept domestic prices for raw sugar at around three times the world level.

The Rural Electrification Administration continues to receive public funds at an interest rate of two percent more than thirty years after its creation and long after the circumstances that originally were deemed to warrant its creation have drastically changed. The maritime industry directly and maritime workers indirectly have long received substantial subsidies and a substantial captive market. Air controller service, a significant part of the cost of operating commercial airlines, is provided by the FAA (Federal Aviation Agency). Resale price maintenance subsidizes high-cost retailers, and the brokerage business is subsidized by the maintenance of minimum commissions on the purchase and sale of securities. In addition to these and other overt examples of subsidy and protection, there are a host of less obvious subsidies scattered throughout such regulated markets as transportation, communications, and public utilities, where

---

[61] Jurisdictional Statement for the United States at 27, *United States* v. *ICC, prob. juris, noted,* 36 U.S.L.W. 3307 (U.S. Feb. 25, 1969).

particular classes of users continually receive services at rates below long-run marginal costs.[62]

Although, as I noted earlier,[63] there are undoubtedly some important areas in which subsidy or a comparable inducement is warranted, there are many situations in which the divergence between private and social costs and benefits is too insubstantial to make corrective efforts worthwhile; and there are many other situations in which the case for subsidizing a particular group or activity is no better than the case would be for subsidizing practically anyone. There is simply no question that much of present protectionism and subsidization is no longer justifiable, if indeed it ever was.

I shall not try to argue here the merits of granting some form of subsidy or protection in particular instances, but I do wish to comment briefly on the further question, namely, if extra governmental help is thought necessary, what is the most suitable method of providing it? All too often, the methods of protection or subsidy are much more costly than alternative methods would be, and too often the methods adopted put the cost of protection or subsidy on the wrong shoulders. The ideal approach would meet three tests: (1) that it minimize the real economic cost of the subsidy; (2) that it minimize the governmental decision-making that goes with it; and (3) that it put the burden of the subsidy where it belongs. Generally speaking, these tests are best met by the method that minimizes interference with the market's mechanism; and generally speaking, these tests are best satisfied by a direct subsidy derived from tax revenues — general revenues when the subsidy is thought to serve the general public interest or by special assessments on a particular area or class when it serves a more particular interest.[64]

In the absence of a count, it is probably a fair guess that the methods of protection and subsidy actually in use rarely meet these tests. Agricultural price supports plainly do not: they greatly multiply the cost of the agricultural subsidy by giving most of the increased agricultural income to farmers who need it not at all; and while a program of direct subsidy is hardly devoid of administrative problems, the problems posed are certainly no greater than those of the price support program and are probably con-

---

[62] It may well be appropriate, and does not constitute a "subsidy," to charge prices below long-run marginal costs but above short-run marginal costs in situations where such a price is necessary fully to utilize temporary excess capacity. Also, I want to make it perfectly clear that I of course do not consider mere price discrimination as establishing a "subsidy" to those paying lower prices.

[63] See pp. 1–6 *supra*.

[64] Thus, where the benefit is to the nation as a whole, as is the case with subsidized activities in fact critical to the national defense, the subsidy is properly paid out of general tax revenues. But as closely as possible, the class taxed should coincide with those benefited by the subsidy. Of course, complete congruence is not the goal, for a subsidy will not lower the cost to consumers and thus increase use when it is derived from a sales tax imposed on the purchase of the product or service concerned. The tax must be payable whether or not the taxpayer buys the subsidized product or service.

siderably less. Oil production-rationing, oil import quotas, and oil depletion allowances are methods of subsidy so inappropriate as to border on the scandalous. Each of them vastly increases the cost of any defensible subsidy. Both production-rationing and import quotas promote inefficiency, and they put state and federal governments in the extremely difficult and treacherous business of allocating valuable rights among a host of clamoring claimants.

Nor does subsidizing particular classes of transportation users by raising the rates to other classes of users meet the tests I have described. There is no good reason why shippers of freight on the Penn-Central railroad should bear the burden subsidizing Westchester County commuters or why transportation users in one area of the country should subsidize users in another. Moreover, on straight economic analysis, recoupment of out-of-pocket losses on some classes of traffic by raising rates on others only further distorts the allocation of economic resources, driving some traffic out of the latter classes by higher costs.[65]

IV. Concluding Comments

Many of the difficulties and mistakes that I have described are in large part due to the fact that economic analysis, even with its limitations, is still a greatly underutilized tool in making public policy. I grant that, even if basic economic principles were thoroughly understood by the relevant policy-makers, many decisions mildly or strongly repulsive to the economist would still be made. There have been, and are, instances where everyone recognizes — at least privately — that no economic excuse exists for regulation or subsidy, but the regulation or subsidy persists because of the political wallop of the beneficiaries. My experience, however, has been that many final decisions are made with only the faintest grasp of the economic consequences of the various alternatives and that we could hope for measurable improvements if this defect were cured. I would also note, parenthetically, that the relative neutrality of economic principles would make decisions based upon them much more palatable than those made without any readily explicable guides and therefore reflecting or appearing to reflect invidious discrimination.

As I have said, it seems obvious that competitive policy has not had the scope it should; that we are overregulating, overexempting, and over-

---

[65] An argument can be made for the proposition that a tariff, all things considered, is the best device for giving moderate protection to a domestic industry (assuming protection is warranted) on the ground that it is much simpler than any other device. It should be recognized, however, that a tariff is virtually certain to be a more costly way of supplying any given amount of protection than is a direct subsidy, because here too, as with any increase in price over competitive levels, the price increase caused by a tariff not only yields profits to those who do not need support but also had adverse effects on allocation of resources.

subsidizing many elements of our economy; and that the aggregate economic cost of these mistakes in terms of the inefficient use of resources is far greater than what it directly appears to be. Not only should we vigorously resist adding to past errors; we should begin to dismantle those schemes which lack adequate justification. But it is vitally important to accept the fact that as a practical matter they simply cannot be abandoned overnight. The financial wreckage and personal suffering would be intolerable.

Consequently, we should devote serious attention to developing and perfecting techniques that will minimize the dislocations caused by radical changes in regulatory and subsidy policy, methods whereby regulation and subsidy may be withdrawn by stages rather than all at once, or withdrawn after lapse of time sufficient to give affected private groups an opportunity to make necessary adjustments in their investing and other economic decisions. As a crude example, I suggest a statute terminating all economic controls over rates and entry in motor-trucking five years after the date of enactment. As another, I suggest a statute directing a ten percent increase in permissible oil import quotas each year for five years, all quotas thereafter to cease.

There is always the possibility, of course, that statutes of this kind would never stick, that pressures would cause repeated postponement of the final termination date. But if we collectively lack the capacity and fortitude to carry through with wise policy, reason can help us no further.

6

Consumer Behavior, Market Imperfections, and Public Policy

*Richard H. Holton**

Information in the Market for Consumer Goods

Economists pursuing the study of consumer demand during the past decade or so have directed their attention primarily to those aspects of the subject significant in macroeconomic models or in understanding the nature of demand for particular categories of goods and services. Thus the savings behavior of consumers is of continuing interest because of its implications, especially for short-range forecasting of economic conditions. Consumers' expectations and buying plans are also studied with care. The characteristics of demand by consumers for housing, for automobiles, and for other specific commodities have been the subject of considerable analysis as well.

This substantial body of literature, however, has afforded little assistance in the recent discussions of public policy concerning one important set of problems in markets for consumer goods. Since 1964 Congress has demonstrated particular interest in what is loosely referred to as "consumer legislation." Hearings, threats of hearings, and actual legislation have drawn attention to "Truth-in-Lending," "Truth-in-Packaging," automobile safety, tire standards, insurance, pharmaceuticals, and other topics bearing on the performance of consumer markets. Although the economic literature on consumer demand is extensive, surprisingly little of it deals with the aspects of demand relevant to a better understanding of these current issues in public policy.

The situation exists because little attention has been directed to what I

* University of California, Berkeley

will call here, for lack of a better term, the *quality* of consumer demand across broad categories of products and services. By "quality," I mean the nature and extent of the information that the consumer brings to bear on a given purchasing decision. For certain consumers in certain purchasing situations, the buyers may have assimilated nearly perfect and complete (by one definition or another) information; such cases may be rare, but they are at least conceivable. The spectrum of cases can run from this ideal version to the opposite extreme, in which the individual faces a purchasing decision with limited or erroneous information in mind. If all markets for consumer goods and services were marked by identical conditions at supply, — that is, by identical characteristics of market structure among sellers — differences in the quality of demand across these markets might nevertheless lead to quite different results in terms of the market's performance.

Studies of market structure and performance in consumer–goods industries typically consider characteristics of supply in the market rather more carefully and completely than those of demand. This paper contends that, by considering the quality of consumer demand across markets, one can understand why certain markets are likely to yield results approximating the competitive model more closely in some cases than in others.

The purpose of this paper is to explore the question of the quality of consumer demand across markets and to develop some tentative conclusions about the impact of the quality of demand on market performance. This exploration may help explain why the architects of public policy are concerned more about the performance of some consumer markets than others. Finally, the paper suggests certain implications for the design of public policy. No doubt the arguments along the way call for more qualifications than will be found in the following material. Full documentation would require far more extensive research into the vast literature on phenomena of consumer behavior than I have attempted, and it would lead to a paper far longer than is appropriate here. Nevertheless, it is hoped that the discussion will suggest questions that might be pursued further.

Information Derived from Consumers' Past Experience

Information that the consumer brings to bear on a given purchasing decision is obtained from a variety of sources. The consumer's own experience is perhaps the most obvious of these. Word-of-mouth information from family, friends, and acquaintances is often of great importance as well. Certainly advertising, defined broadly to include not only advertising through the usual media but also point-of-purchase advertising, is often of major consequence. In some situations, advice from the retail clerk affects the purchasing decison. Finally, some consumers make use of various neutral sources, such as the consumer magazines and governmental reports.[1]

Each of these sources of information is clearly subject to certain weaknesses. One's own experience is likely to be limited, as is that of the people providing the word-of-mouth advice and counsel. The marketer-dominated information is intentionally biased, regardless of whether the marketer is the manufacturer or the retailer. Even the neutral sources are often subject to question. The rating services for consumers work with very small samples of the items tested; the weights they attach to different attributes of the product may differ from the weights the buyer might assign; features of design that are subject to criticism might be altered by the manufacturer soon after the item is rated; and ratings often become obsolete as whole new product lines are developed.

A rough but useful distinction can be drawn between the nature and quality of the information assimilated by the consumer from past experience — information which he has in mind as he considers a purchasing decision prior to additional search — and the nature and quality of the information likely to result from any additional search. At the time the specific purchasing decision is being made, the buyer consciously or unconsciously brings to bear on the decision a set of messages acquired in the past from the various sources of information influencing his decision. These can be drawn from the totality of his past experience and would include not only his experience with the brand being considered but also his impressions of that brand and its competitors gained from past exposure to advertising and the myriad other sources of information. With a memory less than perfect, the purchaser will not even be able to bring to bear the complete past experience, since forgetfulness will have screened out certain of the past information.[2]

If the consumer considers search worthwhile, he may engage in some shopping before making the specific purchase. In other words, the consumer may, by incurring some costs, improve the state of the information at his disposal.

Let us consider first the quality of consumer demand if the state of information is limited to that in the mind of the consumer when the purchase is first considered, that is, prior to any search. Under some circumstances this information can be quite complete. Such would seem to be the case when four conditions are met, namely:

[1] Donald F. Cox has suggested that these sources of information to consumers be classified as "consumer dominated," "marketer dominated," and "neutral." See Donald F. Cox, ed., *Risk Taking and Information Handling in Consumer Behavior* (Boston; Division of Research, Graduate School of Business Administration, Harvard University, 1957), p. 605.

[2] For a full discussion of this aspect of consumer behavior, see Francesco M. Nicosia, *Consumer Decision Processes* (Englewood Cliffs, N.J.: Prentice-Hall, Inc., 1966).

1. The item is bought frequently by the specific buyer in question;
2. The quality and performance characteristics of the product are known to the buyer prior to purchase or are quickly ascertained after the item is used;
3. The rate of technological change in the product is slow relative to the frequency of purchase, and
4. The terms of competing sellers' offers are known and are stable over time.

Under these circumstances the learning process can take place rather quickly. The consumer can conduct his own experimentation with alternative brands and arrive at his own evaluation of which best serves his needs. A few supermarket items might meet, or come close to meeting, all the criteria. Scouring powder or razor blades are a case in point. Various food products might at first glance appear to meet all four tests; however, such subtleties as vitamin content cannot be perceived through use, but only through the label. At the other end of the spectrum are a host of goods and services which fail to meet one or more of the tests. Automobile tires, automobiles themselves, appliances, appliance repair, casualty and life insurance, medical care, pharmaceuticals are only the more obvious cases.

Opponents of legislation for consumers are wont to sing the praises of the quality of competition in consumer markets. "The consumer is no moron, she's your wife," is a favorite quip. The housewife in the supermarket is depicted as a lightning calculator of values; and, the argument runs, the seller who does not measure up will be eliminated from the market if he does not mend his ways. It is interesting, nevertheless, to see how many times the illustrations used to buttress the generalization are drawn from the context of the supermarket, where the learning process can take place at a faster pace than in most other markets. The market for supermarket items comes closer to meeting the four criteria mentioned above than do the markets for most other consumer goods and services.

In general, we can conclude that markets characterized by rapid, accurate learning through experience by buyers in consumer markets may approximate more closely than other markets the competitive ideal on the demand side.

Information Derived from Consumers' Search

The discussion above has been limited to what might be termed the "costless information" case, that is, the case in which the consumer faced with a purchasing decision does not engage in additional search. Considering the case of search as separate from the case of costless information is a bit strained, since the experience relied upon in the first instance is accumulated from a background of previous purchases and exposure to advertising and other signals which can be defined in some broad sense as "search."

Search is rather narrowly defined here as the explicit comparison of alternatives prior to purchase.

If search is carried out with sufficient care, the consumer's state of information about available alternatives can be developed to the same point that might be achieved through extensive experience in those instances where the four criteria listed above are met. But will the search be carried out, and if so, how thorough will it be?

Stigler has noted that the buyer will continue the search to the point where the marginal cost of search is equated with the expected marginal return from further searching effort.[3] He notes that the greater the dispersion of prices, the greater the expected savings from an additional unit of search.[4] One may add that, in the case of differentiated products, the greater the dispersion of each of the quality characteristics, the greater the expected gains from search.

Stigler also points out that "if the correlation of asking prices of dealers in successive time periods is perfect (and positive!), the initial search is the only one that need be undertaken."[5] In this case the present price asked by a dealer is a perfect predictor of his future asking price, and search need not be repeated before future purchases. But he explicitly assumes no changes in quality or in the product's characteristics over time. If this assumption is abandoned in favor of the more realistic assumption that a product's features, real or contrived, do change over time, the life of the information acquired during search is limited. Innovations in a product's design or advertising message — broadly defined to include such features as design of packages and labelling — are of course common. Indeed, the marketing manager for product purchased frequently by the individual consumer is motivated to alter the marketing program for the product in order to attract new buyers, since the brand-loyal consumer presumably will not switch from the product and new buyers might be attracted. This is saying that the new buyers engage in some search when they encounter the change in the advertising "pitch," in the objective features of the product, and so forth. Marketing techniques must surely work to make the consumer's information obsolete more quickly, thus probably increasing the marginal return to the process of search and motivating the consumer to engage in more search than he would were products' characteristics static.

Several observations about the phenomenon of search can shed light on the relationship between search and the imperfections in the markets for consumer goods. First, the problem of search may be worsening over time if the rate of technological change is increasing or if the rate of change in marketing programs is increasing, or if both developments are taking place.

[3] George J. Stigler, "The Economics of Information," *Journal of Political Economy,* LXIX (June, 1961), 216.
[4] *Ibid.,* p. 215.
[5] *Ibid.,* p. 218.

Second, the nature of technological change in many consumer products may now involve a growing number of product modifications that are below the threshold of the consumer's perception. Gasoline additives provide a case in point. Despite agreement that the additives increase the life of the automobile engine, it is doubtful that anyone but the most zealous automobile owner can determine for himself that this is the case. Thus the search must be based increasingly on information which the consumer cannot generate by his direct observation of performance but which instead must come from advertisements and other sources of information.

If we can assume that the higher one's income, the more valuable one's time, increases in income per capita may lead to less search in a social group. Simultaneously, perhaps one of the luxuries which well-to-do people can afford is the luxury of not shopping carefully. For them, the opportunity cost of a bad purchase is not as high as for a low income buyer. If these two forces are in fact at work, they would seem to reduce the level of discipline to which sellers are subjected in the market place for consumer goods and services.

For low-income people, the process of search may be both costly and quite inefficient. The pattern of life of the metropolitan poor may make it difficult and expensive both in terms of time and money to cover alternative sources of goods and services outside the ghetto. Furthermore, the limited education of poor people presumably makes it difficult for them to assess satisfactorily the quality of the offerings of competing sellers. In short, they don't know "what to look for." This suggests that low-income people are likely to favor major brands of consumer goods, since they would look on the brand name as a surrogate for information.

If these possible attributes of consumers at both ends of the income scale apply, they work to reduce price competition in the market place. The impact of such buyers is no doubt offset at least in part by the corps of what we might call "professional shoppers" found across the whole spectrum of consumers. They are the consumers who consider shopping almost a hobby. Their sensitivity to offerings is such that every shopping trip is an information-gathering expedition that may yield impressions of prices and quality for goods which are not immediate prospects for purchase but which may be bought at a later time. For these people the process of search is enjoyable in and of itself. They are likely to be sources of information for their friends who look to them for shopping advice. Thus in their individual capacities and as centers of networks of influence and information, they serve to increase competitive discipline among sellers.

The nature and extent of individual shopping behavior will depend in part on the buyer's perception of the risk involved in the individual purchase. The risk may be related not only to performance of the good being considered for purchase, but to the prospective psychological satisfaction as well. Thus the buyer may check, overtly or otherwise, with his or her social group to determine whether purchase of a particular version of an item would enhance his prestige or acceptability among his peers. The greater the risk of a bad decision, the greater the search for information prior to the purchase.[6]

The process of search is becoming increasingly complicated by two phenomena in particular. One is that the increasing importance of services in the consumer's budget should lead to more time being spent on the searching process for services relative to goods. Yet services are not well standardized and their pricing is a matter of considerable uncertainty for the consumer. Automobile and appliance repair and home maintenance services are prime illustrations of the problem. The difficulty and imperfection of search in these markets no doubt help explain the continual grumbling about these markets. Medical services and insurance are two additional significant cases in point.

A second phenomenon is that the increasing mobility of consumers also operates to complicate the process of search, especially with respect to services. When the buyer moves to a new neighborhood or city, the search for satisfactory services must start afresh. Thus the useful life of the information gathered by the consumer about the sources of service is reduced.

The process of search by the consumer is shared, in a sense, by the retailer; if the retailer selects only certain brands or items to sell, he is conducting search himself, and the consumer chooses retailers in part by the quality of their performance as searchers. Competition among retailers turns not only on this but on their total package of services as well. Nevertheless, we must recognize the role of the retailer in the process of search.

For the many reasons cited above, the difficulties of the searching process may cause a relatively low, and perhaps declining, quality of demand. Nevertheless, the consumers are presumably in equilibrium in the sense that they are equating the marginal cost of search with the expected marginal return. As argued below, however, this does not necessarily mean that public policy should be neutral in the matter.

Consumer Compared with Industrial Purchasing Agent

An appreciation of the quality of demand in consumer markets can be enhanced by comparing the consumer as a buyer with the industrial purchasing agent as a buyer. The parallels and contrasts here are especially interesting because in so many instances the actual purchaser for the household is playing the role of purchasing agent for other members of that household. In a classic article appearing in 1912, "The Backward Art of Spending Money," Wesley Claire Mitchell recognized the difficult role of the housewife as purchasing agent:

[6] For a detailed study of the question of perceived risk among consumers, see Cox, *op. cit.*

She must buy milk and shoes, furniture and meat, magazines and fuel, hats and underwear, bedding and disinfectants, medical services and toys, rugs and candy. Surely no one can be expected to possess expert knowledge of the qualities and prices of such varied wares. The ease with which defects of materials or workmanship can be concealed in finishing many of these articles forces the purchaser often to judge quality by price, or to depend upon the interested assurances of advertisers and shopkeepers. The small scale on which many purchases are made precludes the opportunity of testing before buying, and many articles must be bought hurriedly wherever they are found at whatever price is asked.[7]

Comparing the features of the purchasing situation faced by the household "purchasing agent," on the one hand, and the industrial purchasing agent, on the other, can illuminate the nature of competition in these two kinds of markets and the role performed by the quality of demand in the two cases. Again, it helps to distinguish between the case involving only the information accumulated from past experience and the case involving further search.

The industrial purchasing agent will be motivated to maintain files of information on the experience of the plant or company with competing brands of various inputs. Since to maintain such a system of information is not costless, presumably the industrial purchasing agent will have more complete information on items requiring large annual expenditures than on items of less consequence in the firm's total costs. An exception to this general rule would be the case of the less significant item for which information on performance is easily and quickly collected. The purchasing agent must balance the cost of maintaining such an informational system against the expected benefit in terms of improving purchasing.

The sheer magnitude of the money at stake will lead the industrial purchasing agent to maintain a better system of informational feedback than will the household purchasing agent. Thus the firm operating a fleet of cars or trucks can "afford" to keep records on the performance of the tires purchased. The average motorist, by contrast, buying perhaps two tires a year, is likely to have little more than impressionistic evidence at hand when he ventures forth to buy a tire. Performance records such as rejection rates, "down time" of equipment and the like at the plant can generate for the industrial purchasing agent firm evidence of the quality of inputs. The household purchasing agent, on the other hand, has only the crudest kind of feedback from members of the family.

When search is undertaken, the rational purchasing agent will push search to the point where the expected marginal return from further search is equated to the marginal cost of the search. Thus major expenditures should be subject to more extensive and careful search than minor ones.

[7] Wesley Claire Mitchell, "The Backward Art of Spending Money," *American Economic Review,* II (March, 1912), p. 269.

Since the industrial purchasing agent will be dealing with at least some large purchases, the search will often be undertaken with great care. The contrast with the case of the household is clear. If 10,000 housewives sally forth one day to buy an item for which the expected price is around $5.00 and if each thinks she might possibly save five percent by comparison-shopping, the expected saving of 25 cents will lead to a certain amount of search, varying from individual to individual. On the other hand, if a single industrial purchasing agent is seeking 10,000 units of an item for which he expects to pay about $5.00 per unit and if he thinks he might save five percent by shopping, the $2,500 that might be saved should lead to more careful search than if the purchase is being made by 10,000 separate buyers. This feature of industrial markets clearly leads to greater competitive discipline.

The magnitude of the purchase in the industrial case is frequently so great that the buyer will engage in in-plant testing prior to purchase. This testing is simply an extension of the searching process; the greater the purchase and the greater the expected variability in performance of competing sellers' products, the greater the probability that such testing will be carried out before the commitment to purchase.

The quality of demand is therefore likely to be considerably greater in industrial markets than in consumer markets. It should be added that competitive discipline in industrial markets is especially great if the buyer has the option of making the item for himself. He is then a present or potential competitor on the sellers' side of the market. Furthermore he may be a buyer so large that he can engage in formal competitive bidding.

Stigler notes that

> Of course, the sellers can also engage in search and, in the case of unique items, will occasionally do so in the literal fashion that buyers do. In this — empirically unimportant — case, the optimum amount of search will be such that the marginal cost of search equals the expected increase in receipts, strictly parallel to the analysis for buyers.[8]

Search by sellers may well be empirically unimportant in the case of consumer goods, but it is certainly not unknown. Door-to-door sales of vacuum cleaners, encyclopedias, and certain home improvements like aluminum siding and storm sash are cases of sellers' search — and do not life insurance salesmen engage in sellers' search? On the other hand, search by the salesmen of industrial equipment, process supplies and raw materials surely is not empirically unimportant. The average purchase times the probability of the salesman actually making the sale may warrant maintenance of a sales force that calls directly on purchasing agents or those who influence the purchasing agents' decisions. This brings the buyer into direct contact

[8] Stigler, *op. cit.*, p. 216.

with the manufacturer, a situation unlike that in most consumer markets. Consequently, the feedback from ultimate user to producer can be much more accurate and detailed than is true with those consumer goods going through a retailer and perhaps a wholesaler as well. Buyers' complaints in the latter instance must be filtered back through the marketing channel, unless the buyer writes the manufacturer directly. But here again the contrast between industrial markets and consumer markets is interesting. The consumer may feel that registering a complaint even directly with the manufacturer is not "worth while," especially if the purchase is minor in amount. The industrial buyer, on the other hand, with larger average purchases, is surely more likely to make certain that the supplier hears of his complaint. Furthermore, the manufacturer is inclined to heed the large buyer but not the small one. Hence the manufacturer selling in industrial markets is probably fitting his product more successfully to the needs of the buyer because of more efficient informational feedback than one finds in consumer markets.

The manufacturer of industrial products is not able to afford a sales force — his searching mechanism — which contacts users directly if the average purchase times the probability of making the sale does not return revenue great enough to support the sales force. Thus many process supplies and such items as janitorial supplies may move to the user through industrial wholesalers, whose total product line is broad enough to yield average sales and hence support a sales force. In this case the seller's search is delegated to a middleman, just as the manufacturer of consumer goods may delegate his search to retailers.

Summary and Implications for Public Policy

We can now recapitulate the discussion above and proceed to draw some conclusions about the design of public policy directed toward improving the quality of consumer demand. The magnitude and accuracy of the information assimilated by the consumer from past purchases and other sources of information at the point in time when he is considering a purchase vary widely from individual to individual and, for a given individual, from product to product. Perfect competition assumes that the buyer has perfect knowledge of alternative offers by sellers. The point here is not so much that this knowledge is imperfect; this has never been questioned. More interesting is the wide variation in the state of information across markets.

Prior to the consumer's engaging in incremental search, his knowledge of alternatives is based on accumulated experience, be it great or small. This experience may have generated nearly perfect information if the four criteria mentioned early in this paper are met. Some large percentage of purchasing situations, however, fail to meet one or more of these criteria.

If the buyer feels that his experience is inadequate, he is motivated to search. Search will be extended to the margin where the expected returns from further search are judged equal to the incremental cost of the search. The expected returns will be greater, the larger the dispersion in sellers' offerings of prices, quality and performance; the greater the present value of the stream of purchases of the item the individual expects to make in the future; and the lower the rate of obsolescence in the information the buyer gathers during the search. Among individuals, evaluations of both cost and returns will vary, causing some to search more or less than others.

The gross imperfection in some markets, imperfections which can result from the low quality of consumer demand, is suggested in its extreme form by the life-insurance industry. Data on the yearly net cost per $1,000 of coverage are available for 1959–68 for the 71 companies with $500 million or more of ordinary life insurance in force, figured on insured age 35. The range is from a low of $0.37 per $1,000 for one insurer to a high of $5.95 for another, with an interquartile range of $2.25 to $3.85.[9] Although the terms of the policies are not strictly comparable and the data are subject to other qualifications which we need not delve into here, it is difficult to imagine differences in the "product," however defined, that would explain such price discrepancies. No doubt part of the explanation is that purchasers of life insurance look on the annual premium, rather than the net cost, as the price of the policy. The dispersion of the 10-year premiums for the 71 companies is much narrower, ranging from a low of $212.50 to a high of $266.60. Although the life insurance market is not as imperfect as the dispersion of net cost suggests, the intelligent purchasing of life insurance is so complex that one can conjecture consumers do not engage in extensive search, given their inability to assay the alternatives very completely or satisfactorily.

The individual consumer stands in interesting contrast with the industrial purchasing agent. Although the basic decision rule determining the extent of search will be the same, the returns from both an information system designed to evaluate performance and the larger average size of purchase will lead to more careful search by the industrial purchasing agent than by the consumer. Thus the quality of demand in industrial markets is considerably greater than in consumer markets. Total market performance in the broadest sense is enhanced in the industrial case because search by the seller commonly leads to direct contact between the manufacturer of the product and the buyer who will use, rather than resell, the product.

These points are all subject to more qualification than space permits, but the main thrust of the argument would seem to hold. If this is true, what is its significance for the public-policy discussion of "the consumer problem?"

[9] *Flitcraft Courant* (July, 1968).

First, the complaint that consumers do not have sufficient information available for intelligent decisions on purchasing misses the point. If costless search were possible, consumers could acquire quite complete information in some high proportion of purchasing situations. But even if all conceivable relevant information on, for example, detergents, could be printed on the packages, comparisons of price and quality would still be required. Search calls not only for collecting information on the individual brands and versions of the product in question but for comparing brands as well. What is needed, therefore, is not so much *more* information but rather more *efficient* information, that is, information not only "complete" but also provided in a form which permits comparisons with maximum efficiency. This would lead to a reduction in the incremental cost of search, and so the process would be pushed further than if these conditions were not met.

A second and related point addresses the common charge that consumers do not use the information already available. Marketers have complained, for example, that housewives do not even take advantage of the most accessible information, that is, they do not read the labels on the package. This, too, misses the point. Given the rationale for the search, the quality of demand would be improved and competition enhanced if information presented on the label and elsewhere were presented in a manner minimizing the cost of search and comparison. Consumers would still not make use of all available information, however, because presumably the condition of equilibrium would not always call for such extensive search. Nonetheless market performance would be improved.

A third observation deals with one part of the argument that consumers seem to be content with the quality of performance in consumer markets. Adequate search, however, presumes that the consumer knows what features of the product are important, that is, which pieces of information are relevant for the purchasing decision. In fact, however, some industries have been embarrassed by studies revealing the importance of certain features not previously considered by the average buyer. The furor over automobile safety and the concern about flammable fabrics and the side effects of pharmaceutical products are illustrations. Buyers may have thought they were operating under conditions of information adequate by some definition, but publicity has changed that perception at least to some degree.

A fourth comment concerns the role of consumers' complaints. It is often argued that the unhappy consumer will complain to the retailer or manufacturer and that this serves to discipline sellers. But a complaint carried back to the seller is an extension of the searching process. It will not be carried out unless the expected benefit from complaining is greater than the "cost" of making the complaint. This cost can be high relative to the expected return; the buyer may consider complaining as unpleasant, he may not be sure how strong a case he has; or the time and inconvenience may be significant. Especially in the case of items bought infrequently by the consumer, he may question whether the product really performed less well than competing products. For these various reasons, the complaints actually made may be but the tip of the iceberg, and the unregistered complaints may lead only to an undercurrent of consumers' grumbling.

If the quality of consumers' demand is to be improved, means must be found for increasing the efficiency of search, that is, reducing the cost of search and raising the returns. Better education of consumers is universally praised as one means of doing this. No doubt consumer education in the schools can be improved so that buyers are able to evaluate better the returns from search and carry out the process more efficiently. Outside the schools, however, one does not have the benefit of a captive audience; adults will turn to consumer-education materials only as part of the searching process. Thus the consumers' magazines find that subscribers use their services most frequently when purchasing "big-ticket" items. These services no doubt improve the efficiency of search, but buyers will use them only when warranted by their perception of the expected return.

Greater use of standards holds promise of making search by consumers more efficient, since standards are in substantial part a proxy for information. The recent legislation calling for the establishment of standards for automobile tires should reduce the confusion about the meaning of "first-line" and "second-line," tires. Although the consumer may not know just what features distinguish the first-line from the second-line tire, at least he can assume that the minimum standards met by one manufacturer's first-line tire are higher than those met by another manufacturer's second-line tire.

Use of the term "standards" in the marketing of consumer goods causes considerable confusion because of variations in the meaning of the word. Some products are subject to what we will call legal minimum standards; in other words, certain standards must be met before the item can be marketed legally. Drugs subject to clearance by the Food and Drug Administration provide a case in point. Likewise, standards might be established by law, agreement, or common usage for employing particular terminology, as with octane ratings of gasoline. The recent Truth-in-Lending Act involves this type of standardization in that the annual rate of interest, previously subject to several definitions, will now be used in a consistent manner across virtually all consumers' transactions. Standardization of terminology is not to be confused with what might be called standardized and mandatory specifications. When the need for broader use of standards is discussed, opponents of further regulation often argue that this measure will minimize the range of choice to consumers. It is one thing, however, to have legislation prohibiting the production of tires other than first-line tires; it is something else to have legislation permitting the production of other than first-line tires but limiting the use of the term "first-line" to tires meeting certain minimum requirements.

The Fair Packaging and Labeling Act of 1966 — the so-called "Truth-in-Packaging" Act — is a step toward standardizing not just the nomenclature but the actual sizes of packages for certain consumer goods. The objective here of course is to facilitate search by easing the task of comparing prices. To the extent that this reduces the cost of search, the quality of demand in consumer markets is improved.

Advertising is one source of information to consumers that is subject to a steady barrage of criticism for a variety of reasons. Without delving into the subject in any detail, it is relevant to note that, in the absence of false and misleading statements, advertising is of course a source of information to the consumer. It is imbalanced, though, in that the disadvantages of the product are rarely mentioned; nor can one rely on the advertisements of competing sellers to point out these weaknesses in the products of other marketers. Moves to require certain minimum disclosures in advertising may introduce some qualifications into what may now be exclusively laudatory comments about a product, thus improving advertising as an informational source.

It has been argued above that the quality of consumer demand may be deteriorating. Although consumers are supposedly increasingly well educated, they are also earning higher incomes. Thus the perceived risk of an unsatisfactory purchase is reduced, since the opportunity cost of replacing the item is lowered. The proliferation of products, versions of products, and brands widens the spectrum of consumers' choice. Delightful as this may be on some counts, it does increase the cost of search. As products become more complex, certain characteristics in performance may lie below the threshold of perception even though they are nonetheless important.

If the reasoning set forth here is generally correct, it helps explain why legislative attention has been drawn to such markets as packaged foods, automobiles, insurance, tires and pharmaceuticals. In each of these markets, one or more of the four criteria cited early in this paper are not met, and search is relatively unsatisfactory. Consumer groups and interested legislators sense the imperfections in these markets. This suggests that public policy toward consumer markets will probably continue to move toward making the process of consumer search more efficient.

7

The Competitive Effects of Joint
Bidding by Oil Companies for
Offshore Oil Leases

*Jesse W. Markham**

I The Central Issue

The Nature of Joint Bidding

Joint action by competing firms is surely among the more ancient concerns of antimonopoly policy. Cato the elder is reported to have been bothered by the practice as early as 160 B.C., over 1400 years before the 1285 statute of Edward I prohibiting "forestalling."[1]

More timely legal antecedents to the subject with which this essay is concerned are the familiar cases on interfirm agreements beginning with *Addyston Pipe*[2] and the more recent cases involving *joint ventures*.[3] The two classes of cases, while related, raise somewhat different issues.

The per se doctrine pertaining to interfirm agreements on price and to other terms and conditions of trade, a doctrine born in *Addyston Pipe* and reared in *Trenton Potteries* and *Socony-Vacuum,* derives from the clear substitution of collective for individual action. That is, for every firm becoming a party to the agreement, the number of independent decision-making units on matters the agreement encompasses is reduced by one. Stated more rigorously, we define x as the total number of original decision-

* Harvard University

[1] Fritz Machlup, *The Political Economy of Monopoly* (Baltimore: The Johns Hopkins University Press, 1952), pp. 185–186, citing Frank A. Fetter, *The Masquerade of Monopoly.*

[2] *U.S.* v. *Addyston Pipe and Steel Co.,* 171 U.S.–614(1899); *U.S.* v. *Socony-Vacuum Oil Co.,* 310 U.S. 150(1940); *U.S.* v. *Trenton Potteries Co.,* 2273 U.S. 392(1927).

[3] cf. *U.S.* v. *Penn-Oil Chemical Co.,* 389 U.S. 308(1964).

making units, and n as the number of firms that enter into an agreement to act in unison, the effect of the agreement is to reduce x by $n - 1$.[4]

This relationship is undoubtedly the basis for the almost unanimous acceptance by the United States antitrust fraternity of the per se doctrine on interfirm agreements, even those who have seriously questioned the wisdom of all other aspects of contemporary antitrust policy;[5] the agreement produces no likely procompetitive effects that should be weighed against the obvious reduction it causes in the number of independent decision-making units.

In comparison, the competitive effects of joint ventures, to which joint bidding by oil companies for offshore oil is somewhat more akin, are not so predictable. As traditionally defined, a "joint venture" is an organization of two or more persons or companies for the purpose of carrying out a single or temporary operation. The joint effort makes it possible to engage in certain ventures that are beyond the capabilities of a single firm or individual because such ventures are unusually risky or require unusually large amounts of capital. Examples are the eight companies Henry Kaiser temporarily joined to build Boulder Dam (1931) and the four-company joint venture that built the Toronto, Canada subway system (1953).[6] In theory, and very likely in fact, joint ventures of this sort make it possible to produce outputs that otherwise would not be produced. Moreover, because of their temporary existence, their anticompetitive effects, if any, are likely to be trivial; in any case they are, by definition, short-lived.

The developing antitrust doctrine on recently launched joint ventures pertains to a *different* kind of joint venture. In a contemporary corporate joint venture "two or more companies combine less than all of their assets to create a new entity."[7] The significant difference between the new and the traditional type of joint venture is that the new variety brings into being an entity that contemplates a "continuity of life" commensurate with that of its parents. It is probably the virtual permanency of the entity that has accounted for the application of Clayton Act, Section 7, to joint ventures on the grounds that "[o]ver all, the same considerations apply to joint ventures as to mergers."[8]

[4] The agreement itself is of course one decision-making unit.

[5] *cf.* Robert Bork and Ward Bowman, "The Crisis in Antitrust," *Fortune,* (December, 1963), pp. 138–140, 192–201. The most penetrating and persuasive case for some relaxation of the per se rule can be found in Almarin Phillips, *Market Structure, Organization and Performance,* (Cambridge: Harvard University Press, 1962), esp. chapts. II and XI. Phillips argues that, where the per se doctrine leads to economic inconsistencies, it should be abandoned and that, in any case, price-fixing should not be conclusively presumed from the fact that firms may have entered into an agreement.

[6] Elvin F. Donaldson, *Corporate Finance* (New York: The Ronald Press Co., 1957), pp. 37–38.

[7] Lewis Bernstein, "Joint Ventures in the Light of Recent Antitrust Developments: Anti-Competitive Joint Ventures," *The Antitrust Bulletin,* (January-April, 1965), 25.

[8] *U.S. v. Penn-Oil Chemical Co.,* 389 U.S. 308(1967) 87.

As presently conducted, joint bidding for offshore oil leases is clearly analogous to neither the interfirm agreements traditionally governed by the per se rule nor the corporate joint venture governed by the law on merger. In form, duration, and to the extent it can be ascertained, in purpose, it is more closely akin to joint ventures of the traditional sort. It is a temporary arrangement among two or more oil companies whereby they "pool" their bid money on specific offshore tracts. The joint bidding, at least in some cases, is accomplished through the instrument of a contract whereby all bidding partners agree that the highest bid among them is the prevailing bid.[9] Hence, in these cases, the direct consequence of joint bidding is simply to eliminate several low bids that would not be winning bids anyway. As later analysis shows, the indirect consequences of joint bidding, such as whether, and how, it affects the high bid, the total number of bidders, and other aspects of the lease market, are not easily determined.

Statistical Analysis of Effects of Joint Bidding

It has been estimated that one-third of the 1,307 oil and gas leases awarded between 1954 and mid-1968 in the Gulf of Mexico and Pacific coast regions were awarded to joint bidders.[10] The central purpose of this essay is to determine, through the use of the relevant available data and techniques of quantitative analysis, the effect of such joint bidding on competition for offshore oil leases. Professor Mason's frequently quoted caveat serves as an appropriate preface to this undertaking, and will be kept firmly in mind throughout the analysis: "No one familiar with the statistical and other material pertaining to the business performance of firms and industries would deny the extreme difficulty of constructing from this material a water-tight case for or against the performance of particular firms in particular industries. Few, on the other hand, would deny that with respect to many industrial markets, an informed judgment is possible."[11]

The problem of rendering an enlightened judgment in the case of offshore oil leasing is of more than average complexity because of certain characteristics peculiar to the market involved. In most markets the competitive consequences of interfirm arrangements may be judged from how they affect the price-cost relationships of the sellers. Frequently, as an operational matter, such relationships are inferred from the level of the sellers' profits. We are deprived of the use of these conventional measures of competition in the offshore oil leasing market, since the seller, in this case the federal government, incurs no costs of production. Moreover, because

---

[9] This arrangement makes joint bidding less vulnerable to antitrust.

[10] See Bureau of Land Management, U.S. Department of Interior, *Oil and Gas Lease Data Reports,* 1954–1968.

[11] *Economic Concentration and the Monopoly Problem,* (Cambridge: Harvard University Press, 1957) p. 368.

of the very high risks that attend offshore oil leasing and exploration, it is virtually impossible to check the prices paid for tracts against their "value" as determined by market forces. The bids submitted for any given tract are obviouly affected by each bidder's estimate of the amount of recoverable oil and gas the tract contains, the cost of development, future crude prices, and other relevant variables. But the substantial differences between estimated and actual values are evidenced by the small number of tracts that turn out to be successful commercial ventures and the enormous variation in bids among bidders having access to essentially the same geological data.[12]

Quantitative data do, however, permit the testing of at least four hypotheses that relate directly to the impact of joint bidding on competition in offshore oil leasing:

1. *Joint bidding reduces (increases) the number of bidders and by this means reduces (increases) the average bid price.*

Although the factors affecting bid prices are numerous and their causal relationships complex, a simple positive correlation exists between the number of bids and the magnitude of the highest bid. The effect of joint bidding on the number of bids is therefore a relevant issue, but one that cannot be resolved a priori.

On the one hand, joint bidding may bring into the market bidders who would not be there were they restricted by regulation to solo bidding. The mere fact that joint bidding is so prevalent is sufficiently conclusive evidence that in many instances it is preferred over solo bidding. The possibility of joint bidding is therefore likely to induce some firms to enter bids when they otherwise would not do so. This would have the effect of increasing the total number of independent bids entered for some tracts.

On the other hand, where joint bids are simply substituted for independent solo bids, they reduce the total number of bids. That is, if all the participating firms bid individually on a given tract in any event, joint bids would simply be substituted for a larger number of independent solo bids. If the resulting reduction in total bids is substantial, competition may be adversely affected.

2. *Joint bidding affects the size distribution of firms participating in the bidding and consequently affects competition by raising (lowering) the level of concentration in the domestic petroleum industry generally.*

The transaction prices resulting from some of the recent bidding surely suggest that a large number of tracts would lie beyond the means of the average industrial corporation. For this reason alone, it

---

[12] For a highly informative analysis of the complexities of oil exploration, see James W. McKie, "Market Structure and Uncertainty in Oil and Gas Exploration," *Quarterly Journal of Economics* (November 1960), pp. 543–571. McKie found that the high bids on unproved leases on the outer continental shelf in 1955 were sometimes fifteen times the low bids.

may be inferred that joint bidding enables more of the smaller and medium-sized firms to participate in the bidding process. For example, in 1968 tracts on the outer continental shelf were leased in Santa Barbara Channel, California at an average price of $8.5 million; the price in 1968 for Texas offshore leases of tracts on the outer continental shelf averaged about $4.5 million. In view of the high order of uncertainty concerning the revenues any given tract will yield, a bidder would have to bid successfully on a fairly large number of tracts to be reasonably optimistic about earning a profit. But three or four successful bids per year which proved to be unproductive would seriously tax the cash flow of the average industrial corporation.

The unusually large asset base and cash flow required to carry on explorations are further indicated by the fact that the annual outlay for oil and gas exploration in the United States alone typically amounts to $2 billion; between 1959 and 1965 the total outlay on such exploration in the United States amounted to $14.1 billion.[13] Many of the larger firms also conducted extensive explorations outside the United States. Exploratory expenditures generally equal 30 percent of total expenditures on exploration and production for the industry's operations in the United States.

On the other hand, however, oil companies are not average industrial corporations. Of the twenty largest industrial corporations in terms of assets appearing on *Fortune's* 1967 list of the largest 500, eight were oil companies. The smallest of these eight had total assets in excess of $2 billion. The same list shows that fourteen oil companies each had total assets in excess of $1 billion; these fourteen companies accounted for nearly one-third of all industrial companies in the United States with assets of $1 billion or more. Thus, while a successful program of solo bidding would require firms with unusually large financial resources, oil companies are among the most prominent candidates for this financial category.

3. *Joint bidding increases (decreases) the total revenues the government receives from the leasing of offshore oil tracts.*

The Outer Continental Shelf Land Act of August 7, 1943[14] provides that the federal government may lease public lands under either of two arrangements: (1) it may fix the royalty on the value of oil and gas recovered and determine the initial fixed payment, referred to as "bonus payment," through competitive bidding; or (2) it may fix the bonus payment and let the royalty payment be determined through competitive bidding. The government has used the first of these alternatives, setting the royalty rate at 16⅔ percent.

---

[13] American Petroleum Institute, *et al., Joint Association Survey,* various annual issues.

[14] 43 U.S.C. sec. 1331 *et seq.*

Joint bidding conceivably could affect both the total bonus payments the government receives and the maximum bid on individual offshore tracts but, a priori, it need not affect them by the same magnitude or even in the same direction. For example, it is very possible, indeed very likely, that joint bidding encourages individual oil companies to put up more money for offshore tracts than they would if forced to enter solo bids. Joint bidding may have this result because it would provide a means for each company to spread its risks and "play the averages" by entering bids on more tracts. Since risk and uncertainty inhibit investment, a reduction in risk and uncertainty, all other things remaining the same, should lead to an increase in investment — in this case, an increase in the amount of money individual firms allocate to bidding for offshore tracts. Notwithstanding its committing more money to *all* tracts, the individual firm need not bid higher on every tract than it would if forced to enter only solo bids. In essence, the possibility of joint bids permits each firm to follow a strategy of "play the averages" rather than one of "go for broke."

Were it forced to pursue a "go for broke" strategy, each firm would very likely concentrate its bidding (exposed money) on those few tracts its geological surveys showed to have the highest expected profits. If the geological surveys of all bidding companies tended to agree, all companies would be inclined to concentrate their bidding on a limited number of the most desirable tracts. As a consequence, the few most desirable tracts might sell at higher prices under solo than under joint bidding. This outcome is by no means certain, however. It would depend on whether several companies bidding jointly would come up with a higher total bid than one company concentrating on several such tracts. Almost certainly, tracts other than the most desirable ones would go at lower transaction prices under solo than under joint bidding because most bidding companies would concentrate their bids on the more promising tracts. This expectation is reinforced by the fact that joint bidding very likely increases the total number of independent bids — by making it possible for those firms who may not bid solo to participate in the bidding.

Through the use of simulation techniques, it is possible to compare the total bonus payments made under the present system permitting joint bidding with the payments that would have been made had such bidders been required to bid solo.

4. *Whether joint bidding has affected competition in the leasing of offshore tracts should have been reflected in the rate of return the industry has earned on offshore oil operations.* The data required to test this hypothesis are neither complete nor entirely satisfactory, but they are adequate for crude tests.

II The Quantitative Analysis

Relationship between Total Number of Bids
and Number of Joint Bids

Both the magnitude of the high bid and the number of bids appear to be positively correlated with the estimated value of the tract. Accordingly, it is at least possible that, if the effect of the estimated value of the tract on the price offered by the high bidder could be eliminated, the relationship between number of bids and the high-bid price would be a random one.[15]

The only known attempt to disentangle, and measure, the effects of various factors which logically should influence the bid-price on offshore tracts pertains to 189 leases issued in the 1954 and 1955 Louisiana sales of oil and gas leases.[16] A multiple-regression model of the following form was applied to these data:

$$Y = b_1 + b_2 x_2 + b_3 x_3 + b_4 x_4 + b_5 x_5 + b_6 x_6 + e$$

where: Y = high-bid price
and $x_2, \ldots, x_6$ are, respectively, realized productivity of the tract from time of lease to 1967, depth of water, number of bidders, incidence of high-bid prices in joint bids by the eight largest groups of oil companies, and number of acres per tract (e is the usual error term).

The most significant determinants of high-bid prices turned out to be the number of bidders, productivity of tract, and number of acres in the tract, in that order.

As the study recognizes, the results suffer from several important defects and shortcomings: (1) in view of the age and narrow coverage of the data, the estimates have very limited applicability; (2) the bid-price logically should be much more closely related to the *expected* profitability of the tract than to its subsequent realized output in physical units; that less than one

---

[15] This can be expressed in terms of the multiple-regression problem often encountered in regression analysis. Suppose theory leads us to expect a linear relationship between Y, x_2 and x_3:

$$Y = b_1 + b_2 x_2 + b_3 x_3 + e$$

where: Y = high-bid price
         x_2 = number of bidders
and, x_3 = estimated value of the tract.

If x_2 and x_3 were connected by an exact linear relationship, it would then be impossible to estimate the separate effects on the high-bid price of the estimated value of the tract and the number of bidders.

It might be noted that, as the number of observations of a variable is increased, the expected *range* of its observed values will increase. For this statistical reason, assuming no other influences, we would expect the high-bid price to increase and the low bid to decrease as the number of bids is increased.

[16] See *Study of the Outer Continental Shelf Lands of the United States,* prepared by Nossaman, Waters, Scott, Krueger, & Riordan for the Public Land Law Review Commission, Los Angeles, California, October, 1963.

out of four outer-continent-shelf tracts leased have produced crude oil in economic quantities is persuasive evidence that actual yields vary significantly from expected profitability. Hence, if expected profitability could have been used instead of actual physical output, the number of bidders may have lost some of its relative importance as a determinant of high-bid prices.

Another means of determining the possible effect of joint bidding on the number of bids is to observe the simple statistical relationship between solo bids and joint bids, holding the price of the high bid relatively constant in order to eliminate most of the effect bidders' estimated value of the tracts has on the number of bids. The problem could be stated in the form of a simple linear relationship as follows:

$$Y = a + bX$$

where Y = total number of solo bids

and X = total number of joint bids

When the simple-regression model is applied to data on bids for fairly narrowly defined price ranges, the values of a and b should at least provide an answer to the following question: "Do joint bids tend to be *additive* to solo bids or are they *substituted* for solo bids?" If the latter, a high incidence of joint bids should reduce the total number of solo bids; if the former, the number of joint bids should leave the total number of solo bids unaffected. Relating this theory to the equation, if there were zero joint bids, a would represent the total number of firms participating in the bidding, which in turn would equal the total number of bids, all of which would be solo. If joint bids were merely substitutes for solo bids, b would take on some value significantly different from zero, and its sign would be negative; that is, the total number of solo bids Y would decline as the number of joint bids increased.

The simple regression model $Y = a + bX$ was fitted to the combined data on bids for offshore tracts leased in Louisiana, Santa Barbara, and Texas for the most recent available year.[17] To eliminate as effectively as simple techniques would permit the influence of the estimated value of the tracts on the number of bids, the model was fitted separately to bid data falling in the following ranges: less than $1 million; $1 million to $5 million; $5 million to $10 million; $10 million to $20 million; $20 million to $30 million; $30 million to $40 million; and over $40 million. The results obtained are shown in Table 7–1.

It will be noted that the b values are positive for five of the seven bid-range intervals and, considering the degree of heterogeneity of the data, do not vary substantially from zero. Strictly interpreted, the computed regressions tell us that as joint bids (X) increase total solo bids (Y) remain

---

[17] This was 1967 for Louisiana and 1968 for Santa Barbara and Texas.

Table 7–1 *Computed Relation between Total Solo Bids and Total Joint Bids for Leases on Offshore Tracts in Louisiana, Santa Barbara and Texas Combined, 1968**

High-bid Range ($000,000)	Observations	Computed Relationship	Standard Error
<1	187	$Y = .97 - .04x$	.98
1– 5	113	$Y = 1.65 + .35x$	1.68
5–10	42	$Y = 2.97 + .36x$	2.41
10–20	23	$Y = 2.38 + .21x$	2.43
20–30	10	$Y = 3.75 + .22x$	2.08
30–40	6	$Y = 2.25 - .25x$	.98
>40	7	$Y = 1.34 + .81$	1.77

Source: Computed from data on bids compiled by the Bureau of Land Management, U.S. Department of the Interior.
*1967 for Louisiana.

virtually the same. In brief, joint bids are net additions to total bids rather than substitutes for solo bids. It is obvious, however, from the very large values of the standard error that the regressions do not justify this strict interpretation. One can conclude, however, that the analysis does not support the hypothesis that joint bids are at the expense of solo bids; indeed, if one were forced to guess, the better guess is that joint bids increase, rather than reduce, the total number of bidders. Additional data tend generally to strengthen this latter otherwise very weak conclusion. Figure 7–1 shows the incidence of joint bidding on tracts — those in the three offshore areas combined in the foregoing analysis — by size of high-bid range. It is clear that joint bids as a percent of total bids increase as the high-bid price increases, rising from slightly over one-third of total bids for the less-than $1 million bid class to about two-thirds of total bids for the over $30 million bid classes. This is consistent with the expectations that the very high-price tracts tend to exceed the available resources of at least some of the individual bidding companies. It can therefore be reasonably inferred that the possibility of joint bidding tends to increase the number of bids, and possibly the magnitude of the bids,[18] in the high-price classes. As further evidence of this possible effect, joint bidding has accounted for a much higher percent of total bids on the Pacific Coast than on the Gulf Coast. The average high-bid price has also been significantly higher on the Pacific Coast.[19]

[18] See below for discussion of the possible effect of joint bidding on the high-bid price.

[19] On the Pacific Coast, 54% of the high-bids have been joint bids; in the Gulf Coast only 29% have been joint bids. See *Study of the Outer Continental Shelf Lands of the U.S.*, op. cit., p. 488.

Figure 7-1 *Joint Bids as a Percentage of Total Bids and Percentage of Total Tracts in Each High-Bid Range*

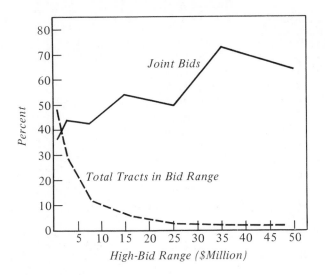

Source: U.S., Bureau of Land Management, Department of the Interior.

Size of Firm and Incidence of Joint Bidding

Joint bidding appears to be relatively more important for small- and medium-size oil companies than for very large companies, although the available statistics on this issue are dominated by Humble-Esso — by far the largest company — with nearly $7 billion in domestic assets. A breakdown of bids by size of firm in the Santa Barbara Channel sale up to February 2, 1968 is shown in Table 7-2. Only 40 of the 399 total bids included in the table were solo bids, of which nearly half were accounted for by Humble-Esso. Union, Shell, and Pan American Petroleum, all three of which are among the top ten largest oil companies, account for all except one of the remaining 21 solo bids.

All bids, by type of bid and size of firm, for the most recent sales in each of the three offshore regions are shown in Table 7-3. The pattern is highly irregular, but there is a perceptible inverse relationship between a firm's size and extent of its reliance on joint bids. Among the top five firms in terms of domestic assets, only Chevron has used joint bids in appreciably more than half the total number of times it has bid. With the single exception of Sun Oil Company,[20] the smallest eight oil companies rely almost entirely on joint bidding.

---

[20] As will be noted from Table 7-2, however, Sun has relied entirely on joint bids for Santa Barbara Channel tracts. Sun's large percentage of solo bidding is attributable to what appears to be its policy of entering at least a small bid on virtually every tract.

Table 7–2 Outer Continental Shelf Santa Barbara
Channel Sale up to February 2, 1968

Rank in order of United States assets 12/31/67		Bids	
		Joint	Solo
11	Atlantic Richfield	26	0
22	Ashland	8	0
9	Continental	18	0
12	Cities Service	14	0
—*	Colorado Oil & Gas	9	0
3	Gulf	25	0
1	Humble	48	19
6	Mobil	34	0
16	Marathon	7	0
7	Pan American Petroleum	19	5
—*	Pauley	11	0
8	Phillips	19	0
4	Standard	51	0
20	Signal	1	1
—*	Superior	4	0
15	Sun	4	0
17	Sunray DX	8	0
5	Shell	0	9
2	Texaco	18	0
10	Union	35	6
		359	40

Source: The Chase Manhattan Bank, *Financial Analysis of a Group of Petroleum Companies*, June 1968; and Bureau of Land Management, U.S. Department of the Interior.
*Small companies with undetermined ranks.

It may be even more meaningful to compare the use of joint bidding by the largest seven firms ranked in Table 7–3 with that of the remaining thirteen, since the most significant break in size occurs between the seventh and eighth largest firms. For the largest seven companies, 51 percent of all bids were joint bids; for the remaining thirteen, 70 percent of all bids were joint bids.

Moreover, data appearing in the *Study of the Outer Continental Shelf Lands of the United States* indicate that the incidence of successful solo bidding has been concentrated in the largest companies.[21] For the entire outer continental shelf, bids have been entered on 1,370 tracts; of the 1,370 high bids, 455 (33 percent) were joint and 915 (67 percent) were solo.

[21] *Op. cit.*, pp. 486–487.

Table 7–3 Joint Bids as Percent of Total Bids
By Size of Company

Company	Domestic Assets ($000,000)	Joint Bids (Per Cent of Total)	Total Assets ($000,000)
Humble	$6,646	28.8	$15,197
Texaco	4,100	26.3	7,169
Gulf	3,195	52.3	6,458
Chevron	3,783	78.6	5,310
Shell	3,421	2.6	3,421
Mobil	3,346	100.0	6,224
Pan Am. Petro.	3,268	58.4	4,058
Phillips	2,324	100.0	2,787
Union	1,845	68.5	2,026
Conoco	1,805	88.8	2,354
Atlantic-Rich	1,692	73.8	1,886
Cities Service	1,674	33.0	1,829
Sinclair	1,628	100.0	1,810
Sun	1,147	5.0	1,529
Getty	948	100.0	1,173
Signal	878	96.8	1,090
Sunray	684	93.1	977
Marathon	616	100.0	749
Skelly	589	100.0	606
American	233	86.6	421

Source: The Chase Manhattan Bank, *Financial Analysis of a Group of Petroleum Companies*, June 1968; and Bureau of Land Management, U.S. Department of the Interior.

The largest eight companies entered 906 of the high bids, the next twelve largest entered 233 of the high bids, and the rest of the industry entered the remaining 231. Since the 906 successful bids entered by the "big eight" exceeded by far the total of 455 joint bids entered by firms of all sizes, it can be concluded that the largest firms entered a very large percentage of the high solo bids.[22] From these data it would appear that the rewards of joint bidding might very well accrue most frequently to small- and medium-

[22] A fitting of a linear regression of the type $Y = a + bX$ to the most recent year's data on bids for Santa Barbara Channel, Texas, and Louisiana yields the following results:

$$(1) \quad Y = 92.7 - 0.01035X_1$$
$$(2) \quad Y = 83.2 - 0.00404X_2$$

where Y represents joint bids expressed as a percent of total bids by Company, and X_1, and X_2 are respectively total domestic assets and total assets (world wide). It will be noted that joint bids as a percent of total bids decreases as the size of firm increases.

size oil companies, although there are some striking exceptions to this generally supportable conclusion. Phillips Petroleum and Mobil Oil, both of which are among the 10 largest oil companies, have used joint bidding exclusively, whereas the significantly smaller Sun Oil company has engaged heavily in solo bidding except for its relying entirely on joint bidding in the Santa Barbara Channel.

The Effect of Joint Bidding on Total Government Realization From Outer Continental Shelf Leases: A Theoretical Analysis

It is obviously impossible to measure directly the effect of joint bidding on the total outlays of oil companies, which are of course the total receipts of the government, in the form of bonus payments for offshore leases. Since there have been no sales in which all oil companies bid singly, it is impossible to make direct statistical comparisons. It is possible, however, to derive from past data on sales the necessary inputs for a theoretical model which can be used for estimating the effect of joint bidding on the government's bonus receipts; that is, the conditions of solo bidding can be simulated. The simulation proceeds as follows:[23]

1. It is possible to calculate the average bid for each tract from actual sales data.

2. All tracts can then be assigned to one of the following four categories according to their average bid:

Category	Average Bid ($000,000)
A	0–5
B	5–10
C	10–15
D	15–

3. It is possible to calculate for each category the average *exposure* — with "exposure" defined as the total money put up in the bidding — and the average number of bids per tract.

4. From observation it can be determined that the probability distribution of bids on a tract tends to be exponential. That is, the probability P that a bid B will not exceed some amount x is given by the formula

$$P(B \leq x) = -e^{\frac{-x}{m}},$$

where m is the mean bid on the tract.

---

[23] I am heavily indebted to Dr. Rudolph C. Reinitz for help on this portion of the paper.

To illustrate, the case of a mean bid of $10 million is shown in Figure 7–2.

The probability of a bid being offered that is less than $5 million is 0.4, while that of a bid being offered that is less than $20 million is 0.86. Thus, given the average bid and the average number of bids in a category, it is possible to calculate the expected maximum bid for the average tract from the formula:

$$\text{average winning bid} = m(1 + 1/2 + \ldots + \frac{1}{n})$$

where n is the average number of bids per tract and m is the average exposure per tract.

5. The total expected government's realization is obtainable by multiplying the expected maximum bid by the number of tracts in the category and summing the results in the four categories.

Figure 7–2

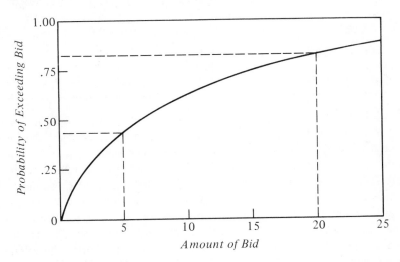

Amount of Bid

Assuming that (1) each company's interest in bidding and (2) the industry's total exposure remain the same under solo bidding as they have in fact been with joint bidding permitted, it is then possible to estimate the effect single bidding would have on expected total governmental realization. The average bid and the average number of bids per tract may be calculated on the assumption that all companies entered solo bids. For example, in the Louisiana sale in 1967, the total amount exposed for all tracts that fell in the $0–$5 million category was $373.3 million. The total number of tracts in that category was 125. The number of bids would have been 620 had each company actually involved in the bidding bid solo. Consequently, the average bid equals \$373.3 million divided by 125, or approximately \$3 million. The average number of bids per tract equals 620 divided by 125, or 5. From the formula in (4), the average maximum bid is:

$$\frac{\$3 \text{ million}}{5} (1 + \tfrac{1}{2} + \tfrac{1}{3} + \tfrac{1}{4} + \tfrac{1}{5}), \text{ or } \$1.37 \text{ million.}$$

To obtain the expected realization for all the tracts in the \$0–\$5 million category, \$1.37 million is multiplied by 125, the number of tracts in that category, thus yielding \$171.3 million. The same operations can be performed for all four categories, and the sum represents the expected realization from the entire sale if all companies bid solo.

The expected realization and the actual realization computed from actual sales data on the three outer continental shelves — Louisiana 1967, Texas 1968, and California 1968 — are compared in Table 7–4.

Table 7–4

Sale	Actual Realization (with joint bids) (Millions of Dollars)	Expected Realization (no joint bids) (Millions of Dollars)
Louisiana 1967	510	427
Texas 1968	593	301
California 1968	602	316

It will be noted that, in the case of each of the outer continental shelves, the government's expected realization under exclusively solo bidding is substantially less than the actual realization has been under a combination of joint and solo bidding. The mathematical explanation, in relatively simple terms, lies in the conditions assumed to hold for the simulation model, the most crucial of which is the assumption that the industry will expose the same amount of money whether firms bid solo or both solo and jointly. Since total exposure is divided by the total number of bidders to derive the average bid, the average bid turns out to be smaller under the relatively larger number of bidders when all firms bid solo. The smaller the estimated average bid, the smaller will be the estimated maximum bid and, hence, the smaller will be the estimated total government realization.

The validity of the foregoing simulated results therefore depends very heavily on the validity of the assumption concerning the total industry's exposure — the assumption that exposure remains the same for the two patterns of bidding. Although data required to test its validity are not available, this proposition can be rendered somewhat less speculative by breaking it down into its component parts. On the one hand, if it might be assumed that firms entering into joint-bidding arrangements would generally bid their independent estimates of the value of the tract if forced to bid solo, joint bidding might be said to "hide" some of the bid money that would be exposed under solo bidding. For example, if firms A and B entered into a joint-bidding contract, and A estimated the tract to be worth $10 million while B estimated it to be worth $5 million, the joint bid of $10 million would "hide" the $5 million which would otherwise have been bid. On the other hand, since joint bidding is an important means of reducing risks, it almost certainly induces individual firms to allocate more funds to the purchase of leases than they would allocate if risks were greater. Moreover, the possibility of joint bidding may both raise maximum bids and induce some firms to bid that otherwise would not bid. These factors tend to offset each other and, although this does not add up to either a validation or refutation of the assumption in question, it weakens any a priori argument that joint bidding tends to reduce total exposure.

For the purpose of observing the relationship between total exposure and the government's realization, we may now relax the assumption that total exposure remains the same under a combination of solo and joint bidding and exclusively solo bidding. One way of doing this is to estimate the amount the industry would have had to expose in the three sales covered in Table 7–4 if the government's realization from the sale were to remain at least as large as it in fact was. Again, the formula appearing in step (4) above may be used.

1. Average winning bid $= m\left(1 + \dfrac{1}{2} + \ldots \dfrac{1}{n}\right)$, which may be approximated as follows:

$$\text{average winning bid} = m\left(0.58 + \log_e n + \dfrac{1}{2n}\right).$$

And, since m, the average exposure per tract, is equal to E, total exposure, divided by the number of solo bids, the formula can be set to solve for E:

2. $E = \dfrac{\text{total amount of winning bids}}{\text{number of tracts}} \times \dfrac{\text{number of solo bids}}{\left(0.58 + \log_e n + \dfrac{1}{2n}\right)}$

The Louisiana offshore sale may be used to illustrate the application of the formula. That sale involved 24 tracts for which the winning bid fell in the $5 million-$10 million category; total government realization from the sale of all tracts in that category amounted to $171 million; and the total number of solo bids, assuming that all firms bidding jointly would have bid solo had joint bidding been impossible, would have been 346, or 14.4 bids per tract. Accordingly, for the $5 million-$10 million category:

$$E = \dfrac{\$171 \text{ million}}{24} \times \dfrac{346}{.58 + \log_e 14.4 + \dfrac{1}{28.8}} = \$746 \text{ million.}$$

Solving for *E* in all categories for all three outer-continental-shelf areas generates the data appearing in Table 7–5. The estimated total exposure required if the government is to obtain the same it in fact obtained under a mixture of joint and solo bidding is $7.8 billion. Actually, the total money exposed in bidding was only $4.5 billion, or 42 percent less than the estimated required exposure. It would therefore appear that joint bidding could have the effect of substantially reducing the total exposure without reducing the total receipts of the government from the sale of outer-continental-shelf tracts.[24]

Table 7–5   *Estimated Exposure Required of Industry under Solo Bidding to Have Government Realization the Same as Actual Government Realization Under Joint Bidding.*

	Estimated Exposure (Billions of Dollars)
Louisiana	1.9
Texas	3.6
California	2.3
Total	7.8

The Rate of Return on Offshore Oil Operations

Economists are in general agreement that profits' rates are among the best indicators of the state of competition in an industry or economic activity.[25] It is true, of course, that such profits' rates must not be used uncritically. It is both theoretically and factually demonstrable that the rate of profit varies directly with the degree of risk and uncertainty confronting the capital investment.[26] Accordingly, any profit rate must be interpreted in terms of the riskiness of the economic activity in which it was earned. Moreover, in addition to risks, factors unrelated to competition and monopoly can affect profits. Successful innovation can produce profits higher than a normal competitive rate, and inefficiencies that go unpunished by market forces can produce low profits. Even with all these qualifications, however,

[24] If in fact total exposure is greater under joint-bidding than it would be under solo, and all other assumptions incorporated in the simulation model were retained, the estimated government realization under solo bidding would be even smaller than that shown in Table 7–4.

[25] For a recent strong argument in support of this point, see W. S. Comanor and Thomas A. Wilson, "Advertising, Market Structure and Performance," *Review of Economics and Statistics,* (November, 1967), pp. 423–40.

[26] The classic theoretical treatment of this issue is Frank H. Knight, *Risk, Uncertainty and Profit,* (Boston: Houghton Mifflin Co.; 1921), for a recent statistical analysis see Gordon Conrad and Irving Plotkin, "Risk/Return: U.S. Industry Pattern," *Harvard Business Review* (March-April, 1968), pp. 90–99, and I. N. Fisher and G. R. Hall, "Risk and Corporation Rates of Return," *Quarterly Journal of Economics,* (Feb. 1969), pp. 79–92.

there is a strong presumption that high rates of return will attract new capital and thereby drive the rates down, and low rates of return repell capital and drive the rates up, to a competitive rate of return with appropriate allowance for risk.

A forceful case can be made that the development of offshore oil leases involves very high risks and very great uncertainty. The data supporting this point are quite persuasive: less than one out of four of the outer-continental-shelf tracts leased from 1954 through 1962 have produced crude oil in economic quantities; in exploration the chances of hitting oil are no better than one out of ten; estimates of the value of a given tract, even for oil companies having available to them essentially the same information, vary enormously; for example, bids on tract No. 334 in the Santa Barbara Channel ranged from $303,000 to $21 million, thus indicating the very high order of uncertainty attending the recoverable crude from the tract.

But in spite of the high risks, the recently issued *Study of the Outer Continental Shelf Lands of the United States*[27] reaches the conclusion that

> the discounted internal rate of return (the interest rate which equates the present values of the future net income and net investment on 1954 and 1955 leases with long production records) . . . is 7.5 percent before taxes. This is substantially below the historical rate of return on oil industry investments. The petroleum refining and related industries earned 13.2 percent return *after taxes* on stockholder equity in 1955. The profit rate had declined to 11.8 percent by 1965. The return on the outer continental shelf oil and gas lease investments is very low relative to normal return. Even if the estimated 7.5 percent rate of return before taxes is 100 percent wrong and the true before-tax yield is 15 percent, this yield is also below the normal yield in investments in the oil industry.

From this it would appear that competition for offshore oil and gas leases has been sufficiently effective to drive up high-bid prices in the aggregate to a level that yields a less-than-normal rate of return. It is very likely that the yield was above this rate for certain tracts, and below it for others, an outcome which is to be expected when considerable uncertainty attaches to the estimated commercial value of each tract.

III Summary and Conclusions

The purpose of this analysis has been to measure the competitive impact of a particular form of joint action among competing firms — joint-bidding for outer-continental-shelf oil leases. In a narrow sense the object has been to test in as quantitative terms as possible two conflicting hypotheses concerning joint action among firms: the ancient view that joint action may enhance competition by encouraging entry that would not otherwise occur,

---

[27] *Op. cit.,* pp. 521–27.

and the contemporary antitrust view that joint action lessens competition by lessening potential competition. In a broader sense, however, the object has been to determine the extent to which the reasonably predictable consequences generally ascribed to joint action also hold for activities characterized by a high order of risk and uncertainty.

Although the available data for measuring the competitive effect of joint bidding leave much to be desired, application of four tests point to the following conclusions:

1. There is no statistical evidence that joint bidding reduces the number of bidders. Consequently, there is no statistical evidence that the average bid price is reduced by joint-bidding. There is weak statistical evidence that joint bidding increases the number of bidders and, consequently, the average bid price.

2. On balance, the small- and medium-sized oil companies appear to rely somewhat more heavily on joint bidding than the very large companies. In the last three outer-continental-shelf sales, the five companies with largest domestic assets made 47 percent of all solo bids but only 19 percent of the joint bids. The percentage of solo bids for the five companies with largest domestic assets is about 60 percent of the total number of bids made by that group, whereas only 28 percent of the bids by the medium and smaller companies were solo bids. For the seven very large oil companies, 51 percent of all bids were joint bids, while for thirteen middle-size and small companies, 70 percent of all bids were joint bids.

3. The expected total of the bonus payments which the government will receive on any sale depends on the number of bids and on the industry's total exposure. It is clear that joint bidding increases the total bonus payments taken in by the government under the assumption that each company's interest in bidding, and hence the industry's total exposure, will not increase under solo as compared with joint bidding. Put differently, the total bonus payments to the government will be higher under joint bidding than under solo bidding unless the industry's total exposure increases. For the three most recent outer-continental-shelf sales, industry's exposure would have had to nearly double (from \$4.520 billion to \$7.800 billion) in order for the government's realization to have been as great (\$1.705 billion) under solo bidding as under a combination of joint bidding and solo bidding.

4. Analysis of the oil industry's profits earned on outer-continental-shelf operations shows that a 7.5 percent rate of return on these operations is below the rate earned on less risky activities.

We close with Professor Mason's caveat on which this essay opened: "No one familiar with the statistical and other material pertaining to the

business performance of firms and industries would deny the extreme difficulty of constructing from this material a water-tight case for or against the
performance of particular firms in particular industries. Few on the other
hand, would deny that . . . an informed judgment is possible." The conclusions to which the statistics used here appear to lead clearly do not add
up to a water-tight case for or against joint bidding as an important competitive factor. But this may be a far more significant conclusion than appears at first blush. The traditional antitrust doctrine eschews joint action
among competing firms. Informed judgment might very well dictate that
this eschewal, though entirely justified when contemplating most industrial
markets, be reexamined and applied with discretion in markets characterized by an unusually high order of risk and uncertainty.

8

"World Oil" and the Theory of Industrial Organization

M. A. Adelman*

A mathematician is said to have boasted that his newly discovered theorem was novel, elegant, and of no practical use to anybody. No such claim may be made for the study of industrial organization, whose only reason for existing is to help predict a market's behavior.

A recently completed study of the world oil market[1] (including all areas outside the United States and the countries of the Communist bloc) suggests that at the border between economic theory and the study of a particular industry may be found some additional insights into both fields of inquiry.

Some Theory Concerning the Firm

As an extreme case, the world oil industry may prove to be a useful educational device. Just as much was learned about human genetics from observation of fruit flies, which compressed into a short time span the evolution of many generations, so "world oil" may throw into strong relief the tendencies that may be missed elsewhere. Most of the output is produced by a few enormous corporations, whose ownership and management are almost completely separate. The companies are staffed with specialists who do much refined planning. They take the long view because the assets they use are typically long-lived. If we are to believe what the specialists publish about their work, its object is to improve the current value of the corporate assets. They usually call this "maximizing profit" and may give it precise mathematical formulation, which they do not confuse with the reality it helps them master.

* Massachusetts Institute of Technology

[1] *The World Petroleum Market* (publication expected 1970).

Maximizing profits. The hint a quarter-century ago[2] that business aimed not at maximum current profits but maximum present value was prophetic. The literature on investment planning and finance has since been transformed beyond recognition by the application of present-value and discounted-cash-flow techniques. Probably no industry has contributed to this development and benefited more from it than oil. The need to live in the future and reckon with expected, not current, variables is by no means peculiar to the oil industry; but it is particularly important to that industry, where an unusual effort must be expended on planning future conduct and commitments and on estimating future expenditures and receipts.

All decisions are made in the present and commit the future. In the conventional supply-demand diagram, the "price" and "cost" on the vertical axis and the "quantity" of output on the horizontal, are nearly always rates per unit of time. Moreover, each rate is an average, such as barrels daily over a month, quarter, year, or decade. In averaging the rates, we need a weight for each observation; and the farther off in time, the less should be the weight. If at some quantity of expected output, "marginal revenue equals marginal cost," we mean that the sums of two discounted streams are equal. (In the limiting case, the time period is so short that it would be pedantic to average rates over it.) If we hold fast to the principle that present values are all we can ever know, we are rid of the awkward pseudo-conflict between long-run and short-run profit-maximizing, on which so much ink has been spilled.

An aggregate of discounted present values is subject to constant change, however, because it is a forecast or prophecy. It depends on expected demand, supply, and degree of monopoly — and on expected range of errors. To have these predictions turn out right would be rather unusual. Business management needs a flow of information on how far its plan is working or not working, how far the original data and expectations are right or wrong, and to what extent the data are changing. The constant jar between reality and its perception is registered in the changing evaluations of the future.

In recent years, linear programming has become a justly popular means of economic analysis and business planning. The systematic exposure of constraints upon the decision-maker shows the rewards for enlarging or removing the constraints. This continual iteration and reiteration of experiments — trial and error — is the true model of business behavior. It may entail a considerable volume of formal calculation and planning. But planning has no more replaced maximum profit, that is, maximum present value, as an objective than jet aircraft have replaced motion. There is no evidence of oilmen trying to maximize growth or security or personal satisfactions or utility functions in five variables. One president of an oil com-

---

[2] Committee on Price Determination [E. S. Mason, chairman], *Cost Behavior and Price Policy* (New York: National Bureau of Economic Research, 1943), p. 274.

pany has said, his indifference lightly tinged with scorn, that there is nothing wrong with adding security and growth to profits as a corporate goal "if you want three goals rather than one, but the latter two are largely implicit in the first."[3]

In the international oil industry some recent theories of the business firm might be expected occasionally to represent a slight correspondence with reality. One nonexample does not dispose of a theory. On the other hand, where the conditions are favorable and yet no evidence supporting the theory is found, we must wonder about the odds of ever finding any.

At close range, the personnel of a large corporation may not give the impression of seeking any particular goal beyond doing the jobs delegated to them. A large corporation is a collective entity, like an army, a church, a university, or a forest, of which we lose sight when we get too close to the trees.

The separation of ownership from management means that the selection of key personnel no longer depends on the accident of heredity, thus ensuring one less deflection from the path of maximizing profits. Nearly half of executive compensation in large firms is provided by ownership interest, which is an incentive to act like an owner.[4] But even were this not so, the executive would improve his own income more easily by improving the income of the corporation. What is good for General Motors is surely good for its president.

Significance of maximizing growth in sales. Much has been heard this last decade of maximizing sales, so long as a "satisfactory" profit is earned. More recently, the objective has been restated as maximizing the rate of *growth* of sales, subject to the constraint of a satisfactory rate of growth of profit.[5] This description is not too unrealistic. In the short run, increased sales usually mean increased profits. Since sales are known much sooner, they are a better indicator of profit than the profit figure itself. In the long run, an increase in sales is a very good proxy for an increase in profit.[6] It

---

[3] John E. Swearingen, "The Executive Decision", *Petroleum Management,* 36, XXXVI (1964), pp. 99–123.

[4] Wilbur G. Lewellen, *Executive Compensation in Large Industrial Corporations* (New York: Columbia University Press for National Bureau of Economic Research, 1968). Indeed, the ownership interest may be seriously understated. Lewellen has translated the various types of deferred and conditional income into present-cash equivalents. Total compensation after tax, in real terms, was no higher in 1963 than 1940. This seems hard to accept. If there is an error, such that the true present-cash equivalent income is really higher than indicated, it must be due to undervaluation of the ownership-tied income; therefore its importance would be greater than Lewellen's calculation indicates.

[5] William J. Baumol, *Business Behavior, Value and Growth* (1959, 1967).

[6] Bevars D. Mabry and David L. Siders, "An Empirical Test of the Sales Maximization Hypothesis," *Southern Economic Journal,* XXXIII (1967); Marc Nerlove, "Factors Affecting Rates of Return on Investments in Individual Common Stocks", *Review of Economics and Statistics,* L (1968).

is not surprising that the pressure of surging demand on limited facilities generates a high rate of use of the expanding capacity and results in high profits, or what Marshall called "quasi rents."

On the other hand, a crucial example is yet to be found of a company's deliberately sacrificing present value for the sake of higher sales. To be sure, one finds in world oil as in other trades quite a few accusations that someone else (it is always someone else) is foolishly and perversely seeking higher sales at the expense of the industry's welfare and profits. Newcomers to oil producing or refining are particularly blamed, as are shipbuilders for buying and building new ships when tanker rates and ships' prices are "too low." A British governmental report calls Japanese prices "unnecessarily low," the result of "ambitions to dominate the world market."[7] No evidence is offered. Nevertheless, the argument is not new; neither is it "wrong." Trade journals often warn their readers not to act independently, not to seek each his own welfare, but to remember that they are all members of one another. "Industrial statesmen" seek the common good, that of the industry as a whole. A monopolist of course *is* the industry as a whole. Industrial statesmanship is thus limited collusion. It can do less for the industry than overt cooperation but more than competition, where each firm must pursue its own profit as it best knows how. A business executive to whom statesmanship is the "natural" or desirable way of life is likely to mistake competition for a renunciation of profit, and those instructed or guided by him will do the same. What looks like a theorem (sales maximizing) turns out to be the value judgment of the industrial statesman.

If the management desires growth above all things, the managers probably know that the money needed for growth is obtained through high retained profits and through the credit-rating brought by high profits that make it easy to borrow or to sell stock. If the managers prefer a quiet life to earnings and growth, the stockholders may have no choice but to sell their shares. As the price per share falls, the firm becomes a tempting prize. The final result may be acquisition by outside interests, or a stockholder suit expelling the old mismanagement, or failure, or absorption by another firm. These are all surface phenomena of a central fact: a company whose management does not aim at maximizing profit or present value has not the same chance of survival and growth as a company which does.

As a general principle, maximizing growth instead of profit is superfluous or mistaken,[8] notwithstanding it holds well for the Soviet economy.[9] But it has enriched the theory of industrial organization by helping draw our attention to a pervasive fact that is intimately joined to profit-seeking and to

[7] *Shipbuilding Industry Committee Report* ["Geddes Report"] (Cmd. 2937, London H.M.S.O. 1966), p. 43.
[8] For an important exception, see below, p. 27.
[9] Edward Ames, *Soviet Economic Processes* (1965).

competition. Maximum present value is not a number to be read from a price-cost table; it is the evaluation of an uncertain future, and reasonable men will differ on what strategy will best promote it. The disparate growth rates of the large oil companies testify to diverse visions of what was around the next bend: they could not all be right, but sometimes they were all wrong.

Hypothesis of a target rate of return. The theory of prices set by a target rate of return on investment need not detain us long. The first known skeptic was Adam Smith, who thought that, when businessmen referred to a sound and reasonable profit, they meant "no more than a customary and usual profit".[10] From this point of view, the target rate of return is merely a guess of what is attainable; it is not a cause but only a surface, and probably inaccurate, reflection of an effect. To give it significance, one must assume that business firms aim at lower rates than the traffic will bear.

Here the petroleum industry serves as an excellent laboratory, for there is a considerable literature on rates of return in the trade and technical journals. In the petroleum industry, if anywhere, we ought to discover some faint hints of *full-cost, target-rate-of-return pricing,* and we do not. The cost of capital is treated as an external datum, like the cost of any other factor, though far more difficult to discern or measure with precision. At no place, so far as I am aware, is the imprecision of the figure made into an excuse for treating it as a free choice of management. Nor is there a hint that a rate of profit will be adhered to even when earnings could be bettered by changing prices up or down or by changing the size of a plant or the rate of depletion of a reservoir. Target rate-of-return pricing, with or without "full cost," is no more to be found in the petroleum industry's trade and technical literature than is heaven in a telescope. (It would be interesting to review the only empirical support of such pricing, that is, the interviews granted by some managers a decade or so ago.[11] One might take those seven cases where target rates of return were specified and compare them with what the companies have done since.)

Predictive value of profit-maximizing hypothesis. That firms maximize profits is not important in itself, but it does permit us to predict their reactions to certain stimuli. Very likely their actions will not be as expected, and the discrepancy cannot be attributed to chance or to errors of observation. Economists, like geologists, should earn their keep by finding

---

[10] Adam Smith, *The Wealth of Nations;* Book I, chapter 9, (New York, Modern Library ed.), p. 97.

[11] Robert F. Lanzillotti, "Pricing Objectives in Large Companies", *American Economic Review,* XLVIII (1958), pp. 921–40. The companies (target after-tax return in parentheses): Alcoa (20), G.E. (20), G.M. (20), Johns-Manville (about 15), Kroger (20 before tax), Sears (10–15), U.S. Steel (8).

and explaining anomalies. Let us therefore consider the failure by the oil companies to import into the United States on a large scale before 1959.

The competitive explanation would be that the incremental cost of expanding capacity had already approached the price. This can be proved untrue, for expanded output and exports to the United States would have been highly profitable to each individual producer acting as an individual.

We can always explain the failure to import as due to "the diverse goals of management of a large enterprise," or "target rates of return," and so forth. If we do not take this easy way out, we must conclude that there was a constraint on individual competitive conduct. Since the sellers were a small, close-knit group, the hypothesis of an understanding among them to limit output and exports to the United States seems confirmed. Unfortunately for the hypothesis, it appears that exports to the United States would have been profitable even for a single Middle East seller. Hence, whatever its truth, the monopolistic hypothesis is not important; it is a nonbinding constraint. There was some other, tighter inhibition: the companies were somehow not free to act as their profit-increasing interests would dictate. This hypothesis is confirmed by the abundant documentary record — starting in 1948 with Congressional hearings — of restraints on imports into the United States, by the Texas Railroad Commission's elaborate system of control, and by the "voluntary" quotas of the national government. The fact that these looser systems all broke down in turn shows that the joint profit-maximizing interest of the companies could not have accounted for the restrictions on imports, because had these governmental measures merely been a convenient vehicle to attain their joint interests and circumvent the anti-trust laws, they would have lasted.

Another anomaly is the so-called downstream losses apparently suffered by integrated companies on their refining operations, especially in Western Europe. These losses have lasted for about ten years, during which time these same companies have invested several billion dollars and tripled their capacity, all without a murmur of reproach from stockholders for apparently throwing so much good money after bad. But if one declines to believe that management will do any such thing, an alternative explanation is needed. "Downstream losses" in a vertically integrated company are computed by subtracting from the sales value of refined products the operating expense plus the value of the crude oil consumed. This value has been approximately equal to the f.o.b. "posted price" of the crude oil, i.e., the price publicly quoted, plus an allowance for maritime freight. But these entries on the books of account have no validity as market facts. Nonintegrated refining companies were presumably selling products at about the same prices as integrated, and they too maintained and expanded capacity. Therefore real arm's-length crude oil prices must have been lower than those posted, and declining over this period, for otherwise the nonintegrated firms would have dwindled and disappeared.

"Downstream losses" are an artifact, not a market datum. Consequently, a computation of the price of crude oil as landed in Western Europe is logically possible by subtracting from prices of the refined product a calculated refining cost, including both capital and operating expenses. This calculation has checked well enough with scattered observations of arm's-length sales to permit an admittedly rough and imprecise tracing of real prices during the 1960's. It also yielded, early in the 1960's, the controversial prediction that, because product prices covered the costs of refining, there was no reason to expect a rise in margins and product prices.[12]

The lesson for research into industrial organization is that a step-by-step application of the profit-maximizing assumption may yield novel and interesting results in history, results which help predict how well the companies will be able to coordinate their prices in later years and whether nonintegrated refiners can exist. Reliance on "discretionary corporate goals" and "full-cost, target-rate-of-return pricing" would have given us nothing.

Competition: A Market's Structure and Performance

Since 1949 it has become customary to analyze a given market in terms of its structure and performance (or behavior). "These measures must be used to complement not to exclude one another."[13] One of our best tests of any hypothesis is to look for the convergence of two independent lines of evidence. Where a market's structure looks competitive yet prices diverge from the competitive model, the evidence is conflicting or insufficient. Where data on structure and performance point in the same direction, the combined weight of the two is more than the sum of the separate parts.

Crude-oil production costs, present and future.   Analyzing performance involves a comparison of prices with incremental costs, whose behavior is rather "orthodox" in production of crude oil and gas. For any given reservoir, unit costs decline over an interval as the production rate is increased by drilling more wells, since overhead — access roads, dwellings, supply dumps, utilities — is spread more thinly. But the more wells drilled, the more output per well decreases by mutual "interference." Because the liquid in the reservoir is finite, the more intensive the development, the greater the cost of recovery: one could drain even the largest pool in a few years, but at prohibitive expense. Hence the development-cost function describes a U shape, although the descending phase is rather brief, and incremental cost is nearly always above average cost. Moreover, in any given reservoir, new wells must be drilled to offset the decline in production.

[12] See my "Les Prix Pétroliers à Longe Terme," *Revue de l'Institut Français du Pétrole*, XVIII (1963).

[13] Edward S. Mason, "The Current Status of the Monopoly Problem in the United States" *Harvard Law Review*, LXII (1949), p. 1265.

Incremental cost is therefore determined not only by higher or lower rates of output planned *ex ante,* but by the new investment needed to *maintain* or increase the current rate of output. There is no such thing as a field "all drilled up" and needing only current operating costs to keep going at the current rates of output.

Looking now at the whole population rather than the single reservoir: the array from lowest-to highest-unit cost is a first approximation to the supply curve. The higher the rate of output planned for any given period, the more must it call on the less productive reservoirs. Finally, exploration for new pools proceeds by arraying prospects in order of promise and investigating the better ones first.

Since the U-shaped cost curve in crude oil production is so well established, how are we to account for the widely, and firmly, held belief that the industry is one of increasing returns or decreasing costs — that is, a natural monopoly? Whatever the reason, the belief has been very important in forming public policy.

As a rough approximation to the industry's incremental cost, we have used the cost (net of all transport cost) in the most expensive of the "Big-Five" producing countries — Iran, Iraq, Kuwait, Libya, Saudi Arabia. This cost is about six cents current operating cost and six cents investment cost, with investment cost defined as the supply price of the necessary capital. In other words, a price of 12 cents per barrel would suffice to pay current operating expenses and provide a stream of receipts whose present value (discounted at 20 percent, taxes paid) would just equal the necessary developmental investment.[14]

However, we need to make due allowance for the replacement value of the oil withdrawn from existing pools.[15] But this cannot be done by forecasting the price, which would be circular as well as impossible in practice. Nor can we estimate finding costs in a mineral industry — there is as yet no basis for doing so. An indirect approach will suffice, however. The

---

[14] Operating cost needs no special explanation. Capital cost is defined as that price at which the needed investment would be barely worth making. A given development requires or implies: I, the investment in drilling wells, installing gathering systems, local pipelines, marine facilities, etc.; q_0 the initial output rate, in barrels daily; a, decline rate of output of the wells; t, time in years; r, the rate of discount or cost of capital taking account of risk; and p', supply price or cost. Then

$$p' = I/365 \; q_0 \int_0^T e^{-(a+r)t} \, dt.$$

Factors used are: $a = 0.01$ at the Persian Gulf, 0.03 in Libya, 0.10 in Venezuela; $r = 0.20$, $t = 20$. The investment per initial daily barrel, I/q, is estimated from a variety of published sources. In the big four producing concessions of the Persian Gulf, the range is about \$75–\$120. The higher end of the range is considered as the marginal investment, since demand could all be satisfied from those concessions plus Libya.

[15] I have had to retract the proposition that replacement cost is zero. See my "Efficiency of Resource Use in Crude Petroleum," *Southern Economic Journal,* XXXI (1964).

process of mineral production is the depletion of a large existing stock — at rising costs, as just seen. Discovery of new mineral bodies is an attempt to offset the otherwise inevitable increase in cost. The maximum economic finding cost (MEFC) is equal to the expected increase in incremental developmental cost. Any finding cost above the level is a waste of resources. Anything less means a new and lower cost function.[16]

We have made a set of assumptions about world petroleum for the period 1967–1983 each assumption biased in the direction of greater production and strain on existing deposits and hence in the direction of higher costs: a high rate of growth in output (implicitly assuming a lower price), no natural gas anywhere in the world market, no nuclear power, no improvement in technology, no new discoveries, and all 1968–1983 production from existing fields. Our long-run projected incremental cost of crude oil for around the year 1983 is thus not 12 cents but about 20 cents per barrel. As a forecast, it is biased and must be above the true figure. Hence 8 cents per barrel may be designated as a generous estimate of MEFC and somewhat between 12 and 20 cents a barrel is the upper limit of where the price would be today under purely competitive conditions.

The study of market competition converges here with the classic problem of a natural resource — the increasing scarcity of a fixed stock depleted at an increasing rate. We cannot tell what it would cost to replace the used-up stock, but at least we can know its value. MEFC is the penalty for doing nothing to replace the stock, the cost of not spending. But the benefit of not spending is both (1) the productivity of using the resources elsewhere in the meantime, and (2) the possible increase in knowledge, whether of discovery techniques, new energy forms, or more thrifty use, which will later give us the same result more cheaply. A discount rate of 13 percent which Denison considers the social rate of return outside agriculture and government[17] is perhaps the lowest we can use; it allows only for (1), not for (2). If MEFC rises to 8 cents per barrel at the end of 12 years, that is, by 0.67 cents per year, its present value is 4.2 cents. What happens after 1983 we do not know, and as of 1969, it does not much matter. It matters more with each year that passes; there is greater need to act but also much less risk of acting wrongly to ward off a scarcity that may keep receding through time as it always has up to now.

Crude-oil prices.   In mid-1969, the price of crude oil at the Persian Gulf may be measured by (1) prices on arm's-length transactions, or (2) refined-product arm's length prices in Europe, less a refining and transport

---

[16] For the early 1980's, we estimate the marginal figure I/q to have risen to around $180, and the decline rate a to around 0.05.

[17] E. F. Denison, *The Sources of Economics Growth* (New York, C.E.D., 1962), p. 33. My colleague Robert M. Solow considers the true social rate of return to be higher. See his *Capital Theory and the Rate of Return* (North Holland, 1963), p. 96.

margin. These two measures coincide in the neighborhood of $1.20 per barrel. Even after a decade of decline, the price is at least ten times as high as current supply price, and six times as high as what it would be if we make a generous allowance for estimated replacement costs. Hence, on the basis of "performance" criteria, we must conclude that there is somewhere in the market a massive block to competition.

Market structure.   The bulk of oil produced in the world market comes from the concessions operated by eight large companies. Concentration has slowly decreased since the end of World War II; the "numbers equivalent" of firms operating has grown from less than five to about nine.[18] The eight largest companies, however, are closely associated in some joint ventures in the Middle East, the combined effect of which is to reduce the independence forced on each participant, who knows the investment and output plans of his rivals. In addition, the high degree of vertical integration has a double significance. First, there is very little room for independent bargaining over crude oil prices with independent refiners desirous, and capable, of carefully examining the range of offers, choosing the best, and trying to play one seller against another. In a market where price is so far above cost, the absence oɪ independent-bargaining centers at the various levels of production slows down the attraction of price toward cost. Perhaps even more important, the companies, who to some extent coordinate their production plans, meet again as rivals in refining and marketing. The conditions in the products markets afford a check on the intentions of a rival — if he is not building additional refineries, he will not be pressing for higher output of crude oil to supply them.

Thus, the two bodies of evidence do not conflict. But the evidence from market structure, however strong a confirmation, does not contribute much more. It would be as compatible with a price which was, say, double the cost, as with the actual price, which is ten times cost. The decline in concentration has been substantial, but can it be made into a prediction to be verified or disproved? Should we have expected a steep or gradual decline in price? Our inquiry is not complete until we look at the history of prices in world oil.

Competition: History of Prices

There is no simple association between the mild decrease in concentration and a turbulent price evolution that included increases as well as decreases in prices. The most drastic price reduction of all came during 1947–49, when the structure of prices was transformed from multiple discrimination to a single f.o.b. price, uniform to all destinations. Under 1949 price levels

[18] See my article, "On the H-Coefficient as a Numbers-Equivalent," *Review of Economics and Statistics,* LI (February 1969).

and the original price structure, the Persian Gulf price would have been $3.81 per barrel. Instead, by December 1949 the single f.o.b. price was $1.65. The Federal Trade Commission portrayed this as a "world oil cartel" operating a "basing-point system," but any market with substantial transport costs reflected in the price structure can be called a "basing-point system," whether the structure is discriminatory or not. A "basing point system," in and of itself, is compatible with any model of competitive or monopolistic behavior, so that further information is needed for a conclusion about the market's structure.

The proximate cause of what was literally a revolution is not in doubt. The United States Government was indirectly the largest single buyer of Middle East Oil and insisted on having "the lowest competitive price," interpreted to mean the lowest price netted back from the farthest destination. A group of consultants appointed by the Economic Cooperation Administrator rendered two brief reports still worth reading today for their artistic economy in saying no more than was absolutely necessary to dispose of the problem before them.[19] Had the government not been in that particular bargaining position, and had it been less ably advised, one cannot say what would have happened. Perhaps like Hamlet and his shipmates, who "put on a compelled valor" when attacked by the pirates, the companies put on a compelled competition when confronted by the United States Government. A careful study by Professor Frank[20] concludes that the government hastened a result which would have come in any case. It may be so. I doubt it, less because of a different view of the 1947–49 events than because of the cost data and what happened when governmental pressure was withdrawn. Prices increased quite substantially during 1952–56, on the order of 20 percent. Since 1957, the price trend has been markedly downward, but with some temporary recovery during 1960–63. Obviously, therefore, declining concentration and vertical integration contribute little to the history of prices and promise even less for the future.

In trying to explain any price increase, we must soon discard the hypothesis of collusion. The companies were highly visible to the antitrust authorities. They were subjected to a set of Congressional and Federal Trade Commission investigations and were sued as a cartel by the United States Department of Justice. The result was a consent decree, which gave them permission to fix prices, divide markets, and limit output on the request of governments or of a supranational organization, which meant OPEC (Organization of Petroleum Exporting Countries). It may sound strange for an antitrust suit to have such a result, but the guiding genius of the law

---

[19] Max Ball, Walter J. Levy, Edward S. Mason, Sumner T. Pike, George W. Stocking, L. S. Wescoat. See Mutual Security Agency, *ECA and MSA relations with international oil companies concerning petroleum prices* (mimeographed, August 15, 1952), pp. 6–8.

[20] Helmut J. Frank, *Crude Oil Prices in the Middle East* (1966).

has always been Mr. Facing Both Ways. The consent of the government shows that they turned up nothing that even resembled collusion.

Let us consider the evolution of price in that sector of the market where competition seemed most keen: heavy or "residual" fuel oil.

Up to 1957–58, the oil companies matched the price of coal, and filled the small gap between availability of coal and total demand for steam-raising fuel. The companies were working as if they were under pure competition, with the price as an outside datum, and they turned out all that was physically possible, given their current refining facilities. Since coal prices rose more than they fell, it was not an uncomfortable state.

Soon after Suez, coal prices were again increased, as usual because of rising labor costs. Consumption of all steam-raising fuel was expanding rapidly. The increased demand for heavy fuel oil was a strong incentive to compete for expanded highly profitable sales. Lacking an assured division of the market, which only an outright collusive agreement could have permitted, the companies responded with increased output fed by new refinery installations. The result was that oil prices declined to the surprise of everyone.

Very much the same thing happened in and after 1966, when the United States removed controls on imports of heavy fuel oil. Despite the efforts of the Venezuelan government and the companies to maintain or even raise the price, it had fallen about 15 percent by the spring of 1969. The prospective reward for aggressive behavior and punishment for excessive prudence overstrained the companies' control of the market.[21]

When the companies' understanding that they would meet but not beat the price of coal broke down in the late 1950's, the expansion of fuel oil output accompanied, and in part caused, an expansion of other refined products, adding to the pressure on price. By 1959, it was clear that the 1957 crude oil price increase, in slavish imitation of the United States, had been a mistake, a textbook example reminiscent of the famous 1931 price increase in cigarettes.[22]

To some extent, impossible to measure, the decline in prices was also furthered by the entry of new producers. Their role must not be exaggerated, for had the old-timers been able to coordinate their plans fully, the wisest course would have been a lordly indifference toward the newcomers. Thereby the old-timers would have lost only a small share of the market, and nothing on price. But they could not do so because any large company losing business to a newcomer had to try to recoup at the expense of its fellows. It is dangerous to become known as the only industrial statesman or industrial "fall guy," and the example of Texas, which has

[21] The effect is not peculiar to oil. In early 1968, for example, it was an increase in the demand for steel that set off the first wave of independence in price-setting the industry had known in nearly 70 years.

[22] William H. Nicholls, *Price Policies in the Cigarette Industry* (1951).

often been forced to bear the brunt of reduction in output, was undoubtedly known all too well. We conclude that effects of informal cooperation were both substantial and limited.

From the late 1950's to the late 1960's, the control over the market in world oil decreased perceptibly. The internal mechanism changed much more quickly.

Changing of the Guard: Governments as Oligopolists

The original tax (or royalty) in the oil-producing concessions was first a per-barrel payment, then a percentage of sales. During the early 1950's the governments that were hosts moved to an income tax, at first 50 percent of profits on the production of crude oil. This required that a crude oil price be established from which to subtract costs; hence those famous "posted prices" which were originally not too far different from real market prices, at least as expected in the near term. It was not in the interests of the producing companies to set them too much higher. For every additional cent by which they might overestimate the real market value of a barrel of oil, they penalized themselves by half a cent.[23]

When it became apparent that the 1957 price increases were not holding and that posted prices were not a reasonable approximation to market prices, the companies tried to reduce their taxes by cutting posted prices in 1959 and again in 1960. Thereupon the outraged producing nations formed OPEC and in effect gave notice that they would tolerate no further reduction. Since 1960 the tax has been almost a pure excise, in cents per barrel, except that changes in tax-deductible costs are reflected in taxable income and hence in tax due. The tax per barrel has increased as a result of two general revisions in the concession agreements in 1965 and in 1967. We may summarize a long story without concluding it: in Saudi Arabia, the tax increased from 18 cents per barrel in 1946 to 88 cents in 1968, escalating to over 90 cents by 1970. It is expected to rise further. Since real prices have been declining, the percentage of profit going to the producing countries has risen very sharply.

One recalls a wonderfully compact, evocative, almost Chinese phrase: "Grande firme, petite nation." In world oil, some of the smallest nations

---

[23] This exaggerates the case because it takes no account of the tax offsets. Percentage depletion gives an American company 0.275 cents' tax credit, or about .137 cents lesser tax liability, for every additional cent of price. Furthermore, the tax paid to the foreign government is directly deductible from United States income tax rather than from taxable income. Hence it seems at first that the rule for an American company would simply be: the higher the price the better, since the company could not help but gain. In practice, the rule is greatly attenuated, to the point where the statement in the text is closer to the truth. One reason is that British and French tax treatment is less favorable. More important, since an American company usually has little taxable income in respect of producing operations, the foreign tax credit offers little help. The companies' attempt to lower posted prices, hence taxes, bears out the hypothesis that a higher posted price means a lower after-tax income.

have overcome the very biggest companies. But the important market fact is that the excise tax serves for the time being as a floor to price and has even been effective at a distance. No prudent management of a company will commit itself to selling oil for less than the sum of tax plus cost plus some allowance for contingencies.

We can now measure the importance of the concentrated market structure and the unspoken understanding among the companies not to lower prices. Let us assume pure competition in world oil, with the host governments collecting their current revenues. Then prices would be lower by perhaps 15 or 20 cents per barrel. Governmental take explains five-sixths or more of the price-cost gap. The companies' ability to hold the line accounts only for the rest. Their once-great influence is now mostly, though by no means wholly, expended.

The price level must henceforth become largely the governments' responsibility. A prediction of the long-run price of crude oil depends on how governments will act as oligopolists, and this is complicated by their being landlords. In 1968 they proclaimed their intention of taking from the companies everything over and above cost, which they were properly careful to define as including the necessary return on investment. The direction of the movement is toward the companies' becoming hired contractors or even buyers but no longer owning and selling oil. As a halfway house, the governments would move back toward an income tax, taking more from those earning more. This implies, however, that those earning less pay less, which dissolves the fixed per-barrel tax as a price floor. Unable to reach a firm agreement, governments will shade taxes so that companies may shade prices to increase total revenues. Indeed the distinction between prices and taxes will become increasingly vague, for some governments will become the full owners while their concessionnaires become contractors, working for a fee. Governments will be oligopolists charging a price ten times cost, not 20 or so percent over cost-plus-tax. The only way to avoid price-chiseling is by removing the incentives, by limiting output and dividing markets. But the governments are drifting into ownership rather than deliberately assuming it, a circumstance which will make it more difficult to reach an agreement.

A lasting agreement among governments to share markets and limit output is unlikely. The technical difficulties of assigning quotas and dealing promptly with surpluses and deficits are great. Mutual confidence and trust are hard to achieve when there is wide dispersion of interests. One favorable element should be recognized, namely, that on our reckoning, there is no great cost diversity among the Big Five. Nevertheless, every government must balance the advantages of larger receipts today, through chiseling on the agreement, against smaller receipts tomorrow, when prices decline. The answer depends most of all on the value of present versus future revenues. The social rate of discount may be very different in a country with water, labor, and land, like Iran and Iraq, than in a small barren area like Kuwait or Abu Dhabi. A small "superaffluent" Arab state must reckon on giving up a portion of its revenues as loans or subsidies to other states or national-ist movements, then investing the remainder in the world's money market. Future revenues may therefore be discounted at perhaps six percent. This is a far cry from Iran, where real GNP (gross national product) has grown by 7 percent annually since 1960 and by 10 percent in 1964–69. The real social return to additional capital investment can hardly be less than 20 per-cent per annum. If so, an additional dollar for the next four years is worth taking even if thereafter one loses over a dollar per year in perpetuity. (Discounted at 20 percent, the present value of an income of one dollar per year for four years is $2.60. A perpetuity would be worth $5.00.) Hence large amounts of additional oil sold at an incremental low price might well be a very desirable transaction even if they served to lower prices and tax receipts a few years hence.

The general principle stated earlier, that sellers can only maximize pres-ent values, holds here as well. Rational behavior differs as between the two governments-turned-oligopolist sellers. Under competition, if each owned a stock of oil resources, his urge to expand output would be blunted (1) by rising unit costs at higher rates of output and (2) by the higher present value of revenues sacrificed when diverting investment to oil production. Indeed, since the social rate of discount reflects the investment opportunities available, the seller with the higher discount rate would probably be *more* reluctant to expand if higher sales would require diversion of investible funds from projects promising the higher rates of return.

We need not resolve this issue because Middle East-North African oil prices are so far above developmental cost that cost increases incident to higher rates of output and faster stock depletion are negligible or unimpor-tant. All that matters is the faster receipt of revenues. A determination to press for higher output rates and let the price structure sink is bad policy for one oil-producing country, good policy for another. It has brought a staggering rate of growth and inflow of revenue to Libya, and if the govern-ment of Iran is able to follow suit, it is difficult to anticipate much com-bined influence by the producing countries on the price level.

Moreover, all governments in the producing countries are bringing in new concessionaires. The more sellers, the greater the difficulty of moni-toring the constant flow of bargains and arrangements to see to it that prices are not inadvertently set lower than the prevailing level. There are so many terms of the bargain that anyone tempted to chisel for the sake of incre-mental profit finds he can use numerous dimensions of the transaction.

The national oil-producing companies being set up by the producing nations may become the first authentic sales-maximizers. They want to show the world that Western companies are not the only ones able to run a large business. Nevertheless, they need not operate at a loss; indeed for a time it will be impossible to avoid a profit because they will subtract from the price, not tax-plus-cost but only the minor fraction, cost.

The price decline is likely to remain slow, however, because the consuming country governments will continue to restrict competition and hence blunt the incentive to independent search for greater sales volume even if it will lower prices. All the important consuming nations think of themselves as producers also — and in some instances as primarily producers. They are beginning to gradually eliminate their respective coal industries, but this will take another decade, and in the meantime some nations will replace coal with high-cost nuclear power needing protection against cheap oil. A large program is well advanced in Britain. Moreover, some governments of the most important consuming countries are directly involved in oil or gas production and sale, and others are doing their best to follow the example. The general assumption of a fuel scarcity is firmly rooted and will only disappear with the current generation of policy-makers. The same is true of the obsession with "security," a word used as a code and having a meaning different from its customary usage. Since governments own national companies or subsidize private firms, the golden rule is: the company must not lose money lest the government lose face. Hence there is no prospect of competition growing quickly in the consuming nations nor, therefore, of a considerable decrease in price in a short time.

A slow price decline need not be smooth, however. Some producing country's governments will carefully "chisel" on the tax, hence indirectly cutting the price, while their national companies cut prices directly. Other governments will display reluctance turning into anger. Disappointed expectations will make them difficult to live with, and some will demand more of the companies than the companies can give.

Here we confront again the essential imprecision of present values, which summarize the imperfectly forecasted stream of payments and receipts. In company-government negotiations, each cent bargained over represents many millions of dollars. Neither side knows how far the other can be pushed; perhaps it does not even know its own reservation price. Hence we must expect tense negotiations, with a government threatening to expel a company, or the company threatening to leave. For the most part, these disputes will somehow be settled and never come to public attention. Some may result in a confrontation of governments versus companies. A commodity agreement under UNCTAD (United Nations Conference on Trade and Development) is a possible outcome and might slow the rate of price decline.

Afterthoughts on Competition

1. Whatever the respective merits of structure and behavior (performance) as standards for antitrust law or policy, for analysis structure is little more than a check on conclusions drawn from behavior. It is simply too imprecise. Even with market boundaries quite clearly defined, the number of sellers and their distribution by size is compatible with a wide variety of results.

Whether sellers are few or many in really only an index of the degree of independence of sellers, which tends to vary with numbers but shows very great dispersion. Large numbers are a sufficient, but not necessary, condition for independence.

2. Again aside from antitrust law, it may be simply meaningless to pin a label of "competitive" or "monopolistic" on a given market. We have been forced to use two opposing hypotheses because, without both, we cannot begin to understand what has been happening. Only the hypothesis of competition can explain why oil prices have declined so much. And only a hypothesis of monopoly, i.e. of some massive block to the competitive process, can explain why they are still ten times cost. Our prediction of a continued price decline rests on an evaluation of the strength of the opposing forces, which is surely the more important as well as the more interesting task.

3. The do-nothing strategy, which was the best the oil companies could do, is of peculiar importance in a progressive economy. Improved products, processes, or sources of supply (of which Persian Gulf oil is merely an extreme case) mean in the first instance a wider profit margin. The ability to hold the line and not pass on savings in cost requires no more than the understanding that nobody intends to reduce the price until somebody else reduces it first; it may take quite a while before anybody reduces it at all. But this profitable inaction obviously needs a group whose members trust each other. It helps if they are few and can take soundings frequently in various markets to be reassured that others are not gaining by price shading.

4. The distinction between "price-makers" and "price-takers" is useless. In the world oil trade, nearly all arm's-length prices are negotiated. Only at the retail level are they "administered." Even there they have changed frequently, to the pleasure or pain of the sellers, in response to changing competitive conditions. It would be improper to cite posted prices as an example of "administered" prices disregarded in practice. The posted prices are simply not prices, not market facts, at all. Nevertheless, they are for many the symbol, or somewhat vague hope, of a "normal" price level to which some day actual prices will return, hence evidence of a state of mind. As with fancied scarcity and insecurity, the conflict between what is and what is imagined, helps explain what is to be.

5. A term recently coming into wide use is "discretion" or "discretionary power" in price-output decisions. Two ideas seem to be included. First, in a competitive market, the individual firm has no choices. It follows that companies with any discretion over price or output have market power. Second, the firm with discretion is free to pursue goals other than profit-maximizing — it may be content with a lower rate of return, or go in for conspicuous lavish display or political influence, or whatever.

But a little reflection shows market power is neither necessary nor sufficient for discretionary spending. Mr. Aristotle S. Onassis does much discretionary spending. The tanker trade, however, is purely competitive. Its low concentration and price-cost behavior leave no other conclusion even remotely possible. On the other hand, it has stayed very far from long-run equilibrium, that is, it is very *imperfectly* competitive. Innovation has been massive. The work-horses of the fleet during the 1970's will be 10–15 times as large as the T-2 of World War II, which itself was larger than the then prevailing size. The quicker and more venturesome shipowners have reaped huge fortunes. (The supposed conflict between "static efficiency under competition and dynamic innovation favored by monopoly" is hard to reconcile with this industry.)

With this we may contrast an overripe oligopoly, where market power has sufficed for higher than competitive prices but not for preventing eventual excess investment by old or new competitors. Excess capacity forces the return on investment down to normal or subnormal levels. Sellers do no discretionary spending; here the wages of market power are the pauper's fate.

Although pure competition is no bar to higher profits, it is no relief from the pain of choice, i.e., the ever-present need to decide whether or not to commit resources on the basis of one's guess on prices and costs a week, month, or years hence. This is very different from the choice of higher or lower output to affect prices.

Unlike "administered prices," "discretionary" conduct is not an empty phrase. On the other hand, it adds nothing to the idea of monopoly or market power, and it can be misleading.

6. When the stormy tripartite history of the relations of companies with two sets of governments comes finally to be written, our profession may take some small share of the blame for the multi-billion-dollar misunderstanding. Among the literate public, which includes advisers of companies and government, the usual view today is that large firms have great "power" and that they can do whatever they want by Planning, thus disregarding The Market rather than planning to best exploit it. Companies do not try to maximize profits. Therefore, they have always a handy reserve price-raising power. If they argue that they cannot raise prices at some time or other, this only shows their bad faith. These theories have become clichés which, being familiar, give the illusion of being clear. Sometimes divertingly written and other times mathematically refined, they are all variations on the one theme: wishing will make it so. Oil companies and governments will for the most part find out the truth the hard way.

9

A Sherman Act Precedent for the
Application of Antitrust Legislation
to Conglomerate Mergers:
Standard Oil, 1911

*Samuel M. Loescher**

At least through 1968, our antitrust agencies have been reluctant to challenge conglomerate mergers[1] and thus have permitted to snowball the greatest merger movement and trend toward aggregate economic concentration in America since the turn of the Twentieth Century. Consequently, I believe that it is time to re-examine the dissolution in 1911 of the Standard Oil of New Jersey holding company.

The Antimerger Law of 1950 has been little applied to conglomerate mergers, despite a legislative history authorizing use of the law's amended section 7 of the Clayton Antitrust Act to halt increases in the trend toward economic concentration caused by any type of merger likely to substantially decrease competition. Both the original, and revised, section 7 of the Clayton Act were designed to reduce relative to the Sherman Antitrust Act the weight of evidence (which might be) necessary to find that combinations of firms alleged to restrain competition were illegal. The 1950 revision of section 7 removed any question that the original Clayton Act might have been intended to exempt mergers achieved solely by the acquisition of assets or to exempt mergers of firms not competing directly in the same market.

Until May 1969 officials responsible for policy-making in our antitrust agencies may have concluded that ordinarily even large conglomerate mergers could not be proved to reduce competition substantially. The

* Indiana University

[1] Excluding some dramatic and controversial exceptions, such as Procter and Gamble — Clorox and Consolidated Foods — Gentry.

officials may also have been sidetracked from a powerful precedent by George Stigler's contention that an effective remedy for oligopoly within a specific market will only be realized when we "regain the 1911 level of use of the remedy of dissolution."[2]

What apparently has been overlooked, at least with respect to the 1911 instance of Standard Oil, is that despite the allegedly greater weight of evidence required to find corporate mergers in violation of the Sherman Act, the specific mergers challenged in Standard Oil's holding-company combination were essentially averred, and found, to destroy potential competition. Moreover, the court's affirmation of the government's original and sole petition for relief, appended to the initial bill of complaint, did nothing to reduce directly and immediately the shares of the oligopolistic firms in "the relevant markets." Indeed, following a detailed analysis of both the market and ownership organization of the dissolved corporations, the decree may more properly be described as having restored a potentiality for potential competition — that is, potential potential competition — while substantially reducing the aggregate concentration of economic power.

Market power in oil for the Standard Oil group rested largely on refining and marketing, while Standard's strategic position in pipelines and in bargaining with railroads served to place both existing, and potential, outside rivals at a serious cost disadvantage. Had the charge been focused squarely on Standard's status as the partial monopoly (dominant firm) in refined products within each and every geographical part of the country — a status nevertheless predicated upon illegal combination — the requested relief might have been expected to fashion a form of dissolution that, acknowledging the limits of economic feasibility, was designed to increase the number of actual competitors within every section of the United States.

Tables 9–1 and 9–2 show respectively the exclusive marketing territories of Standard Oil's marketing corporations and the refinery locations of Standard Oil's refining corporations. Out of the properties of the three large, exclusively marketing companies — Continental, Waters-Pierce, and Kentucky Standard — a "patchwork scramble" of bulk stations might have been assigned to a number of marketing companies so as to increase immediately actual competition in every section of the country. In smaller cities and towns, of course, only a single bulk station would have been available for assignment. A like assignment of bulk stations might have been made in the remaining territories serviced by the integrated refiner-marketers: Jersey Standard, New York Standard, Atlantic Refining, Ohio

[2] "Discussion on Report of the Attorney General's Committee on Antitrust Policy," *American Economic Review, Papers and Proceedings,* Vol. 46, No. 2, pp. 504–507, esp. p. 507. On the other hand, most of us have failed to heed the clue of Eugene Rostow: "The place of the *Standard Oil* case in the history of the Sherman Act is so important that far too little attention has been given to its possibilities in the development of remedies for enforcing the Sherman Act," in his *A National Policy for the Oil Industry* (New Haven: 1948), p. 6.

Table 9-1 Domestic Marketing Territories Allocated to Standard Oil's Leading Refining and Marketing Companies, 1892–1911

| Company | Marketing Territory Inherited as of April 1, 1892, Following Dissolution of Standard Oil "Trust" (Ohio) | Transfers of Marketing Territories 1892-99 During Coordination by "Standard Oil Interests" | | Transfers of Marketing Territories 1899-1906 Following Recombination into Standard Oil Holding Company (N. J.) but Prior to Filing of Antitrust Suit | | Transfers of Marketing Territories 1906-11 Following Filing of Antitrust Suit but Prior to Dissolution | |
		Acquired	Relinquished	Acquired	Relinquished	Acquired	Relinquished
Atlantic Refining (Refining and Marketing)	Pennsylvania, Delaware, southern New Jersey, western Maryland, southeastern Ohio, part of West Virginia		(1894) to Jersey Standard—southern New Jersey and Delaware		(1906) to Jersey Standard—remainder of West Virginia and remainder of Maryland (1906) to Ohio Standard—southeastern Ohio		
California Standard* (Refining and Marketing) *Successor in 1906 to Iowa Standard	Arizona, California, Nevada, Idaho, Oregon, Washington, western Montana		(1896) to Continental Oil—western Montana and Idaho				
Continental Oil (Marketing only)	Colorado, Wyoming, eastern Montana, Utah, and New Mexico			(1906) from California Standard—western Montana and Idaho			

Company	April 1, 1892	1892-99 Acquired	1892-99 Relinquished	1899-1906 Acquired	1899-1906 Relinquished	1906-11 Acquired	1906-11 Relinquished
Indiana Standard (Refining and Marketing)	Northern Illinois, Minnesota, Wisconsin	(1896) from Kentucky Standard—western Missouri, Iowa, Nebraska, Kansas		(1899) from Ohio Standard—northern Indiana and Michigan (1906) from Kentucky Standard—southern Illinois, southern Indiana	(1906) to Nebraska Standard—Nebraska		
Jersey Standard (Refining and Marketing)	Northern New Jersey, eastern Maryland, District of Columbia, Virginia, eastern North Carolina, eastern South Carolina, part of West Virginia (Charlestown, Huntington)	(1894) from Atlantic Refining—Delaware and southern New Jersey (1895) from Kentucky Standard—western North Carolina, Georgia, and Florida		(1906) from Atlantic Refining—remaining part of West Virginia, western Maryland	(1906) to Kentucky Standard—Georgia and Florida		
Kansas Standard* (Refining only) *Created 1896							
Kentucky Standard (Marketing only)	Western North Carolina, western South Carolina, Georgia, Florida, Alabama, Mississippi, eastern		(1896) to Jersey Standard—western	(1906) from Jersey Standard—Georgia and	(1906) to Indiana Standard—southern		(1909) to Louisiana Standard—eastern

157

Table 9-1 (continued)

Company	April 1, 1892	1892-99 Acquired	1892-99 Relinquished	1899-1906 Acquired	1899-1906 Relinquished	1906-11 Acquired	1906-11 Relinquished
	Louisiana, Kentucky, Tennessee, southwestern Ohio, southern Indiana, southern Illinois, northern Missouri, Iowa, Kansas, Nebraska, and South Dakota		North Carolina, western South Carolina, Georgia, Florida (1896) to Indiana Standard—northern Missouri, Iowa, Kansas, Nebraska, southeastern Indiana, southern Illinois, and South Dakota	Florida	Indiana and southern Illinois (1906) to Ohio Standard—southwestern Ohio		Louisiana (1910) to Louisiana Standard—Tennessee
Louisiana Standard* (Refining and Marketing) *Subsidiary of Jersey Standard created 1909						(1909) from Kentucky Standard—eastern Louisiana (1910) from Kentucky Standard—Tennessee	
Nebraska Standard* (Marketing only) *Created 1906				(1906) from Indiana Standard—Nebraska			

Company	April 1, 1892	1899-1906	
		Acquired	Relinquished
New York Standard (Refining and Marketing)	New York and New England States		
Ohio Standard (Refining and Marketing)	Northern and central Ohio, northern Indiana and Michigan	(1905) from Atlantic Refining—southeastern Ohio (1906) from Kentucky Standard—southwestern Ohio	(1899) to Indiana Standard—northern Indiana and Michigan
Solar Refining (Refining only)			
Vacuum Oil (Refining only)			
Waters-Pierce (Marketing only)	Southern Missouri, Arkansas, Oklahoma, western Louisiana, and Texas		

Source: R. Hidy and M. Hidy, *Pioneering in Big Business, 1882–1911* (Harper, 1955), pp. 292–293 and pp. 460–461, and *Record* in *Standard Oil Co. of New Jersey v. U.S.*, 221 U.S. 1 (1911).

159

Table 9–2   Refining Facilities Assigned to Standard Oil's Leading Refining and Marketing Companies in Standard Oil's "Trust" Dissolution and Reorganization of 1892; Refining Capacities in 1906 and 1911; and the Apparent Sources of Refined Product from Standard Oil For Standard Oil's Domestic Marketers in 1911.

Company	1892 Plants	1906 Plants	1906 Daily Capacity (Bbls.)	1911 Plants	1911 Daily Capacity (Bbls.)	1911 Apparent Sources of Supply (from Standard Oil's Refineries) for Standard Oil's Domestic Marketers
Atlantic Refining (Refining and Marketing)	Philadelphia, Pa.	Philadelphia, Pa. Marcus Hook, Pa. (Jointly operated; Marcus Hook Plant acquired with Bear Creek Refining Company and Crescent Pipe Line from Mellon Family in 1895)	41,100	Philadelphia, Pa. Marcus Hook, Pa. (Jointly operated)	43,600	Atlantic Refining Jersey Standard
	Franklin, Pa. (Assigned Eclipse Refining Co.) Pittsburgh, Pa. (Assigned Pennsylvania Standard)	Franklin, Pa. Pittsburgh, Pa.	8,000 2,000 ⎯⎯ 51,100	Franklin, Pa. Pittsburgh, Pa.	9,000 2,800 ⎯⎯ 55,400	
California Standard* (Refining and Marketing) *Successor in 1906 to Iowa Standard		Richmond, Cal.	28,700 ⎯⎯ 28,700	Richmond, Cal. Redondo Beach, Cal.	25,700 15,000 ⎯⎯ 40,700	California Standard
Continental Oil (Marketing only)	Florence, Colo. (Minority Interest in Florence Refining Co.)	Florence, Colo. (Minority Interest)	Unknown, but small	Florence, Colo. (Minority Interest)	Unknown, but small	Florence Refining
Indiana Standard (Refining and Marketing)	Whiting, Ind.	Whiting, Ind. Kansas City, Kansas	22,500 16,000 ⎯⎯ 38,500	Whiting, Ind. Kansas City, Kansas North Alton, Ill.	37,200 18,000 10,300 ⎯⎯ 65,500	Indiana Standard Kansas Standard Indiana Standard

160

Company	1892 Plants	1906 Plants	Daily Capacity (Bbls.)	1911 Plants	Daily Capacity (Bbls.)	1911 Apparent Sources of Supply
Jersey Standard (Refining and Marketing)	Bayonne, N. J. Communipaw, N. J. (Assigned Eagle Oil Co.) Brooklyn, N. J. (Assigned Bush and Denslow)	Bayonne, N. J. Communipaw, N. J.	33,600 9,000	Bayonne, N. J. Communipaw, N. J.	44,700 11,200	
	Baltimore, Md. (Assigned Baltimore United)	Baltimore, Md.	6,000	Baltimore, Md.	6,700	Jersey Standard
	Parkersburg, W. Va. (Assigned Camden Consolidated)	Parkersburg, W. Va.	2,700	Parkersburg, W. Va.	2,600	
				Linden, N. J.	17,200	
			51,300		82,400*	
				*(Does not include Baton Rouge, La., 7,000 Bbls./day refinery of Louisiana Standard subsidiary listed separately)		
Kansas Standard* (Refining only) *Created 1896		Neodosha, Kansas	8,800	Neodosha, Kansas	12,000	
Kentucky Standard (Marketing only)						Indiana Standard Louisiana Standard
Louisiana Standard* (Refining and Marketing) *Subsidiary of Jersey Standard Created 1909				Baton Rouge, La.	7,000	Louisiana Standard

161

Table 9-2 (continued)

Company	1892 Plants	1906 Plants	Daily Capacity (Bbls.)	1911 Plants	Daily Capacity (Bbls.)	1911 Apparent Sources of Supply
Nebraska Standard* (Marketing only) *Created 1906						Indiana Standard
New York Standard (Refining and Marketing)	Long Island, N. Y. Brooklyn, N. Y. (Assigned Pratt Mfg. Co.) Brooklyn, N. Y. (Assigned Sone and Fleming) Buffalo, N. Y. (Assigned Atlas Ref. Co.) Olean, N. Y. (Assigned Acme Oil Co., N. Y.)	Long Island, N. Y. Brooklyn, N. Y. Brooklyn, N. Y. Buffalo, N. Y.	5,300 4,300 10,300 3,100 ——— 23,000	Long Island, N. Y. Brooklyn, N. Y. Brooklyn, N. Y. Buffalo, N. Y.	4,300 3,700 13,700 4,000 ——— 25,700	New York Standard Vacuum Oil
Ohio Standard (Refining and Marketing)	Cleveland, Ohio	Cleveland, Ohio	5,800	Cleveland, Ohio	3,400	Ohio Standard
Solar Refining (Refining only)	Lima, Ohio	Lima, Ohio	5,100	Lima, Ohio	6,400	Solar Refining
Vacuum Oil* (Refining only) *Entered general refining sometime between 1899-1906, when Olean, N. Y., plant was transferred	Olean, N. Y.	Olean, N. Y.	4,500	Olean, N. Y.	5,400	

162

Company	1892 Plants	1906 Plants	1906 Daily Capacity (Bbls.)	1911 Plants	1911 Daily Capacity (Bbls.)	1911 Apparent Sources of Supply
from New York Standard to Vacuum. Part of Olean, N. Y. output for years had been shipped as feedstock to Vacuum's lubrication plant in Rochester, N. Y.						
Water-Pierce (Marketing only)						Kansas Standard Indiana Standard [Magnolia]
Excluded: Magnolia Oil* (Refining only) *Formed in 1911 and technically and legally adjudged not to be a Standard Oil unit.†		Corsicana, Texas (Navarrow Ref.) Beaumont, Texas (Security Ref.)	2,000* 8,000* 10,000*	Corsicana, Texas Beaumont, Texas	2,000* 8,000* 10,000*	
			*Estimated		*Estimated	

Source: R. Hidy and M. Hidy, *Pioneering in Big Business* (Harper, 1955), esp. pp. 102–105 and pp. 416–417 and *Record* in *Standard Oil Co. of New Jersey v. U.S.*, 221 U.S. 1 (1911).

†Following the Supreme Court's opinion in *Standard Oil v. U.S.*, Magnolia Oil was formed by the presidents of Jersey Standard and New York Standard to suceed to a company which, "as individuals," they had created in 1909, and principally controlled thereafter, to acquire and operate the assets of Navarrow Refining (previously named Corsicana) and Security Oil. Navarrow and Security had been ordered to liquidate by Texas courts in 1909 for having violated the state antitrust law.

Navarrow (Corsicana) had been formed in 1899 by some executives of the Standard Oil holding company, with funds supplied by National Transit (a Standard subsidiary), to operate in Texas as a producer, pipeline, and refiner. Security was formed by a London corporation, with funds supplied by Anglo-American Oil (a Standard foreign subsidiary) and on loan from New York Standard, to operate in Texas a pipeline and refinery from a different producing field.

163

Standard, Indiana Standard, and California Standard. Greater access to markets would have been provided both to non-Standard refiners and to three nonintegrated refiners divorced from Standard: Vacuum Oil, Solar Refining, and Kansas Standard.

Of perhaps even greater importance, in various sections of the country, refineries could have been extracted from all multiple-refinery companies, so that each refinery company would have been left with a single unit, while the other units would have provided the basis for creating new refining companies disconnected from the Standard group. The number of separate refining companies could have been increased — in the coastal region of the Middle Atlantic states, from three to eight; in Ohio-western Appalachia, from six to seven;[3] in the Middle West from northwest Indiana to eastern Kansas, from two to four; in California, from one to two; and in east Texas-Louisiana, from one to two.[4]

In contrast with the above steps, the only relief ever sought, and that ultimately granted, was aimed at divesting Standard Oil of New Jersey of *going corporate-unit* subsidiaries — in other words, at "demerging." The initial target was seventy subsidiaries, but it was ultimately reduced, without governmental objection, to thirty-three.[5] Most of the thirty-three subsidiaries ordered divested had been transferred to Standard Oil of New Jersey either immediately preceding the technical dissolution of the trust in 1892 — in truth, only a partial dissolution — or consequent to the grand consolidation of 1899. A few units represented "outside" acquisitions or subsidiaries newly created by Standard Oil of New Jersey in the years either immediately preceding or following the 1899 amendment of its corporate charter.

In essence, the government had prayed that the Standard Oil Company of New Jersey would merely divest itself of control over defendant subsidiaries and that these subsidiaries would be enjoined from paying dividends to the holding company, a procedure implicitly forcing divestitures. For three reasons the government was scarcely in a position to object when the circuit court specifically decreed that the New Jersey Corporation was not prohibited from distributing ratably the stocks of the subsidiaries found to be parties to the combination: (1) The government's principal theory of

[3] Increasing the total number of separate refining companies in the Northeast (from Ohio and western Virginia east to Baltimore and New York City) from 6 to 15.

[4] Security and Corsicana had allegedly been liquidated, but the two refineries had in fact been transferred to the Magnolia Oil Co., "ownership" of which was assigned to the presidents of Jersey and New York Standard (See G. Gibbs, and E. Knowlton, *The Resurgent Years — 1911–1927: History of Standard Oil Company (New Jersey),* (New York, N.Y.: 1955), p. 20.

[5] Eliminated were (1) many subsidiaries which had been liquidated either prior to the complaint or during the course of the litigation, (2) many subsidiaries in which the New Jersey corporation held only a minority interest, and (3) many natural gas subsidiaries, since the bill of complaint and evidence assembled had not been broadened to embrace the business of natural gas within the oil industry.

the case, to be explained in detail later, was that the combinations into both the trust of 1882 and the holding company of 1889 permanently suppressed potential competition among corporations, which were admittedly commonly owned. A ratable distribution would restore direct ownership by the stockholders in the separate corporations, so that time would be permitted to diversify the stockholders' interests in the separate corporations and active competition could come to pass. (2) The legal theory of the combination rested heavily upon the decision and decree in *Northern Securities*. The decree in that case specifically permitted the dissolution to be made on a ratable basis.[6] (3) The Federal government had limited authority in antitrust cases to interfere in a detailed way with the organization and ownership of property of a corporation created by a state. After all, Justice Harlan had written in his majority opinion in the case, used as a paradigm for Standard Oil: "The Federal court may not have power to forfeit the charter of the Securities Company; it may not declare how its shares of stock may be transferred on its books, nor prohibit it from acquiring real estate, nor diminish or increase its capital stock. All these and like matters are to be regulated by the State which created the company. But . . . Congress may prevent that company, in its capacity as a holding corporation and trustee, from carrying out the purposes of a combination formed in restraint of trade . . . [and can] prevent the two competing railroads here involved from cooperating with the Securities Company in restraining commerce . . . All this can be done without infringing in any degree upon the just authority of the States."[7]

Each of the above considerations had undoubtedly also recommended caution to the government with respect to praying for more than a quarter loaf of remedy, as by also requesting property reorganization of either the divested subsidiaries or the remnant of New Jersey Standard — in order to deconcentrate the inherited "relevant economic markets" in which the parent and each of its foster children engaged, usually exclusively.

An Economic Analysis of the Market Status of the Separated Standard Companies

Market activities, classified by function and territory, had, not unexpectedly, been specially tailored by Standard Oil for each corporate unit, so that virtually no competitive-market overlap and duplication existed among Standard Oil's subsidiaries and operating parents. Geographical divisions of market territory, coupled with rational assignments of capital equipment,

---

[6] The permitted ratable distribution was somewhat surprising because a complete community of interests in the two railroads replaced what prior to the merger had merely been common stockholding by a group able to exercise minority control of the two railroads.

[7] *Northern Securities Co.* v. *U.S.*, 193 U.S. 197, (1904) at 346.

like bulk stations, for serving such territories, kept corporate divisions from easily competing with each other. Such territorial divisions prevented this competition even when several corporate units happened to operate at an identical functional level and irrespective of the vertically integrated status of a corporate unit. (See Table 9–3.)

Some minor market overlap was permitted to persist in a few instances. Some persisted in products of lubricating works, despite efforts to promote product specialization. But even here, for example, Galena-Signal was given the exclusive right to supply railroad lubricants, sold consequent to induced reciprocal purchasing. Jersey Standard's Pennsylvania Lubricating Co., a nondefendant, exclusively supplied steel mill lubricants. The footloose nature of tanker-shipping suggests that the three Standard units that were vertically integrated into tankers might readily have become active competitors in delivering to common foreign ocean ports when their stockholder ownership became diverse. The market for ocean tanker services, however, was growing so rapidly relative to economies of scale in supplying tanker services that effectively competitive conditions could probably be expected in this line of commerce in any event. Some overlap also existed among the several companies in crude production, particularly in the Appalachian field, but market concentration was so low in crude production in every field that this functional branch may be passed over.

Some market overlap existed among the severed pipelines. Two severed pipelines, one of which had been acquired from Mellon in 1893, ran from the Appalachian oil field to the greater Philadelphia area. Another two severed pipelines, which ran from Appalachia to the New Jersey shore of York Harbor, had been deprived of any possibility of becoming actual competitors in 1906, when Jersey Standard separately incorporated the portions running across New Jersey from their respective entry points at Centerbridge, Pennsylvania and Unionville, New York in an effort to forestall the applicability of common-carrier status by the pending Hepburn Act. Finally, only minor market overlap, at most, existed among the refiner-marketers.[8]

The peak coordinators of Standard between 1896 and 1906 had been periodically reassigning capital facilities and market territories to the corporate units marketing kerosene and gasoline, whether these units were integrated into refining or not. Such reassignments were especially active in the years preceding 1906. By this time, the entirety of every state, excepting Missouri, which continued divided by an east-west line between Indiana Standard and Waters-Pierce, was assigned to an exclusive marketer

---

[8] I exclude from discussion the bogus major and minor operators which Standard employed in some areas and at some times prior to 1906 to harass other independent marketers. Republic Oil Co. from 1901 to about 1906 was operated as a powerful bogus independent, allegedly succeeding to a considerable territory in Ohio, Indiana, Illinois, and Missouri vacated by Scofield, Shurmer & Teagle, following its acquisition by Standard Oil in 1901. Most of the remaining bogus independents were jobbers, or merely only tank-wagon peddlers, operating in a local, or sublocal, market.

of Standard. Standard's objective was frankly a "legalistic" one of seeking to challenge under the "commerce clause" the alleged interstate nature of its marketing trade by eliminating from the crossing of state lines all but a trickle of the final transport in tank wagons of refined products from bulk stations to retailers. One corollary for the future would be the impossibility of Standard's refiners as corporate units, if subsequently really divorced, to market effectively *on a vertically integrated basis* in a rival's territory without incurring some major capital investments for new bulk-station locations and for supporting systems of tank wagon delivery.

Of course, New York City lay across New York Harbor for the Bayonne and Linden, New Jersey refineries of Jersey Standard, while Newark and Jersey City were similarly accessible to the Brooklyn and Long Island refineries of New York Standard, but this situation was exceptional. Although virtually all of New York State and New England, which were New York Standard's exclusive preserve, and all of Pennsylvania and Delaware, which were the preserve of Atlantic, were technically accessible to the refineries of Jersey Standard, these refineries could not be effectively reached without major capital commitments for the establishment of a multitude of bulk stations and tank-wagon routes. And save for Jersey Standard's subsidiary Louisiana Standard — founded after the antitrust suit was filed, and apparently left unchallenged — which might conceivably easily supply Alabama, Mississippi, Arkansas, and east Texas from its Baton Rouge refinery, most of the remainder of the United States, which was marketed by Ohio Standard, Kentucky Standard, Indiana Standard, Waters-Pierce, Continental, and California Standard, could not be effectively reached by product transported from Jersey Standard's existing refineries. To become actively competitive with refined products in most of the country, Jersey Standard, the largest of the surviving refiner-marketers would need to establish, not only a vast and capital-intensive network of marketing facilities, but also additional refineries in several other parts of the United States.

It is true that most Standard refiners, following the ratable distribution of their stocks would be converted from a unified status to that of potential *actual* competitors in the procurement of crude oil. Excepting California Standard, a market analysis would show that two or more of the several refiners obtained crude from each of the major crude-oil pools: Appalachia, Ohio-Indiana, Illinois, Mid-Continent and Gulf. But no convincing evidence exists that, when purchasing crude oil, subsidiaries were ordinarily[9]

---

[9] The Commissioner of Corporations suggested that the Standard combine retarded its purchases in the Ohio field in 1888–90 to depress temporarily the acquisition prices of oil wells. While Standard kept the Ohio producers of high-sulfur oil unaware of both Standard's development of the Frasch refining process and Standard's ongoing construction of the huge Whiting, Indiana refinery to process Ohio Oil, Standard purchased half the Ohio producing capacity. Thereafter Standard sharply advanced its posted price and purchase rate of Ohio crude. See *Report on the Petroleum Industry, Part II, Prices and Profits* (Washington, 1907), pp. 94–95.

Table 9–3 Vertical Stage(s), or Function(s), Operated in 1911 by Companies Ordered Separated From Standard Oil Holding Company

Vertical Stage, or Function, Operated	Companies Operating in the Stage	Nonintegrated Companies	Integrated Companies and the Additional Stage(s), or Function(s), Operated (by Coded Symbol)*								
				(C)	(P)	(R)	(M)	(L)	(F)	(S)	(T)
(C) Crude Production	California Standard		California Standard	n.a.	x	x	x	x	x	x	x
	Jersey Standard		Jersey Standard	n.a.	x	x	x	x	x	x	x
	Ohio Oil		Ohio Oil	n.a.	x						
	Prairie Oil		Prairie Oil and Gas	n.a.	x						
	South Penn Oil	South Penn Oil									
	Washington Oil	Washington Oil									
Number of Companies	6	2	4								
(P) Pipeline and Storage	Buckeye Pipe Line	Buckeye Pipeline									
	California Standard		California Standard	x	n.a.	x				x	
	Crescent Pipeline	Crescent Pipeline									
	Cumberland Pipeline	Cumberland Pipeline									
	Eureka Pipeline	Eureka Pipeline									
	Indiana Pipeline	Indiana Pipeline									
	Jersey Standard		Jersey Standard	x	n.a.	x	x	x	x	x	
	National Transit	National Transit									
	New York Transit	New York Transit									
	Northern Pipeline	Northern Pipeline									
	Ohio Oil										
	Prairie Oil and Gas										
	Southern Pipeline	Southern Pipeline									
	South-West	South-West									
	Pennsylvania Pipeline	Pennsylvania Pipeline									
Number of Companies	14	10	4								

Table 9–3 (continued)

Vertical Stage, or Function, Operated	Companies Operating in the Stage	Nonintegrated Companies	Integrated Companies and the Additional Stage(s), or Function(s), Operated (by Coded Symbol)*							
				(C)	(P)	(R)	(M)	(L)	(F)	(S)	(T)
(R) Refining	Atlantic Refining		Atlantic Refining	x	x	n.a.	x				
	California Standard		California Standard			n.a.	x			x	
	Indiana Standard		Indiana Standard			n.a.	x				
	Jersey Standard		Jersey Standard	x	x	n.a.	x	x	x	x	
	Kansas Standard	Kansas Standard									
	New York Standard		New York Standard			n.a.	x			x	
	Ohio Standard		Ohio Standard			n.a.	x		x		
	Solar Refining	Solar Refining									
	Vacuum Oil		Vacuum Oil			n.a.		x			
Number of Companies	9	2	7								
(M) Marketing	Atlantic Refining		Atlantic Refining	x	x	x	n.a.				
	California Standard		California Standard			x	n.a.			x	
	Continental Oil	Continental Oil									
	Indiana Standard		Indiana Standard			x	n.a.				
	Jersey Standard		Jersey Standard	x	x	x	n.a.	x	x	x	
	Kentucky Standard	Kentucky Standard									
	Nebraska Standard	Nebraska Standard									
	New York Standard		New York Standard			x	n.a.			x	
	Ohio Standard		Ohio Standard			x	n.a.		x		
	Waters-Pierce		Waters-Pierce				n.a.		x		
Number of Companies	10	3	7								

Table 9–3 (continued)

Vertical Stage, or Function, Operated	Companies Operating in the Stage	Nonintegrated Companies	Integrated Companies and the Additional Stage(s), or Function(s), Operated (by Coded Symbol)*								
				(C)	(P)	(R)	(M)	(L)	(F)	(S)	(T)
(L) Lubricant, or Other Specialty Product—Manufactured or Distributed	Borne, Scrymser; Chesebrough Mfg.; Galena-Signal Oil; Jersey Standard; Swan and Finch; Vacuum Oil	Borne, Scrymser; Chesebrough Mfg.; Galena-Signal Oi; Swan and Finch	Jersey Standard	x	x	x	x	n.a.	x	x	
			Vacuum Oil			x		n.a.			
Number of Companies	6	4	2								
(F) Foreign Marketing	Anglo-American Oil; Colonial Oil; Jersey Standard; New York Standard; Vacuum Oil; Waters-Pierce	Colonial Oil	Anglo-American Oil	x					n.a.	x	
			Jersey Standard	x			x	x		x	
			New York Standard			x	x	x		x	
			Vacuum Oil			x	x	x			
			Waters-Pierce				x				
Number of Companies	6	1	5								
(S) Shipping Tankers	Anglo-American Oil; California Standard; Jersey Standard; New York Standard		Anglo-American Oil	x	x	x	x	x	x	n.a.	
			California Standard	x	x	x	x	x	x	n.a.	
			Jersey Standard						x	n.a.	
			New York Standard						x	n.a.	
Number of Companies	4	0	4								
(T) Tank Cars	Union Tank Line Co.	Union Tank Car Co.									
Number of Companies	1	1	0								

Source: R. Hidy and M. Hidy, *Pioneering in Big Business* (Harper, 1955) pp. 324–325 and *Record* in *Standard Oil Co. of New Jersey* v. *U.S.*, 221 U.S. 1 (1911).
*n.a. = not applicable.

restricted in their procurement by dint of the Standard combination. A Standard refiner purchased as much crude as it wished, upon considering quality from the field (usually fields) at which the refiner could obtain the lowest delivered cost, a cost based upon the field price posted — and initially paid by the Crude Purchasing and Carrying Department — plus transportation charges, plus a trivial commission of one-fourth cent per barrel.[10] The monopolistic power possessed, and exerted, by the Standard combination in refined products through Standard's exclusive territorial allocations of the dominating marketing position to a particular Standard marketing corporation elevated consumer prices, and reduced consumer purchases, of refined products. As a corollary, such exertion of monopolistic power in the product market reduced input requirements of the marketing corporations and, of course, reduced crude prices.

There is no reason to believe, however, that Standard's dominating position in the procurement of competitively-supplied crude oil provided the Standard group with the long-run power, and motivation in terms of maximizing present value, to depress crude prices monopsonistically. Standard Oil's barriers to entry, and to expansion by existing rivals had primarily resided in its access to favored transportation costs — principally pipelines but also railroads. This advantage was supplemented by some differential savings in processing cost because of large-scale refineries and by a differential ability, and willingness to direct its superior wealth and geographical conglomeration toward discriminatory sharpshooting in segmented oligopolistic markets in order to disadvantage particular rivals it wished to contain.[11]

[10] R. Hidy and M. Hidy, *Pioneering in Big Business, 1882–1911: History of Standard Oil Company (New Jersey)*, (New York: 1955), pp. 279–280, 333–334, 629–630.

[11] In a soon-to-be-completed complementary piece, I shall contest the thesis, evidence, and implications of the much cited article by John McGee, "Predatory Price Cutting: The Standard Oil (New Jersey) Case, *Journal of Law and Economics,* I (October, 1958), 137–169. Combination-by-merger was the central issue, especially the ultimate conglomerate-type mergers of 1899, not unfair competition. To the extent that "unfair competition" was an issue — one designed both to bolster the inferences of intent to restrain trade and to perpetuate the effectiveness of the restraint — possession and application of power to generate differential advantages in transportation cost constituted the principal forces of the exclusionary charges. The charges of localized sharpshooting discrimination constituted but a subsidiary, though nontrivial, element in the charge of unfair competition.

A reinterpretation of conglomerate-type "deep pocket" power suggests that Standard Oil possessed an incentive to employ such tactics, not to bankrupt rivals, but to contain the expansion of rival sales by limiting access to local markets characterized by relatively substantial economies of scale for bulk-station and tank distribution. Both the record and later historical studies show that the Standard Oil combination did employ, and at times quite dramatically, some discriminatory sharpshooting. That the record is not loaded much more heavily with a compilation of such practices, not to mention Standard's documents explaining purpose and intention, may be attributed primarily to: (1) the major thrust of the charge — combination into a holding company to restrain potential competition, (2) the aged character of many inci-

The Standard combination, conscious of the strictly limited height of the barriers to entry and expansion by rivals afforded by its advantageous position, practiced limit-pricing.[12] It sought to take advantage of the dynamically elastic, long-run demand in its markets for refined products, a demand which possessed the potential for both a rapid absolute growth of refiners as a whole and a rapid rise in the relative share of non-Standard occupancy. Should Standard raise its highly satisfactory targets for profit margins above levels "guesstimated" — nonuniformly for the various regions, and even subregions, exclusively supplied by a designated Standard marketing company — to retard expansion of the share secured by outsiders in the rapidly growing market, its own growth would have declined. To have elevated profit margins to levels consistent with strictly short-run profit-maximizing adjustments of the classic, dominant-firm type of price leader would have so stimulated expansion by rivals as to substantially reduce the average annual rate of growth of Standard's profits. In this classic type of price leadership, the dominant firm in each successive period makes static-like decisions based upon the (successively applicable) particular residual demand — computed by subtracting from the estimated given aggregate market demand schedule the estimated given aggregate supply schedule of outsiders.

Standard foresaw the possibilities of a greater present value to the combination by gearing its profit-margin policy to levels that dampened their magnetic impact upon the incentives of rivals to expand their capacity.[13] "Through-puts" of crude in American refineries grew on average at a compounded rate of 8.6 percent per year during the decade of 1874–84 when the Standard Oil combination became well established; they grew almost as fast, at an average rate of 7.6 percent per year during the next thirty years, 1884–1914.[14] The Standard group sought, and substantially succeeded, in maintaining its participatory share in market growth.

Standard had no desire to press its monopolistic power to the hilt in product markets, by charging prices that would be calculated merely by the price elasticity of the *industry* rather than by its own dynamically estimated demand for refined products. It had even less desire to elevate profit margins still further by exerting its residual power over demand in procurement markets so as to reduce monopsonistically the prices of crude oil.

To be sure, the government charged the Standard combination with the possession and exercise of substantial power to fix the price of crude in

---

dents, and (3) an inability of government to make an unrestricted search of the file and to make more than modestly successful use of its powers of subpoena in a civil action conducted before a special examiner.

[12] See R. Hidy and M. Hidy, *op. cit.*, pp. 194 and 448–450.

[13] See Allan Nevins, *Study in Power* (New York: 1953), II, 66–67.

[14] Calculated from tables in Harold Williamson, et al., *The American Petroleum Industry,* I, 489 and 633 and II, 111.

most American oil fields. But the Justice Department also followed the lead of the Commissioner of Corporations in attributing the creation and maintenance of the Standard group's excessive margins between the prices of crude and refined products *principally* to the suppression of competition among members of the combination in the markets for refined products and *collaterally* to the power of the combination to maintain substantial barriers against the expansion of refinery capacity by rivals, an expansion which would otherwise have reduced prices for refined products.[15]

Apparently no persisting horizontal combination in procurement for the purpose of depressing crude prices had existed among Standard's refining companies. The several defendant refiners essentially operated as uninhibited (competitive) quantity-adjusters of crude inputs at the estimated market-clearing prices posted in the various fields, for everyone, by Standard's purchasing department. An enhancement in competitive buying by Standard's refiners — and higher crude prices — would not result from dissolution, even allowing time for disbursement of symmetrical stock-ownership, so long as the severed marketing companies maintained exclusive marketing territories for the outputs of the refining companies without reducing prices of refined products in these marketing territories. Reduced product prices in any of these exclusive territories would increase the demand for output from supplying refineries; the collateral increase in demand from supplying refineries (Standard's refineries and others) for required inputs would increase crude prices. But product prices would be reduced in the exclusive marketing territories only (1) as actual competition increased in marketing the product; or (2) as the heirs to market dominancy and price leadership perceived, consequent to a gradually emerging divergence in stockholders' interests, an enhancement in the threat of potential competition at former profit margins, particularly from Standard's several neighboring refinery companies, but also from "independent" refiners and marketers.

The corporations designated to be separated from what I choose to call a "conglomerate holding company" included many subsidiaries that were additional to those exclusively in marketing and that contemporary analysis would label "vertically related": notably pipeline subsidiaries, but also the Union Tank Car Company. It was the combination in refining, however, and its associated suppression of competition through territorial division of marketing, that was alleged to have created power for the Standard group to gain control in transportation. By spinning off these units, the government apparently hoped to improve competitive conditions in five ways: (1) increase for non-Standard shippers the accessibility to the shipping facilities of the severed pipelines — and at reasonable minimum tenders and comparable rates; (2) remove from the severed refinery companies a

---

[15] Commissioner of Corporations, *op. cit.,* pp. 3, 99–100, 614–669.

major source of excess profits that financed subsidization of losses in local tank-wagon markets; (3) enlarge and solidify the interest of refiners in generating countervailing pressure for regulation to reduce pipage rates; (4) enhance the threat to pipelines of potential competition from severed refinery (and crude-producer) subsidiaries; and (5) enhance the threat to refineries of potential competition from severed pipeline subsidiaries.

The varieties of potential competition reduced by vertical combination are substantially equivalent to those reduced by combining firms that occupy unrelated markets — the narrowly-defined conglomerate combination — when the markets are ineffectively competitive in either instance. Little purpose appears to be served in classifying vertical combinations separately from the conglomerate. Both types of combination contain the wherewithal for disciplinary price squeezes to contain existing, more specialized rivals and to raise entry barriers against new rivals. Both types eliminate the possibility of future competition among firms which might expand into each other's market. At most, vertical mergers might be treated as a special case of conglomerate merger, wherein possession of a preexisting source of supply or market outlet and, respectively, an inherited familiarity with the business of a supplier or customer may, especially in the short run, make substantially more credible the threat of potential competition by vertically related firms.

Nevertheless, given the *long-run suppression of potential competition* that was charged, and found to have resulted from combining commonly owned firms of "Standard Oil Interests" first into a trust (1882) and then into a corporate holding company (1899) — a long-run potential competition which was to be restored by the requested, and granted dissolution — I conclude that there is little merit to analyzing separately the litigated issue of potential competition in this conglomerate combination in accordance with whether the potential competition was vertical or otherwise. Neither did counsel for the litigants.

In reality, the decree sought by the Justice Department, and ultimately approved by the courts, sought merely to restore a *potentiality for potential competition.* The form of potential competition that the prayer for relief most clearly and capably contemplated concerned restoration of the potentiality for potential competition *among* the corporate units to be separated from the supersized Standard Oil holding company. But the very process of time, which was relied upon to convert eventually the *potential into an actual* potential competition among Standard's former affiliates, was also relied upon to enhance the potentiality for effective competition from both (a) the group of smaller and more specialized existing rivals and (b) new entrance by firms substantially smaller and more specialized than Standard's combination. By reducing the extent to which the pooled interests of affiliates' owners could be marshalled to generate substantial unfair competition against nonsubservient outsiders, eventual weakening of the bonds of solidarity among the former affiliates was expected to reduce barriers against expansion and against entrance by outside rivals.

Development of the Government's Bill of Complaint

The Standard Oil of New Jersey case, from the filing of the initial bill of complaint and prayer for relief in November 1906 until its conclusion in 1911, was managed by a talented and prominent Saint Paul, Minnesota attorney, Frank B. Kellogg, who today is best remembered for his later role as a Secretary of State in promoting the 1929 Kellogg-Briand Pact to outlaw war. Kellogg had become a confidant of President Theodore Roosevelt both on the midwest political climate and on industrial and railroad regulation. In return, the president pressed Kellogg in to taking a fee-plus-cost assignment as a special assistant to the attorney general to direct the government's antitrust actions against both the Standard Oil of New Jersey holding-company combination and the Union Pacific-Southern Pacific combination. For victories in these actions, he gained a now-forgotten national reputation as "The Trust Buster,"[16] election to President of the American Bar Association in 1913, and election to the United States Senate from Minnesota in 1916.

Kellogg cautiously and *conservatively* marshalled his bill of complaint and prayer for relief substantially on the model of the government's successful charge of illegal combination in Northern Securities. But Northern Securities was a railroad case; no governmental success had been achieved in dissolving a tight combination in manufacturing before the complaint against Standard was filed, or indeed until Kellogg's victory before the Supreme Court in 1911 — almost twenty-one years after the passage of the Sherman Act. In 1909, following two exhausting years of collecting a record of exhibits and testimony that extended to twenty volumes and while awaiting the circuit court's decision in the case, Kellogg confessed his worries that the Sherman Act would be interpreted by the court to nullify his labors.[17] At the final conclusion of the case in 1911 and in answer to criticisms of the decree, Kellogg explained his reasons for believing that the dissolution accomplished all that was authorized by the Sherman Act. He contended, moreover, that the decree accomplished something far more important than the dissolution of the great holding company in the oil industry:

[16] Kellogg had already gained a reputation among newspaper publishers as a trust buster during 1905–1906 when he forced a collapse of a common sales agency which controlled the marketing of newsprint produced in Wisconsin and Minnesota. See David Bryn-Jones, *Frank B. Kellogg, A Biography* (New York: 1937), Chs. V–VII.

[17] See Kellogg Papers at Minnesota Historical Library, letter to his law partner, C. A. Severance (November 8, 1909).

The decree of the court was necessary to establish the power of any regulative body like a commission which Congress might establish. This battle had to be fought first because these corporations, entrenched behind State charters, claimed immunity from federal control. It would have been idle to legislate further upon this subject until the power to do so and to enforce legislation was clearly sustained by the Supreme Court, as it has been done.[18]

The government's bill of complaint essentially charged that the 1899 absorption by the Standard Oil of New Jersey holding company of all other corporations owned by Standard interests constituted the ultimate and perpetual unification of a continuing combination of seventy-one named defendant corporations and a conspiracy of seven named principal individuals to restrain and monopolize commerce, a combination that had its origins in 1870. A loose alliance of refinery companies, based on exchanges of stock and supplemented by additional purchases of refineries and pipelines during the early part of the 1870's, was alleged to have provided the strategic buying power that made it possible for the alliance to win unfair advantages in freight rates from railroads. These advantages in turn induced most other refineries and pipelines to either participate in a pooling of stockownership, sell out to a Standard corporation, or expire. The outcome of such combining provided the Standard interests with 90 percent of the nation's refinery capacity by the end of the decade.

Because Standard Oil of Ohio was not permitted to hold stock in other corporations, various individuals were holding "in trust" title to stock that had been acquired by exchange or purchase by Ohio Standard. In 1879, an interim trust was created to bring together, and hold title to, all of the stock which Ohio Standard had acquired but to which it lacked title. The trustees were instructed to distribute such acquired stock ratably to stockholders in Ohio Standard. The instructions were not executed.

The government charged that a penultimate unification of commonly owned but "separate and independent" corporations was created by the formation of the Standard Oil Trust of 1882. According to this agreement, stockholders surrendered to a management trust, in return for Standard Oil Trust Certificates, their shares of Ohio Standard stock and their proportional entitlement to the shares of other companies held by the 1879 trust. The management trust was to assume responsibility for directing and supervising the conglomeration of corporations held by Standard interests.

The complaint charged that, following the formation of the Standard Oil Trust of 1882, several new corporate subsidiaries, such as New York Standard Oil and New Jersey Standard, were created to absorb and coordinate respectively many businesses that had already been acquired in the Northeastern seaboard, excepting Pennsylvania, where existing Atlantic

[18] Frank B. Kellogg, "Results of the Standard Oil Decision," *Review of Reviews,* XLV, (June, 1912), p. 729.

Refining was employed for a like purpose. Several previously acquired corporations which marketed in the South were absorbed into, or made corporate subsidiaries of, a newly created Kentucky Standard.

The complaint alleged that a massive wave of acquisitions was no longer necessary to maintain Standard's dominance of 80–90 percent of the purchasing, pipeline transportation, refining, and marketing of petroleum products. The dominance was, thereafter, allegedly maintained both by the periodic acquisition of strategic refiners, pipelines, and marketers and by the formation of new corporations, which were "taken into the combination," to market in the West (Continental and Iowa Standard), to refine later discoveries of non-Appalachian crude (Solar Refining, Indiana Standard, Kansas Standard, and California Standard[19]), or to transport crude by pipeline from newly discovered fields (Indiana Pipeline and Prairie Oil and Gas).

Technically, the Standard Oil Trust of 1882 was "partially" dissolved in 1892 and superseded by a tightly knit community of interests — and identical body of liquidating trustees — that coordinated Standard's corporations in loose combination. The Supreme Court of Ohio, upon an action initiated by the state's attorney general, had found Standard Oil of Ohio to have violated (1) the corporation laws of Ohio by permitting a trust, rather than its stockholders, to exercise control over the corporation and (2) the common law of Ohio on the ground that the trust was unreasonably restraining trade and monopolizing. The charter of Ohio Standard was not revoked, but the Standard Oil Trust was given only four months to discontinue its control of Ohio Standard. Preceding the "formal" dissolution of the trust, the eighty-four corporations controlled by the trust were consolidated into twenty by transferring the remaining sixty-four to a subsidiary status, principally in New Jersey Standard, New York Standard, and Atlantic Refining. Upon "liquidation," only ten of the largest stockholders — including all the trustees who remained until 1899 the liquidating trustees — and their families, constituting a bare majority in ownership, converted their certificates to become directly holding stockholders, in common, of the reconstituted twenty corporations. The liquidating trustees continued to pay dividends on close to half of the trust certificates that remained unconverted.[20] Some strategic firms were acquired in the name

[19] Strictly speaking, California Standard became the successor company to the Pacific Oil Co., a large producer with a modest pipeline and refinery, which the Standard holding company acquired in 1901. But California Standard began construction of a large refinery and, shortly thereafter, replaced Iowa Standard as the West Coast marketer.

[20] Several individuals, with an interest of 10 to 20 thousand shares, which were worth, on a conservative capital-stock basis, at least $1 to $2 million, were among those who did not liquidate. Standard had suggested that the nonliquidaters were simply holders of a trivial number of certificates, who would have been entitled to only a fraction of a share of the separated corporations consequent to the ratable distribution.

of Jersey Standard or Atlantic Refining during the period of guidance by the tightly knit community of interests: in 1893 an important lubricating works, Borne, Scrymser; in 1895 the budding Mellon complex — including 302 miles of gathering lines in Western Pennsylvania, the Crescent Pipe Line (a trunk line to Marcus Hook in Greater Philadelphia), and a nearly completed large refinery at Marcus Hook; and, also, in 1895 the Union, Mutual, and International refineries, which were part owners and shippers of the struggling United States Pipe Line (and predecessor of Pure Oil), which Standard was seeking to acquire.

The government alleged that a troubled concern persisted among the controllers and founders of the Standard complex as to whether solidarity and coordination could be maintained within the system of partial dissolution, should deaths or some personal disagreements among key stockholding families produce sales of stocks and generate powerful minority, or even majority, interests in particular Standard companies which would diverge from the community of interests. Notwithstanding the 1895 *E. C. Knight* decision, this concern was undoubtedly increased by the threat that various states would initiate their own antitrust actions to compel a *bona fide* distribution of stock to all the owners of trust certificates. Indeed, in the fall of 1897, Ohio's attorney general initiated contempt proceedings against Ohio Standard for having failed to divorce itself from the Standard Oil Trust. Moreover, a year later the same attorney general initiated *quo warranto* proceedings against all four Standard units chartered in the state — Buckeye Pipe Line, Ohio Oil, Solar Refining, and Ohio Standard — for both violating a newly enacted Ohio antitrust statute and for conspiring to assist Ohio Standard to evade the 1892 decree ordering Ohio Standard to sever its relations with the Standard Oil Trust.

Given the many threats to the continued unity of the "Standard Oil Interests," — the expression by which the controlling group unofficially referred to the interim partial combination — the government alleged that the liquidating trustees instructed Standard Oil of New Jersey to seek an amendment of its charter under the liberalized laws of New Jersey, an amendment that would replace its existing $10 million of common stock with an authorized $100 million capitalization of new common shares and that would allow it to engage in a conglomeration of business activity.[21] In June 1899 the New Jersey holding company began to exchange one new $100 share of common stock for every $100 trust certificate or for an equivalent bundle of fractional shares in the twenty companies previously distributed to persons who had converted their trust certificates.

[21] The charter read: "to do all kinds of mining, manufacturing, and trading business; transporting goods by land or water in any manner; to buy, sell, lease, and improve lands; build houses, structures, vessels, cars, wharves, docks and piers; to lay and operate pipe lines; to erect lines for conducting electricity; . . . to carry on its business and have agencies in all parts of the world, and to hold, purchase, mortgage, and convey real estate and personal property outside the State of New Jersey."

The government charged that the ultimate combination of these nineteen sister corporations of Jersey Standard into the New Jersey holding corporation created a perpetual unification and a perpetual suppression of competition. The charge rested essentially upon an alleged illegal combination in restraint of trade,[22] but the government alleged throughout that the defendants also monopolized by means of the same specified combinations.

To bolster its charge of monopolization, the government asserted that Standard possessed power — and cited numerous instances in evidence of its application — to generate unjustified discrimination against rivals in both railroad services and pipeline services, which were dominated by Standard subsidiaries. The government also alleged that barriers against entry by rivals resulted from Standard's unfair practices in obstructing the construction and successful operation of independent pipelines and in obstructing through geographical price discrimination, the access of rival refiners to markets.

Finally, to demonstrate both the substantiality of the combination to restrain trade and the exertion of its power to monopolize, the complaint made two allegations. (1) The combination had realized monopolistic profits, citing the record of Standard's great profits and dividends from the period of the trust of 1882 through the year preceding the filing of the complaint in 1906. (2) The combination had divided the country into separate territories, each of which was assigned to a designated marketing corporation and excluded other defendant corporations.

Parallel with Northern Securities

The final 1899 combination of twenty oil companies into the Standard Oil holding company sufficiently paralleled the 1901 combination of two railroads into the Northern Securities holding company so that the Sherman Act precedent from the *Northern Securities*[23] case could be employed to find the Standard Oil Company of New Jersey an illegal combination in restraint of trade. Nevertheless, some modest differences with respect to Northern Securities existed in regard to: (a) the origin of the stockholders' community of interest in the respective companies to be joined, (b) the degree of symmetry in the respective stockholders' community of interests, and (c) the purposes to be served by the formation of the respective holding companies.

[22] Hugh B. Cox, a former chief in the Antitrust Division, recently contended that all of the early Sherman Act dissolutions were essentially brought, and decided, on the basis of illegal combination in restraint of trade. "From the very beginning of the act's history the tendency of the Department of Justice and of private plaintiffs has been to treat Section 2 as ancillary or supplementary to Section 1." See "Competition and Section 2 of the Sherman Act," *ABA Antitrust Section,* Vol. 27 (1965), p. 72.
[23] *Northern Securities Co. v. U.S.,* 193 U.S. 197 (1904).

Cooperation between the Hill and Morgan groups in managing the two railroads began in 1895. In that year the Hill-Morgan coalition arranged to have Hill's Great Northern acquire 50 percent of the financially weak Northern Pacific's stock in return for guaranteeing the Northern Pacific's bonds. This effort at collaboration was frustrated by an unhappy minority stockholder in the Great Northern, who was sustained in a suit which he had brought under a Minnesota statute prohibiting a merger of competing railroads (*Pearsall* v. *Great Northern R. Co.*).[24] Active competition had ceased, however, and in 1897 Hill and his associates made directly substantial purchases of Northern Pacific stock, thereby strengthening the controlling, though minority, position of the Hill-Morgan group in Northern Pacific. Meanwhile, the Hill group continued to maintain majority control in the Great Northern. Finally, the two railroads negotiated a joint takeover in 1901 of virtually the entire common stock of the Burlington railroad, a transaction which assured the acquiring roads of access to Chicago. But the Burlington takeover also deprived Harriman's Union Pacific of one of its feeder lines at Omaha and Kansas City to the East. When, in retaliation, Harriman sought to purchase majority control of the Northern Pacific, the Hill-Morgan group sought by formation of the Northern Securities holding company to escalate the cost and thereby frustrate Harriman's quest for control. To be sure, the Hill-Morgan group appealed to the independent stockholders in Northern Pacific to exchange their stock for Northern Securities on the grounds that competition would be reduced consequent to a permanent unification of the economic interests of the northern lines.[25]

The Eighth Circuit Court, which initially tried the case and whose decision was upheld on review by the Supreme Court, clearly recognized that a "community of interests" had controlled the two railroads and had rationalized their competition prior to their absorption into the Northern Securities holding company. But save for some opening casual remarks concerning the public having "ever regarded" the two railroads as competing and concerning the roads having competed for "some years, at least, after they were built" and their being "natural competitors,"[26] the court proceeded, and continued, to repeat the language of the complaint which charged an illegal combination of "competing and parallel roads." By failing to amend the language of the complaint in the interest of accuracy to read "potentially competing," yet still finding the combination one that *permanently* restrained trade, the Supreme Court was also channeled into upholding a loosely worded charge directed against a combination of "competing and

[24] 161 U.S. 646 (1895).

[25] See William Letwin, *Law and Economic Policy in America,* (New York: 1965), pp. 182–217 for an extended analysis of the events preceding the Northern Securities combination.

[26] *U.S.* v. *Northern Securities Co.,* 120 F. 121 (8th C.C., D. Minnesota, 1903), at 722.

parallel railroads," thus providing Standard with the foundation upon which Standard would seek to construct the heart of its defense.[27]

Standard's principal contention was that formation of the New Jersey holding company in 1899 combined commonly owned, noncompeting corporations. Standard was also to emphasize the perfect symmetry of the ownership interest of Standard stockholders in the corporations controlled by the Standard group, which owned one hundred percent of all but a small minority of corporations possessed by the group, a situation in marked contrast to the Hill-Morgan "community of interests." Furthermore, Standard would contend, indirectly, that virtually none of the pairs of defendant Standard corporations possessed the market characteristic of "natural competitors" comparable to that of parallel railroads.[28] Finally, Standard was to contend (1) that combinations which were illegal among competitive railroads — a field uniquely affected with a public interest — would be legal in the *private* oil business and (2) that, in the instance of Standard, the purpose of corporate acquisitions was not to restrict competition but to contribute to an efficient and economical subsequent natural growth, which principally benefited the public and only incidentally, and inconsiderably, restricted competition.[29]

The Government's Theory of the Case

As finally developed by Frank B. Kellogg for presentation first to the Eighth Circuit Court and then to the Supreme Court, the government's theory of illegal combination constituted at heart a series of theories of the case. The series of theories allowed for lines of retreat should the courts be unwilling to accept the grounds upon which the earlier and simpler formulations were constructed. The government trusted, however, that the grounds for erecting the simpler formulations would, if required, be employed as

[27] Compare William Letwin, *op. cit.,* pp. 210–227, 253–254.

[28] Standard was to emphasize that none of Standard's companies owned refineries in the same state (excepting New York Standard and Vacuum Oil in New York and Ohio Standard and Solar Refining in Ohio) and that none of Standard's marketing companies marketed in the same state (excepting Indiana Standard and Waters-Pierce in Missouri). See Defendant's Brief in Circuit Court for the Eastern Division of Missouri, *U.S.* v. *Standard Oil Co. of New Jersey,* 173 F. 177 (8th C.C., E.D. Mo., 1909) Part I, p. 3, Part IV, pp 143–48. Standard was also to argue that its pipelines should be excused from any dissolution since they were not competitive with, but wholly complementary to, refinery subsidiaries. Likewise it was to argue somewhat inconsistently in denying the potentiality of competition that divested pipelines would become vulnerable, and valueless, consequent to an expected integration by refineries into a transport function historically supplied by commonly controlled affiliates. See Brief for Appellants in the Supreme Court for the United States, *Standard Oil Co. of New Jersey* v. *U.S.,* 221 U.S. 1 (1911), pp. 156–159.

[29] Defendants' Brief, *op. cit.,* Part IV, pp. 36–70; Appellants' Brief, *op. cit.,* Part II, pp. 88–98.

evidence by the courts so as to infer an illegal intent and to interpret the probable effect of charges of a more contemporary standing. In brief, and with only modest simplifications, the government's argument incorporated the following steps:

(1) During 1870–82 a loosely organized combination, and conspiracy, through an alliance of individuals who had exchanged stocks in respective companies unreasonably restrained trade under federal common law by suppressing competition among pipelines, refineries, and marketing corporations handling 90 percent of the nation's refined product.[30] Contributing to the combination's unreasonable restraint of trade was the systematic application of its combined power in pipelines, and against railroads, to force many other refiners into the combination, into sale to the combination, or into extinction. (At the time of the complaint in 1906, the going combination of the New Jersey holding company was merely a vastly enlarged, continued, and permanently cemented suppression of potential competition that violated the Sherman Act for reason of its illegal origin under the common law.)

(2) In 1882 the common owners, who had previously suppressed competition among corporations in the alliance, made almost permanent — "for the life of the trustees, their successors, plus nine years" — this suppression of potential competition among separate and independent corporations by transferring all of the owners' common shares, in exchange for trust certificates, to trustees who would manage and rationalize the business of these corporations. This elimination of the previously existing "potential" competition, which could have later developed into actual competition, constituted an illegal combination in unreasonable restraint of trade in violation of federal common law, even if the prior combination into a "community of interests" did not violate federal common law. (The going combination of the New Jersey holding company was merely a vastly enlarged, continued and permanently cemented suppression of potential competition that violated the Sherman Act for reason of its illegal origin in 1882 as an almost permanent suppression of potential competition in violation of the federal common law.)

(3) In July 1890, with passage of the Sherman Act, the continued existence of the Standard Oil Trust, which almost permanently suppressed potential competition, constituted a combination in restraint of trade in violation of section 1 of the Sherman Act, even if no federal common law existed with respect to unreasonable restraint of trade or monopolization in interstate commerce. (The going combination of the New Jersey holding

[30] "It is said that this company simply acquired properties in the usual course of business. No company in this country ever entered into a business in which able men were engaged and suddenly sprang from 10 percent to 90 percent of the business by natural growth." Transcript of the Oral Argument of Frank B. Kellogg on Behalf of the United States, in the Supreme Court of the United States, *Standard Oil Co. of New Jersey* v. *U.S.*, 221 U.S. 1 (1911), p. 25.

company was merely a vastly enlarged, continued and permanently cemented suppression of potential competition that violated the Sherman Act for reason of its illegal origin in, and continued operation beyond July 1890, of the 1882 trust, whose maintenance violated section 1 of the Sherman Act for reason of its almost permanent suppression of potential competition.)

(4) In 1899 the Standard Oil Company of New Jersey, which already held many corporate subsidiaries — most of which were transferred to it in the 1892 partial dissolution of the 1882 trust — acquired nineteen major corporations including their subsidiaries, nearly all of which were commonly, and completely, owned by former and present certificate holders in the 1882 trust, which was partially dissolved in 1892. This supercombination into the New Jersey holding company perpetually suppressed potential competition among these twenty corporations and among many of their subsidiary corporations that may be deemed to have joined this supercombination in violation of section 1 of the Sherman Act. Combining anew in 1899 was illegal, even if merely continuing the effects of a trust created before July 1890, would not have been deemed to violate section 1 of the Sherman Act.

Of course, the new combination of 1899 was not merely one whereby a going Standard Oil Trust from 1882–99 effected newly ratified legal arrangements to merge all of its other corporations into one member serving as a holding company, so that the almost permanent suppression of perpetual competition by the trustees became perpetual by the vehicle of a holding corporation with eternal life. In the years preceding 1899, various state governments were demonstrating increasing hostility to the trust form of control over corporations created by their particular state. Some other states would almost assuredly have initiated legal proceedings to force a dissolution of the legally questionable trusteeship if the State of Ohio had not already, as of 1892, ordered a dissolution to effect the restoration of direct stockholder control to Ohio Standard. The upshot, of course, is that a *bona fide,* rather than a solely partial, dissolution of the Standard Oil Trust in 1892 would indeed have restored direct ownership, albeit with commonality, following a ratable distribution in the stock of even more corporations. Hence such dissolution would have created the status of potential competitors for even more corporations than were eventually granted this status in 1911 under the Sherman Act. But even the partial dissolution forced a distribution of stock to stockholders owning a majority of outstanding shares of twenty reconstituted corporations. The subsequent act of combining these twenty corporations perpetually suppressed the possibility that any of these potential competitors would ever engage in active competition against another. (The going combination of the New Jersey holding company was an enlarged and continued combination that violated the Sherman Act for reason of its illegal origin as a perpetual suppression of potential competition in 1889 in violation of the Sherman Act.)

(5) As of the date at which the complaint was filed against it, November 1906, the New Jersey holding company was in fact a combination that actually exerted its power to restrain trade, and nontrivially. This restraining of trade was illegal even if a showing that the act of combination of 1899, which created centralized power perpetually to suppress potential competition, was not a sufficient offense to constitute a violation of section 1 of the Sherman Act.

Perhaps a showing of the substantial ineffectiveness of competition in the oil business, in terms of either conduct or performance, would suffice to persuade the court that an enhancement in potential competition was required and that any diminution of potential competition in most fields of the oil business indeed constituted a combination in restraint of trade. The following considerations evidenced the exertion of power over price: (a) Since the 1899 formation of the holding company, several important acquisitions of independent pipelines, refining companies, crude producers, and marketers had been made by an enterprise which continued to transport by pipeline, to refine, and to market over 80 percent of the refined products in the United States. (b) The holding company actually suppressed competition among its marketing corporations by assigning the territory of an entire state — except Missouri, which is divided along an east-west line — to a particular marketing corporation while excluding all its other affiliates. (c) The high ratio of profit on investment provided convincing evidence that power over price was in fact exercised, and the vast absolute level of profits made it improbable that the market was so limited in size relative to operating economies of scale that the rate of return was merely an inevitable return to superior efficiency obtained by a firm whose past acquisitions had made such efficiency possible.

(6) Particularly when it was recalled that Standard occupied in excess of 80 percent of most oil markets, the contentions raised in points (1) through (5) were sufficient to find the New Jersey holding company to be monopolizing illegally by combination, under section 2 of the Sherman Act, even if none of the contentions raised above would have constituted an illegal combination in restraint of trade.

(7) The vast size of the New Jersey holding company, and its nationwide domination of the oil industry in all regions and in virtually all branches, provided power to wrongfully, but not necessarily illegally, exclude others, particularly from nondiscriminatory access to the pipeline transport of crude oil and the railroad transport of refined products, but also from nondiscriminatory access to particular geographical market outlets. Such a power to exclude constituted illegal monopolizing in violation of section 2 of the Sherman Act. Proof of this power to exclude others, that is, to raise barriers to entry, was bolstered by the assemblage of some substantial evidence that the power to exclude had been actually exerted to deny

nondiscriminatory access. The possession, and exercise, of power to exclude wrongfully enabled Standard not only to maintain and elevate its power over price and its control of supply but also to delimit opportunity for the exercise of new initiatives, such as those which independents had pioneered and proved feasible, first with crude pipelines and then with product pipelines. Monopolizing based on the possession and exercise of the power to wrongfully exclude, was alleged to violate section 2 of the Sherman Act, even if monopolizing that was merely consequent to combination did not violate section 2.

Findings and Decision of the Circuit Court

The Eighth Circuit Court, meeting in St. Louis, reached its decision upholding the government's complaint on grounds that remarkably paralleled the Supreme Court's decision in *Northern Securities*. (Indeed two justices in the four-judge panel were among the panel of the Eighth Circuit Court, meeting in Minneapolis, which had earlier found the Northern Securities holding company to be an illegal combination.) The main differences were two: (1) The test required for illegal restraint of trade consequent to combination was that of a "direct *and substantial* restriction of competition."[31] (italics added.) (2) A substantial restriction could be found in a combination which perpetually united "potentially competitive corporations,"[32] not just in a combination that united actually competitive members. Indeed, in the light of the fact that Hill, Morgan, and their associates had gained control of both roads long before they placed their stock in Northern Securities, the court corrected its prior description of the market status of the two railroads to that of being "natural and potential competitors."[33]

The circuit court focussed its decision essentially upon the elements of combination in the formation of the Standard Oil of New Jersey holding company. The court decided that it was unnecessary to determine whether combinative acts preceding July 2, 1890 violated the common law. It held, however, that such prior acts could be used as evidence of the dominant purpose and probable effects of forming and continuing the operation of the "stockholding trust of 1899," since the effects of earlier combination would have violated the Sherman Act had they been undertaken after July 2, 1890. The court's findings of fact suggest that the court was impressed with the growth in the par value of the capital stock of the combined companies from $100,000,000 in 1899 to over $150,000,000 in 1908 — a rate of growth substantially below that for net worth, as the court was undoubtedly aware.

---

[31] *U.S.* v. *Standard Oil Co. of New Jersey,* 173 F. 177 (C.C., E.D. Mo., 1909) at 188.
[32] *Id.,* at 189.
[33] *Id.,* at 186.

The court was also impressed with the fact that the principal corporation and its more than thirty chief subsidiaries possessed such a vast ownership of refining capacity, gathering and trunk-pipeline mileage, and bulk selling stations as to enable the combination to hold a commanding proportion of the entire nation's business in many branches of the oil business — pipeline transport, refinery production, tank-car shipment of manufactured products, domestically marketed illuminating oil and naphtha (gasoline), and lubricating oil for railroads.

The court found that the principal corporation was using the power acquired along with the commanding volume of business in oil to prevent competition among its subsidiaries and between the subsidiaries and itself, and that the corporation thereby controlled the purchase price of crude oil, rates for its transportation, and the selling prices of its products. The court also found that *many* of the combined companies "were capable of competing with each other" and "would have been actively competitive if they had been owned by different individuals or different groups of individuals."[34] It proceeded to illustrate the situation by the instance of the principal company with refineries in New Jersey, Maryland, and West Virginia and of the subsidiary company, New York Standard, with refineries in New York, where both companies drew crude oil from, and marketed much of the refined product outside of, "the states in which their refineries were located."[35] It found that these companies and many other pairs of companies had been prevented by the formation of the holding company from competing in each other's territory or industrial branches.[36]

In reaching its decision, the circuit court rejected the two major propositions of the defendants: (1) The competition-restraining effect of combination among private manufacturing corporations lacked a substantiality analogous to combinations among railroads, which owed a duty to the public. (2) any restraint of trade resulting from the 1899 transfer of stock to the Standard Oil of New Jersey holding company was neither direct, immediate, nor substantial because the owners of that stock had exercised the same powers of restraint before the transfer.

The circuit court summarily disposed of the first contention by referring to the power and purposes of Congress to regulate interstate and foreign commerce in all fields. It dramatized its point by again referring to size. "The mischief against which the law was leveled is not less threatening from a vast combination of private corporations owning and using in interstate

---

[34] *Id.,* at 185.

[35] *Id.,* at 185.

[36] Consciously, or otherwise, the circuit court was employing "capable of competing" or potentially competing in two senses: (1) New Jersey Standard and New York Standard would, probably, eventually be owned by stockholders of divergent interests, and (2) either would, probably, thereafter establish bulk marketing stations in the previously exclusive marketing territory of the other, thus making the companies "actively competitive."

and foreign commerce property worth hundreds of millions of dollars than from a combination of two railroad companies."[37]

The circuit court devoted more effort and creativity to meeting the "persuasive force" with which the defendants offered their second and most important contention. It focused its answer and legal determination upon long-run considerations, namely, the perpetual suppression of potential competition among the combined companies. It sideswiped the "immediacy" point by asserting, undoubtedly correctly, but assuredly less importantly, that the power vested in a holding company to manage the fixing of prices, coordinate the division of responsibility, and prevent competition "was greater, more easily and quickly exercised, and hence more effective than it could have been in 3,000 scattered stockholders."[38] The court shifted to longer-run competitive effects by drawing a parallel between the permanent suppression of potential competition accomplished by the trust agreement of 1882 and that accomplished by the holding-company combination of 1899. Combinations formed by the transfer of ownership are "less liable to be destroyed, more reliable and permanent that those springing from the joint ownership of 3,000 stockholders of each corporation. There is much more probability that corporations potentially competitive will separate and compete, when each of their stockholders has a separate certificate of his shares of stock in each corporation, which he is free to sell, than when a majority of the stock of each of the corporations is held by a single corporation, which has the power to vote the stock and to operate them."[39]

The absolute power conferred on the Standard Oil Company of New Jersey to prevent competition permanently among, and with, the corporations acquired by the stock transfer of 1899, many[40] of which were potentially competitive, constituted grounds for finding a "direct and substantial restriction of competition"[41] and hence an illegal combination in violation of section 1 of the Sherman Act.

The circuit court's handling of the charge under section 2 was anticlimactic and essentially double counting. The court waved aside, as moot, the government's averments concerning the wrongful exclusion of others — averments based upon the achieved possession of the power to exclude and

---

[37] *U.S.* v. *Standard Oil Co. of New Jersey,* 173 F. 177 (C.C., E.D. Mo., 1909), at 188.

[38] *Id.,* at 189. We must recall that pressures were mounting by the end of 1897 to complete a *bona fide* liquidation of the trust, only partially undertaken in 1892 when ten dominating families converted their bare majority of outstanding trust certificates for a proportionate distribution of stock in the 20 Standard companies which had been consolidated out of 84.

[39] *Id.,* at 189.

[40] The Northwestern Ohio Natural Gas Co., one of the 19, along with other natural gas companies were not proved to be engaged in petroleum, the field in which the combination was charged in the complaint.

[41] *U.S.* v. *Standard Oil Co. of New Jersey,* 173 F. 177 (C.C., E.D., Mo., 1909), at 189.

upon concrete acts of actual exclusion. Possibly the court did so because the exceedingly long record of hotly contested facts and interpretation of facts, had been generated by the court's appointed special examiner — not the trial judges of the court.

The court held that the gist of the violation of the second section was not monopolizing by a single corporation, but combining to monopolize. Since the evidence was uncontested that the Standard Oil of New Jersey holding company secured, and continued to enjoy, a very substantial part of the commerce in petroleum products, and since the defendants were found to have combined illegally, the court necessarily also found that the Standard Oil of New Jersey holding company was a combination to monopolize in violation of section 2 of the Sherman Act.

The decree ordered by the court mirrored the one which the earlier Eighth Circuit Court had directed at the Northern Securities combination and which the Supreme Court had affirmed. Standard Oil Company of New Jersey was not prohibited from distributing ratably among its shareholders the stock of thirty-seven subsidiary companies found to be parties of the combination.[42] To produce assurance that the holding company would divest itself of ownership in these companies, the holding company was enjoined from voting the stock of the thirty-seven named subsidiaries and from exercising any control or supervision over these subsidiaries, while the thirty-seven named subsidiaries were enjoined from paying any dividends to the holding company and from permitting the holding company to vote their stock or exercise any control whatsoever over their corporate acts.[43]

Thus the government had been granted all the essential relief it had requested. Frank B. Kellogg was completely satisfied.[44]

Standard's Appeal to the Supreme Court

The defendants immediately appealed to the Supreme Court. Standard's principal contention was that neither the trust of 1882 nor, more importantly, the formation of the holding company of 1899 constituted a combi-

[42] The bill of complaint was dismissed with respect to 33 of the original corporate defendants for want of sufficient proof of their participation in the combination in the field of petroleum. Of the dismissed companies, 16 were natural gas companies, 10 had actually been liquidated prior to the filing of the bill of complaint, and 7 were companies in which the holding company failed to own a majority of shares. The government protested none of the exclusions, although the government may have been displeased with New Jersey Standard's continued holding of 42% of the stock of Tidewater Oil Co. — a major East Coast refiner with a pipeline to Appalachian crude.

[43] *Id.,* at 92–93.

[44] Kellogg wrote to his friend in Africa, the former President Theodore Roosevelt: "The opinion was . . . unanimous . . . It was a complete victory, the decree granting the Government everything asked . . . I feel [so] sure that the judgment is based on sound principles of law as well as wise and farseeing principles of public policy and economy that I fail to see how it can be reversed." See David Bryn-Jones, *op. cit.,* p. 65.

nation in restraint of trade since there was no "combination of *independent or competing* concerns or corporations."[45] Counsel for Standard contended that the circuit court's reasoning with respect to illegal combination represented an erroneous and "entirely new interpretation" of the Sherman Act, since the reasoning was based solely on the proposition that "the various corporations were *potentially* competitive, and the probability of their becoming actually competitive was lessened by the substitution of the ownership of the stock of the separate companies by [Standard Oil Co. of New Jersey] for their ownership by three thousand or more stockholders."[46] Standard's counsel objected further that "potential competition is a term borrowed from economics and means that the field is open to newcomers," a term that "the Court below used to express the fact that two corporations engaged in the same business are *naturally* competitive regardless of their origin and ownership."[47]

Counsel for Standard had already proposed that the strictures against combinations in restraint of trade were limited to contractual combinations working through executory agreements,[48] except for competing quasi-public corporations, such as transcontinental railroads, which assumed an implicit obligation to maintain a separate and independent existence.[49] But even if the unification of the ownership of manufacturing corporations might be held to restrain trade, such would be true only if the firms combined were in actual competition. The defendant corporations, which were combined into Standard Oil Company of New Jersey in 1899, were all *commonly owned* — excepting some minor instances, in which the common owners held less than 100 percent of the ownership — and *noncompeting* corporations, as was also the situation prior to formation of the trust of 1882. "A transaction which makes the joint ownership of properties of a single business, and therefore non-competitive [business], more convenient, effective, reliable and permanent is condemned because its *tendency* is to obstruct its disintegration into diverse ownerships of the various corporations, and thereby *possibly* bring competition between them into play."[50] (Italics added.)

In oral argument, John G. Johnson, Standard's Philadelphia lawyer, contended that for years Standard Oil had been essentially a single business. The reasons why a single corporation had not been formed in lieu of the trust of 1882 "was that one corporation, as the policies of the state then were, could not have sufficient capital to own the whole; and some of the States would not permit them to own a pipeline or do such business under a corporate charter."[51] After offering some hypothetical examples, Johnson

---

[45] Brief for Appellants in the Supreme Court, *op. cit.*, Vol. I — Law, p. 16.
[46] *Id.*, p. 73.
[47] *Id.*, p. 73.
[48] *Id.*, p. 49.
[49] *Id.*, p. 70.
[50] *Id.*, p. 75.
[51] *Oral Argument on Behalf of Appellants, op. cit.*, p. 100.

reached his climax: "And now we come to the very heart of the government's contention . . . the destruction of potential competition. Such destruction is only a wrong to the State if the State is entitled to the competition. Here were these people with a property which it was necessary for them to hold together in order that they might get out of it the best value. And because of that purpose and that purpose alone — not to monopolize, not to restrain; they had nothing to gain from that, but in order that the title might be vested in them — they did this thing, they committed an offense, because they deprived the government at some future time of potential competition!"[52]

Concerning "potential competition," Johnson reasoned . . . "Government has no right to speculate upon a dismemberment or a destruction of the value of my property by my death . . . . The argument comes to this: It is not wrong in the present; but simply because, while not monopolizing anything at the present; at some future time I may be so unfortunate as to want to sell and be obliged to sell my property, I shall have to sell it in a ruinous way. Is it likely that these people will sell their property so it will be disintegrated?"[53]

Counsel John Milburn had made the first half of Standard's pleading, by proposing that the enterprise's forty-year history had to be viewed in terms of a vast endeavor by a fully legal combination to organize, rationalize, and continually reorganize the petroleum industry so as to reduce costs and prices while elevating quality. Milburn had concluded by questioning whether the cost of sacrificing the efficiencies of coordination would be compensated by the dubious benefits of dissolution. "Should stockholdings of such immense total value [estimated at $600,000,000] be revolutionized merely to convert an equitable ownership of thirty-seven corporations into a legal ownership?"[54]

As a second point, Standard strenuously contended that the decree for dissolution should not have been made to apply to several corporations which Standard created either preceding the formation of the 1899 holding company, such as Indiana Standard, or afterwards, such as Prairie Oil and Gas. The final major but lower-keyed thrust to Standard's appeal concerned its objection to the circuit court's basis for determining a violation under section 2 of the Sherman Act. Counsel for Standard contended that the offense of monopolizing, whether done individually or pursuant to combination or conspiracy, was directed solely at "the exclusion of others from a trade by *illegal* means."[55] (Italics added.)

The foundation stone of our contention [said counsel] is that the acquisition of existing plants or properties, however extensive, though made to

[52] *Id.,* p. 103.
[53] *Id.,* pp. 103–104.
[54] *Id.,* p. 62.
[55] Brief for Appellant, *op. cit.,* Vol. I — Law, p. 85.

obtain their trade and eliminate their competition, is not a monopoly at common law or monopolizing under the Sherman Act, in the absence of exclusion of others from the trade by conspiracies to that end or contracts in restraint of trade on an elaborate and effective scale, or other systematic, wrongful, tortious or illegal acts, and that when such monopolizing is present the remedy of the Act is to prohibit the offending conspiracies, contracts and illegal acts or means of exclusion, leaving the individual or corporation with the properties or plants that have been acquired or created shorn of the monopolizing elements in the conduct of the business.[56]

Noting that the circuit court had made no findings with respect to the issue of illegal means of exclusion but had simply found that illegal unification produced an illegal combination to monopolize, defendants' counsel concluded that the only established basis for the circuit court's decision and decree would disappear under section 2 if the defendants' position denying illegality of combination under section 1 were upheld. "But so much has been said, and will no doubt be said in the presentation of this case respecting monopolization," that counsel felt it was justified "to travel far enough outside the actual decision" to discuss the issue of alleged exclusion.[57] Counsel contended the record would show that Standard had not engaged in any *illegal* means of exclusion in any of three principal classes alleged: (1) control of pipelines, (2) railroad discriminations, and (3) unfair competition.

The Government's Argument to the Supreme Court

On appeal, the government based its major argument on the key finding of the circuit court to the effect that the 1899 absorptions by the New Jersey holding corporation constituted an illegal combination in restraint of trade, by effecting a perpetual and substantial restriction of potential competition among the combined firms. To be sure, in the course of oral argument, the government contended that the trust agreements of 1882 and the only partial dissolution of 1892 — in response to the judgment of violation of both Ohio's corporate law and common law on monopoly — provided allegedly illegal vehicles whereby was preserved a common ownership of separate corporations that were not actually competing, and of which so much was made by counsel for the defendants.

The government additionally contended that the combination's power to elevate price and restrict output, a power consequent to the restraint of competition among the constituent corporations, was enhanced by the presence of combination in *all* sections of the country and in *most* branches of the industry. But since evidence with respect to power to exclude rivals by denying them nondiscriminatory terms (in shipping crude by pipeline

[56] *Id.,* pp. 98–99.
[57] *Id.,* p. 112.

and both crude and finished products by railroad) and equal opportunities (to construct gathering and trunk lines, purchase crude from local oil pools, and market refined products in local bulk station and tank-wagon markets) overlaps with the argument on these points under the charge of monopolization, we shall temporarily defer discussion.

The government constructed a line of strategic retreats in its arguments. Indeed, its basic contention on appeal constituted in itself a retreat from an original proposition that it tactically attempted to readvance at one point in its oral argument: The trust of 1882 constituted a combination in unreasonable restraint of trade under federal common law because what violated the common law on monopoly in the intrastate trade of Ohio from 1882 to 1892 must have violated the federal common law of monopoly in interstate trade.[58] Considering the fact that no decision ordering dissolution of a manufacturing combination had been rendered by the Supreme Court during the first twenty years of the Sherman Act, it is perfectly understandable that the government employed a strategy embracing multiple theories of the case.

In line with its strategy of retreats in its theory of the case, the government argued that, even if the evidence of dominance — power to control price — achieved merely by acquisitions rather than pure natural growth could not be found to constitute an illegal combination in restraint of trade, it could be found an illegal combination to monopolize. That is, the charge of combination to monopolize could rest solely on the acts of fusion, where the result "tends to monopoly." In the words of the government, "The monopoly most commonly known in this country, and which debates in Congress show were intended to be prohibited by the act, were those acquired by combination (by purchase or otherwise) of competing concerns."[59] Acts of wrongful exclusion, let alone illegal exclusion, need not be shown to meet the condition of illegal combination to monopolize under section 2 of the Sherman Act, but the government was prepared to meet such a collateral condition, if necessary.

In support of the circuit court's finding of illegal combination in restraint of trade, Frank B. Kellogg sought to stress in a number of ways the substantiality of the restriction of competition that had been going on ever since potential competition among the original and additionally acquired corporations had been permanently suppressed by the trust of 1882 and its successors — the merely *partial* dissolution from 1892–99 and the holding company's absorptions since 1899. Kellogg attributed the great growth in profits, dividends, and net worth in the combination to the power of the enterprise to control price, a power based on the original combination and

---

[58] *Transcript of the Oral Argument of Frank B. Kellogg on Behalf of the United States, op. cit.,* p. 20.

[59] *Reply Brief for the United States, op. cit.,* p. 39.

its subsequent acquisitions.[60] Kellogg argued that, contrary to "romances," the present size of Standard was not "the result of natural growth in business, guided by a master mind."[61] Both the export business of refined products and gathering pipelines had been well developed by independents in 1872. The feasibility of constructing long-distance pipelines over the Allegheny Mountains to transport crude and refined products were first demonstrated by independents.[62]

Kellogg stressed that the potential competition permanently suppressed by the trust of 1882 was that of the separate — albeit, frequently 100 percent commonly owned — but powerful corporations of the Standard alliance of the 1870's. The corporations unified into the trust of 1882 had gained supremacy over outsiders by acquiring a dominant position in gathering lines, acquiescence of the Tidewater Oil Company and its Tidewater Pipe Line Company, and a dominating position over the structuring of railroad rates with respect to members of the alliance and independents. The country was divided up so as to assign an exclusive marketing territory to each of the firms in the trust, and thus potential competition was permanently eliminated. Moreover, whenever an important independent pipeline, refinery, or marketer emerged — integrated or otherwise — efforts were made, very frequently successfully, to lure its sale to the trust, or its successors — the partially dissolved trust and the New Jersey holding company.

Basing his oral argument most heavily on the charge under section 1, Kellogg contended that Standard exaggerated in distinguishing the degree of common ownership and control in the Standard corporations from that in the Great Northern and Northern Pacific. First Kellogg contended that a ratable dissolution of Northern Securities was in fact carried out following the Sherman Act decrees but that no one suggested the succeeding symmetrically positioned common owners of each road were thereby entitled to effect a new holding corporation combining the two roads. Second, Kellogg pointed out that 30 percent of the shares of both Waters-Pierce (Standard's marketer in the Southwest) and Galena-Signal (Standard's specialist in railroad lubricants) were owned by outsiders, thus technically preventing the thirty-seven defendant companies from being fully owned in common. In the case of both Northern Securities and Standard Oil Company of New Jersey, a holding company "was able to take the place of a large number of stockholders, who might sell out or whose power might be destroyed by death, and perpetuate in a Jersey corporation the power to control."[63]

[60] *Id.*, p. 6.
[61] *Id.*, p. 2.
[62] *Id.*, p. 11.
[63] *Id.*, p. 70.

With respect to section 2, the government's argument on the charge of monopolization was essentially that monopolization was secured through combination and was perpetuated through the power to exclude provided by the size and scope of the combination. "We believe that the defendants have acquired a monopoly by means of a combination of the principal manufacturing concerns through a holding company; that they have, by reason of the very size of the combination, been able to maintain this monopoly through unfair methods of competition, discriminatory freight rates, and other means set forth in the proofs."[64]

In the course of oral argument, Kellogg reviewed both the contemporary and more ancient patterns of discriminatory freight rates, several of which had already been found improper, and even illegal, by decisions of either the courts or the Interstate Commerce Commission. Kellogg suggested, however, that regulations and injunctions would be of only limited effectiveness in curbing the power of a unified Standard to obtain favored treatment by the railroads. Kellogg cited an instance of what today would be called reciprocal buying. At very high rates of profits for one subsidiary, Standard supplied 97½ percent of all railroad lubricating requirements despite strenuous competitive efforts, at lower prices, by independents. The Tidewater Railroad, owned by a Standard principal, Henry H. Rogers, was the only railroad cited by Standard to be lubricated by another concern.[65]

Standard was charged with having denied access to its trunk pipelines, particularly by erecting so-called delivery points for repiping at villages on the borders of Pennsylvania with New York, New Jersey, and Maryland to avoid compliance with the Hepburn Law.[66] Kellogg cited the expensive harassment that Standard had practiced to thwart construction of both the Tidewater Pipe Line Company and the United States Pipe Line Company, the predecessor of Pure Oil. Standard acquired refineries that otherwise would have received their crude through the Tidewater Pipe Line Company and would have shipped their product through the United States Pipe Line Company. Strips of real estate across the planned rights of way were acquired by Standard to delay construction. Furthermore, the railroads in New Jersey, where no right of eminent domain existed for pipelines kept the independent pipelines, but not Standard, from reaching New York harbor. By contrast, the Prairie Oil and Gas Company was built on the railroad's right of way virtually the entire distance from Oklahoma to Standard's refinery at Whiting, Indiana.[67] Finally, the price of Appalachian crude for the western Pennsylvania suppliers and owners of the United States Pipe Line was elevated sharply relative to the price of export kerosene for ap-

[64] *Reply Brief for the United States, op. cit.,* p. 39.
[65] *Transcript of the Oral Argument of Frank B. Kellogg, op. cit.,* p. 44.
[66] *Id.,* p. 37.
[67] *Id.,* pp. 31–34.

proximately an entire year in an effort, which proved unsuccessful, to generate a regional price squeeze that would force a union with Standard.[68]

The Standard Companies in California, first Iowa Standard, then California Standard, took a sharp loss in Southern California during 1902–04, when the independents were doing 15 to 33 percent of the business.[69] Kellogg stressed in this regard what today would be called the conglomerate nature of Standard's operation: "Why, the business of Standard Oil Co. of California is absolutely foreign to the business of the other [Standard] companies as my business is to that of any other counsellor of law. [Standard] is holding together in corporate form these companies scattered all over the country, through which they may put the price so low in one place as to ruin a competitor, while raising it in another."[70] Kellogg contended that "great power enables [Standard] to use the unfair methods and to do acts, some of them perhaps illegal and some not illegal in and of themselves, which would not be [socially] harmful in the hands of the corner-grocery man as against his neighbor."[71]

Kellogg opposed, however, on two grounds any relief that would be limited solely to enjoining wrongful acts: (1) Potential competition would remain suppressed among members of the combination.[72] (2) The regulatory method is not likely to be adequately effective, and it involves an excessive "degree of paternalism."[73] Kellogg's advice was to take away the power by separating "the companies which Standard Oil of New Jersey controls by stock ownership; and no one of them is big enough or covers territory enough to enable it to carry on this sort of predatory competition."[74]

Kellogg noted that Standard Oil companies had been excluded from the states of Texas, Tennessee, and Missouri for violating state antitrust laws, but with little effect. Only particular Standard companies could be excluded from conducting intrastate business. The Standard combine could still ship into these states and market with another Standard company.[75] The inherent ineffectiveness of state antitrust provided additional grounds for Kellogg to urge that the Court reexamine the purpose of Congress with respect to combinations and trusts in enacting the Sherman Act.

Basically, the monopolizing abuses consequent to combination, which by raising barriers to potential competition from outsiders, served to maintain,

---

[68] *Id.,* p. 34.
[69] *Id.,* pp. 27–29.
[70] *Id.,* p. 30.
[71] *Id.,* p. 30.
[72] *Id.,* p. 31.
[73] *Id.,* p. 29.
[74] *Id.,* p. 68.
[75] E.g., Louisiana Standard took over marketing in Tennessee when Kentucky Standard was banned.

and even accentuate, power to control price, merely increased compulsion for dissolving the combination, which perpetually suppressed potential competition among participating corporations within the combination. As the government argued in its final brief, "so far as this case is concerned, we believe the court has power under Section 1 to declare illegal the combination, thereby causing the [seven individual] defendants to sever their various corporations. This would destroy the monopoly."[76]

Finally, the government contended that no valid reason existed for excusing from the decree those defendant corporations, such as Indiana Standard and Colonial Refining, which were created by the trustees during the years of the invalid trust. The government's proposition, based on a number of legal precedents, was that such corporations were "still separate corporate entities, engaged in business, and by joining the conspiracy their action partook of the same illegality as though they were original parties to it."[77]

This legal issue was never argued orally by either party before the Supreme Court. But the public policy implications might have been interesting had Kellogg contended the following proposition for the government: Corporations or trusts of vast size and substantial market power are legally authorized to create new corporate subsidiaries with productive facilities to supply new markets more effectively and profitably, *provided* that such corporations are "spun off" by a ratable distribution of their stock to shareholders of their creator, so that the created corporation might eventually become a potential competitor of its own creator. Kellogg would undoubtedly have admitted that the Standard group's creation of a major refinery at Whiting, Indiana in 1890, which was designed to process Ohio-Indiana crude, accelerated a substantial reduction in the resources required to distribute, if not the prices charged for, refined products in the Middle West. Given this element of natural growth, he probably would have agreed that Standard's stockholders were entitled to benefit for a time from the lucrative profits made possible by Indiana Standard's unique location. But he is also likely to have urged that the newly created Indiana Standard be immediately freed from ownership by the "combination," in keeping with the public policy of hastening opportunities for more competitive conditions — directly in the Middle West and indirectly elsewhere — and also of increasing opportunities for independent business leadership.[78]

[76] *Reply Brief for the United States, op. cit.,* p. 41.
[77] *Id.,* p. 21.
[78] "The combination of wealth, or corporate acquisition may go to that extent where the individual right and freedom of the citizen may be in danger. It is of the highest importance in the preservation of society, in development and elevation of the race, that the right to earn a livelihood, to engage in any commerce, employment, or labor be kept free and untrammeled. It is not sufficient that the citizen be given merely an opportunity to earn a livelihood; the avenues of commerce and trade should be kept open." Brief for the United States, *op. cit.,* p. 354. See also Frank B. Kellogg, "Results of the Standard Oil Decision," *op. cit.,* p. 729.

Prelude to "The Rule of Reason"

Contrary to Chief Justice White,[79] the government did not contend that *every combination* in restraint of trade violated section 1 of the Sherman Act. The government's proposition was that *every instrumentality,* thus including combinations as much as contracts, which restrained trade by suppressing competition was inhibited by the Sherman Act. "The real point is, not the instrumentality or the scheme used to suppress the competition, but whether competition is thus suppressed and trade restrained and monopolized."[80] The government identified suppression of competition with power "to control the supply and to regulate prices."[81]

The government did not contend that every acquisition of property, including that which merely incidentally eliminated a competitor, constituted a violation of the law. "Each [acquisition] must be determined by its own circumstances and conditions. The oft repeated argument that this construction of the law prevents the formation of partnerships and the legitimate consolidation of business enterprises is fallacious; for the reason that such construction has no application where an enterprise is formed with the honest and legitimate intent to pursue a lawful business and not go beyond the bounds of legitimate combination or directly or *substantially* suppress competition. But whenever that acquisition is a mere cloak to cover the intention of monopolizing commerce, or for the purpose of using it as a weapon to strike down competition, it is illegal. It follows from this that the acquisition of the same property might under some circumstances be legal while under other circumstances it would be illegal."[82] (Italics added.) Shortly preceding its differentiation of legal from illegal acquisitions, the government's brief set forth the additional point: "If the antitrust act is to be made effective, if monopoly is to be stopped, if corporations or holding companies are not to be permitted through their aggregate wealth and power to control all the industries of the country, *the court must adopt a broad and reasonable construction of this act* which will not permit monopoly in whatever form it may be organized."[83] (Italics added.)

In oral argument before the Supreme Court, Kellogg contested the proposition of the defendants that Standard Oil "simply acquired properties in the usual course of business" and by what could be called "natural growth."[84] He pointed out that Standard had acquired at least 225 concerns — 137 refineries and lubricating works; 64 exclusively marketing

---

[79] *Standard Oil Co. of New Jersey* v. *U.S.,* 221 U.S. 1 (1911) at 63.
[80] Brief for the United States, in the Supreme Court of the United States, *Standard Oil Co. of New Jersey* v. *U.S.,* 221 U.S. 1 (1911), p. 304.
[81] *Id.,* p. 353.
[82] *Id.,* p. 355.
[83] *Id.,* p. 353.
[84] *Transcript of the Oral Testimony of Frank B. Kellogg on Behalf of the United States, op. cit.,* p. 26.

contrary to the instructions of this Court, to insert before the words, "re-

Indeed, one of the counsel for Standard, John G. Johnson, in an oral argument before the Supreme Court, accused the government of attempting, contrary to the instructions of this Court, to insert before the words, "restraint of trade," the word "reasonable."[86] Counsel Johnson had previously quoted from a brief apparently offered by the government in the circuit court, "We do not maintain that every sort of restraint of interstate or foreign commerce is denounced by the Sherman Act . . . But when . . . the restraint is a direct consequence of . . . combination . . . and also of a material and substantial character, it is clearly within the meaning of the statute." Immediately thereon, he snapped, "There is the plainest possible statement that the Government does not maintain that every sort of restraint of interstate trade is contrary to the Act; and it must be of a material and substantial character. But why did Congress insert that word "every"? In order to get a definition that was never intended by the legislature, they are obliged to state the definition and withdraw some incidents that would go with it."[87]

In truth, it was Standard's counsel that had pressed "every" in one of its own briefs, hopefully as a means of nullifying the strictures of the Sherman Act with respect to combinations, as distinct from contracts and conspiracies. But a review of the arguments from the bench in *Northern Securities* on the concept of illegal combination in restraint of trade is necessary to fully appreciate the implications.

The Northern Securities holding company had been found to be an unlawful combination in restraint of trade by a mere 5 to 4 decision, and the majority was sustained only with the assistance of Justice Brewer's delimiting concurring opinion. Fearing "that broad and sweeping language of the opinion of the court might tend to unsettle legitimate business enterprises and stifle or retard wholesome business activities,"[88] Brewer distinctly asserted his strongly held view that the Sherman Antitrust Act included not all, but only "unreasonable restraints of trade." "That act, as appears from its title, was leveled at only unlawful restraints and monopolies Congress did not intend to reach and destroy those minor contracts in partial restraint of trade."[89] Brewer had no difficulty in finding unreasonable the destruction of competition consequent to the unification of control of two large railroads. Unification came not via "investment of a single individual of his means" but by the combination of several individuals which employed the "mere instrumentality" of an "artificial person," to hold their stock in the two railroads. "A corporation" reasoned Brewer, "is not en-

---

[85] *Id.* About half of the 225 concerns were acquired before 1882.
[86] Oral Argument on Behalf of Appellants, *op. cit.,* p. 91.
[87] *Id.,* pp. 90–91.
[88] *Northern Securities Co.* v. *U.S.,* 193 U.S. 197 (1904) at 364.
[89] *Id.,* at 362.

dowed with the inalienable rights of a natural person." Brewer contended
that upholding the legality of this $201,000,000 corporation would in effect
authorize a process of further pyramiding of holding companies through
combination and that by means of this process "three or four parties would
be in practical control . . . of the whole transportation system of the
country."[90] Brewer concluded with a final consideration, possessing particular relevance to the Standard Oil of New Jersey's conglomerate holding
of monopolistic subsidiaries: "It must also be remembered that under present conditions a single railroad is, if not a legal, largely a practical monopoly, and the manner by which the control of these two competing roads was
merged in a single corporation broadens and extends such monopoly. I
cannot look upon it as other than an unreasonable combination in restraint
of trade."[91]

Both Justice Harlan, who spoke for the majority, and Justice Holmes,
who spoke for the minority of four in the more important of two dissents,
agreed that Congress had been concerned with vast size in passing the
Sherman Act. But the major contention rested on "every" and "any."
Harlan conceded that many believed "the general business interests will be
best promoted if the rule of competition is not applied. But there are
others who believe that such a rule is more necessary in these days of
enormous wealth than it ever was in any former period of our history."[92]
He went on to repeat phraseology of the Court in *Joint Traffic* to explain
why Congress enacted "the rule of competition" for interstate commerce:
"It is the combination of these large and powerful corporations, covering
vast sections of territory and influencing trade throughout the whole extent
thereof . . . that constitutes the alleged evil."[93] Preceding his review of
state court decisions designed to "show the circumstances under which the
Anti-Trust Act was passed," Harlan remarked, "It may well be assumed
that Congress, when enacting the statute, shared the general apprehension
that a few powerful corporations or combinations sought to obtain, and,
unless restrained, would obtain such absolute control of the entire trade and
commerce of the country as would be detrimental to the general welfare."[94]
Harlan seized on the "every" of section 1 to reach combination through
fusion as well as combination through agreement (contract or conspiracy).
Harlan asserted a number of propositions: (1) The Sherman Act embraces
"every contract, combination or conspiracy, in *whatever form, or whatever
nature*" which directly operates to restrain interstate "trade or commerce."
(Italics added.) (2) The act is not limited to restraints that are unreasonable in their nature, "but embraces *all* direct *restraints* imposed by any

[90] *Id.,* at 363.
[91] *Id.,* at 363.
[92] *Id.,* at 337.
[93] *Id.,* at 338.
[94] *Id.,* at 337.

combination, conspiracy or monopoly,"[95] including combinations of man-ufactures as well as railroads. (3) Every combination that would extinguish competition is made illegal.[96] To establish a violation, it need not be shown that the combination "will result in a total suppression of trade or in a complete monopoly, but it is only essential to show that by its necessary operation it tends to restrain interstate or international trade or commerce or tends to create a monopoly in such trade or commerce and to deprive the peoples of the advantages that flow from free competition."[97]

At several junctures in his dissent, Holmes conceded that Congress was primarily concerned with combinations of size. He contended, however, that by its draftsmanship Congress failed to include only combinations which were large, significant, and unredeemed by social economies, thus including combinations which were small, insignificant, and of potential social benefit. "There is a natural inclination to assume that [the statute] was directed against certain great combinations and to read it in that light. It does not say so. On the contrary, it says 'every' and 'any part.' "[98] And having employed such instances as a merger of two small grocers in inter-state trade and the combination of men into a corporation to build and run a single railroad down a narrow valley between two states, he wrote: "There is a natural feeling that somehow or other the statute meant to strike at combinations great enough to cause just anxiety on the part of those who love their country more than money, while it viewed such little ones as I have supposed with just indifference. This notion, it may be said, somehow breathes from the pores of the act, although it seems to be contra-dicted in every way by the words in detail."[99] To prevent the act from "being construed to mean the universal disintegration of society into single men, Holmes chose to deny that the outlawed "combinations" embraced communities of interest; he held that they only embraced "every" com-binative activity directed at "keeping rivals out of the business and ruining those already in."[100]

Circuit court Judge Sanborn of the trial court in the Standard Oil case arrived at a position in interpreting section 1 of the Sherman Act with respect to combinations that in effect would reach the category of principal Congressional concern — great combinations among powerful corporations which tended to restrain competition — but would concurrently exclude the small, insignificant, or socially useful. After declaring that the purpose of the Sherman Act was to prevent the stifling and *substantial* restrictions of competition in interstate and international commerce, Sanborn asserted the following test of the legality of a combination: "If its necessary effect is but

[95] *Id.*, at 331.
[96] *Id.*, at 331.
[97] *Id.*, at 332.
[98] *Id.*, at 402.
[99] *Id.*, at 407.
[100] *Id.*, at 405.

incidentally or indirectly to restrict competition, while its chief result is to foster the trade and increase the business of those who make and operate it, it is not a violation of the law. But if its necessary effect is to stifle, or directly and *substantially* to restrict free competition . . . it falls under the ban of the act." (Italics added.)[101] It is difficult to read the circuit court's decision in Standard Oil without receiving the impression that the magnitude of the combination supplied the ingredient of *substantiality* necessary to make illegal a combination that conferred power to prevent perpetually *potential* competition among the commonly owned corporations which became subsidiaries of a foster parent, Standard Oil of New Jersey.

Contrary to the strawman erected by Chief Justice White, partly to rationalize his protracted lecture on the necessary use of "the rule of reason" to be used in interpreting violations under the Sherman Act, there exists no convincing indication that the government proposed an interpretation of "every" that would have required "applying its prohibitions to every case within its literal language." Although, in his role as special confidant and advisor to Roosevelt, Kellogg had submitted to the president in the latter part of 1907 a memorandum recommending expanded attacks against major aggrandizements, he had scored the "theorists" who asserted "that all combinations of capital are void under the Sherman Act".[102] Not only had the present appeal been from a circuit court which had ruled a combination to be illegal only when it "directly and substantially" restricted competition; not only had the entire thrust of the government's presentation been to emphasize the scope and magnitude of Standard's history of acquisitions in order to demonstrate the perpetuation of Standard's overwhelmingly substantial powers to restrict competition; but finally, a careful legal craftsman, such as Kellogg, would have shaped his pleading before the supreme court in an effort to win support, rather than hostility, from the three remaining dissenting judges so as to effect a coalition of support with the three judges remaining from the majority in *Northern Securities.*

As we have previously shown, Kellogg's brief, upon defendants' appeal, was unequivocally reasonable with respect to proposing a method for distinguishing legal from illegal suppression of competition associated with the combination of competitors. The government had also urged that, for a full understanding of the congressional meaning of "combination" in 1890, "resort must be had to the history of the times in which it [the statute] was passed. In construing statutes the Court will consider the previous condition of the commerce of the country and the political and social conditions against which the remedial statute is directed."[103]

Kellogg suggested that the Court read the investigation of committees of both state legislatures and Congress as well as the New York State and

[101] *U.S.* v. *Standard Oil Co. of New Jersey,* 173 F., 177, at 188.
[102] David Bryn-Jones, *op. cit.,* p. 79.
[103] *Brief for the United States, op. cit.,* Vol. 1, p. 228.

Illinois State anti-combination opinions in the cases of the sugar and gas trusts, cases which preceded the congressional session of 1890. Indeed, the last two of seventy-odd printed transcript pages of Kellogg's oral argument constituted a plea to the Supreme Court to discover what was disturbing the Congress.

"The Rule of Reason" and Unreasonable Combination

By his recommendation, Kellogg appears to have consciously or unconsciously, spawned Chief Justice White's evocative (but now forgotten?) preface to his famous discourse on the meaning to be accorded the Sherman Act, a preface which begins by referring to the debates of Congress. The antitrust legislation was "thought to be required by . . . the *vast* accumulation of wealth in the hands of corporations and individuals, the enormous development of corporate organization, the facility for combination which such organizations afforded, the fact that the facility was being used, and that combinations known as trusts were being multiplied, and the widespread impression that their power had been and would be exerted to oppress individuals and injure the public generally."[104] (Italics added.)

The "Rule of Reason" holds that undue restraints of trade violate the Sherman Act; but since White concluded that all contracts and combinations which unduly restrict competition — by tending to enhance prices, rather than develop trade — unduly restrain trade, the rule scarcely changed going interpretations with respect to *contracts* in restraint of trade.[105] It may be concluded that the "Rule of Reason" was therefore enunciated, to distinguish combinations which merely incidentally eliminated a competitor, only trivially limited competitive conditions, and reasonably forwarded the development of trade from those which eliminated one or more substantial competitors, unreasonably limited competitive conditions, and merely incidentally forwarded the development of trade.

White's reading of the history of the period to ascertain the purposes of Congress in passing the antitrust law strongly suggests that Congress deemed the preservation of competitive conditions to be a major means for thwarting a growing accumulation of corporate wealth and power. The "process of reasoning" suggests that combinations involving a corporation with a "vast accumulation of wealth" and business would more readily be deemed by White "unreasonably restrictive of competitive conditions" and less readily entered into or performed for the purpose of reasonably forwarding personal interest and developing trade."[106] Where they were not alleged

[104] *Standard Oil Company of New Jersey* v. *U.S.*, 221 U.S. 1, at 50.

[105] The nature and character of the contracts in both *Freight Association* (166 U.S. 290 [1897]) and *Joint Traffic Association* (171 U.S. 505 [1898]) was such, as White saw them, that "reasoning" created a conclusive presumption as to their "unreasonableness" in purpose and effect — the enhancement of price. 221 U.S. 1, at 64–65.

[106] *Id.*, at 58.

to create economies of scale in processing costs or product improvements, such combinations would face still greater difficulty in rebutting the *prima facie* presumptions of "tending to bring about the evils, such as enhancement of prices, which were considered to be against public policy."[107] Indeed, even a modest tendency to enhance prices — say, that resulting from a combination which suppresses merely potential competition — might be reasoned to create a *prima facie* presumption difficult to rebut where "surrounding circumstances" evidence both that (a) the existing competition is insufficient and (b) the business of the combination is "vast."[108]

Unreasonable Combination and the Standard Oil Decision

The unanimous decision of Chief Justice White[109] is thoroughly permeated by his repeated reference to the "vast" size of the combination, which he cannot attribute to "natural growth." Indeed, he employs the descriptive term "vast" on five different occasions: "vast accumulation of property which it owns and controls";[110] "vast business which the defendants control";[111] "vast amount of property and the possibilities of far reaching control";[112] "enlarging the capital stock of the New Jersey company and giving it the vast power";[113] and "the unification of power and control over petroleum and its products which was the inevitable result of the combining in the New Jersey corporation . . . of the stocks of so many other corporations, aggregating so vast a capital."[114]

In a manner which outdid the circuit court, the Chief Justice made the extensiveness of the combination all the more compelling by devoting parts of three pages to listing the corporations that became parties to the trust agreement of 1882,[115] parts of four pages to the corporations and their capitalizations held by the trust in 1888,[116] and parts of two pages to the

---

[107] *Id.,* at 58.

[108] Incidentally, economic logic would support the use of volume of business in selecting cases and reaching decisions concerning the substantiality of effect if resources for enforcement and redress are to be economized. Both "consumer surplus" and the "deadweight loss of monopoly" are functions of both volume of business and price-cost margins. Even a modest reduction in the price-cost margin can effect a substantial gain in consumer welfare if the volume of business is great. Moreover, the discounted stream of benefits of the possibly long-delayed benefits from restoring, or maintaining, increments of potential competition will be functionally related to the volume of business.

[109] Justice Harlan merely objected to the "Rule of Reason." 221 U.S. 1 (1911), at 82–106.

[110] *Id.,* at 47.

[111] *Id.,* at 48.

[112] *Id.,* at 70.

[113] *Id.,* at 71.

[114] *Id.,* at 75.

[115] *Id.,* at 34–36.

[116] *Id.,* at 37–40.

corporations and their capitalizations held with majority control by the New Jersey Corporation as of 1906.[117]

On the other hand, in sharp contrast to the circuit court, White supplied surprisingly little information on the percentage of the market occupied by Standard Oil in various branches of the petroleum industry. The only specific reference to share of the market appeared as part of his recapitulation of averments in the government's bill of complaint to the effect that the combination between 1870 and 1882 "had obtained a complete mastery over the oil industry, controlling 90 percent of the business of producing [sic! purchasing?], shipping, refining, and selling petroleum, and thus was able to fix the price of crude and refined petroleum."[118] To be sure, Standard's dominance in the market of the oil industry in all branches (save for crude production) and all sections of the country was common knowledge, but only one other reference was made by White to control over price. In a final paragraph of his decision, prior to taking up a discussion of the remedy, he wrote: "As substantial power over the crude product was the inevitable result of the absolute control which existed over the refined product, the monopolization of the one carries with it power to control the other . . ."[119]

White was impressed with the substantial growth in assets that had occurred in the ten years following the already extensive consolidation of properties into the New Jersey holding company, "despite enormous dividends and despite the dropping out of certain corporations enumerated in the decree below."[120] In White's judgment, the implicitly high profits[121] which made possible such a growth in Standard's property gave to the New Jersey Corporation as compared with the trust "an enlarged and more perfect sway and control over the trade and commerce in petroleum and its products."[122] Such were the considerations, said White, which caused the court below to hold that the transfer of stock and of control over other Standard corporations to the New Jersey Corporation "operated to destroy the 'potentiality of competition' which otherwise would have existed [among the commonly owned corporations] to such an extent"[123] as to be a combination in restraint of trade and also to be "an attempt to monopolize and a monopolization bringing about a perennial violation of the second section."[124]

[117] *Id.*, at 72–73.
[118] *Id.*, at 33.
[119] *Id.*, at 77.
[120] *Id.*, at 71.
[121] John G. Milburn, in oral argument for Standard, stated that Standard averaged a 14 percent rate of return on net worth from 1882–97 and 25 percent after 1900. Oral Argument on Behalf of Appellants, *op. cit.*, p. 59.
[122] 221 U.S. 1, at 71.
[123] *Id.*, at 74.
[124] *Id.*, at 74. The circuit court had actually asserted, by a process which I referred to above as double counting, that the gist of the government's charge under the

White reasoned that the conclusions of the lower court were especially correct because the unification of power and control over petroleum in the New Jersey corporation, consequent to the combination of so many other corporations with so vast a capital, gave rise at least to the *prima facie* presumption, "not of normal methods of industrial development," but of an intent to use the new means of combination to gain greater power than would have been obtained with normal methods, a power obtained by excluding[125] others from the trade and by centralizing perpetual control in a combination over petroleum.

White found no countervailing circumstances to overcome the *"prima facie* presumption of intent to restrain trade, to monopolize, and to bring about monopolization." Instead he found reinforcing considerations for judging it conclusive. First, there was the long history of conduct preceding the formation of the New Jersey corporation, from which could be inferred an unmistakable intent to restrict competition. Second, such an intent was

---

second section was "combination to monopolize." Perhaps Justice White coupled the charge of "monopolization" with "combination in restraint of trade" for two reasons: (1) to signify the presence of a stronger element of both intent and power to suppress competition (possibly also subsuming the competition of "outsiders", but his only reference to excluding outsiders [at 78] concerns the period prior to the trust of 1882); and (2) to emphasize that merely injuctive relief, such as that granted in *Swift* v. *U.S.* (196 U.S. 375 [1905]) against a combination would not suffice where the monopolization was "perennial." But I am not strongly persuaded by these explanations of mine. The tight combination into a holding company in Standard Oil could only be effectively corrected by dissolution, and an economically, and socially corrosive intent to suppress competition unduly could be inferred equally strongly from the magnitude of tight combination in restraint of trade, unless "monopolization" was merely a synonym for the condition of ongoing ineffectiveness of competition against which the elimination of potential competition might have been, and its restoration might be, judged "substantial." The coupling of multiple phrases of offense with the Sherman Act suggest more the comfortable habit of a "litany" to this investigator.
In his discourse on the "Rule of Reason," White had suggested no differing tests, as distinct from acts, in distinguishing illegal restraints of trade from illegal monopolizing. "In other words, having by the first section forbidden all means of monopolizing trade, that is, unduly restraining it by means of every contract, combination, etc., the section seeks, *if possible,* to make the prohibitions of the act all the more complete and perfect by embracing all attempts to reach the end prohibited by the first section, that is restraints of trade, by any attempt to monopolize, or monopolization thereof, even although *the acts* by which such results are attempted to be brought about or are brought about be not embraced within the general enumeration of the first section." (*Id.,* at 61, italics added) See also Hugh B. Cox, *op. cit.*
125 I would have to presume that White was primarily referring to others, distinct from the "community of stockholder interests," who would eventually have gained control of various Standard corporations consequent to sales of stock in individual companies held directly by their owners. But White may have also taken judicial notice of the averments in the government complaint (and collected record of supporting evidence which was pressed both in the government's briefs and the oral testimony of Frank B. Kellogg) concerning the possession, and application, of power by the Standard combination to exclude parties outside the combination. Save for a reference to the period preceding 1882 (*Id.,* at 76), White, like the circuit court, had made no specific findings on these matters.

also shown in the way the holding company exercised the power it had obtained, namely, by (1) acquiring, here and there, every efficient means through which competition could have been asserted (2) slowly, but relentlessly, absorbing and bringing under control means of transportation,[126] and (3) adopting a system of dividing the market according to which a designated corporation was assigned a specific territory of the country while other members of the combination were excluded.

The terms of dissolution decreed by the circuit court were sustained, but four additional defendants were excused on grounds that Standard already had liquidated them.[127] The Supreme Court did permit some requested modifications in the interpretation of collateral provisions in the decree to provide assurance that various divested corporations would be permitted to contract with one another — particularly the various pipelines, which were interconnected with each other or with divested refineries in supplying transportation services.[128] But the modifications were not to be interpreted to permit "any device whatever, recreating directly or indirectly the illegal combination which the decree dissolved."[129]

The Aftermath of Dissolution

The deconcentration in economic power of the Standard Oil Company of New Jersey was immediately exceedingly popular. On the other hand, the extremely slow pace at which the potential competition — truly, potential potential competition — converted itself into actual competition in the oil industry produced considerable disillusionment for a number of years thereafter among both the public and many antitrust officials. They had not sufficiently appreciated the perceived constraint under which Kellogg was forced to labor in mobilizing his complaint and in petitioning for relief. (No previous tight combination in manufacturing had been found to violate the Sherman Act; and, of course, the only previously decreed dissolution

---

[126] Again, I assume that White was primarily referring to the 1899 acquisitions of the important Manhattan Oil Co. in the Indiana-Ohio oil field and of the new 180 mile pipeline of the Indiana Pipe Line & Refining Co. from the Indiana oil field to Kankakee, Illinois for supplying a newly completed refinery, as well as to the 1901 acquisition of a short, but strategic, pipeline of the Pacific Oil Co. in California. But White may have also referred to the "internalization" of the pipeline which was constructed by the Prairie Oil and Gas subsidiary from the midcontinent oil field to Whiting, Indiana and to pressures which continued to be exerted on the railroads, including the inducement of reciprocal buying of railroad lubricants.

[127] Iowa Standard, Manhattan Oil, Corsicana Refining, and Security Oil. The latter two, following action by the State of Texas which banned them, as we have previously noted, had actually been reorganized as the Magnolia Oil Co., — with its controlling stockownership transferred to the Presidents of Jersey and New York Standard.

[128] 221 U.S. 1, at 80–81.

[129] *Id.*, at 81.

had specifically permitted an identical ratable stock distribution in the northern railroad lines.)

After carrying out the decree, the Department of Justice in October 1912 appointed Charles B. Morrison, who had assisted Kellogg during the entire Standard Oil litigation, special assistant to the attorney general. Morrison's sole task for almost the next decade, when an eye ailment forced his retirement, was to oversee the implementation of the objectives of the decree.[130] His regular reports to the attorney general reflect an increasing frustration on his part to generate proposals to convert the dissolved Standard Companies into *bona fide* potential competitors, let alone actual competitors. Separate boards of directors and officers had been established for each of the dissolved companies. But the continued substantiality of commonality in the stockholders' positions, particularly considering the large blocks held by Rockefeller, Payne, and others, made it improbable that officers of the respective companies would initiate invasions of the market preserves of others. The major exception was the Waters-Pierce Company, in which Pierce had always possessed a large minority position. Obtaining the assistance of the state of Missouri, which had earlier won state antitrust action against the Standard companies, Pierce prevented the Rockefeller interests from using their majority control to place former officers of Indiana Standard in charge of the company. The Rockefeller interests shortly thereafter sold their stock in Waters-Pierce. In turn, Indiana Standard and Magnolia (a virtual joint-subsidiary of Jersey and New York Standard), hastily established marketing stations in separate sections of the former exclusive territory of Waters-Pierce.

Morrison did find that unfair competition was considerably reduced. The discriminatory pattern, in Standard's favor, of railroad rates on refined products from particular refining points to marketing points were modified but not entirely discarded. He also found much less evidence of regional and local patterns of price discrimination against independents.[131]

Nevertheless, he found that the nonintegrated refiners, namely, Vacuum Oil, Solar Refining, and Kansas Standard, were continuing to deliver all their refined kerosene and gasoline to New York Standard, Ohio Standard, and Indiana Standard, respectively, for marketing. He noted that Kentucky Standard, despite the presence of crude oil within Kentucky, continued to engage solely in marketing — obtaining its refined product from Jersey Standard (Parkersburg, West Virginia); Indiana Standard (Whiting, Indiana); Ohio Standard (Cleveland, Ohio); Louisiana Standard (Baton Rouge, Louisiana) and Magnolia Petroleum (Corsicana and Beaumont,

[130] See Department of Justice File #60–57–0. (Standard Oil Co. of New Jersey) in the National Archives, Washington, D.C.
[131] *Ibid.* Report from C. B. Morrison (February 28, 1913).

Texas). Moreover, Kentucky Standard had not begun to market in any territory of its suppliers, nor had any of its suppliers begun to market in its territory. Indeed, Kentucky Standard had not moved back into Tennessee — a vacancy in its marketing territory which Louisiana Standard had filled when the state of Tennessee compelled Kentucky Standard to vacate several years before.[132] Finally, the dissolved pipelines were found to continue service exclusively to the Standard refineries, a situation which prompted Morrison to write a congratulatory letter to Attorney General McReynolds upon his Supreme Court victory declaring Prairie Oil and Gas to be a common carrier, subject to the Hepburn Act.[133]

Throughout the remainder of Morrison's assignment, there was insufficient indication of active competition. Similar reports were filed by his successors at the "Standard Oil post" in the Department of Justice. As late as 1924, the current occupier of the post was proposing that the government initiate a new equity suit against the Standard Oil companies, although some weakening of the community of interests had appeared in marketing territories and California Standard's personnel were found to be chafing at the deference shown to New Jersey Standard, a deference which prevented California Standard from retaining a greater percentage of the profit on their tanker exports.[134]

In the meantime, in 1915, the Federal Trade Commission had issued a report on gasoline, which included a key chapter on the "Position of Standard Companies in the Industry." The dominating and exclusive position of a hereditary Standard company was documented and explained in terms of a "community of interest" of common stock ownership. The expanding, and more rationally shaped marketing boundaries of such independents as The Texas Company, Gulf Oil Corporation, Indian Refining Company, and National Refining Company were contrasted with the rigid state boundaries of successor Standard marketers. The Federal Trade Commission avoided criticizing the decree, by suggesting that "The decree may be regarded as an experiment."[135] Among the commission's final recommendations to Congress were proposals to place "Effective limitation upon common ownership of stock in *potentially* competitive corporations by withdrawing the power of voting and control."[136] (Italics added.)

Yet some weak elements of potential competition were already beginning to convert themselves into actual competition as early as 1915. During 1914–15 Magnolia invaded with bulk stations Louisiana Standard's Arkansas and Continental's New Mexico. But the major breakthrough came in

---

[132] *Ibid.*

[133] *Ibid.* Letter from Morrison (June 23, 1914).

[134] *Ibid.*, Memorandum prepared by J. R. Kelly, Special Consultant to the Attorney General (Nov. 24, 1924).

[135] Federal Trade Commission, *Report on the Price of Gasoline in 1915,* Ch. VII, esp. p. 158.

[136] *Ibid.*, p. 163.

1915–16 when Atlantic Refining invaded with bulk stations New York Standard's Connecticut, Rhode Island, and Massachusetts.[137]

Following World War I, invasions became somewhat more frequent. Atlantic Refining built a refinery in Georgia and began to market against both Jersey Standard and Kentucky Standard in their respective portions of the Coastal Atlantic states. Atlantic Refining also marketed in Ohio Standard's Ohio, and Jersey Standard marketed in Atlantic Refining's Pennsylvania. Net additions to active competition were admittedly exaggerated by many of the invasions of the 1920s, since many of them were a consequence of acquisitions. For example, Jersey Standard's 1919 entry into Texas came through its acquisition of Humble Oil and Refining Company, a major crude producer that did some marketing. Indiana Standard's 1921 entry into Continental Oil's Rocky Mountain territory came through its acquisition of Midwest Refining Company in Wyoming, and its 1925 entry into the South and South Atlantic came through its acquisition of Pan American Petroleum and Transport Company and its subsidiary, American Oil Company. Continental Oil's 1924 entry into Indiana Standard's prairie portion of the Midwest came through its acquisition of Mutual Oil Company. New York Standard's 1925 entry into Texas and the Southwest came through its acquisition of semirelated Magnolia, and its 1925 entry into California came through its acquisition of General Petroleum Company. Jersey Standard's 1929 entry into New England came through its acquisition of the marketer, Beacon Oil Company.[138]

Moreover, during the 1920s, both Ohio Oil and Prairie Oil and Gas — companies that previously operated solely in production and pipelines — vertically integrated into refining and marketing. Ohio Oil marketed in Ohio Standard's Ohio and in Indiana Standard's Michigan and Indiana. Prairie Oil and Gas marketed in Continental Oil's Refinery Mountain states and in Indiana Standard's Illinois, Indiana, Iowa, and Minnesota.[139] In addition, two formerly nonintegrated refiners began to market: (1) Kansas Standard in Indiana Standard's Kansas and Missouri and (2) Vacuum Oil in Atlantic Refining's Pennsylvania. Finally, the crude producer, South Penn Oil, began to refine and market in Ohio Standard's Ohio.

The upshot was that by 1928 single successors of Standard Oil marketed in only five states — Nevada, North Dakota, South Dakota, Wisconsin, and Wyoming. As of 1926 the shares of the market controlled by most invaders were still found to be modest even in comparison with "independents" — Gulf Oil Company, Texas Company, Shell Oil Company, Sinclair Oil and Refining Company — but their potential competition had become actual.[140]

---

[137] Harold F. Williamson, et al. *op. cit.,* p. 234.

[138] *Ibid.,* p. 496.

[139] *Ibid.,* pp. 495, 497.

[140] U.S. Senate, *Petroleum Industry — Prices, Profits and Competition,* A Report of the Federal Trade Commission (Washington: 1928), pp. 225–227.

A considerable conversion of potential competition into actual competition also came during the 1920's when dissected refiners vertically integrated into transportation — most notably with reference to the strategically positioned Prairie Oil and Gas Company's pipeline, which delivered from Oklahoma and central Texas to Indiana Standard and, by way of interconnections, to other "separated" Standard refinery companies in the East. To bypass Prairie's efforts to maintain high pipage rates, Atlantic Refining constructed a pipeline from west Texas to the Gulf and shipped by tanker to its Philadelphia and Georgia refineries, while New Jersey Standard and New York Standard used the pipelines of their respective acquisitions, Humble Oil and Refining Company and Magnolia Petroleum Company, to move Texas crude to the Gulf for tanker shipment to New York Harbor. Further ramifications of these tanker movements hit Prairie; for the National Transit Company began to ship crude oil from eastern ports to refineries immediately west of the Alleghenies, while Jersey Standard reversed the flow of its nondivested Tuscarora pipeline and also converted it to a products line, carrying gasoline to western Pennsylvania and Ohio. Finally, various separated Standard refinery companies were induced to form joint ventures with "independents" to bypass the rate structure of Prairie's pipeline to midwest locations. Indiana Standard and Sinclair Oil and Refining Company formed two joint ventures — one from Oklahoma and Texas and another from the Wyoming field to Kansas City and Chicago. Jersey Standard and Ohio Standard joined with Pure Oil Company to build the Ajax — the largest capacity of the new pipelines — to carry crude from Oklahoma to Woods River, Illinois, and then by eastward connections of the Illinois Pipe Line to refineries of the owners in Ohio, West Virginia, and Canada. Moreover, large "independents" entered to bypass Prairie — such as the Cities Service Oil Company-Texas Company's joint venture from Oklahoma to Chicago and as the Gulf Oil Company's line from Oklahoma to Cincinnati, with connections to Pittsburgh and Toledo, for supplying Gulf's first entry into this territory with new refineries in each of these cities.[141]

A final clue to disintegration in the "community of interests" among the dissolved companies came in January 1929 when John D. Rockefeller, Jr. succeeded in ousting Colonel Robert Stewart, who had been implicated in the Teapot Dome Scandal, from the helm of Indiana Standard only after one of the most ambitious solicitations of proxy support in American corporate history.[142]

Twenty years is a long time to convert potential competitors to potential and actual competitors, and almost sixty years later some of the potential competitors are still transforming themselves into actual competitors with some of the other descendants of the dissolved holding company. But few would deny that both American society and the economy were bettered by

[141] Harold F. Williamson, et al., *op. cit.*, pp. 339–350.
[142] Paul Giddens, *Standard Oil Company* (*Indiana*) (New York: 1955), Ch. XIV.

the 1911 conglomerate-type antitrust suit against Standard Oil Company of New Jersey.

Entry by descendant corporations with both refinery and marketing investments into territories of other descendants has undoubtedly helped reduce the economic concentration of ownership of refinery capacity in various refining regions. It has also helped reduce the economic concentration of shares at the level of distribution in the growing state and local bulk and retail markets.

The discovery and expansion of the midcontinent and gulf oil fields would have contributed markedly in and of themselves to the growth of "independents" in the oil business, as would the emerging entrepreneurial arteriosclerosis of the holding company.[143] It appears highly probable, however, that the gradual erosion of solidarity among the dissolved companies — as an attenuating "community of interests" among their stockholders converted the separated companies into true potential competitors — reduced their power to contain the entry and expansion of companies lacking a common inheritance. This factor appears particularly important with respect to the greater access to nondiscriminatory pipeline and railroad services — including elimination of the varieties of discrimination hidden by induced reciprocal buying of high-profit-margin railroad lubricants — and with respect to the fewer obstacles in the construction of pipelines by "independents." Likewise, independent refiners and marketers, who sought to increase their shares in oligopolistic local markets and in regional collections of local markets, must also have been less fearful of discriminatory attack for disciplinary purposes.

Finally, a substantial reduction was made in aggregate economic concentration in the American economy. To gain some crude approximation of the position of the Standard Oil Company of New Jersey relative to the entire economy in 1906, when the case was filed, we can compare its recorded net assets (sales data are unavailable) with gross national product (meaningful aggregate net wealth data are unavailable). The holding company's net assets were $359 million; the gross national product was $28.7 billion; the ratio between the two was 1.25 percent. This compares with the 1967 net assets of the largest industrial corporation, Standard Oil (New Jersey), of $9.45 billion and a 1967 gross national product of $789.7 billion, resulting in a ratio of 1.20 percent. The ratio of the average net worth in 1906 of the thirty-four separated companies to gross national product in that year is 0.0368 percent. This ratio corresponds to the 1967 ratio of net assets to

---

[143] Many students contend that the Standard organization was slow to develop a refining mix and marketing channels to capitalize upon the explosive development of the automotive market for gasoline. See, for example, Robert S. Eckley, The United States Petroleum Industry in Transition, 1910–1920, unpublished doctoral thesis (Harvard University, Cambridge: 1949), p. 83; and Warren C. Platt, "40 Great Years — The Story of Oil's Competition," *National Petroleum News* (March 9, 1949), p. 46.

gross national product of the industrial corporations Castle and Cook, Eastern Gas and Fuel Associates, and Potlach Forests, each of which owned net assets of approximately $290 million and ranked respectively 229th to 231st on a net-assets basis for 1967 in the *Fortune* list of the 500 largest United States industrial corporations.[144] Several of the corporations ordered separated to restore "potential competition" were much larger than the group's average — most notably, Jersey Standard, but also New York Standard, Indiana Standard, California Standard, Prairie Oil and Gas, National Transit, and Ohio Oil. Some, however, were substantially smaller — Borne, Scrymser Company, Chesebrough Manufacturing Company, Swan and Finch Company, Washington Oil Company, and Nebraska Standard. These were, in order, three small lubricating and specialty works, a small crude producer, and a marketer in a single state of modest population.

Precedents for the 1969 Model of an Anticonglomerate Merger Policy

On June 6, 1969 the attorney general of the United States spelled out formally the Nixon "Administration's policy toward current corporate merger trends," with special reference to conglomerate mergers.[145] The attorney general's announcement followed several earlier warnings by his assistant attorney general for antitrust and came almost immediately upon the filing of two complaints, one against Ling-Temco-Vought's plan to acquire Jones and Laughlin Steel and the other against Northwest Industries' plan to acquire Goodrich (B. F.) Rubber. The 1906 antitrust complaint to demerge from the Standard Oil Company of New Jersey's holding company a large number of corporate subsidiaries, most of which had been acquired in 1892 or especially in 1899, provides important precedents for both (A) the current legal theory of the anti-competitive effects of conglomerate mergers and (B) the current public purpose in allocating antitrust resources for carrying out an enforcement policy against conglomerate mergers.

A. Legal theory

The 1969 model, like its 1906 counterpart, essentially takes as given the property structure of incorporated enterprises in so far as this structure immediately affects the existing degree of market concentration in individual markets occupied by the combining corporations and by others. In both models, the mergers are attacked on essentially identical grounds. Various

---

[144] "The Fortune Directory," *Fortune* (June, 1968).

[145] Address by Hon. John N. Mitchell, Attorney General of the United States, delivered before the Georgia Bar Association, Savannah, Ga. (June 6, 1969). Department of Justice Release, p. 1.

theories are offered concerning their alleged *long-run* tendency "substantially to lessen competition" or "unreasonably to restrain trade." Four basic considerations are raised in the 1969 model.

1. Potential competition.   The already large conglomerate, "with its broad financial base, should have the capability to become a new and effective competitor in a spectrum of industries."[146] Taking a long-run view, very large corporations may be expected over time — in a dynamic environment of developing technology and evolving market potentials — to acquire new managerial, technical, and marketing talent and competence thereby making such corporations truly potential competitors with many other corporations, in whose markets they could not readily become actual effective competitors today merely through budgeting new investments, notwithstanding their favorable access to capital funds. Such potential competitors are truly "potential potential competitors," analogous to the demerged Standard corporations, which did not truly become potential competitors until sufficient time had expired to erode the symmetrically common ownership in the merged Standard corporations, an ownership restored by the ratable stock distribution permitted in the dissolution. Only after a considerable lapse of time did a community of interest among the stockholders dissipate, thus creating freedom for the managements of the demerged companies to utilize their newly gained status of potential competitors in making capital investments by which they would become actual competitors in markets occupied by former members of the combination.

Given ineffective competition in the markets currently occupied by the merging firms, for reasons of concentrated oligopoly (1969) or monopolistic dominancy (1906), the long-run benefits from maintaining competition may be substantial. They probably will be substantial if the aggregate size of markets occupied by the merging firms is large.

2. Unfair competition and reciprocity.   The 1969 model charges that "Large conglomerate mergers also pose dangers to free competition by the expansion of nationwide marketing structures, capital resources and advertising budgets. Such a structure may offer a diversified firm a physical advantage over its competitors in terms of volume discounts on transportation and advertising."[147] Because the major thrust of this entry-inhibiting charge appears to rest upon the differential advantage of large buying power in generating favorable terms from oligopolistic suppliers, I shall lump with it the power to induce reciprocal buying by oligopolistic suppliers. For example, in lieu of additional discounts, the supplier may be induced to "subsidize" the greater profitability of conglomerates by reciprocal purchases of products produced by the conglomerate in oligopolistic markets.

[146] *Ibid.*, p. 11.
[147] *Ibid.*, p. 12.

"Reciprocity," but not by that name, was also charged in the Standard Oil combination.

Vast capital resources coupled with "satisfactory" flows of profit from multiple markets played a major role in the charge that the Standard conglomerate possessed a differential advantage ("power") in obtaining preferential terms on transportation services, in obstructing the endeavors of others to construct pipelines, and in denying to others, by discrimination, an efficient distributed share in local oligopolistic bulk station tank-wagon markets. But both the circuit and Supreme courts found it unnecessary to make findings on these charges in the 1906 complaint. The decision of substantial injury to competition rested upon the theory that potential competition among parties to the combination had been suppressed.

3. Concentration of industrial and financial assets in the hands of the few The 1969 model refers to the Celler-Kefauver Act's purpose of combatting the trend toward increasing aggregate concentration. That Congress had the same purpose in the passage of the Sherman Act was alleged by the government in 1909–11, upon presenting its case, based upon the 1906 complaint, to the courts. Chief Justice White, who agreed at length concerning the purpose, interwove continual references to aggregate size in presenting his findings and in reaching his conclusions. Furthermore, in terms of my analysis of his "Rule of Reason" with respect to mergers, White relied upon the element of size in evaluating the degree to which combination could eliminate competition without constituting an unreasonable restraint of trade. But this argument essentially coincides with the brief economic analysis that I introduced immediately above to conclude my discussion of "1. Potential competition."

B. Policy

The Justice Department in 1969 perceives itself as substantially constrained in slowing, or reversing, the trend toward aggregate economic concentration by proceeding directly to the restructure of the property of existing corporations in order to deconcentrate oligopolistic markets. The Sherman Act has yet to be tested with respect to its power to compel the fragmentation of corporations occupying a specific market characterized by ineffective competition because of an inherited situation of concentrated oligopoly. Moreover, vast commitments of limited resources in antitrust manpower would be required to staff these "big cases" and, if successful, to supervise the division of each single corporation into two or more. Finally, unless the relevant economic market selected was exceedingly large, such as the market for automobiles (and unlike the market for shoe machinery), no substantial impact upon the trend toward increasing aggregate economic concentration would be accomplished.

An even greater constraint confronted the government in 1906 than in 1969. The alternative uses of antitrust resources would then have been against "contracts" and "conspiracies"; and the impact of the alternative allocation on aggregate economic concentration would have been virtually nil.

Yet Congress in 1890, and again in 1950, asserted as a national priority a public policy to retard the growing total concentration in economic power, although not, to be sure, to the exclusion of other public policies for promoting competition. Antitrust policy was meant to be used to retard growing overall economic concentration even when the *immediate* anticompetitive effects of certain combinations, that is to say, Mergers, was slight. Congress was seriously concerned with the social and political "externalities" that accompany the growth of aggregate economic concentration.

Probably there is no inconsistency between promoting the political and social objectives of retarding the growth in aggregate economic concentration and in procuring the maximum long-run economic benefits of enhanced competition. If considerable economic concentration already exists in the markets of merging conglomerates and if the conglomerates are themselves very large, a fact which implies a very large size of sales for the sum of the markets occupied, the long-run benefits of increased "consumer surplus" or reduced "deadweight loss of monopoly"[148] — benefits that are undoubtedly measured hypothetically — might greatly exceed those benefits associated with the immediate and substantial reduction in price-cost margins which, in a *small* market and for a *short period* of time, may follow the successful antitrust attack on an *ephemeral* overt price-fixing scheme.

The economic benefits gained by demerging the conglomerate Standard Oil holding company were indeed excessively delayed, principally because of the ratable stock distribution, but also because of other perceived constraints upon antitrust action, constraints which impeded a reorganization of the property structures of, and the market occupied by, the separated companies. On the other hand, few would deny that these strictly economic benefits from increasing competition throughout the full sweep and history of the oil industry were not worth the endeavor.

Moreover, except for the erosion of social and political pluralism ground out "externally" by giantism, what other form of environmental pollution can be reduced at probably a negative economic price?

---

[148] Not to mention the even more conjectural: (a) "efficiency gains" which could arise from enhanced competitive pressure and (b) "progressiveness" which could arise from the enhanced variegation of more decision-makers.

10

Should Commodity Taxes be Levied
on Manufacturers or Retailers?

*Robert L. Bishop**

The choice between levying excise taxes at the manufacturing or retailing stage has been discussed mostly with reference to the possible pyramiding of a tax levied at the earlier stage. A surprisingly neglected aspect of the question, which will be considered here, concerns the influence of market structure at each stage.

As to pyramiding, one kind involves the added working-capital cost in later stages when the tax is imposed at an early stage. Another, more debatable kind rests on an alleged adherence by retailers to a rigid percentage-markup pricing policy, with the result that a price increase attributable to a tax at an earlier stage is itself marked up as a part of the retail price. Both these phenomena will be ignored initially in favor of concentrating on the influence of market structure under static, profit-maximizing conditions. Costs of tax collection and other administrative considerations will also be neglected. The discussion will embrace a series of alternative cases, the last of which will concern percentage-markup pricing as opposed to profit-maximization.

I A Monopolistic Manufacturer and
Purely Competitive Retailers

Let us assume that a purely competitive industry of retailers faces the demand-price function $p = p(q)$. Let us also assume that its supply-price function $s = s(q)$ takes the special form of $s = a(q) + w$, where the parameter w is the wholesale price and the variable a is the industry's supply price of the retailing service — with $a = a(q)$ assumed to be independent of w. The demand-price function confronting the monopolistic manufacturer is then $w = w(q) = p(q) - a(q)$.

---

* Massachusetts Institute of Technology

216

In the case of a specific tax t, it does not matter whether the tax is levied on the manufacturer or his retailers. When imposed on the retailers, their net demand price as a function of the quantity sold is $p^* = p(q) - t$, and the corresponding function facing the monopolist is

$$(1) \qquad w^* = p(q) - a(q) - t.$$

Since this same function also applies when the tax is imposed directly on the manufacturer, the effects are obviously the same.[1]

The situation is very different, however, in the case of ad valorem taxes. If an ad valorem tax is levied at the rate r_1 on the gross price charged by the competitive retailers, the total-revenue function of the monopolistic manufacturer becomes:

$$(2) \qquad R_1 = (1 - r_1)p(q)q - a(q)q.$$

Alternatively, if an ad valorem tax is levied directly on the monopolist at the rate of r_2, his total revenue function is:

$$(3) \qquad R_2 = (1 - r_2)[p(q)q - a(q)q].$$

The respective marginal-revenue functions in the two alternative situations are then:

$$(4) \qquad R_1' = (1 - r_1)(p + qp') - a - qa',$$
$$(5) \qquad R_2' = (1 - r_2)(p + qp' - a - qa').$$

We must now find the relationship between r_1 and r_2 that will make those two alternative taxes "equivalent," in the sense that they would have the same effects on retail price and quantity. In other words, for some given value of r_1, we seek the corresponding value of r_2 that will result in the same q and p. Since this requires that R_1' and R_2' must be equal at the monopolist's equilibrium output, we set the two equations equal to one another and then solve for:

$$(6) \qquad r_2 = \frac{r_1(p + qp')}{p + qp' - a - qa'}.$$

[1] In his article, "The Effects of Ad Valorem and Specific Taxes on Prices," *Quarterly Journal of Economics,* LXXIX (1965), 649–50, Paul Taubman came up with the wrong answer to this problem, because he confused it with the comparative effects of a given specific tax on a monopoly or a purely competitive industry under comparable demand and cost conditions. Taubman first refers to Richard Musgrave's demonstration in the case of linear demand and cost (See R. A. Musgrave, *The Theory of Public Finance: A Study in Public Economy* [New York, 1959], pp. 289, 295, and 297) that a given specific tax will raise a monopoly's price by only half as much as it would raise a competitive price. Taubman then concludes in the case of "a monopolistic manufacturer and an industry of perfectly competitive retailers," under conditions where the monopoly's price would be increased by no more than half the tax, that "less of a tax will be passed along if the tax is imposed on the monopolist since the retailers will, at the most, pass along their cost increases." Clearly, Musgrave's comparison cannot be extended to cases involving a vertical relationship.

To compare the tax revenues per unit of output, $v_1 = r_1 p$ in the one instance and $v_2 = r_2 w = r_2(p - a)$ in the other, we first substitute the above value of r_2 in the expression for v_2:

$$v_2 = \frac{r_1(p + qp')(p - a)}{p + qp' - a - qa'}.$$

It is then implied that $v_2 > v_1$ when this expression is greater than $r_1 p$, or when

$$(p + qp')(p - a) > (p + qp' - a - qa')p.$$

That inequality readily reduces to:

(7) $$pa' > ap'.$$

This is always the result when $a' \geq 0$, since $p' < 0$ (as will be assumed throughout). The inequality also holds, moreover, when $a' < 0$ and the elasticity of the retail-demand function is smaller in absolute value than the elasticity of the retailing-cost function. That is to say, from the above inequality,

$$p/p' > a/a',$$
(8) $$-E_{qp} = -p/qp' < -a/qa' = -E_{qa}.$$

Conversely, of course, $v_1 > v_2$ when $a' < 0$ and $-E_{qp} > -E_{qp}$. At best, this possibility is rather academic, since it requires external economies that are strong enough to make the industry's supply curve of retailing service less elastic than its demand curve. With that implausible exception, then, an ad valorem tax on the monopolistic manufacturer raises more revenue than the equivalent ad valorem tax on his competitive retailers.[2]

For a further insight into the relationships of v_1 and v_2, it should be noticed that in the normal case the industry demand confronting the competitive retailers is more elastic at any given output than that facing the monopolistic manufacturer. Bearing in mind that $w = p - a > 0$ and $w' = p' - a' < 0$, we may prove this as follows:

$$pa' > ap',$$
$$pp' - ap' > pp' - pa',$$
$$\frac{p - a}{p' - a'} > \frac{p}{p'},$$
(9) $$-E_{qw} = -w/qw' < -p/qp' = -E_{qp}.$$

---

[2] It is a familiar theorem, furthermore, than an ad valorem tax on a monopolist raises more tax revenue than the equivalent specific tax in the proportion that price (p) bears to marginal revenue (R') in the post-tax equilibrium (See Musgrave, *op. cit.*, pp. 304–5, n. and R. L. Bishop, "The Effects of Specific and Ad Valorem Taxes," *Quarterly Journal of Economics*, LXXXII (1968), p. 204). In a purely competitive industry, by contrast, the two types of tax are interchangeable. That is also why, under our present assumptions, it would not make any difference where either type of commodity tax was imposed if the manufacturing and retailing stages were both purely competitive.

Since the less elastic the demand, the more revenue a tax yields per unit of induced contraction of output, it follows in this normal case that taxing the monopolist is more productive than taxing his retailers. In the abnormal case, by contrast, when we subtract from a given retailers' demand-price function a negatively sloped and less elastic supply-price function, the resulting demand function facing the monopolist is more elastic than the one facing the retailers.

II Purely Competitive Manufacturers and a Monopolistic Retailer

In this opposite situation, let us again designate the retail demand-price function by $p = p(q)$; but we now designate the total cost of the monopolist's retailing service as $A = A(q)$. The supply-price function of the purely competitive manufacturers is denoted by $s = s(q)$. The monopolistic retailer is thus also a monopsonist in his role as purchaser of the wholesale product; and his total-cost function is $C = s(q)q + A(q)$.

Again it makes no difference whether a specific tax is levied at the wholesale or retail level, since the monopolist's total-profit function is then, in either case:

$$\text{(10)} \qquad \pi = p(q)q - s(q)q - A(q) - tq.$$

When an ad valorem tax at the rate r_1 is imposed on the monopolist's gross retail price, his total-profit function is:

$$\text{(11)} \qquad \pi_1 = (1 - r_1)p(q)q - s(q)q - A(q).$$

Alternatively, when the competitively supplied product is taxed, it is convenient to specify the ad valorem rate r_2 as applying to the *net* wholesale price. The monopolistic retailer's total-profit function is then:

$$\text{(12)} \qquad \pi_2 = p(q)q - (1 + r_2)s(q)q - A(q).$$

This means, in turn, that the monopolist's marginal-profit functions are, respectively:

$$\text{(13)} \qquad \pi_1' = (1 - r_1)(p + qp') - s - qs' - A'.$$
$$\text{(14)} \qquad \pi_2' = p + qp' - (1 + r_2)(s + qs') - A'.$$

By equating these functions and solving for r_1, we establish the relationship of r_1 to r_2 if the two alternative taxes are to be equivalent:

$$\text{(15)} \qquad r_1 = \frac{r_2(s + qs')}{p + qp'}.$$

It now follows that $v_1 = r_1 p > v_2 = r_2 s$ when

$$\frac{r_2 p(s + qs')}{p + qp'} > r_2 s,$$

which reduces to:

(16) $$ps' > sp'.$$

The analogy of this result to the critical inequality (7) in the preceding case is apparent. Clearly, the inequality holds when the competitive industry's supply slope $s' \geq 0$; and it also holds when $s' < 0$ provided that the elasticity of the retail demand is less in absolute value than the elasticity of the wholesale supply, since the above inequality then implies that

(17) $$-E_{qp} = -p/qp' < -s/qs' = -E_{qs}.$$

It is again normal, therefore, for the ad valorem tax on the monopolist to raise more tax revenue than the equivalent tax on the competitive industry. Now, of course, since it is the retail stage that is monopolized, the more productive ad valorem tax is levied there in the normal case. In that normal case, the elasticity of the retail demand facing the monopolist is smaller in absolute value than the likewise negative elasticity of the net demand, $p - s = p(q) - s(q)$. Only when the relative values of those elasticities are reversed is it more productive to tax the competitive manufacturers.

III   A Monopolistic Manufacturer and a Monopolistic Retailer: Collusive Behavior

Each of the two preceding cases had a unique solution because the passive price-taking behavior of the purely competitive stage raised no challenge to the monopolist's or monopsonist's role as price-quoter. When both stages are monopolized, however, there is a relationship of bilateral monopoly between them; and this opens the door to a multiplicity of possible outcomes.

If the manufacturer and retailer maximize their joint profit and share it in some manner, thereby behaving in effect as a single integrated firm, the only safe method of ad valorem taxation would be to tax the retail product, since the wholesale price w would then be wholly arbitrary and might even be set at zero to frustrate any attempt to tax it. On the other hand, if side payments are prohibited and the manufacturer's profit must be obained in the normal manner, an ad valorem tax may again be appropriately imposed at either the retail or the wholesale level, despite the fact that the retail tax would be compatible with maximizing joint profit while the wholesale tax would not. Collusive behavior in either case calls for the firms' operation on the relevant contract curve, where for any given attainable profit of one seller, the other's profit is a maximum. As before, our analysis concentrates on ad valorem taxes, since equivalent specific taxes at either the wholesale or the retail level have fully equivalent effects.

Let us designate the retailer's and manufacturer's profit by π_r and π_m, respectively. The retail demand is again $p = p(q)$ and the wholesale price is w, a negotiated price consistent with a contract-curve solution. The retailer's total revenue is $R = pq$, and his average and total costs of the retailing function are $a = a(q)$ and $A = aq$. The manufacturer's average and total costs are designated by $c = c(q)$ and $C = cq$.

If an ad valorem tax is levied on the retail product at the rate r_1, the respective profit functions — distinguished by asterisks from the profit functions that are designated farther on — are:

$$\text{(18)} \qquad \pi_r{}^* = (1 - r_1)R(q) - A(q) - wq,$$

$$\text{(19)} \qquad \pi_m{}^* = wq - C(q).$$

The joint profit π is then independent of w, which merely governs the distribution of profit between the two claimants:

$$\text{(20)} \qquad \pi = (1 - r_1)R(q) - A(q) - C(q).$$

For maximum π, then,

$$\text{(21)} \qquad \pi' = (1 - r_1)R' - A' - C' = 0.$$

When an ad valorem tax is levied on the wholesale product at the rate r_2, the respective profit functions become:

$$\text{(22)} \qquad \pi_r = R(q) - A(q) - wq,$$

$$\text{(23)} \qquad \pi_m = (1 - r_2)wq - C(q).$$

Here the joint profit, for any given $r_2 > 0$ and $q > 0$, is a linearly decreasing function of w:

$$\text{(24)} \qquad \pi_r + \pi_m = R - A - C - r_2wq.$$

This is not a maximum except when $w = 0$.

To be on their contract curve, for any given value of r_2, the two firms must choose associated values of q and w so that their isoprofit curves, of the form $\pi_r = \pi_r(q,w)$ and $\pi_m = \pi_m(q,w)$, will be tangent. From the implicit-function rule, the slopes of those curves are:

$$\left(\frac{dw}{dq}\right)_{\pi_r} = -\frac{\partial\pi_r/\partial q}{\partial\pi_r/\partial w} \qquad\qquad \left(\frac{dw}{dq}\right)_{\pi_m} = -\frac{\partial\pi_m/\partial q}{\partial\pi_m/\partial w},$$

where

$$\begin{aligned} \partial\pi_r/\partial q &= R' - w - A' & \partial\pi_m/\partial q &= (1 - r_2)w - C' \\ \partial\pi_r/\partial w &= -q & \partial\pi_r/\partial w &= (1 - r_2)q. \end{aligned}$$

Accordingly, setting the isoprofit-curve slopes equal to one another yields the equation for the contract curve:

$$\text{(25)} \qquad (1 - r_2)(R' - A') - C' = 0.$$

Since w drops out of this expression, q is the same everywhere on the contract curve for any given r_2. We can then readily determine the profit frontier — that is, the associated values of π_m and π_r on the contract curve — by substituting $wq = R - A - \pi_r$ from equation (22) in equation (23):

$$(26) \qquad \pi_m = (1 - r_2)(R - A - \pi_r) - C.$$

Clearly, this is linear with a slope of $d\pi_m/d\pi_r = -(1 - r_2)$.

In order to compare the relative tax revenues, $v_1 = r_1 p$ and $v_2 = r_2 w$, we first find the related values of r_1 and r_2 that would have the same effect on q from equations (21) and (25):

$$(27) \qquad r_1 = \frac{(R' - A')r_2}{R'}.$$

Secondly, we define the operator $k = \pi_r/\pi_m$ to allow for the different proportions in which profits may be shared along the contract curve and profit frontier. Then, since the profit equations (22) and (23) imply that

$$R - A - wq = k[(1 - r_2)wq - C],$$

we solve for:

$$(28) \qquad w = \frac{p - a + kc}{1 + k - kr_2}.$$

It now follows that the tax at the retail level will be the more productive when $v_1 = r_1 p > v_2 = r_2 w$, or when

$$\frac{(R' - A')r_2 p}{R'} > \frac{(p - a + kc)r_2}{1 + k - kr_2}.$$

This inequality reduces to:

$$k(1 - r_2)(R' - A')p - A'p > R'(kc - a).$$

Substitution from equation (25), however, gives:

$$(29) \qquad p(kC' - A') > R'(kc - a).$$

It is easiest to interpret this inequality in the extreme cases, when k is either very low or very high. As $k \to 0$, the criterion approaches:

$$(30) \qquad \frac{p}{R'} < \frac{a}{A'}.$$

To interpret these ratios in terms of the respective elasticities $E_{qp} = p/qp'$ and $E_{qa} = a/qa'$, we note that

$$\frac{p}{R'} = \frac{E_{qp}}{1 + E_{qp}} \qquad \frac{a}{A'} = \frac{E_{qa}}{1 + E_{qa}},$$

where $E_{qp} < -1$ and $E_{qa} > 0$ or $E_{qa} < -1$. Our inequality may then be restated as:

$$(31) \qquad E_{qp} > E_{qa} \text{ when } E_{qa} > 0,$$

$$(32) \qquad E_{qp} < E_{qa} \text{ when } E_{qa} < -1.$$

Clearly, the first of these inequalities never holds, and the second holds only in the possible, but rather unlikely, circumstance where the demand elasticity is greater in absolute value than the likewise negative retailing-cost elasticity.[3] Hence, when $k \to 0$ and π_m represents the lion's share of the joint profit, we conclude that normally $v_2 > v_1$, and it is therefore normally more productive to tax the manufacturer.

The reverse is true as $k \to \infty$, when it is π_r that absorbs essentially all of the joint profit. Then the inequality (29) approaches:

$$(33) \qquad \frac{p}{R'} > \frac{c}{C'}.$$

Except for the substitution of the manufacturer's average and marginal costs for those of the retailer, this is strictly analogous to the case just considered. Here the criteria become:

$$(34) \qquad E_{qp} < E_{qc} \text{ when } E_{qc} > 0,$$
$$(35) \qquad E_{qp} > E_{qc} \text{ when } E_{qc} < -1.$$

Now the first inequality always holds, and the second holds except when the manufacturer's average-cost curve has a sufficiently pronounced negative slope so that the curve's elasticity is smaller in absolute value than that of the retail-demand curve.[4]

More generally, when k is positive and finite, the inequality (29) becomes:

$$(36) \qquad \frac{p}{R'} > \frac{kc - a}{kC' - A'} \text{ when } kC' > A'.$$

$$(37) \qquad \frac{p}{R'} < \frac{kc - a}{kC' - A'} \text{ when } kC' < A'.$$

In the special case when $kC' = A'$, however, the inequality (29) becomes:

$$(38) \qquad kc < a.$$

Similarly, when $kc = a$, it becomes:

$$(39) \qquad kC' > A'.$$

[3] It would be inconsistent with a maximized non-negative profit for demand to be more elastic than full average cost at the equilibrium point; for then $p \geq c$ and $R' = C'$, from which it follows that $-E_{qp} \leq -E_{qc}$. The abnormal relationship mentioned in the text is possible only because it involves merely a partial cost. On the other hand, since we are now dealing with a monopolist, a negatively sloped average-cost curve is not at all abnormal, in marked contrast to a negatively sloped supply curve of a purely competitive industry. Nevertheless, the close analogy of the present case to that in section I should be noticed. Here, if $\pi_r = 0$, the retailer's price is $p = a + w$, just as it was earlier; and he supplies his retailing service on the same basis of barely covering cost as in pure competition.

[4] Just as the preceding case was pointed out in n. 3 to be analogous to that in section I, this one is analogous to that in section II; for, when π_r absorbs essentially all the joint profit, the manufacturer has a passive, cost-covering attitude analogous to that of a purely competitive industry.

When $a = a(q)$ and $c = c(q)$ have equal elasticities, such that $a = hA'$ and $c = hC'$, where $h > 0$ and $E_{qa} = E_{qc} = h/(1 - h)$, there is a critical value of k where $kC' - A' = kc - a = 0$. It is then implied that $v_1 = v_2$, and it does not matter whether the retailer or the manufacturer is taxed. Otherwise, however, the criteria (36) and (37) now become:

(40) $$\frac{p}{R'} > h \qquad \text{when } kC' > A'.$$

(41) $$\frac{p}{R'} < h \qquad \text{when } kC' < A'.$$

When k is large enough so that criterion (40) applies, that inequality is fulfilled, provided only that the tax on the retailer would not altogether eliminate the joint profit. Thus, provided that

$$(1 - r_1)p > a + c,$$

and since, from equation (21),

$$(1 - r_1)R' = A' + C',$$

it follows that

$$\frac{p}{R'} > \frac{a + c}{A' + C'}.$$

Then, because

$$h = \frac{a}{A'} = \frac{c}{C'} = \frac{a + c}{A' + C'},$$

it is established that the inequality (40) holds. By the same token, when k is small enough so that criterion (41) applies, that inequality does not hold. To put the matter in a nutshell in this case of equally elastic average costs, it is more productive to tax the retailer or the manufacturer according as $kc/a = kC'/A'$ is greater or less than one; that is, it is more productive to tax the firm whose average and marginal costs, so weighted, are the lower.

When these cost functions have different elasticities, $kc - a$ and $kC' - A'$ cannot both be zero. When either is zero, however, such that either criterion (38) or (39) applies, it becomes:

(42) $$\frac{c}{C'} < \frac{a}{A'}.$$

This is also the criterion for taxing the retailer when $kc - a$ and $kC' - A'$ are of opposite signs. In that event criterion (36) is surely fulfilled when it applies, and criterion (37) is never fulfilled when it applies. Similarly, criterion (42) is then always satisfied in the former instance and never in the latter.

The same tendency toward taxing the retailer when his marginal cost is relatively low and his average cost relatively high is quite general. As an inspection of criterion (29) reveals, it is fulfilled for any positive, finite values of k, p, and R' whenever A' is sufficiently low relative to C' and a is sufficiently high relative to c.

In summary, taxing the retailer tends to be the more productive method when: (a) his share of the joint profit is high (when $k = \pi_r/\pi_m$ is high); (b) the average and marginal cost of the retailing service is relatively low ($a/kc = A/kC' < 1$ being the dominant consideration when $E_{qa} = E_{qc}$); and (c) the ratio of the retailer's average cost to his marginal cost is high relative to the corresponding ratio for the manufacturer ($a/A' > c/C'$ being the dominant consideration when $kc - a$ and $kC' - A'$ are of opposite signs or when one of them is zero).

There is also a large measure of symmetry in the situation. Thus, if it is equally likely for k to be greater or less than $1/k$, if $a = a(q)$ is equally likely to be greater or smaller than $c = c(q)$, and so on for their derivatives and elasticities, there is no *a priori* presumption in favor of taxing either the retailer or the manufacturer. There is one inherent element of asymmetry, however, in that the profit frontier of equation (26), when the tax is levied on the manufacturer, has the relatively unfavorable slope for him of $d\pi_m/d\pi_r = - (1 - r_2)$. For example, if the bilateral monopolists have utilities that are linear functions of their profits and behave in accordance with Nash-Zeuthen-Harsanyi rules, their equilibrium will be at the midpoint of the profit frontier. This would mean, of course, that the retailer's profit would be the greater, with $k > 1$. Hence, in an otherwise neutral situation, it would be more productive to tax the retailer.

IV   A Monopolistic Manufacturer and a Monopolistic Retailer: Noncollusive Behavior

When the manufacturer and retailer do not collude, they may behave in a variety of ways. For example, besides exerting his monopoly power as a seller, the retailer may be able to act as a monopsonist toward the manufacturer, who in turn behaves as a passive profit-maximizer with respect to a wholesale price fixed by the retailer. This Bowley-Stackelberg case is closely analogous, however, to that in section II, when the retailer was a monopsonist toward his purely competitive suppliers; so there is no need to treat it further. On the other hand, it is worth exploring the other Bowley-Stackelberg case where the retailer, though exerting his monopoly power as a seller, is a passive profit-maximizer with respect to a wholesale price set by the manufacturer, who is thereby in a position to exert his monopoly power too. This case is especially interesting because of its analogy to another, more prevalent, one where monopolistically competitive retailers are passive price-takers in buying from one or more manufacturers who also possess monopoly power.

It may first be observed that this species of noncollusive behavior is more restrictive of output than the collusion analyzed in the preceding section. With the same basic notation as before, the retailer's profit function and the first-order condition for its maximization are, in the absence of any tax:

(43) $$\pi_r = R(q) - A(q) - wq,$$
(44) $$\pi_r' = R' - A' - w = 0.$$

Hence the demand-price function confronting the manufacturer is:

(45) $$w = R' - A',$$

where

(46) $$w' = R'' - A'' < 0.$$

The manufacturer's profit function and the first-order condition for its being maximized are then:

(47) $$\pi_m = wq - C(q) = (R' - A')q - C(q),$$
(48) $$\pi_m' = R' - A' - C' + q(R'' - A'') = 0.$$

Comparing this with the corresponding condition for a maximized joint profit when $r_1 = 0$ in equation (21) and noting the inequality (46), we see that this noncollusive case requires a greater restriction of output, until $R' = A' + C' - q(R'' - A'')$, than the case of maximized joint profit, where $R' = A' + C'$.

Once again, a specific tax has the same effects whether it is levied on the retailer or the manufacturer; so we go on immediately to ad valorem taxes. When such a tax is levied at the rate of r_1 on the retailer's product, his profit function and first-order maximizing condition are:

(49) $$\pi_r = (1 - r_1)R(q) - A(q) - wq,$$
(50) $$\pi_r' = (1 - r_1)R' - A' - w = 0.$$

The demand–price function facing the manufacturer is then:

(51) $$w^* = (1 - r_1)R' - A';$$

and his profit function and maximizing condition are:

(52) $$\pi_1 = (1 - r_1)R'q - A'q - C(q),$$
(53) $$\pi_1' = (1 - r_1)(R' + qR'') - A' - qA'' - C' = 0.$$

Alternatively, when an ad valorem tax is levied at the rate r_2 on the manufacturer's product, equations (43)–(46) apply at the retail level; and the manufacturer's profit function and maximizing condition are:

(54) $$\pi_2 = (1 - r_2)(R' - A')q - C(q),$$
(55) $$\pi_2' = (1 - r_2)(R' - A' + qR'' - qA'') - C' = 0.$$

Equations (53) and (55) then establish the relationship or r_1 and r_2 when the two alternative taxes would have the same effect on q:

(56) $$r_1 = \frac{(R' - A' + qR'' - qA'')r_2}{R' + qR''} = \frac{(w + qw')r_2}{p + qp' + qR''}.$$

It now follows that it is more productive to tax the manufacturer when $v_1 = r_1 p < v_2 = r_2 w$, or when

(57)
$$(w + qw')p < (p + qp' + qR'')w$$
$$pw' < w(p' + R'').$$

The significance of this inequality depends on the relationship between p' and R'' — the slopes of the retailer's average-revenue (AR) and marginal-revenue (MR) curves. Consequently, let us define the operator

$$z = \frac{p' + R''}{p'} = \frac{3p' + qp''}{p'} = 3 + E_{p'q}.$$

where $E_{p'q} = qp''/p'$ is the elasticity of the slope of the demand or AR curve with respect to quantity. Criterion (57) may then be rewritten as

(58)
$$pw' < zwp'$$
$$-E_{qp} = -p/qp' > zw/qw' = -zE_{qw} = -(3 + E_{p'q})E_{qw}.$$

This inequality is fulfilled, implying that it is more productive to tax the manufacturer, when the wholesale demand that he confronts is sufficiently less elastic than the retail demand. This resembles criterion (9) in the case of a monopolistic manufacturer selling to purely competitive retailers; but the two cases differ in that now the verdict depends not only on the comparative values of $-E_{qw}$ and $-E_{qp}$, but also on z or $E_{p'q}$. There is also the difference that here $w = R' - A'$, in contrast to $w = p - a$ in the earlier case.

When the retail demand is linear, $E_{p'q} = 0$ and $z = 3$. Furthermore, $E_{p'q}$ is positive or negative and z is greater or less than 3 according as that demand is concave from below or above. When the retail demand is constant-elastic, such that $p = mq^{-1/n}$ and $-E_{qp} = n > 1$, it follows that $z = (2n - 1)/n$ and therefore that $1 < z < 2$. Finally, if we waive the rather academic possibility that a monopolist might be in equilibrium with positively sloped MR (and an even steeper MC), we may take it as a kind of limiting case where $R'' = 0$, $z = 1$, and $E_{p'q} = -2$. As long as $R'' < 0$, however, $z > 1$; and in all such cases criterion (58) will call for taxing the manufacturer only when $-E_{qp}$ exceeds $-E_{qw}$ by some ratio greater than unity.

Within an output range where $z = 1$ and R' is a constant, we have the following implications: $p = R' + b/q$ (where b is a positive constant); $p' = - b/q^2$; and $-E_{qp} = 1 + (R'q/b)$. Since $-E_{qp} \to 1$ as $q \to 0$ and $E_{qp} \to \infty$ as $q \to \infty$, there is clearly ample room for criterion (58) to be either fulfilled or not fulfilled; for in this case it is more productive to tax the manufacturer when $-E_{qp} > -E_{qw}$, and the only limitation on the latter term is that $-E_{qw} \geq 1$ when $C' \geq 0$. There would similarly be room for criterion (58) to go either way in all other cases where $-E_{qp}$ is an increasing function of q.

When the retail demand is the constant-elastic $p = mq^{-1/n}$ criterion (58) becomes

$$(59) \qquad\qquad -E_{qp} = n > -\frac{2n-1}{n} E_{qw}.$$

Hence it is more productive to tax the manufacturer only when the retail demand is more elastic than the wholesale demand by a factor between 1 and 2, depending on n. Clearly that criterion could readily go either way.

The case of linear demand illustrates the remaining possibility that $-E_{qp}$ may be a decreasing function of q. Here, since $z = 3$, criterion (58) becomes:

$$(60) \qquad\qquad -E_{qp} > -3E_{qw}.$$

Now the retail demand must be more than three times as elastic as the wholesale demand if it is to be more productive to tax the manufacturer. With demands that are concave from below, such that $z > 3$, the retail demand must be still more elastic than the wholesale demand if criterion (58) is to be fulfilled. In these cases, the verdict could again go either way.

Whether criterion (58) is, or is not, fulfilled depends to a considerable extent on the relative values of A' and C' — the marginal cost of the retailing service and the manufacturer's full marginal cost. To see this, we may first use equations (45) and (46) to recast criterion (58) as:

$$(61) \qquad\qquad -E_{qp} > \frac{z(R' - A')}{-q(R'' - A'')}.$$

Then, by further substitution from equation (55), the criterion becomes:

$$(62) \qquad\qquad -E_{qp} > \frac{z(R' - A')}{R' - A' - C'/(1 - r_2)}.$$

Now, as $C' \to 0$ (and as the equilibrium value of $-E_{qw} \to 1$), criterion (62) approaches:

$$(63) \qquad\qquad -E_{qp} > z.$$

This is always fulfilled when $z = 1$; for, even if A' were zero, the retailer's full marginal cost of $A' + w = R' > 0$, so that $-E_{qp} > 1$. In the same manner, this inequality is also likely to be fulfilled when z is only moderately greater than one; and, especially when A' is relatively large, it may be fulfilled even when z is large. On the other hand, as $C'/(1 - r_2)$ increases relative to $R' - A'$, the righthand expression in the inequality (62) grows larger; so there is increased likelihood that the inequality will be reversed. As we have also noticed in analogous earlier contexts, the upshot is that the lower a firm's marginal costs, the more its eligibility to be the one taxed. In addition, the curvilinear properties of both retail demand and retailing cost are also involved, as reflected by the appearance of R'' and A'' in equilibrium condition (55); but, since C'' does not make any appearance in the analysis, C' itself is the only relevant aspect of manufacturing costs.

A particular case of special interest is the one where retail demand is the constant-elastic $p = mq^{-1/n}$ (such that $-E_{qp} = n > 1$) and the average and marginal costs of the retailing service are the constant a. This is the case where, since $p/R' = n/(n-1)$, an increase in w (like a specific tax at the retail level in the absence of any vertical interdependence) causes the retail price p to rise by $n/(n-1)$ times the increase in w.[5] This is also the case where, apart from the consequences of vertical interdependence, an ad valorem tax would increase price by exactly the amount of the tax.

The demand confronting the manufacturer is then

$$(64) \qquad w = R' - A' = \left(\frac{n-1}{n}\right) mq^{-1/n} - a;$$

and this has the elasticity,

$$(65) \qquad -E_{qw} = -\frac{w}{qw'} = n - \frac{an^2 q^{1/n}}{(n-1)m}.$$

Furthermore, the manufacturer's first-order condition for a profit maximum when the tax is imposed on him, $(1 - r)(w + qw') = C'$, is:

$$\left(\frac{n-1}{n}\right)^2 mq^{-1/n} - a = \frac{C'}{1 - r_2}.$$

$$(66) \qquad q^{1/n} = \left(\frac{n-1}{n}\right)^2 \frac{m}{a + C'/(1 - r_2)}.$$

Substituting this in equation (65) then gives that elasticity's equilibrium value:

$$(67) \qquad -E_{qw} = n - \frac{a(n-1)}{a + C'/(1 - r_2)}.$$

Since criterion (59) may be rewritten as

$$\frac{n^2}{2n-1} > -E_{qw},$$

substitution of equation (67) shows our criterion to be:

$$(68) \qquad \frac{a}{C'} > \frac{n}{(1 - r_2)(n-1)}.$$

Since $n/(n-1) > 1$, this inequality is never fulfilled when $a < C'$; and in that event, of course, it is more productive to tax the retailer. It is more productive to tax the manufacturer only when a exceeds C' by more than the factor of $n/(1 - r_2)(n-1)$ — a ratio that exceeds unity by an in-

---

[5] This implication prompted Ursula Hicks to identify this case with percentage-markup pricing and the associated "pyramiding" of taxes levied at earlier stages. (See U.K. Hicks, *Public Finance*, 2nd ed., [London, 1955], 151.) The question is discussed in the next section (see especially n. 6).

creasing amount as the tax rate goes up or as the elasticity $-E_{qp} = n \to 1$. As $n \to \infty$, however, it pays to tax the manufacturer when

$$a/C' > 1/(1 - r_2).$$

Another interesting special case is the one where $p = p(q)$ and $a = a(q)$ are both linear. Let us specify, accordingly, that

(69) $$p = h - kq,$$

(70) $$a = m + nq,$$

where $h > m \geq 0$, $k > 0$, $k + n > 0$, and $km + hn > 0$ (lest, if $n < 0$, the marginal cost of the retailing service be less than zero within the relevant range of positive marginal revenue). It then follows that

(71) $$w = R' - A' = h - m - 2(k + n)q.$$

The elasticities of the retail and wholesale demand, which depend solely on the ratio of q to the q-axis intercepts of the respective demand schedules ($q = h/k$ and $q = (h - m)/2(k + n)$, respectively), are then:

(72) $$-E_{qp} = \frac{h}{kq} - 1$$

(73) $$-E_{qw} = \frac{h - m}{2(k + n)q} - 1.$$

The manufacturer's first-order condition for a profit maximum when the tax is imposed on him, $(1 - r_2)(w + qw') = C'$, is:

$$h - m - 4(k + n)q = \frac{C'}{1 - r_2}$$

(74) $$q = \frac{h - m - C'/(1 - r_2)}{4(k + n)}.$$

Hence, by substituting this in equations (72) and (73), we get the equilibrium values of the elasticities:

(75) $$-E_{qp} = \frac{3h + m + 4hn/k + C'/(1 - r_2)}{h - m - C'/(1 - r_2)}$$

(76) $$-E_{qw} = \frac{h - m + C'/(1 - r_2)}{h - m - C'(1 - r_2)}.$$

Criterion (60) then becomes:

(77) $$2\left(m + \frac{hn}{k}\right) > \frac{C'}{1 - r_2}.$$

To interpret this, notice that $m + hn/k$ is the ordinate of $a = m + nq$ when $q = h/k$, which is the q-axis intercept of $p = h - kq$. This is also the same as the ordinate of $A' = m + 2nq$ when $q = h/2k$, which is the q-axis intercept of $R' = h - 2kq$. Hence the inequality (77) is fulfilled when twice that ordinate is greater than the manufacturer's tax-augmented marginal cost, $C'/(1 - r_2)$. Again, it is more productive to tax the firm whose costs are relatively low, since high values of the retailer's cost parameters (m and n) tend to fulfill the inequality and a high value of the manufacturer's marginal cost (C') tends to reverse it. A high tax rate r_2 also tends to reverse the inequality; and high values of the retail-demand parameters (h and $-k$) work either for or against fulfilling it according as n is positive or negative.

When $n = 0$ and $a = m$ is a constant equal to the equilibrium value of C', the verdict of criterion (77) is for taxing the manufacturer, provided only that r_2 remains less than 50 percent. With constant-elastic demand, by contrast, criterion (68) favors taxing the retailer under the same cost conditions. These contrasting biases run counter to what we might have been led to expect from the contrasting values of z in criterion (58), since $z = 3$ for linear demand and $1 < z < 2$ for constant-elastic demand.

V   *The Consequences of Percentage-Markup Pricing*

If, as frequently alleged, retailers set their prices by marking up wholesale prices by some fixed percentage, this practice involves a pyramiding of the increase in wholesale price attributable to a tax levied prior to the retail stage. By contrast, a tax levied at the retail stage is supposed not to be pyramided. Therefore, it is concluded that retail taxes are preferable to those levied earlier.

On this theory's own terms, as we shall see, the conclusion is eminently correct that a retail tax is more productive than an equivalent tax levied at the manufacturing stage, whether the latter is competitive or monopolistic. On the other hand, the theory also rests on a behavioral hypothesis inconsistent with profit-maximization. The major source of that inconsistency is the assumption that a retailer will react differently to an increase in wholesale price than to an equal increase in some other component of marginal cost — such as that occasioned by a specific tax levied on his product. Except in very special circumstances, moreover, percentage-markup pricing is itself inconsistent with profit-maximization.

Percentage-markup pricing implies that the retail price is related to the wholesale price by a constant markup factor, $k > 1$:

(78) $$p = kw.$$

Let us see when this would be consistent with profit-maximizing behavior by a monopolist. When full marginal cost is the retailing marginal cost $A' = A'(q)$ plus the constant w, the first-order condition for a profit maximum implies that

$$w = R'(q) - A'(q).$$

Substituting this in equation (78) then indicates the special form that

$A' = A'$ (q) must take if percentage-markup pricing is to be consistent with profit-maximizing:

(79) $$A' = R'(q) - p(q)/k.$$

This condition is consistent with a nonnegative A' when $R' > w$, since $w = p/k$.

Perhaps the most obvious of such special cases is the one where the monopolist faces a constant-elastic demand and $A' \equiv 0$. As observed earlier, when $p = mq^{-1/n}$ and $-E_{qp} = n > 1$, it is implied that

$$p = \frac{n}{n-1} R'.$$

Hence, when marginal cost is just w and that is equated to R', the result is obviously consistent with equation (78):

(80) $$p = \frac{n}{n-1} w.$$

On the other hand, when A' is a positive constant, the equilibrium condition that

$$p = \frac{n}{n-1} (A' + w)$$

is not the equivalent of percentage-markup pricing of the wholesale price, even though it does imply such a relationship of price to the full marginal cost.[6]

Even if percentage-markup pricing by a retailer or group of retailers happened to be coincidentally consistent with profit-maximization, the practice is still a rule of thumb that takes the place of systematic profit-maximizing. Furthermore, the significance of the pyramiding implied when a tax is levied at an earlier stage appears only in contrast to the alleged nonpyramiding when the tax is levied on the retailer himself. It is this contrast, as already mentioned, that is basically inconsistent with profit-maximizing. Let us now examine its implications, first with respect to specific taxes.

If a specific tax t_1 is imposed at the retail stage, with the result that

$$p = kw + t_1,$$

the implied demand-price function at the manufacturing stage is:

(81) $$w^* = \frac{p(q) - t_1}{k}.$$

---

[6] Mrs. Hicks's identification of this case with percentage-markup pricing and with pyramiding has already been mentioned, in n. 5. Since her discussion is based entirely on the profit-maximizing principle, it should be stressed that, in that context, there is only an illusory connection between a monopolist's motive to raise price by more than the increase in his marginal cost and the kind of pyramiding that would militate against imposing specific taxes at earlier stages.

With purely competitive manufacturers, if their supply-price function is $s = s(q)$, their equilibrium condition of $w^*(q) - s(q) = 0$ implies that

(82)
$$t_1 = p - ks.$$

If, alternatively, a tax of t_2 is imposed at the manufacturing stage, where the demand-price function is now $w = p(q)/k$, and equilibrium implies that

$$\frac{p(q)}{k} - s(q) - t_2 = 0,$$

it follows that

(83)
$$t_2 = \frac{p - ks}{k}.$$

Clearly, since $t_1 = kt_2$ and $k > 1$, the specific tax at the retail level always raises more revenue than the equivalent tax levied earlier; and it does so by precisely the factor of the retailer's percentage markup, k.

This is also true when the manufacturing stage is monopolized. When the tax t_1 is levied on the retailer, the manufacturer faces the demand-price function (81); so his total revenue is

$$R_1 = w^*q = \frac{p(q)q - t_1 q}{k} = \frac{R(q) - t_1 q}{k},$$

and his marginal revenue is

(84)
$$R_1' = \frac{R' - t_1}{k}.$$

When the tax t_2 is levied on the manufacturer, however, and he faces the demand $w = p(q)/k$, his total and marginal revenues are:

$$R_2 = (w - t_2)q = \frac{p(q)q}{k} - t_2 q = \frac{R(q)}{k} - t_2 q,$$

(85)
$$R_2' = \frac{R'}{k} - t_2.$$

Equating R_1' and R_2', so that the alternative taxes will be equivalent, we again see that $t_1 = kt_2$. Naturally, this failure of specific taxes to be fully equivalent whether levied at the retail or manufacturing stage, in contrast with all of our preceding cases, is squarely attributable to the departures here from the principle of profit-maximization.

The story is much the same with ad valorem taxes. If such a tax is levied at the rate r_1 on the retailer, with the result that

$$(1 - r_1)p = kw,$$

the demand-price function at the manufacturing level becomes:

(86)
$$w^{**} = \frac{(1 - r_1)p(q)}{k}.$$

Equating this with the supply-price function of an industry of purely competitive manufacturers, $s = s(q)$, implies that

$$(87) \qquad r_1 = \frac{p - ks}{p}.$$

Alternatively, when an ad valorem tax is levied at the rate r_2 on the wholesale price, $w = p(q)/k$, the equilibrium condition, $(1 - r_2)p(q)/k = s(q)$, implies that

$$(88) \qquad r_2 = \frac{p - ks}{p}.$$

In other words, when $r_1 = r_2$, the alternative taxes would have the same effects on p and q. This also means, however, that $v_1 = r_1 p > v_2 = r_2 w$; and specifically, since $p = kw$, it follows that $v_1 = kv_2$.

The same thing is again true with a monopolistic manufacturer. When the tax is imposed on the retailer, the manufacturer's total and marginal revenues are:

$$R_3 = w^{**}q = \frac{(1 - r_1)p(q)q}{k} = \frac{(1 - r_1)R(q)}{k}$$

$$(89) \qquad R_3' = \frac{(1 - r_1)R'}{k}.$$

Alternatively, when the tax is levied on the manufacturer, the corresponding functions are:

$$R_4 = (1 - r_2)wq = \frac{(1 - r_2)p(q)q}{k} = \frac{(1 - r_2)R(q)}{k}$$

$$(90) \qquad R_4' = \frac{(1 - r_2)R'}{k}.$$

Once again, obviously, the alternative taxes are equivalent when $r_1 = r_2$. Also, $v_1 = r_1 p > v_2 = r_2 w$; and, specifically, $v_1 = kv_2$.[7]

[7] In the article mentioned in n. 1, Taubman rejects as "incorrect for ad valorem taxes" the statement by John Due that "the retail form of tax avoids the pyramiding of burden which is inevitable with any tax levied prior to the retail level, when distributors use percentage-markup pricing methods." (See Taubman, *op. cit.*, p. 650.) Clearly, if Due's assumptions accord with those made here, Taubman's criticism is wrong.

Taubman seems to base his argument (Taubman, *op. cit.*, pp. 652–53) on the fact that a profit-maximizing monopolist who has constant marginal cost and faces a constant-elastic demand would raise price by an amount equal to an ad valorem tax but by an amount greater than a specific tax (see above, p. 229). As already mentioned (n. 6), this has a dubious connection with the phenomena of percentage-markup pricing and pyramiding. More fundamentally, although Taubman is specifically concerned with the comparative effects of taxes imposed on retailers or manufacturers, under both profit-maximization and percentage-markup pricing, he does not really analyze at all the vertical interdependence that is essential to such comparison. See also A. J. Vandermuelen, "The Effects of Ad Valorem and Specific Taxes on Prices: Comment," *Quarterly Journal of Economics*, LXXXI, (1967) 158–160.

In a fully profit-maximizing context, we know that an ad valorem tax raises the same revenue as the equivalent specific tax under pure competition but p/R' times as much under monopoly. Interestingly enough, exactly the same contrast also applies here when the alternative taxes are imposed on the percentage-markup retailers, according as the supplying industry is competitive or monopolistic. When the taxes are imposed on the supplying industry, however, the ad valorem tax is more productive than the specific tax in the competitive case and still more productive in the monopolistic one.

When the manufacturing industry is purely competitive, the alternative taxes on the retailer are equivalent provided that equations (82) and (87) relate to the same magnitudes of p and s. In that event, it is implied that $v_1 = t_1$, so the alternative taxes would raise the same revenue. Similarly, when the manufacturing supplier is a monopolist, equations (84) and (89) show the alternative taxes to be equivalent when $t_1 = r_1 R'$; and, comparing this with $v_1 = r_1 p$, we see that $v_1 = (p/R')t_1$.

When the manufacturing industry is competitive and the alternative taxes are levied there, equations (83) and (88) establish that $v_2 = kt_2$. Similarly, when a monopolistic manufacturer is taxed, equations (85) and (90) imply that $kt_2 = r_2 R'$, which in turn establishes that $v_2 = (kp/R')t_2$. Thus, when the manufacturing stage is taxed, this increases the ad valorem tax's revenue-raising advantage over the specific tax by the factor of k, as compared with the situation when it is the retail stage that is taxed.

The main conclusions of this section are that, with percentage-markup pricing by retailers and profit-maximizing by manufacturers, retail taxes are always more productive than the corresponding equivalent taxes on manufacturers. When the manufacturing stage is purely competitive, it does not matter whether the retail tax is specific or ad valorem; but with a monopolistic manufacturer, the ad valorem tax is the more productive.

VI Conclusion

Although this is a suitable stopping point for a first installment in the analysis of the vertical effects of taxes, extensions of it would be clearly desirable. It would be especially useful to investigate the implications when monopolistically competitive groups operate in either the retailing stage, the manufacturing stage, or both. That analysis promises to be difficult and much too lengthy to deal with in an essay.

Only a brief recapitulation of the more important results of the foregoing analysis will be attempted. It should be recalled that our analysis abstracts from certain administrative considerations, such as the costs of tax collection, and treats the cost of the retailing service as independent of the wholesale price.

Except in the aberrant case of percentage-markup pricing, then, it does not matter whether a specific tax is levied at the retailing or manufacturing stage, irrespective of the competitive or monopolistic character of each. With an ad valorem tax, however, it typically does make a difference.

When one stage is monopolized and the other is competitive (as in sections I and II), it is almost surely more productive of tax revenue, for any given contraction of output, to put an ad valorem tax on the monopolist rather than on the competitors, whether it is the manufacturing or retailing stage that is monopolized. Only if a negatively sloped supply schedule of the competitive industry were actually less elastic than the retail demand would that verdict be reversed.

When both stages are monopolized, generalization is more difficult. The situation is essentially symmetrical, however, when the bilateral monopolists behave collusively but without side payments (section III). It then tends to be more productive of tax revenue to impose an ad valorem tax on one firm rather than the other to the extent that (a) its share of the joint profit is high, (b) its marginal cost is relatively low, and (c) the ratio of its average cost to its marginal cost is relatively high.

Similar, but still more complex, generalizations also apply when the retailer, though exerting monopoly power in the retail market, is a passive price-taker vis-à-vis the monopolistic manufacturer (section IV). Again it appears that the lower a firm's marginal cost, the more eligible a candidate that firm becomes for ad valorem taxation. Furthermore, the more elastic the retail demand relative to the wholesale demand, the greater the likelihood that taxing the manufacturer will be more productive than taxing the retailer. In all of the ordinary cases, however, the verdict goes that way only when the retail elasticity exceeds the wholesale elasticity by a factor greater than one. That factor, in turn, is the greater, the more steeply downward-sloping is the retail marginal-revenue curve relative to the retail demand.

When a retailer practices percentage-markup pricing, so that a tax imposed at an earlier stage is pyramided but a tax at the retail stage is not (section V), it is always more productive to tax the retailer, whether the tax is specific or ad valorem and whether the manufacturing stage is competitive or monopolistic. Furthermore, the ad valorem tax is more productive than the specific tax if the manufacturer is a monopolist, but the two taxes are equally productive if the manufacturing stage is purely competitive The behavior assumed in this section is, of course, inconsistent with profit-maximization.

REFERENCES

[1] Bishop, R. L. "The Effects of Specific and Ad Valorem Taxes". *Quarterly Journal of Economics,* LXXXII (1968), 198–218.

[2] Hicks, U. K. *Public Finance* (2d ed., London, 1955).

[3] Musgrave, R. A. *The Theory of Public Finance: A Study in Public Economy* (New York, 1959).

[4] Taubman, P. J. "The Effects of Ad Valorem and Specific Taxes on Prices". *Quarterly Journal of Economics,* LXXIX (1965), 649–56.

[5] Vandermeulen, A. J. "The Effects of Ad Valorem and Specific Taxes on Prices: Comment". *Quarterly Journal of Economics,* LXXXI (1967), 158–160.

11

The Impact of Uncertainty on the
"Traditional" Theory of the Firm:
Price-Setting and Tax Shifting

*John Lintner**

Uncertainty is an inescapable fact. All significant decisions are forward-looking. Many or all of the relevant consequences of any decision cannot be foreknown with precision at the time the decision is made. The purpose of the present paper is to illustrate a few of the far-reaching consequences of these facts for the traditional theory of the firm.

As these consequences are more fully explored by economists over the next few years, the resulting "uncertainty revolution" in the body of doctrine may confidently be expected to be marked by later historians of the discipline as a watershed comparable to the "Chamberlinian revolution." This theoretical work should also lead to as much important empirical research as the constructs of Monopolistic Competition, which in the hands of an Edward Mason, spawned the whole field of Industrial Organization in its modern form. Important new dimensions of analysis for "industry studies" will be opened up, and new results of major consequence will surely be obtained.

Some theoretical work along the lines proposed has, of course, already been done. The work of Shubik and others using the theory of games has surely enriched our understanding of oligopolistic interactions. Models of stochastic dynamic programming have had a substantial impact upon business practice with respect to inventory policy and production scheduling, and they have greatly increased our understanding of the effect of uncertainty upon these specific short-calendar-time policies. Mills[1] in particular

* Harvard University

[1] See Mills [12]. (Throughout this essay the numbers in brackets in footnotes refer to items listed in the essay's bibliography.)

has dealt with the effect of uncertain demands upon the prices charged by firms concerned with losses on unsold inventory, and Nelson[2] and others have examined the impact of uncertainty on prices in a setting of purely competitive equilibrium. But it seems fair to say that these contributions have had relatively little, if any, impact upon the hard core of the traditional theory of the firm — upon the major concerns of a Chamberlin or a Mason with the price and output policies of the modern corporation operating under less than purely competitive conditions so that price as such becomes an important decision variable to the firm. Closer in spirit to the thrust of the present paper are contributions of Fellner and others that introduced risk aversion as such into the analysis. More detailed comment on these latter papers will be made below.

The Empirical setting. Our analysis will be specifically concerned with the impact of uncertainty upon the prices, and the profit margins over direct (marginal) costs, established by firms satisfying the following characteristics:

1. They are *price-setters* and *price-leaders* as distinct from price-takers and price-followers. We are dealing with the pricing decisions of firms which have substantial discretion with respect to their price policy. In the standard taxonomy of Industrial Organization theory, these firms have substantial degrees of *market power*.

2. At the time prices are determined, the quantities of output which can be sold at any one of the possible prices during the model or calendar year (or other price-planning period) are highly uncertain. Expected unit demand varies inversely with price, but there are substantial variances in expectations about the quantities which will in fact be sold conditional on any price.

3. The outputs of the firms that interest us are generally produced by particular "processes" in the programming sense, and a substantial literature confirms that — over wide ranges of outputs and to a very good approximation — marginal production costs are essentially constant with respect to output.

4. In view of the market power enjoyed by these firms, they are able to increase the expected quantities of output which can be sold at any given price by increasing their outlays on advertising and other promotion — more salesmen, displays at trade shows, and the like. In the present paper, however, we will treat advertising budgets as

---

[2] See Nelson [13]. While the present paper was in galley, I learned of Ira Horwitz' new text *Decision Making and the Theory of the Firm* (Holt, Rinehart and Winston, 1970), Chapter XIII of which deals with some of the issues raised in this paper. At substantially the same time, I also received an elegant unpublished paper "The Theory of the Firm Facing Uncertain Demand" by Hayne Leland of Stanford University which should be noted, both for its independent derivation of some of the results presented below and for the other significant propositions it develops.

exogenously fixed and concentrate upon prices and outputs subject to the given level of advertising outlay.

5. The products produced and sold are such that the economical "lot sizes" for separate production runs are moderate or small relative to expected sales over the calendar period for which announced prices are expected to hold without change. Since several "production periods" occur within each "pricing period," questions of optimal carry-over stocks from the final production run, and of the extent of price-cutting necessary to move out the final units in a model year, have relatively little bearing upon selection of a price to be quoted at the beginning of the pricing period. Total production before the next change in model or price can be rather easily lined up with the actual market demand by adjustments in the final production run before the change. Consequently, we ignore the usual inventory problem as a second- or third-order qualification. Since the firms in which we are interested plan capacity well ahead of current demand, we also assume that any output actually demanded can be supplied from available capacity.

6. At the time a new price is to be announced, management knows that, during the model year (or period during which the newly announced price will be in effect), there may be some occasions when average unit revenues fall short of quoted unit prices; and there is always some uncertainty concerning the level of unit variable costs which will be incurred in producing the outputs sold. But for the dominant price-setting firms in the industries we have in mind as prototypes — notably automobiles and other major consumer durables, trucks, most road equipment, standardized motors and many other industrial products not produced to order — their uncertainties regarding unit sales at any price seem to be relatively very much greater than their uncertainties regarding price-realizations and variable costs.[3] In section II we ignore the latter, more minor uncertainties

---

[3] These dominant price-setting firms are well known for their modern and efficient systems of cash-budgeting and cost-controls. Increases in productivity are projected with considerable accuracy in such firms. Wage rates are determined by contracts running much longer than the product's (usually annual) pricing period, and when labor contracts are to be renegotiated within the product's pricing period, rather good advance estimates of the cost of the final settlement can usually be made. Materials are usually contracted in advance with substantial foreknowledge, if not outright control, of price in the event of new contracting within the product's pricing period. It should also be noted that *planned* increases in discounts or bonuses to dealers over the course of a price-planning period (as in the auto industry) do not constitute an uncertainty, and are consequently extraneous to the concern of this paper. In a broader historical sweep, the evidence presented by Ruggles [16], Neal [14] and Lanzillotti [8], [9], clearly indicated the *relatively* high degree of control over, and hence predictability, of profit margins.

In contrast, uncertainties about quantity are almost uniformly very substantial, both absolutely and relatively. Moreover, this is true both in historical time series and in

by treating prices and variable costs as being known in advance. We return to them in section III, which examines the effects on prices and expected outputs of uncertainties regarding realized net prices and levels of variable cost.

7. In the present paper, we will concentrate upon the comparative statics of optimal "short run" behavior — in the Marshallian sense — with respect to prices and outputs. We will ignore interperiod dependencies in demand functions and other dynamic considerations, and we will treat the stock of capital and the level of fixed costs as given data throughout. To focus most sharply upon the impact of "uncertainty-cum-risk-aversion" on the price-output decisions of immediate interest, we will also ignore any "portfolio aspects" of the interrelations between these decisions and the firm's other operations along with their associated uncertainties.

8. For purposes of the analysis in this paper, we will simply assume that pricing decisions are made on a fully rational profit-maximizing basis subject to risk aversion with respect to the uncertain profits involved. It should perhaps be emphasized that, in making this assumption, we do not intend to imply any judgment that profit-maximization-cum-risk-aversion is a behaviorally *sufficient* description of the goal that in practice determine all decisions on price and advertising within firms having a more or less significant degree of market power.[4]

There is ample evidence, however, that earnings and profits are usually one of the most important considerations at the highest levels of corporate policy-making and that uncertainties regarding the effects of different policies on profits are a major concern of top management. The traditional theory of the firm, based on profit-maximization as such, urgently needs at least to be generalized to incorporate the observable facts that profit-seeking managements are very much aware of risks to profits and that these risks do significantly affect decisions. Such generalization is the primary purpose of the present paper.

---

data on major products (autos, refrigerators, television sets) for individual firms, and especially data on individual models requiring separate *ex ante* pricing. The author knows of forecasting errors in recent years of well over 50% on sales of particular models and products in the field of consumers' durable goods.

[4] Dollar sales, market shares, management's own empire-building or emoluments, and various other nonprofit elements may well belong in a complex multivariate utility function, which on the basis of subsequent research, would turn out to more adequately describe the range of decision-making in modern corporations. But our results in this paper show that several of the qualitative effects ascribed by others to non-profit criteria may simply be due to uncertainties and risk aversion within an otherwise more tranditional profit-maximizing context. Our exploration of profit-maximizing under risk-averse reactions to uncertainty will thereby sharpen and hopefully stimulate badly needed research on the *distinctive* content and empirical significance of the various theoretical suggestions (made in a context of certainty) presented in the "revisionist" literature.

The objective function.   Our assumption that decisions are made on a profit-maximizing basis subject to risk aversion with respect to the uncertainties involved is a special case of assuming in our one-period context that decisions are made to maximize the expected utility of the firm's uncertain end-of-period wealth $\tilde{W}_1$. We specifically assume that each firm behaves in accordance with the Ramsey-de Finetti-Savage axioms of rational decision-making under uncertainty with respect to wealth and that its preference (or von Neumann-Morgenstern utility) function is risk averse in the standard sense. In other words, the firm prefers options with greater expected returns — net increments to wealth — provided that risks are no greater, and it prefers options with lesser risks if expected returns are at least as high. Effectively, this requires that $U'(W_1) > 0$ and $U''(W_1) < 0$, that is to say, positive but diminishing marginal utility for successive increments to wealth. As Pratt[5] and Arrow[6] have shown, the *degree* of risk aversion is $r(W_1) = -U''/U'$ and may be interpreted as twice the dollar insurance premium which, as a matter of indifference, would be paid to avoid incurring each dollar of variance in uncertain outcomes.

Now there are reasonably persuasive grounds for believing that the degree of risk aversion is generally a declining function of the wealth of a particular decision-making unit and that for "large" decisions — such as capital investments and the planning of long-term strategies for continuing growth[7] — this inverse functional dependence of risk aversion on wealth is strong enough that it needs to be taken explicitly into account in theoretical work on these "large" decisions. On the other hand, the degree of curvature in the utility function within the relevant range of variation involved in various "small" decisions — such as short-term production scheduling and inventory policy — is sufficiently small to indicate that an analysis based on an "expected monetary value" — and hence entirely ignoring risk aversion *per se* — is generally adequate for most practical purposes. In effect, for these "small" decisions, conclusions are not significantly distorted by substituting the tangent (an "as if" *linear* utility) for the utility function. But this is true only because large differential sums of money — amounts relative to total assets or wealth — are not involved in the individual decisions and because errors, surprises, and new information can readily be allowed for in short order.

We regard the pricing decisions of the firms in which this paper is interested as falling in an "intermediate" category of decision-making with respect to risk aversion. Our price leaders with substantial market power announce prices which they will not, or do not expect to, change over substantial calendar periods in the face of highly uncertain unit demands. Under these conditions, they clearly regard the dollar-profit uncertainties involved in price announcements as being very much greater than those

[5] See Pratt [15].
[6] See Arrow [1].
[7] See for instance Lintner [10].

involved in deciding on the batch size of a particular production run. For this reason, risk aversion is much more important in pricing decisions than in production-scheduling and in setting individual targets for inventory in the short run. At the same time, individual pricing decisions for these firms do not involve nearly as large dollar commitments and uncertainties as do major programs of capital investment and the formulation of broad policies and strategies for continuing growth — in part because announced prices can be changed in a matter of several months while these more portentous decisions usually involve relatively inflexible commitments over periods of several years at a time.

Just as the assumption of a constant elasticity in the utility function on wealth — a form of the function which implies constant *proportional* risk aversion — is probably a much better approximation than other mathematically convenient forms of the utility function for theoretical work on the latter "large" and more portentous decisions, it seems reasonable to adopt an exponential utility function as the prototype for analyzing "intermediate" decisions — such as, specifically, pricing in the context of the present paper. This function is simple and convenient to use,[8] and it effectively builds any given degree of risk aversion into the analysis. The *measure* of risk aversion $r(W_1)$ may be set at whatever level is appropriate to any particular company after taking into account its assets and wealth at the time. On the other hand, the use of this function holds the assigned level of risk aversion fixed over the entire range of random outcomes relevant to the decision in question. To this extent, like all convenient theoretical models, the function involves an approximation, but a good one for present purposes. Even though the dependence of $r(W)$ on conditional values of wealth is important for probative analysis of "large" decisions with major multiperiod consequences for the firm, this dependence may reasonably be regarded as a matter of only second-or even third-order significance for "intermediate" decisions in the comparative static, short-run context of the present analysis.[9]

[8] The obvious, equally simple, alternative utility function would be the quadratic, which has been rather commonly used in related work. But the quadratic has several anomolous and undesirable properties — most notably a *perverse* relation of $r(W)$ and W, which implies that *less* will be paid for a given dollar risk, the greater the wealth. See Pratt [15].

[9] In more detail for interested readers, let the true utility function over very broad ranges of $\widetilde{W}$ be $U(\widetilde{W}) = f(W)$, with $r(W) = -f''(W)/f'(W)$ and $r'(W) < 0$. If the level of wealth expected at the end of the year is $\overline{W}_1$, the argument in the text may be stated in three parts. First, for "small" decisions, $U(W)$ may be satisfactorily approximated by $U^*(\widetilde{W}) = a + f'(\overline{W}_1)\widetilde{W}_1$, with $f'(\overline{W}_1)$ treated as a constant, so that $r[U^*(\widetilde{W})] = 0$. The company thus acts "as if" it were neutral to risk and makes such decisions effectively on an expected-money-value basis.

Second (of immediate relevance to this paper), this approximation is satisfactory only if the range of $\widetilde{W}_1$ affected by the decisions is small enough that the variation in $f'(\widetilde{W}_1)$ over this range of $\widetilde{W}_1$ is truly negligible. We argue that $U^*(\widetilde{W})$ is *not* good enough for the "intermediate" decisions we are concerned with here, which involve considerably larger ranges of possible outcomes. For these, the variation of $f'(W)$

When the degree of risk aversion is effectively constant over the relevant range of outcomes under consideration, the firm's utility function may be written

(1) $$U(\tilde{W}_1) = a' - b'e^{-2\alpha\tilde{W}_1},$$

where the measure of risk aversion is $r(W) = -U''/U' = 2\alpha$. Since a risk-utility function (like centigrade and Fahrenheit temperature scales) is unique only up to a linear transformation, a' can be *any* finite number ($-\infty < a' < \infty$) and b' can be *any positive* finite number ($0 < b' < \infty$) without affecting the choice of decisions that will maximize expected utility.

Decisions are, of course, affected by the degree of risk aversion 2α and also by the assessments made of the relevant distributions of the uncertain outcomes associated with any action. The simplest and most convenient form of probability distribution to use with our exponential utility function is the normal or Gaussian distribution. Since it can be shown that all the principal results obtained below with normal distributions will also hold over a broad range of other distributions (including the rectangular), we use a normal probability distribution $f(\tilde{W}) = N[\overline{W}, \sigma_w^2]$, and find that[10]

(2) $$E[U(\tilde{W})] = a' - b'E[\{\exp(-2\alpha\tilde{W})\} f(W)dW]$$
$$= a' - b'[\exp(-2\alpha[\overline{W} - \alpha\sigma_W^2])].$$

Since expected utility varies directly with the value of the interior bracket, it follows that the decisions which maximize the certainty equivalent $\hat{W} = \overline{W} - \alpha\sigma_w^2$ will also maximize expected utility.

In order to focus specifically upon the implications of uncertainty and risk aversion for firms otherwise maximizing profits, we will regard the uncertain end-of-period wealth $\tilde{W}_1$ as being equal to its initial wealth plus its uncertain profits during the period

(3) $$\tilde{W}_1 = W_0 + \tilde{\Pi}_1.$$

Other things equal, $\overline{W}_1$ is thus taken to be a constant W^0 plus *expected*[11]

---

over the relevant range is so large that $f''(W)$ and $r(W)$ cannot properly be ignored or set to zero. But for this class of decisions, it does seem appropriate to ignore the variation of $r(W)$ over the relevant "intermediate" range of possible outcomes. We consequently give $r(W)$ its value at the point of expected wealth $\overline{W}_1$ and treat this value as a constant in our analysis of *these* decisions, a procedure which results in the "exponential" utility function used in the text with $2a = r(\overline{W}_1)$. Finally, we argue that for "large" decisions involving substantially greater ranges of possible $\tilde{W}$, $r(W)$ can no longer be treated as a constant, and *its* variation over the broad range of W must also be built into the analysis of these *other* "larger" issues.

[10] The expected value of an exponential utility function of a normally distributed argument is readily found by completing the square in the exponent under the integral or by referring directly to the moment-generating function for the formal distribution. See any good introductory text in mathematical statistics.

[11] This simplification enables us to derive the major conclusions of most interest for this paper in the simplest possible form. In a more extended treatment, I have shown that the same qualitative results are obtained when the change in wealth during the period is a multiple, or a rising function, of the level of current profits.

profit Π. Moreover, since as already noted, we are ignoring in this paper any "portfolio interactions" with other decisions and policies in order to focus on the price-quantity implications of risk aversion and uncertainty, we set $\sigma_w^2 = \sigma_\pi^2$. We thus consider only the profits arising from the price-output decisions of immediate concern and find the optimal mix of these decisions by seeking to maximize the certainty equivalent of profits

$$\text{(4)} \qquad\qquad \hat{\Pi} = \bar{\Pi} - \alpha\sigma_\pi^2$$

where α is half the risk-aversion coefficient in the primary utility function.

II The Price-Setting Firm: Uncertainty About Quantity

Uncertainty about demand independent of price.

Some of the most significant effects of risk aversion and uncertainty upon the prices established by the important class of firms described in paragraphs (1) through (7) above can most readily be seen by considering the simplified case in which (a) all uncertainty is confined to the quantities which will be sold at different announced prices, and (b) this uncertainty is the same at all possible levels of prices (or expected quantities sold). Dependence of demand uncertainty upon expected quantities is introduced in subsection 3 below, and uncertainty with respect to realized prices and the level of marginal costs will be introduced in section III.

The usual theory of the firm under certainty assumes that the demand for the firm's output is a declining function of the price set by the firm and that management knows the functional relation between price (p) and quantity (q). With uncertainty recognized, we correspondingly assume that the firm knows the probability distribution governing the demand for its product:

$$\text{(5)} \qquad\qquad \tilde{q} = f(p, \tilde{u}) = h(p) + \tilde{u}, \qquad h'(p) < 0,$$

where u is a random term, and tildes denote random variables. We will assume that $\tilde{u}$ (and hence $\tilde{q}$) are normally distributed with an expected, or mean, value $\bar{u} = 0$ and a variance σ_u^2. Total revenues or sales receipts will also be a normally distributed random variable defined by

$$\text{(6)} \qquad\qquad \tilde{R}(p, \tilde{u}) = p\tilde{q} = pf(p, \tilde{u}).$$

In this section we ignore any uncertainties in the costs of producing any given output. Conditional on quantity produced, production costs have no random term. Even under these conditions, however, actual total costs are a random quantity, since at the time price is set, the quantity of product that will be produced and sold is a random variable defined by (5). The distribution of even determinate functions of normally distributed random variables can be very complicated, but a simple form is quite appropriate in our case, given the evidence that in practice marginal costs are essentially constant over the relevant ranges of output for the types of firms being studied here. We thus specify the cost function as

(7) $$C(\tilde{q}) = F + v\tilde{q},$$

where $v = C'(\tilde{q}) > 0$ is some constant. The fixed, nonvariable costs F will include the exogenously established level of advertising outlay along with all overheads and administrative expenses.

In general, the functional relation between profits and price will be given by

(8) $$\tilde{\Pi}(p, \tilde{u}) = \tilde{R}(p, \tilde{u}) - C(\tilde{q}) = p\tilde{q} - C(\tilde{q}).$$

Expected profits are

(8a) $$\bar{\Pi}(p) = \bar{R}(p) - v\bar{q} = (p - v)\bar{q} - F,$$

and the variance of profits is

(8b) $$\sigma_\pi^2 = (p - v)^2 \sigma_u^2.$$

Upon substituting (8a) and (8b) in (4), our proximate criterion function derived in the previous section becomes

(9) $$\hat{\Pi} = \bar{\Pi} - \alpha\sigma_\pi^2 = \bar{R}(p) - v\bar{q} - \alpha(p - v)^2\sigma_u^2 - F$$
$$= (p - v)\bar{q} - \alpha(p - v)^2\sigma_u^2 - F.$$

Since price is our decision variable, we determine the optimum by examining the derivatives of (9) with respect to price. If we consider a firm as initially thinking of announcing a relatively high price and then progressively reducing this price so long as the benefits of the price reduction outweigh the costs of the reduction, we can write the derivatives of (9) in the following way:

(10) $$\frac{\partial\hat{\Pi}}{\partial(-p)} = \frac{\partial\bar{\Pi}}{\partial(-p)} - \alpha\frac{\partial\sigma_\pi^2}{\partial(-p)}.$$

Futher reductions in price are desirable so long as the entire expression on the right-hand side of (10) is positive, and the optimum price will be that for which this full expression is zero.

1a. Illustration with a linear demand function. Because the implications of equation (10) come out in particularly transparent form if we specify a linear form of the demand function (5), we will for the moment let the demand function be

(5a) $$\tilde{q} = a - bp + \tilde{u}, \qquad a, b > 0,$$

which makes the expected quantity $\bar{q} = a - bp$, a form often used to illustrate traditional price theory. When this expression is substituted in (9), the critical derivative in (10) becomes

(10') $$\frac{\partial \hat{\Pi}}{\partial(-p)} = 2bp - a - bv + 2\alpha(p - v)\sigma_u^2.$$

Consequently, the optimal price is

(11a) $$p_u^* = \frac{a + bv + 2\alpha v\sigma_u^2}{2(b + \alpha\sigma_u^2)} = v + \frac{a - bv}{2(b + \alpha\sigma_u^2)} \; ;$$

and the optimal gross margin over variable cost is

(11b) $$m_u^* = p_u^* - v = \frac{a - bv}{2(b + \alpha\sigma_u^2)} ,$$

while the optimal percentage margin is

(11c) $$m_u^{0*} = \frac{p_u^* - v}{p_u^*} = \frac{a - bv}{a + bv + 2\alpha v\sigma_u^2} .$$

As a matter of notation, we will use an asterisk to represent optimum values and a subscript *"u"* to represent a value under uncertainty. We distinguish between gross "dollar" margin, $m_u = p_u - v$, and the *percentage* margin, $m_u^0 = (p_u - v)/p_u$, by adding a superscript "0" to the latter variable.

1b. Some initial conclusions. When there is no uncertainty, the equilibrium prices and margins are given by (11 a-c) after setting $\sigma_u = 0$. (Note that $a > bv$ is a condition for any output to be produced even under certainty.) It is also obvious that an increase of either α or σ_u^2 in the denominator in equations (11) will reduce the value of the ratios for any fixed values a and b (specifying the demand function) or v (the marginal cost of output). Consequently, under the conditions specified in the first paragraph of section II.1:

1. *prices will be lower,* (a) *the greater the uncertainty* concerning the quantities which will in fact be sold over the pricing period at any announced price, and (b) *the greater the risk aversion of the company.*
2. *gross margins measured in dollars and cents per unit also vary inversely with both the degree of risk aversion and the amount of uncertainty in the estimates of quantity.*
3. risk aversion and uncertainty about quantity *also reduce percentage margins over variable costs.*

For simplicity, these results have been illustrated with linear expected demand functions, but we can readily establish that they are much more general.[12] The first-order condition for the maximum of (9) is simply

---

[12] Elsewhere we have taken derivatives with respect to price reductions $(-dp)$ rather than to price itself, since the heuristic interpretation seems more direct in this form. But the present, more general, proof relies on second derivatives, which are more readily interpreted when taken with respect to price itself rather than the negative of price.

$\partial\hat{\Pi}/\partial p = 0$, and the second-order conditions for a true maximum require that $\partial^2\hat{\Pi}/\partial p^2 < 0$ — a condition we show later to be less restrictive than the corresponding condition under certainty. When uncertainty is confined to quantities sold, the total differential of the first-order condition is

$$\left(\frac{\partial^2\hat{\Pi}}{\partial p^2}\right) dp + \left(\frac{\partial^2\hat{\Pi}}{\partial p \partial\sigma_u^2}\right) d\sigma_u^2 = 0,$$

so that

(12)
$$\frac{dp^*}{d\sigma_u^2} = -\frac{(\partial^2\hat{\Pi})/(\partial p \partial\sigma_u^2)}{(\partial^2\hat{\Pi})/(\partial p^2)} < 0,$$

since $\partial^2\hat{\Pi}/\partial p^2 < 0$ and $\partial^2\Pi/\partial p \partial\sigma_u = -2\alpha(p - v) < 0$ for all $p > v$. Since α and σ_u^2 enter the criterion only as elements multiplied together, the conclusion that optimal prices will be lower, the greater the uncertainty also holds for the degree of risk aversion α. It also holds for margins $m^* = p_u^* - v$, since variable costs were held constant in proving our proposition that prices are lowered by uncertainty and risk aversion. Similarly, the conclusion holds for *percentage* margins, since $m^{0*} = (p_u^* - v)/p_u^*$ rises or falls with prices for fixed variable costs.[13] Q.E.D. for propositions (i), (ii), and (iii).

1c. An explanation. Before proceeding to point out further implications of this model, it seems appropriate to fill in the rationale for these perhaps surprising or even seemingly paradoxical results. The explanation becomes clear if we look back at the form of expression in equation (9) for the certainty equivalent of profits. In the limit as $\sigma_u^2 \to 0$, the certainty equivalent becomes simply the profits which would be realized under known data in the standard analysis assuming certainty. But, given uncertainty, there is a (utility) cost attached to uncertainty of profits — in our case, a constant "marginal cost" for any dollar of profit variance, with this "marginal cost" measured in terms of a dollar *expected* profits. Since the profit variance is the product of the quantity variance and the square of the (gross) profit margin — announced price less constant marginal production cost — any reduction in price not only has the usual effect on *expected* profits, but it *also reduces the amount of profit variance* attributable to any quantity variance σ_u^2. This latter "utility gain" leads to greater price reductions than would be profitable ceteris paribus if it were known that expected values would be realized with certainty.

Specifically, under certainty, the firm would stop searching for lower prices when $\partial\hat{\Pi}/\partial(-p)$ in (10) became zero. (In terms of our linear demand illustration, the resulting p_c^*, m_c^*, and m_c^{0*} will be given by [11 a-c]

[13] Note that $\partial m^0/\partial p = v/p^2 > 0$. Since $dm^0/d\sigma_u^2 = (\partial m^0/\partial p)(dp^*/d\sigma_u^2)$, the sign of the change in percentage margins induced by changes in uncertainty (or risk aversion) must be the same as that of price itself.

with $\sigma_u^2 = 0$.) But in the face of uncertainty, the derivative in the second term in (10) with respect to price reductions is negative and will remain so as long as price remains above marginal production costs, since

$$\frac{\partial \sigma^2}{\partial(-p)} = -2(p - v)\sigma_u^2 < 0, \qquad \text{if } p > v.$$

With prices and margins at their "certainty" levels, this continuing reduction in "uncertainty costs," costs which are being subtracted in our objective function, means that prices will continue to be reduced until the marginal sacrifice in *expected* profits — that is $\partial \overline{\Pi}/\partial(-p)$ — becomes large enough to offset the gain from further risk avoidance represented by the second term in (10). At the resulting optimum point, the marginal losses from further price reduction will no longer be less than — and hence will equal — the marginal gains from risk avoidance by means of any further price reduction.

Formally, we have

(10a) $$\frac{\partial \hat{\Pi}}{\partial(-p)} = \frac{\partial \overline{\Pi}}{\partial(-p)} - [-2\alpha(p - v)\sigma_u^2].$$

And at the optimum under uncertainty,

(10b) $$\frac{\partial \overline{\Pi}}{\partial(-p)} = -2\alpha(p - v)\sigma_u^2,$$

rather than zero.

1d. Reinterpretation in terms of traditional "MR" and "MC." It will be noticed that we have consistently taken our derivatives with respect to price p, since this is the decision variable of interest in the situation we are analyzing. In an adaptation of the economist's usual marginal language, we can translate our statement of the firm's optimum or equilibrium position in (10c) as saying that "the marginal *expected* profit (loss) *with respect to price* equals the marginal value of differential risk with respect to price."

Even under certainty, once one leaves the subset of purely competitive markets, price becomes the decision variable,[14] and quantity sold is derived from price by way of the demand function. In keeping with this approach, elasticities of demand are consistently defined in terms of the responsiveness of quantity to change in *price* as the action variable. Nevertheless, the usual prescription of a monopolist's price equilibrium under certainty calls for price to be set so that marginal profit is zero, or $MR = MC$, when marginal profits, marginal revenues, and marginal costs are all defined *with respect to quantity*, not price.

This orientation of marginal revenues and costs to changes in quantity

---

[14] Except, of course, when inventory decisions and production schedules are at issue.

rather than price is understandable, as well as traditional,[15] and makes no difference under certainty.[16] It is instructive to consider our results with uncertainty from a corresponding point of view.

We should first note that it simply makes no sense to try to find a maximum by equating a derivative with respect to a random variable to zero. Specifically, it would be nonsense to try to set $\partial \hat{\tilde{\Pi}}/\partial \tilde{q} = 0$, which might be taken to correspond to the usual maximizing condition under certainty: $\partial \Pi/\partial q = \partial R/\partial q - \partial C/\partial q = MR - MC = 0$. In our context, once chosen, p is a constant with respect to volume, and we have assumed constant marginal production costs. In this case, $\tilde{\Pi}(p,q)$ varies directly with each unit change in *actual* volume by a constant amount $(p - v)$ — that is, $\triangle\tilde{\Pi}(p,\tilde{q}) = (p - v) \triangle\tilde{q}$. It would consequently be impossible to bring marginal profit to zero (or any level other than $(p - v)$) by varying $\tilde{q}$ — *even if $\tilde{q}$ could in fact be determined in advance.* But the essence of the situation in more general terms is that $\tilde{q}$ is a *random* variable whose actual *ex post* value is not subject in advance to direct choice or control by the company. Only the *parameters of the distribution* of the random variables — quantity sold, and hence revenues and profits — are subject to control or choice in advance. In the simple case being treated, announced price is the only control variable.

We can, however, both legitimately and fruitfully take derivatives of expectations or other moments of random variables with respect to expectations, or the underlying parameters (such as price) of the distributions of our random variables. Recognizing that $\bar{q} = \bar{q}(p)$ in our criterion (9), we have

$$(13) \qquad \frac{\partial \hat{\tilde{\Pi}}}{\partial(-p)} = \frac{\partial \bar{R}}{\partial(-p)} - v\frac{\partial \bar{q}}{\partial(-p)} - \alpha\frac{\partial \sigma_\pi^2}{\partial(-p)} = 0.$$

The right-hand equation is equivalent to

$$(14) \qquad \frac{\partial \bar{R}}{\partial \bar{q}}\frac{\partial \bar{q}}{\partial(-p)} - v\frac{\partial \bar{q}}{\partial(-p)} - \alpha\frac{\partial \sigma_\pi^2}{\partial(-p)} = 0$$

or

$$(14a) \qquad \frac{\partial \bar{R}}{\partial \bar{q}} - v = \alpha\frac{\partial \sigma_\pi^2}{\partial(-p)}\left(\frac{\partial \bar{q}}{\partial(-p)}\right)^{-1}$$

[15] The practice doubtless reflects the economist's proper and traditionally primary concern with the allocation of resources, a study for which the theory of the firm has supplied the little black boxes needed for the general equilibrium system. The practice also clearly reflects the fact that costs pertain to output, not price, and marginal revenues are then denominated in terms of quantity for symmetry.

[16] Since $\partial\pi/\partial p = (\partial\pi/\partial q)(\partial q/\partial p) = 0$ and because $\partial q/\partial p \neq 0$, our first order condition implies the usual formula $\partial\pi/\partial q = \partial R/\partial q - \partial R/\partial q = MR - MC = 0$. With normal demand functions, that is with $\partial q/\partial p < 0$, the signs involved in the second order conditions also carry through.

or

(14b)
$$\frac{\partial \overline{R}}{\partial \overline{q}} = v - 2\alpha(p - v)\left(\frac{\partial \overline{q}}{\partial(-p)}\right)^{-1}\sigma_u^2,$$

where $\partial \overline{q}/\partial(-p) = -\partial \overline{q}/\partial p > 0$. In words, the optimal announced price is the price at which the marginal *expected* revenue with respect to *expected* quantity equals marginal production cost *less* the marginal value of induced change in gross-profit variance with respect to *expected* quantity. Although it is thus possible to restate our equilibrium conditions in terms of an adaptation of the usual $MR - MC$ criterion of certainty, it is more convenient and straightforward to state the optimizing condition in terms of the decision variable price, as in our previous formulation.

1e. Further implications of the model.   Our model carries several further implications of normative and predictive significance beyond the three noted above in section III.1b. In particular, as mentioned above:

4. Once quantity uncertainty is recognized, determinate solutions are found under conditions of *expected* demand which would produce indeterminancies or "explosions" if the same expectations were held with certainty. More formally stated, *the second-order or "stability" conditions for a true maximum are less restrictive than the corresponding conditions under certainty — and the admissible upper limits increase with both the degree of risk aversion α and the extent of quantity uncertainty σ_u^2.*

To see this, note that the first-order condition for a maximum of (9) is

(15)
$$\frac{\partial \hat{\Pi}}{\partial p} = \frac{\partial \overline{\Pi}}{\partial p} - \alpha\frac{\partial \sigma_\pi^2}{\partial p} = (p - v)\frac{\partial \overline{q}}{\partial p} + \overline{q} - 2\alpha(\overline{p} - v)\sigma_u^2 = 0,$$

and that the second-order conditions thus require only that

(16)
$$\frac{\partial^2 \hat{\Pi}}{\partial p^2} = \frac{\partial^2 \overline{\Pi}}{\partial p^2} - \alpha\frac{\partial^2 \sigma_\pi^2}{\partial p^2} = (p - v)\frac{\partial^2 \overline{q}}{\partial p^2} + 2\frac{\partial \overline{q}}{\partial p} - 2\alpha\sigma_u^2 < 0,$$

i.e., that

(17)
$$\frac{\partial^2 q}{\partial p^2} < 2\left(\alpha\sigma_u^2 - \frac{\partial \overline{q}}{\partial p}\right)\bigg/ m > 0,$$

using $m = p - v$. With declining demand curves, both terms in the numerator on the right are positive, as is the denominator. Our proposition follows from the fact that the entire expression on the right is an increasing function of both α and σ_u^2, since the numerator is so, and we have proved above that the optimal margins m_u in the denominator decline with α and σ_u^2. Q.E.D.

5. *The expected quantity to be produced and sold will be greater,* (a) *the greater the uncertainty* regarding sales and volumes *and* (b) *the more risk averse the management.* With normal declining demand

functions, this follows as a *corollary* to proposition (1) that risk aversion and quantity uncertainty reduce prices, *ceteris paribus*.

6. Other things equal, *Lerner's classic measure of monopoly power will vary inversely with the degree of risk aversion and the amount of uncertainty concerning unit sales in the market.* This follows as a corollary to proposition (3) above, since Lerner's index is equal to the percentage gross profit margin on sales $m^0 = (p - v)/p$.

7. As a further corollary to (5) and (6), *risk aversion and quantity uncertainty on the part of "monopolists" — and, more generally, in the minds of the dominant firms in oligopolistic markets — reduce the severity of the "monopolistic distortions" traditionally ascribed to such markets* in the traditional analysis made under assumptions of certainty.

8. In the traditional analysis under certainty, a necessary and sufficient condition (following Scitovsky[17]) for monopoly power to be greater in periods of high prosperity than in weak markets is for the elasticity of demand to vary countercyclically. In our model, any countercyclical variation in either the degree of risk aversion or in the variance of unit demands would have the same consequence.

1f. Relation to models of Fellner and Baumol. Some two decades ago at the height of the "marginalist" controversy, Professor Fellner[18] suggested that "mark-up" pricing was an entirely rational pattern of behavior for firms having market power and faced with uncertainty. Our analysis, however, shows that, when the uncertainties are dominated by lack of precise estimates of unit sales conditional on any price, *"safety margins"* (over *average* costs) *will neither be maximized nor* (as he held in later versions[19] *will they be optimized*) at levels *higher* than those which would prevail in the absence of uncertainty. In our analysis, (a) *margins over variable* (not average) *costs* will be optimized, and (b) *the optimizing margins so determined will be lower* (not higher), the greater the risk aversion and uncertainty. As confirmed below,[20] the difference in conclusions arises because Professor Fellner in effect considered only the consequences of uncertainties regarding the prices which would in fact be realized, and the costs which would in fact be incurred, before announced prices would be changed. But for dominant firms in a very wide range of markets who *set* prices (rather than being mere "price takers" as in traditional competitive models) their uncertainty regarding *how much* will *in fact be sold* at any price is probably very much greater than their uncertainties regarding price realization or marginal costs over the price-planning period.

[17] See Scitovsky [17].
[18] See Fellner [5].
[19] See Fellner [6] and [7].
[20] See below, section III.

Although our results thus differ from Fellner's, readers familiar with the literature will also have noted the marked similarity between our conclusions and those drawn by Professors Baumol [2], Williamson [18], Marris [11] and other recent writers who have emphasized nonprofit objectives in the firm's (or management's) goal structure. Our conclusions thus open for empirical investigation the possibility that *uncertainty and risk aversion in a profit-maximizing context may account for many of the phenomena so far ascribed in the "revisionist" literature to other goals,* like sales maximization, as distinct from profit maximization, or management's concern for its emoluments and personal empire-building. This possibility is strengthened by the implications of our model with respect to the consequences of corporate income taxes — to which we now turn.

2. The Effects of Corporate Income Taxes.

One of the central theorems of the traditional theory of the profit-maximizing firm asserts that, in the short run, taxes on corporate profits are irrelevant in determining optimal price and quantity. With given demand and cost functions, any unit of output for which marginal revenue exceeds marginal cost before taxes will add some fraction of the difference to profits taken after taxes. The marginal unit that adds nothing before tax adds nothing after tax. The prices and quantities which exhaust the available incremental profits before tax will thus also do so after tax and be unaffected by the change in the tax.

This central tenet of the traditional theory of the firm is no longer valid once uncertainty and risk aversion are admitted into the analysis. It is perfectly rational for profit-maximizing, but risk-averse, managements who are uncertain of sales volumes to shift forward any increase in taxes on corporate profits. It should be emphasized that *this conclusion holds in the strict Marshallian short run, and it does not depend on "bad" accounting* (improper identification and measurement of "true" earnings in the economic sense) *or on irrational, nonoptimizing, or "satisficing" behavior either before or after the change in taxes.* (In particular, Galbraithian situations in which higher prices would have been profitable before the tax increase are specifically not relied upon or involved in any way — nor is nonoptimizing mark-up pricing). Likewise, the conclusion does not invoke the position of regulated industries that secure rate increases to maintain after-tax returns. Neither does it involve any assumption that the tax laws fail to allow deductions for all relevant costs. Nor, it should also be emphasized, does it rely on any hypothesis of sales maximization or on the introduction of any such nonprofit goals as managerial emoluments or empire-building into the criterion or effective utility function.

The proof of the statement is simple. After the introduction of a corporate income tax, the relevant utilities of a profit-maximizing, but risk-averse, corporation depend on after-tax profits, and the certainty equivalents of our basic equation (9) must be denominated in profits after tax Π_t rather than profits before tax Π:

(19)
$$\hat{\Pi}_t = \bar{\Pi}_t - \alpha\sigma^2_{\pi_t} = (1 - t)\bar{\Pi} - \alpha(1 - t)^2\sigma^2_\pi$$
$$= (1 - t)[(p - v)\bar{q} - F] - \alpha(1 - t)^2(p - v)^2\sigma^2_u.$$

Setting the derivative of this expression to zero, we find the condition for optimal price to be

(20)
$$\frac{\partial\hat{\Pi}_t}{\partial(-p)} = (1 - t)\frac{\partial\bar{\Pi}}{\partial(-p)} - \alpha(1 - t)^2\frac{\partial\sigma^2_\Pi}{\partial(-p)} = 0$$

(20a)
$$\frac{\partial\hat{\Pi}}{\partial(-p)} = \frac{\partial\bar{\Pi}}{\partial(-p)} - 2\alpha(1 - t)(p - v)\sigma^2_u = 0,$$

which is *not independent of the tax rate* so long as there is any risk aversion ($\alpha > 0$) and uncertainty ($\sigma^2_u > 0$). But (20a) differs from the corresponding condition (10a), when taxes were ignored, *only* by *either* (a) substituting $(1 - t)\sigma^2_u$ for the uncertainty term σ^2_u in the earlier formulation, *or* (b) leaving the uncertainty term σ^2_u unchanged and substituting $(1 - t)\alpha$ for the risk-aversion term in the previous formulation. We consequently have established the following propositions with respect to the impact of corporate income taxes upon the optimal policies, other things being the same, of profit-maximizing, but risk-averse, firms faced with uncertainty concerning sales volume:

1. *An increase in corporate income taxes has the same effects on the price decisions of price setters as either a reduction in their risk aversion α or a reduction in their assessment of the relevant risk σ^2_u in a given situation.*

2. As a corollary to proposition (1) in the previous subsection, *an increase in corporate profits taxes will rationally be shifted forward by increasing the prices which otherwise would be announced, ceteris paribus.*

3. As a corollary to our earlier propositions (2) and (3), *corporate profits taxes increase the profit margins $m^*_u = p^*_u - v$ of price setters,* and

4. *profits taxes also increase their optimal percentage margins $m^{0*}_u = (p^*_u - v/p^*_u$ over variable costs.*

5. Given declining demand functions, on a partial-equilibrium *ceteris paribus* basis, *corporate income taxes reduce the expected quantities which will be produced and sold by dominant price-setting firms — and by the industries whose prices levels they control or influence strongly.*

6. *Corporate income taxes consequently increase the severity of the "monopolistic distortions" traditionally ascribed to such markets.*

7. Other things equal, *corporate income taxes increase the degree of monopoly power exercised by dominant price-setting firms as measured by Lerner's standard index.*

3. Conclusions When Demand Variances are a Function of Expected Quantity (or Price).

To this point, we have treated the uncertainty regarding actual demands as a datum unaffected by the decisions reached. We have seen that a given degree of demand uncertainty reduces the prices and margins set by risk-averse, but otherwise profit-maximizing, firms and leads to expected quantities greater than would be found if demands were known with greater precision. We now need to allow for the fact that the degree of uncertainty, measured in units of demand, is itself likely to increase to some greater or less degree with the *expected* quantity of unit sales.

It might seem that, since a given unit variance leads to lower optimal prices and larger expected unit sales, any tendency of uncertainty to rise with unit sales would compound the tendencies already found and lead to still lower prices — possibly even to an unstable regress with no determinate solution. It turns out, of course, that the solution *is* stable,[21] but that, contrary to heuristic presumptions, a positive dependence of demand uncertainty upon the level of *expected* demand dampens the extent of the price reduction and tax shifting which would otherwise occur. Nevertheless, if we continue to assume that unit variable costs are known data, constant with output, and that there is no uncertainty with respect to realized price (after any price announcement), we can then establish that all the conclusions previously stated continue to be valid when quantity variance σ_u^2 increases with expected quantity, so long as the increase in σ_u^2 is less than fully proportional to $\bar{q}^2$.

In other words, if we consider the standard deviation of quantity to be related to expected quantity by $\sigma_q = \bar{q}^\gamma$, all our qualitative conclusions in subsections 1 and 2 continue to be valid so long as $\gamma < 1$. And there is an important mass of empirical evidence that this is indeed the generally relevant range in practice. For instance, Robert G. Brown of Arthur D. Little, Inc. reports[22] that "the standard deviation of forecast errors for several thousand items stocked by a large equipment manufacturer is proportional to some power of the forecast and that the power is frequently between 0.7 and 0.9 (occasionally higher or lower powers have been noticed)." Although the bulk of such empirical evidence arises in the context

---

[21] The stability of the solution on the basis of Samuelson's classic proposition is obvious from the fact that observed prices and margins over variable costs in markets dominated by quantity uncertainty are positive. The certainty equivalents must be "concave downward."

[22] See Brown [3], p. 294.

of inventory planning, there are good reasons to believe that the same sort of inelasticity in the uncertainties of forecast will also hold over the longer periods generally involved in price-planning. Indeed, an increase in uncertainty *less* than fully proportional to the increase in expected quantity — that is, $\gamma < 1$ — is precisely what one would observe whenever the total quantity uncertainty reflects some random elements whose effect is largely (if not fully) independent of the expected level of total demand, along with some random elements whose effect is fully proportional to expected total quantities.[23]

The fact that all our previously stated conclusions continue to apply when uncertainties increase with expected quantities, so long as $\gamma < 1$, follows as a special case of the following more general *Theorem:* Let u in the demand function (5) be specified by

(21) $$\tilde{u} = [h(p)]^{\gamma} \cdot \tilde{\epsilon} = \bar{q}^{\gamma} \cdot \tilde{\epsilon},$$

where $0 < \gamma < \infty$ and $\tilde{\epsilon}$ is normally distributed with mean zero and variance $\sigma_{\tilde{\epsilon}}^2$, an exogenous constant, so that the variance of unit volume $\sigma_u^2 = (\bar{q}^{\gamma})^2 \sigma_{\tilde{\epsilon}}^2$. *Then:*

(22) $$p_u^* \lessgtr p_c^* \quad \text{as } \gamma \lessgtr 1,$$

where p_u^* is the price which maximizes equation (9) when the uncertainty of demand is given by (21) and p_c^* is the "certainty price" which maximizes (9) in the limit as $\sigma_{\tilde{\epsilon}}^2 \to 0$.

The proof follows directly from recalling that the maximization of (9) requires that

(10a) $$\frac{\partial \hat{\bar{\Pi}}}{\partial(-p)} = \frac{\partial \bar{\Pi}}{\partial(-p)} - \alpha \frac{\partial \sigma_{\pi}^2}{\partial(-p)} = 0;$$

p_c^* is the value of p for which $\partial \bar{\Pi}/\partial(-p) = 0$; and p_u^* is the value of p for which $\partial \bar{\Pi}/\partial(-p) = \alpha[\partial \sigma_{\pi}^2/\partial(-p]$.

We also know by Samuelson's classic argument that $\hat{\bar{\Pi}}(p)$ is a concave function; stability conditions must always be satisfied because we never observe negative, or infinitely high, prices. Consequently,

(23) $$p_u^* \lessgtr p_c^* \quad \text{as } \left(\frac{\partial \bar{\Pi}}{\partial(-p)}\right)^* \lessgtr 0 \quad \text{as } \left(\frac{\partial \sigma_{\pi}^2}{\partial(-p)}\right)^* \lessgtr 0,$$

where asterisks indicate optimizing values satisfying (10a). To complete the proof of the theorem and to validate equation (22), we thus need only show that

---

[23] Formally stated, $\gamma < 1$ is implied by a model in which total uncertainty is made up of any weighted sum or average of a proportional and an independent component. Let $\tilde{q} = \alpha \tilde{K} \bar{q} + (1 - \alpha)\tilde{\epsilon}$, where $0 < \alpha < 1$, $\tilde{\epsilon}$ and $\tilde{K}$ are normal with $\bar{\epsilon} = 0$ and $\bar{K} = 1$, with variances of σ_K^2 and σ_{ϵ}^2 so that $\sigma_q^2 = \alpha^2 \bar{q}^2 \sigma_K^2 + (1 - \alpha)^2 \sigma_{\epsilon}^2 + 2\alpha(1 - \alpha)q\sigma_{K\epsilon}$. Then, $d \log \sigma_q / d \log q = \gamma < 1$.

(24)
$$\left(\frac{\partial \sigma_\pi^2}{\partial(-p)}\right)^* \lessgtr 0 \quad \text{as } \gamma \lessgtr 1.$$

But from $\sigma_\pi^2 = m^2(\bar{q})^{2\gamma}\sigma_\varepsilon^2$, we have

$$\frac{\partial \sigma_\pi^2}{\partial(-p)} = -2m(\bar{q})^{2\gamma}\sigma_\varepsilon^2 + 2\gamma m^2(\bar{q})^{2\gamma-1}\sigma_\varepsilon^2(\partial\bar{q}/\partial(-p))$$

(25)
$$= -2m(\bar{q})^{2\gamma}\sigma_\varepsilon^2[1 - \gamma(m/\bar{q})(\partial\bar{q}/\partial(-p))]$$
$$= -2m(\bar{q})^{2\gamma}\sigma_\varepsilon^2[1 - \gamma m^0 \eta],$$

where $m = p - v$ and $m^0 = (p - v)/p$ as before, and $\eta = (p/q)$ $(\partial q/\partial(-p))$ as usual. It is readily established that, in the limit under certainty,[24] as σ_ε^2 (or σ_u^2 or σ_π^2) $\rightarrow 0$, the optimal percentage margin $m_c^{0*} = \eta^{-1}$. Suppose the corresponding certainty price p_c^* were established when $\sigma_\varepsilon^2 > 0$. Then, if $\gamma = 1$, $\partial\sigma_\pi^2/\partial(-p) = 0$, and $p_u^* = p_c^*$. But if $p = p_c^*$ and $\gamma > 1$, the bracket in (25) is negative, and $\partial\sigma_\pi^2/\partial(-p) > 0$; by (23) and (24) and the stability conditions, the initial "certainty" price would have to be raised to satisfy (10a). Consequently, $\gamma > 1 \rightarrow p_u^* > p_c^*$. Correspondingly, if $\gamma < 1$, the bracket in (25) is positive and $\partial\sigma_\pi^2/\partial(-p) < 0$ with $p = p_c^*$, and this initial price would have to be lowered to satisfy (10a); therefore, $\gamma < 1 \rightarrow p_u^* < p_c^*$. Q.E.D.[25]

With constant risk aversion applied directly to profits, as we have assumed for pricing decisions,[26] optimizing prices under uncertainty will thus be lower than those under certainty, and all the conclusions in the earlier sections of the text continue to hold whenever $0 < \gamma < 1$. But all these conclusions would have to be reversed in situations where the elasticity of uncertainty with respect to expected quantity is greater than unity — for example, optimizing prices and margins and degrees of monopoly power

[24] Set $\sigma_u = 0$ in the optimizing equation (15) and divide through by q. The result is
$$1 + \left(\frac{p - v}{p}\right)\left(\frac{p}{q}\frac{\partial q}{\partial p}\right) = 1 - m_c^{0*} n = 0.$$
[25] The proof given in the text emphasizes the intermediate steps in the economic logic involved. For a more formal and succinct proof, let
$H(p) = (p - v) h'(p)/h(p)$ where $\bar{q} = h(p)$, $h'(p) < 0$,
and
$C(p) = 2\alpha(p - v)\sigma_\varepsilon^2 h^2\gamma(p)$. Then if we set the derivatives of (9) with respect to p equal to zero, we find that p_c^* satisfies $1 + H(p_c^*) = 0$ and p_u^* satisfies
$\hat{\pi}'(p) = h(p)[1 + H(p)] - C(p)[1 + \gamma H(p)] = 0.$
If we evaluate $\hat{\pi}'(p)$ at p_c^*, we get
$\hat{\pi}'(p_c) = C(p_c^*)[1 - \gamma].$
Since $\hat{\pi}(p)$ is concave, $\hat{\pi}'(p)$ is a decreasing function. Consequently,
$p_c^* <(>) p_u^* \leftrightarrow \gamma <(>) 1.$ Q.E.D.
[26] Indeed in a more advanced treatment, it can be shown that our conclusion with respect to quantity uncertainty continue to hold on very reasonable assumptions for (bounded) values of γ significantly greater than unity. In particular, this will be true (a) if constant risk aversion holds but the relevant increment of wealth is the change in equity market values attributable to those profits, rather than merely the current profits themselves as assumed in equation 1 above; and (b) if risk aversion in fact decreases with increasing wealth (or profits).

would be raised, and income taxes would be "reverse shifted." *Strictly* proportional uncertainty would have no effect regardless of the degree of such aversion to risk. In this special case, the conclusions of the standard certainty analysis would be valid, and income taxes would not be shifted.

We have thus proved that quantity uncertainty *does* make a difference in the prices established by risk-averse price setters with "market power," except in a special limiting case. Those who believe that quantity uncertainty leads to increased prices and increases in the "degree of market power availed of" must also believe that an increase in corporate income taxes *ceteris paribus* will lead to *lower,* and not higher, prices. The implausibility of such an inference, together with the empirical evidence cited earlier, seems to be a persuasive reason for believing that the quantity risks relevant for pricing decisions in a broad range of market power rise *less* than proportionately with expected quantity within any given decision period — in other words, that the case with $0 < \gamma < 1$ which has been relied upon in the earlier text is indeed the generally relevant one, and that the qualitative conclusions stated in section II, subsections 1 and 2, above are those which should be expected (predicted) in practice.

III   The Price-Setting Firm: Uncertainty over Variable Cost and Realized Price

To this point we have been concerned with the impact of risk aversion upon the price policy of price-setting firms with considerable market power who were uncertain only of the quantity they would in fact sell at any given price. Although this quantity uncertainty probably dominates the uncertainties with respect to cost and price realizations (conditional on announced prices), the latter uncertainties are generally present to some degree; and we now examine their impact on the pricing decisions and tax shifting of the subject firms. It will be found that, if independent of the price quoted, the effect of uncertainties with respect to costs, realized prices, and profit margins are qualitatively opposite to those found for quantity uncertainty — an important fact which seems to have been overlooked in the literature.

To bring out the essential results of this section most simply, we will assume for the moment that, conditional on an announced price, the quantity that will be sold is known. In terms of the previous section, we will set σ_q^2 and σ_u^2 equal to zero. We now allow, however, for the net realized price p_r to be somewhat uncertain even when the announced price p is fixed and the quantity sold is known. We also allow the variable costs associated with any quantity to also involve some random variation — that is, we assume that variable costs v will be constant with respect to output but that there is uncertainty regarding their level. Our cost function (7) thus becomes

$\tilde{C}(q) = F + \tilde{v}q$, where $\tilde{v}$ is normally distributed[27] with mean $\bar{v}$ and variance σ_v^2. After allowing for corporate income taxes, the functional relation between profits and announced price p is now

(8′) $$(1 - t)\tilde{\Pi} = (1 - \tau)[\tilde{m}_r q - F];$$

expected profits are

(8a′) $$(1 - \tau)\bar{\Pi} = (1 - \tau)[\bar{m}_r q - F];$$

the variance of net profits is

(8b′) $$\sigma_{\pi_t}^2 = (1 - t)^2 \sigma_{\tilde{\pi}}^2 = (1 - t)^2 q^2 \sigma_m^2$$

And the objective function to be maximized is, of course,

(19) $$\hat{\Pi}_t = (1 - t)\bar{\Pi} - \alpha(1 - t)^2 \sigma_{\tilde{\pi}}^2,$$

as before but now using (8a′) and (8b′).

1. Uncertainty Concerning Profit Margins (Realized Price or Variable Costs, or both) Independent of Announced Price.

The maximum of (19) occurs when

$$\frac{\partial \hat{\Pi}}{\partial(-p)} = (1 - t)\left[\bar{m}_r \frac{\partial q}{\partial(-p)} - q\right] - 2\alpha(1 - t)^2 q \sigma_m^2 \frac{\partial q}{\partial(-p)} = 0.$$

or

(26) $$\frac{\partial \bar{\Pi}}{\partial(-p)} = 2\alpha(1 - t)q\sigma_m^2 \frac{\partial q}{\partial(-p)} > 0.$$

By the logic of subsections II.1.c and II.2 above, it is immediately apparent that

    1. *The effects of uncertainties regarding the level of variable costs, realized prices, and realized profit margins all*[28] *run counter to the effects of quantity uncertainty in the demand function.*

    2. *In particular, these uncertainties, ceteris paribus, each tend to reduce output,*[29] *and to raise announced prices, expected margins, degree*

[27] As a technical point, we should note that we continue to assume normal distributions for the uncertainties in order to maintain simple mathematical forms for our results. It may easily be shown (with more complex algebra) that the same qualitative results would be found if we had used other distributions (such as truncated normals, gammas, or rectangular distributions) which permit only "down-side risk" on price and only uncertain increases in costs.

[28] The effects of uncertainty regarding realized price (conditional on any announced price), or regarding variable costs separately, are given by substituting σ_{pr}^2 or σ_v^2 for σ_m^2 in (27). Where both p_r and v are uncertain, of course, $\sigma_m^2 = \sigma_{pr}^2 + \sigma_v^2 + 2\sigma_{vpr}$.

[29] In [4], Dhrymes has considered the impact of uncertainty on the price-setter's behavior when the uncertainty is confined to price realized (cf. his eq. (25)). Although his equations (46)-(47) are correct, his verbal conclusion that an increase in risk aversion will increase output is incorrect because of an inadvertent misinterpretation. (His α is the negative of our own.)

of monopoly power availed of, and the severity of the monopolistic distortions usually ascribed to less-than-purely competitive markets.
3. *These effects all become more severe, the greater the degree of risk aversion and extent of this kind of uncertainty.*
4. *These effects are reduced, however, by corporate income taxes.*
5. If risk-averse companies were only uncertain about the level of their marginal costs, *an increase in corporate taxes would tend to reduce prices.*

2. Conclusions When the Variance of Margins Is a Function of Announced Price.

To this point we have treated σ_m^2 as a datum. It is clear that any tendency of the variance of margins to increase with quantities sold — or with lower announced prices — would reinforce the above conclusions. Any uncertainty regarding realized price is likely to be less, the lower the announced price, however, while uncertainties concerning the level of variable costs may either be independent or provide less than a full offset. It is consequently of interest to consider the case where the standard error of forecast of margins varies directly with the announced price — that is, when $\partial \sigma_m / \partial p = -\partial \sigma_m / \partial(-p) > 0$. If we form the elasticity coefficient $\eta_{sp} = (p/\sigma_m)(\partial \sigma_m / \partial p)$ for this relation between price and margin-uncertainty, and let η_{pq} represent the usual price-quantity elasticity, we find that when the quantity q is nonstochastic, the maximization of (19) occurs when

$$
(27) \qquad \frac{\partial \bar{\bar{\Pi}}}{\partial(-p)} = 2(1-t)\left[2q\sigma_m^2 \frac{\partial q}{\partial(-p)} + 2q^2\sigma_m \frac{\partial \sigma_m}{\partial(-p)}\right]
$$
$$
= 2(1-t)q^2\sigma_m^2[\eta_{pq} - \eta_{sp}]/p.
$$

We therefore conclude that *uncertainty regarding realized prices, variable costs, and margins serves to raise quoted prices above their "certainty levels," except when margin-uncertainty varies directly with announced price and has an elasticity greater absolutely than the price-elasticity of demand. With the same exception or qualification, uncertainty regarding profit margins leads risk-averse profit maximizers to lower their prices when corporate income taxes are increased, and vice versa.*

3. Conclusions When Both Margins and Quantities Sold Are Uncertain.

As shown in the proof of the theorem in section II, subsection 3 (and in the derivation of the immediately preceding results), the prices announced in the face of uncertainty by risk-averse, profit-maximizing price setters with market power will be lower or higher than "certainty" prices, depending upon the sign of $\partial \sigma_\pi^2 / \partial(-p)$: if reductions in prices reduce the variance of profits, price will be lower in equilibrium; if reductions in prices raise the variance of profits, then risk-aversion an uncertainty lead to higher prices and margins. We have also seen that taxes on corporate profits will be shifted forward in an uncertain environment when uncertainty as such lowers the equilibrium price (section II, subsection 2), but these taxes will be "reverse shifted" in the contrary case. We have also found that uncertainty concerning quantity sold will reduce prices, and lead to forward shifting of income taxes, whenever $0 < \gamma < 1$, as empirical evidence confirms. On the other hand, uncertainty over margins as such has contrary effects except when the uncertainty regarding margins falls off rather rapidly with lower prices.

When both uncertainties regarding quantities sold and net realized margins are simultaneously present, the *net* effect of the total uncertainties depends of course upon the relative amounts of each kind of uncertainty and the parameter values relevant to the particular case. More specific results can be obtained by noting that, apart from a constant, $\tilde{\Pi} = \tilde{m}\tilde{q}$ so that[30]

(28) $$\sigma_{\tilde{\pi}}^2 = \bar{m}^2\sigma_q^2 + \bar{q}^2\sigma_m^2 + \sigma_m^2\sigma_q^2 + 2\bar{m}\bar{q}\sigma_{mq} + (\sigma_{mq})^2.$$

Our results in section II were based on using the first term on the right; those in section III, subsections 1 and 2, the second term. In view of the complexity of the full formula for $\sigma_{\tilde{\pi}}^2$ when both types of uncertainty are involved, it is instructive to consider first (subsection 3a below) the combined impact on prices of σ_q and σ_m when q and m are independent of each other and of announced prices. We then add (in subsection 3b) the incremental effects of the dependence of both on announced prices, and finally (in subsection 3c), we determine the impact of any covariance σ_{mq} that may be present in any given situation.

3a. Combined effect of uncertainties in quantities and margins when they are independent of each other and of announced prices. We combine the results of subsection II.1 and III.1 by examining the derivatives of the first two terms in (28) when σ_q and σ_m are treated as exogenous. In this case,

(29)
$$\frac{\partial\sigma_{\tilde{\pi}}^2}{\partial(-p)} = 2m\bar{q}^2\left[\frac{\sigma_m^2}{qm}\left(\frac{\partial q}{\partial(-p)}\right) - \frac{\sigma_q^2}{q^2}\right] = 2m\bar{q}^2\left[m^0\eta_{qp}\left(\frac{\sigma_m}{m}\right)^2 - \left(\frac{\sigma_q}{q}\right)^2\right]$$

Now suppose $\sigma_q/q > (<) \sigma_m/m$; if a price $p = p_c^*$, the certainty level were set, we would have $m^0\eta_{qp} = 1$ and the entire bracket would be negative (positive); by the concavity of $\hat{\Pi}$, this initial price would have to be lowered (raised). Consequently, whenever the covariance σ_{qm} is negligible and σ_m^2 and σ_q^2 do not depend on announced prices, we have

[30] This convenient, exact formula for the variance of the product of two jointly normal random variables is taken from some unpublished work of Professor John Bishop.

(30) $$p_u^* \gtreqless p_c^* \quad \text{as} \quad \sigma_m/m \gtreqless \sigma_q/q;$$

and in particular, risk aversion and uncertainty will reduce prices below certainty levels and lead to forward short-run tax shifting whenever the coefficient of variation of unit volume is greater than that of realized margins.

3b. Combined effect of uncertainties in q and m when $\sigma_{qm} = 0$ *but* σ_m^2 *and* σ_q^2 *depend on p.* If we take the derivatives with respect to the first terms in (28), and let σ_m^2 and σ_q^2 vary with the announced price p, we have

$$\frac{\partial \sigma_\pi^2}{\partial(-p)} = -2m\sigma_q^2 + 2\overline{m}^2\sigma_q \frac{\partial \sigma_q}{\partial(-p)} + 2\overline{q}\sigma_m^2 \frac{\partial q}{\partial(-p)} + 2\overline{q}^2\sigma_m \frac{\partial \sigma_m}{(\partial - p)}$$

(31)
$$+ 2\sigma_m \sigma_q^2 \frac{\partial \sigma_m}{\partial(-p)} + 2\sigma_m^2 \sigma_q \frac{\partial \sigma_q}{\partial(-p)}$$

$$= +2m\overline{q}^2 \left\{ \left[m^0 \left(\eta_{qp} - \eta_{sp} \right) \left(\frac{\sigma_m}{\overline{m}} \right)^2 - \left(1 - \gamma m^0 \eta_{qp} \right) \left(\frac{\sigma_q}{\overline{q}} \right)^2 \right] \right.$$

$$\left. + \left[m_0 (\gamma \eta_{qp} - \eta_{sp}) \cdot \left(\frac{\sigma_m}{\overline{m}} \right)^2 \left(\frac{\sigma_q}{\overline{q}} \right)^2 \right] \right\}.$$

Now the sign of $\partial \sigma_\pi^2 / \partial(-p)$ will be essentially determined by the sign of the expression within the first bracket, since the second bracket involves the triple product of the *squares* of the respective coefficients of variation with the percentage margin m^0. If price were initially set at the certainty level $p = p_c^*$, we know that $m^0 \eta_{qp} = 1$; and the first bracket will be negative if

$$(1 - \gamma) \left(\frac{\sigma_q}{\overline{q}} \right)^2 > (1 - m^0 \eta_{sp}) \left(\frac{\sigma_m}{m} \right)^2$$

(32)
$$\text{or} \quad \frac{\sigma_q}{q} > \left(\frac{1 - m^0 \eta_{sp}}{1 - \gamma} \right)^{\frac{1}{2}} \left(\frac{\sigma_m}{m} \right).$$

If η_{sp} is small, as seems probable, and γ is .75, as Brown's data suggests, it follows by our now standard concavity argument that $p_u^* < p_c^*$ so long as $\sigma q/\overline{q} > 2(\sigma_m/\overline{m})$. Even if γ is as high as .9 in a particular situation, prices under risk-averse uncertainty would be lower than competitive prices so long as the coefficient of variation of the forecasts of quantity sold were more than 3.2 times that of realized profit margins. The general observations made on pages 239–41 of our introduction surely indicate that these conditions will probably be satisfied by a comfortably wide margin for a large number of the more important products supplied by the companies of interest in this paper.

3c. The effect of covariance between realized margins and quantity sold. It remains to consider the net effect of the final two terms in (28).

We first note that the *effect of a given level of positive (or negative) covariance will accentuate* (*or run counter to*) the discrepancy between p_u^* and p_c^* produced by the earlier terms of (28). This is true because

(33) $$\frac{\partial \overline{m}\overline{q}\sigma_{mq}}{\partial(-p)} = \sigma_{mq}\left[-\overline{q} + \overline{m}\frac{\partial q}{\partial(-p)}\right] = \overline{q}\sigma_{mq}[m^0 n_{pq} - 1].$$

The sign of the contribution of this covariance term is controlled by sign of the bracket. But as shown in section II, subsection 3, this bracket is negative (positive) as $p_u^* < (>) p_c^*$, and negative impacts on the variance of profits reduce announced prices. Q.E.D.

Finally we note that any dependence of the covariance on the level of prices will tend to offset (or support) the combined impact of the earlier terms if $\gamma \eta_{qp} > (\text{or} <) \eta_{sp}$ since

(34) $$\frac{\partial \sigma_{mq}}{\partial(-p)} = \frac{\partial \rho \sigma_m \sigma_q}{\partial(-p)} = \rho\left[\sigma_q \frac{\partial \sigma_m}{\partial(-p)} + \sigma_m \frac{\partial \sigma_q}{\partial(-p)}\right]$$
$$= \sigma_{mq}[-\eta_{sp} + \gamma \eta_{qp}].$$

In summary, to the extent that covariance is negative and tends to become more so as price is lowered in a given situation, an additional positive term is introduced on the right side of our basic condition (32). From the general empirical evidence available to date, it nevertheless appears that the augmented inequality will usually be satisfied in practice for major products of the major price-setting firms being considered. Pending possibly contrary indications from future empirical research, the provisional conclusion seems justified:

> The combined effects of uncertainties regarding realized margins and quantities sold lead risk-averse profit-maximizing firms with substantial market power to set prices below the "certainty" level and to shift corporate income taxes forward within the context of a Marshallian short-run equilibrium for the firm.

IV Conclusions

This paper has explored some of the consequences of uncertainties upon the price-quantity behavior, market performance, and tax shifting of risk-averse profit-maximizing price setters with significant market power. It has been shown that, except in special limiting cases, uncertainties and risk aversion do change prices, margins, degrees of market power availed of, and the extent of the market distortion usually ascribed to such markets. It has also been shown that, again waiving special limiting cases, the combination of risk aversion and uncertainty means that rational profit-maximizing behavior does lead to strictly short-run shifting of taxes on corporate profits.

Empirical evidence indicates that the uncertainty of price setters regarding quantity sold is inelastic with respect to expected quantity. Such uncertainty was shown *ceteris paribus* to lower market prices, margins over marginal costs, the Lerner index of monopoly power, and the degree of monopolistic distortion usually ascribed to such markets. It also was shown to produce forward tax shifting in the strict Marshallian short-run, and in consequence, to make the degree of monopolistic distortions of resource allocations vary directly with corporate income tax rates.

We also noted that, under risk-averse profit-maximization, these effects of uncertainty concerning unit sales parallel the effects of nonprofit goals, such as sales maximization or management's concern with its own emoluments and empire-building, emphasized in the recent "revisionist" literature by Baumol, Williamson, and others. The results in the present paper concur with the conclusions of such authors concerning the need for revisions and extensions of the traditional theory of the firm. On the other hand, our results suggest that, after the traditional profit-maximizing theory has been revised and extended to incorporate risk aversion and uncertainty, the incremental contribution of the other nonprofit revisionist goals may be less significant than previously expected. But only careful and extensive empirical research, which hopefully will be stimulated by the present paper, can settle such issues.

Another major conclusion of the present paper has been that the qualitative, as well as the quantitative, effects of uncertainties on the behavior and performance of risk-averse profit-maximizing price setters with substantial market power depend upon which variable is uncertain and how its uncertainty varies with price and expected quantities sold. In particular, we have also shown that any uncertainty over realized prices and any uncertainty over the level of variable (marginal) costs have effects which are the reverse of those produced by uncertainty concerning quantities sold.

Whether uncertainties over quantities sold or those regarding realized margins in fact dominate pricing decisions is an empirical issue, and one not to be resolved by theory. The author's impression, based on the evidence available so far, is that for the firms of interest the relative uncertainties of management concerning unit sales will very probably be found to dominate the other uncertainties considered. In this event, the qualitative conclusions of our section II will be the most generally relevant ones in a positive or descriptive sense and for considerations of public policy.

The broadest conclusions of the present paper, however, is that research adequate to settle the empirical issues raised is badly needed. The present exploration of the consequences of introducing uncertainty and risk aversion into the traditional theory of the firm will have served its purpose if it stimulates further research on these exciting dimensions, which are so pregnant with far reaching consequences for the economic theory of the firm, for the corpus of industrial organization as we have known it, and for public policy.

BIBLIOGRAPHY

[1] Arrow, Kenneth. *Aspects of the Theory of Risk Bearing.* Helsinki, Finland: Yrjo Jahnssonin Saatio, 1965.

[2] Baumol, William. *Business Behavior, Value and Growth.* New York, 1959.

[3] Brown, Robert G. *Smoothing, Forecasting and Prediction.* Englewood Cliffs, New Jersey: Prentice-Hall, Inc., 1962.

[4] Dhrymes, Phoebus. "On the Theory of the Monopolistic Multiproduct Firm under Uncertainty," *International Economic Review* (September, 1964), pp. 239–57.

[5] Fellner, William. "Average Cost Pricing and the Theory of Uncertainty," *Journal of Political Economy* (June, 1948), pp. 249–52.

[6] ————. *Competition among the Few.* New York: Alfred A. Knopf, 1949. Esp. pp. 146–58.

[7] ————. *Probability and Profit.* Homewood, Illinois: Richard D. Irwin, Inc., 1965, pp. 173–80.

[8] Kaplan, A. D. H.; Dirlam, Joel B.; and Lanzillotti, Robert F. *Pricing in Big Business.* Washington, D.C.: The Brookings Institution, 1958.

[9] Lanzillotti, Robert F. "Pricing Objective in Large Companies," *American Economic Review* (December, 1958), pp. 459–77.

[10] Lintner, John. "Optimal Dividends and Corporate Growth under Uncertainty." *Quarterly Journal of Economics.* (February, 1964), pp. 49–95.

[11] Marris, Robin. *The Economic Theory of Managerial Captialism.* New York, New York: The Free Press of Glencoe, 1964.

[12] Mills, Edwin S., "Uncertainty and Price Theory," *Quarterly Journal of Economics* (February, 1959), pp. 116–29.

[13] Nelson, Richard R. "Uncertainty, Prediction and Competitive Equilibrium," *Quarterly Journal of Economics* (February, 1961), pp. 41–62.

[14] Neal, Alfred C. *Industrial Concentration and Price Flexibility.* American Council of Public Affairs, 1942.

[15] Pratt, John W., "Risk Aversion in the Small and in the Large," *Econometrica* (January-April, 1964), pp. 122–36.

[16] Ruggles, Richard. "The Nature of Price Flexibility and the Determinants of Relative Price Changes in the Economy," *Business Concentration and Price Policy.* Princeton, New Jersey: Princeton University Press, 1955, pp. 441–95.

[17] Scitovsky, Tibor. *Welfare and Competition.* Homewood, Illinois: Richard D. Irwin, Inc., 1951. Esp. chap. XIII.

[18] Williamson, Oliver E. *The Economics of Discretionary Behavior: Managerial Objectives in the Theory of the Firm.* Englewood Cliffs, New Jersey: Prentice-Hall, Inc., 1964.

12

Competition Between Cables and Satellites: The Single-Entity Proposal for International Telecommunications

*Merton J. Peck**

One simple maxim of economics is that competition is good and monopoly bad. Yet, thinking on policy in international telecommunications has moved in an opposite direction to that simple precept, for the President's Task Force on Communications Policy has recommended a single entity to operate the long-distance portion of international telecommunications.[1]

"Single entity" refers to the ownership by a single firm of the cable and satellite facilities through which overseas telephone and record messages are transmitted. The proposal of the Task Force would limit the single entity to long-distance transmission, prohibiting vertical integration into equipment manufacturing and affiliation with domestic carriers. Creating a single entity would bring together the overseas transmission functions of the Communications Satellite Corporation (Comsat), American Telephone and Telegraph (AT&T), and the record or telegraph carriers — Western Union International (WUI), Radio Corporation of America (RCA), and

* Yale University

[1] *Final Report: President's Task Force on Communications Policy* (submitted December 7, 1968; released May 20, 1969). Henceforth cited as *Task Force Report* with page references to the mimeographed version.

The author wrote this essay while a staff member of The Brookings Institution and with financial assistance from a Ford Foundation grant to the Institution. He was a member of the President's Task Force on Communications Policy from February 15, 1968 to January 20, 1969, and the ideas presented here benefited immensely from the staff papers prepared for the Task Force. William Capron of The Brookings Institution, Leland Johnson of the Rand Corporation, Roger Noll of the California Institute of Technology, and Harvey Levin of Hofstra University read drafts of this paper; and the author is much in their debt for their extensive comments. The views expressed are, of course, the sole responsibility of the author. A summary of this paper was presented at the meetings of the American Economic Association, December 1969, and appears in the Association's *Papers and Proceedings,* May 1970.

International Telephone and Telegraph (ITT). Comsat is the sole United States participant in the ownership and operation of satellites through Intelsat, an international organization. AT&T and the record carriers jointly own the cables, although AT&T alone installs and operates most of such installations.[2]

The Task Force offers five reasons for recommending a single entity:[3]

1. To promote the system's efficiency and enable realization of the available economies of scale.

2. To further United States foreign policy objectives.

3. To resolve the anomalies of Comsat's role and function.

4. To help to resolve the various problems of the international record industry.

5. To improve the prospects of effective governmental regulation.

This essay focuses on the first reason, which raises a more general question, that of the industrial organization of diverse, but closely rivalrous, technologies. In most industries, the market has been permitted to decide this question, and often new companies have come into being to exploit each new dramatic shift in technology. As Professor Schumpeter put it, "In general, it is not the owner of stage-coaches who builds railroads."[4] There are significant exceptions; thus most manufacturers of home radios successfully made the transition to the production of television sets. In the regulated industries, however, the question must be faced more explicitly. A common American answer is to have each technology in separate firms with public policies to regulate the resulting competition. Thus railroads were sharply restricted in the extent to which they might own truck lines in order to promote the development of trucking and to encourage competition between the two modes of transport.

There have been some notable exceptions to the policy of rivalry, one of which is described in Edward Mason's first book, *The Street Railway in Massachusetts*. He reports that "In many communities motor busses operated in competition with the street railway. A law of 1918 (Chapter 226) had, however, authorized street railways to purchase and operate busses and, in the course of time, assisted by a hesitating and slowly developed policy of exclusion of competition adopted by state and local authorities, the public transportation facilities in each locality were concentrated in the hands of a single agency."[5]

The proposal for a single entity in international telecommunications involves shifting from the rail-truck precedent to that of the street car-bus.

---

[2] The present organization of the United States international communications industry is described in greater detail in *Task Force Report*, chap. 2, pp. 3–6.

[3] *Task Force Report*, chap. 2, pp. 27, 29, 31, 32, and 35, respectively.

[4] Joseph A. Schumpeter, *The Theory of Economic Development* (Harvard University Press, 1934), p. 66.

[5] Edward S. Mason, *The Street Railway in Massachusetts* (Harvard University Press, 1932).

The gains of such a move depend in great part on (1) how well the present system of regulated competition operates and (2) the cost functions of the competing technologies.

I Failure of Regulatory Policy to Choose between Cables and Satellites

Present situation. At present overseas telephone calls travel by means of domestic telephone lines (primarily the AT&T system) to either cable-heads or satellite earth stations.[6] The calls are then transmitted overseas on either cables — of which the American portion is owned jointly by AT&T and the record carriers — or over satellite circuits leased from Comsat by AT&T and the record carriers. Record and mixed-voice record traffic follows a somewhat similar pattern, with Western Union or telephone lines carrying messages to the offices of the international record carriers on the two coasts and from there to cableheads and satellite ground stations. Note that in neither instance does Comsat lease circuits directly to users; its role is limited to that of a "carriers' carrier" by Federal Communications Commission (FCC) ruling, a point discussed subsequently. For most traffic, cable and satellite transmissions are perfect substitutes; the exceptions are discussed in the next section.

Relative prices or costs play no direct role in allocating traffic between cable and satellite. The individual placing the call has no choice about whether his voice travels across the ocean by cable or satellite; indeed, he probably never knows which way it went and the charge is .identical with either form of transmission.[7] AT&T and the record carriers allocate the traffic between cable and satellite, but their decisions are not guided by a per-message charge. There is no mechanism by which consumer choice or relative prices, as expressed in a market, guide decisions on investment. In a sense, the situation is economics upside down, namely, the investment decisions influence the division of output rather than the other way round.

FCC ruling in case of ITT Cable & Radio, Inc. The distribution of investment is determined largely by FCC rulings. How these operate can be illustrated by a classic instance in which cable and satellite clashed head-on: the case of service between Miami, Florida and Puerto Rico and the Virgin Islands.[8] In 1965, ITT Cable & Radio, Inc.-Puerto Rico (a sub-

---

[6] A small volume of traffic is sent overseas by high frequency radio circuits operated by ITT and RCA.

[7] Television signals are sent by satellite because of the broad band of the frequency required.

[8] *In the Matter of ITT Cable & Radio, Inc.-Puerto Rico, et al.,* 5 FCC 2nd 823 (Dec. 7, 1966). Facts cited in the following paragraphs are from the *Opinion.* Note that, for the purposes of this essay, such service may be considered international even though it is between points in the United States.

sidiary of ITT) filed an application with the FCC to construct an earth satellite station in Puerto Rico. Shortly thereafter AT&T filed an application for authority to lay a 720-circuit cable. ITT, WUI, and RCA requested ownership participation in the AT&T cable, with their capital contribution being assigned on the basis of expected use. Comsat then applied for an earth station with a capacity "well in excess of the 720-circuit cable."

Faced with this rivalry, the FCC decided to authorize both cable and satellite service. The FCC further directed division of earth station ownership among Comsat and the record carriers, and of cable ownership among AT&T and the record carriers. As a result, every applicant won something even though none was granted his original request. And the consumer gained improved service, clearly needed additional capacity, and lower rates; for AT&T and ITT advised the FCC that once the cable was in operation rates would be reduced by 25 percent.

Indeed, this happy outcome of everyone being a gainer may explain why the applicants eventually appeared willing to compromise. According to the *Opinion,* "Originally all [applicants] appeared to share the view that only one of the two types of applications [cable or satellite] should be granted or justified on economic grounds. However, as the carriers made more detailed reviews of the available data, including expected projections from past experience, their views changed."[9] All applicants shifted to the view that both cable and satellite would be needed. AT&T and ITT volunteered to lease satellite circuits, despite the fact that their cables would be markedly under-utilized for years to come. Furthermore, as indicated above, the ownership of each mode became divided, with at least the acquiescence of all the parties.

The difficulty is that the outcome was uneconomic; costs and hence rates were higher than necessary. Although users paid lower rates than prior to the expansion of capacity, the rate reduction could have been much greater without the cost of the excess capacity created by the FCC-approved compromise. Based on the estimated circuit requirements attached to the *Opinion,* either the proposed cable or satellite service could meet the demand until 1973. For six years or so, international transmission costs will be about twice as high as with one facility.

FCC's reasons for authorizing both facilities. The FCC *Opinion* lists three reasons for authorizing both facilities. First, the potential revenues are sufficient to support two systems. This fact shows only that it is possible to support two systems without injury to investors, but it does not justify authorizing both.

Second, cable and satellite were said to be necessary as insurance against service interruptions. The *Opinion* states, "If only one (cable or earth

[9] *Ibid.,* p. 829.

stations) were to be authorized, we could soon be confronted with a situation where an interruption or a failure abruptly eliminates service for 400 or 500 voice circuits with no alternate facilities available. Thus thousands of users who have come to rely upon these facilities for their needs could be deprived of an essential service for days or weeks."[10]

Yet the probabilities of "days or weeks" of service interruptions if only the satellite had been authorized is very low. The sole satellite failure occurred when the Atlantic Intelsat III was out-of-service for one month in the summer of 1969. Most service was maintained during the period of the malfunction by greater reliance on Intelsat II satellite and by placing the Early Bird back into service. (Early Bird, one of the earliest satellites, had been in "orbital retirement" since January 1969.)[11] As this example indicates, spare satellites can provide insurance against failures and generally at significantly lower costs than cables. As for cables, the older Puerto Rican cable has never been out since it went into operation in 1960. The Puerto Rican cable is particularly fortunate in that it is in waters more sheltered from storms than the Atlantic and Pacific cables, and the major hazard, trawler fishing, does not occur in the Caribbean. Finally, the failure of either the proposed cable or satellite service would not entail the total cessation of communication service between Puerto Rico and the United States. There were 213 cable and high-frequency radio circuits prior to the proposed cable and satellite facilities, capacity sufficient to service about one-fifth of the 1975 demand. The possible loss, then, is the cost of returning to the 1960 level of communications for periods ranging from an hour or two each year (a satellite ground station failure) to a very unlikely two to four weeks (a cable or satellite failure). This kind of situation does not seem to warrant the doubling of costs by authorizing both cable and satellite.

The third reason offered in the *Opinion* was that the public interest requires the continued development of both cable and satellite technologies. In 1966, this may have been a reasonable consideration, given the more unproved character of the satellite; but it is questionable whether promoting two technologies required the approval of both facilities. Cable and satellite were being used in other areas, providing a market elsewhere for each.

FCC's authorization of TAT-5. The decision to authorize both facilities for Puerto Rico might be considered a single instance, explainable by the early stage of satellite development. Yet this ruling has been followed by an FCC decision in 1968 to authorize a fifth transatlantic cable (TAT-5) with an initial investment of some $70 million, a venture which will require $250

---

[10] *Ibid.* p. 831.
[11] See August 1 Press Release of the International Telecommunication Satellite Consortium.

million in revenue over its life to amortize the investment, pay the allowed rate of return, and cover operating costs.[12] Since more Intelsat satellites are soon to be launched, considerable excess capacity again appears likely. Approval of the cable was conditioned on the doctrine of "equal proportional fill," that is, cable and satellite capacity will be utilized at the same rate, thus dividing the traffic in the presence of excess capacity. To be sure, this decision was complicated by the need for additional capacity in 1971, before Intelsat IV was certain to be available, but there was no exploration in the *Opinion* of the relative cost of meeting the circuit requirements with a satellite.[13]

Issues raised by authorization of TAT-5. The TAT-5 Opinion has led to concern that the FCC is embarked on a policy of dividing the market and allowing the expansion of both cable and satellite despite the added cost. Clearly, the pressures on the FCC to follow this policy must be very great. In these decisions, the FCC is caught between the claims of two powerful rival groups of firms. On one side is AT&T, RCA, ITT, and WUI, generally considered progressive, well-managed firms and unlikely to be without political influence. On the other side is Comsat, to which all these statements would also apply. Choosing one over the other would condemn the loser to a lesser role in the expanding business of international communications. Given such a powerful conflict of interests, it is not surprising that the FCC has avoided the choice and developed compromises that allow both modes to prosper, despite the higher cost to the consumer.

The pressures on the FCC are likely to continue. Clearly, Comsat will remain an aggressive advocate of satellites, its only business. As both the Puerto Rican and TAT-5 cases show, the carriers are aggressive advocates of additional investment in cables, despite the resulting excess capacity and higher costs. Such behavior is easily explained by the incentives to invest in cables under the industry's present organization.

Higher costs associated with excess capacity resulting from investment in cables are passed on to consumers in higher rates, so that the main loss to the carriers is the lower volume of traffic occasioned by higher prices. Against this loss are several potential benefits to the carriers from continued investment in cables. International telecommunication is a rapidly growing and profitable business; hence the carriers might be expected to be loath to relinquish any part of it. Furthermore, the carriers may feel more com-

---

[12] *Task Force Report,* chap. 2, p. 10.

[13] It is possible that, with no slippage in satellite launchings, there would be no gap between demand and capacity. But if a high premium is attached to guarding against a gap in service, then a 1970 launching of an additional Intelsat III satellite using present technology might have been substituted for the cable at a lower cost. Another solution would be some form of peak-load pricing to reduce the demand. Neither of these possibilities is examined in the FCC Opinion.

fortable by keeping part of the transmitting process directly under their own control. And AT&T and ITT have cable-manufacturing affiliates for which continued investment in cables provides sales.[14]

The American communications industry is, of course, regulated, a fact which brings to the fore the role of the rate base in providing incentives for cable investment. The regulatory determination of profits is through a rate of return on assets devoted to the regulated service. As a well-known article by Harvey Averch and Leland Johnson has shown, the greater the rate base, the greater will be the allowed profits, creating an incentive for regulated firms to expand their rate bases.[15] In such situations, then, regulated firms will have a greater preference for capital-intensive means of production than competitive firms. There is much dispute about just how empirically important the tendency is. But in comparing the use of a cable owned by a carrier with a satellite circuit leased by the carrier, the alternatives become a considerable rate base versus almost none at all.[16]

In this situation, even a weak profit-maximizing assumption would indicate that the carriers preferred cable, particularly the record carriers, which have 60 percent of their rate base represented by cable investment. Since the preponderance of AT&T's investment is in domestic telephone facilities, the relative effect on AT&T would be much less. If international operations alone are considered, however, AT&T's situation is comparable to that of the record carriers.

Carriers, however, also have ownership interests in the satellite system. They hold jointly some 40 percent of the stock in Comsat; but this investment is excluded in computing the rate base, and earnings from the investment are also excluded in determining allowable returns. To be sure, the carriers will benefit by Comsat's earnings on its rate base, but such earnings are diluted by their fractional ownership. And, in any case, the carriers obviously gain by having both cable and satellite investment approved rather than only one or the other.

The importance of the rate base is reflected in FCC rulings assigning the carriers a half ownership in the satellite earth stations, which is included in

[14] Pressure for cables may also originate from the foreign communication entities at the other end of the service. These entities may prefer cables since their shares of ownership and influence in the operation are likely to be greater than with satellites. Some European countries also have cable-manufacturing industries. In addition, countries in which cables are landed realize revenue from transit cable traffic.

[15] Harvey Averch and Leland L. Johnson, "Behavior of the Firm under Regulatory Constraint," *American Economic Review*, LII (December, 1962), 1052–69.

[16] One solution would be to allow the capitalization of long-term leases of satellite circuits and add the capitalization to the rate base rather than have such lease payments treated as current costs. Although this might reduce the incentives of carriers to promote the expansion of cables, it would create the awkward problem of allowing the rate of return twice — once to Comsat and once to the lessees. Since the rate of return is presumed to represent payment for the use of capital, this solution seems unacceptable and costly.

their rate bases.[17] In part, the FCC so ruled in order that the carriers might have a rate-base interest in satellites. Lacking such joint ownership, the FCC said, "They [the carriers] would be faced with the prospect of ever diminishing rate base, both in the absolute as well as relative senses, and would be driven to seek alternative means, not necessarily dictated by efficiency but their need for survival."[18] This statement would seem to be an implicit acceptance of the Averch-Johnson hypothesis.[19]

There is an offsetting factor that could make the use of satellites rather than cables more profitable to the carriers in the short run. If the cost of leasing satellite circuits is less than that of owning cables, the carriers would make greater total profits at any given level of rates by using such circuits. And since there is no investment involved, the difference in profit rate will, of course, be considerably greater. Yet in the long run, cables are the more profitable because regulation would require that rates be lowered until profits no longer exceeded levels allowed by the rate base. The short and long runs are separated by the regulatory lag — the length of time between the realization of excess profits and the ordering of rate reductions. The FCC has not had a formal hearing on international-communications rates since 1958, but this fact alone is a poor measure of the regulatory lag. The carriers have regularly initiated rate reduction, often under FCC pressure.[20]

Given these two considerations, the carriers would be likely to rely primarily on satellites only if their costs in so doing fell radically relative to the costs of using cables and if regulation worked slowly enough to let the carriers realize profits from such cost reductions. To date these factors have not led to any apparent desire by the carriers to forego investment in cables.

II   Comparing Cables and Satellites

At present neither market forces nor regulation economically resolves the problem of how to mix cable and satellite investment. The economical make-up of this mix turns, of course, on costs.

[17] 5 FCC 2nd 812 (December 8, 1966). For a good and very comprehensive discussion of earth station ownership and the general problem of international communications, see Herman Schwartz, "Comsat, the Carriers, and the Earth Stations: Some Problems with 'Melding Variegated Interests,'" *Yale Law Journal,* LXXVI (January 1967), 441–84.

[18] 5 FCC 2nd 815.

[19] The rate base involved in the earth stations is still considerably less than in cable. The ownership share of AT&T and the record carriers in the six earth stations is about $30 million as compared with their overall international rate base — largely in cables — of several hundred million dollars. Thus the gain from using cables instead of satellites in terms of rate base, and hence long-run profits, is considerable.

[20] For example, in a decision involving the carriers' leasing of satellite circuits, the FCC said, "We therefore expect the common carriers promptly to give further review to their current rate schedules and file revisions which fully reflect the economies made available through the leasing of satellite circuits. Failure of the carriers to do so promptly and effectively will require the Commission to take such actions as are appropriate." (4 FCC 2nd 434)

Relative costs. The Task Force requested the National Academy of Engineering to establish a Committee on Telecommunications that would examine the relative costs of satellites and other long-haul modes of transmission. The studies of this group as well as other literature indicate that the costs of cable and satellite have the following characteristics.[21]

1. There are now very great economies of scale in both cable and satellite, and these economies are increasing markedly. In the mid-sixties, the Atlantic basin — the area with the largest traffic volume — had about a thousand circuits divided equally between cable and satellite. By comparison, TAT-5 will have 720 circuits; and Intelsat III satellite, launched in December of 1968, has about 1,000 circuits. But the estimated cost per circuit of these two new installations is a third to a fifth below the cost per circuit of their immediate and much-lower-volume predecessors. Intelsat IV satellite, now planned for launching early in 1971, will have about 5,000 circuits, five times that of Intelsat III. After 1975, the Committee of the National Academy of Engineering anticipates an Intelsat IV-A with about 20,000 circuits and cables with about 3,000 circuits.[22]

2. The short-run marginal costs for long-distance transmission by either cable or satellite are extremely low. Investment in major equipment represents about two-thirds of the system's cost for satellites and even more for cables. The remaining costs are for maintenance, unaffected by volume, and for operations, determined mainly by the number or hours in service.

3. Satellite costs are lower than those of cable for long distances and high traffic densities. The Committee of the National Academy made a specific comparison between the TAT-5 cable and a modified Intelsat III-A system. The costs were roughly comparable for the two facilities, but the cable had 720 circuits and the satellite 10,000 circuits. The Committee states, "It may be concluded that up to 720 circuits may be provided for up to 20 years for trans-Atlantic traffic at approximately the same annual costs, whether a satellite or cable system is used. . . . However, if more than 720 circuits are required, the satellite has a decided cost advantage."[23] Since circuit demand is growing rapidly, the satellite is clearly the low-cost mode, even at present. Furthermore, satellites have two qualitative advantages. Their life is around five years compared to twenty for the cable. Hence

---

[21] Committee on Telecommunications, National Academy of Engineering, *Report on Selected Topics in Telecommunications,* (Final Report to the Department of Housing and Urban Development under Contract No. H.952, November 1968; revised, December 1968.) Henceforth cited as *Academy Report.* Also, "The Satellite Confrontation," *The Economist,* CCXXX (Feb. 22, 1969), 58–59; Herman Schwartz, *op. cit.,* 450–51; *In the Matter of American Telephone and Telegraph, et al.,* FCC 68 569 (May 27, 1968); and *Task Force Report,* chap. 2, 21–29.

[22] *Academy Report,* p. 108.

[23] *Ibid.,* p. 101.

satellites can more readily take advantage of a rapidly evolving technology. Second, satellites can collect signals from a number of ground stations, can thus serve wide areas, and so capitalize on their economies of scale. Indeed, world-wide communications can now be provided by only three satellites. In contrast, cables are inherently point-to-point service. Cables have two advantages. First, they require no radio spectrum; but this drawback of satellites can be minimized by locating ground stations away from metropolitan areas and bringing the signal from the ground station over telephone lines. Second, cables are cheaper for short distances, though it is uncertain just how far their zone of advantage extends. Estimates range from 600 to 1,200 miles, depending in part on the traffic density.

If the only problem were devising a cost-minimizing system, then the preceding points suggest its nature. The *Task Force Report* concludes: "A single satellite will soon have the capacity to handle all traffic on several international routes (perhaps even whole ocean basins), probably at lower cost than alternative techniques."[24]

Cost estimates by the Committee of the National Academy support a stronger conclusion. Since the FCC has already authorized sufficient cable and satellite to meet the anticipated demand in the Atlantic basin until 1975, the Committee has examined the costs of three alternative investment strategies if the anticipated demand beyond that time grows at 10 percent per year.[25] The results are shown in Table 12–1. Concentrating all the investment in satellites, as in strategy one, is half as expensive as dividing the additional traffic between cables and satellites, as in strategy three.

Criteria other than costs. If costs were the only criteria and if the system were being built *ab initio,* then the optimum transoceanic system would be entirely satellite. As always, however, there are complications.

First, cables and satellites are not perfect substitutes for some kinds of traffic. Telephone conversations via a satellite involve a time delay which becomes particularly noticeable with transmission via two satellites, such as a Tokyo-London call that passes through both a Pacific and Atlantic satellite. The time delay with satellites also involves a higher rate of error for high-speed transmissions of data, though this may be correctable by the redesign of transmitting and receiving equipment. These two kinds of traffic are considerably less than the capacity of existing cables, so that although the traffic does not create a case for added cable capacity, it does create a case for retaining the existing capacity.

---

[24] *Task Force Report,* chap. 2, p. 21.
[25] The Committee has also examined a situation in which demand grows at 20 percent annually. A satellite-only investment strategy is still the cheapest, though a mixed cable-satellite strategy carries a smaller cost premium — about 50 percent, since the faster growth of demand means that the mixed strategy has less excess capacity.

Table 12–1   Costs of Various Investment Strategies for an Annual Growth in Demand of Ten Percent during 1976–85

Strategy	1985 Traffic via Satellite (percent)	Cumulated Annual Costs 1976–85 ($ millions)*
1. All incremental investment in satellites	85	90
2. Incremental investment primarily satellites but with some cable	70	127
3. Incremental investment divided between satellites and cable	48	184

Source: *Academy Report*, p. 109.
*Costs are those occurring each year which are associated with the planned investment for 1976 through 1985. These include annual maintenance, capital cost amortized in a straight-line fashion over the life of the investment, and an interest charge of six percent on the net investment.

Second, there is the problem — noted above in connection with Puerto Rico — of insurance against interruption in service. Satellites have proved to be exceptionally reliable. To be sure, there are service interruptions due to atmospheric conditions, but these are short and infrequent. Nonetheless, there has been one satellite failure; and the Intelsat program provides for spare satellites, both in orbit and on the ground, an arrangement which is a cheaper way of providing back-up capacity than the cable. There are also failures in ground-station circuits, but these now amount to less than one percent of operating time and never last more than a few hours. Spare capacity in ground stations is again cheaper insurance than laying cables.[26]

Nevertheless, there remains a view that insurance against service failure must be provided by an alternative mode, namely, cable. This view reflects a folk wisdom that diversification is good: don't put all the eggs in one basket. Yet the specific insurance that cable can provide is limited to relatively short interruptions in service of satellite communications due to atmospheric conditions that blank out transmission.

The United States Department of Defense is one customer that prizes continuous service. The Department so values reliability in communications that it maintains its own system, involving high-frequency and troposphere radio as well as its own satellites. All of these media still go through the atmosphere, and one can imagine jamming of frequencies by unfriendly nations. Here cables would be highly valuable, though they are subject to

[26] Note also that a cable has its own problems of service interruption, problems on which we comment subsequently in the text.

cutting by "trawler operations." The Department of Defense has supported the laying of TAT-5 on grounds of national security, as this would provide the only direct cable service to Spain and Portugal.

Yet if cable is so essential, it would be better to have the Department of Defense directly subsidize its construction. At present, defense officials simply state a national security requirement without providing any direct financial payment. The Department of Defense pays only a share of the added costs through higher rates; most of the costs are borne by other users. Hence the national security costs of having a cable are not evaluated relative to the costs of using resources to contribute to national security in other ways. Furthermore, it is economically irrational to levy on communication users a special contribution for national security. Such a procedure is analogous to having steel buyers pay for the steel used for defense purposes. A better way to meet the requirement of national security would be for the Department of Defense to make direct payments to insure cable facilities.

Other users might conceivably pay something to insure against interruptions of communication, but these might be such low-volume or intermittent users that they would find paying to maintain cable circuits an uneconomical insurance device. There seems to be no easy way to collect an insurance premium in advance from just those users who value reliability.

It is unlikely, however, that consumers would pay a great deal in order to insure a large cable capacity. Satellite reliability has improved so radically in the last decade that now cables have become the device more prone to service interruption. For all of the United States overseas cables, service interruptions from cable failures averaged one per year per cable during 1967 and 1968, with the median duration of service interruption being four days and the longest twelve days.[27] Cable was the principal method of transoceanic communication from 1956 to 1965; the only alternative was a limited number of high-frequency radio circuits. Thus, with their shorter service interruptions, satellites alone represent a marked gain over the reliability of just a few years ago. That consumers would value even further gains in reliability to the extent of being willing to pay a great deal more to insure extensive cable facilities is improbable.

Yet it does seem plausible that they would pay something more to insure some cable service so that at least limited service would be available as a hedge against satellite failure. This insurance can be provided at a relatively small cost by maintaining existing cables, since the investment to lay them has already been made.

A final complication arises from the possibility that the cost of cables might overtake the cost advantage of satellites. The lead of the satellites now seems so great as to make this unlikely. Nevertheless, it should be noted that some experts in communication are still persuaded that cable and satellite costs are even now very close and that future developments

---

[27] Based on data from the FCC cable service log. This source covers only cables with United States terminals.

might place cables in the lead. This view receives some support from the fact that, in the early sixties, cable costs fell sharply with the development of the transistorized cable and there was speculation that the cable might become cost competitive with satellites. The Committee on Telecommunications of the National Academy of Engineering recommended that research on the technology of both satellites and undersea cables should be supported.[28] Although such a point is difficult to assess, its economic implications are that it may pay for an indefinite period to maintain some cable development and manufacture. If the uncertain prospects for cables deter existing cable manufacturers from such research, a gap between the value from the development of cable technology expected by any one manufacturer and that expected by the communications system as a whole may justify some financial support by the latter.

These complications strongly suggest that an adequate international telecommunications system would include maintaining existing cable capacity. It may also be desirable to replace that capacity at some future date and to insure continued development of cable technology. On the other hand, the lower costs of satellites combined with their great economies of scale suggest that international telecommunications should be primarily a satellite system.

III   The Single-Entity Solution for an Economical Mix of Cable and Satellite Investment

As noted earlier, regulatory policy now avoids the choice between satellite and cable. The outcome is the parallel expansion of each mode, resulting in a system very far from the one just described.

The Task Force examined four alternatives to the present system: (1) establishing competing entities, each owning both cable and satellite facilities; (2) promoting more effective competition between cable and satellite transmission; (3) substantial changes in present regulatory policies without a change in the existing structure of ownership; and (4) the single entity.[29]

The first alternative, competing bimodal entities, would be a costly one because of the very great economies of scale in both cable and satellite transmission. The competitive solution is thus limited to the second alternative: competition between a cable entity and a satellite entity. This solution would require two major changes in existing regulatory policy.

The first change is that the two firms would be free to compete on a price basis for the traffic of the few big users leasing circuits directly, because it

[28] *Academy Report,* p. vii.

[29] *Task Force Report,* chap. 2, 21–28. The *Report* contains a detailed discussion of each alternative, which parallels in part the discussion in this section. The Task Force, however, being concerned with matters other than satellite and cable competition, such as the implications for United States international relations, has additional reasons for rejecting all but the alternative of the single entity.

would not be sufficient to have the cable and satellite firms compete only for traffic originated by the carriers. The FCC has discouraged rate-cutting to specific users in its "30 circuits decision," which involved a Comsat contract with the Department of Defense for a block of circuits in the Pacific. In that instance, the record carriers had offered to lease at a monthly charge of $10,000 to $12,000 per half circuit; Comsat's offer was $4,000 and initially it was awarded the contract. The carriers protested to the FCC and, in connection with its decision in that case, the Commission ruled that Comsat was a "carriers' carrier" and thus precluded from serving users directly except in special circumstances.[30] The effect of this decision was to remove competition for the leasing of circuits to large users.

The second change in regulatory policy required by the competitive solution is that cable ownership would have to be divested from AT&T and the record carriers. Otherwise, these companies, which originate most of the traffic, would have incentives to favor cable. A parallel action would be divestiture of the carriers' ownership interest in Comsat as well as termination of their representation on Comsat's board of directors.

Yet even with these measures, competition would be either transitory or limited in scope, depending on how the cable and satellite entities reacted to their mutual interdependence. If they behaved like pure competitors, always cutting price as long as the short-run gains exceeded short-run costs, prices would be driven down to the low level of marginal costs, given the excess capacity inherent in the large indivisible investment in both cable and satellite. Funds both for new investment and for recoupment of past investment would then be unavailable. One firm would eventually become bankrupt, and there would be pressure to allow its merger with the other. If the financial staying power is equally distributed between the two firms, the satellite firm, with the low-cost technology, should be the winner. The final outcome would be the multimode single entity.

That outcome, however, seems unrealistic, for it assumes that each duopolist would fail to recognize that its price cut will be matched by its rival and hence yield no immediate increase in its share of the market. With a recognition of mutual interdependence, the outcome would be what the Task Force called a "live-and-let-live" attitude toward pricing and the rival's expansion.[31] The final outcome might be very similar to that produced by the present situation: parallel expansion of cable and satellite.

The third alternative, better regulation, is clearly a necessary condition

---

[30] *Authorized Users,* Memorandum Opinion and Statement of Policy, 4 FCC 2nd 421 (July 20, 1966); *Authorized Users,* Memorandum Opinion and Order, 6 FCC 2nd 593 (Feb. 1, 1962); *ITT World Communications, et al.,* Memorandum Opinion, Order, and Certificate, 6 FCC 2nd 511 (Feb. 1, 1967). The carriers subsequently proposed a composite rate, based on a mix of leased satellite circuits and cable circuits. The proposed rate was $7,100 per month per half circuit, and at this rate the contract was awarded to the carriers.

[31] *Task Force Report,* chap. 2, p. 23.

for improvement, but is it a sufficient condition, without a change in the existing structure of ownership? The Task Force lists several key steps that might be taken under this alternative:

> The rates of AT&T and the record carriers could be set on the basis of the most efficient and lowest cost transmission medium regardless of ownership; government review could be strengthened to enable rigorous scrutiny and evaluation of adversary proposals for new facilities and choices which avoid overbuilding; and the international carriers could be subjected more rigorously to the test of the market by giving others direct access to international circuits by modifying the authorized-user rulings.[32]

Although these measures would go far to improve the situation, the Task Force doubted "the practicality of such steps."

Regulation could produce the socially optimum solution. But the difficulties of regulation alone as a solution are most apparent in the case of setting rates on the basis of the low-cost medium of transmission. This would be transmission by satellite; and the resulting rates would not only preclude further investment in cables, they might also preclude earning a "fair return on a fair value" for existing cables. In the nonregulated portion of the economy, the investor, of course, bears the loss from the emergence of a better technology. In the regulated portion, there is a clear tendency to fetter the introduction of new technology when it threatens established firms. It may be desirable to face that tendency by paying compensation rather than to restrict the use of new technology. Paying compensation has a further justification in that returns of regulated industries are held down on the grounds that such industries are relatively risk-free. Finally, compensation for shifts in regulatory policy is merely a subcase of the general proposition of compensation for changes in public policy. This type of compensation is exemplified by adjustment assistance for those adversely affected by tariff changes, as provided in the 1962 trade legislation. And, apart from the economic logic, provision for compensation would increase the political feasibility of changes in policy.

The creation of a single entity would provide an occasion for compensation to cable owners through the purchase of present cable assets.[33] It would no longer be necessary to keep satellite rates at a level high enough to insure the recovery of investment in cable operations.

The single entity would also increase the likelihood of the "rigorous scrutiny and evaluation of new investment" mentioned above. The FCC would be free of the conflicting claims of proponents of cables and satellites,

---

[32] *Ibid.*, chap. 2, pp. 26–27.

[33] If Comsat served as the nucleus of the single entity, it would have considerable capital with which to purchase cable assets. At present, only a third of its $200 million initial capital is invested in satellite communications, with the remainder in securities. This excess liquidity came about because the initial financing was for a system of many random orbiting satellites with very complex earth stations. Technology soon made possible a synchronous system with fewer satellites and less complex earth stations, and hence much lower capital requirements.

and it would no longer be faced with crucial decisions determining the fate of two technologies and powerful companies. The denial of an application for either a cable or satellite would no longer remove one set of firms from a growing and profitable market.

On the other hand, creating a single entity is no solution for the problem of rate-base expansion, the Averch-Johnson effect. The single entity could still increase profits through a rate-base expansion from parallel cable and satellite investment, or indeed from any other form of excess capacity. The defect is inherent in the method of rate regulation, and the solutions lie in a radically different way of regulation or more vigorous regulatory control of investment. Still, it may be easier to grant a single entity an authorization for either a cable or satellite than to deny either of two applicants its only way of expansion.

A more inherent advantage of the single entity is that it provides the most straightforward way of dealing with the complications of the interrelationship between cable and satellite indicated earlier. Existing cables should be maintained and in due time perhaps replaced, both to provide diversity in the overall system of communication — a diversity intended as a special insurance against service interruptions for a fraction of the traffic — and to serve traffic ill-suited to satellite transmission. A single entity could also fund the development of cable technology and be in a position to capitalize on such progress should the balance of advantage shift back toward cable. Although the special traffic preferable for cable might be charged higher rates, the other two aspects — a limited degree of diversity and the continued development of cable — involve benefits for the system's users in general. A single entity permits internalizing these benefits and recouping the costs from all the system's users. With a cable entity alone, it might be necessary to hold satellite rates at a level high enough to keep a small amount of cable capacity financially viable.

These advantages of the single entity are bought at the cost of foregoing the existing rivalry between Comsat and the carriers for the function of long-distance international telecommunication. Although this rivalry generates excess capacity and added costs, it still appears to be a significant factor in the very rapid technical progress of both cable and satellite technology. In the case of satellites, however, the rapid progress originated largely with the manufacturers of satellite equipment and with the military and space programs. These sources of progress would still remain, for the single entity could be precluded from vertical integration into equipment manufacture. On the other hand, there is the possibility that, without competition, a single entity may be a bit less vigorous in applying new technology.

The loss of competition could be partially offset by insuring that the single entity would be free of ownership and control by the domestic carriers. The carriers would no longer be proponents of cable. Rather, they would have a strong interest in lower rates for the international traffic they originate. Under the Task Force proposal, the single entity would sell only transmitting capacity, with AT&T, WUI, and other firms retailing the service. Although countervailing power is often considered a weak reed in offsetting monopoly AT&T may represent a special case, The Task Force concluded. "And we suspect that the entity's principal carrier customer — AT&T, representing most users of international communications — would be quite able to ensure adequate performance from it."[34]

The major drawback to the single entity is more conjectural; nonetheless it could be quite decisive. This potential hurdle is not inherent in the single entity per se but rather in the problem of moving from the present situation to that industrial structure. The present regulatory problem arises because the existing firms are unwilling to relinquish a growing and profitable market and they are in a position to protect their role in international telecommunications. The same reluctance and the same political pressures would be present during the creation of the single entity. There would be the same pressures now present in the regulatory process to devise some way of sharing the market, with the sharing process not necessarily confined to international telecommunications. One could visualize some particular change in the domestic market — say, the assignment of domestic satellite operations to the carriers — that might compensate for the loss of the international market and thus buy their support of the single entity. But such an arrangement might well be too costly in terms of the opportunities foregone for improvement elsewhere. The single entity for international telecommunications, itself, is an improvement; but at a stiff enough price, it may no longer be worthwhile.

The thesis of this essay may be summed up by a paragraph from Edward Mason's work, *The Street Railways in Massachusetts,* by substituting for the words in italics those in brackets.

> The replacement of *rail* [cable] by *motor service* [satellite] over a considerable part of the *street railway territory* [international telecommunications market] was, of course, inevitable. But the decision between these alternative methods of *transport* [communications] ought to be made on the basis of their comparative costs. Such a decision is impossible under a system of regulation which imposes *heavy burdens and responsibilities on one type and not upon the other* [divides the markets between the two modes]. Furthermore, there are great economies to be had in concentrating the operation of all *public transportation within a locality* [international telecommunications] in one company.

Only time will tell whether Edward Mason's next sentence will be needed. "Public regulation in *Massachusetts* [the United States] appears to have been unnecessarily slow in recognizing these facts."[35]

[34] *Task Force Report,* chap. 2, p. 39.
[35] Mason, *op. cit.,* p. 132.

13

Uncertainty, Market Structure and Performance: Galbraith as Conventional Wisdom

*Richard E. Caves**

In *The New Industrial State,* Professor John Kenneth Galbraith argues that the characteristic form of economic organization in our industrial society is the giant corporation, usually diversified into many product markets and owing its size to economies of scale and the complexity of modern technology. It is organized bureaucratically; and it is run by, and largely for, its managers and their subordinate departmental heads, technicians, and other white-collar specialists who share the authority and information that make them undisputed chieftains in their domain. Although easily securing the sullen acquiescence of the stockholders, the managers and their subordinates run the corporation to serve their own objectives of freedom from uncertainty and outside interference; the attainment of growth; and the display of "technological virtuosity," or what the more sanguine would call technological progressiveness. This cadre, or "techno-structure," largely succeeds in controlling the corporation's environment for the purpose of achieving these ends. Thus, the corporation integrates backward to control the supply of needed raw materials; it "cuts in" the trade unions to assure a labor supply that is compliant except for ritualistic haggling; it rigs the price of its product and manipulates demand to assure that the market will take what it produces at that price; and it cons the government into assuring a high and stable level of aggregate demand. The corporation spreads through the land the gospel of the goodness of material things and rising incomes, raising aspirations for private consumption even when the thinking man can plainly see that we are sated with material goods and starved of leisure and public consumption.

* Harvard University

283

Economists who reviewed the book have at best received it with faint praise. Most of the attacks have centered on Galbraith's views about the extent to which the large firm controls its political and economic environment. An armchair strategist may suspect that the author's flat and frequent assertions about the firm's freedom from constraints are calculated to win compromising consent from doubters to the weaker proposition that the firm *somewhat* controls its environment. In any case, the jousting in this corner of the arena has diverted attention from the rest of the show and in particular from Galbraith's analysis of the motives of corporate managers and their effects on the firm's behavior. Several reviewers have passed off his propositions on the firm's structure and motivation as "old hat" before they squared off to trade innuendos and assertions concerning the firm's control of its surroundings. Yet Galbraith has reacted hotly to the charge that his model of the inner workings of the large corporation is casual or unscholarly.[1] I shall maintain that, in one of his arguments, he has touched upon an important and oft-ignored aspect of the large firm's behavior: that a significant portion of the potential profits latent in its position of market power is taken in the form of avoiding uncertainty, with important allocative effects on the economy. Specifically, the following sections will maintain that:

1. The available evidence on the profit performance of the large firm is consistent with this bias affecting its behavior;

2. Many strategies employed, and allocative decisions made, by the large firm may embody this avoidance of uncertainty;

3. The implications of the pattern of corporate behavior that we observe, and its allocative effects on the economy, have received little attention.

I   Profit Data and Avoidance of Uncertainty by Large Firms

Let us assume with Galbraith that the managements of large firms, operating in a world frequently afflicted by random disturbances, act to avoid uncertainty. Their evasions could take many forms. They could systematically forego economic activities — markets, production processes, inputs, and so forth — that yield a high but variable rate of return. They could eschew changing their plans in order to seize new profit opportunities which might, or might not, prove transitory.

Why should large firms display these forms of uncertainty-avoidance in greater measure than small firms? There are two possible reasons. First, large firms more frequently occupy positions of market power than small firms. Thus the former enjoy the option of trading off some excess profits

[1] See [13]. The bracketed number or numbers in this and subsequent footnotes refer to entries in the essay's bibliography.

for an increased amount of the "quiet life." The small firms often lack the chance to earn other than the opportunity cost of capital and so cannot shift to more certain alternatives yielding a lower return.[2] Second, managerial personnel may distribute themselves between large and small firms on the basis of differing marginal rates of substitution between the level of returns — whether profits or direct managerial rewards — and their variance. These two explanations of why uncertainty-avoidance is concentrated in the large corporation raise very different normative questions but predict the same general patterns of behavior. Large firms would press farther than would small firms with actions tending to reduce uncertainty while lowering and stabilizing the level of reported profits.[3]

A similar problem in weighing the significance of uncertainty-avoiding behavior in the large corporation arises because most specific actions or policies that reduce uncertainty about the decision variables with which management is preoccupied also reduce the uncertainty of the profit stream to the shareholders. It is thus impossible in practice to distinguish between managerial actions which reduce uncertainty in the service of optimizing the risk-return package for the stockholders and — what Galbraith postulates — *additional* uncertainty avoidance undertaken to provide a quiet life for the techno-structure. Which motive predominates does not greatly affect one's assessment of the consequences of uncertainty avoidance for general economic welfare, but the question of motivation is, of course, interesting on its own. I would merely advance two general arguments suggesting that uncertainty avoidance demonstrated by large firms in concentrated industries to some extent serves managerial self-interest. First, it is widely conceded that managerial behavior can be described and analyzed as a process of utility maximization. If uncertainty avoidance is an argument of personal utility function of management, one would in general expect that managers enjoying some behavioral options would avoid uncertainty to a greater extent than is needed to maximize the value of the shares. Second, it is well to remember that stockholders trade as pure competitors, whether in the

---

[2] I abstract here from lenders' risk, which would raise this opportunity cost for firms systematically exposed to greater risks. The terms "risk" and "uncertainty" will be used interchangeably through much of this paper. I shall consider, however, the extent to which alleged uncertainty-avoidance by the large firm really involves the pooling of risks.

[3] The "Chicago school," e.g., Alchian and Kessel [1], would rule out the first explanation, holding that the choice of any degree of risk-aversion other than that which maximizes the value of the equity shares will result in a takeover raid. They urge that this threat deters firms with market power from excessive risk avoidance, just as free entry keeps the pressure on competitive firms to maximize profits. Aside from doubting the indicated omniscience and omnipresence of raiders, I would note that this influence should work on any publicly traded corporation whether "competitive" or "monopolistic." Unrestricted entry usually affects only competitive markets, however. At the least, the line of reasoning in the text may be justified by arguing that competitive corporations face pressure for maximization from both raiders and market rivals; firms with market power, only from the raiders.

shares of companies enjoying market power or of those lacking it. Suppose that the former firms, by virtue of their ability to avoid uncertainty, offer stockholders lower-variance dividend streams, and that these streams command a higher value per dollar of dividends. This would imply that the cost of capital is lower to firms enjoying market power, and in turn raise a question about the observed persistence of large sectors of small, reasonably competitive enterprises in the economy. This argument cannot be pushed too far for numerous reasons, but it does suggest that an assertion that large corporations avoid uncertainty extensively *and* pass the benefits along to their stockholders entails some odd implications.

Clearly this proposition as stated can be given no straightforward test. It calls for comparing two sets of observable data not with each other but with hypothetical alternatives: profit patterns of actual small firms with those of hypothetical profit-maximizing small firms, and likewise for actual giant corporations. Indeed, the recorded profits of actual small and large firms cannot be appropriately compared without taking account somehow of differences in potential rates of return due to the greater market power of the large firms. Grounds for despair over making proper allowance for differences in potential rates of return come quickly to mind. Nonetheless, I shall argue that the abundant evidence on the profit performance of large and small firms is consistent with this proposition.

Consider, as a starting point, the relation between profit rates — on equity or assets, before or after taxes — and size — measured by assets — that has been shown in various studies of data for the United States gathered by the Internal Revenue Service and Federal Trade Commission-Securities and Exchange Commission.[4] Firms' average profit rates rise until some relatively modest size is attained and then remain roughly constant: Sherman's recent study puts the size at which the increase halts between $500,000 and $2,500,000 for most measures of profit.[5] If one compares only those corporations reporting net income, however, average profits decline as size increases. The two findings are consistent because a larger proportion of small corporations report losses, and report proportionally larger losses. Hence, the result for all corporations taken together is an increase of average profits with size. (The studies that have reached the opposite conclusion often seem to employ samples biased toward the overrepresentation of profitable enterprises.) A corollary is that the variance of profit rates among firms declines substantially as one goes from small to large corporations. The above conclusions hold either for all corporations or for corporations in manufacturing alone.

These facts are obviously consistent with the hypothesis that large firms succeed in reducing uncertainty, but, of course, they are also compatible with other explanations of the influence of a firm's size on profitability. One

---

[4] See [2], [27], [29], and [30].
[5] See [27], chap. 2.

explanation in particular requires attention, since it suggests that the fall in the variance of firms' profit rates as we move to larger-size classes may be a purely statistical phenomenon. Large firms are in the broadest sense more diversified than small firms — producing and selling not only more products but also more varieties of any given product, operating a greater number of plants, and selling in a greater number of geographically segmented sub-markets. The large firm, then, may be viewed as an aggregate of n small firms, each of them $1/n$ its size. The variance of the profit rates for the large firms should then be approximately $1/\sqrt{n}$ of the variance of the profit rates of firms $1/n$ as large, since the variance of the means of samples of size n is reduced in approximately this proportion from the variance of the sampled population.[6] Now, if the assumptions about large firms that underlie this hypothesis could be verified independently *and* the variance of large firms' profits found to be reduced by *more* than the predicted proportion, we would have independent confirmation of the effects of uncertainty-avoidance by large corporations. Unfortunately, no test of this sort has proved possible. The variance of firms' profits in fact declines with increasing size in a proportion significantly less than that predicted by the hypothesis, at least for firms reporting assets greater than $500,000.[7] Furthermore, the assumptions of the hypothesis are clearly false insofar as they imply roughly that a large firm operating in n well-defined submarkets typically occupies no greater share of any of them than firms $1/n$ its size operating in single markets. One could prove something about uncertainty-avoidance by the large firm from the data on the variance of profits only through comparison with some direct measure of the relative variability of profit opportunities — the extent of diversification, the extent of sales fluctuations, and the like. Nothing of this sort seems available or within the realm of easy construction.[8]

This relation between the variability of profits and a firm's size can be analyzed in other ways, however, to test for the effects of uncertainty-avoidance. Let us switch from the variance of profits among firms in any given time period to measures of the variability (or stability) of profit rates over time for firms of various sizes. In a sample of 186 companies in the United Kingdom, Samuels and Smyth have found that the variability of profits over time — variance around their time trend — decreases as their size increases, just as the variance of profit levels among firms.[9] This fact

---

[6] See [2].

[7] See [27], p. 120.

[8] Ferguson [8] has studied the relation of business size to the stability over time of a number of variables, including profits, sales, employment, and the rate of growth. Unfortunately for present purposes, his technique of testing for significant relations between stability and size — rank correlation over relatively small samples of firms in individual industries — does not allow statements about whether the stability of one variable increases more rapidly with size than the stability of another.

[9] See [26].

alone could simply reflect once more the correlation between size and diversification. However, they also classify 116 of their 186 firms by industry and plot the variability of profits against concentration of sellers in the respective industries as measured by the share of the market held by the top three firms. The distribution suggests a split with significantly lower variability for firms in industries where the top three control more than 30 percent, and this split proves statistically significant. Although other causal factors could be responsible for it, the result is certainly consistent with the proposition that positions of market power might be exploited in part for the enjoyment of greater stability and freedom from uncertainty.

One can examine the variability over time of aggregate profits for firms in various size classes as well as the variability of the returns of individual companies. Sherman's recent study of data from the United States Internal Revenue Service for the years 1931–61 concludes that the profits of small firms in the aggregate vary significantly more over the business cycle than those of large corporations. The cyclical amplitude of the total profits of small firms is systematically higher than the amplitude of the profits of large firms, whether for all corporations or for manufacturing only.[10] These findings usefully supplement those of Samuels and Smyth in that the greater variability over time of aggregate profits of small than of large firms cannot be caused by any difference in the extent of diversification: aggregate profits for a given size class reflect the experience of the whole "diversified" group of firms in that class and are unaffected by the degree of diversification attained by the individual firms.[11]

Another test of profit data for evidence of uncertainty-avoidance can be made by noting how firms' rates of return change with increases in the variance of those rates, both within size classes and between groups of small and large firms. One would expect that, among firms of a given size and with comparable degrees of market power, the rate of return for the firm would be an increasing function of its variability over time. Fisher and Hall[12] confirm this prediction for a sample of giant firms from the 500 listed in *Fortune*.[13] For a complete population of corporations or a sample covering the observed range of sizes systematically, however, uncertainty-avoidance, as well as diversification, by large firms might well swamp the normal risk/return relation and produce a negative relation between the level of profits and their variability over time. Samuels and Smyth report just this result for their sample of United Kingdom companies.

---

[10] See [27], chap. 7.

[11] Sherman argues quite reasonably that small firms may systematically undertake risks involving greater expected cyclical fluctuations of profits, but his discussion tends to confuse this with the pooling of risks *per se* in the large firm (pp. 182–83).

[12] See [9].

[13] They note (pp. 79–80) that their sample includes medium-size as well as giant firms from the *Fortune* list but also that "since earnings patterns for large firms have atypical characteristics, no assertion is made that the results can be generalized to cover all firms."

Analogous to the relation between the level of profits and their variability, one expects that profit rates will reflect the riskiness of the capital structure chosen by a firm. Specifically, a higher ratio of equity to total assets should be associated with a lower rate of profit on equity if no other influences intrude. If large firms forsake some above-normal profits to avoid exposure to risk, however, this relation might be reversed in a sample that includes large and small firms or large firms with, and without, significant market power; the favored firms could enjoy both higher profits and lower leverage. The results reported by Hall and Weiss for a sample drawn from *Fortune*'s 500 confirm this prediction.[14] The simple relation between profits on equity and the ratio of equity to total assets is positive and significant. However, when dummies are introduced into the regression equation to allow for class intervals of seller-concentration ratios, the relation of profits on equity to equity/assets becomes negative. This is consistent with the use of market power to buy the tranquility of low leverage.

Each of these relations between profits and risk can be explained by hypotheses other than the use of market power by managers to purchase freedom from uncertainty. But they are rather impressively consistent with this hypothesis. To pursue the matter further, it is necessary to seek direct evidence of the extent to which patterns of conduct might signal the efforts of large firms to avoid risk.

II Patterns of Market Conduct to Avoid Uncertainty

The avoidance of uncertainty by large firms can potentially take numerous forms, and this section will restrict itself to some principal varieties that seem reasonably well documented. Many varieties are associated with patterns of market conduct typical in oligopolistic industries. As we shall see, some involve not an unqualified reduction of uncertainty for the firm, but rather a swap of one form for another. These switches and transformations of risks will be noted here and considered more fully in the following section, where I discuss the significance of this behavior for the absorption of disturbances in the economy at large.[15]

1. Oligopolistic pricing. The sticky behavior of list prices in oligopoly now seems too well established to demand extensive documentation. Given continual disturbances in either demand or cost, price rigidity implies frequent discrepancies between the prevailing price and the price that would maximize oligopolists' joint profits or that would attain the profit rate implicit in a mutually agreeable entry-limiting price. The reality of this effect

[14] See [16], pp. 328–29.

[15] With this suggestion I necessarily part company with Galbraith's proposition that giant corporations succeed in fending off all uncertainties, in which case no shifting would be necessary. It is worth noting, though, that his assertion about their ability to control the quantity of their output that is purchased refers to their long-run prowess in market research, not to the short run [12, pp. 202–3].

depends only on the existence of *some* rigidity; its significance of course is limited by price-shading and off-list sales, flexibility of a product's quality, and the like. In any case, the evidence seems to reveal the relative stability of an oligopoly's prices over the business cycle and the periodic appearance of unexploited monopolistic profits during periods of inflation.[16]

The significance of price rigidity is that, in oligopolistic markets with partial collusion or imperfectly recognized mutual dependence, the immobility reduces the risks of misunderstanding and subsequent "destructive competition" in the process of adjusting prices. When rigidity imposes a lag in the pursuit of the profit-maximizing price, it is clear that some cumulative sacrifice of maximum profits to the avoidance of uncertainty occurs. The same holds for the profits of the initial group of oligopolists maintaining an entry-limiting price, if their conjecture is correct about entry ensuing from a price that exceeds the limit. Price rigidity, of course, is a policy that may reduce overall uncertainty for the firm, but it may not reduce every type of uncertainty that the firm faces; the expected variability of production or inventory levels, or both, would in general be increased.[17]

2. Stability of market shares. Other forms of uncertainty-avoidance implement oligopolists' strategies for reducing the uncertainties of coordinating market behavior. Apart from the stabilization of price, sellers may reach either tacit or express understandings that tend to stabilize their shares of the market. This may involve no more than the disuse of some market policies which might upset these shares or no more than caution about actions that would change them at an unacceptable speed. Any such understandings should reduce profits for some firms in an oligopoly and stabilize them for the group as a whole, but the understandings would not necessarily reduce profits for the industry in the long run. Gort has reported an investigation of market shares that strongly supports the prediction of their greater stability in concentrated markets.[18] Working with data from the 1947 and 1954 Censuses of Manufactures, he calculated for each of 205 four-digit industries two measures of the stability of market shares for the top 15 firms in each industry: (1) the correlation coefficient between 1947 and 1954 shares, and (2) the geometric mean of the regression coefficient of 1947 shares on 1954 shares and the reverse regression of 1954 on 1947. Using either measure, a strong relation appears between stability and the initial level of sellers' concentration for the top-four firms. Concentration among sets of firms other than the top four failed, however, to show a significant relation to market-share stability. As research on the relation be-

[16] See references cited in Sherman [27, pp. 178–81].

[17] Note the complementary conclusion reached by John Lintner's paper in this volume: that the oligopolist certain of his price-cost margin but uncertain about the quantity to be sold at that price will rationally choose a lower price than he would if this uncertainty about the quantity sold were absent.

[18] See [14].

tween concentration and profits suggests, a necessary and sufficient condition for the effective recognition of oligopolistic interdependence seems to be a minimum level of top-end concentration. Other parameters of the size distribution of firms add little to the explanation of behavior or performance.[19]

Possibly this result lends misleading support to our hypothesis. The 15 largest firms classified within a four-digit industry also typically qualify as large in absolute size. It is often urged that size itself impedes rapid change, that the sapling can with ease proportionally outgrow the mighty oak. Market shares in concentrated industries might be stable just because the dominant firms were large. Fortunately, Gort tested absolute size as an additional explanatory variable for the stability of concentration.[20] Although absolute size proves significant, it adds little to the explanation of stability provided by concentration alone. This conclusion gives important support to Galbraith's argument that large absolute size provides a special motive to avoid uncertainty but requires market power to take significant action for avoidance.

3. Stability in rates of growth.   If positions of market power are managed so as to stabilize market shares in a growing market, then the growth rates of firms in concentrated industries should show a smaller variance than those of firms in unconcentrated sectors.[21] This is merely another way of exploring the question of market-share stabilization. In this form the hypothesis has received at least one direct test by Hymer and Pashigian.[22] They analyzed the growth of the 1,000 largest manufacturing firms publishing financial data between 1946 and 1955. In their study, these firms were classified into three-digit industries, and the standard deviations of firms' growth rates in these industries were regressed on the industries' growth rates, concentration ratios, and average initial (1946) sizes of firm. Their principal result is that the growth rates of firms in fast-growing industries diverge more than those in slow-growing industries. As expected, the relation between the standard deviation of firms' growth rates and the level of concentration is negative; but the relation is below the level of statistical

---

[19] Gort [14, p. 56] shows that concentration for firms ranking 5 . . . 8 or 5 . . . 20 in an industry appears related to market-share stability only in industries where these measures of concentration are highly correlated with concentration for firms ranking 1 . . . 4. This positive correlation can occur only in industries with relatively low concentration of sellers. Where top-end concentration is high, by arithmetical necessity only a small share of the total market remains for the smaller firms, and the correlation must ultimately become negative.

[20] See [14], pp. 57–58.

[21] Studies of oligopolistic industries customarily dredge through patterns of market conduct in the mutual adaptation of short-term pricing decisions, for the purpose of establishing the extent and character of parallel action. Yet they almost always ignore the question of parallel action in investment decisions and the adjustment of firms' productive capacity, although these long-run decisions set important constraints within which the price is fixed.

[22] See [18].

significance. Since the test is probably biased against the hypothesis, the result is still not without interest.[23] That firms in concentrated markets effect some parallelism in their growth policies as a means of reducing uncertainty remains likely if, nonetheless, unproved. The proposition also enjoys some general support from other investigations, such as the demonstrations that the turnover in the 50 or 100 largest industrial firms has apparently declined since the late 1920's.[24]

4. Stability of employment and composition of workforce. One of the means employed by Galbraith's technostructure to assure its stability and independence is to buy off the workers, paying high wages and accepting unions in return for peace.[25] Others, of course, have argued that labor or other suppliers of inputs might bargain away a portion of a monopoly's profits; and they have rationalized the prediction without recourse to any desire of the managers to avoid uncertainty. On the other hand, the evidence on wages and concentration is rather impressively consistent with the hypothesis of uncertainty-avoidance; and some interesting incidental findings emerge from studies that have dealt with the effect of concentration on wages.

The data recently surveyed by Lester confirm Galbraith's conjecture that average hourly earnings for production workers in given occupations normally increase with size of establishment, although the increase is less in strongly unionized sectors.[26] Census data, which do not standardize wage figures for differences between large and small establishments in the composition of an industry's workforce, also reveal this pattern. Fringe benefits differ even more in favor of workers in large establishments, a difference consistent with a desire of large corporations to deal in amenities and buy stability in their labor force. Casual inspection of Lester's breakdowns by industry suggests that the wage differentials in favor of large establishments may be greater in more concentrated industries, although he himself is unimpressed by this explanation.[27] He does note that large size-of-establish-

---

[23] Collinearity among the independent variables appears to be a serious problem in their regression covering "pure" three-digit industries [18, Table 6B]. Concentration and the industry's growth rate are significantly and positively correlated, yet these variables are predicted to have opposite effects on the standard deviation of firms' growth rates. Another study covering about the same time period found a significant negative relation between these variables [21]. Both independent variables are also significantly and positively correlated with the average size of a firm.

[24] See [6] and [10].

[25] See [12], pp. 264–65.

[26] See [19].

[27] "The character of competition could hardly be a key factor with wide influence, since a significant differential exists in other industries characterized by a preponderance of small firms producing for a wide market, such as food and wood products." (Pp. 60–61) He also mentions the fact that small plants are often located in low-wage small towns; the pressure of public opinion on the managers of large enterprises; and scale economies in the administration of benefit plans, economies that may favor compensation by fringes in large establishments.

ment differentials prevailed prior to the unionization of most manufacturing industries.

The evidence of studies that deal directly with the influence of concentration on wages is somewhat mixed. Rapping has attempted to estimate the size of monopolistic rents per man-hour of labor input as a measure of the spoils potentially available to labor and thus as an explanatory variable for wage differentials among two-digit industries.[28] One proxy for these rents relates to total after-tax profits per man-hour, while another employs the industry's concentration ratio in a formulation derived from the Lerner index of concentration. Both proxies in fact display some explanatory power, although only the second is significant when the extent of unionization is also taken into account. Furthermore, Allen's study of annual wage changes 1947–1964 in four-digit industries shows a significant relation between the *level* of concentration and the change in wages.[29] This relation, which is not clearly predicted on the basis of the assumptions we have been considering, holds through the 1950's for all years except those of wartime and very high employment (1949–51, 1955–56) but breaks down in the early 1960's. It is consistent with several divergent explanations, among them the use of wage increases as an excuse for the adjustment of sticky prices in pursuit of unexploited monopolistic profits.

Weiss' important study of concentration and labor earnings throws findings like these into a new perspective.[30] Using the 1/1000 sample data from the 1960 Census of Population, he shows that the significant relation between concentration and earnings disappears when personal characteristics of the labor force are taken into account: education, race, region, urban residence, and so forth. This finding may be given two nonexclusive interpretations. First, it may confirm Becker's discovery of a positive relation between monopoly and discrimination[31] or at least a broader propensity of the proprietors of large corporations to restrict their hiring to "nice people."[32] Second, the problems of supervision and coordination in a large enterprise may give cause for hiring workers who by education and background are adaptable, require little close personal supervision, and will readily internalize the goals set by the organization.[33]

What do Weiss' findings indicate about uncertainty-avoidance by the large enterprise? Although the findings are easily explained by other attributes of business size, they also seem consistent with the goal of reducing

---

[28] See [24].
[29] See [3].
[30] See [33].
[31] See [4].
[32] See [1].
[33] To reverse this comparative-advantage proposition, the small enterprise may secure relatively higher productivity from workers of below-average education or adaptation to the pace of factory work. This explanation is also consistent with the proposition that more capital-intensive establishments are likely to employ higher-skilled and thus higher-paid workers [31, pp. 96–98], considering that large enterprises are typically more capital-intensive than small ones.

the uncertainties of organizational operation notwithstanding the possible sacrifice of some margin between cost and price. One interesting incidental conclusion of Weiss' research is that the insertion of variables representing the steadiness of employment (freedom from temporary unemployment and short weeks) cuts sharply into the significant influence of concentration on earnings.[34] Since there is no reason to think that oligopolies enjoy more stable demands for their products than do competitive industries, this means that the bargains struck by large enterprises with their employees include the fringe benefit of stabilized employment.[35] Uncertainty about the regularity and reliability of the labor force is reduced, presumably at the expense of greater uncertainty about inventories and possibly about profits.

5. Conglomerate mergers and diversification.   The current boom in mergers, strictly channeled away from horizontal acquisitions by the amended Clayton Act, section 7, has run heavily to what are broadly called conglomerate mergers. The recent wave of mergers plus the obviously high incidence of diversification — by merger or otherwise — in giant firms may stem in part from the motive of avoiding uncertainty. Besides, there is some evidence that diversification is pursued with more vigor, the larger the size of firms or the more their primary activity is in an industry with a high concentration of sellers. Gort found that the *number* of nonprimary activities of a firm increased with its size, although over his sample the *proportion* of its employees in nonprimary activities did not.[36] The extent of diversification (measured in any of several ways) increased with the level of sellers' concentration in the firm's primary activity. This tends to suggest hedging by firms that enjoy market power, although the result may have been due to the high correlation between absolute size and sellers' concentration in the primary activity.

Conglomerate mergers and diversification are potentially consistent with practically any type of entrepreneurial motivation — the maximization of profits, growth, or utility as well as the reduction of uncertainty about the consolidated rate of return. Although any merger or diversification tends to convey some advantage in reducing uncertainty or pooling risk, only with respect to the small minority of conglomerate mergers that lack "concentric" elements — common inputs, technologies, channels of distribution, and so forth utilized by the combining companies — can the motive of avoiding risk be isolated to some degree. Even here, competing explanations, such as economies of scale in finance, may intrude.

[34] See [33], pp. 109–10.

[35] Strong evidence that the greater stability of employment in giant firms does not rest on the mixing of industries comes from Ferguson's study [8], which shows greater employment stability in large firms than in small firms in the same industries. Another relevant bit of evidence is the finding [32, Table 3] that quit rates for workers may be negatively related to size of establishment.

[36] See [15], chap. 4.

In order to contain these doubts, we may note some evidence that tends to narrow the primary motives for mergers to a subset including uncertainty-avoidance. Reid's data indicate that the profit performance of firms in the largest 500 has been inversely related to the extent of their merger activity during 1951–1961; and this finding survives, although weakly, when the sample of firms is broken down by industrial group. Reid also classified his firms by the primary type of merger in which they engaged; his tables suggest, more weakly still, that those specializing in conglomerate mergers reported poorer profits than the average of all others; but the result is probably not significant.[37] Whether or not conglomerates make a significant sacrifice in their average rate of return, they do appear to attain a degree of freedom from risk that compares reasonably well with the performance of mutual funds that undertake purely financial diversification.[38] In short, the evidence is consistent with some giant firms' undertaking conglomerate mergers for avoiding risk even at the cost of maximum expected profits, but the statistical case hangs by slender threads.

6. Vertical integration.   One method for reducing uncertainty would be vertical integration into an activity in which a stoppage or disturbance could significantly disrupt the firm's operations in its principal markets. A firm enjoying excess profits in its principal market would be willing to integrate into such an "essential" secondary activity even at a normal or lower rate of return, if it could not otherwise protect itself against the associated uncertainty through its inventory holding or through a futures-market. Oi and Hurter cite as examples integration into tanker transportation by the international oil companies and into Great Lakes ore carriers by the major steel producers.[39] Likewise, "tapered integration" by the automobile manufacturers and others — a system of producing a portion of their requirements of a given component but buying the remainder — may be explained on this basis. The integrated producers appear to accept a lower rate of return in the self-supplying activity while attaining some freedom from exogenous disruption of supply; at the same time, the lower rate of return is a more certain one, since the "taper" allows shunting the risk of fluctuations in output onto the independent producers.

7. Research and development and product strategies.   A good deal of evidence, ranging from quantitative analysis through case studies to gossip, has accumulated on the policies and achievements of large firms in managing the resources they devote to research and development (R&D). Conceding the perils that beset objective judgment in this area, the impression remains that these policies are consistent with a strong aversion to risk

[37] See [25], chaps. 8, 9.
[38] See [28].
[39] See [23], pp. 45–49.

in research and innovation. Large firms' research activities are conservative in the sense of being strongly oriented toward protecting existing positions of market dominance in the sale of differentiated products. This means that much effort, and expenditure, is devoted to minor improvements of products and the extension of product lines rather than to basic research or the improvement of processes.[40] Such conservatism is consistent with the use of short pay-out periods for a substantial portion of R & D commitments. Large firms indicate an explicit preference for safe over risky projects. Probably the more important point, however, is that they undertake lines of research that are risky in direct payout but risk-avoiding in providing a hedge against surprise discoveries or innovations by others, developments that might undermine the firm's share of the market or increase its exposure to the threat of entry. This suggests another example of a pattern noted above: large firms undertake some risky activities, perhaps with a low expected yield, in order to reduce uncertainty about their continuing ability to defend their market shares.

One alleged consequence of such policies in research and development is that the research laboratories of giant firms produce a relatively modest proportion of what turn out to be major innovations.[41] This pattern carries over into the placing of innovations on the market and the diffusion of innovations among firms. Innovation in oligopolistic markets may be delayed because of the uncertain consequences from rivals' reactions; a recent study of the automobile industry has suggested that some innovations — as, for example, the compact car in the 1950's — may have been postponed until the potential market would allow each of the industry's Big Three to enter it profitably.[42] Several studies seem to suggest that the best innovative performance flows from industries containing a mixture of large- and medium-size firms. The larger firms undertake investments in innovations entailing proportionally low risks though perhaps large absolute commitments of resources. The smaller firms, with less to lose of established market positions, undertake the research and innovations that involve large market risks.

8. Investment criteria.   A corporate management giving effect to its desires to avoid uncertainty might be expected to change its procedure for ranking the alternative investment opportunities open to it. Donaldson has suggested that the avoidance of uncertainty and other motives might lead a corporate management to prefer holding a larger portion of resources in liquid form — because of the resulting gain in flexibility for dealing with contingencies — than profit maximization would warrant. The simple pay-back-period criterion for business investment decisions embodies just this

---

[40] See [22], chaps. 3, 4.
[41] See [17].
[42] See [34], chap. 11.

bias toward liquidity and away from rate of return in its selection of projects. Donaldson argues that the payback period is widely used, despite the availability of more sophisticated techniques of investment analysis, and that the reason lies not in ignorance but because the payback approach "tells management what it wants to know: How long will it have to wait before the cash to be committed to the investment will be available for reinvestment?"[43] This proposition amounts to informed observation, rather than hard evidence, and the retention of *some* assets in liquid form is of course fully consistent with long-run profit maximization. Nonetheless, the fact that the vitally important investment decision may so plausibly be affected by the avoidance of uncertainty is suggestive.

This list of forms of uncertainty-avoidance on the part of the large corporation possessing market power could be extended further, but it tends to trail off into specific examples taken from extant studies of individual industries. One impression I draw from this list is that forms of risk avoidance frequently represent in effect transformations of risk into a new type or exchanges of one form for another. Furthermore, the type of risk reduced to the greatest extent is typically associated with imperfectly recognized mutual dependence among oligopolists; and it is reduced either by deferring, or avoiding, decisions that could involve misunderstanding or by taking action to raise barriers to entry. Thus, the manufacturers of metal containers used "requirements contracts" committing themselves to supply all the tin cans required by their customers.[44] This action presumably increased inventory costs and fluctuations for the producers of metal containers, but it reduced the threat of entry by shrinking the open market for containers and increasing the entry costs of newcomers. Likewise, the use of annual changes in model by makers of consumers' durable goods may be rational, even if the change fails to increase total demand, because of the fixed costs of converting the model and of advertising that the change imposes on new or small producers. Thus the change reduces the uncertainty of market rivalry but of course tends to increase the fluctuations of demand over time and thus augment that form of uncertainty.

To conclude this section, probably no pattern of behavior described above can be defended as consistent with significant aversion of risk by large firms *and with no other explanation*. Nonetheless, the range of behavior consistent with this hypothesis seems impressive. Specifically, it suggests that risk avoidance by large corporations in the United States economy may affect resource allocations enough so that any substantial change in the size distribution of firms could make a difference in the condition and reactive properties of the economy. It also suggests that not all monopolistic profits appear on the income statement, and it may explain some of the difficulty

[43] See [7], esp. p. 122.
[44] See [20].

economists have encountered in isolating them statistically.[45] Let us now consider what welfare importance attaches to these forms of uncertainty-avoidance.

III   Effects on Welfare

The topic of uncertainty has been much studied by economists in recent years, but the bulk of the resulting literature is remarkably unhelpful for dealing with the questions of policy raised by the risk-avoidance behavior of large firms. Optimizing strategies for individual decision units facing uncertain alternatives have been propounded with breath-taking subtlety and sophisticated attention to all aspects of the problem, except possibly the decision unit's informational requirements. Within the framework of pure competition, a theoretical answer is always ready for any question about how markets would cope efficiently with any given form of uncertainty. Nonetheless, this literature strikes me as offering only limited assistance in answering the operational questions of policy raised by uncertainty-avoidance in the large firm.

A fruitful way of approaching these questions is perhaps to borrow from Professor Friedman's classic discussion of the case for flexible exchange rates.[46] Disturbances will continually impinge on the economy in the form of demand shifts, changes in factor supplies, displacements in input-output relations, and the like. Putting aside any fully, and correctly, anticipated trends or shifts, some of these disturbances will be essentially random, but some will augur unanticipated longer-term changes. These winds of change impose subjective or objective, or both subjective and objective, costs of adjustment and response somewhere in the system. Most important, these disturbances can be responded to in various ways, and the pattern of response dictated by any given set of economic institutions — by the existing size distribution of firms, for example — may, or may not, be the most efficient attainable. In avoiding uncertainty, giant corporations may shift the burden of adjustment to units which, ideally, would enter into mutually profitable trade to rid themselves partially of the burden. They may locate the burden with units that have a poor betting record in distinguishing random disturbances from unanticipated permanent shifts, either dawdling over response to a long-term change or jumping the gun in adjusting to a random disturbance. Of course, corporate giants do the economy no favor however they deal with those forms of uncertainty, such as price warfare, that are *created* by imperfect recognition of mutual dependence within oligopolistic markets.

I do not read Galbraith as offering any strong view on the good or evil associated with avoidance of uncertainty by large firms. In light of his

[45] See [5], chap. 2.
[46] See [11].

general tone of disapproval, however, it seems proper to stress that the one clear conclusion about the welfare effects of these forms of risk avoidance is their diversity: some reduce the rate of economic progress or cause an outright waste of resources; some increase welfare through the pooling of risks; and some have primarily redistributive effects, the value of which depends on one's own views of the better and the best. Let me suggest a few examples of each type of cost or benefit, keeping in mind for comparison an alternative hypothetical economy marked by smaller divergences among both the absolute sizes of firms and their shares of the market.

Forms of risk avoidance which entail real costs to the economy include most of those associated with familiar patterns of conduct in oligopolistic industries. Price rigidity in the face of varying sectoral or aggregate-demand pressure implies greater investment in inventories or excess capacity, or both, than would be required with more flexible prices, or else it implies the costs of queuing and rationing for consumers. Risk avoidance in research and development is usually held to starve basic research, to deter quests for substantial novelty, and to waste research resources in the search for trivial and defensive improvements of products. The risks avoided by these policies and practices would in more atomistic markets presumably be absorbed in ways involving lower real costs to society.

Some of the efforts by large firms to avoid uncertainty, on the other hand, may provide a net reduction of uncertainty to the economy through the pooling of risks. Diversification is the obvious example. If n equally profitable single-market enterprises, with the random components in their profit rates imperfectly correlated, are merged at no cost and with no side effects, the owners as a group enjoy the same rate of return as before and a smaller variance. Corporate diversification could thus be efficient, both as against a situation of no risk-pooling and as against alternative pooling methods, such as mutual funds. Whether or not corporate diversification can claim these virtues depends on the level of the transaction- and coordination-costs associated with combining diverse activities and running them by means of a single management, not to mention any side effects that diversification or conglomerate merger may have.

Finally, there are the cases in which the large corporation shifts uncertainty between itself and another group of decision units, or between other groups or markets. Consider the large corporation's impact on the labor market. It apparently absorbs uncertainty from its own employees, since their employment seems more stable than that of other industrial workers. Because its hiring also seems influenced by workers' personal characteristics, the large corporation may thus bring about a discrimination among groups in the labor force in regard to the stability of employment as well as the level of hourly earnings. Other important shifts of uncertainty may occur between the large corporation and the small firms that are its suppliers, competitors, and customers. The displacement of uncertainty to small competing suppliers by the practice of tapered integration was mentioned above. A similar transfer could occur between the large firm and small firms that compete in its principal product market, if the dominant firm tends to hold its list price through weak and strong markets, letting the queue lengthen in good times.

The diversity of the effects on welfare of risk avoidance by the large firm thus seems to be established. One is left to wonder how to devise a world in which the costly forms of uncertainty-avoidance are altered or abandoned but the valuable ones sustained; in which undesired redistributions due to risk avoidance are blocked or compensated, and desired ones encouraged. Ways of offsetting any particular costly form of risk avoidance are in principle not difficult to conceive. They would include not only controls affecting the size or market occupancy of firms, but also taxes or subsidies affecting their reactions to various types of uncertainty. But they raise the threat of throwing out the "baby" of pooled risk along with the "bathwater" of resource-wasting conduct in the market.

Perhaps it seems quixotic even to raise this question in a paper drawing its text from *The New Industrial State,* which tends to regard the hegemony of the large corporation as inevitable as the changing of the seasons. Economies of scale and the need for planning — the latter in large part to control uncertainty — render the large firm the characteristic form of economic organization. "The size of General Motors is in the service not of monopoly or the economies of scale but of planning. And for this planning . . . there is no clear upper limit to the desirable size."[47] This is a call for passivity, perhaps with a patrician sigh. From this I must politely but firmly demure. Several reviewers have challenged Galbraith's invocation of planning as a rationalization of the present size of enterprises: the fact that giant firms plan means only that large organizations must act in purposive fashion to accomplish their objectives, not that the need for planning has necessarily called industrial giants into existence. Casting about for examples of giants whose growth and success are due primarily to the efficient substitution of planning for the allocative mechanism of the market, I have come up with only one class: the large retail chains of grocery, drug, and notions stores, which substitute administration and planning for the market in placing their many items of trade on the shelves of the neighborhood stores. Somehow these do not strike me as the technostructural core of the new industrial state.

BIBLIOGRAPHY

[1] Alchian, Armen A., and Reuben A. Kessel. "Competition, Monopoly, and the Pursuit of Pecuniary Gain," Universities-National Bureau Committee for Economic Research, *Aspects of Labor Economics.* National Bureau of Economic Research, Special Conference Series, No. 14. Princeton, New Jersey: Princeton University Press, 1962. Pp. 157–75.

[47] See [12], p. 76.

[2] Alexander, S. S. "The Effect of Size of Manufacturing Corporation on the Distribution of the Rate of Return," *Review of Economics and Statistics,* XXXI (August, 1949), 229–35.

[3] Allen, Bruce T. "Market Concentration and Wage Increases: U.S. Manufacturing, 1947–1964," *Industrial and Labor Relations Review,* XXI (April, 1968), 353–65.

[4] Becker, Gary S. *The Economics of Discrimination.* Chicago: University of Chicago Press, 1957.

[5] Collins, Norman R., and Lee E. Preston. *Concentration and Price-Cost Margins in Manufacturing Industries.* Berkeley and Los Angeles: University of California Press, 1968.

[6] ————. "The Size Structure of the Largest Industrial Firms, 1909–1958," *American Economic Review,* LI (December, 1961), 986–1011.

[7] Donaldson, Gordon. "Financial Goals: Management vs. Stockholders," *Harvard Business Review,* XLI (May-June, 1963), 116–29.

[8] Ferguson, C. E. "The Relationship of Business Size to Stability: An Empirical Approach," *Journal of Industrial Economics,* IX (November, 1960), 43–62.

[9] Fisher, I. N., and G. R. Hall. "Risk and Corporate Rates of Return," *Quarterly Journal of Economics,* LXXXIII (February, 1969), 79–92.

[10] Friedland, Seymour. "Turnover and Growth of the Largest Industrial Firms, 1906–1950," *Review of Economics and Statistics,* XXXIX (February, 1957), 79–83.

[11] Friedman, Milton. *Essays in Positive Economics.* Chicago: University of Chicago Press, 1953.

[12] Galbraith, John Kenneth. *The New Industrial State.* Boston: Houghton Mifflin, 1967.

[13] ————. "A Review of a Review," *The Public Interest,* No. 9 (Fall, 1967), 109–19.

[14] Gort, Michael. "Analysis of Stability and Change in Market Shares," *Journal of Political Economy,* LXXI (February, 1963), 51–63.

[15] ————. *Diversification and Integration in American Industry.* National Bureau of Economic Research, General Series, No. 77. Princeton, New Jersey: Princeton University Press, 1962.

[16] Hall, Marshall, and Leonard Weiss. "Firm Size and Profitability," *Review of Economics and Statistics,* XLIX (August, 1967), 319–31.

[17] Hamberg, D. "Invention in the Industrial Research Laboratory," *Journal of Political Economy,* LXXI (April, 1963), 95–115.

[18] Hymer, Stephen, and Peter Pashigian. "Firm Size and Rate of Growth," *Journal of Political Economy,* LXX (December, 1962), 556–69.

[19] Lester, Richard. "Pay Differentials by Size of Establishment," *Industrial Relations,* VII (October, 1967), 57–67.

[20] McKie, James W. *Tin Cans and Tin Plate: A Study of Competition in Two Related Markets.* Cambridge, Mass.: Harvard University Press, 1959.

[21] Nelson, Ralph L. "Market Growth, Company Diversification and Product Concentration," *Journal of the American Statistical Association,* LV (December, 1960), 640–49.

[22] Nelson, Richard R., Merton J. Peck, and Edward D. Kalachek. *Technology, Economic Growth and Public Policy.* Washington, D.C.: The Brookings Institution, 1967.

[23] Oi, Walter Y., and Arthur P. Hurter, Jr. *Economics of Private Truck Transportation.* Dubuque, Iowa: Wm. C. Brown, 1965.

[24] Rapping, Leonard A. "Monopoly Rents, Wage Rates, and Union Wage Effectiveness," *Quarterly Review of Economics and Business,* VII (Spring, 1967), 31–47.

[25] Reid, Samuel Richardson. *Mergers, Managers, and the Economy.* New York: McGraw-Hill, 1968.

[26] Samuels, J. M., and D. J. Smyth. "Profits, Variability of Profits and Firm Size," *Economica,* XXV (May, 1968), 127–39.

[27] Sherman, Howard J. *Profits in the United States: An Introduction to a Study of Economic Concentration and Business Cycles.* Ithaca, New York: Cornell University Press, 1968.

[28] Smith, Keith V., and John C. Schreiner. "A Portfolio Analysis of Conglomerate Diversification," *Journal of Finance,* XXIV (June, 1969), 413–28.

[29] Stekler, H. O. *Profitability and Size of Firm.* Berkeley, California: Institute of Business and Economic Research, University of California, 1963.

[30] _____. "The Variability of Profitability with Size of Firm, 1947–1958," *Journal of the American Statistical Association,* LIX (December, 1964), 1183–92.

[31] Stigler, George J. *Capital and Rates of Return in Manufacturing Industries.* National Bureau of Economic Research, General Series, No. 78. Princeton, New Jersey: Princeton University Press, 1963.

[32] Stoikov, Vladimir, and R. L. Raimon. "Determinants of Differences in the Quit Rate Among Industries," *American Economic Review,* LVIII (December, 1968), 1283–98.

[33] Weiss, L. W. "Concentration and Labor Earnings," *American Economic Review,* LVI (March, 1966), 96–117.

[34] White, Lawrence J. "The American Automobile Industry in the Postwar Period." Unpublished Ph.D. dissertation, Harvard University, 1969.

PART TWO

Economic Development and International Trade

Lloyd G. Reynolds

David E. Bell

Charles P. Kindleberger

Stefan H. Robock

Sidney S. Alexander

Emile Despres

14

Is "Development Economics" a Subject?

Lloyd G. Reynolds*

A striking feature of postwar economics has been the "development boom." In 1945 anyone scanning library shelves for a book on economic development would have found only Schumpeter's works. There was probably not a single university course under this heading. Today there are dozens of such courses, several standard textbooks, scores of monographs, and hundreds of articles and governmental reports. Development economics is among the two or three most popular specialties for graduate students.

Yet it is not at all clear that development economics constitutes a distinct subject. Specialists in older branches of our science view this intruder in the curriculum with considerable reserve. This is partly because work on the less-developed countries has been heavily problem-oriented rather than analytically oriented and partly because there is no substantial body of theory about early economic growth comparable to that available to the student of public finance or international trade. It may be useful, therefore, to look at the work of the past twenty years in perspective. Is development economics a subject, actual or potential? If so, what is its scope and shape?

A word first on language. The countries in which we are interested will be called "less-developed countries" (LDC's). The industrial nations of North America, Europe, Australasia, and Japan will be called "more-developed countries" (MDC's). The study of LDC's will be termed "development economics." This is not an ideal term, being somewhat imprecise and implying that growth in output is the sole object of study. "The eco-

The author wishes to express his gratitude to All Souls College, Oxford, and to the Guggenheim Foundation for fellowship support during the period in which this paper was drafted.

* Yale University

nomics of less developed countries" would be better. But it is not worthwhile to quibble over what has become a reasonably accepted terminology.

Our problem may now be posed as follows: Does economic analysis of the LDC's, including, but not limited to, the study of early economic growth in these countries, constitute a distinct kind of work within economics?

We shall approach the problem from three directions: First, does research on the LDC's involve mere application of established tools of "Western economics," or does it also involve new tool-building? Second, what are the most promising lines of further research on these economies? Third, what seem at present the most plausible hypotheses about early economic growth?

I The Relevance of "Western Economics"

Economists and students from the LDC's often assert, with varying degrees of strength, that the economic theory taught in British and American graduate schools is not very relevant to their own economies. Some Western economists fall in with this assertion, while others react strongly against it. The issue is clearly important to our present concern. If a Western-trained economist can employ his usual tool-kit as effectively in Thailand as in Germany, if he in fact finds no need for additional tools, the case that study of the LDC's constitutes a distinct specialty becomes less convincing.[1]

It is often not clear what critics of Western economics really mean. One possible meaning may be eliminated at the outset. Use of Western economic analysis is sometimes identified with a particular stance on policy — with idealization of the market mechanism and a suspicion of governmental activity. This identification is simply confusion. There is no reason why such concepts as utility, preference, production possibilities, or opportunity cost should be identified with any one institutional setting. Since the work of Lange and Lerner in the 'thirties, it has been accepted that the apparatus of microeconomics can be redirected toward management of a socialistic system.

Setting aside this misunderstanding, a statement about the limited relevance of Western economics may mean at least four different things: (1) that *quantitative relations* among economic variables are different and will need to be reestimated in the LDC's; (2) that *personal behavior* is "less economic" in the LDC's, so that one cannot assume the usual responses to material incentives; (3) that the *priority of problems* is different in the LDC's, with a consequent difference in the relative importance of analytical

---

[1] This issue has been examined by Hla Myint, "Economic Theory and the Underdeveloped Countries," *Journal of Political Economy* (October, 1965), pp. 477–491; see also by the same author, "Economic Theory and Development Policy," Inaugural Lecture at the London School of Economics (London: G. Bell and Sons, Ltd., 1967).

tools; (4) that, because of *structural differences* in the economy and society, one has to develop new tools for purposes of explanation and policy.

The truth of the first statement is self-evident. For the Western economies, we know a good deal about price and income elasticities of demand, input-output relations, returns to labor and capital, consumption and investment functions, and so on. This knowledge is not directly transferable to an economy operating at a much lower level of income, and with different factor supplies, technology, and organization. Functional relations must be estimated anew by painstaking research, as is still being done in the MDC's. Because of the fragmentation of the less-developed economies, greater attention should be directed to particular sectors and industries, and greater skepticism maintained about the stability of aggregative coefficients, than is needed in a more integrated economy.

These differences in quantitative relations are not damaging to the logical structure of economics. On the other hand, the second kind of statement, which alleges noneconomic behavior, would be decidedly damaging. But how convincing is this allegation?

Tests of economic rationality must be framed with care. It is not sufficient to show that individuals' preference systems are different in the LDC's. The relevant questions are, first, whether material welfare is prominent among the criteria of decision, and second, whether the direction of reactions is "normal" in the sense that higher levels of material satisfaction are preferred over lower levels.

Much evidence supports an affirmative answer. As regards peasant-producers, several research workers have concluded that, given the techniques they know, peasants apply labor and capital to land as far as it is reasonable to do so, that is, until marginal rates of return have fallen to a low level. Moreover, where peasants produce for market and where two or more crops are open to them, there is evidence of marked responsiveness to changes in relative product prices. If one crop becomes more advantageous than before, the proportion of acreage devoted to this crop rises with only a short time lag.[2]

[2] See, for example, E. R. Dean, "Economic Analysis and African Responses to Price," *Journal of Farm Economics* (May, 1965), pp. 402–409; V. Dubey, "The Marketed Agricultural Surplus and Economic Growth in Underdeveloped Countries," *Economic Journal* (December, 1963), pp. 689–702; W. Falcon, "Farmer Response to Price in a Subsistence Economy: the Case of West Pakistan," *American Economic Review, Proceedings* (May, 1964), pp. 580–591; W. D. Hopper, "Allocation Efficiency in a Traditional Indian Agriculture," *Journal of Farm Economics* (August, 1965), pp. 611–624; R. Krishna, "Farm Supply Response in India-Pakistan: a Case Study of the Punjab Region," *Economic Journal* (September, 1963), pp. 477–487; Carl C. Malone, "Some Responses of Rice Farmers to the Package Program in Tanjore District, India," *Journal of Farm Economics* (May, 1965), pp. 256–269; M. Mangahas, A. E. Recto, and V. W. Ruttan, "Price and Market Relationships for Rice and Corn in the Philippines," *Journal of Farm Economics* (August, 1966), pp. 685–703; D. E. Welsch, "Response to Economic Incentives by Abakalike Rice Farmers in Eastern Nigeria," *Journal of Farm Economics* (November, 1965), pp. 900–914.

As regards labor, there is little doubt that workers prefer higher-wage jobs to lower-wage ones But it is sometimes asserted that their limited view of the possibilities for consumption sets a low ceiling on aspirations for income. Once the ceiling is reached, the amount of labor offered varies inversely with the hourly wage — the labor supply curve bends backward. The writer was at some pains to test this hypothesis regarding new factory workers in Puerto Rico, a group which is untypical only because of the strong demonstration effect of readily available American consumer goods. For this group, there was convincing evidence that income aspirations were quite elastic. Workers wanted more money, knew what they would do with it, and were willing to work longer hours to obtain it wherever factory schedules permitted. Elliot Berg has reported similar findings from studies of African workers.[3]

There are probably two reasons why the notion of the backward-bending supply curve is widely accepted. First, it has long been a standard argument offered by employers, particularly foreign employers of indigenous labor, in defense of a low-wage policy. Nor is this defense at all new. Two centuries ago, early English industrialists argued that higher wages would lead to greater idleness, a conclusion challenged by Adam Smith.[4] Second, the argument is associated with the peculiar circumstances of migratory labor in certain parts of Africa. Here the family does not accompany the worker to his place of wage-employment, the wife does not become a consumer, and the normal pressures for a higher scale of *household* expenditure are inoperative. It is not surprising, then, that men work only long enough to acquire a few readily transportable consumer goods — bicycles, radios, and the like — or to accumulate the customary bride-price in their area. On a world view, however, this system of employment is quite untypical.

It is perhaps unnecessary to argue that businessmen, in the LDC's as elsewhere, respond strongly to monetary rewards. This is not disproved by the observation that many LDC businessmen prefer commerce or moneylending to manufacturing, prefer quicker speculative gains to slowly maturing projects, and prefer to hold land and buildings rather than intangible assets. Given the politico-economic milieu, this behavior may be quite as economic as the differing behavior of American or European businessmen. Such behavioral differences reflect, not a difference in basic motivation, but a difference in the structure of incentives. There is much evidence that, when the

---

[3] See Lloyd G. Reynolds and Peter Gregory, *Wages, Productivity, and Industrialization in Puerto Rico* (Homewood, Illinois: Richard D. Irwin, Inc., 1965); Elliot J. Berg, "Backward-sloping Labor Supply Functions: The African case," *Quarterly Journal of Economics* (August, 1961), pp. 468–492.

[4] "A plentiful subsistence . . . it has been concluded, relaxes, and a scant one quickens their industry. That a little more plenty than ordinary may render some workmen idle cannot be doubted; but that it should have this effect on the greater part . . . seems not very probable." (*Wealth of Nations*, Everyman Edition, Volume I, p. 74.)

government of a LDC makes a calculated effort to redirect incentives so as to favor long-term fixed investment, there will be an appropriate (and predictable) response from the business community.

The third line of criticism — that priority with respect to issues of policy differs as between MDC's and LDC's — is on firmer ground. The following areas, for example, seem to deserve a *higher* relative ranking in the LDC's: agricultural organization and productivity; demography and population growth; the economics of small-scale industry; the microeconomic aspects of taxation and public expenditure; and international trade and capital movements.

To the extent that economics is viewed as providing instruments for policy, then, there is a corresponding reranking of the usefulness of analytical tools. The basic tools of microeconomics are highly useful in the LDC's, whether applied to agricultural production, the economics of industry, the impact of taxation, or cost-benefit analysis of public-sector projects. Western macroeconomics is considerably less useful. Paradoxically, the modern theory of growth has little to offer economies in which growth is the most urgent practical problem. Post-Keynesian theories of income determination and economic fluctuations have some transfer value in semi-industrialized countries, such as Mexico, Argentina, and Brazil. Their usefulness diminishes, however, as one moves toward the more fragmented and institutionally underdeveloped economies with a very small modern sector.

The fourth question posed above is the most fundamental. Does analysis of the less developed economies require simply a reshuffling of the same instruments, a lifting of different tools from what remains essentially the same tool-kit? Or does it require also a significant amount of new-tool construction?

The answer depends somewhat on the level of abstraction. Such concepts as individual preference systems or production functions are so fundamental that any kind of economic reasoning must take them as a point of departure. At this level one may argue that economics is independent of time and space. But economics does not consist solely of such basic ideas. There is a hierarchy of theoretical constructs, ranging from the simple and general to the quite complex and specific — from, say, the concept of profit maximization to a model of investment decisions in the steel industry in contemporary United States. As theory comes closer to grappling with a specific body of phenomena, its structure becomes more elaborate, specific, and empirically oriented.

At some stage of elaboration and specialization, the kind of theory required to explain a certain range of economic phenomena is a LDC — the variables to be included, the presumed relations among them, the specific hypotheses to be tested — begins to differ significantly from the one relevant to the MDC's. Experience in having worked on similar problems in a MDC may be useful as background. But it is only background, and does not obviate the need for new theoretical constructs and for new research design.

This situation can be illustrated from a variety of fields. We have noted that the kind of growth theory relevant to the LDC's is considerably different from that currently being developed for the advanced industrial countries. This dissimilarity of theories extends also to short-run macroeconomics. The fact that fluctuations in the LDC's are usually externally induced and that they impinge on economies with a small public sector, a primitive monetary system, and serious inelasticities of supply changes both the analysis of fluctuations and the nature of stabilizing measures.

Although Latin American theories of "structural inflation" may be partly an apologia for fiscal laxity, they are not wholly that. Monetary processes and price behavior do differ from the corresponding processes in the MDC's. Brazilian inflation is not to be explained, or corrected, in the same manner as inflation in Sweden or Canada.

There has been a strong reaction in the LDC's, most marked again in Latin America, against the standard theory of international trade. Even if some of the counterreasoning advanced from the LDC's may appear implausible, the deficiencies of trade theory are undoubtedly real. Work has focused on comparative advantage and optimal trade patterns at a point in time, with given factor supplies and identical production functions in each trading nation. But the assumption of identical production functions between MDC's and LDC's is unacceptable by definition. How to import technology, and what technology to import, is a major issue. The problem of the LDC's, as Chenery[5] and others have shown, is to define dynamic comparative advantage under conditions in which tastes, relative factor supplies and prices, and technology are all subject to rapid change. Analysis of the dynamics of trade relations, which in the MDC's may appear merely interesting, is for the LDC's a vital necessity.

In agriculture, theorizing about the production-consumption behavior of peasants' households[6] is significantly different from the production economics of a midwestern American farm. In industry, models of the isolated profit-maximizing firm, or of the interaction of firms in a competitive industry, are useful but by no means sufficient. There are problems of distinguishing private from social profitability, of estimating returns to a complex of interrelated investments ten or twenty years in the future, of devising efficient sequences of investment à la Hirschman. These kinds of analysis are similar in being time-related, forward-looking, and extending beyond the bounds of a single industry. They rest in a sense on standard concepts of microeconomics. But these concepts must be manipulated in new ways

[5] Hollis B. Chenery, "Comparative advantage and development policy," *American Economic Review* (March, 1961), pp. 18–51.

[6] See, for example, A. K. Sen, "Peasants and dualism, with or without surplus labor," *Journal of Political Economy* (October, 1966), pp. 425–450.

to explore, not optimal resource allocation at a moment, but optimality over extended periods of time.

Thus an industrial economist, or agricultural economist, or international economist will find himself becoming a different kind of economist as he works on the structure of the LDC's. He will have a certain expertise not possessed by those who have never strayed outside the developed world. He will necessarily have to make theoretical contributions to achieve significant research results. In this sense, there *is* something new about development economics.

II The Positive Study of Less-Developed Economies

We turn now to our second main theme. What are the most fruitful lines of research on the less-developed economies? What are the outlines of the body of systematized knowledge that one might hope to see emerging in the years ahead?

We must distinguish first between basic and applied studies. The LDC's face grave problems of economic policy, problems which cannot wait on the results of basic research. Policy-makers must use the imperfect information and tools presently available. Experienced economic advisers can mobilize and analyze relevant information, and they can help raise the rationality of decision-making. There is no intent here to minimize the importance of these policy-related activities, to which Professor Mason and his colleagues have contributed so much in a number of countries. But given the limitations of space and my own competence, I propose to concentrate on the longer-range task of improving our understanding of the less-developed economies, an understanding desirable both in itself and as a firmer basis for future policy-making.

Thinking in these terms, four main lines of activity suggest themselves: building abstract models of early economic growth; analyzing the movement of actual economies over time; cross-country studies designed to test specific hypotheses; and microanalysis of particular sectors or particular topics within a country.

Models of Early Economic Growth

During the past twenty years there has been a spate of neo-Keynesian and neo-classical growth models. A recent survey lists upwards of a hundred contributions.[7] Most of this work, however, is not relevant for present purposes. The standard assumptions of growth theory — one or at most two products, full mobility of factors, competitive pricing, constant returns to scale, constant elasticity of labor-capital substitution along well-behaved

[7] F. H. Hahn and R. C. O. Matthews, "The Theory of Economic Growth: A Survey," *Economic Journal* (December, 1964), pp. 779–902.

production functions — are quite unrealistic even for the MDC's. For the LDC's, they verge on a fantasy. Particularly restrictive is the common assumption of a single output and a single production function. The essence of underdevelopment is a sharp cleavage between "modern" and "traditional" production. Nor can one get round this by applying the standard growth theory only to the modern sector, leaving the much larger traditional sector in residual status. The behavior of the traditional sector as factor supplier and product demander, including its gradual transformation and annexation to the modern sector, is an integral part of early economic growth.

The neglect of land and the primacy of capital in modern growth theory also stamps the theory as industrially oriented. A theory of early economic growth must explain what is happening in agriculture, which remains the largest sector of the economy for many decades after growth begins. The initial land-labor ratio, the organization of farm production, the nature of production functions and of producers' responses, the rate and factor-bias of technical change, are key features of any usable growth model.

Moreover, much of the recent work has been normative in character. Much ingenuity has been exercised on the stability or instability of hypothetical growth paths, the "golden rule" of saving, and the optimization of consumption over time. Whatever potential application such work may have for "developed" countries, its usefulness in the low-income countries approaches zero. For a country struggling to lift its net saving rate to 5 percent of national income, it is not helpful to be told that a 20 percent saving rate would maximize the satisfaction of all future generations.

When we ask what kind of growth theory *would* be useful in a less-developed country, there are several possible answers. First, theory might aim at explaining how economic growth gets started in a previously stagnant economy. What are the minimum institutional prerequisites? Given a favorable environment, what kinds of stimuli may set the mechanism of expansion in motion? Is export-led growth a frequent case? Study of the preconditions of growth involves noneconomic variables, some of which are difficult to quantify; and so economists tend to hold back from it.[8] But there is little indication that political scientists, social anthropologists, or others are going to produce adequate theories of how economic growth begins. Economists, who in recent decades have tended to define the boundaries of their discipline more and more narrowly, should be venturesome enough to conduct some forays into this difficult area.

---

[8] A notable exception is Professor Everett Hagen. See his two volumes, *On the Theory of Social Change: How Economic Growth Begins* (Homewood, Illinois: Dorsey Press, 1962); and *The Economics of Development* (Homewood, Illinois: Richard D. Irwin, Inc., 1968). See also the work of Irma Adelman and Cynthia Taft Morris in this area.

Second, there is theorizing of a "biological" character. This emphasizes the alternative ways in which the monetary economy may penetrate a system of household production, and the changes in personal behavior, economic organization, and exchange relations that occur in the process. Institutional transformation occupies the center of the stage; input-output relations are rather in the background. The process often starts with sale of one or more export products for cash; but if this is all that happens, the economy remains underdeveloped. Only in so far as dealings in cash, specialization in production, and trading relations spread gradually *within* the country can it be regarded as developing. Its degree of development is measured by how far it has moved toward full specialization, sale of products and factor services for cash, and economic integration through markets. Myint's work[9] is especially rich in suggestions about how and why an economy may move, or fail to move, in this direction.

Third, there are theories in which quantitative relations in production play a central role. These theories are mechanical in the sense that, given one or more sectoral production functions and given the rates of increase in inputs, certain rates of increase in output follow automatically. Economic growth has already begun "before the curtain rises," and the problem is to determine its rate and direction. This kind of work, exemplified in the models devised by Lewis and Fei-Ranis, is promising because of its quantitative character and the potentiality of statistical testing.

Growth models adapted to the LDC's, however, are still in an early stage of development. Attention has been focused mainly on the fully settled, heavily populated, "surplus labor" economy. The result is what Myint has termed an "Indian model." But this is only one possible kind of situation. Many countries, particularly in Africa and some parts of Latin America, have unutilized land of good quality, so that for some time land and labor inputs can increase together. Some countries, too, have virtually unlimited access to foreign resources because of rich oil or mineral deposits.

Growth models tend to emphasize maximization of output. This is natural, since growth is usually defined in terms of output. But most LDC's also face a serious employment problem, which is tending to increase over time. Maximizing employment in the naive sense of minimizing productivity is not a sensible objective. But up to a point, "capital shallowing" to accommodate more labor per unit of capital will raise total output; and it may be desirable on political or distributional grounds to push even farther in a labor-using direction.

The key fact is that labor-capital-output ratios, and the technical feasibility of changing these ratios, differ widely among sectors and industries. An interest in employment, then, leads in the direction of disaggregated

[9] See in particular Hla Myint, *The Economics of Developing Countries*, (London: T. W. Hutchinson, 1964).

growth models, which make it possible to explore the implications of different technologies and different patterns of sectoral expansion.[10]

Finally, most existing growth models are closed-economy models.[11] Trade and capital movements, however, are central facts of life in most of the LDC's; and so any plausible growth model must include a foreign sector.

In view of these complications plus the inherent heterogeneity of the less-developed world, we should not expect to come out a generation from now with a *single* model of early economic growth. One should expect rather a "family" of growth models. These will be similar in that they focus on economies starting from a low level of income and a near-zero rate of growth and in that they try to trace the interaction among major sectors as growth proceeds. But they will differ as regards the initial resource situation, the openness of the economy, and the sectoral pattern of increase in employment and output.

The Movement of Economies Through Time

A second kind of research analyzes how particular economies have grown, or failed to grow, over time. This is an area in which the Economic Growth Center at Yale has now had considerable experience. A half-dozen monographs on countries have already appeared, and some twenty others are in progress. The intent is to analyze the growth experience of each country, paying special attention to the post-1945 period but going back in some cases to 1900 or beyond.

This kind of work poses numerous difficulties and challenges. An obvious but time-consuming necessity is to construct a quantitative picture of what has been happening in major sectors of the economy. This can usually be done with fair success for foreign trade, the governmental sector, commercialized agriculture, and modern industry. On the other hand, the picture of household production for its own use is decidedly cloudy, and so is the picture of traditional trade, service, and artisans' activities. Because much of national output ends up unmeasured, large uncertainties are introduced into such aggregates as gross national product and gross capital formation. Even for the measured parts of output, price distortions may pose a serious problem. For example, where import substitution is proceeding behind a protective wall, domestic prices of manufactures may be well above world prices, and the divergence may grow over time. The growth rate of manufacturing output measured in domestic prices will thus appear higher than if output were valued at world prices.

---

[10] For fuller development of this theme, see my paper "Development With Surplus Labor: Some Complications." *Oxford Economic Papers* (July, 1969).

[11] See, however, the work of Chenery and others on the role of foreign capital; and the work of Johnson, Bhagwati, Meier, and other trade theorists on the interrelations of growth and trade.

Beyond such statistical difficulties lie challenging intellectual problems. In economies that appear to have been growing, where has the growth been coming from? To what extent has it been export-induced, to what extent generated domestically? What have been the flow of resources among sectors? How has a higher level of capital formation been organized and financed? In what ways has government played an initiating, facilitating, or, possibly, retarding role?

In the end the analyst has to construct his own, county-specific, model of early economic growth. This may turn out to resemble one or another of the models developed by theorists and may thus serve to test their explanatory value. Or it may be something quite different, and it may suggest the need for new model construction. Progress will doubtless come through an interaction of theorizing and investigation, with speculative hypotheses serving as a guide to research, which in turn suggests new or refined hypotheses.

An interesting possibility suggested by the Yale program is the comparative study of similar, or contrasting, economies. Examples include the oil-rich countries of Iran and Venezuela; the ex-French Ivory Coast and the ex-British Ghana and Nigeria, which are similar in factor endowment but differ in their colonial heritage; Taiwan and South Korea, which have relatively well-educated populations operating with meager natural resources and which may be following a "Japanese path" of development; and small export-oriented economies, such as Colombia and the three East African countries, versus more self-contained economies, such as Pakistan and Brazil.

Comparative Statistical Analysis

Spatial limitations compel only brief mention of two other types of research. Suppose one is interested in a particular sector or in a particular set of economic relationships, and suppose further that one hopes to develop generalizations for a large number of LDC's. Then one will probably turn to testing hypotheses by cross-country econometric analysis.

A good deal of such work has already been done. For example, Chenery has analyzed the relation between a country's pattern of manufacturing output, its population, and its per-capita income. Chenery and others have tried to test intercountry similarity in production functions. Thorne and others have tested the relation between a country's per-capita income and the size and composition of governmental budgets. Houthakker has made an intercountry analysis of personal, corporate, and governmental saving.

The scope for such investigations is as broad as economics itself; but several cautions are in order. The first relates to difficulties in data. It is common practice, for example, to use GNP per capita as an explanatory variable in cross-country analyses. But there are many reasons why GNP is presently a very imprecise statistic for most of the LDC's: inability to measure subsistence and traditional output, lack of adequate price deflators, distortion of price relationships, exchange-rate conversions based on artificial exchange values, index-number and market-basket problems, and so on. Regression results involving GNP measures cannot be taken very seriously until the basic data have been substantially improved.

Second, regression analysis assumes some degree of homogeneity in the universe being studied. This is less plausible for intercountry than for intracountry analysis. It may be sensible, for example, to assume that the same variables are relevant to an explanation of investment by 60 different manufacturing industries in the United States from 1945–70. But it may not be sensible to suppose that a few variables can explain differences in governmental saving in 60 LDC's with quite different economic structures and political systems.

Third, research in the more-developed countries has shown that cross-section results often differ substantially from those derived from time series, requiring further work to reconcile the two. But in most LDC's the time series are still too short to warrant firm conclusions; and defects in data, of course, are quite as damaging for time-series work as for cross-section analysis. One is bound to conclude that our understanding of the economic mechanism of the LDC's will remain imperfect until we have both more years of experience and data of substantially higher quality.

Microanalysis of Economic Behavior

Let me mention finally what will doubtless, in sheer volume, be the largest kind of research activity in the less developed countries. This is detailed analysis of limited problems in a particular sector of a particular economy. A venturesome scholar may try to encompass the whole economy of Brazil. But we shall not really understand Brazil until there have been scores of studies of agriculture, manufacturing, banking and finance, and other sectors of the economy. An agricultural economist set down in the middle of Thailand or Ceyon could easily make a long list of high-priority research topics and so could a labor economist or a student of public finance. Moreover, he would find that on most topics very little is presently known. As compared with the more-developed countries, the research frontier in most LDC's is rich, and the marginal yield of research effort is high.

The fact that much of the research needed in the LDC's relates to particular sectors has interesting implications. Economists have traditionally specialized in sectoral subjects, such as agriculture, labor, monetary economics, or public finance; and their work has been confined largely to the economies of North America and Western Europe. It may be argued, however, that to be a thoroughgoing student of, say, public finance, an economist should embrace every kind of economy in his investigations —

socialist economies and less developed economies along with the Western mixed economies. In this sense, any sectoral specialist can become something of a development economist as well.

Some would go farther to argue that, if all these sectoral specialists are doing their job, this exhausts the content of economics. There is no need and no logical room for specialists in "types" of economy — MDC's, LDC's, or socialist economies. The writer would not agree with this view, for reasons suggested in Section 1. Working on agricultural organization in the USSR or Thailand is not the same as working on agricultural organization in Canada. There is some overlap in tools and problems, but far from complete correspondence. Moreover, there are economy-wide problems which do not fit into sectoral specialties.

It may be conceded, however, that in the present formative stage of development economics, to announce oneself as a specialist in the LDC's comes close to calling oneself a general practitioner, a claim that may well seem overambitious. Many economists will probably prefer to combine an interest in the LDC's with expertise in some sectoral subject.

III Some Hypotheses About Early Economic Growth

From World War II until the early sixties, thinking about economic growth was heavily tinged with worship of capital. This came about partly because the spectacular economic recovery of Western Europe in the wake of Marshall Plan aid encouraged an assumption that capital could work equal miracles in other parts of the world. Moreover, the leading growth model at the time was the Harrod-Domar model, in which capital-formation rates and capital-output ratios play a key role. On a superficial view, this model appeared applicable to the LDC's; and it came to be used both as an explanation of economic growth and as a rationalization of foreign aid.

Experience over the past two decades, however, has been disillusioning. The yield of capital has turned out to be quite variable from country to country and time to time. In some countries, large investments have yielded minimal returns.

As faith in the efficacy of physical capital has diminished, there has been a tendency to seek other keys to economic growth — for example, "human capital formation." It would be unfortunate, however, if a fixation on physical capital were to be succeeded by an equally myopic concentration on human capital or, indeed, on any other single element. Rather, we should recognize that growth is an extremely complex, multicausal process, whose nature we have scarcely begun to understand.

We know little enough about early economic growth in the older industrial countries, even though economic historians have been working on them for generations. We have little idea how far conclusions drawn from eighteenth- and nineteenth-century growth are applicable to a quite different range of economies in the late twentieth century. We do not have a long enough record for today's LDC's to determine which have embarked on a sustained path of growth and how this happened.

This is not to say that we are without ideas. It will be useful to advance a few hypotheses about early economic growth in today's LDC's — ideas which do not seem to run counter to present knowledge but which can be tested only by much additional research.

1. Economic growth is not homogeneous.   The countries which we label LDC's are quite heterogeneous. No generalizations about economic structure and behavior apply equally to all. If one looked carefully at the MDC's in the era when their accelerated growth began, their heterogeneity would doubtless appear equally great. Consider England in 1750, the United States of America in 1830, Japan in 1870. Growth itself gradually smooths out many differences and produces considerable resemblance among "mature" economies; but this is not true in the incipient stages.

If countries enter on economic growth with different internal structures and under different external circumstances, it follows that what happens in the early stages of growth will differ from one case to the next. True, output per capita rises, capital formation rises as a percentage of national product, and so on. But this is purely definitional — this is what we *mean* by economic growth. It does not indicate that the initial factor endowment, or the stimuli to growth, or the leading and lagging sectors, or the attendant institutional transformation was similar from case to case. One should not expect, then, to arrive at a *single* theory of early economic growth.

2. Economic growth is gradual.   It is not accomplished by a single "big push," nor is it compressed into a Rostovian "take-off period" of two to three decades. Rather, output per capita at first rises slowly, sometimes almost imperceptibly. The growth rate then gradually increases, and so does the capital-formation rate, though there is no indication of a close relation between increments of capital and output. This acceleration continues for perhaps 50 to 75 years before the growth rate, the capital-formation rate, and, possibly, the rate of increase in population settle down on a kind of plateau. To a mediaeval historian, 75 years may seem a short period; but it is much longer than the take-off periods visualized in much of the literature on development.

Reasons for the inevitability of gradualness are not hard to find. In a new country, it may take decades to establish secure political leadership, orderly procedures for the transfer of power, internal law and order, and other prerequisites for economic progress. Gradualness is inherent also in the time required to lay down the physical infrastructure of a modern economy and in the subsequent lag before other productive activities have "grown up" to the point of utilizing these facilities fully. Perhaps equally important is the slow turnover of human populations. It is a truism that the most important product of economic modernization is a different kind of person, and that this different person is required for effective operation of the new facilities. If one starts today to educate all children aged 6, it will be twenty years before these children have reached full productive efficiency. The higher the occupational level, the longer the gestation period. It may be thirty or forty years before highly-educated business managers, political leaders, agriculturalists and civil servants have taken over from their less well-educated forbears.

It is often said that poor nations today are determined to develop more rapidly than their predecessors, and optimistic projections are often embodied in "perspective plans." But future projections are less persuasive than past accomplishments. Where are the LDC's that have succeeded in modernizing their economies and achieving a sustained growth rate of, say, 2 percent per capita per year in less time than was required by the richer nations? One can point to Israel and Taiwan, but these are special cases. Both countries imported large quantities of human capital — administrators, business men, technicians, teachers — in the first case from Europe and in the second from mainland China. Both countries received foreign funds which, relative to their small populations, were very large. In order not to grow, they would have had to be remarkably wasteful and inept. The growth of these two countries resembles the postwar reconstruction of Japan and Western Europe, economies which, given a rich endowment of human capital plus substantial imports of physical capital, were able to restore their productive capacity in a remarkably short time.

3. Economic growth depends mainly on internal effort. The classic cases of almost completely self-financed development are Britain, Japan, and more recently the USSR. Some of the European countries, such as Sweden, received limited amounts of capital from abroad. The most substantial nineteenth-century capital movements, however, were to the frontiers of settlement in the United States and the British Dominions. This was part of a vast transfer of human beings as well as capital goods, combined with continual settlement of new land and exploitation of additional natural resources. Had the component of foreign capital been missing, expansion might have been slower, but it is very unlikely that it would have been stopped. The willingness of British bankers to market American railroad bonds can scarcely be considered the key to the dramatic expansion of the American economy.

It would be useful to compare contemporary growth rates in the LDC's data and to correlate these with various measures of foreign-capital inflow. Even if such an exercise indicated a positive relation, one could not infer that the foreign capital was the source of more rapid growth. It is more likely that countries with a superior institutional framework and internal leadership, which are able on this account to grow faster than others, are considered superior credit risks and are able to attract larger amounts of foreign funds. Capital typically flows toward those who need it least.

4. Economic growth involves a diversified increase in output across a broad front.   Some lines of production naturally grow faster than others, and there may even be a sensational spurt in one field (British cotton goods, 1780–1820, or Swedish timber, 1830–80). But these are not "leading sectors" in the sense of an engine pulling an inert mass. Rapid growth in one sector both requires and encourages growth in related activities. Unless conditions in the economy are *broadly* favorable to growth, as they were in the British and Swedish cases, expansion in a single sector will prove abortive. The colonial type of enclave-economy illustrates this point. Although a substantial rate of expansion may be achieved within the enclave, this typically fails to communicate itself to the mass of the population and to activate a process of general growth.

It is now generally recognized that increases in agricultural output are an indispensable feature of early economic growth. The industrialization of the MDC's was typically accompanied, or preceded by, substantial agricultural progress. In many of today's LDC's, too, the behavior of agriculture is a key indicator of capacity for growth. The reason is not just that higher agricultural output is essential in an expanding economy, but also that inability to activate agriculture is symptomatic of weaknesses in governmental leadership and administration. Anyone can order a steel mill, but the intransigent problems of agriculture are a crucial test of innovational ability.

5. Output can usually be expanded substantially by absorbing previously unused resources.   In the conventional view, economic growth is held back by scarcities in resources, and particularly by a shortage of capital. It is more accurate to say that, in a stagnant economy, the resources needed for a higher level of output are *present but underutilized*. There is often cultivable land that is not already under cultivation. Many workers may be unemployed or underemployed, and they can be induced to work longer hours in industry or agriculture. Management and entrepreneurship may also be present but underutilized.

There are also indications that many LDC's have unused saving capacity. It is not that investment is being held back by unwillingness to save. Rather, people who could save perceive only limited investment opportunities attended by high risk. If the outlook changes and the prospective yield of capital rises, saving will be undertaken. There is also unused saving potential in the fiscal mechanism. Lewis has argued that no country is too poor to collect, say, 20 percent of national income in taxation. If actual revenues are small, and if the proportion of revenues devoted to investment is also small, the main reason may be weak government and poor public administration.

The view that capital shortage is not a major barrier to early economic growth is supported by the experience of the MDC's. Close students of early industrialization in Britain and Western Europe are of the opinion that finance did not seriously limit industrial development. Habbakuk, for example, states that perceived investment opportunities typically *generated* the necessary capital, rather than vice versa.[12] Deane and Cole express the opinion, with respect to early eighteenth-century England, that "the limiting factors to an increase in capital formation seem to have operated more from the side of investment than from the side of saving."[13]

If there is any basic scarcity in the LDC's, it is a scarcity of leadership, of ability to innovate in both the private sector and the public sector. This limitation has been heavily, and in our view correctly, emphasized by Hagen and Hirschman.

6. Economic growth involves a transformation of politico-economic institutions. The relevant economic institutions are those which affect markets in factors and products. In labor markets, this includes adequate training facilities, encouragement of desirable mobility, and modernized wage-setting practices. In capital markets, it includes private and public banks, insurance companies, and other savings institutions. In industry and commerce, it means a gradual superseding of the small family business by large enterprise and professional management. In agriculture, it means marketing facilities, sources of credit, availability of "modern" inputs, and technical assistance.

It is unnecessary for a country to have a full panoply of such institutions before growth can begin. It need not have a stock exchange, or a social security system, or much corporate enterprise. To a large extent development of "modern" economic institutions is a by-product of economic growth. It was so in the older industrial countries, and it will be so in the LDC's. At the same time, some minimum institutional base must exist quite early. The make-up of this minimum base is surely one of the key problems in the economics of growth.

The governmental structure must also be broadly favorable before economic growth can begin. But again, we do not know what this means in concrete terms. Economists have skirted the issue, and political scientists have not met it head-on. Moreover, orientation of government toward economic objectives, and improvement of its technical efficiency to attain those objectives, seems to be in good measure an accompaniment of long-

[12] See in particular his essay on "The Historical Experience on the Basic Conditions of Economic Progress," in L. Dupriez (ed.), *Economic Progress* (Louvain: Institut de Recherches Economiques et Sociales, 1955).
[13] Dupriez (ed.), *op. cit.,* p. 260.

sustained growth. Once economic modernization is underway, the political milieu becomes modified in a way progressively more favorable to continued growth. This "virtuous circle" can be traced in societies as diverse as those of Britain, the USSR and Japan.

Discussion of the role of government in today's LDC's is afflicted by opposing dogmas. On one side is the neoliberal view that, if government will stand out of the way, private initiative will mobilize increased resources and direct them toward the most productive uses. On the other side is the planning technician's view that government can generate growth through administrative actions and can predict and regulate its pace. In most LDC's, however, 80 to 90 percent of national output comes from the private sector. Here government can not compel expansion but must induce it by creating a structure of incentives that will lead producers to respond in the desired way.

It would be helpful if speculative and ideological discussion of these matters were replaced by careful analysis of experience. What did governments in the MDC's contribute to early acceleration of growth in those countries? What have governments in selected LDC's been doing over the past generation, and with what consequences? What kinds of action seem to have contributed to growth, and what policies have led to stagnation? There can in the end be no substitute for such a detailed, case-by-case analysis of the historical record.

A Concluding Comment

During the fifties and early sixties, development economics was prematurely policy-oriented. It offered an abundance of prescriptions with a minimum of diagnosis. The debates of this era — over balanced *versus* unbalanced growth, over the preconditions for a take-off, over the feasibility of a big push, over investment criteria and optimal savings rates — probably served some useful purpose. If nothing else, they attracted able graduate students into development economics under the mistaken impression that the subject already existed.

But those who entered the field under an illusion have done much to transform the illusion into reality. Over the past decade there has been an impressive flow of doctoral theses, journal articles, and monographs, deriving usually from field experience in the LDC's. We can now mount a varied and rigorous reading list for graduate courses. It is predictable that, as the subject is elaborated by further scientific work, it will occupy an increasingly solid place in the curriculum of economics.

This emerging specialty, however, will not be symmetrical with the older sectoral specialties. It is concerned with total economies in certain regions of the world and at an early stage of economic evolution. Work on these economies requires an assortment of existing macroeconomic and microeconomic tools plus new tools which remain to be invented. In this respect development economics resembles the study of socialist economies or the study of economic history. It interpenetrates the sectoral specialties rather than stands alongside them.

There should not, however, be any rigid dividing line between "development economists" and economists in general. It is highly desirable that economists in the traditional specialties extend their range of interests and activities to the less-developed world. A labor economist can study wage structures in Chile as well as in Sweden. An agricultural economist can fit production functions for wheat in West Pakistan as well as in North Dakota. This will not only advance our understanding of the LDC's, but will produce broader economists and more interesting courses throughout the economics curriculum.

15

On the Future of Technical Assistance

David E. Bell*

The thesis of this paper is that certain changes occurring in the less developed countries, and in our understanding of the process of development, call for important modifications over the next decade in the policies and methods of operation under which technical assistance is provided by foreign-aid agencies — both bilateral and multilateral. These changes are (1) the rapid rise in the number of well-trained, competent professionals and technicians in the less-developed countries; (2) the continuing steady increase in nationalistic attitudes and policies in many developing countries; (3) the increasing awareness of the need for research in dealing with problems of economic and social development; and (4) the increasing convergence between many problems of less-developed countries and those of more-developed countries. The following pages outline some of the modifications in the character and quality of technical assistance which should follow, in my opinion, from these changing conditions.

A word must be said about concepts and terminology. "Technical assistance" is a phrase customarily used to describe advisory services and training and demonstration activities that are provided as part of a foreign-aid program to a less-developed country. The argument in the present paper does not require great precision, but there are two important aspects of the concept as I shall use it which should be made explicit at the beginning.

First, "technical assistance" is often defined as the transfer of ideas from more-developed to less-developed countries.[1] Such a definition can be highly misleading if understood to mean that the ideas needed to solve

* The Ford Foundation

[1] "Technical assistance is the diffusion of ideas from a technically rich society to a technically poorer society." Sidney C. Sufrin, *Technical Assistance-Theory and Guidelines,* (Syracuse, N.Y., Syracuse University Press, 1966) p. viii.

problems in developing countries already exist in advanced countries. By and large, this is not so, and the notion that economic growth and social change can be speeded up by transferring to less-developed countries institutions, policies, and programs devised to meet the needs of the more-developed countries is not only erroneous but pernicious. In reality, virtually every problem in developing countries requires a novel solution, worked out in those countries to meet their conditions, and the transfer of a solution worked out for an advanced country may set back the evolution of correct answers.

What can usefully be transferred are not solutions but methods of analysis, insights based on experience, the confidence and energy to tackle deep-rooted difficulties. These are the qualities brought by good foreign advisers, and it is the application of these qualities in the less-developed countries, in the search for new solutions, that is the heart of the technical-assistance process.

Accordingly, in using the term "technical assistance", I mean to place emphasis on the cooperation between professionals and technicians from advanced countries or international organizations and their colleagues in developing countries in designing solutions for the problems of those countries; on the training necessary to produce people competent to join in such work; and on the research, demonstration, testing, and evaluation necessary to find such solutions.[2] For this reason, I find the term used by the United States Agency for International Development — "technical cooperation and research" — preferable to the more customary "technical assistance." In this paper, I shall use all these terms loosely and interchangeably, with the general meaning indicated above.

Second, although commonly contrasted with capital assistance, technical assistance is rarely effective separately, and in fact most useful examples of foreign assistance consist of some appropriate combination of capital and technical assistance — buildings and equipment along with teachers and researchers in a university; fertilizer and credit along with new varieties of wheat seed; jeeps and supplies along with family planning experts. I believe there is a sense in which technical advances are the principal cause of rapid development, but technical advances normally require capital to put them into effect. Therefore my focus on technical assistance in this paper is not intended to derogate the importance of capital assistance.

---

[2] Sufrin comes closer to this concept when he says, "Technical assistance is an aspect of cultural diffusion in that the problem is the transference or origination, by means of advice, of new ways of social behavior." *Ibid.* The difficulty I find with this way of putting it is that it makes the foreign adviser the source of the origination, whereas I think the emphasis should be on the cooperative process by which foreign adviser and local professional or technician discover solutions — and indeed, ideally establish a process by which steadily better solutions will be found as time goes on, experience is gained, and foreign advisers are no longer needed.

I.

The number of well-trained, experienced professionals and technicians in less developed countries has risen spectacularly over the past two decades. This is no surprise; it has, after all, been a major objective of the governments of developing countries and of foreign-assistance agencies. The sources of increased sophistication have been mainly three: the working of training institutions in the less developed countries; the large flows of trainees sent from less-developed countries to educational courses of one kind and another in advanced countries; and, perhaps most important, the effect of experience in the exercise of responsibility.

I know of no summary figures which describe these changes effectively, but anyone who has visited the developing countries over any span of years will confirm the observation. Many thousands of persons from developing countries have been sent abroad over the past twenty years for periods ranging from a few weeks to several years; and one encounters them in many, perhaps most, positions of responsibility in governmental agencies, educational institutions, the larger banks and businesses, and other organizations in less-developed countries. Larger numbers have been trained in the hundreds of institutions that have been set up or greatly enlarged in developing countries in relevant fields — public and business administration, agriculture, education, the social sciences, engineering, and so forth. And one has only to talk with present-day leaders in developing countries to realize the greater sureness of their grasp of developmental processes and priorities, a sureness which has come from the experience of responsible management.

An illustration may be useful, from a field I have followed closely. Today, there are a dozen heads of development planning organizations in less-developed countries who are among the world leaders in this exacting profession — men like Widjojo Nitisastro of Indonesia, Edgar Gutierrez of Colombia, and Philip Ndegwa of Kenya. Men like these are well-trained in the social science disciplines relevant to their jobs, experienced in applying technical knowledge to issues of national policy, sophisticated in the intricate interplay between political interests and analytical results that leads to public policy decisions in all countries. A decade ago, the leadership of the planning agencies in developing countries was very different — often made up of able men, but lacking the breadth of academic background and analytical competence today's leaders have.

What is true of planning agencies is largely true of other agencies central to the making of economic policy — Ministries of Finance, Central Banks, Ministries of Economic Affairs. These have been traditional centers of power, which have always attracted strong and able men. The difference today is that so many of these men have had good modern training in economics, in planning, and in other relevant disciplines, plus solid experience on the job. Consequently, they are able to deal much more as equals with the highly qualified professionals of the International Monetary Fund, the International Bank for Reconstruction and Development, and the finance and foreign-assistance agencies of the more-developed countries. In addition to the change in the quality of senior leadership in planning and economic agencies, there is a change in the middle and junior staff, with far larger numbers of better-trained men in those positions.

I have no wish to exaggerate the degree of difference. Looked at in absolute terms, compared to the size and complexity of the problems faced, the number of competent professional and technical men dealing with developmental problems in less-developed countries is pitifully, often desperately, small. Moreover, the availability varies from country to country and among different fields of development. Even where good men are available, they are often not used properly for reasons of politics, archaic administrative patterns, or other obstacles.

But looked at in relative terms, compared to the situation ten and twenty years ago, the number of well-trained and experienced men is very large. This constitutes a major change in the circumstances of the less-developed countries. What are the consequences for foreign-aid agencies? First, the greater the competence of managers and leaders of developmental organizations in less-developed countries, the greater the chances for rapid economic growth and social change, and the greater the opportunities for technical assistance. Foreign aid agencies can expect their outlays for well-designed projects to have a bigger impact in the future because there will be more local talent to work with.

Second, the increasing competence of professional and technical leadership in developing countries changes the nature of the need for foreign help. In many cases in the past, the foreign professional or technical adviser had to be in fact, if not in name, the policy-maker and chief manager of the aided enterprise. Today in more and more cases, the aid-receiving country has men who are capable of playing the leading roles.

The relationship between external professional and technical personnel and those in the aid-receiving country, therefore, is increasingly one of technical collaboration and support rather than one of foreign technical leadership. This change should make for better results. It will mean that decisions on sensitive matters of policy in developing countries will be made increasingly by persons who share the historical and cultural background and the nuances of value systems and political interests that are necessarily involved. Moreover, the increase in local competence will offer a sounder basis for collaboration between foreign and local personnel — collaboration which truly reflects a joint effort to discover the best solutions for problems rather than a one-sided effort by a foreign expert to apply in a new and strange environment what he has learned elsewhere.

A third consequence of the increasing degree of competence in developing countries is that, in the future even more than in the past, foreign-aid agencies will have to strive to obtain talent of the highest quality when providing foreign advisers. It has been recognized since the days of Point IV, the United Nations Technical Assistance Board, and other early technical assistance efforts, that the problems of developing countries are extraordinarily difficult to solve and that first-class talent is needed to deal with them. In practice, foreign assistance agencies have naturally attracted talent of varying quality, and there may have been a tendency in some of the national and international bureaucracies dealing with foreign aid over the years for some of the less able to stay and gain seniority while some of the more able departed for other career opportunities.

The increasingly competent leadership in developing countries will place great pressure on foreign-assistance agencies in this regard. Young, well-trained Ph.D.'s from Iowa State or Harvard, returning to their own countries to work in governmental ministries or university faculties, will be quick (indeed, sometimes overly quick) to identify, and object to, what seems to them mediocre competence in foreign advisers.

The only effective response is for the foreign aid agencies to insist on strengthening their own personnel systems and raising the level of talent they command. This may require strong action both in national agencies like the Agency for International Development (AID) and in international agencies like those of the United Nations. Past patterns of seniority and career service are likely to work against the results needed. It may in some cases be easier to obtain the competence required through contractual arrangements which permit highly able people to be associated with foreign-aid organizations and projects on a relatively short-term basis, while on leave from more permanent careers. However accomplished, the rising competence in developing countries will have to be matched by higher quality in technical advisers.

A fourth question raised by the growth in competence in less developed countries is more difficult to answer. Will there be larger or smaller requirements for foreign advisers? Although the data are far from unambiguous, there seems in recent years to have been a substantial rise in the number of technical advisers going to less-developed countries under foreign-aid programs.[3] This trend, however, reflects in part the continuing wave of new countries becoming independent, notably in Africa, a wave which has continued well into the 1960's and which has naturally resulted in new requests for outside help. It also reflects the continuing increase in

---

[3] The number of "experts and volunteers" financed by the governmental aid agencies of Development Assistance Committee members rose steadily from 86,000 in 1964 to 111,000 in 1967. Report by Edwin M. Martin, Chairman of the Development Assistance Committee, *Development Assistance, 1968 Review* (Paris, OECD, December, 1968), p. 273.

Peace Corps volunteers from the United States and similar volunteers from other advanced countries.

I have not found any useful analysis of the requirements for technical assistance that reflects clearly the effects of growing local competence. One would assume this would have two somewhat opposite effects. On the one hand, as local competence grows, local professionals and technicians can fill posts held till then by foreigners. This is one familiar effect, and intention, of most technical-assistance projects.

On the other hand, as local competence grows, new initiatives are possible that may require additional foreign advisers. When an economics faculty begins to acquire trained local faculty members, displacing foreign professors who helped establish the teaching program, it may be feasible to begin significant research programs that in turn may require foreign advisers on research methodology until the local staff has gained competence in the new field. When the senior officers of a ministry of agriculture gain a better understanding of what is needed to achieve rapid change in agricultural output, they may press for improvements in a stagnant local research organization, opening opportunities for technical assistance that until then were blocked by inertia or other obstacles.

Successful technical assistance, that is to say, to some extent creates further requirements for technical assistance, often of a more advanced and sophisticated type. And whether the increased requirements stemming from this follow-on effect, will be larger or smaller than the decreased requirements stemming from the displacement effect, is not clear. My own hunch is that the opportunities will become somewhat fewer in number but will call for somewhat better trained people. The subject would, I think, repay more careful study than it has received.

II.

A second change evident around the world is a steady increase in the spirit of nationalism in the less-developed countries. The causes seem complex, at least to this observer. They evidently include an intense desire for freedom from what appears in many countries — especially to the young people — to be foreign domination, whether by the United States, France, Japan, China, or some other country. There is plainly also an insistent demand for regional, communal, religious, and language group independence, a demand which affects advanced countries like Canada and Belgium as well as less-developed countries like Nigeria and India.

Whatever the causes, the virus is strong, and the impact on foreign assistance agencies is likely to be substantial. There has always been tension between the desire of developing countries — particularly those with recent colonial experience — to exercise the full powers of independence and the clear necessity for them to seek and accept external assistance, which necessarily carries with it both a flavor of dependence and some degree of intervention by the aid donor in the policy-making of the aid receiver. The current steady rise in nationalistic attitudes exacerbates this tension, increases the sharpness with which it is expressed, and makes it more difficult to work out acceptable aid relationships.

What sort of technical-assistance activities can retain legitimacy in the surroundings of a strongly nationalistic political environment? What adjustments in past practice can meet this growing problem?

The first element in an effective response is to make sure that each foreign-assistance project is aimed accurately at real problems in the less developed countries. The point of attack by spokesmen for nationalistic views is usually the claim that external assistance conceals ulterior motives, and is only a mask for attempts to achieve commercial advantage, acquire intelligence information, or accomplish something else in the interest of the aid giver.

Much can be done to make sure — and to make plain — that technical assistance in fact is focussed sharply on solving the problems of the less developed countries, and that solving those problems is the guiding interest of the giver in providing the assistance. Inviting experts from aid-receiving as well as aid-giving countries to participate in project selection will add both to the substance and to the appearance of the process. Both donors and recipients can emphasize that control over all projects is in the hands of the governments of aid-receiving countries. Foreign advisers and technicians can stress the "low posture" that is appropriate for would-be helpers from outside. Where research or studies are involved, collaboration by local scholars or specialists, assurance of publication of the results in the aid receiving country, and other measures can help make plain the usefulness and reliability of the work.

Nevertheless, serious problems may be expected to continue in the light of the passion and pride so easily aroused in developing countries, where assistance from the advanced countries can appear as a combination of conscience money and an effort to maintain foreign domination. (The tangle of emotional attitudes surrounding the assistance relationship is increasingly familiar within the United States as we establish developmental programs for our own disadvantaged groups.)

A second way to modify foreign-aid activities to fit them better into an increasingly nationalistic world, is to place more emphasis on building networks of constructive and mutually supporting relationships among professionals and technicians in different countries. Such relationships, based on mutual confidence and trust among men who know each other through common participation in serious work, may provide modest countervailing forces to the excesses of nationalistic pressures. International and regional associations of economists, urban planners, rice specialists, and the like;

international and regional research efforts in which researchers in less developed countries are full partners; international and regional conferences and seminars in which participants from developing countries share fully, are all illustrations of the point.

Constructive relationships among professionals and technicians in more-developed and less-developed countries are not easy to build. Those from less-developed countries inevitably fear that they will be dominated by their older and more experienced colleagues from more-advanced countries. The right beginning in some cases may be to establish relationships first among the professionals in less-developed countries — as is beginning to happen in many fields in Latin America — with the later prospect of building ties with advanced countries.

A third possible adjustment to the rise of nationalistic sentiment would be to provide more technical assistance through international organizations which, it is argued, are less vulnerable to charges of serving the national interests of aid donors. In the field of capital assistance, a system has been growing in recent years under which international agencies, principally the World Bank, through consortia and consultative groups that include the major aid-giving nations, take the lead in working out the amount and terms of capital assistance required by each major aid-receiving country in the light of its developmental plans and policies — its "self-help" measures. Bilateral aid donors then provide capital assistance within this multilateral framework. Would it be sensible to aim at similar arrangements in the field of technical assistance?

I suspect that the analogy is not persuasive. In contrast to capital assistance, technical assistance is inherently diffuse, and lacks relatively simple unifying concepts like the balance of payments, the budget, the program of developmental investment, all expressed in monetary terms that have a reasonably clear meaning. So far, technical assistance has not found similar frameworks for comparison and measurement; a set of technical assistance projects includes a bewildering array of requirements whose most important dimensions are skills, not money. We are just beginning to have some idea of how to design a program for developing, over a period of years, the skills needed in a sector, say agriculture, of a less-developed country. As yet, however, we do not know how to put together a useful national program for developing technically skilled individuals and institutions.

Consequently, there is no basis at present for any international agency to perform the service for the technical assistance field that the World Bank performs in the capital assistance field, namely, to examine a country's plans and proposals and reach conclusions on the volume and nature of foreign assistance that are warranted, conclusions which can then guide aid donors. We need urgently to develop better techniques and arrangements for doing this for technical assistance, but at present we are at a relatively primitive stage.

Furthermore, there is at present no international organization in the field of technical assistance that commands the authority and respect the World Bank does in the field of capital assistance. The United Nations Development Program (UNDP) comes closest, but its lack of clear authority in relation to the specialized agencies, and the consequent difficulty in achieving a consistent and logical program of technical assistance even within the United Nations group, are serious obstacles to any leading role for the UNDP. Furthermore, the United Nations technical-assistance agencies have been criticized on grounds of inefficiency.

The United Nations development assistance system in 1969 was under intensive review by Sir Robert Jackson, who was appointed a special Commissioner for the purpose. Depending on the reception given to his recommendations, the United Nations may in the future be in a position to play more of a leading role.

Nevertheless, it remains true that international technical-assistance agencies are somewhat less vulnerable to nationalistic criticism than are national agencies. This reinforces the conclusion that strong efforts should be made to improve the efficiency of the United Nations technical-assistance agencies, and of other international technical-assistance activities such as those of the Organization of American States. It may be desirable also in the future to divert some technical assistance funds from the United States bilateral aid agencies toward international agencies, although there would be strong resistance in the United States Government toward any substantial shift of funds to the United Nations technical-assistance program until the efficiency of the latter has been raised.

III.

A third and very important change which is occurring — this one in our understanding of the developmental process — is to give much greater weight to research focused sharply on the conditions and problems of less-developed countries, in contrast to the attempt to apply the results of research conducted for the purposes of the advanced countries.

We have all learned much from the recent experience with new varieties of wheat, maize, and rice, produced by scientific research conducted in tropical countries with the specific objective of finding varieties which would, under the growing conditions of those countries, produce several times as much per acre as traditional types. The results, so far, have been spectacular. These new varieties have led to radical increases in output in Pakistan, India and other countries, begun to have major effects on the economies of the countries concerned, and altered sharply the prospects for food supplies to feed the world's growing populations.

The lessons for foreign-aid agencies seem plain. The first is to give much higher weight than they have in the past to the support of research specifically directed at finding technology suitable for less developed countries. The needs are enormous. Only a beginning has been made in agriculture. Little research has been conducted on education, or on many other vital subjects.

Most important of all is the field of population. Current governmental attitudes in many countries strongly favor the rapid expansion of family planning programs, but the technology available for preventing births is poorly adapted to conditions in low-income countries. It is clearly necessary to give first priority to the research necessary to find better and cheaper contraceptive technology.

The second lesson is to conceive "research" properly. Judging from the experience of the Ford Foundation with agricultural and population research, the essential requirements are (1) to point the research sharply at specific goals of high priority, and (2) to accompany the research with strong parallel efforts to develop practical applications of the scientific findings, test them, evaluate the results, and train the necessary personnel, all to the end that the research is tied continually and directly to the practical work of applying better technology in practice.[4]

It is important to note that the kind of research called for is not "applied" research in the older sense of seeking engineering applications for the results of "pure" or "basic" research. What is needed is to use basic and applied science in whatever combination is required to deal with the problems. In the case of birth regulation, for example, in order to find better contraceptives it is currently necessary to undertake much basic research on reproductive biology — a field which has been seriously neglected by scientists in the past — as well as to undertake applied research and testing of potential new contraceptives.

The recent appreciation of the importance of research and its application for solving problems in developing countries should lead to a major increase in the resources made available for these purposes by aid-giving agencies. In many instances, this will require radical changes in the application of their funds.

For example, the United Nations Development Program has been effectively barred from using any of its funds for research activities outside the

---

[4] The terminology here is not easy. The term "research" is understood in many developing countries to mean scientific experimentation or writing aimed more at scholarly journals than at practical problems. The term "research and development" is often used in the United States to mean goal-oriented research carried through the stage of experimental application and testing, but it has obvious difficulties in a context where "development" is used much more broadly. "Research, development, testing and evaluation" is a phrase which has received some usage in the U.S. Government but seems too complex for wide adoption. "Research, development, and application" has been suggested as a preferable phrase by Professor Raymond Carpenter of Pennsylvania State University and has much to commend it. On the whole, I prefer to use the single word "research" but understood to meet the standards set out in the text above.

boundaries of developing countries, or for the activities of international, as opposed to national, research organizations. This has prevented UNDP funds from being used to support research on reproductive biology in advanced countries, and has even prevented them from being used to support such high-payoff research centers as the International Rice Research Institute in the Philippines or the International Center for Maize and Wheat Improvement in Mexico.

Expenditures on research by the bilateral aid agencies have also been very limited. A research provision was included in the AID legislation in 1961, largely through the efforts of a group of physical and social scientists from universities, and the provision has been administered with the help of a distinguished Research Advisory Committee. But the funds available for research under the AID legislation have always been very sharply limited by the United States Congress — a limitation that looks increasingly outmoded and damaging to the basic purpose of the aid program. One promising step in the right direction is the announced intention of the Canadian Government to establish a quasi-independent foundation for international development, financed largely with governmental funds, which will greatly increase the share of Canadian aid funds used to support development-oriented research.

IV.

A fourth major change affecting the future of technical assistance is the growing convergence between the problems of less-developed countries and those of more-advanced countries. Examples are easy to cite. It is increasingly evident that the urbanization problems of Calcutta or Lagos or Lima, while sharply different in degree from those of Los Angeles or Tokyo, are not different in kind. The problems of rural groups suddenly set down in urban settings, the problems of obsolete governmental machinery, the problems of retaining a sense of the small community in the impersonal metropolis — these and many other difficult issues are faced alike in the more-developed and the less-developed countries.

A less familiar illustration is the difficulty of teaching young children in languages which are not those of the home. This problem, it turns out, is not markedly different in Kenya, where the home language is tribal and the school language is Swahili, from what it is in Texas where, for many children, the home language is Spanish and the school language is English. Likewise in agriculture, when peasant agriculture gives way to market-oriented agriculture, as is now happening in much of Asia, the problems that arise are markedly similar to those of more advanced countries: the storage and marketing of larger crops, the maintenance of incentive price levels, the difficulty of achieving export markets, and so on.

All this suggests that many of the problems of development are in fact common to more advanced and less advanced societies and that as modernization begins to be more widespread, the problems encountered in the process of economic growth and social change are more similar than we had assumed a few years ago. In consequence, there is plainly much to be gained from the interchange of ideas and experience.

I believe that something more — something deeper — is beginning to come to light. There is a real sense in which advanced and less-developed countries are both struggling with issues neither has yet found a way to solve. The problems of early childhood education are not well handled in most advanced countries. The problems of urban development have proven to be beyond the capacity of the ablest city planners in the more advanced as well as in the less-developed countries. The problems of pockets of rural populations bypassed by modernization are acute in Appalachia as well as in the Deccan.

In these circumstances, do we not need to find ways to apply the best talent available anywhere in the world to theoretical and practical issues whose solution is of great concern everywhere? Economists have long argued that the benefits to advanced countries of economic growth in less-developed countries would be found not only in new opportunities for international trade and investment, but even more in the larger numbers of persons in the world who would then be capable of finding the technological innovations and breakthroughs that are the heart of economic progress.[5] In the same sense, there is great potential benefit to the more advanced countries in the social and political innovations and breakthroughs that may be found in the process of struggling to solve the problems of development in low-income countries.

What does all this signify for the process of technical assistance? In my opinion, it suggests that technical assistance — or technical cooperation and research — will increasingly need to be thought of as a two-way process, with mutual benefits in view. This viewpoint has implications for individuals; more of the ablest physical and social scientists may become interested in problems of developing societies when they see that gains can be achieved for their own societies as well. It has consequences for the organization of technical assistance; the advance planning and the follow-up of technical-assistance projects ought to take account of the possible gains at both ends of the relationship. Much more can be done to understand the meaning and significance for problems in advanced societies of research and innovation in less-developed countries. There will also be increasing opportunities for parallel or comparative research, focused simultaneously on problems of advanced and less-developed countries and combining the talents of research scientists from both.

[5] I believe I first heard this idea stated by Professor Simon Kuznets in a seminar at Harvard in the early 1950's.

V.

In a sense, all the changes identified in this paper point toward the desirability of similar responses: to base technical-assistance relationships more than in the past on cooperation between professionals and technicians in advanced and developing countries, to place greater emphasis on research and innovation as the heart of the process of technical advance, and to think of the results of technical assistance in terms of their possible value to advanced as well as to less-developed countries.

One is tempted to go further, and project a future when "technical assistance" will not be needed, a time when the less developed countries have sufficient scientific and technological strength to be thought of in some sense as self-sustaining — a concept akin to that of self-sustaining economic growth, under which economic interchange continues and increases, not on the basis of foreign aid, but on the basis of normal financing through trade and investment. So in the field of technical and professional relationships among scientists, researchers, educators, and others in advanced and in less-developed countries, cooperation and mutually beneficial arrangements would be realized on a permanent and growing basis without depending on the extra stimulus of foreign aid.

But such a time for most less-developed countries must be judged to be still a considerable distance in the future. Despite the growing number of skilled and competent people in those countries, it will be years before most of them have sufficient strength in the many disciplines and professions important for development to do without foreign technical assistance.

For the next decade or so, at least, it would seem that the right way to think about the problem is to search for changes in the present system of technical assistance that will result in higher quality and more efficiency. For most countries, the question of what comes after technical assistance can be deferred.

16

Less-Developed Countries and the International Capital Market

Charles P. Kindleberger*

I Introduction

The collapse of the international capital market in 1930, plus the realization that less-developed countries needed foreign capital for economic growth, led to the development after World War II of new institutions for the provision of aid and governmental loans, alongside private equity capital. Sufficient problems have been encountered in aid, governmental loans, and private direct investment, however, to make it timely to raise the question whether the resurrection of the international capital market is in order.

The simple-minded solution of Bretton Woods was to replace the international capital market with an International Bank for Reconstruction and Development (IBRD), which would stand, with governmental guarantees and some governmental funds, between private investors and borrowing governments. In one respect this solution has been streamlined: the IBRD was freed by means of post-UNRRA (United Nations Relief and Rehabilitation Administration) relief, Interim Aid, and the European Recovery Program (Marshall Plan) of the necessity to concern itself with reconstruction from wartime economic dislocation. In every other respect, however, the solution has been rendered more complex. Capital is provided to the less-developed countries, not only by the IBRD, but by aid grants; by aid loans — for example, the Development Loan Fund (DLF); by "soft loans" (International Development Agency (IDA)); by the regional banks for Latin America, Asia, and Africa; and by regional agencies, such as the European Overseas Development Bank. In addition to private direct investment, there is an international agency for the provision of equity capital, the Interna-

* Massachusetts Institute of Technology

tional Finance Corporation (IFC), along with an assortment of national and international guarantee programs which add the investing country's credit to the warranty of the country where the investment is undertaken.

Despite this array of machinery, the provision of foreign capital to the less-developed countries to assist in their growth cannot be said to be proceeding satisfactorily. Aid is in trouble; soft loans are running dry. The IBRD has taken on a new quantitative upsurge under the leadership of Robert McNamara, but there is criticism of its "project basis" for loans. There is also criticism of the "program basis" for lending with which the aid agencies have replaced the project basis. Direct investment is more and more under attack for the foreign control it exerts over host-country resources. In a world increasingly attracted by decentralization and local responsibility, the possibility of returning to the impersonal forces of the international capital market inevitably suggests itself. If the complex apparatus of intergovernmental and governmental aid and lending is not working satisfactorily, perhaps the time has come to revive the mechanism which it replaced. If the second-best machinery is poor, can we repair the broken first-best?

In the short run, a revival of international private lending to the developing countries in debt form is needed as a supplement to official aid and lending. In the long run, it is desirable that such private lending should, and conceivable that it could, replace some or most of such aid and lending.

II The Collapse of 1930

The collapse of the international capital market in 1930 can be quickly disposed of. London was replaced by New York as the world financial center in the 1920's because of the payments difficulties of the pound, which were associated with overvaluation and deflation. Savings were limited and needed for use in the United Kingdom or the Commonwealth. New York discovered the foreign dollar bond with the flotation of the Dawes Loan in 1924. In five years, it produced a sizeable volume of loans, primarily for Germany and Latin America, but for Canada and other European countries as well. Then, as suddenly, the volume dried up in 1928 when the call-money market attracted investors interest in the stockmarket boom. Foreign dollar bonds declined precipitously. A brief revival took place in 1930 but failed to endure. Revelations of high-pressure tactics of Wall Street investment houses, some even selling bonds after the receipt of telegrams from the borrower telling of default of debt service, put the instrument into disrepute. Preferred borrowers, such as Canada on a commercial basis and Israel on a basis part commercial and part eleemosynary, continued to claim access to the dollar bond. Not until 1958, however, did lending take place for other borrowers on a substantial scale. In 1963 the Interest Equalization Tax was levied — with an exemption for Canada and the less-developed countries, including Israel — and transferred the action to the Euro-dollar bond market across the Atlantic.

III Problems in Governmental Lending

Three main problems arise with respect to loans by international institutions, which we may take as representing all governmental loans: the allocation of the loans by countries, the conditions on which the loans are granted, and the extent to which the terms of the loans approach arms-length commercial terms. These problems are, of course, interrelated, but they are apart from the overriding issue, the volume of loans.

As concerns the first problem, international lending is somewhat like awarding prizes at a children's party, there must be something for everyone. To preserve the aura of an arms-length commercial transaction, the "children" have been divided into two groups: (1) the good boys and girls who can borrow at the IBRD because they had good credit records, and (2) the poor credit risks who have access only to soft loans, repayable after many years in local currency. In time, of course, mixed loans — partly IBRD and partly IDA, or partly DLF and partly grant in the bilateral aid from the United States — blurred the distinction between the good risks and the poor, or perhaps made it less sharp.

The World Bank (IBRD) early took the line that there was no shortage of loanable funds, only a shortage of lendable projects. Few countries acceded to this proposition, however, and regional groupings banded together to increase the volume of capital available to them, at the expense of the rest of the world. The Inter-American Development Bank (IADB) was the first such group. In the World Bank, more for one country meant less for other countries and other areas; and the bank's allocations were made on a world-wide basis. The IADB was an attempt to get a prior allocation for Latin America, an allocation which would be proof against undermining by diversion to other continents. The attempt led to the formation of new banks for Asian and African development. It may be argued that the cycle was useful in adding more funds for development and producing a new set of authorities with local knowledge and responsibility. It cannot be doubted, however, that it reduced flexibility in allocating loan funds where they would make the greatest contribution to economic development.

The second problem relates to the issue of intervention. In an effort to justify its procedures to the financial community, the IBRD early adopted a program of project-lending. It made funds available only for well-engineered projects which would effect a notable contribution to the economic growth of the country. Economists argued that it made little difference whether the funds in a particular project were well used if parallel resources in the economy were being wasted. They maintained that partial-equilibrium analysis was useless in a general-equilibrium problem and that what mattered was the use of all resources, not the bank's monies. At the United States Agency for International Development, for example, an alternative "program" approach was developed which sought to trace through, not the flow of the agency's lending, but the flow of all resources, including those produced locally as well as those borrowed from abroad.

Albert Hirschman and Richard Bird have raised a point in behalf of the project, and against the program, approach.[1] The program approach, they contend, involves a more thorough-going intervention in the affairs of a country than the project approach and is to that extent more subversive of the values of independence and self-reliance. It is paternalistic in an age of youthful revolt. The foreign-aid agency intrudes on the political life of the borrowing country in ways which give rise to an accusation of neo-colonialism or neo-imperialism.

The third problem — the terms of the loans — relates to hard loans, because a soft loan may be regarded as in part a grant, or gift, and in part a hard loan. David Horowitz, the Governor of the Bank of Israel, has put forward a suggestion for making all loans a blend by taking the amount of "profit" earned by the IBRD on past loans and using it to subsidize the interest rate of hard loans. This subsidization may have distributional effects through lowering the rate of interest paid by countries previously borrowing at high rates and through reducing the funds available for soft loans from IDA. It is difficult to see how it can increase the amount of loans overall. Instead of lending part at commercial rates and part at very low rates, approaching grants, all loans under the Horowitz plan would be subsidized to achieve an amalgam *ex ante* instead of *ex post*.

The problem nonetheless remains. Intergovernmental and governmental bodies lending on hard terms produce a singular external diseconomy insofar as these units resist default for fear of "domino effects." Among the classic rules of economics is "Bygones are bygones." For Ghana, which borrowed sizeable resources from the DLF and the IBRD under Nkrumah and wasted them, default on these obligations is strenuously opposed on the ground that other countries would be tempted to follow suit. The same is true of Indonesia and the obligations accumulated under Sukarno. Debts are rolled over, and their present discounted value reduced by substantial percentages. But "debt illusion" persists; for not everyone has the sophistication to calculate the present discounted value of a contractual stream of debt service or to reckon by how much the present value has been reduced when immediately due payments are postponed a decade or so. To the government and people, what is evident is that a previous government has borrowed monies and wasted them, which the new and struggling government is asked to requite. The possibility of writing down the capital amount, and

---

[1] Albert O. Hirschman and Richard M. Bird, "Foreign Aid — A Critique and A Proposal," in *Essays in International Finance,* No. 69 (Princeton: Princeton University Press, July, 1968).

scoring a loss on the books of the lender, is excluded by the fewness of lending agencies, all closely interconnected and, along with the debtors, guilty of "asset illusion" and, in addition, fearful of precedent. A healthier relationship would exist if the lenders as well as the borrowers were a disparate lot.

Horowitz's suggestion for subsidizing the interest rate on World Bank loans is paralleled by the proposal that national governments subsidize developing countries' borrowing in the private capital market. One form of the proposal is that national governments contribute some substantial portion of the market rate of interest. It is doubtful, however, that this measure would be effective so long as the risk of default was substantial. If governments were to guarantee repayment at the end of the contract, their guarantee might suffice to lower interest rates to levels approaching those on the issues of the developed countries, themselves, as the experience of the British government with colonial issues demonstrates. Such guarantees might usefully increase the available resources of the developing countries, provided the guaranteeing governments took an optimistic view of the current discounted value of their future contingent liability and did not reduce aid and governmental loans by the same amount that they guaranteed. But it fails to satisfy the need for reducing the tutelary role of the developed countries vis-à-vis the developing. No country is likely to be willing to underwrite another's obligation without some influence on economic policies. In the nineteenth century, guarantees of another country's external debt was a badge of colonialism. Today it would seem to imply neo-colonialism, which may make it politically unacceptable.

During the Eisenhower administration in the United States, from 1952 to 1960, there was an up-surge of opinion that, through direct investment, private investment could cope with the capital needs of the less-developed countries. The advantages of direct investment were taken to be (1) those derived from the cyclical variability of servicing capital investment and (2) the accompaniment of capital with technology and management. The cyclical-variability advantage proved illusory since the world has been spared serious depression, a situation in which fixed-interest obligations weigh heavily on the debtor and equity earnings are sharply reduced, thus lightening their burden on the balance of payments. To the extent that direct investment has occurred, its earnings have on the whole been high and their transfer burdensome.

A further objection to reliance on direct investment for economic growth has been its unavailability except in rare instances, for the kinds of social and economic-overhead capital which most countries appear to need for development. Few private corporations invest in roads, railroads, schools, universities, hospitals, utilities, ports, and the like. Occasionally, large companies investing in small and primitive countries may make some investment of this sort. In these cases, the problem of control, to be discussed, is increased. For the most part, however, private enterprise can provide only a fraction, though a substantial one, of the foreign capital needed for development.

The major objection to direct private investment in today's state of opinion is its control. More and more countries are wondering whether they cannot hire the capital and the technology while they themselves furnish the management. To the extent that the management is technical, it too may be hired from abroad while the domestic variety is being produced. Foreign technical skills must be bought in any event, if only to advise the country on the reasonableness of terms for concessions to private foreign investors. Once one-sided, the bargaining between direct investors and less-developed host countries is rapidly becoming an intense, evenhanded negotiation in which the country is assisted by foreign experts working in its interest. It may not be possible to dispense with foreign direct investment, if the scarce resource provided by the foreign firm — technology, management, access to foreign markets, or massive amounts of capital, as in aluminum projects — cannot be obtained alternatively. But local pride and determination to manage the nation's destinies provide a strong incentive for resisting direct foreign investment, à la Japan, when the cost is not too high and sometimes even when it is.

Thus it cannot be said that today's arrangements for providing capital to the less-developed countries are optimal. Supplementing existing methods with other means would improve the welfare of the less-developed countries, whether by enlarging the capital resources available to them, by furnishing them a preferred alternative, or possibly only by making a rejected alternative available. Before concluding that access to a private market for debt capital would assist the less-developed countries, however, it is necessary to review the arguments against such an international capital market.

IV   The Bretton Woods Agreement

The Bretton Woods Agreement drew a sharp distinction between current and capital accounts in balances of payments. It forbade intervention in the former, but readily permitted intervention in the latter. It assumed, without explicit demonstration of the generalization, that intervention in trade and service payments led away from Pareto-optimality, whereas controls over capital movements were at least as likely to be in the direction of desirable resource-allocation as away from it.

The experience of the 1930's, in which capital movements had been attracted to the United States — the country with the most abundant savings — rather than from it, suggested to the majority of economists that private-capital flows might well be repressed and replaced by governmental movements in the obviously desirable direction. This view still prevails widely. The report by the Organization for European Co-operation and Development (OECD) on balance-of-payments adjustment may be summarized as stating that the remedy for balance-of-payments maladjustment arising from excessive or deficient spending is macroeconomic measures to curtail or expand spending; the remedy for structural disequilibrium is exchange-rate adjustment; and the remedy for balance-of-payments disequilibrium from capital movements in the wrong direction, or in excess amount, is foreign-exchange control. Controls over the current-account are ruled out, over the capital account accepted.

The development of economic theory in the last twenty years since the war has made clear that, although private capital movements may be in the wrong direction and lead away from Pareto-optimality, so may measures to expand trade. The theory of the second-best makes clear that, under circumstances where there are discrepancies between private and social values, private trade may lead in the wrong direction — away from an optimum for a given distribution of income or toward a worsening distribution for a given, or even somewhat enlarged, level of income. The presumption of improving welfare through reducing trade barriers has been weakened substantially in the ivory tower, even though it remains sanctified in the market place. Academic economists nonetheless favor a general presumption that lower tariffs are better than higher. For some reason, however, this presumption is not extended to restrictions on capital movements.

Private capital movements may lead away from, rather than toward, Pareto-optimality because of tax differences between states and because of risks which threaten, or are perceived to threaten, private capital. Portfolio diversification improves private welfare; it is an open question whether this improvement for the investor adds to national welfare or constitutes an external diseconomy. It is hard even to determine whether there is a presumption in favor of consonance between the private and the general welfare. In what follows, however, it is assumed that there is such a presumption and that private capital movements improve general welfare unless the contrary is evident. Thus a gross flow of capital from a country where capital is scarce may be tolerable in some limited amount on the ground of portfolio diversification, provided that the net flow of capital is inward. A country like Canada, which borrows on balance from the United States, will benefit from permission to its private investors to acquire growth stocks on the New York Stock Exchange, even though the gross flow departs from the desired direction of the net. Such portfolio-balancing, involving substantial gross movements of capital, is a normal part of the process of international financial intermediation that provides investors with diversification and liquidity and thereby improves their welfare. So long as net movements of capital are in the direction dictated by basic capital abundance or scarcity and are in some appropriate volume — a magnitude difficult to determine — the movements in the opposite direction are not only tolerable but serve a significant economic function.

The second aspect to control of capital movements is its efficiency. Short of complete foreign-exchange control, there is doubt whether restrictions work. The IMF (International Monetary Fund) rule that the current account should be free, even though capital movements are restricted, fails because of leads and lags, which can only be eliminated if the control authority regulates the credit terms of merchandise exports and imports. Underinvoicing of exports and overinvoicing of imports is another current-account loophole. The United States attempt to control capital movements flowing through a limited number of conduits demonstrated how fungible capital is. The Interest Equalization Tax on security issues had to be followed by action to block capital outflows through short-term bank loans, long-term bank loans, direct investment, the Canadian gap, and the pension-fund gap; and such action still left the foreign-owned-securities gap. Under this last, as interest rates rose in Europe relative to the United States, foreign owners of dollar securities would sell their low-yield issues in the United States and buy Euro-dollar bond issues abroad, thus joining the two markets in still another way. To prevent capital flows means surveillance of all sources, including foreign-exchange control over current-account transactions. Even such surveillance is unlikely to be more than 67–75 percent efficient against determined attempts to export capital. To the doubt about the desirability of controlling capital movements must be added the doubt about its feasibility.

V   *Advantages of a Private Market*

In these circumstances, there is a possible point in policies designed to revive the private international capital market for the less-developed countries. The difficulties are imposing: to relax restrictions on lending in the capital-rich countries and to bring potential borrowers to the state of credit worthiness that makes certain their obligations will attract investors. (More is said on both issues in section VI below.) But the advantages are considerable. The allocation of a portion of internationally available capital would be made by a market process — the "invisible," rather than the "visible hand" — thereby relieving the political process of a disagreeable task. Conditions for borrowing would be determined by neither projects nor programs that were imposed by the lenders and that interfered with the sovereignty of the borrowing country. These conditions would be volunteered by the borrower, and they would be in accord with the market's requirements as determined by the borrower and the investment bankers underwriting its loans. Where the market misjudged the credit worthiness of a borrower and default occurred, private negotiations of the Council-of-Foreign-Bond-holders type would ensue without the external diseconomy implied by a single cohesive set of lenders whose condoning of one default implied license for all.

More significant, perhaps, the sensible fiscal management needed to restore credit worthiness in the international capital market is the same management needed for effective economic growth. Applied impersonally, rather than by paternalistic officials of international institutions, such management and governmental borrowing from the private international capital market raise a prospect of enlisting local capital in national growth efforts, initially in roundabout, and ultimately in direct, fashion. Latin American funds are said to abound in Switzerland and to be available for investment in Euro-dollar bond issues. If interest rates are competitive, these monies may be invested in the issues of the home country. In this way, the gross capital outflow might be reduced to a net of zero, and domestic capital mobilized for use at home through the intermediation of foreign capital markets. The equity of giving certain capitalists the security of a foreign-exchange guarantee for their loans may be questioned; but to the extent that these savers export their capital in any event, they acquire the guarantee anyhow. There is no question of offering or withholding the guarantee, but only one of acquiring or not acquiring the use of the capital.

If additional domestic capitalists in less-developed countries were attracted to invest in their country's obligations in foreign currencies because of borrowing abroad, one should not focus only on the problem of matching the capital outflow with the capital inflow and the incurring of a foreign-exchange obligation by the borrowing entity without a gain of foreign exchange for the country. In addition to this effect, which is negative for the borrower's country, the borrower has presumably contracted for his loan at a lower rate of interest abroad than at home and at a narrower underwriting spread in the more competitive market. Via foreign capital markets, the domestic lender obtains a more liquid asset, denominated in a more stable currency, but he gives up several percentage points of interest. The borrower incurs an international obligation in a harder currency, but he benefits from reduced debt service.

With respect to debt service, it is probably impossible to claim any advantage for the private capital market over official and semiofficial intergovernmental and international institutional lending. Some observers believe that a number of countries, having already overborrowed or about to borrow too much in relation to their capacity to service external obligations, are headed for trouble with present institutions. The private market would not regard these countries as credit worthy and would not lend to them. For the most part, governmental and international institutions recognize the dangers confronting loans to such countries, but they feel obliged to throw soft money after hard to avoid domestic crises in international payments and domestic growth. Debts are rolled over and thus reduced in present, if not in nominal, value.

Private rather than official lending would increase the willingness to recognize past error through default only where a country had achieved credit worthiness at one time and then lost it, whether through internal revolution or through a drastic change in economic conditions, such as the collapse of the price of an export staple. Here the capacity of the private market to adjust to reality should be superior to that of official lenders because of the preoccupation of international institutions with dangerous precedents. Official institutions are obliged to keep on lending to the less-developed countries in some fashion; the private capital market is not. The less-developed countries may on this score have a greater incentive to maintain their credit rating on the private market than to meet debt service regularly to the IBRD and DLF. Too much should not be made of the point, however, since the difference in incentives is small.

VI Requirements for Reviving a Private Market

There are thus positive advantages in reviving the private international capital market for the less-developed countries. These advantages are perhaps moderate, so that the problem is not at the top of developmental priorities. Nonetheless, as stated, the advantages are positive and more than trivial. To achieve them, action is required on three fronts: the less-developed countries must be interested in establishing their credit worthiness; the lending countries must take action to stimulate the international capital market; and various governmental and institutional actions may be initiated, or extended, to stimulate the appetite of private investors for the obligations of developing countries.

The interest of the developing countries in establishing their credit standing is best illustrated by the experience of Mexico, which has borrowed in the New York open market through private placements with an American insurance company and in the Euro-dollar market. These were all strictly arms-length business issues, unlike Israeli debentures sold in the United States on a quasi-charitable basis and the bonds of dependencies, or former dependencies, sold in the French, Belgian, Dutch and British markets, in the first case with the explicit guarantee of the French government and in the other cases with implicit guarantees of the governments concerned. A United Nations study states that the international bond market has shown no signs of revival for the developing countries since 1930.[2] This seems too negative a conclusion in the light of figures to be cited presently. The separate issues of a number of countries — Colombia, Venezuela, Liberia,

[2] United Nations, *Foreign Investment in Developing Countries,* Sales No. E.68. II.D.2, (New York, 1968), para. 176.

the Philippines, and the Federation of Rhodesia and Nyasaland — issues which where not followed by further flotations, support the negative conclusion. But the Mexican example of continual borrowing in one form or another offers encouragement. Here is a country that wants to reduce its dependence on governmental and international lending and that explores a variety of means of borrowing private funds.

Mexico's attraction for investors throws light on the conditions of credit worthiness. The country is developing; its balance of payments is in good shape; and it adjusts its issues to the conditions of the market, shifting a small issue from New York to the Euro-dollar market in an effort to broaden its appeal for investors.

Argentina set out on such a course with small issues sold in Switzerland (were they perhaps sold to Argentine holders of numbered accounts?) and in Germany. But political difficulties at home cut off the flow. To ongoing development, a favorable payments position, and financial aptitude must be added domestic tranquility, if a country is to attract investors. The formula is a difficult one. Yet, it may be possible to achieve it in one or another country, and it has merit on its own, quite apart from the exigencies of the foreign investor.

The requirement in the creditor countries for a larger flow of capital to developing countries is acceptance of the desirability of building an international capital market. It is not sufficient to exempt the developing countries from restrictions on lending to developed countries and from the Interest Equalization Tax (I.E.T.), the Mandatory Credit Restraint Program and so forth. The United Nations report cited claims that the United States exemption for developing countries was effective, since the volume of bonds sold on the United States market rose from $97 million in 1963 to $203 million in 1964 and $221 million in 1965. These amounts, however, are small in relation to the need. What is required is a substantial general growth of the international capital market, a growth which will spill into the less-developed countries. Investors are creatures of fashion and habit; the development of the foreign bond, well under way until 1963 when the I.E.T. was applied, would in due course probably have carried loans for developing countries to much larger totals. Economies of scale predominate in financial markets. The short-run gain of the developing countries from the cutting off of loans to developed countries is likely to lead nowhere because the market will dry up. Thus a major condition in the development of a private capital market for the developing countries is the removal of restrictions on lending in general.

This is not the place to argue the case against United States restrictions on capital outflows based on an unusual concept of balance-of-payments equilibrium, a concept which takes into account the normal function of an international financial center in lending long and borrowing short to provide the world market with liquidity. To do so would take us far afield. I assert, however, that with this different definition of equilibrium in the balance of payments widely accepted, it would be possible to relax the restrictions on international lending and that the payments system would be efficient and sustainable. One reason for moving to the superior balance-of-payments concept, in fact, is that the move would permit the world to embark on the task of building an international capital market.

Finally, there are various specific actions for stimulating private lending to the developing countries. Many of these have been pursued in the past, but they tend to be neglected because of the slowness in developing a broader international capital market. Short-term credits extended by the Export-Import Bank, Export Credit Guarantees Department, Kreditanstalt fuer Wiederaufbau, and similar institutions could be resold to the private market and ultimately turned over to it. The IBRD pattern of selling to the private market, without guarantee, serial notes of early maturity might be pushed further. The IBRD officers might explore private placement of foreign bonds with insurance companies, like the $100 million Mexican loan sold to the Prudential Life Insurance Company in the late 1950's. In Europe, the long list of restrictions placed on foreign capital issues and intended to give priority to national governments' capital requirements should be removed, as called for in the reports on the capital market by the EEC (European Economic Community) and OECD. In the United States, a major task that might be worth undertaking — not as a first step, however, unless the policy of lending were more generally agreed on — is the task of introducing and passing state legislation that raises present low limits on the purchase of foreign bonds by insurance companies. Such a campaign was successfully undertaken in the 1940's to enable the securities of the IBRD to qualify for investment by insurance companies. IBRD obligations with the guarantee of the capital-market governments are evidently an investment superior to debtor governmental securities in general. Nonetheless, restrictive laws passed at a time when investing by insurance companies approached scandalous levels, unduly inhibit sensible policies of investment today. To build a broader market for foreign bonds requires removal of restrictions in both Europe and the United States that have outlived their usefulness and appropriateness to a shrinking world.

Providing subsidies on interest rates and guarantees on repayment of principal may also be worth consideration, but as indicated earlier, the writer is sceptical about the efficacy of these measures.

VII Conclusions

The foregoing argument is largely asserted rather than demonstrated. Many of the steps in the reasoning rest on instinct instead of solid propositions. It is justifiable therefore to take a stand in opposition and to maintain that the provision of capital and aid to the developing countries is best carried on at the intergovernmental and international-institution level. Planning, centralized accumulation of savings and their allocation, along with assistance to the statesmen and technicians of developing states in overcoming the resistances to development they face at home by imposing explicit conditions on them from abroad, this approach may be the better path to development and improved welfare. Perhaps. It is not without its successes in Taiwan, Korea, Israel. And the international capital market is prone to excess and collapse, most recently in 1930 but, prior to that, on many occasions in the nineteenth and earlier centuries.

Nevertheless, the path of independence and the "invisible hand," — that is, the market test and a minimum of controls — is not without its attraction, as Adam Smith demonstrated in 1776. "External diseconomies" prevent easy acceptance of the view that the market outcome is optimal. Some guidance is needed, however, as to how to behave in the absence of explicit recognition of externalities that call for intervention in market processes. I have a hard time accepting a presumption that such externalities are absent as a rule in merchandise trade but abound in capital movements. It is possible for the instinct of others to maintain this position. Not mine.

17

Industrialization Through Import-Substitution or Export Industries: A False Dichotomy

*Stefan H. Robock**

Narrow or biased solutions result from a narrow or biased structuring of a problem. A case study in point has been the matter of strategies for industrialization in the less-developed countries (LDC's). This essay argues that a persistent tendency to consider the issue within a limited foreign-exchange framework has long inhibited and frequently misdirected the efforts of the less-developed countries to industrialize.

To be sure, the foreign exchange problems of the LDC's have been critical. Furthermore, foreign exchange can be a vital constraint on industrialization, and industrialization can be an important element in programs to improve a country's foreign-exchange situation. But despite the overlap, the issues relating to foreign exchange policies and those relating to industrialization policies need separate, though harmonic, attention. Each set of issues involves singular factors and special expertise.

Over the recent past, the myopia caused by excessive concern with foreign exchange led to wide support for *import-substitution industrialization* (ISI). More recently, many enthusiasts for import substitution have become disenchanted,[1] and they have been urging that export industries be promoted as a preferred alternative. The priorities have shifted, but the dominance of a foreign-exchange framework persists. The preference for export industries has emerged largely out of disappointment with the foreign exchange results of ISI.

* Columbia University. The research for this article was supported by Resources for the Future.

[1] See Albert O. Hirschman, "The Political Economy of Import-Substituting Industrialization in Latin America," *The Quarterly Journal of Economics* (February, 1968), pages 1–4, for a discussion of the disenchantment with import-substitution industrialization.

From the point of view of industrial development, to present the matter of strategies as a choice between import substituting and export industries is to pose a false dichotomy. Specific industries cannot be meaningfully classified as inherently *import substitution* or export types. Many factors other than the type of product determine whether the output of a factory actually substitutes for imports or is exported out of a country. Such additional factors include the locational characteristics of the industry as determined by technology, the size of the national market relative to the economic size of plant, the levels of production and marketing efficiency being achieved, and many other elements.

An aluminum plant, for example, is a materials-oriented type of industry. Given present technology, it is invariably located near sources of low-cost electric power. When located in a country whose market is too small to absorb the output of a plant of economic size, an aluminum plant will be an export industry. When located in a country with a large enough domestic market, an aluminum plant will be an import-substitution industry.

To portray the choice of industrialization strategies as between policies that encourage import substitution and those that encourage exports is a false dichotomy. Not only does the approach segregate the domestic from the foreign market, but it fails to take into account the historically verified process by which many countries have become important exporters of industrial products.[2] For example, Japan first imported manufactures from the more advanced countries, then began producing domestic substitutes, and eventually became an important exporter of these same products. At first Japan's exports of manufactured goods tended to move to countries less developed than Japan. Later on, Japan was able to export to the industrially advanced countries as its labor force gained experience, the quality of its products improved, and the marketing ability of its businessmen became more sophisticated.

A great deal of technical information is available on direct approaches to industrial development, most of which recognize foreign exchange as a constraint.[3] But in recent years, such information has not been adequately exploited because the "foreign-exchange myopia" continues to dominate deliberations on policy and research on industrialization. This essay will critically examine the prevailing views on ISI and its reciprocal, export industries (EI), in the hope that a greater share of the relatively scarce resources for planning and research still being devoted to the ISI-EI syn-

---

[2] William V. Rapp, "A Theory of Changing Patterns under Economic Growth: Tested for Japan," *Yale Economic Essays* (Fall, 1967), pp. 69–135.

[3] For example, see the excellent study on *Processes and Problems of Industrialization in Under-Developed Countries,* (New York: United Nations, 1955). More recently, the work of the United Nations Industrial Development Organization (UNIDO) is contributing greatly to a balanced and comprehensive approach to industrial development. See *Report of the International Symposium on Industrial Development,* (New York: United Nations, 1969).

drome may be shifted toward more fruitful directions. Generally, in order to gain acceptance for new directions, it is necessary to challenge and weaken prevailing views.

Import Substitution and Industrialization

"Import substitution" has been defined as the process by which a growing proportion of the total consumption of a given country is satisfied by domestic production.[4] "Import-substitution industrialization" refers to governmental actions that ban or restrict imports through tariffs, foreign-exchange controls, import quotas, and similar measures and thereby encourage the establishment of domestic production to supply substitutes.

Actually, ISI is more a new label than a new concept. Providing protection against imports has long been a foundation stone of the "infant industry" approach to industrialization. Using imports to identify new possibilities for industries with market-oriented types of production has been a traditional and logical technique of those planning industrial development. And there is little new in the idea of increasing the availability of foreign exchange through substituting local production for imports.

Nevertheless, import substitution as a strategy for industrialization burst onto the scene in the early 1950's, mainly through the efforts of the Economic Commission for Latin America, with an aura of originality as part of a broad and attractive development ideology. The sharp focus on ISI emerged from Dr. Raul Prebisch's analysis of the trade problems of the developing nations. He emphasized the need for developing countries to diversify their economies and embark upon a process of "development from within"[5] because of the limited prospects for expanding traditional exports and enlarging their earnings of foreign exchange. Basically, this meant industrialization through substitution of imports.

At least in Latin America, it is doubtful that the concept of ISI resulted in new affirmative and comprehensive strategies for industrialization (a subject discussed below) or even changed significantly the policies of industrial promotion already being pursued. Yet the concept ascended rather quickly to a position of great popularity among scholars and public officials as a rationalization of past history and as a basis for recommending future policies. In the process, an impressive pseudological technical apparatus was spawned to support the historical interpretation and future recommendations.

This interesting intellectual phenomenon can be illustrated by the almost universally accepted conventional wisdom on Latin American industrializa-

[4] Various meanings have been given to the term "import substitution," and the definition used above is one of the highly simplified forms. For a comprehensive discussion of the matter of definitions, see "The Growth and Decline of Import Substitution in Brazil," *Economic Bulletin for Latin America* (March, 1967), pp. 4–9.

[5] *The Economic Development of Latin America and Its Principal Problems* (New York: United Nations, 1950).

tion as articulated by the Economic Commission for Latin America (ECLA). Recent ECLA studies identify import substitution as having been "one of the prime movers of industrial development." Yet, "its chances of continuing to be in the future are increasingly slender."[6] The pessimistic view of the future, and the genesis of the emphasis on export industries, is supported by the arguments that the growth rate of established import-substitution industries has been slowing down, that the possibilities for additional import-substitution industries appear to be drying up, and that import-substitution has resulted in many high-cost industries that do not have export possibilities because of their small size and inefficiency.

The slowdown in the growth rate of import-substitution industries has been observed to be an inherent tendency of the process. New industries expand rapidly during the initial stage when domestic production is substituting for previously imported goods. After the stage of substitution, it is argued, the growth rate tends to slow down to the relatively slower pace of growth in domestic demand.

According to the prevailing views, the exhaustion of new opportunities for import substitution has occurred because the easy possibilities — involving small plants, simple technologies, and low capital requirements — are first exploited. The product lines in which possibilities of import substitution still remain are much more difficult, and even impossible, because they require large markets, complex technologies, and large investments.

A capstone argument used in Latin America against import substitution is that "the region as a whole now has an exceptional low import coefficient of only slightly more than 8 percent, which can scarcely be reduced any further."[7] The import coefficient is the relationship between the value of imports and the value of total domestic product.

This is the background in abbreviated form for the polemic of import substitution versus export industries and for the evolution from import substitution to export industries as the favored strategy in industrialization. The discussion assumes that ISI was widely adopted as a deliberate industrializing strategy. It argues that past results were unsatisfactory to a large degree and that future prospects of ISI are not bright. It advocates as a solution that emphasis be shifted to export industries. For Latin America, it also urges that efforts at regional economic integration be accelerated so as to open new prospects for import substitution by enlarging the market.

Has Import Substitution Been a Deliberate Industrializing Strategy?

A critical examination of the evolution from import substitution to export industries as the favored strategy for industrialization might begin by ques-

---

[6] *Economic Survey of Latin America, 1964* (New York: United Nations, 1966), Sales No. 66.II.G.1, p. 151.
[7] *Ibid.*, p. 151.

tioning the prevailing interpretation of recent history. A foundation stone of the preference for export industries is that import substitution was widely adopted as a deliberate industrialization policy and "failed."

The Latin-American experience, which may be representative, suggests that few, if any, countries had formulated coherent industrial development programs until quite recently. Furthermore, import-substitution measures appear to have been devices to cope with balance-of-payments problems rather than conscious instruments for promoting industrialization. Thus a more accurate interpretation of recent history is that the strategy of industrialization alleged to have been tried and found wanting had in fact rarely, if ever, been adopted as a strategy of industrialization.

As Dr. Prebisch recently observed, "Usually industrialization has not been the result of a programme but has been dictated by adverse external circumstances which made it necessary to restrict or ban exports; . . ."[8] In the case of Argentina, according to Professor David Felix, "Whether ECLA's efforts did much more than change the vocabulary of the industrial promotion effort is not clear. . . There the phrases 'import substitution' and 'saving foreign exchange' appear explicitly in the industrial promotion laws and decrees after 1950, whereas previously 'anti-dumping,' 'diversification,' and 'economic independence' had predominated. But the industrial promotion policies pursued in the 1950's did not vary in essence from those of the previous decade."[9] Furthermore, "The policy of import substituting industrialization during 1943–55 was not an integrated and thought-out plan. Rather, it seemed to proceed from one improvisation to another, reacting to short run economic and political pressures."[10]

In Brazil, "the prime objective in the late nineteen forties and early nineteen fifties was coping with the balance-of-payments disequilibrium. This also provided the protection needed to stimulate new industries. Only in the middle nineteen fifties did exchange rate and tariff protection become more conscious instruments for the promotion of industrialization than just devices to cope with balance-of-payments problems."[11]

This is not to suggest that governments were generally passive with respect to industrialization. Many positive actions were taken, such as implementing a national desire for a steel plant or encouraging industries that would further process materials before export. But, almost without exception, such positive actions were not part of an overall coherent strategy

[8] Raul Prebisch, *Towards a New Trade Policy for Development* (New York: United Nations, 1964), pp. 21–22.

[9] David Felix, "The Dilemma of Import Substitution — Argentina" in *Development Policy, Theory and Practice,* edited by Gustav F. Papanek (Cambridge: Harvard University Press, 1968), p. 57.

[10] Carlos F. Diaz Alejandro, "An Interpretation of Argentine Economic Growth Since 1930. Part II." *Journal of Development Studies,* (January, 1967), p. 158.

[11] Werner Baer, *Industrialization and Economic Development in Brazil* (Homewood, Ill.: Richard D. Irwin, Inc., 1965), p. 79.

of industrialization or of a comprehensive program for industrial development. Insofar as partial plans emerged, some were dominated by balance-of-payments considerations and many others were not.

Import Substitution as a Process

Another aspect of the debate over import substitution that deserves critical examination has been the failure to differentiate between import substitution as a process and import substitution as a strategy for industrialization. As an observed phenomenon, import substitution *for the economy as a whole* results from many development activities other than industrialization. It may result from increased domestic production of petroleum, minerals, or agricultural products. Also, an expansion of nationally owned facilities for ocean transportation or an expansion of commercial services may substitute for imports. Thus, the widely used coefficient of import substitution, which relates total imports to total domestic production, reflects many forces other than industrialization.

How a major import-substitution effect may result from developmental efforts other than industrialization is illustrated by the case of petroleum in Brazil. In 1955, Brazil produced only 2 million barrels of oil domestically while it imported 28 million barrels. By 1966, after an aggressive program of exploration and production, domestic output had expanded phenomenally to 42 million barrels annually, although imports had increased also to a level of 83 million barrels. But domestic crude production in the later year accounted for 33 percent of national consumption as compared to 7 percent in 1955.

The substitution of domestic for imported crude was complemented by the expansion of local refineries, thereby permitting crude oil to substitute for imports of refined products. The overall result was that imports of both crude oil and refined petroleum products, which represented 24 percent of Brazil's total imports in 1955, fell slightly in absolute value and even more as a share of total imports — 15 percent in 1966 — while the consumption of petroleum products in the country more than doubled.

Even when related to industrialization, import substitution can be a result of exogenous forces, inherent patterns of development, or positive policies not directed toward import substitution. In other words, *the fact that import substitution occurs coincident with discussions or actions to promote industrialization through import substitution should not necessarily be interpreted as a cause and effect relationship.*

An example of exogenous forces is the import substitution that occurred on a major scale in Latin America during World War I and World War II, when imports from the industrialized nations could not be secured. An example of natural market forces that result in import substitution largely independent of ISI programs is the establishment of units for producing market-oriented products in a country or in a region within a country when demand grows to the point that a plant of economic size can be justified.

The motivation for establishing new market-oriented plants in growing markets is generally the decision of a business enterprise responding to the economics of location. The economics of location, of course, may be influenced by governmental measures to encourage import substitution. Nevertheless, the normal strategy of many international business firms is to develop a foreign market through exports and, at a later stage, establish productive facilities in the market area *so as to minimize transportation costs and expand demand through providing better service.* The phenomenon of decentralizing market-oriented production is well known to students of industrial location and regional development, but it has not received much attention, as is true of locational economics in general, in discussions of import-substitution industrialization.

Resource-based industries as well as market-oriented types of manufacturing can become established in a country for motives other than import substitution, but import substitution may be a major effect. Another Brazilian example may be used to illustrate the point. In the mid-1940's, the Brazilian government provided a major impetus to its domestic iron and steel industry by establishing the first integrated plant at Volta Redonda. Endowed with rich deposits of iron ore, Brazil had long nurtured a national desire to have a major iron and steel industry. This intense desire was supported by a popular belief that the presence of iron ore provided a sound economic base and by the conviction of certain influential military leaders that Brazil needed such an industry for reasons of national security. The United States assisted in the realization of this goal through loans from the Export-Import Bank, in part at least because of Brazil's military support during World War II. The effect was import substitution but the governmental decision to establish an iron and steel industry was mainly a response to quite different issues.

In brief, import substitution for the economy as a whole involves much more than industrialization. Even in the case of industrialization, import substitution as a process may be primarily a result of forces other than governmental measures to encourage import substitution.

The Coefficient of Import Substitution

A related issue is the widely accepted conclusion for Latin America that prospects for future industrialization are poor because the region as a whole and specific countries in particular already have low import coefficients "which can scarcely be reduced further." The overall coefficient to which this statement refers is a ratio of total imports to gross domestic production.

As a ratio, the coefficient can vary with differential changes in the two components and with divergent trends in the prices of imports and domestic products. A reduction in the coefficient does not necessarily imply a reduction in the absolute value or quantity of imports.[12] In the case of Mexico and Brazil, for example, the coefficients declined while the value of imports expanded significantly. In 1929, Mexico's imports totalled $465 million and its coefficient of import substitution was 14.2 percent. By 1960, Mexico's imports had more than tripled to $1,416 million, but the coefficient had dropped to 7.3 percent because of the more rapid growth of gross domestic product. Comparable figures for Brazil are imports of $898 million and a coefficient of 11.3 percent in 1929 as compared to $1,658 million and 5.8 percent in 1960. The imports in both countries and for both years are stated in 1960 dollars.[13]

The principal empirical work underlying the conclusion that the import coefficient for Latin America has been declining sharply has been that of the Economic Commission for Latin America. On the basis of this work, ECLA states in its recent study of industrialization that the import coefficient for Latin America declined from between 20 and 25 percent in 1929 to about 10 percent in 1963.[14] The actual statistical analysis is not presented in the published report, but it is available in an unpublished annex, which has been summarized in Table 17–1.

A comparison of the two selected years, one at the beginning (1929) and one at the end (1963) of the thirty-four-year period supports the conclusion of a sharp decline in the import coefficient. But over the decade and a half following the end of World War II, only a slight downward trend, at best, might be discerned in the data. In general, imports and the import coefficient seem to be closely associated with the availability of foreign exchange. The high ratios for imports in 1947 and 1948 reflect the immediate postwar tendency to make up for the shortage of imports during the war years. The rise in 1951 was most likely due to the greater availability of foreign exchange as a result of the Korean War; in 1954, of the high prices of coffee; and in 1957, of the effect of the Suez Crisis on Venezuela.

Another problem with the ECLA data is that the import component of the coefficient, following the standard system of classification in balance-of-payments accounting, includes such items as foreign travel expenditures by residents of the country and income paid to foreigners on their direct investment in the exporting country. In the case of Mexico, for example, payments for travel abroad and direct investment by foreigners were almost

---

[12] See *El Proceso de Industrializacion en America Latina* (Nueva York: Naciones Unidas, 1965), No. de venta: 66.II.G.4, pp. 29–41, especially Grafico IV on p. 31.

[13] *The Process of Industrialization in Latin America, Statistical Annex, St/ECLA/-Conf. 23/L.2/Add.2, 19 January 1966, (Mimeo),* Table I–5 for import coefficients and Table I–7 for imports.

[14] *El Proceso de Industrializacion en America Latina* (Nueva York: Naciones Unidas, 1965), No. de venta: 66.II.G.4, p. 29.

Table 17–1 Latin America: Import Coefficients 1929, 1939, 1946–1963

Imports of Goods and Services as a Percent of
Gross Domestic Product at Market Prices

Year	Latin America	Argentina	Brazil	Chile	Colombia	Mexico	Venezuela
1929	n.a.*	17.8	11.3	31.2	18.0	14.2	n.a.*
1939	n.a.*	10.0	5.6	12.9	12.9	5.9	24.5
1946	9.5	6.4	5.9	11.7	11.0	11.1	25.7
1947	12.4	11.7	8.7	12.6	13.8	10.6	34.3
1948	10.8	10.5	6.8	10.8	11.5	8.8	37.8
1949	9.6	6.7	6.4	12.2	9.6	8.2	37.8
1950	9.9	7.3	7.3	9.0	11.4	8.0	35.4
1951	11.3	7.8	10.3	10.5	10.4	9.2	32.3
1952	10.3	6.0	8.9	9.5	10.1	8.9	31.9
1953	9.5	4.6	6.6	8.9	13.4	8.4	35.1
1954	10.0	5.0	7.4	8.7	14.0	7.9	35.0
1955	9.4	5.4	5.4	9.3	13.7	7.4	34.2
1956	9.5	4.9	5.5	9.8	11.5	8.2	34.1
1957	10.5	5.9	6.1	10.1	8.9	8.2	43.0
1958	9.3	5.6	5.4	8.8	7.4	7.4	38.0
1959	8.9	5.1	5.6	9.0	7.6	6.9	35.3
1960	8.8	6.2	5.8	12.5	9.3	7.3	24.3
1961	8.7	7.2	4.9	14.7	9.2	7.2	24.0
1962	n.a.*	7.1	4.5	11.3	8.8	6.8	21.4
1963	n.a.*	5.5	4.4	12.8	8.2	7.0	19.4

Source: Economic Commission for Latin America, *The Process of Industrialization in Latin America, Statistical Annex.* (Santiago, Chile: 19 January 1966), ST/ECLA/Conf. 23/L.2/Add. 2. Tables 1–5, p. 5. Note: These coefficients represent the relationship between the c.i.f. value of imports of goods and services in dollars at 1960 prices and the gross domestic product at market prices in terms of 1960 dollars, calculated for each country at the parity exchange rates applied in the present study. The data on imports are based on the foreign trade yearbooks of the various countries, and the series used as a basis for determining the gross domestic product were obtained from the national accounts of the countries concerned.
*n.a. = not available.

one-third of the total "imports" in 1963. To say the least, the relevance for a policy on industrialization of including outflows for such items as travel and investment in calculating an import-substitution coefficient is not apparent.[15]

Despite the uncertainties of the data used to describe import substitution, the growth rate of imports has been less than the overall growth rate for Latin America during the postwar period. Thus, the observation that im-

[15] The same technique of comparing imported goods *and services* is used in the much quoted article on "The Growth and Decline of Import Substitution in Brazil," *Economic Bulletin for Latin America* (March, 1964), Table 4, p. 15.

port substitution has occurred could be supported statistically. But the growth rate of *exports* has also been less than the overall economic growth rate for Latin America. And a conclusion that *export substitution* has occurred could also be supported. Thus, the question arises as to how meaningful such concepts are for studies of industrialization.

Obviously, some minimum limit on imports exists for a specific country, although the case of the Soviet Union suggests that under special circumstances the minimum may be close to zero. But a much more complex analysis than the conventional coefficient of import substitution is required to identify this minimum. The minimum will vary with many factors, such as endowment of resources, success in exploring for resources, technological trends in utilization of resources, size of country, stage of development, economic structure, and so forth. Also, the minimum as expressed by a coefficient may be lower when growth is rapid than when gross domestic product increases slowly. In short, the general conclusion is too general and cannot be accepted as a significant and firm indication of prospects for industrial development in Latin America.

Is There an Inherent Tendency for Import Substitution to Slow Down?

Although my general conclusion is that the import-substitution, export-industry framework is inadequate for strategies of industrialization, it is hard to resist the temptation to challenge the view that import-substitution industries have an inherent tendency to slow down.[16] This phenomenon has occurred frequently, but it may have resulted more from poor implementation of policy than from inherent weaknesses. The impact on industrialization and the duration of the dynamism of import-substitution industries will vary greatly with the way in which the import-substitution policy is applied.

If the industries being given protection are legitimate infant industries and have potentialities for becoming economically viable, they can retain a high rate of growth by eventually becoming export industries. Furthermore, the conclusion that, after the rapid spurt of substituting for imports, the growth of new industries will slow down to a pace commensurate with the growth of domestic demand overlooks several possibilities for enlarging domestic demand.

The conventional view implicitly assumes that demand is fixed for a specific product at each level of gross domestic product. Yet, demand may be price elastic. And after a learning period, an import-substitution industry may be able to reduce its prices and maintain a rapid growth in output. Also, demand may be stimulated through encouraging complementary in-

---

[16] The continuing importance ascribed to this aspect of the import-substitution, export-industry polemic is demonstrated by the comprehensive and highly sophisticated analysis of David Felix, devoted almost exclusively to the "diminishing dynamics of ISI" and published as recently as 1968. See David Felix, *loc. cit.*

stitutional changes. For example, in an early stage, a domestic automobile industry may be able to expand its sales rapidly even though adequate facilities do not exist for consumer financing. As the pent-up demand becomes satisfied, the market can be enlarged by providing consumer financing, so that a rapid rate of growth in production can be maintained. A wide range of other possibilities for enlarging the market may also exist through advertising, promotion, and the improvement of the distributive system.

The point is that inherent weaknesses in the process are not necessarily there if the industries are well selected and if opportunities for enlarging the market through pricing and other marketing techniques are exploited. Furthermore, if the import-substitution industries are well selected in terms of backward and forward linkages, a slowing down in demand for the initial industry may be offset by the rapid growth of a supplier's or user's activity that has become viable as a result of the growth of the initial industry.

Import Substitution and the Infant-Industry Approach

In terms of implementation techniques, import substitution is similar to the traditional protectionist and infant-industry approach to industrialization. The infant-industry approach argues that the late-comer countries must provide a period of protection to infant industries for the time-consuming learning process and for the development of an efficient scale of production.[17] The infant-industry approach generally assumes implicitly, if not explicitly, that the new industries have a potential for becoming economically viable without protection after the learning period and after reaching a feasible scale of operations.

Thus, the protectionist and infant-industry approach is generally directed toward encouraging industries expected to become economically viable or to yield returns to the nation in terms of increased employment or other benefits that outweigh the subsidy that might be required on a continuing basis. In practice, the import-substitution approach with its balance-of-payments genesis has emphasized the industries' savings potential in foreign exchange and has frequently overlooked the question of long-run viability of the industries being established.

Being neither a comprehensive approach to balance-of-payments problems nor to industrialization, import-substitution programs have resulted in poorly conceived efforts at industrial development as well as inadequate balance-of-payments programs. Arising out of adverse external circumstances, as Dr. Prebisch notes, "these measures have been applied especially to non-essential imports that can be dispensed with or postponed.

---

[17] Still one of the most eloquent arguments for protecting an infant industry is Alexander Hamilton's, *Report on Manufactures,* communicated to the House of Representatives (December 5, 1791).

Thus home production of these goods has been encouraged, absorbing scarce production resources, often regardless of cost." He then goes on to suggest, "A more rational policy would have given priority to import substitution in respect of goods which could be produced under more favorable conditions than others, not only consumer goods, as has generally been the case, but also raw materials and intermediate and capital goods."[18] He might also have added that a more rational import-substitution program would have included agricultural development, minerals development, planning of external debt, and a wide range of new industrial possibilities for saving or earning foreign exchange.

That import-substitution policies have been poorly implemented in terms of both industrialization and foreign exchange objectives is not unique to Latin America. Professor Mason's study of economic development in India and Pakistan concludes that industrialization in both India and Pakistan has laid heavy emphasis on import substitution and that the import-substitution policies paid little attention to considerations of comparative advantage. "In shaping the incentives offered to particular types of domestic production, there is little evidence that the terms on which domestic resources are likely to be exchanged for foreign resources were seriously taken into account in either country. In fact, it is only a slight exaggeration to say that, in India, official opinion holds that no domestic cost is too high a price to pay for import saving."[19]

Reinterpretation

This brief reexamination of the debate on industrialization through import substitution versus export industries suggests a set of conclusions somewhat different from those widely accepted, particularly in Latin America.

1. The desire in less-developed countries to accelerate industrialization has been translated only gradually into comprehensive programs of industrial development. In fact, the recent experience of most countries in industrialization has been characterized more by an absence of a coherent and long-range plan for industrialization than by import substitution as an affirmative strategy of *industrialization*.

2. Continuing concern over persisting balance-of-payments problems and foreign-exchange shortages has resulted in actions which were taken primarily for balance-of-payments reasons, but which had the effect of encouraging import-substitution industries. The implementation of these foreign-exchange measures, however, was generally not accomplished by expertise in industrialization. Thus, many shortcomings from the standpoint of industrialization — such as the foster-

[18] Raul Prebisch, *op. cit.*, pp. 21–22.
[19] Edward S. Mason, *Economic Development in India and Pakistan* (Cambridge: Center for International Affairs, Harvard University, September, 1966), p. 42.

ing of high-cost, inefficient plants producing luxury-type goods — [20] may be ascribed to inadequacies in planning and implementation rather than to inherent defects in the policies.

3. As an event, import substitution results from many factors other than governmental measures for import substitution. Thus, the popular tendency to evaluate import substitution as a strategy for industrialization by measuring the total amount of import substitution that has occurred in a country is highly questionable.

4. The balance-of-payments framework for discussions on policy has led to a preference for export industries as a logical alternative for import substitution, whereas a direct approach to industrial development results in a different and broader range of alternatives.

A Direct Approach to Industrial Development

If the import-substitution, export-industries framework has been of questionable validity and effectiveness for orienting efforts at industrialization, as has been argued above, what are the implications of the analysis? Are the observations merely interesting or do they have practical significance for the less-developed countries?

The available resources for development planning are relatively scarce, and the capacity for decision-making and implementation is limited. A practical issue, therefore, is whether the scarce resources still being allocated to the ISI-EI approach are likely to produce better results if shifted toward other directions. Such a shift may be difficult because of the large vested intellectual interest in the foreign-exchange framework.

If new directions are indicated, what should they be? One major change might be for planners of industrial development to give more attention to issues of economic viability and potentials for efficient operations than to targets of specific products or industries. Much activity in industrial identification has been based on an industry's short-range effects on foreign exchange rather than on an industry's long-term potentials for growth, as the one-time proponents of import substitution are now recognizing. Similar activity has been stimulated by subjective preferences for "basic industry," however defined — on the grounds that whatever is "basic" is better than the opposite, "nonbasic," I suppose — or by priorities for "dynamic" rather than "traditional" industries.

Programs of industrial development should also recognize that growth can be secured by encouraging fuller utilization of existing industrial capacity and by the expansion of established industries. The tendency all too often

---

[20] For an outstanding, but not necessarily representative, case of import-substitution shortcomings, see Leland L. Johnson, "Problems of Import Substitution: The Chilean Automotive Industry," *Economic Development and Cultural Change,* Part 1 (January, 1967), pp. 202–216.

is to concentrate heavily on the identification and encouragement of new industries.

A greater concern for the general encouragement of industrial efficiency may lead to a wide range of possibilities for effective governmental action. Many of the crucial factors affecting industrial efficiency in the less-developed countries have to do with the external environment and external economies. Governmental action to improve communications and transportation, to expand the training of workers and business executives, to provide more efficient capital markets and reduce the cost of money, to modernize the legal system, to stimulate competition — even by reducing tariffs — and to improve the efficiency of governmental regulation may be extremely productive in creating conditions under which either existing or new industries can operate efficiently.

Programs of industrialization should recognize that entrepreneurship is a key requirement and often an extremely scarce resource. Consequently, the strategy must include a comprehensive program that creates favorable conditions for indigenous entrepreneurships to emerge and become effective, that supplies entrepreneurship in some cases through governmental enterprise, and that makes use of foreign private enterprise as a source of, and training experience for, local entrepreneurship. In other words, the guidelines for industrialization should become economic viability, potentials for expansion, and industrial efficiency with emphasis on external economies and the encouragement of entrepreneurship.

Foreign-exchange planning should receive major but separate attention. It should consider tourism, the flight of domestic capital, the control and scheduling of foreign debt, potentials for export expansion, and even the pros and cons of attracting foreign private investment from the standpoint of the balance of payments. Export expansion may indicate a need for market research, better quality control and adaptation of design, as well as the development of a capacity for export sales and distribution. In some cases, export incentives may be effective and justified. In other situations, the export marketing ability of international business firms may be sought through encouraging the establishment of jointly owned ventures or even wholly foreign-owned operations in the country. But a necessary condition for securing self-generating industrial growth and maximum possibilities of export is to promote and achieve high levels of industrial efficiency.

Both the ISI-EI and the direct approach to industrialization have the same ultimate goal — that of accelerating overall economic growth. But the recommended paths to be followed, the relative importance of the criteria used as guidelines, and the patterns of industrialization actually achieved can differ greatly.

The ISI-EI approach starts from the conviction or assumption that foreign exchange is the principal and overriding constraint on economic growth. It has seized upon the industrial sector as a field of action where rapid and relatively easy results for the balance of payments appear feasible; and in the process, it has generally neglected many other possibilities outside the industrial sector for improving the situation in foreign exchange. The approach segregates the domestic from the foreign market, thus failing to take into account the historically verified process whereby industries can begin by substituting for imports and later evolve into significant exporters. The choice of industries to be encouraged has been based upon their past or present importance as users of foreign exchange. Even though the ISI-EI has increasingly shown concern for the economic viability, prospects of expansion, and potential efficiency of types of industries being encouraged, foreign-exchange goals, generally short-range, almost invariably prevail as the decisive consideration.

The patterns in industrialization resulting from the foreign-exchange approach are likely to be characterized by broad diversification and a high degree of self-sufficiency. For a large country, diversification may not be detrimental because the large domestic market may justify productive units of efficient size. But for small countries, the pattern of industrialization may mean small, uneconomic units producing at high costs and with limited possibilities for becoming competitive in foreign markets.

In contrast, the direct approach to industrial development is more likely to bring about specialization in a smaller number of fields selected on the basis of comparative advantage. Industries to be encouraged are identified on the basis of comparative advantage in locational factors, such as availability and proximity to sources of raw materials, manpower, or markets. The concept of the market used to evaluate possibilities for industrialization is not segregated as to domestic or foreign markets, and promising prospects for industrial expansion may be based on a combination of both domestic and foreign markets or on an evolution over time from one to the other.

The important difference from the foreign-exchange approach, however, is that the direct and comprehensive industrial-development approach leads governments into a much wider range of actions beyond manipulating tariffs, quotas, and other protective devices. The direct approach focuses heavy attention on the many opportunities for governmentally supported activities that can increase industrial efficiency, such as: educational programs for workers and management; development of capital markets; making facilities for transportation and communications more efficient; and expanding the capacity of electric power systems so that industries need not rely on their own high-cost, small independent power units.

The devotees of the foreign-exchange approach will defensively respond, "Isn't it true that the foreign-exchange bottleneck is generally the major constraint on development, and won't any type of strategy for industrialization still end up facing this problem?" The widely held conviction that foreign exchange is the principal bottleneck may or may not be true, depending upon the country. And it may have become a self-fulfilling prophecy in some cases because the foreign-exchange authorities have been devoting their attention to planning industrialization rather than to taking advantage of the potentials outside of the industrial sector for improving the situation in foreign exchange, such as better scheduling of external debt. But even accepting the conventional wisdom on foreign exchange, the strong possibility exists that the direct approach to industrial development implemented by experts in industrial development can solve the foreign-exchange problem better than the ISI-EI approach. An industrial sector characterized by efficiency, specialization, and comparative advantages can be both an effective substitute for imports and a promising contributor to foreign-exchange earnings through exports. To structure the issue of strategy for industrialization as a choice between import substitution or export industries is indeed a false dichotomy.

18

The Interaction of Economic, Political, and Social Aspects of Development in Egypt and the Fertile Crescent

*Sidney S. Alexander**

We in the United States, however much we reject Marxism, have come to hold, not by conversion but by instinct born of our national experience, a Marxist interpretation of history, a belief that economic factors are the driving forces in social and political development. Nowhere is that belief more clearly evident than in our foreign policy, which has strongly relied on economic measures for at least a generation. In the 1930s and 40s Cordell Hull made the freeing of international trade a prime instrument of American diplomacy until means became ends and the merit of a policy came to be rated by its efficacy in reducing trade restrictions. After World War II, as we became more deeply involved as a global power, development aid became a cornerstone of our foreign policy. Just as, in the inter-war period, Britain and France, their world primacy presumably attributable to their democratic institutions, helped propagate parliamentary government throughout the underdeveloped world in response to the aspirations of the indigenous societies, so the United States after World War II is engaged in sharing with the underdeveloped world the secret of our own success, growth of per capita income, eagerly desired by the peoples concerned.[1] After its manifest success in the Marshall Plan, aid in economic development came to be viewed as a sound policy for the United States in all the underdevel-

The author prepared this manuscript under the RAND-Resources for the Future Research Program on the Middle East, supported by the Ford Foundation.

* Massachusetts Institute of Technology

[1] I owe this observation to Morroe Berger, *The Arab World Today,* Doubleday, New York, 1962 and 1964, pp. 296–7 (1964 ed.).

oped world, in the Middle East as well as elsewhere, without any thorough-going analysis of the general mechanisms presumed to be at work.[2] It is the object of this paper to investigate the interaction of economic factors with political and social in the development of Egypt and the Fertile Crescent since 1800.

The area under consideration, labeled on American maps as "The Bible Lands," is now occupied by six countries: Egypt (United Arab Republic), Iraq, Israel, Jordan, Lebanon, and Syria. The territory occupied by the last four countries may also be referred to as Greater Syria, which, together with Iraq forms the Fertile Crescent. At the end of the eighteenth century, as our drama opens, these lands were outlying districts of the decaying Ottoman Empire, supporting altogether a population of only some 5 million people, about 2½ million in Egypt, and a little over 1 million each in Greater Syria and Iraq (Table 18–1). Compared to their golden ages in the past, they were depopulated. In Roman times Egypt supported about 8 million people, and Greater Syria 5 or 6. In the eleventh century of the Christian era, Iraq alone had a population estimated at 15 million; its more fervent nationals often claim it to have had 30.[3]

Economic Development

At various times in the nineteenth century, these countries embarked upon a course of modern development that will have brought their aggregate 1970 population close to twelve times that of 1800, as compared with a ten-fold increase in world population over the past 2000 years.[4] While we have no statistical measure of their per capita incomes until recent years, it can nevertheless be inferred that, low as they are, they are now from 2 to 2½ times what they were in 1800; the aggregate regional product is, accordingly, 25 to 30 times as great.[5] Although these countries are still under-developed as measured by their 1965 per capita GNPs ranging from $158

[2] See Nadav Safran, *From War to War*, Pegasus, New York, 1969, p. 132 for the philosophy underlying the aid policy to the UAR in the Kennedy administration.

[3] Charles Issawi, *The Economic History of the Middle East, 1800–1914*, University of Chicago Press, Chicago 1966, p. 3, for Syria and Egypt. The 15 million population figure for Iraq "in ancient times" is attributed to Seton Lloyd, a former director of antiquities in Iraq, (Kurt Grunwald and Joachim O. Ronall, *Industrialization in the Middle East*, Council for Middle Eastern Affairs Press, New York 1960, p. 45). The 30 million figure for ancient Iraq is very frequently encountered, for example Lowder-milk (also quoted in Grunwald and Ronall, loc. cit.,) and El-Hadithy and El-Dujaili of the Ministry of Agrarian reform, Baghdad, in Mohamad Riad El-Ghonemy, *Land Policy in the Near East*, FAO, Rome 1967, p. 218.

[4] W. S. Woytinsky and E. S. Woytinsky, *World Population and Production*, N.Y., 1953.

[5] Charles Issawi, in "Economic Growth in the Arab World Since 1800: Some Observations," *Middle East Economic Papers* 1964, Economic Research Institute, American University of Beirut, hazards the guess that per capita incomes in the Arab world may have doubled over the last hundred or one hundred and fifty years. (p. 27).

Table 18–1   Population in the Central Middle East

	Egypt	Greater Syria	Iraq	Total
	(Millions)			
In Antiquity	8	6	15	29
1800	2.5	1.2	1	5
1850	4.5	1.4	1.2	7
1900	10.0	3	2	15
1938	16.4	5.4	3.9	25
1970	34.5	14	9.7	58

Sources:
Egypt
Antiquity: Charles Issawi, *The Economic History of the Middle East* 1800–1914, University of Chicago Press, Chicago and London, 1966, p. 3.
1800: Alfred Bonné, *State and Economics in the Middle East*, Routledge and Kegan Paul, London, 2nd ed., 1955, p. 162; also Patrick O'Brien, "The Long-Term Growth of Agricultural Production in Egypt: 1821–1962," in P. M. Holt, ed., *Political and Social Change in Modern Egypt*, Oxford University Press, London, 1968, pp. 174–5, based on Jomard.
1850: 4.46 in 1846 according to Régny (O'Brien, loc. cit.)
1900, 1938: Official censuses, interpolated.
1970: U.N., *Provisional Report on World Population Prospects as Assessed in 1963*, N. Y., 1964 (ST/SOA/SER.R/7)
Greater Syria
Antiquity: Issawi, loc. cit., "five to six million."
1800: Author's conjecture; Issawi, loc. cit.: "perhaps two million," Bonné, loc. cit., 0.8 for Syria (presumably includes Lebanon) and 0.3 for Palestine; Kurt Grunwald and Joachim O. Ronall, *Industrialization in the Middle East*, Council for Middle Eastern Affairs Press, New York, 1960, p. 39, give 0.5 for (modern) Syria, 0.3 for Palestine (pp. 39, 45, 46).
1850: Author's conjecture; Philip K. Hitti, "The Impact of the West on Syria and Lebanon in the 19th Century," in Guy S. Metraux and Francois Crouzet, *The New Asia*, The New American Library, New York and Toronto, 1965, p. 95, gives 1¼ million for 1840.
1900: Author's estimate; Grunwald and Ronall, op. cit., give 1.5 for (modern) Syria, 0.75 for Lebanon, 0.6 for Palestine, presumably excluding Transjordan; Hitti, loc. cit., gives 4 million; Bonné gives 2.4 for Syria (presumably including Lebanon) and 0.6 for Palestine.
1938: Grunwald and Ronall, op. cit., give 2.8 for (modern) Syria, 0.85 for Lebanon, 1.5 for Palestine (1940), to which we may add about 0.35 for Transjordan.
1970: U.N., op. cit.
Iraq
Antiquity: Seton Lloyd, quoted in Grunwald and Ronall, op. cit., p. 45; a figure of 30 million is frequently encountered.
1800: Bonné, loc. cit. Grunwald and Ronall, op. cit., p. 44.
1850: Author's estimate. Hasan in Issawi, op. cit., p. 155 gives 1.28 for 1867.
1900–1938: Hasan, loc. cit., (interpolated)
1970: U.N., op. cit.
Total
Rounded summation of country figures.

in Egypt to $437 in Lebanon, with Syria, Iraq and Jordan at $200 to $300,[6] they have nevertheless come a long way from their state in 1800.

Why was the area able to support, by 1938, a population five times that of 1800? That the population in 1800 was less than a fifth of what it was in ancient times may give us a lead to the most important factor in the nineteenth century increase of output and population. The depressed and stagnant economies of the region at the end of the eighteenth century can be attributed to the low state into which the institutional structures of the Ottoman Empire had fallen. In particular, the older feudal arrangements whereby the local fief-holders (sipahis, literally horsemen) furnished the Sultan a stipulated number of horsemen in proportion to the lands subject to their control, had been shifted to a system of monetary payments through tax farms, which were auctioned off for periods limited to the lifetime and satisfactory performance of the successful bidder.[7] It was in the tax farmer's interest to get as much out of the peasantry as possible during his tenure, with no afterthought to the long run preservation of the tax base. The consequences are exactly those predicted in the literature of political economy — long term interests were sacrificed for short, and in human terms, villages were abandoned and the countryside depopulated. Furthermore, the Bedouin, who constantly put pressure on the sedentary population, had, during the period of relative weakness of the central authority, extended their area of control and driven back the frontier between the desert and the sown. In Egypt the quarrels among the Mamluks for tax power over various areas had the same deleterious effects.[8] The major part of the sixfold increase in economic production in the nineteenth century is accordingly to be attributed to the greater security afforded to agriculture. While primary emphasis is usually placed on security against the Bedouin, security from rapacious tax-collectors and quarrelling overlords was probably far more important in the aggregate.

Other factors worked in the same direction. The opening up of trade with the West stimulated agriculture throughout the region, and afforded opportunity for realizing comparative advantage through specialized crops for export. In Lebanon silk production was expanded through the extended culture of the mulberry tree. In Egypt the outstanding development was the widespread adoption of cotton production for the world market as well as a general increase of output of other agricultural products based partly on the extension and improvement of irrigation and partly on better agricultural techniques.

[6] AID, *Statistics and Reports Division, Near East and South Asia: Economic Growth Trends,* November 1967, Table 1.

[7] Bernard Lewis, *The Emergence of Modern Turkey,* Oxford University Press, London, 1967 and 1968, p. 33 (1968 ed.).

[8] See Stanford J. Shaw, "Landholding and Land-tax Revenues in Ottoman Egypt" in P. M. Holt, ed., *Political and Social Change in Modern Egypt,* Oxford University Press, London, 1968, p. 102.

Some statistical evidence is available for Egypt, though its quality is suspect, indicating that agricultural production during 1872–78 was 5.6 times that of 1821.[9] Labor inputs about doubled over the period, and the cropped area increased by about 80%, partly through multiple cropping and partly through a 56% increase in cultivated area. The greatly increased value yields per acre cropped and per man, at constant prices, are partly to be explained by a large shift in the composition of output toward higher-valued crops, in particular toward cotton from grains. Had it not been for the shift toward cotton the value-weighted volume of agricultural production would have quadrupled rather than increasing over fivefold.[10] But that implies that output per acre cropped in grains must have more than doubled, which seems incredible against the background of other information on the conduct of agriculture over that period.

The transformation of Egypt from a grain subsistence economy to one dominated by a cash export crop is usually credited to Muhammad Ali (1805–49). He abolished tax farming, so that peasants came to pay their taxes directly to the government. He undertook irrigation works and opened the clogged canals; he encouraged, indeed commanded, the planting of long-staple cotton.[11] On the other hand, Muhammad Ali established, among other monopolies, a monopoly in the purchase of cotton from farmers at prices fixed well below the international price. Whether there might not have been an equally strong, though possibly a slower, response of cotton culture in Egypt to the world demand if the high world prices had been transmitted to the local markets without the whips of Muhammad Ali's men, we cannot know. In any case, the basic economic conditions which made it highly remunerative for Egypt to specialize in cotton were strongly reinforced by the direct political action of the government commanding expansion of cotton acreage. There were, however, extensive increases in the production of other products, not commanded by the government. Wheat production is estimated to have increased by 1872–8 to 3.3 times the 1821 production; corn (maize) to 6.7 times its 1821 output, and barley and beans to have more than doubled their 1821 output.[12]

While agricultural production, valued at constant prices, was increasing

[9] This is a rough estimate of the comparative values of output at fixed prices, based on data for various crops presented by Patrick O'Brien, in Holt, op. cit., p. 179. O'Brien's index derived therefrom showing a twelvefold increase over this period greatly exaggerates the increase, because he weighted quantity relatives by average value of production over a late period instead of the initial period. The above estimate was derived from a rough calculation weighting the reported physical production by representative prices of the products in the 1920s.

[10] O'Brien estimates (p. 184) that it would only have tripled, but this seems inconsistent with his basic data.

[11] Charles Issawi, *Egypt in Revolution,* Oxford University Press, London and New York, 1963, p. 22.

[12] The 1872–8 estimates may be on the high side. See O'Brien, op. cit., p. 167, comments on 1875 figures.

more than fivefold from 1821 to the decade of the 1870s, the total population was doubling as was the rural population. If, as would seem likely, average productivity increased in non-agricultural as well as in agricultural activities, aggregate output must have at least quadrupled and output per capita would then have increased to well over twice its 1821 level.

After the 1870s, the rural population seems to have grown faster than agricultural output, so that output per farm worker was lower in 1939 than in the 70s. Aggregate output per capita of the economy at large apparently also failed to show an upward trend from the late nineteenth century until after World War II. This generally held view can be substantiated for the period from 1919 to 1943 for which modern estimates are available.[13] From 1956 to 1965, however, output grew at about 5½ percent a year and population at 2½ percent. Only for the half century after 1821 and for the decade after 1956 is there evidence of any substantial growth of income produced per capita above previous peak levels. For the rest of the time the growth pattern was Malthusian. In the meantime, new classes arose, and the middle class was expanded, so that a sustained or even an increased average per capita income might well be consistent with a deterioration of conditions at the lowest level, that of the fellahin. Some authors judge that just this occurred from 1914 to 1960.[14]

Even less quantitative information is available on the economic development of the Fertile Crescent up to World War II, but it seems that a similar pattern was followed, though with local variations. The principal exception was Lebanon, where output presumably grew substantially more rapidly than population, so that its current output per capita is well over twice that of Egypt, and substantially higher than Syria's or Iraq's, especially if oil output is excluded from the latter's national product. In all cases there was a great increase of output consequent on opening up market sectors whose expansion was accompanied also by growing security of the producers. But the other countries had nothing to match the cotton boom of mid-century Egypt.

For the period after World War II, indicative national accounts for four of the Arab countries of the area are shown in Tables 18–2 through 18–5. In all four countries output grew much faster than population. Lebanon had a similar development. Jordan's economic growth was most rapid in proportional terms, but its initial base was very small. Even Syria, whose growth rate was lower, doubled its output from 1953 to 1968, on the top of substantial growth from 1939. In each country agriculture remained, in the

---

[13] Bent Hansen and Girgis Marzouk, *Development and Economic Policy in the UAR (Egypt)*, North Holland Publishing Co., Amsterdam, 1965, p. 3. Riad estimates a substantially unchanged per capita income 1882–1914, and 1914–1960, but this reflects assumptions more than independent evidence; see Hassan Riad (pseud.), *L'Egypte Nasserienne;* Les Editions de Minuit, Paris, 1964, p. 163.

[14] Riad, op. cit., p. 163. See also Charles Issawi, *Egypt in Revolution*, Oxford University Press, London and New York, 1963, p. 121.

Table 18-2 United Arab Republic: Industrial Origin of Gross
Domestic Product at 1959-60 Prices

(£E Millions)*

	1952-3	1964-5
Agriculture	337	477
Industry and Electricity	175	407
Construction	28	77
Transport, Communications and Storage	58	158
Trade and Finance	101	152
Dwellings	59	80
Other Services	228	333
(including Government and Public Utilities)		
Total Gross Domestic Product	986	1,684
Population (millions)	21.7	29.0
GDP per capita (£E)	45.5	58.1

*£E1 = $2.84 (1959-60)
Sources:
1. 1952-53: Donald C. Mead, *Growth and Structural Change in the Egyptian Economy*, Irwin, Homewood, Illinois, 1967, Table I-A-8, derived from Bent Hansen and Donald Mead, "The National Income of the U.A.R. (Egypt), 1939-1962," Memo No. 355 (Cairo: Institute of National Planning, July 1963), Table 8. The source figures have been adjusted to 1959-60 prices from 1954 prices by use of sectoral "implicit deflators" derived from the ratio of the figure for each industrial sector in 1959-60 at 1959-60 prices, as given in source (2) to the corresponding figure for 1959-60 in 1954 prices from source (1). This procedure embodies in the "implicit deflators" not only the difference in the price levels concerned, but also differences in the definitions of the industrial sectors. In effect, the 1952-3 figures are extrapolated backward from the 1959-60 figures from source (2) on the basis of the sectoral growth rates from 1952-3 derived from source (1).
2. 1964-65: Bent Hansen, "Planning and Economic Growth," in P. J. Vatikiotis, ed., *Egypt Since the Revolution*, Praeger, N.Y. 1968, pp. 22 and 24.

early 1950s, the leading single industrial sector (except for oil in Iraq), but non-agricultural activities, in the aggregate, came to account for a major, and rapidly increasing, share of total output.

It would be misleading to say these countries were being industrialized, although manufacturing industry did expand in all of them — not quite enough to overtake agriculture even in the United Arab Republic, and it was far behind in Syria, Iraq and Jordan. But there was a general fleshing out of the economy, with almost all sectors gaining on agriculture. "Services and Government" including defense expenditures typically grew most rapidly, but other "modern" sectors grew vigorously as well.

It is clear that there is in all these countries a dynamic radically different from that of earlier years. With governments dedicated to modernization, and often with the aid of capital from abroad, output at last has been able to grow even faster than the accelerated rate of population growth, an acceleration partially a consequence of the growth of output itself. More generally, the accelerations of both output and of population are the con-

Table 18–3   Iraq: Industrial Origin of Gross Domestic Product at 1962
Factor Costs

*(Millions of Iraqi Dinars)**

	1953	1966
Agriculture, etc.	112	156
Mining and Quarrying	113	302
Manufacturing	17	61
Construction	13	19
Trade and Finance	23	67
Transport, Communications		
Water and Power	28	69
Property Income	12	18
Public Administration	29	96
Services	21	57
Gross Domestic Product (at factor cost)	368	846
Less: Factor Cost paid abroad	61	138
Gross National Product at Factor Cost	307	708
Gross Domestic Product		
excluding mining and quarrying	255	544
Population (millions)	5.6	8.4
GDP per capita (ID)		
excluding mining and quarrying	45.5	64.7

*ID1 = $2.80 (1962)
Sources:
1. 1966: Central Bureau of Statistics, Ministry of Planning, Iraq, preliminary unpublished study of August 1968.
2. 1953: U.N., *Yearbook of National Accounts Statistics*, 1966. Data at 1956 factor
costs were adjusted to 1962 factor costs and sectoral definitions of source (1) by "implicit
deflators" derived from the ratio of the 1962 figure for each sector at 1962 factor costs
from source (1) to the corresponding 1962 figure at 1956 factor costs from source (2).
1953 "factor cost paid abroad" scaled up from 1953 current factor cost figure of 57.6 in
rough proportion to the adjustment in gross domestic product.

sequences of those social, political and economic changes which we are
calling "development." Let us turn next to the social and ideational transformations that accompanied that development.

Social and Ideational Aspects

The political and economic aspects of development are usually described
in terms of what is built up, the social in terms of what is broken down. The
old traditions and social links that bind the society together must be broken,
it seems, before new ones more in keeping with the new economic and
political conditions can be forged. Yet, the social changes in Egypt that
accompanied development in the nineteenth century "changed only partly
the life and organization of Egyptian society. The traditional family and

Table 18–4 Jordan: Industrial Origin of Gross Domestic Product at Current Prices[1]

*(Millions of Jordanian Dinars)**

	1954	1966
Agriculture	13.5[2]	27.2[2]
Mining, Manufacturing and Electricity	4.0	19.5
Construction	1.5	9.3
Transport, Trade and Banking	15.6	46.1
Ownership of Dwellings	3.5	11.2
Public Administration and Defense	8.5	22.0
Services	4.2	13.9
GDP (at factor cost)	50.8[2]	149.3[2]
Population (millions)	1.4	2.1
GDP per capita (JD)	36.3	71.2

*JD1 = $2.80 (1966)
Sources:
Michael Mazur, unpublished dissertation materials, M.I.T., Spring 1969, derived from:
1954: R. S. Porter, Economic Trends in Jordan 1954–1959, Beirut, 1961 (mimeographed).
1966: Government of Jordan, Department of Statistics, *The National Accounts 1959–1966*, Amman, 1967.
[1] Price rises were not significant in Jordan over this period so these figures may be taken as reasonable approximations to measures of growth in real terms.
[2] Agricultural figures at 1964 prices, smoothed to eliminate estimated effect of rainfall variability, so these figures differ slightly from figures in original sources.

religious community remained intact and the position of women in society did not change. Neither wealthy Egyptians nor the lower classes acquired the mentality of an industrial society. The social change brought about consisted almost entirely in the destruction of the traditional socio-economic framework, the dissolution of the tribe and the village community, the disappearance of the guilds and the abolition of slavery. Most of these developments occurred during the last two decades of the century."[15]

In the Fertile Crescent as well, possibly with a partial exception for the Christians in Lebanon, the process was similar. The socio-economic framework changed, as did the political, while the family and religious structures and the mental outlook were relatively stable, except among the urbanized middle and upper classes, principally in the twentieth century.

The transition to the market economy, we are told, did involve the dissolution of the village community with the consequent elimination of the "security formerly enjoyed by all peasants."[16] But the village community

[15] Gabriel Baer, "Social Change in Egypt: 1800–1914," in P. M. Holt, ed. *Political and Social Change in Modern Egypt*, Oxford University Press, London 1968, p. 160.
[16] Charles Issawi, "The Arab World's Heavy Legacy" *Foreign Affairs*, April 1965 reprinted in J. H. Thompson and R. D. Reischauer, *Modernization of the Arab World*, Van Nostrand, Princeton, New Jersey 1966, p. 17.

Table 18–5   Syria: Industrial Origin of Net Domestic Product at 1963
Factor Costs

(Millions of £S)*

	1953	1968
Agriculture	842	1,047
Industry (including Mining)	242	517
Construction	51	136
Transport	120	451
Commerce	391[1]	489
Finance	24	118
Dwellings	107	367
Administration and Defense	61	569
Services	130	342
Net Domestic Product	1,968	4,034
Population (millions)	3.7	5.7
NDP per capita (£S)	531	706

*£S1 = $0.26 (selling rate, 1962–1964)
Sources:
1. 1968: Central Bureau of Statistics, Syria, as reported in *L'Economie et les Finances des Pays Arabes*, April, 1969.
2. 1953: *U.N., Yearbook of National Accounts Statistics*, 1966. Data at 1956 factor costs were adjusted to 1963 factor costs and the sectoral definitions of source (1) by "implicit deflators" derived from the ratio of the 1956 figure for each sector at 1963 factor costs from source (1) to the corresponding 1956 figure at 1956 factor costs from source (2).
[1]This figure is suspect. It seems to me at least 25% too high relative to 1968.

survived with strong vitality down to our days, and it still survives. Its community was dissolved only in the technical sense that in previous days the village lands were periodically redistributed among the villagers and "the village was collectively responsible for the payment of a fixed tax quota imposed on it and for the supply of labor for public works,"[17] while now land ownership and tax liability are personal, in the western style. As a result, social mobility increased, and as only part of the population increase was absorbed in the extension of cultivation and the increase in its intensity, a large remainder found its way to the growing cities. There the pressure of the new in-migrants on the labor market together with the willingness of foreign entrepreneurs to hire laborers where they could get them cheapest led to the breakdown of the guild system which had formerly organized the economic life of the towns. The introduction of new techniques also worked powerfully in the same direction.[18]

The influx of European goods also contributed to the erosion of the handicraft guilds, while the dispersion of retail trade throughout the town

[17] Baer, op. cit., p. 142.
[18] Ibid., p. 144.

broke up the merchants' guilds, and the town-quarter lost its significance as a social unit. With the growing strength of the central government and its agent, the municipal government, the need for the security afforded by these gated town-quarters disappeared; furthermore, the high degree of autonomy they previously enjoyed would have interfered with efficient municipal administration, and with a more mobile population, the social homogeneity of the town-quarters was diluted. In general, the social and political structures came into a new equilibrium with the new economic arrangements and possibilities.

The migration to the cities which at various times in their respective developments occurred in all these countries reflected not only the pull of economic opportunity in the city but also the push of the miserable conditions in the country as population outran agricultural opportunities. The drive toward the city was not entirely economic, however. The classic reply of the Baghdad slum dweller to the question of why he stays under these terrible conditions is that here there is no oppressive shaykh.[19] Because of these economic and social pressures, we find in the cities not only those occupations which we should expect from the residence there of the bureaucracy and the rich landowners with an elaborate economic substructure to serve the needs of these classes as well as of those who serve *them,* but also a large class of people without any fixed employment.[20] It is estimated that in Cairo in 1962, about 37 percent of the population was in this social group.[21] This class along with other groups in the lower economic levels formed the basis of a mob which usually suffered quietly, but at critical junctures might come to play an important political role, as they did in helping to usher in revolutionary governments. In Egypt they participated in burning Cairo in January 1952, so helping to demonstrate the breakdown of government, and setting the stage for the military takeover. In Iraq they helped consolidate Kassim's position at the time of the 1958 coup and thereafter, and in Syria they played a similar role. With the ascendancy of military leadership, and with the development of "stage management" of the street mob, its independent influence seems to have been reduced, though it may still be a useful adjunct of one military faction as against another.

Urban development in Arab countries has frequently been characterized as "lopsided."[22] Instead of the general tendency known as Zipf's law, in

---

[19] Fuad Baali, "Social Factors in Iraqi Rural-Urban Migration," *American Journal of Economics and Society,* v. 25, No. 4, October 1966, p. 362. See also Doris G. Phillips, "Rural-to-Urban Migration in Iraq," *Economic Development and Cultural Change,* July 1959.

[20] Baer, op. cit., p. 156.

[21] Hassan Riad, (pseud.), *L'Egypte Nasserienne,* Les Éditions de Minuit, Paris 1964, p. 41.

[22] United Nations Economic and Social Office in Beirut, *Studies on Selected Development Problems in Various Countries in the Middle East,* United Nations, New York 1967 (67.II.C.9), p. 34.

which the ratio of the largest city to successive cities on a list arranged in decreasing order of size roughly follows the pattern of successive integers, we find that there is in each country one or two very large metropolitan centers relative to that country's total population and then a few smaller cities and a mass of very small rural localities. The one or two leading cities play a strong political role, Cairo and Alexandria in Egypt, Beirut in Lebanon, Damascus, Aleppo, Homs-Hama in Syria, Baghdad, and possibly also Mosul and Basra in Iraq. Domestic politics in Arab countries is typically city politics, even though the population is predominantly rural.

One transformation that was political, economic and social all in one was the change in land tenure — the shift from tribal and village ownership subject to tax farming to private property Western style. In Egypt the first intermediate step was taken by Muhammad Ali, who massacred the Mamluk leaders and abolished the tax farms. He gained control of almost all the land of Egypt, by confiscation where claims were doubtful or insecure, otherwise with compensation "real or promised."[23] He redistributed the land to peasants in life estates subject to land tax. Some estates were granted his retainers, a practice continued by his successors. As the latter failed to exercise their powers in nearly so forceful a way as Muhammad Ali, there developed a group of powerful landowners with political influence and power of their own. These great landowners apparently consolidated their position between 1850 and 1870.[24] By the late nineteenth century there was, in effect, private property in land in Egypt with a high concentration of ownership in city-dwelling landlords.

In Syria and Iraq, the same result was reached by a different route. Largely in the period of foreign domination there was a tendency to replace the ancient village or tribal forms of land tenure by title registered in the name of individuals. The old system of land tenure was distorted to fit the new categories, and in the distortion the shaykhs, the local village or tribal chieftains, managed to get the land registered in their names. Today in Iraq "shaykh" means landlord rather than tribal chief.[25] Alternatively, the peasants might for various reasons, sometimes associated with the avoidance of military conscription, or perhaps with their illiteracy and relative ignorance, have an agent in the town register the land in his own name rather than in theirs. Through one process or another, the great bulk of the land in most of these countries came to be held in large estates, although there were also numerous small holdings which accounted for only a small proportion of the cultivable land. The exception was Lebanon where a sturdy independent peasantry seems to have developed.

In this process too the economic relationship was consequent upon the political. In Iraq, for example, the position of the local chieftain was trans-

[23] J. N. D. Anderson, "Law Reform in Egypt: 1850–1950," in Holt, op. cit., p. 209.
[24] Riad, op. cit., p. 196.
[25] Baali, op. cit., p. 359.

formed from being first among others in an egalitarian village or tribal society to being the political boss of a district in a national polity. The parliament was essentially an assembly of sheikhs or their creatures who proceeded to vote themselves into a new system of land tenure, ironically, by legislation purporting to assure the peasant in his holding.

One of the most important social changes wrought by the economic and political development of these countries is the appearance of a new set of urban classes — the bourgeoisie. The newly developing economic and political activities required tradesmen and merchants, manufacturers, bureaucrats, and professional men. These urban middle and upper classes play a principal role in the development process. They developed the new life styles and the new ways of thought, as well as the political and intellectual leadership, that in interaction with the colonial powers transformed the political structures during the colonial period. In the subsequent, current, period of military rule, a small subset of these classes have become the military rulers, while a large subset became the "new class," the officials and the managers who run the political and economic administration under the military authority.

While a deep study of the development of thought patterns in these countries is beyond the scope of this paper, the main outline of the new outlook of the middle-class intelligentsia may be briefly characterized. Many, educated in the West, or in western schools in the area, adopted an essentially western intellectual outlook, conditioned of course by their Middle East origin and viewpoint. At first, these converts to western ways of thought were apostles of western liberalism and democracy which they wished to imitate in their own countries in cooperation with the West. Then, about the first quarter of this century, while imitation persisted, opposition to the West increasingly replaced the idea of cooperation.[26] This was clearly a direct ideological reaction to the experience of colonialism. However beneficial that experience may have been on the economic plane, the political context was one of humiliation for the Arabs, and their reaction was a struggle for self-respect in the form of anticolonialism. This feeling later combined with anti-Zionism into an Arab nationalism which was much stronger in its animus against colonialism and Zionism than in its drive for cohesion among the Arab countries. Then, especially after World War II, Arab nationalism gradually merged with Arab socialism so that the period up to 1939 has come to be called, somewhat nostalgically, "The Age of Liberalism" as a sign of a by-gone orientation. Arab socialism was attained pragmatically in Egypt as the Nasser regime felt impelled to follow up the "Egyptianization" of foreign owned enterprises with the thoroughgoing nationalization of all but the smallest Egyptian firms. It has since been fitted

[26] H. A. R. Gibb, "Near East Perspective: The Present and the Future," in T. Cuyler Young, *Near Eastern Culture and Society,* Princeton University Press, Princeton, New Jersey, 1951, p. 230.

out with an extensive rationalizing ideology. But its underlying ideational base is, quite simply, the desire for rapid industrialization, coupled with the belief that only an authoritarian government in full ownership of large scale enterprise can achieve this end.[27] These ideas are widespread, almost universal, among Arab intellectuals with the partial exception of the Lebanese.

The political, economic and social transformations which constitute the development process we are considering generated powerful strains against the fabric of Islam. The very basis of Islam was challenged by the western demonstration of military superiority.[28] Islam had thrived on conquest and on the feeling of superiority of the power granted by Allah, but it was very hard to believe that Allah had granted to the unbeliever the power that he came to exercise in the Arab lands. The Islamic version of "Render unto Caesar" is that to him who has power obedience is due. This doctrine, which we find rather curious, automatically converts *de facto* power into *de jure*. Actually, the recognition that Allah bestows dominion on whomever he wishes was acceptable to the religious establishment so long as political power was traditionally used only to maintain order, appoint qadis, and collect taxes, while the regulation of almost the entire conduct of life was left to the religious law, (the Shari'ah, or "straight path").[29] Thus the official doctrine amounted to "let him have power who has it, as long as you follow the Shari'ah." But now that the state was taking authority over aspects of life previously governed entirely by the religious law, and so challenging the Shari'ah, a new strain was developing, a conflict between the political power and the commands of the religious law itself.

The problem is intensified by the inflexibility of Islam, whose truths were revealed once and for all in full perfection, together with its comprehensiveness — covering both the spiritual and temporal. The temporal constraints of Islam on all forms of human behavior inhibited the social change required for adaptation to the new economic and political conditions. It is testimony to the vigor and adequacy of Islam that it has been an effective integrator of folkways for thirteen centuries. In the nineteenth and twentieth centuries, however, the strains began to tell.

One type of solution, the separation of church and state and the adoption of a secularist social policy, was actually achieved by force in Turkey, at least in urban areas. But even the radical Arab governments have not made a frontal assault on religious constraints on social behavior; they have offered lip service to religion while promoting secular institutions — so perpetuating the religious-secular dualisms that developed in the social, legal

[27] See Charles Issawi, "The Arab World's Heavy Legacy," *Foreign Affairs,* April 1965, reprinted in Thompson and Reischauer, op. cit.; also Yusif A. Sayigh, "Development: The Visible or the Invisible Hand?" *World Politics,* July, 1961.

[28] W. C. Smith, *Islam in Modern History,* Princeton University Press, Princeton, N. J. 1957, Ch. 1.

[29] Nadav Safran, *Egypt in Search of Political Community,* Harvard University Press, Cambridge, Massachusetts, 1961, p. 40.

and intellectual spheres in the late nineteenth and early twentieth centuries.

In the social sphere, the upper and middle classes met the problem by the modification or abandonment of the traditional life where it conflicted with the new economic and social conditions, while the lower classes continued to be bound by the old ways. In the intellectual sphere there was a comparable separation of paths, symbolized by Cairo University over against al-Azhar. The great majority of Arab intellectuals are now being educated in the secular tradition. In the law, the dualism took the form of parallel secular and religious codes and courts. New civil, penal, and commercial codes were promulgated by the governments, to be adjudicated in governmental courts, while the Shari'ah courts continued to apply the sacred law in the old traditional way, though increasingly confined to matters of personal status.[30] However, even those matters were eventually codified by the governments. The requirements of the new economic and social arrangements were thus accommodated while at least a nominal, and for a long while a substantial, role for Islamic doctrine and institutions was preserved.[31]

Political Development

Under the Ottoman Empire, the traditional local structures consisted of villages, town-quarters, town guilds and tribes functioning essentially as autonomous units. Only minimal administrative functions were vested in the local leadership of these units because tradition and Islamic law, or the laws and customs of the sects and minority groups organized into their respective "millets," prescribed the responsibilities and duties of all, so that, essentially, the society was self-administering. Each tribe, village, guild, or town-quarter had a shaykh, who was the sole upward link to higher authority and also the only downward link except for the qadi, or local magistrate. The latter was usually appointed by higher authority although his remuneration was derived from fees and bribes from the parties to adjudication, and his responsibility was to Islamic law embodied in the Koran and the Tradition, rather than to the appointive authority.

The central government's principal function was to exercise military power supported by, and supporting, a system of taxation. It fulfilled this function through appointed governors and subgovernors (pashas and amirs) who in turn had subadministrators (beys) under their appointment and, in particular, tax farmers (multazims) who were, by the eighteenth century, in many parts of the empire, selected by auction of the tax farms. The tax farmers would normally deal only with the shaykh or headman of the village or tribe who would then see to the allocation of the tax burden

[30] Anderson, op. cit., p. 217.
[31] See Richard H. Nolte, "The Rule of Law in the Arab Middle East," *The Muslim World*, October 1958, reprinted in Richard H. Nolte, ed., *The Modern Middle East*, Atherton Press, New York 1963.

within the community. Under the example of the West, and motivated principally by a desire to acquire the sort of military strength the West had demonstrated, there was gradually established in the nineteenth century a more pervasive influence and control of the central government. In Egypt this increased central control was initiated as a clear break with the past, through a revolutionary transformation of governmental arrangements by Muhammad Ali early in the century. In the rest of the Ottoman Empire it was approached by more gradual central reforms and local developments over the course of the century.

In the "colonial" period dating from 1882 in Egypt, and from 1918 in the other areas under consideration, the powers and the administrative capacity of the central government were further strengthened, and local autonomy correspondingly attenuated. Essentially, the western style of government was adopted, though many traces still remained of the earlier pattern of organization. Modern and traditional institutions existed side by side, sometimes in an ill-fitting coordination.

By the beginning of World War II these countries had governments of varying degrees of national autonomy, but with strong influence still exercised by the western powers. Domestic authority was theoretically vested in a parliamentary system, but was actually operated as a two or three sided system with power balanced between a parliamentary oligarchy, the palace where there was one, and the colonial power, or as it became in this period, the "treaty power." In Egypt, nominally independent since 1922, defense and foreign affairs were reserved by treaty to the British until a new treaty in 1936 terminated British occupation except for the Canal Zone. The British ambassador continued to exert invisible influence, however, which became visible to all in 1942 when British armed forces were used to force the King to accept a government he did not want. Similarly, Iraq, independent since 1932, was bound by a 1930 treaty to have "full and frank consultation with Great Britain in all matters of foreign policy." This treaty, not abrogated until the formation of the Baghdad Pact in 1955, gave Britain such rights and duties as wartime defense of the country and the use of bases and transit. It was the basis of a three-weeks war between Britain and Iraq in 1941.

Lebanon became a republic in 1929, Syria in 1930, though still under French mandate. Both constitutions protected the French position by reserving to the mandatory power military and foreign affairs and public security.

In Syria and Lebanon, as in Egypt and Iraq, there were moves and countermoves throughout the interwar period focusing on treaties redefining their relationships with the semicolonial power. The French never ratified the treaties worked out with Syria and Lebanon, and genuine independence came to these countries only with the evacuation of French and British troops in 1946 after a wartime showdown with France in each country.

Egypt and Iraq also came to be completely independent after World War II, Egypt after the 1954 agreement on withdrawal of the British from the Canal Zone, and Iraq after its 1958 revolution. In the meantime, Transjordan had become Jordan, politically independent but still fiscally dependent on foreign subsidies, a dependence shifted from Britain to the United States after 1957, and from the United States to the Khartum contributors after the June War of 1967. Israel too had come into existence, but its line of development has been so distinctly different from that of the Arab countries in the area that we shall not follow it here. For the Arab countries then, the general tendency has been toward greater independence of the colonial powers realized in form between the wars and in substance after World War II.

Independence, when achieved was discovered not to be the panacea for all the ills besetting these countries: the defects and limitations of the oligarchic governments became apparent, and they were, one after the other, swept away by military coups. The principal transforming force at this stage was ideational on the part of army officers ready to overthrow governments failing to sustain their country's honor. Thereafter they lightly borrowed the intellectuals' ideologies as needed for their pragmatic policies.

The question is sometimes raised why the Arab bourgeoisie, which gradually took power as independence was being fought for and won, lost it to the military in the postwar period of complete independence.[32] The prior question may be raised of how it happened to have power in the first place. Except in Lebanon, it had no real power base. Its political power grew up in the colonial period because the colonial authorities felt obliged, under the impact of anticolonial and liberal feelings among the local bourgeoisie and its intellectuals, to institute parliamentary forms, and once these were established, the bourgeoisie and the large landowners could take them over and operate them, while the colonial power controlled the military. The leading families in each area or group gained ascendancy over a segment of the electorate, and the parliamentary process largely consisted of combinations and permutations among the oligarchy, a continuous shuffling of a small deck of cards.[33] There was no feeling among the people that their interests were served or in any way represented in the parliament. The popular attitude toward government in the area is expressed in the proverb: "The camel driver has his concerns and the camel his." The leading politicians were regarded, often with justification, as corrupt and self-seeking, and the people danced in the streets at the overthrow of the parliamentary regimes. Sometimes, as in Iraq in 1958, the dance was a macabre one, with

[32] Arnold Hottinger, "How the Arab Bourgeoisie Lost Power," *Journal of Contemporary History III,* No. 3, July 1968, pp. 111–28.

[33] This figure of speech is attributed to a remark of Nuri al Said to Wendell Willkie, who reported it without identifying the source. Cited by Abid A. Al-Marayati, "Modern Iraq," *Middle East Forum* (Beirut), XLIV No. 4, 1968, p. 27.

human sacrifices. In Syria in 1949, the story ran, the leader of the coup, Zaim, had the deposed and apparently surprised President Quwatli taken for a ride through the streets in an armored car to see the people celebrating his fall.[34] The story is probably untrue but certainly well-founded, for the ancient tradition in these lands is to rejoice at the loss of a master in the hope that the next will be better.

As the colonial powers relinquished their control of the armed forces, and as the parliamentary governments demonstrated their inability to meet the problems they faced, and as officer recruitment was opened to the lower middle classes, colonels, and even generals, began to question whether the governments they served had the right to exist, and the question once raised, a negative answer was not long in forthcoming. So there developed a willingness on the part of those who could gain command of the critical instruments of power to use those instruments to transform the constitutional structure.

While shortcomings of the existing governments were most clearly revealed by the defeat in Palestine in 1948, the critical coups were more immediately associated with local evidence of breakdown, or threat thereof. In Syria there was a cooking fat scandal in quartermaster supply. In Egypt, there was the breakdown of power evidenced by the Black Saturday of January, 1952 when Cairo was burned by mobs. The familiar pattern of a three-cornered struggle between the royal dynasty, the middle class parliamentary party, the Wafd, and the British, led, by 1952, to the loss of strength of all three. Faruq was dissolute, the Wafd was demonstrably ineffective and tainted by corruption, and the British were the enemy, so the Free Officers, temporarily enjoying the sympathy, if not the cooperation, of the Muslim Brotherhood as well, encountered no effective resistance from any of the three rivals for power. The failure of the prerevolutionary government to make progress on the economic front, or in terms later adopted by Nasser, to advance the social revolution, was also claimed to be a motive for the coup.

The oft-mentioned political power of the landlords proved to be a weak thing, significant under the old regime as a basis for parliamentary strength, but nothing that had any strength of its own to match that of the army after the coup. Only in some local resistance to the implementation of land reform did landowner power show itself, and such demonstrations, as in the murder of a land reform official, usually sufficed to bring conclusive counteraction from the central government. The power base the large landowners did have in Egypt was apparently terminated by the land reform, and similarly in Iraq and Syria. In any case, the shift to military control in these countries did not leave much room for political power to be derived from landownership.

[34] Patrick Seale, *The Struggle for Syria,* Oxford University Press, 1965, p. 45.

The primary perception of the Free Officers, common to their otherwise highly diverse viewpoints, was of a regime that was failing to do what needed to be done to modernize the society and the economy and to remove the humiliation of Egypt's backwardness, principally exemplified by the defeat in Palestine, but also by the social state of the country. Their initial presumption was that it would be necessary only for them to clean up the government and then to be a watchdog against any subsequent failure of the sanitized government to work in the interest of the people. They felt that they were the vanguard of the Egyptian masses, and it was with wistful disappointment that they found, as expressed in Nasser's famous phrase, that there were no masses forthcoming to fall behind the vanguard "in serried ranks."[35] Whether the officers could not in fact find civilians capable of leading an Egyptian government toward modernization, or whether having once tasted power they were not anxious to return to their barracks as they had originally intended, it is impossible to say.[36] In the end they compromised by staying in power but taking off their uniforms. Ultimate power then came to lie between the armed forces and Nasser, who could, after Suez, supplement his leadership of the armed forces, which apparently he delegated to Amer, by his charismatic leadership of the entire Egyptian people, and indeed, the Arab people.

In Iraq, Kassim's 1958 coup that terminated the Hashemite reign there, as well as the close alliance with Britain, came during an expansion of the Iraqi economy which had doubled the real national income in eight years.[37] It clearly indicates that economic progress is not enough to make a regime secure, as has more recently been demonstrated in Pakistan and Libya as well. Here again, economic motives do not seem to have played a major part. A British observer ascribes the revolution to the corruption of the government of Nuri-al-Said,[38] but it is more generally recognized that it was Nuri's policy of working closely with the British that was the principal target of the nationalist opposition. He was a nationalist too, but he felt that Iraq could do best by cooperating with Britain. The opposition hardly distinguished between the procolonialist stand of the government and its corruption. In their opinion, these were just two aspects of the same phenomenon.

The revolution was dedicated to Arab solidarity, but that desire was not sufficient to bring the new regime together with Cairo, with whom, after

[35] Gamal Abdul Nasser, *Egypt's Liberation; The Philosophy of the Revolution,* Public Affairs Press, Washington, D.C., 1955, pp. 32–33.

[36] On this point, see Maxime Rodinson, "The Political System," in P. J. Vatikiotis, ed., *Egypt Since the Revolution,* Praeger, 1968, p. 89.

[37] Based on a linkage of Fenelon's and Haseeb's estimates of national income at 1956 prices, 1950–1958. See K. Haseeb, *The National Income of Iraq,* Oxford University Press, London and New York, 1964, p. 31. See also OECD, *National Accounts of Less Developed Countries,* Paris, July 1968, Table A.

[38] Caractacus (pseud.), *Revolution in Iraq: An Essay in Comparative Public Opinion,* London 1959.

some early internal purging of the Nasserists, particularly Arif, it entered into intense rivalry. The conspirators, or at least the most important of them, seem to have been motivated not only by Arab nationalism, and possibly more strongly by anticolonialism, but primarily, like the Free Officers in Egypt, by a lack of respect for the regime, and by the conviction that the government was unworthy of sustaining the dignity and aspirations of Iraq. That the predominant oligarchy under the monarchy was composed of old Ottoman officers out of tune with the new developments intensified this feeling.[39]

Kassim's declared aim was to rid his country of imperialism and to restore it to the people. He was intensely anticolonial, and bent on achieving unity, strength and dignity for Iraq, as well as power for himself. He was practical enough to avoid interrupting the flow of oil revenues, and so refrained from nationalizing the oil industry. The economic development of the country was hardly his primary objective, though he did attach great importance to it in his speeches. As part of his anti-imperialist stereotype he presumed that the great wealth of the country, which had formerly been exploited for the benefit of foreign imperialists, would now be devoted to the welfare of the people. From the limited information available, accordingly, it appears that the motivation for the 1958 revolution was primarily the opposition to imperialism and to the composition of the Hashemite regime, with a general presumption that once these evil forces had been destroyed, the nation would enjoy liberty and prosperity and happy union with brother Arabs elsewhere. This rather naive ideology was combined with a highly shrewd and practical appraisal of the realities of the power struggle. The revolutionaries, and Kassim in particular, could afford to be naive in their ideology, for that was a luxury. The bread and butter of their political existence was command of the power structure and manipulation of the various factions. Of course, even in this sphere Kassim's skill bought him only five years of power, and then death in the next coup.

Most of the many coups in Iraq and in Syria can best be understood, if at all, as factional disputes in a struggle for power among the military leadership. While alliance was occasionally made with doctrinaire socialists of the Ba'th variety, the latter were carried on the shoulders of the military rather than vice versa. Within these struggles local, sectarian, and personal loyalties and disloyalties counted for a great deal more than ideology or broad political orientation.

It is easy to identify the factors which have led to a stable military based government in Egypt and unstable ones in Syria and Iraq.[40] Egypt is more homogeneous. It has a highly developed bureaucracy. The military there

[39] See Elie Kedourie, "Reflexions sur l'Histoire du Royaume d'Irak" (1921–1958), *Orient* (Paris) no. 11, 1959 for a development of this theme.

[40] See Ayad al Qazazz "Military Regimes and Political Stability in Egypt, Iraq and Syria," *Berkeley Journal of Sociology,* December 1967.

were independent of outside political groups when they made their coup, while in Iraq and Syria there was frequently an alliance with an outside political group when a coup was made. Finally, the Egyptian coup was organized over a longer time and much more solidly than the Iraqi and Syrian coups.

But it is not easy to be satisfied with these explanations of the difference. As usual, they raise more questions than they answer. But the difference exists; at any moment it is a much better bet that there will be an Iraqi or Syrian coup d'etat within the next twelve months than that there will be an Egyptian one. Possibly most important is the fact that the Egyptian regime had developed, at least between Suez and the June War, strong popular support through convincing the people that it was working hard and sincerely for ends which the people shared. It did not gain the further and critical test of legitimacy, that of public support for whatever the government does, rather than for doing what the people want, but that may be too much to ask.[41] In Syria and Iraq the broad masses of the people see in each government just another tyrant. The politically conscious regard the governments as power seeking factions and nothing more, a judgment widely shared by western observers. The more highly developed pattern of loyalty to the common good in Egypt, working in the first instance through the loyalties and support of the military officers, operates more as a constraint on the actions of the Egyptian government, but, as long as that constraint is respected, gives the government greater stability.

In Jordan, a parliamentary government never achieved full power. By 1957 however, the parliamentary government was threatening to challenge the King's power and its leadership attempted, with certain segments of the army, a coup to achieve that end. The high military officers cooperating in the coup were not, fortunately for the King, in troop command. The troops, largely Bedouin, were loyal, while the staff and other officers sympathetic to the coup were mostly Palestinians and townsmen who could not, at the critical moment, command the troops to follow them against the King. King Hussein thus succeeded in maintaining the loyalty of the army and seized power from the parliamentary government in 1957, thus forestalling a revolt on Arab nationalist lines. Since then, the King, with army support, has represented the actual center of power. A parliamentary government operates subject to that power, but, essentially, the rule is in the palace. Subject to that rule an oligarchy flourishes with important influence on the government.

It was British financial support in the early 20s that permitted Abdullah to consolidate his rule over Transjordan by buying off the principal leader-

---

[41] Malcolm H. Kerr, "The United Arab Republic: The Domestic Political Background of Foreign Policy," (Forthcoming publication of the RAND-Resources for the Future Research Project on the Middle East).

ship of the tribes and driving out with a British organized and officered Arab legion those tribal leaders who remained unreconciled. From 1957 to 1967 American budgetary aid directly or indirectly supported military strength loyal to the King, and since the summer of 1967 the Khartum contributors have taken over this function.

The United States seems still disposed to support Hussein, however, though there is some question of what it can do besides continuing to sell him arms. The threat to his government is great; the strength of popular enthusiasm for the Fedayeen forces Hussein to allow the commandos freedom of action likely to bring forth retaliation from Israel. This he must avoid however, or at least keep within tolerable limits. The monarchy has a reasonable chance for survival principally because the Fedayeen are apparently better off with it than they would be after taking over the government of Jordan themselves. For then, by their own principles, they would have to convert their irregular war against Israel to a regular war, with defeat likely. Nor are they in a position to engineer the accession of a third party that would preserve their irregular status but be more favorable to their activities. Meanwhile, Hussein must do his best to contain them without going into such strong opposition to the main body of the Fedayeen as to put his command of the situation to the test. Palace rule has survived in Jordan while it succumbed in Egypt and Iraq possibly because the Jordanian monarchs were more skillful, but also because the political structures were even less developed, the army better organized and drawn principally from the Bedouin who were not sympathetic to the opposition, the demands of the external powers less onerous, and their support much more generous. But it continues in a delicate balance.

The case of Lebanon is especially instructive for there the army not only refrained from making a coup d'etat but twice came to the rescue of the middle class government, for all its failings the most sensitive to considerations of public welfare of any parliamentary government in the area, when it tended to fall apart under the stress of functional tensions. And there may be a third time.

Lebanon is democratic in its own peculiarly Lebanese fashion. There, men are citizens, as they are not in neighboring Arab states; until recently the Arab language did not even include "citizen" in its vocabulary. The basic ideology of Lebanon is free private enterprise in the economic sphere and its correlatives in the political: parliamentary democracy with extensive checks and balances, minimal governmental activity or control, maximum personal freedom. The Lebanese constitution is based upon the famous Lebanese genius for compromise, a genius not conspicuous in the rest of the Arab world. The Lebanese commitment to democracy derives fundamentally from the pluralism of the society, a conglomeration of minorities. Just as in the United States of 1789, or in Switzerland with which Lebanon is so often coupled in metaphor, each group is ready to subscribe to those constitutional measures that will protect it from the tyranny of the rest. Yet other countries, such as Syria and Iraq, have ethnic and sectarian divisions that could profit by a comparable constitutional protection but do not attain this protection.

When the Lebanese parliament attempted, in 1943, to abrogate those articles of the constitution that gave France control of the army and foreign policy, and the French took counteraction leading to the political turmoil which the Lebanese regard as their war of independence, the Christians and Muslims united against France in an unwritten "national pact" which has been somewhat precariously maintained ever since, and whose symbol is the tradition that the President of the Republic is to be a Maronite, the Prime Minister a Sunni Moslem, the President of the Chamber a Shi'i. Political power in Lebanon is balanced not only among confessional groups but also among geographical interests, economic interests, secular ideological interests, and the personal interests of the small group of bloc leaders and family notables who constitute the inner circle of parliament from which cabinet ministers are drawn.[42]

In the threat to the Lebanese government that arose in 1969 from the Fedayeen insistence on operating against Israel from Lebanese territory, the army is in fact more immediately engaged against the Syrian-backed Fedayeen than is the government, since the troubles take the form of clashes between the Fedayeen and the army. Under such circumstances, as in the two earlier crises, the government seems simply to dissolve. If Lebanon is to remain democratic and independent, the army will probably have to be a counterweight to what is now the officially unacknowledged Muslim majority of the country, which is certainly sympathetic with the Fedayeen, but also not without commitment to the preservation of Lebanese democracy. Most critical of all seems to be Egypt's role in limiting the influence of Syria on Lebanese developments.

The Sources of Instability

It is often argued that the instability and tensions of the Middle East are the consequences of the widespread poverty in the area. Speiser, for example, maintained in the 50s that the immediate cause of the basic troubles in the near East was "the familiar chain reaction of extreme and chronic poverty on a mass scale." The vast majority of the population are poor and landless, while the governments are weak, and therefore under the necessity of diverting the attention of "the long-suffering masses from the ills within to some convenient target outside. . . . In a climate such as this

[42] Malcolm H. Kerr, "Political Decisionmaking in a Confessional Democracy" in Binder, op. cit., p. 191.

it is primarily as instruments of diversion that xenophobia and obsessive nationalism spring up and prosper."[43]

Albert Hourani declared that "this theory is not wholly false but by itself it is not a sufficient explanation of what is happening in the Middle East today. . . . Why, for example, should we take it for granted that political problems only derive their reality from economic problems and that the whole complexity of life in common can finally be reduced to a single factor — the desire of the individual to increase his own material welfare?" He asked whether the Middle East's resentment of the West really reflects irrational xenophobia or was it not rather a legitimate opposition to some things which some foreigners do. "Is there an essential connection between poverty and national unrest, or would it not be truer to say that the Asiatic countries become more opposed to Western influence in proportion as they gain economic strength?"[44] He identified the source of the troubles between the East and the West as the new moral relationship which sprang up from the assumption of political control of the Middle East by the Western Powers. The control was not established primarily for the sake of the inhabitants themselves, but "as an incident in the unceasing, all-embracing internecine strife of the Western nations. They occupied the Middle East in order to go somewhere else, or to prevent their rivals doing so, or to obtain assured outlets for their surplus goods or capital, or else — once the exploitation of oil became important — to obtain fuel or to prevent their rivals from obtaining it."[45] Finally, the control was imposed by force and maintained by force. The consequences were what could be expected whether it is Westerners who impose themselves upon Asiatics, or Christians upon Muslims, or one Western people upon another.

Eventually, the strengthening of the economy and the society which took place throughout the area during the period of foreign control generated conditions which made that control harder to bear. New classes arose which adopted from the West notions of liberty and independence, and with their own education and advancement found the rule of foreigners humiliating in a way that had not previously been felt. The Arabs had been subject to humiliating treatment by one master or another for centuries. But those Arabs had not had the benefit of a higher standard of living and of sharing Western culture. Imbedded in that Western culture was the spirit of nationalism which gradually became a part of the Arab culture, primarily in the form of anticolonialism. The process here is an ideational one stemming largely out of political relationships. Economic development played

[43] E. A. Speiser, "Cultural Factors in Social Dynamics in the Near East," in Sydney Nettleton Fisher, ed., *Social Forces in the Middle East,* Cornell University Press, Ithaca, New York, 1955, pp. 9–10.

[44] Albert Hourani, "The Decline of the West in the Middle East," in Nolte, op. cit., pp. 31–2.

[45] Ibid., p. 40.

its part, but as a conditioning variable operating principally through the rise of economic classes that could sustain the spirit of nationalism, typically secular in the upper classes and Islamic fundamentalist in the lower.

The foregoing argument, which flourished some fifteen years ago, over the internal sources of tension between the Middle East and the West, now seems somewhat outdated. For the tensions generated internally in the Middle East, whether in the form of political unrest within the Arab countries or of antagonisms among them, or between them and the West, take on their importance in posing a threat to world peace primarily because of a condition external to the area — the rivalry of the superpowers.

Local conflicts in the area may not remain localized principally because the spheres of influence, both geographical and political, of the superpowers in the region are not stably defined, but are subject to competitive redefinition.

The Middle East is the strategically significant area closest to the Soviet Union in which there is not a well-defined political alignment. Since the middle 50s, the Soviet Union has been building up its political position there, and the United States, as Britain's successor, has been correspondingly on the defensive. The opportunities for Russia to increase its influence do, of course, proceed from the internal political tensions, not only the Arab-Israeli quarrel but also inter-Arab rivalries and ideological differences. It is often said, and with substantial truth, that if Israel did not exist the threat to the world peace from the Middle East would be about the same. For it would still be an area where the influence of the superpowers was not clearly defined but a subject of competition. There would still be rivalries and dissensions there such that one side could look to the United States for support, and the other to the Soviet Union, probably along the line of cleavage between the radical Arab states and the conservative ones. Under these conditions, whether Israel exists or not, the tensions of the area are magnified into tensions between the superpowers themselves, whose actions and orientations feed back to intensify the strains in the area, and pose a continuing threat of enlarging local antagonisms into a superpower confrontation, possibly a cataclysm.

The local governments are insecure, primarily because they have no solid basis of support in the fundamental loyalty of their people, but have at best transient popular support, and at worst, merely army support. They depend on control of the armed forces for the continued maintenance of their power, which means the loyalty of a few key military men who may switch at any time. Such fundamental loyalties as do have political significance run either to small subgroups such as families, sects, or ethnic groups, or to a mythical supergroup — the Arab nation as a whole. Consequently, each government must operate under the constraints imposed both by a loyalty that transcends its sovereignty, and by local group loyalties that may undermine its control. Each government must try to meet a set of unattainable demands upon it — for effective action against Israel, for support of Arab unity, for attainment of domestic unity, and for a dramatic rise in living standards. The three radical states, Egypt, Iraq and Syria also have a self-imposed commitment to promote social revolution in the rest of the Arab world, along with like-minded regimes in Algeria, Libya, Sudan and the Yemens. Meanwhile each regime must also deal with the aspirations for greater participation in the governmental process by excluded groups, largely the urban middle class, for whom students are the vocal spokesmen. These demands for the impossible become threats to the government in power in ways that vary from country to country, with correlative implications for the client-patron relationship with the superpower of its choice.

The need to show progress against Israel lies heaviest on Egypt, but is potentially threatening to the governments of Syria, Iraq and Jordan as well. Until Egypt acts strongly however, these other governments are relatively immune, and even then they may avoid real commitment by being slow to come into action, as Syria was in 1967, and as Hussein must wish he had been. In Jordan and Lebanon, however, the Israel issue also translates into the threat the Fedayeen raise, in their different ways, to the maintenance of the authority of the government, a potential threat elsewhere as well.

For all but Lebanon, arms supplies are of the highest order of importance, and the direction of superpower orientation is signalled by the lines of flow of armaments. But the superpower's willingness to supply arms does not, by itself, govern the orientation of these countries toward the superpowers. Should they switch partners, the losses of arms supply can correspondingly change. The orientations are the result of a complex of factors which govern where the country's interest is deemed to lie. Egypt turned toward the Soviet bloc first for arms without strings, then for development aid under positive neutrality, and most recently for political as well as arms support. Iraq and Syria turn more or less intensely toward Russia according to the current state of their revolutions. Jordan and Lebanon, along with Saudi Arabia and Kuwait, are likely to continue to be reluctant to turn toward the Soviet Union as long as they are ruled by their present regimes, whose chances of survival seem better with the West. These orientations are primarily political, rather than either ideological or economic, although consideration of arms supply at a critical moment shifted Egypt eastward, and ideological revolutions shifted Syria and Iraq. The conservative states, however, have adequate access to arms from the West. Their natural political, as well as commercial, orientation is toward the West, but is rendered difficult by the Israel issue.

The necessity to support Arab unity is closely bound up with the struggle against Israel. Together these impose lines of action which may be close to self-destructive — such as Nasser's conduct leading up to the June War, apparently required by Arab unity in view of the insecurity of the Syrian regime — and Jordan's joining that struggle in response to its duty to Arab unity. For a superpower patron, these objectives of its client impose at least the political duty of defending the client's interests in impossible situations, a burden principally carried recently by the Soviet Union, with the United States' relative freedom from that burden purchased at the expense of its attenuated influence over the radical Arab countries. If political support should not be enough, the clients would, naturally, like military support. Given the irreconcilable Israel-Arab conflict, and the necessity for these governments at least to appear to be doing something about it, or preparing to do so, there is the making of an armed conflict any time the superpower patron is prepared to support it. Short of that, there appears to be a readiness to exert as much threat of military pressure as the patron is willing to permit. So the actualization of the threat to world peace depends on how far the superpowers are ready to let things go. The local parties are ready to fight for their ends. Neither superpower wants a confrontation but, in the absence of a détente not yet reached, neither is apparently willing to cut its arms support to the point that would preclude another war. Once the arms are delivered, the local client has the power of deciding whether to use them. If war breaks out, one of the superpowers, probably Russia, would be faced with the problem of how far to get involved in limiting the losses of the loser.

The third necessity — of showing dramatic economic progress — also imposes on each government tasks that are likely to be beyond its unaided power. Economic aid will accordingly be expected from its superpower patron, except by Lebanon whose situation is special, and possibly by Iraq whose oil revenues could cover the requirements if the government could only function effectively. Concern for economic development might, it could be hoped, act as a restraint on the other objectives, and so work toward the avoidance of costly military ventures. To a certain extent, and for limited periods, this tendency can be recognized; always in Lebanon; sometimes in Egypt, as during 1957–61; but at critical junctures it is overwhelmed by the requirements of Arab unity, as in 1967, or of social revolution as in Egypt's Yemen policy, or of governmental insecurity, as in Iraq and Syria.

The compulsions on the governments are, accordingly, primarily political in nature, compounded of their impossible tasks on the top of their basic insecurity. For the immediate future at least, it would seem that the necessity of doing something effective on the Israel front, together with the probable impossibility of doing just that, will lead to unsettling turbulence, while economic development will be sought to the extent permitted by the overriding demand for action against Israel. So long as the priorities run this way, economic development aid is not likely to be a principal instrument of superpower influence on these countries. Rather it will be a secondary demand upon whatever superpower is meeting the primary demand for arms supply and for political support in the world arena. The demand on the superpower will, of course, be for residual aid required over and above the Khartum payments.

It is not impossible, though it is unlikely, that the 1960 situation may reappear, in which the Israel front becomes quiet enough, for development aid, either direct or in such indirect forms as P.L. 480 food, to assume a significant role, but once again vulnerable to eclipse by political demands which have higher priority.

The basic threat to world peace from the Middle East thus proceeds from the superpower involvement in the area, with primary, though uncertain, leverage through arms supply to their clients. If the superpowers should come to a well defined demarcation of their spheres of influence in the area, the internal tensions would no doubt remain, but they would be "defused" from the point of view of world peace. In this drama, economic development has a part to play, but it is no Hamlet.

The Interactive Process

The broad features of the interaction of economic, political and social factors in the development of the Middle East in the nineteenth and twentieth centuries, closely resembling the pattern of modernization of undeveloped areas elsewhere, should now be clear. Political forces got the process started. The local potentates, impressed by the power of the West, opened their countries to Western contacts, commercial, technological, and cultural, in order to strengthen their own military power. To this end they also instituted internal reforms, revolutionary in Egypt and gradual in the rest of the Ottoman Empire. These increased the strength, stability and effectiveness of local governance, with the significant, if incidental, effect of securing agricultural producers in their tenure and in their share of produce.

Economic forces then took over, and a mighty upsurge of economic output ensued. This resulted partly from the switch from a subsistence to a market economy with access to world markets, partly from the use of new products, new facilities and superior techniques, but primarily from the full realization of productive potentialities consequent on the security afforded by stable local governments.

The growth of output was accompanied by an almost, but not quite, proportional increase of population in a Malthusian pattern that was broken only at the very outset of development and in the recent postwar period. When the Malthusian pattern was broken it was not, as in the West, by a socially conditioned decline of the reproduction rate, but by economic growth rates so accelerated as to run ahead of the reproduction rates, still among the highest in the world.

Trade with the West, following the lines of comparative advantage, involved the export of those primary products suited to the resources of the area and the importation of manufactured goods which displaced the products of local craftsmen. The growth of production for the market stimulated development of new commercial and financial activities and the transformation of the socio-economic structures. In particular, land tenure was shifted from the old forms to private property, and an urbanized middle class arose. Most prominent in that class were the great native landowners. Important commercial and financial roles were played by special groups, typically foreigners in Egypt, and minority groups elsewhere (except for Lebanon where the Christians were in a majority).

Extensive social and ideational changes were part of the modernization process. The example and the political influence of the West led to the adoption of Western ways of thought and Western political and economic institutions to which the indigenous societies adjusted by dualistic arrangements that permitted the coexistence of modern and traditional modes of life, of thought, and of law. Gradually the traditional mode in each sphere gave ground to the modern, a process which is still going on.

As elsewhere in the undeveloped world paramount political power came to be exercised by the then leading world powers, France and Britain, sometimes through influence and sometimes through colonial or semi-colonial control. The economic, social and political developments nurtured by the colonial experience brought forth a class that could eventually challenge the control of the colonial powers themselves. During the colonial period, indigenous political leadership was taken everywhere by lawyers, journalists, teachers and doctors closely associated with the large landowners. Faced by their nationalist demands, France and Britain first helped to establish parliamentary institutions, but eventually found it necessary to devise means of continuing their control over military and foreign affairs by granting independent sovereignty to native political leadership, qualified by treaty with the colonial power. The modification of these treaties became the principal focus of contention between the colonial powers and the local governments during the interwar period. Finally, the semi-colonial treaties were abrogated after World War II as France and Britain lost their international power and their will to rule.

As long as the colonial power maintained its influence, the defects of the newly nurtured parliamentary institutions were not lethal. However, as control of the armed forces shifted from the supporting external power to an indigenous military leadership that could at times challenge rather than support, the weakness of the parliamentary structures was revealed, as was their inadequacy to satisfy the new social and nationalist demands. As real independence was won the military took over and ruled through a compliant bureaucracy, sometimes in an unequal partnership with civilian political leaders.

Throughout the entire period the directly operative forces were political, indeed ideational, with the strength and composition of the ideational forces based largely on economic and social developments. The process was initiated by the belief of Viceroy or Sultan that modernization would bring military strength. Parliamentary government was initiated in response to the belief of the middle class intelligentsia that it was required for respectable nationhood. The external power was forced to shift from colonial to treaty status, and eventually to withdraw, in response to the nationalists' belief that colonial influence was intolerable. Finally the coups which overthrew the parliamentary regimes were based on the belief among army officers that the old-line nationalists were incapable of achieving dignity for their nation and social justice for their people. But economic and social, as well as political developments brought about the situations in which these beliefs flourished and became politically effective.

After World War II there appeared in the area an economic promise and a political threat. The promise, afforded by the demonstration of rates of economic growth previously unattained, was that of breaking out of the Malthusian trap of the preceding century and a half. Favorable foreign export and aid conditions together with domestic commitment to development underlay that postwar performance.

The threat is of political instability, both domestic and international, proceeding out of three sets of conflicts affecting the area: Arab-Israeli, inter-Arab, and United States-Soviet. Concern for economic development takes second place, in national policies, to concern for these conflicts. The hope that the promise can be used to avert the threat seems slim. There is greater danger that in the immediate future the threat will stifle the promise.

19

Stabilization and Monetary Policy
in Less Developed Countries

*Emile Despres**

This essay expounds some thoughts about inflation which I developed during a two-week visit to Brazil in the summer of 1966. Rather than expose my ignorance by saying much about the specific case of Brazil, I shall concentrate on some theoretical reflections about inflation applicable mainly to less developed countries, but not all confined to them, and shall use Brazil as the principal example. The subject is a hoary one and my justification for setting these thoughts down is my view that most of the writings about inflation in Latin America skirt a real analysis of the central points. As a result of inadequate analysis, the anti-inflation or dis-inflation efforts there are to a large extent misdirected and likely to fail.

As one goes through the literature on the monetarist versus the structuralist views, the hardest thing to figure out is what the question is. It is like the game that certain "in" groups played a few years ago in which you give the answer and it is up to the other fellow to figure out what the question was. The best example is "The answer is 9-W." The question is, "Do you spell your name with a 'V,' Herr Wagner?"

The other thing that the controversy reminds me of is the observation of Frank Ramsey's that most debates follow the pattern of A's saying "I went to Granchester the other day," and B's saying, "No, I didn't." This is the same variety of discourse.

This essay is a revision of the transcript of a talk given to the Economics staff of the Agency for International Development on May 1, 1967. My trip to Brazil in 1966, which stimulated the thoughts here expressed, was financed by the University of California's Brazilian Development Project. I thank Arthur B. Laffer, Walter S. Salant, and members of my family for converting the transcript into a publishable product.

* Stanford University

I want to begin with a simple theoretical construct of a neutral or nearly neutral inflationary path, using it to provide a basis for analyzing the effects of a particular inflationary process in a particular country.

"Neutral" Inflation

One can conceive of a neutral, or more accurately, a nearly neutral inflation. I will state later on why I use the qualification "nearly." By a "neutral" inflation I mean an inflationary process which has no effect on any real economic magnitudes — output, employment, composition of output and employment and so on. It is possible to conceive of such an inflation. It is probably very difficult to realize it in practice.

Two sets of conditions would be necessary for the realization of this kind of neutral inflation. One is a set of subjective conditions and the other a set of objective conditions.

Subjective conditions.   These conditions relate to the state of expectations, and when you consider expectations in this context, three aspects are relevant.

1. First the question of the uniformity or diversity of the expectations of individual economic entities — firms and households — in the economy. Do individual firms and households expect approximately the same degree of inflation in the future? Do they have the same future inflationary path in mind, and if not, is the diversity of expectations great or small?

In an open economy the expectations of foreigners who are engaged in trade and financial operations with this economy are also relevant. An example of the importance of the expectations of foreigners is the European inflations after World War I and the accompanying exchange depreciation. In the early stages of these inflations there was a very widespread expectation that European currencies in due course would be restored to the pre-World War I parities. And I recall seeing estimates that in the early stages, Germany got about a billion dollars from ill-advised foreign speculators and foreign bull speculators in marks. This was a form of unintended private foreign aid.

2. The second aspect of expectations that is of importance is the precision or fuzziness of the expectations of each decision-making entity regarding future price level behavior, or, to be a little more formal about it, whether the variance of expectations is high or low.

3. The third aspect is *ex ante* versus *ex post*. Suppose the expectations were uniform and each entity's state of expectation could be thought of as having a sort of mean value. Is this expectation vindicated by the result, or is the inflation greater or less than was foreseen? If the inflation has been generally underestimated or over-estimated, there will be windfall gains and losses.

So far as the subjective conditions are concerned, the neutrality or near-neutrality of an inflation depends upon expectations being (a) highly uniform as among economic entities, (b) precise, i.e., held with low variance, and (c) vindicated in practice, with the expected path turning out to be the realized path.

Incidentally, why avoidance of inflation is a good thing is a question which many people do not bother to ask. A large part of the case for price level stability is that, as a practical matter, it is rather hard to imagine that the subjective state of expectations that is required for neutrality could be fulfilled around a sharply rising price level. Thus the case for price level stability is that it is probably a prerequisite for coalescence of expectations.

Objective conditions. On the objective side, the condition for near-neutrality of inflation is that markets have to behave in such a way that prices equate supply and demand.

When you come to apply this notion to Latin American economies — indeed, to economies generally — you confront the fact that, with or without inflation, prices do not equate supply and demand in these countries, anyway. So a more expedient statement — although just what it means I do not know — of the objective condition is that the price distortions for near-neutrality of inflation should be no different from what they would be under price-level stability.

An illustration of what I have in mind when I state the objective condition in this way is that, with or without inflation, the level of urban real wages for common labor is often above that which clears the market. And, I suspect that the level of interest rates paid by borrowers is often below that which would clear the market without rationing if financial institutions were adequate to make credit accessible to all sectors of the economy. Under these circumstances, clearly, all price distortions cannot be blamed on inflation. That is why the objective condition for neutrality of inflation is fulfilled if the under-pricing of finance and the over-pricing of common labor in urban markets are merely no greater than they would be without inflation.

If both subjective and objective conditions are fulfilled, then inflation is nearly neutral. The reason for saying "nearly" is that there would still be two departures from neutrality. The first is that under the sort of equilibrium-inflation path that I have in mind, while holders of bank deposits would receive a nominal rate of interest at least high enough to offset the inflation, it is hard to see how interest could be paid to holders of currency. As a result, the distribution of money holdings between currency and bank deposits would be altered a little bit. The significance of that point is probably not very great.

The second departure from full neutrality is more important. The function of money as a unit of account under this kind of nearly neutral inflation would be seriously impaired. Children, in order to equip themselves for the economic decisions they have to make during their lives, would have to memorize a log table instead of a multiplication table. The point is that the key function of accounting is to measure gain and to separate recurrent gain or profit from non-recurrent capital gain. In accounting under neutral inflation, all the items would have to be dated and deflated and expressed in units of account having the purchasing power of a given date, and people would have to learn to think this way; they would have to penetrate the veil of money in order to make economic decisions. Although people accustomed to living in inflationary environments manage to do it quite well, even without memorizing log tables, this is a serious inconvenience. To the extent that accounting falls short of perfection the inflation will not be wholly neutral.

This is a rather long theoretical disquisition. The usefulness of this notion of a neutral inflation is that it gives some rigor and precision to the cliché that the harmful results of inflation are due to the distortions caused by inflation.

Distortions

What does the word "distortions" mean? "Distortions" means essentially departures from the two sets of subjective and objective conditions.

Apply this, for example, to the notion of forced saving. Forced saving occurs when wealth is transferred from those who would have consumed or used for non-productive capital flight a high proportion of what is being taken away from them to those who will use for these purposes a smaller proportion of this exaction which is being imposed on the rest of the community.

In Brazil it seems that the chances are very good that forced saving was quite substantial for a time during the 1950's. In the late 1950's and early 1960's, I suspect that forced saving, measured in real terms, declined markedly. There are a number of reasons. Probably the diversity of expectation among economic entities has been very greatly lessened and, as a result, there are fewer suckers. This is the principal reason why forced saving is much more difficult to extract through inflation.

There is a widespread notion that inflation lowers real wages. But in the case of a country like Brazil, or most of the South American countries, I do not see how one can possibly tell. There is not much money illusion left. In fact, there are rather good grounds for believing that the growth and strengthening of labor organizations in urban areas has been in part a product of inflation, and it is possible to argue that real wages are higher than they would have been without inflation. It is just as easy to argue the opposite, however. Everybody has very strong opinions about this, and nobody has evidence that is worth very much.

The significant transfers of wealth in Brazil are now not based upon diversity of expectation or money illusion or anything of this sort. They are based upon inequality of access to scarce resources. I have in mind particularly finance, credit and foreign exchange.

One of the general points that I am trying to make is that there cannot be a general theory of the effects of inflation. The distortions, the departures from the equilibrium path, are of a different sort in different stages of inflation in a particular country, and there are also differences among countries. You can have a general theory of how to analyze the consequences of inflation, but not widely applicable generalizations about the consequences of inflation.

Now, so far as the price distortions are concerned, I propose to talk chiefly about two prices, or two sets of prices; one is interest rates, and the other is foreign exchange rates. I want to emphasize that other price distortions may also be associated with inflation. Quite often there is a lag in the upward adjustment of some prices, particularly in public utility rates and railroad rates; subsidies may be used to keep these prices down. Other things also may be subsidized and you may have rent controls, but I think the most important prices are interest rates and foreign exchange rates.

So far as foreign exchange rates are concerned, currency over-valuation — that is, the underpricing of foreign exchange — is not inherent in inflationary situations. It is generally present, however, in South American inflations. One may perhaps also say it is inherent under inflationary conditions in members of the IMF that adhere to the Articles of Agreement, because under the Articles you are not supposed to devalue until after it is too late — that is a short summarization of IMF — and, of course, if you adhere to that rule under inflationary situations there will be a tendency toward chronic overvaluation of the domestic currency. But in European inflations after World War I and in the later phases of the inflations in Europe during the 1920s, there was in a number of countries a tendency for the external depreciation of the currency to lead the domestic depreciation of the currency.

I said that inflation is advantageous to those who have the most favored access to scarce resources. If you are thinking about South America, this means the government. It also means large firms, especially firms that own banks, and to a large extent it means foreign firms. Foreign-owned firms are particularly favored borrowers, especially from foreign-owned banks but also from some of the domestically owned banks.

I said that the government enjoys favored access to resources. It certainly does in the sense of being able to borrow from the central bank, create money, and so on. When finance is under-priced, one may say it should be the goal of any rational economic entity which is trying to get ahead in the world to be a net debtor. It would seem that the government, when it can borrow from the central bank, is in the best position of all to make itself a net debtor.

It has been widely believed in Brazil and other South American countries that the government, with its control over the instruments of foreign exchange regulations and deficit finance, is singularly well equipped to mobilize the resources for a development program. In fact, however, much of the foreign exchange and capital controlled by the government is dissipated through indirect subsidies to buyers of commodities, such as petroleum products, which are favored by foreign exchange, import licensing and tariff policies, and to users of public utilities, such as the railroads, whose chronic operating deficits are covered by government loans.[1] So although the government is favored by privileged access to finance and control over foreign exchange, it is also burdened by public policies and private practices which greatly deplete the supply of government-controlled resources actually available for investment in a development program.

Finance and Credit

Let me now enumerate some of the financial features in Brazil as of the summer of 1966 that seem to me of key importance.

I gathered that banks were charging the equivalent of about 35 percent per annum interest to borrowers on, typically, very short-term loans. No interest was paid to demand depositors, and a low interest rate was paid on time deposits. While I was there they were changing over to a system of paying somewhat higher interest rates. I think the rate on time deposits had been 4 percent. They were adding a so-called monetary adjustment of around 8 percent. But the volume of deposits eligible for such supplementary interest payments was narrowly restricted. They were very afraid that if they did not restrict these payments the system would be too popular. These higher rates were specifically for small savings and so on.

The demand for credit vastly exceeds the amounts that the banks lend at the 35 percent interest rates, so that bank lending is very much a ration-

---

[1] In addition to dissipating the resources it does control, the government is also constrained from enlarging its development program by a tax system whose weak administration and inelastic structure fail, especially under inflationary conditions, to maintain the government's share of national revenues. One curious phenomenon which illustrates how minor deficiencies of the tax system are amplified by inflation is the prevalence of open refusal to pay taxes. Under the traditional tax laws, direct taxes are assessed, and the assessment can be protested. Moreover, as long as a protest is kept alive, none of the tax liability must be paid. Of course, the lawyer's fee rises as inflation proceeds, but it is still worth dragging out the case until the legal costs equal the gain expected from the continuing reduction in real tax liability, then drop the case and pay the by-now negligible tax. The proliferation of practices of this sort nourished by inflation, makes administration costly, reduces even further the elasticity of government revenues, and limits the government's ability to mobilize resources by the conventional means of taxation.

ing process, not only when efforts are made to tighten credit, but even when the Brazilians are being loose about it. They are never truly loose except to certain favored borrowers and typically, even then, loans are very, very short-term.

Commercial banks lend only to urban borrowers. The Bank of Brazil is both the central bank and the main source of credit for agriculture — actually for very little more than agricultural marketing. In addition to the commercial banks and the Bank of Brazil, there are so-called finance companies which draw upon their time drafts, drawn upon business firms. Their lending rate in effect was about 70 percent per annum, and they sold their paper — their lifetime certificates of deposit, if you will — in the form of bills of exchange, at yields of about 35 percent per annum to the investor. The volume of such credit was equal to about 15 or 20 percent of the outstanding amount of bank credit.

In addition to these forms of credit, there is a colossal amount of inter-firm credit, and this is important to keep in mind. The firms that can borrow from banks do so for one or two months and they sell on four to six month credit, so that this financing is all in the form of trade bills similar to the European method of financing rather than accounts-receivable financing, but it amounts to the same thing. The typical large firm's balance sheet will include a certain amount of bank borrowing, and on the asset side very little cash and a volume of accounts receivable, which is — like the accounts payable — a high multiple of the amount of bank borrowing. It is interesting to trace out the effects of attempts to restrict bank credit.

A firm adjusts to restriction of its accustomed availability of bank credit, apart from whatever it does to inventory, by curtailing the amount of credit it will extend to its trade customers, by seeking to reduce its accounts receivable and by delaying payment on its accounts payable. Bank credit is the narrow apex of the pyramid which supports a substantially multiplied volume of inter-firm credit, as well as consumer credit. If the authorities try to contract bank credit, a domino theory is applicable, because the leverage is very high.

If government steps on the credit brake, the demand for credit will not abate, even if the public believes that the rate of inflation will soon be retarded and hence revises its expectations in some subjective sense. The demand for credit increases for the same reason that the late Ivar Kreuger kept going deeper and deeper into the hole long after he knew that it was virtually impossible to get out of it.[2] He made his bankruptcy more and

---

[2] Ivar Kreuger was the managing director of the Swedish Match Company after World War I. He arranged loans totaling more than £50,000,000 to various European governments in exchange for monopoly rights. His operations expanded in the inflationary environment of the 1920's but with the depression and financial contraction of the 1930's, he resorted to increasingly complex and fraudulent financial activities, including falsifying balance sheets, setting up dummy companies and forging securities of various governments. When his initially high reputation came into

more utter. This effect reflects the very simple principle that if you must choose between committing suicide today or tomorrow, you prefer tomorrow over today. Even though there is only a very low probability that you can avert disaster, you prefer disaster later — if it is some sort of ultimate disaster — to disaster now. This preference operates very strongly when the amount of real wealth represented by financial intermediaries' credit is very, very small. Another effect might operate to increase the demand for credit even more. With funds exceptionally tight, those who still have unused borrowing power will borrow so that they will have sufficient funds in case they might need them later when credit is even tighter.

There is no long-term capital market except the long-term credit that may be provided by the government development bank. What is the obstacle to long-term lending and borrowing? One would suppose that if there is any diversity of long-term expectations, there would be a market for long-term loans. If I believe that the average annual rate of inflation over the next twenty years is going to be 20 percent per annum and you believe it is going to be 30 percent, why do I not lend to you at, let us say, 25 percent per annum? We both ought to be happy, given this state of expectation, so there ought to be a market. But there is not. The reason is that the diversity of expectations is really less than the uncertainty of each individual's expectations. That is, if my belief that inflation is going to proceed at the rate of 20 percent really means that I believe it will be between zero and 40 percent and your belief that it will be 30 percent really means a range of 10 to 50 percent and we are both risk-averters, then there is no interest rate at which a loan can take place. The lender wants to be assured against this high variance of his expectations, and so does the borrower. This is why long-term loan markets dry up.

Please note that the revival of long-term lending and borrowing is not an instantaneous result of a year of approximate or even complete stability of the price level. In most European countries today the appetite for life insurance or other long-term obligations fixed in domestic currency is rather low because it takes a long time to obliterate — I don't want to sound Jungian about it — historical memories. And all this depends upon attitudes about political stability, too.

In Brazil the failure to develop a long-term domestic capital market has been accompanied by the failure to develop a significant long-term market in dollars. A dollar market has not been completely prohibited and there are five-year export credits for the purchase of machinery and that sort of thing. But I think there is no inclination on the part of lenders — American private lenders, let us say — to lend dollars in this kind of environment. Even though the borrower is willing to sign the obligation, the

---

question and Swedish banks refused him further credit unless they could investigate his affairs, he shot himself. His death in March 1932 and the collapse of his fraudulent operations ruined many investors.

government's willingness to release foreign exchange for this purpose is equally important. The lenders must be prepared to gamble on this willingness for five years or so. They will do so when the loan is tied to export sales, but they have no taste for simple long-term loans, although I am sure borrowers do.

There is another point to make about the financial situation. Although it would seem that commercial banking should be an enormously profitable business where no interest is paid on demand deposits and interest earned on loans is 35 and 40 percent per annum, the payments mechanism has become so costly that the net profit may not be as great as these wide gross margins would lead one to suppose. Certainly the bankers allege — although I do not cite this as evidence — that their costs are so great that they could not afford to pay much interest to depositors. The reason is that the payments system is extremely costly. Banks do not pay interest on demand deposits, but on the other hand they do not impose service charges.

The currency situation also contributes to high costs. The largest denomination note is the local equivalent of a dollar or a dollar and a half and a great many notes in circulation have the purchasing power of a tiny fraction of a cent. One of the greatest absorbers of salaried labor is the activity of counting out money. It has to be counted in the retail shops and then it has to be counted again when it is sent to the bank, and so on. This, of course, is due to the fact — true in central banks the world over — that the fellow who orders a new supply of bank notes has no foresight at all. He does not extrapolate the inflation. He orders little if any more than would be enough at today's price level. By the time the notes are delivered four months later, it is far too little. And these old notes keep circulating.

The combination of high costs and inconvenience in handling currency and the absence of service charges on checks means that everybody has bank accounts like American college students, with an average balance for the month of $15.00 and 150 checks for an average amount per check of 65 cents. The velocity of money is high; the total amount of money in real terms is very low. The banks open branches like mad in order to compete with each other in attracting deposits. It is an example of the standard case of monopolistic competition without barriers to entry, similar to having four gasoline stations on every corner, except that in Brazil they are bank branches. I emphasize this because it is an important practical obstacle to doing what I think ought to be done.

In short, my general impressions regarding Brazil were, first, that inflation was no longer very effective as a device to obtain forced saving. Second — and this is more important — inflation very greatly inhibits the development of a capital market. The amount of saving mobilized through financial intermediaries is very, very small.

Saving and Profits

In orthodox economics there are two notions about the capital market. In classical political economy, capital accumulation takes place through the reinvestment of profits, including what we call interest on the owner's capital. The equalization of profits, after allowance for risk, among alternative uses of capital was conceived of as being carried out by the little entrepreneur's shifting his own capital out of Business A where profits were lower into Business B where profits were higher. Since the capital was mostly working capital anyway and since he was small, the shift was easy to accomplish.

In this classical view, the saving was really done by the fellow who is expanding the capital used in his business, and therefore the rate of capital accumulation depended directly on the amount of profits. The competition in the system depended upon the mobility of the businessman as well as upon the mobility of his capital from one line of business to another. When you apply this to the modern world, even in underdeveloped countries where in the modern sector the average size of firms is large and a good deal of fixed capital is employed, if you do not have a capital market, a loan market, and you want capital accumulation — you have to have some kind of internal mechanism that assures the large firms growing profits. What I am really saying is that monopoly in these countries is important chiefly because they have no capital market. The absence of the capital market is a barrier to entry, except by foreign firms. The large firms that do exist derive their profits to a large extent from favored access to the under-priced and scarce resources, and their entrepreneurship is devoted mostly to increasing their share of the scarce resources. In this system, lacking any kind of competitive spur to efficiency, profits are bound to be much too easy.

The Failure of Traditional Policies

The disinflation policy in Brazil, as I observed it, seemed to me doomed to failure. It had three facets. One was reduction of the budgetary deficit. That is okay. The second was holding back on money wage increases, following the utterly irresponsible splurge of the predecessor of the military dictatorship. This was, at least for a time, appropriate. They may have tried to overdo it, but the imposition of such restraint is a normal part of what one would try to put into an anti-inflation package.

The third facet was credit control. The whole empasis on the credit control side, so far as extension of bank credit to the private sector was concerned, was one of blowing hot and cold. In the latter part of 1965, while the fiscal and wage-rate control portions of the disinflation program were going forward, bank credit was allowed to expand at an exceptionally high rate. The officials gave some technical reasons for this which I will not go into. The credit expansion crept up on them accidentally because the Bank of Brazil finances some purchases of coffee under the price-stabilization arrangements, and they had to pay out more than they expected. That increased the credit base for the commercial banks. The officials were aware at the time of what was going on, but felt that the anti-inflation measures should be moderate, that they should dampen inflation gradually. As a result, during that period, they were doing only two of the three things they ought to do.

Then, in the first part of 1966, they were restricting credit expansion. They were able to get away with it because the previous splurge of credit was being absorbed into the system. But it was fairly clear by the time I left that they would soon take their foot off the brake. And the foreign advisers keep saying: "What's the matter, are you chicken?"

The simple fact is that a bank experiencing net withdrawals must, in the absence of a money market, resort to rediscounting to keep its doors open. No bank goes to the Bank of Brazil and says "I want to borrow, I want to rediscount in order to make some loans I would not otherwise have made." They always say "I have to rediscount because I have an adverse balance at the clearing house." The adverse balance at the clearing house may be a result of loans already made, but the Bank of Brazil is faced with the question whether it wants this bank to close its doors, just as the commercial banks, in dealing with their customers, have to confront the agonized groans of borrowers that they will be insolvent if the loans are not made to them. The significant fact that the authorities must face is that these groans are not bluffs. Unless one is prepared to trigger a chain reaction of financial and commercial insolvencies and bankruptcies embracing the whole economy, one cannot appreciably reduce the rate of expansion of bank credit. In the background is the inertia of inflationary expectations. Everybody who ever got his balance sheet into a shape appropriate to expectations of inflation at a given rate is very vulnerable to a substantial retardation of inflation below that rate.

And, as I pointed out in mentioning the Ivar Kreuger phenomenon, even if the government does make people think that inflation may slow down, the impact effect of doing so through credit restrictions is, if anything, to make demand for credit increase, not decrease.

An Alternative Proposal

One general conclusion to which these considerations lead me is that halting the inflation is the wrong goal, or the wrong immediate goal. The immediate goal should be to eliminate the major distortions arising from the inflation, to make the inflation more nearly neutral. If you succeed in doing that, you can probably swing gradually over to the target — which I regard as a secondary and more remote target — of dampening and perhaps finally terminating the inflation.

The essence of eliminating the major distortions is to make the holding of domestic financial assets attractive in the face of the inflationary expectations that prevail. More specifically, this involves two things. One is to raise the price of foreign exchange to a point where an increased number of its holders think it a good thing to sell. In other words, one must make repatriation of capital attractive, undervalue the domestic currency to induce capital repatriation.

You may say that this will cause an accumulation of gold or foreign exchange reserves, which is a waste of resources. I think that the correct way to meet that is to offset the undervaluation by a substantial reduction of import barriers so that the repatriated capital, instead of adding to gold reserves, adds chiefly to the supply of imported goods.

The other thing needed to make holding of domestic financial assets attractive is to raise interest rates sharply. By this I do not mean the interest rates charged to borrowers; I mean the interest rates paid to depositors and lenders by financial institutions. They should be raised so that the combination of the high interest rate paid to depositors and the high price of foreign exchange will increase greatly the demand for domestic bank deposits and other domestic financial assets. To state it in other terms, strong inducements should be provided to increase the domestic propensity to save in domestic financial form. This has been done in South Korea.

Such action will have some negative effects in the goods market. Automobiles and household appliances were being sold on installment credit at interest rates of 100 percent per annum and above. The people who were buying at these terms were buying not primarily because they prized a dishwasher or a Volkswagen this year rather than a year hence so much that it was worth 100 percent per annum to have them this year. A large part of the demand for such consumers goods reflects their desire to accumulate wealth in this form and their expectation that prices and their money incomes are going to rise enough so that they are getting a better buy now than by paying cash, let us say, a year hence. If these expectations are disappointed or revised, there will be at least a transitional slump in the household appliance and automobile markets. But, at the same time, with adequate depreciation of the external value of the local currency, there will be an export stimulus with an increase in saving. You will have an expansion of the flow of real saving through the banking system and some industrial investment, so that the automobile companies can make some capital goods instead of durable consumer goods. I mention this to make clear that I am not saying that the adjustment will be painless. Rather, I think a policy that seeks not to restrict credit, but to increase the desire to save is almost the only kind of adjustment that can be made.

The *ex post* measure of success of the kind of financial stabilization measures that I have been talking about would be growth in the *real* volume of bank credit. The goal is not so much to retard the rise in the price level as it is to remove major distortions. A good *ex post* index of success would be a reduction in the velocity factor in the equation of exchange. This means that bank credit would increase faster than the price level goes up.

So far as concerns price stability as a long-range goal, I have two things to say about it. One, as I have already said, is that price stability is probably the only way to get expectations to coalesce fully. However, with unstable governments and all the other difficulties, even price stability for a couple of years would not be sufficient to achieve the ideal state of expectations. But, the second point is that, one must not demand perfection in these matters. It is not necessary to achieve this ideal state; therefore do not think price-level stability is very important. The chances are very good that you can change the state of expectations gradually toward expectations of smaller price increases, and that you can, rather painlessly, get down to lower rates of inflation and finally price-level stability. That is, provided you accept inflationary expectations as a fact of life and set as the initial goal just bringing prices, especially interest rates and the price of foreign exchange, into equilibrium with this state of expectations. That is 90 or 95 percent of the problem. Then, after that, you play it by ear.

One result of removing or greatly reducing the distortions induced by currency overvaluation and import substitution would be to make the allocation of investment much more productive. The substitution of a loan market for the present classical pattern of capital accumulation means that you will have a much more competitive economy and that much more attention will be paid to efficiency and productivity.

Another result is that if countries like Brazil or Argentina or Chile could "put their houses in order" financially, in this sense, I see no reason why they should not be able to attract a great deal of foreign private loan capital — probably not long-term, but short and intermediate term.

I regard foreign loan capital as a much better buy, from the point of view of the developing countries, than foreign direct investment. Although foreign direct investment may be worth the 15 to 30 percent per annum rate of return — where the effects of innovation, teaching of know-how, and so on, are great enough — much of this foreign investment merely exploits the wholly inappropriate profit opportunities that the underdeveloped countries create by their import-substitution policies. To have foreign investors borrow at 7 percent and invest at 18 percent in an economy where prices have something to do with scarcity values, with true rates of transformation, is very beneficial. But direct investment that earns a return of 20 percent in a manufacturing activity where the value added may well be negative and where the investment is profitable only because of distortions in the import structure is not such a good form of external capital inflow.

Do not misunderstand me. I am not attacking American corporations who take advantage of these artificial profit opportunities. It is the unwise policies of the underdeveloped countries that create them. Nevertheless, I am saying that very often such investment does not contribute much to real development.

Further Problems

Given that a rash of bankruptcies would follow if inflation were eliminated under the present conditions in Brazil — following my earlier analysis — how then could inflation ever be eliminated without an outbreak of bankruptcies? Expectations may coalesce at some high rate of inflation and a non-distortive equilibrium path may exist. In that case, how could a country move from one non-distortive equilibrium path with inflation to another with price stability and still avoid running into the bankruptcy problem?

If you accept that there is much inertia of inflationary expectations, then you would not want the actual behavior of the price level, the actual rise in the price level, to fall far short of expectations. What you want is gradually to change expectations and change the price level, too. But I would say, whatever the state of expectations may be — this has to do with the subjective conditions — it is desirable to have interest rates and a price of foreign exchange which more nearly clear the markets than the present ones do. With all the fuzziness, and undoubtedly also some diversity, of expectation, there is a level of interest rates and foreign exchange rates that will result in a markedly increased desire for domestic financial assets. I think that that is a desirable thing by itself.

The coalescence of expectations is a very gradual process, so far as the long-term loan market is concerned, and I would not expect a domestic long-term loan market to revive, to develop very fast in any event, whether the price level is rising or is stable for a few years. But I do think it is possible to get a sufficient coalescence of expectations to expand quite considerably the real amount of saving flowing into investment through short and intermediate term loans. The state of expectations is doubtless going to be very blurred for a long time, no matter what happens. In the existing situation, the desire of every economic entity is to be a net debtor. The closed-economy identities, of which we economists are so fond, tell us that everybody can not be a net debtor, but everybody can try to be one. In the situation that has prevailed for some time, with negative real interest rates, anybody who has maintained a balance sheet which by our normal standards would seem financially prudent has long since ceased to have any economic importance. Having such a balance sheet is a sure way to go broke during conditions of inflation. A precondition to paving the way for a damping down of inflation is to get firms' and households' balance sheets in what we would consider more respectable shape.

With the enormous incentives to being a net debtor reduced or removed, one can imagine that balance sheets of economic entities will approach what we regard as financially prudent. If, at that time, the rate of inflation were to diminish we would not expect to find many Ivar Kreugers. The first step is to get prices, interest rates, and exchange rates, into such a shape that being a net debtor is not so enormously attractive as it seems to be at present.

A difficult problem may be the feasibility of having banks pay high interest rates, given the fact that they have opened so many branches. I do not know enough about the size of their net profits to know how serious this problem is. I think it is probably serious and that, over time, many bank branches should be closed down. But if the approach I suggest works, their real volume of earning assets will substantially increase, so even though the net profit per unit is smaller, there will be a larger profit base, if you will. But I rather suspect that in the transition period the government may have to put some supplementary capital into the banks in order to ease them over the transition.

In South Korea, where the kind of program that I have been, in effect, recommending for South America was tried, there was the advantage that the banks were government-owned. And, for a time at least, they paid higher interest rates to depositors than they charged to borrowers. (In theory, you could go around to the loan window, borrow some money, and deposit it, and make a profit. I am told this was not a widespread practice because people knew ways to make greater profits without depositing the money.) Clearly, I do not think it necessary to go that far. But nevertheless, payment of high rates to depositors may present problems for banks.

I do not think any program can do anything about the subjective conditions quickly. You can do something about the objective conditions. But you can not improve the objective conditions by being even tighter in your credit rationing. That, if anything, makes things worse rather than better.

After this description of my proposal, a relevant question might be, "Is this all you have to do?" No. I think you have to do other things to promote real capital formation. I think that this proposal will greatly increase the *real* amount of bank credit expansion and that short-term commercial loans will develop, but many other things are needed for the development of a capital market. I would say about most of these other things that in an environment where there is no private appetite to accumulate wealth in domestic financial forms, there is no opportunity to develop a capital market.

Alternative Policies

If you want to weigh alternative courses of action, I think my program should be considered against a revalorization-of-debts program, which operates on the same principle. That is, instead of trying to restrict credit, to carry out overnight a general revaluation of debts as a substitute for a chain reaction of bankruptcies — the kind of thing that was done in stabilizing the German mark after World War I and in Belgium and Germany after World War II. You announce and put it into effect over the weekend so it is in effect by Monday morning, and people's bank balances after the write-down are so low that they want to accumulate financial assets despite their inflationary expectations. It is another way of achieving the same ends. Although this is another possibility, I think it is likely to be very strongly resisted and therefore can hardly be taken seriously as a policy that these governments would be disposed to carry out.

The alternative of forced saving is pretty well excluded for the reasons I gave earlier. These countries cannot resume development by going back to inflation as a means of forced saving. To the extent that forced saving is a possibility, the part of it that goes into private profits is often used in capital flight. The propensity of the beneficiaries of forced saving to save out of their windfalls may be no greater than that of the people who are squeezed in this process. The part of forced saving that goes to the government does not yield much productive investment.

Domestic public saving, i.e., an excess of tax revenues over current operating expenses, is also pretty well excluded, not because taxes can not be raised — many countries have raised tax revenues — but because most countries tend to expand public ostentation expenditures as fast as they can raise taxes, so that they are never going to have enough tax revenue left over for the productive investment that they need.

In short, I think both forced saving and public saving are pretty well excluded. All that is left to fall back on, it seems to me, is the capital market and you can not do much about this until after you have removed or substantially reduced the distortions I have talked about. When that has been done, it would be appropriate to have development banks that borrow short from the banking system and make some long-term loans. There is also a need for agricultural credit, and agricultural credit institutions. I think in the Brazilian case — and I suspect this will be true in many countries — these are the two things that are most needed.

There is a great deal of talk about developing domestic markets for equity securities. I think the importance of doing so is vastly exaggerated. It takes a very long time to establish habits of disclosure and the other things that are needed before a corporation really can be what we regard as a public corporation in the sense that outsiders have equity interests in them. In the United States, disclosure is sufficiently great so that outsiders think that they are not at so great a disadvantage as to be crazy if they own common stocks. In other countries, there is a long way to go before that state of confidence concerning equity securities is achieved, so I do not think that an effort in that direction has much practical importance. When I talk about a capital market, therefore, I am talking about a loan market.

Some Consequences of the Proposal

It is not at all clear to me that, with development of a loan market, financial intermediaries would have to charge higher interest rates. Although one cannot know in advance, my guess is that they might well be able to lower the interest rates charged to borrowers.

One must remember that some of the forms in which individuals accumulate wealth are very costly. For example, doctors keep five Volkswagens in the back yard because wealth is safer in the form of Volkswagens. But, of course, the Volkswagens depreciate. People build houses and take five to eight years to do it. As soon as they have a little surplus cash, they order another load of lumber and dump it on their property. The next time they have a little surplus cash, they hire a carpenter right away. They have to get the lumber embodied in that house. That is not a good form of wealth accumulation, but under present conditions it may be better than keeping wealth in the form of money. If the interest rate paid on bank deposits were, say, 25 percent, however; and if appropriate service charges were made for the use of check payments; and if, at the same time, the foreign exchange rate were allowed to float, import barriers were reduced and the foreign exchange value of the currency were forced down to a level that induced repatriation of capital, I feel quite sure that the combination of price pulls would increase the lending power of the banks a good deal. The banks might then find it appropriate to lower the interest rates charged on borrowing, although nothing that I have said is conclusive about which way such rates should change. The first thing, certainly, is to narrow gradually the spread between rates paid to lenders and rates charged to borrowers and then to see, with a narrow spread, which way you want interest rates to go.

If my proposal were enacted, there would be a major structural shift in the economy. Although the present desire to flee from money affects the demands not only for automobiles and TV sets but also for nondurable goods like textiles, I venture the guess that the effects on the consumer good industries other than durable goods would be fairly small. I do not think that the flight-from-money component of the demand for these goods is very great in relation to the demand for them based on desire for consumption proper.

I also think that consumer stocks are not so big that the transition would be hard for other consumer goods industries. The exchange depreciation would create larger export opportunities. Even though accompanied by relaxation of import barriers, it would provide some protection, and while some industries producing import substitutes would be hurt, other industrial opportunities would be opened up by the exchange depreciation and by import liberalization. But there may have to be some financing to ease the transition. To make this possible you would have to put capital into the banks and you might also have to provide some other financing to ease the transition. If, for example, you expanded agricultural credit and increased the availability of credit to industry, the automobile industry could begin to make tractors and trucks instead of merely passenger cars, and other industries could also shift output to capital goods.

One cannot be sure that the proposed set of policies would work. The difficulties of transition under them may not be too great, however, and they are certainly much less than those of putting on the brakes a little and taking them off, which creates a kind of perpetual stagnation. I think you could not revive the Brazilian boom by going back to all-out inflation, and that you could not revive it by credit restriction. Maybe it could not be revived by my program, either, but I would say that of the three methods, mine is certainly the least unpromising.

If this proposal were undertaken along with import liberalization and exchange depreciation, a theoretically very difficult kind of dynamic problem would arise: How do expectations change and what further adjustments become necessary after the initial steps? An answer involves a dynamic model. I would rather administer the second steps than write about them; I think playing by ear is not so hard, but writing out the symphony before you play it is impossible. If the government's macro-targets are expansionary, they are more likely to be realized or more nearly realized, by following these lines than by doing what governments are in fact doing. I admit that the dynamics of the proposal is hard. The value of this analysis is that it shows that dynamics is what is really involved.

Index